MOTO
& CAM

An IPC Inspire Focus publication, published by IPC Inspire Focus, part of IPC Media Ltd
Caravan, *Motor Caravan* and *Park Home & Holiday Caravan* are IPC Inspire Focus magazines

Distributed by Marketforce, Blue Fin Building, 110 Southwark St, London SE1 0SU. 020 3148 3333.
Distributed to the book trade by Orca Book Services, Stanley House, 3 Fleets Lane, Poole, Dorset BH15 3AJ. 01202 665432

Annuals Editor Kate Taylor
Art Editor Jason Taylor
Database Manager Martine Derwish
Group Ad Manager Beverley Meliniotis
Ad Sales Jill Kelf
Ad Production Manager Gina Mitchell
Publisher Clive Birch
General Manager Niall Clarkson

Editorial and Advertising
Britain's Best Caravan Parks, IPC Media Ltd, Leon House, 233 High Street, Croydon, Surrey CR9 1HZ
Tel: 020 8726 8000

Printer Positive Images UK, 44, Wates Way, Mitcham CR4 4HR

Front cover Main picture: Cheddar. Top right: Gordale. This page: Broadway

HOW TO USE YOUR GUIDE

Welcome to the 2009 edition of Motor Caravan & Camping Parks, which contains details of no fewer than 2028 parks in the UK, Ireland, The Isle Of Man and The Channel Islands. It is published in association with Motor Caravan magazine and is essential reading for motorhome and tent users.

To make it easy for you to find a suitable park in your chosen area or holiday spot, we use a system of colour coding for the various regions (turn the page for a map of these areas). Whatever your needs, you are bound to find a park that suits you. The parks are listed under countries, counties (or unitary authorities or administrative areas) and then under the villages, towns or cities nearest to them. Information for each park, where possible, includes directions, postal addresses, phone numbers, names of owners and websites. Our comprehensive guide and key to the facilities available on or very near to each park is second to none, but remember, standards and facilities can still vary from park to park. A few parks do not accept tents, and a handful will not take motor caravans. We have highlighted these. Please note, inclusion in this guide does not imply recommendation by the publishers.

KEY TO SYMBOLS AND ABBREVIATIONS

 This symbol on a listing entry means the site is one of the Top 101 Sites in the country, as voted for by *Caravan* and *Motor Caravan* readers across 2007/8. You can vote for your favourite at www.caravanclub.co.uk or www.motorcaravanmagazine.co.uk. Here you will also find details of the prizes you could win just for making your favourites known to us!

(5m) Distance to nearest village/town
BH&HPA Brit Hol & Home Parks Assoc.
NCC Member of National Caravan Council
CaSSOA Member of Caravan Storage Site Owners' Association
T Touring caravan pitches
MC Motor caravan pitches
S Privately-owned caravan holiday-homes
H Caravan holiday-homes for hire
L Lodges
LH Lodges for hire
Motor caravans welcome
WCs
Toilet emptying point
Facilities provided for disabled people

Park open all year
Mains electricity hook-ups available
Dogs allowed
Takeaway meals
Swimming pool
Shop on site or close by
Cafe or restaurant
Bottle gas supply
Laundry facilities
Showers or baths
Bus service nearby
Rail station nearby
Tradesmen call
Farm produce available
Games room   Fishing

PARK HOLIDAYS UK

TOURING BREAKS FROM £12 A NIGHT

Even more choice means better value - for you!

DISCOVER GREAT FUN-FILLED FAMILY HOLIDAYS FROM £99 PER BREAK

Park facilities can include:
- Heated leisure pool
- Family Bar
- Kids' Club
- Sky TV in bar
- Wi-Fi internet access
- Entertainment Venue
- Children's Play Area
- Mini Mart Store
- Restaurant/Takeaway

CALL THE HOLIDAY HOTLINE OR BOOK ONLINE
0845 815 9797

www.ParkHolidaysUK.com

Country Parks UK
Where peace of mind comes as standard

Dream Holiday Locations

Craigielands Country Park
Beattock, Moffat, Dumfries & Galloway, DG10 9RB

Located within the village of Beattock, just one mile west of junc 15 off the M74 situated in an idyllic woodland setting in Scotland.

This beautiful Caravan Park has 56 Acres of rural parkland including a 6.5 acre Loch, which has been stocked with both brown and rainbow trout, just waiting for you to catch.

With something for the whole family to enjoy Craigielands is the ideal location for your family holiday this year. And don't forget, we have static holiday caravans and log cabins available for friends or family who don't have their own caravan or motorhome.

www.countryparksuk.com or call 01683 300591

YOUR COLOUR-CODED PARK FINDER

REGIONS AND COUNTRIES

1 **Cumbria** .... page 6

2 **East Anglia** .... page 13
Bedfordshire, Cambridgeshire, Essex, Hertfordshire, Norfolk, Suffolk

3 **Heart of England** .... page 24
Gloucestershire, Herefordshire, Shropshire, Staffordshire, Warwickshire, West Midlands, Worcestershire

4 **Middle England** .... page 32
Derbyshire, Leicestershire, Lincolnshire, Northamptonshire, Nottinghamshire, Rutland

5 **North-West England** .... page 40
Cheshire, Greater Manchester, Lancashire, Merseyside

6 **Northumbria** .... page 43
Durham, Hartlepool, Middlesborough, Tyne & Wear

7 **South-East England** page 47
Kent, London, Surrey, E and W Sussex

8 **Southern England** .. page 54
Berkshire, Buckinghamshire, East Dorset, Hampshire, Isle of Wight, Oxfordshire, Wiltshire

9 **West Country** .... page 70
Bath, Bristol, Cornwall, Devon, Isles of Scilly, Somerset, West Dorset

10 **Yorkshire/Humberside** .... page 105
E Yorkshire, N Yorkshire, S Yorkshire, W Yorkshire

11 **Scotland** .... page 116

12 **Wales** .... page 134

13 **Northern Ireland** .... page 155

14 **The Islands** .... page 162

READ WHAT THE EXPERTS WRITE
IPC Focus Network publishes monthly magazines covering all aspects of caravanning.
WHY NOT SUBSCRIBE NOW?
You can place an order for *Caravan* or *Motor Caravan* magazine on the telephone or online.

☎ **0845 676 7778**

www.caravanmagazine.co.uk. or www.motorcaravanmagazine.co.uk

CUMBRIA

CUMBRIA

ALSTON

(2m). Horse & Wagon Caravan Park, Nentsbury, Alston, Cumbria CA9 3LH. 01434 382805. Owner: Mr W Patterson. On A689, 3m E of Alston. Quiet, country location in an Area of Area of Outstanding Natural Beauty. Near golf, fishing, horseriding, lead mining centre and England's highest narrow-gauge railway. Open March 1-Oct 31.

AMBLESIDE

Chapel Stile Campsite, Bayesbrown Farm, Great Langdale, Ambleside, Cumbria LA22 9JZ. 01539 437150. Owner: David Rowand. From Ambleside SP for Great Langdale to Elterwater. Carry on to Chapel Stile, go through Chapel Stile, about 300yd on L past school. Site is set at the beginning of Langdale Valley. Central to most attractions. Open Feb-Nov.

(5m). Hawkshead Hall, Hawkshead Hall Farm, Hawkshead, Ambleside, Cumbria LA22 0NN. 01539 436221. Owner: M Brass. S of Ambleside on L. Open March 1-Nov 15.

Low Wray Campsite, Ambleside, Cumbria LA22 0JA. 01539 432810. Owner: The National Trust. SP from B5286 Ambleside to Hawkshead road. Small camper vans welcome. No power boats. No cars on grass. No caravans. Arrivals 1-8pm. No groups of more than 4, unless a family group with children. Open Easter-end Oct.

(8m). National Trust Camp Site, Great Langdale, Ambleside, Cumbria LL22 9JU. 01539 437668. www.langdalecampsite.org.uk. Owner: National Trust. W of Ambleside via B5343. Stunning setting amid mountains. Walks from site – easy to strenuous. 3 areas: general, families, groups. Family & group fields can be booked. All other campers – first come, first served. SAE.

(5m). The Croft Caravan & Camp Site, North Lonsdale Road, Hawkshead, Ambleside, Cumbria LA22 0NX. 01539 436374. www.hawkshead-croft.com. Owner: W Barr. On B5286 at Hawkshead village. Rose Award 2005. Showers, shaving and hairdryer points. TV room. Laundry. Shops in village also Beatrix Potter gallery and Wordsworths Grammar school. Open March-Nov.

APPLEBY-IN-WESTMORLAND

(1.5m). Hawkrigg Farm, Colby, Appleby-in-Westmorland, Cumbria CA16 6BB. 01768 351046. Owner: F A Atkinson & Sons. In Colby, take the Kings Meaburn road. Halfway up first hill, turn R, this brings you to farm. Shops, PO, doctor, swimming pool, golf, takeaway meals, café/restaurant, laundry facilities available in 1.5m.

(3.5m). Wild Rose Park, Ormside, Appleby-in-Westmorland, Cumbria CA16 6EJ. 01768 351077. www.wildrose.co.uk. Owner: Harrison Leisure UK Ltd. SE of Appleby. From Appleby on B6260 to Orton. In 1.5m turn E on Ormside and Soulby road. At first crossroad turn L to Ormside. After 600yd turn R into lane, then a further 600yd into drive to site. Recreation room. Heated outdoor swimming and paddling pools. TV. Play areas with safety surfaces. Launderette. Off licence. Restaurant. Takeaway. Indoor nursery room. Licensed mini-market. Pitch & putt. Reduced facilities in winter. Superb mountain views. Golf course 5m. GS. Open 50 weeks a year.

BARROW-IN-FURNESS

■ (5m). South End Caravan Park, Walney Island, Barrow-in-Furness, Cumbria LA14 3YQ. 01229 472823/471556. www.walneyislandcaravanpark.co.uk. Owner: Kath Mulgrew. Take exit 36 from M6, A590 to Barrow. From Ramsden Sq follow Walney signs, 3m S of Bridge. Gas supplies. Family run park with indoor swimming pool and club house. Close to beach. Tennis court, bowling green, children's playground. Open March 1-Oct 31.

BECKERMET

(4.5m). Tarnside Caravan Park, Braystones, Beckermet, Cumbria CA21 2YL. 01946 841308. www.ukparks.co/uk/tarnside. Owner: Mrs A Lockhart. A595 S of Egremont. 2m S of Egremont follow tourist signs on B5345. Overlooks sea, close to Lake District. Clubhouse and restaurant on site. Coarse fishing available.

BRAMPTON

Irthing Vale Caravan Park, Old Church Lane, Brampton, Cumbria CA8 2AA. 01697 73600. www.ukparks.co.uk/irthingvale. Owner: Mrs OR Campbell. 0.5m N of Brampton off A6071. Flat, well-drained site. Near Hadrian's Wall and 9m NE from cathedral city of Carlisle. Lake District, Solway coast and Scotland in easy reach. Open 1 March-31 Oct.

CARLISLE

(6m). Camelot Caravan Park, Sandsyike, Longtown, Carlisle, Cumbria CA6 5SZ. 01228 791248. Owner: Mrs M Fyles-Lee. On A7. 1m S of Longtown, 4m N from J44, M6. Sheltered, level site ideal for Hadrian's Wall, historic Carlisle, north lakes, Borders and Gretna. AA 2 pennant. Dog exercising field. Shops, PO, doctor in Longtown 1m away. Open March 1-Oct 31.

(4m). Dalston Hall Caravan Park, Dalston Hall, Carlisle, Cumbria CA5 7JX. 01228 710165. Owner: Nigel, Elizabeth, Ricky, Dion and Kelly Holder. Off M6 exit 42 to Dalston Village on B5299, direction Carlisle 1m N of Dalston. Small, well maintained, family run park set in 94 acres of wooded park; in easy reach of Lake District, Solway Firth and Border Counties. 9-hole golf course. Clubhouse. Laundry. Playground. Hot showers. Fishing. Hardstandings. Open March 1-Oct 31.

(4m). Dandy Dinmont Caravan & Camping Site, Blackford, Carlisle, Cumbria CA6 4EA. 01228 674611. www.caravan-camping-carlisle.itgo.com. Owner: Mrs B Inglis. Leave M6 J44. Take A7 Galashiels road, park is about 1.5m N on the R after Blackford village sign. Good base for visiting Carlisle. Only 45mins from Lake District. An ideal overnight halt. Superstore, PO, horse riding in 2m – golf, hospital in 4m. Open March 1-Oct 31.

(6.5m). Englethwaite Hall Caravan Club Site, Armathwaite, Carlisle, Cumbria CA4 9SY. 01228 560202. www.caravanclub.co.uk. Owner: The Caravan Club. See website for directions. A tranquil site, located in the Eden Valley. No sanitation. Dog walk and exercise field on site. Non-members welcome. No tents. MV service point. Great for walkers. All hardstanding, part sloping, gas, gaz, information room, storage, quiet and peaceful off peak. Open March-Nov.

(10m). Glendale Caravan Park, Port Carlisle, Carlisle, Cumbria CA5 5DJ. 01697 351317. Owner: Wryeside Caravans. On B5307. Licensed club, dancing weekends. Bar meals. Play area. Open March-Nov.

Hylton Park Holiday Centre, Eden Street, Silloth, Carlisle, Cumbria CA7 4AY. 01697 331707. www.stanwix.com. Owner: E&RH Stanwix. On A596 at Wigton take B5302 to Silloth. In Silloth follow

6 MOTOR CARAVAN & CAMPING PARKS 2009

CUMBRIA

See page 5 for key to symbols and abbreviations

signs to Hylton Park, 0.5m. Ideal base to tour lakes and Borders. Sister park to Stanwix. Full facilities available to Hylton Park holidaymakers. Brochure. AA 4-star rating, 70%. 18-hole golf course 1m. Open March 1-Oct 31.

(8m). Oakbank Lakes Country Park, Longtown, Carlisle, Cumbria CA6 5NA. 01228 791108. 1m N of Longtown on the A7. 60-acre site with 4 lakes; carp and trout. Salmon and sea fishing available. Bird sanctuary. Game bird breeding unit.

(4m). Orton Grange Caravan Park, Wigton Road, Carlisle, Cumbria CA5 6LA. 01228 710252. www.barton-parkhomes. co.uk. Owner: Barton Park Homes Ltd. On A595. Camping accessory shop. Outdoor heated pool. TV lounge. Pay-phone. Automated laundry. Play area. Hardstandings. Dish-washing sinks. Children allowed.

COCKERMOUTH

(4m). Wheatsheaf Inn, Low Lorton, Cockermouth, Cumbria CA13 9UW. 01900 85268. www.wheatsheafinnlorton. co.uk. Owner: Mr M Cockbain & Miss J Williams. On B5289 towards Buttermere and Loweswater. Fishing available: coarse, trout, salmon and sea trout. Cocker and Derwent rivers. Shops, doctors, PO in 4m. Greta 8m. Open March-Nov.

(4.5m). Whinfell Caravan Park & Campsite, Lorton Vale, Cockermouth, Cumbria CA13 ORQ. 01900 85260. r.a.mcclellan@talk21.co.uk. Owner: Mr RA McClellan. Off B5289 through Low Lorton, SP. Small, secluded park, well-placed for the western lakes and fells and set in the tranquility of the Vale of Lorton. 3m to nearest lake. 4m to Cockermouth town centre. Open March 15-Nov 15.

(0.5m). Wyndham Hall Caravan Park, Old Keswick Road, Cockermouth, Cumbria CA13 9SF. 01900 822571. www.wyndhamholidaypark.co.uk. On old A66 Keswick to Cockermouth, turn R at Castle Inn sign (end of Bassenthwaite Lake) then bear L to Embleton-Cockermouth, entrance on L on outskirts of Cockermouth. Tents & tourers welcome. 10 cabins and 8 holiday caravans for hire. Licensed club. Pool tables, table tennis etc. Children's swings. Shower and toilet blocks. Holiday caravans for sale. Nearby swimming pool and sports centre. Shops and PO are 0.5m away and in walking distance. Open from 1 March-31 Oct.

CONISTON

(1m). Coniston Hall Campsite, Hawes Bank, Coniston, Cumbria LA21 8AS. 01539 441223. Owner: Mr Wilson. S of Coniston village centre. Turn off A593 at Hawes Bank towards the lake. Size of site: 20 acres. Open March-Oct.

(3m). Cook Farm Camping Site, Torver, Coniston, Cumbria LA21 8BP. 01539 441453. Owner: Mrs J Leeson. S of Coniston via A593. Quiet site close to Lake Coniston and surrounding countryside. Cold water tap only. Snacks available on request. Breakfast on request. B&B guest house on site.

(3m). Hoathwaite Farm, Torver, Coniston, Cumbria LA21 8AX. 01539 441449. Owner: Mrs J Wilson. A590-3m S of Coniston on Torver road turn L at green railings. Turn L again over first cattle grid. Farm site with basic facilities, near lake. Open seasonally for static privately owned vans. Lake fishing; shops, doctor, PO 3m; golf 10m. Open all year for touring and motorhomes — numbers limited unless you have own chemical toilet. Dogs welcome by arrangement.

(1.25m). Park Coppice Caravan Club Site, Coniston, Cumbria LA21 8LA. 01539 441555. www.caravanclub.co.uk. Owner: The Caravan Club. See website for directions. Set in 63 acres of National Trust woodland with facilities for young families, inc junior orienteering, nature trail and toddler's play area. Near lake for sailing and watersports. Advance booking essential. Non members and tent campers welcome. Toilet block and laundry facilities. MV service point. Fishing. Ideal for walking. Open March-Nov.

DENT

(4m). Ewegales Farm Caravan Site, Ewegales Farm, Dent, Cumbria LA10 5RH. 01539 625440. Owner: Mr JW Akriag. Leave M6 at J37 on to A684 to Sedbergh. Site 4m E of Dent. Shower. Good for fishing – flat field by river.

High Laning Caravan Park, High Laning, Dent, Cumbria LA10 5QJ. 01539 625239. www.highlaning.co.uk. Owner: Mrs M Taylor. M6, J37 SP Sedbergh A684. Dent is a further 5m from Sedbergh. Adjacent to Dent picturesque, historic, cobbled village in the Yorkshire Dales National Park.

ESKDALE

Fisherground Farm Campsite, Eskdale, Cumbria CA19 1TF. 01946 723349. www.fishergroundcampsite. co.uk. Owner: Mr & Mrs Parkin. Leave M6 J 36, follow A590 to Barrow, turn to Workington A5092. R to Ulpha, L to Eskdale, R at King George. Site on L. In this quiet valley peace is the watchword. Camp fires allowed. Hard access road. Member of Cumbria Tourist Board. Adventure playground. Miniature railway. Pets welcome. AA 3 pennant. AA 'Award for Excellence'. ETB 3 rosettes. Open March-Nov.

GRANGE-OVER-SANDS

(4m). Greaves Farm Caravan Park, Field Broughton, Grange-over-Sands, Cumbria LA11 6HU. 01539 536329. Owner: Mrs E Rigg. M6, J36 follow A590 SP Barrow. About 1m before Newby Bridge, L at cross roads Cartmel/Staveley. Site 1m on L before church. Small, quiet, family-run, grassy site with 6-berth luxury fully-serviced caravans. Ideal for exploring the lakes. Personal supervision. Booking essential. Calor Gas. AA 3 Pennant. Open March-Oct.

(3.5m). Lakeland Leisure Park, Moor Lane, Flookburgh, Grange-over-Sands, Cumbria LA11 7LT. 01539 558556. www.lakeland-park.co.uk. Owner: Bourne Leisure Ltd. M6, J36 on to A590. Turn L on to A6/A590 for Barrow-In-Furness. B5277 through Grange-over-Sands, then Allithwaite and into Flookburgh. Turn L at the village square and travel 1m down this road to the park. Convenience store. Entertainment complex, arcade, restaurant. Indoor and outdoor heated pools. Tennis courts. Pony-trekking, stables on park. Welcome Host Award, Investor in People. David Bellamy Gold Conservation Award. Open Mar-Nov.

(0.5m). Lingwood Park, Middle Fellgate Farm, Cartmel Road, Grange-over-Sands, Cumbria LA11 7QA. 015395 32271. Turn R off B5277 SP Cartmel Road. In 0.5m call at Middle Fellgate Farm. Site 200 yards on R. Open March 1-Jan 10.

(2.5m). Meathop Fell Caravan Club Site, Grange-over-Sands, Cumbria LA11 6RB. 01539 532912. www. caravanclub.co.uk. Owner: The Caravan Club. See website for directions. An ideal base for N Lancashire and southern Lake District. Gas. Advance booking essential bank hols, Xmas and New Year. MV service point, playground. Non-members welcome. No tents. Toilet blocks with privacy cubicles, laundry facilities and baby/toddler washroom. Golf nearby. Ideal for families.

www.motorcaravanmagazine.co.uk MOTOR CARAVAN & CAMPING PARKS 2009 **7**

CUMBRIA

(4.5m). Oak Head Caravan Park, Ayside, Grange-over-Sands, Cumbria LA11 6JA. *01539 531475*. Owner: Mrs A Scott. M6, 36,14m on A590 to Newby Bridge. 2m to Lake Windermere. 4.5m to Grange-over-Sands railway station. Follow signs for Ayside along new A590 bypass. Garage, shops, PO, café/restaurant, dairy produces, fishing, golf within 4m Open March 1-Oct 31.

HOLMROOK

(9m). Camping & Caravanning Club Site – Eskdale, Boot, Holmrook, Cumbria CA19 1TH. *01946 723253*. Owner: Camping and Caravanning Club. When approaching from A6, J38 allow plenty of time, follow the road numbers A590-A5092-A595. Eskdale boasts England's highest peak and deepest lake. Walking distance from site is Hardknott Fort, Stanley Gill Waterfall and Muncaster Castle, licensed shop and car hire available. Open March 3-Oct 31.

(2m). Seven Acres Caravan & Camping Park, Holmrook, Cumbria CA19 1YD. *01946 725480*. 1m S of Gosforth on A595 west Cumbria coast road. Flat, grassy, sheltered park. Payphones. Playground. Golf, fell walking, mountain climbing, fishing, boating, rambling, horseriding all available nearby. PO, shops, pubs, restaurants and cafés in Gosforth. Open March-Oct.

(2.5m). The Old Post Office Camp Site, Santon Bridge, Wasdale, Holmrook, Cumbria CA19 1UY. *01946 726286*. www.theoldpostofficecampsite.co.uk. Owner: SR & J Bucknall. A595 to Holmbrook, 2.5m to Santon Bridge, over bridge from Bridge Inn. Small level touring site beside the river Irt. Fishing on site. Mobile van daily. Bridge Inn/Hotel nearby. Close to miniature railway and ancient castle. 2.5m from Wasdale Lake, 5m from sea, golf and doctor. 3m from PO, shops, riding, diving. Mobile van daily. Laundry, washer, dryer now available. Open March 1-Nov 15.

KENDAL

(2m). Camping & Caravanning Club Site – Kendal, Millcrest, Shap Road, Kendal, Cumbria LA9 6NY. *01539 741363*. www.campingandcaravanningclub.co.uk. Owner: Camping & Caravanning Club. 1.5m N of Kendal; on the R of A6. N of nameplate 'Skelsmergh'. A good base for touring the Lake District. Near forest of Bowland and Leighton Moss Bird Reserve. All units accepted. Non-members welcome. Site shop has essentials. Deals for families and backpackers. Open March-Oct.

(2.5m). Camping & Caravanning Park – Windermere, Ashes Lane, Staveley, Kendal, Cumbria LA8 9JS. *01539 821119*. www.campingandcaravanningclub.co.uk. Owner: The Camping & Caravanning Club. Signed off A591. 0.75m from roundabout with B5284 towards Windermere. The site is in an unrivalled rural location of the Lake District. Overlooking the fells of South Lakes. Set in 22 acres and located 5m south of Windermere, close to the village of Staveley. Non-members welcome. All unit accepted. Deals for families and backpackers. On site facilities include a licensed bar, take-away, dedicated packbackers facilities, laundry, toilet and showers, play area and dog walk. Fishing, golf, horse riding and watersports available locally (3-5m). Loo Of The Year (5 stars). David Bellamy Gold Conservation Award. Open March-Jan.

(3m). Low Park Wood Caravan Club Site, Sedgwick, Kendal, Cumbria LA8 0JP. *01539 560186*. www.caravanclub.co.uk. Owner: The Caravan Club. See website for directions. Peaceful location on National trust land, with several walks from site. River fishing (permits available). Gas. Advance booking essential weekends, Bank Holidays, July and Aug. Dog walk. Non-members welcome. No tents. Toilet blocks with laundry facilities. MV service point. Ideal for families. Varied bird life. Open April-Nov.

(3m). Pound Farm Park, Crook, Kendal, Cumbria LA8 8JZ. *01539 821220*. www.northdales.co.uk. Owner: North Dales LLP. M6, J36 follow A591 to roundabout. Exit roundabout on to B5284, Pound Farm 1.8m on L. Sheltered park 5m from Lake Windermere. Newly developed pitches available for lodges. Golf, cinema & town for shopping 3m. Open March 3-Oct 31 (camping & touring), March 3-Jan 6.

(3m). Ratherheath Lane Caravan Park, Chain House, Kendal, Cumbria LA8 8JU. *01539 821154*. www.lakedistrictcaravans.co.uk. Owner: David Wilson. Exit M6, J36 follow A591 for Windermere. Take B5284 to Crook. Park is 1.5m on the R. Close to all Lake District attractions. Small, suits couple. Open March 1-Nov 15.

(6m). Waters Edge Caravan Park, Crooklands, Kendal, Cumbria LA7 7NN. *01539 567708*. www.watersedgecaravanpark.co.uk. Owner: Water's Edge Caravan Park Ltd. 0.75m from M6 junction 36 (follow A65 Kirkby Lonsdale and then A65 Crooklands at roundabout) site is on R before Crooklands hotel. Family run park with modern facilities. Easy access to Lakes, Yorkshire. Morecambe Bay lounge and licensed bar. Restaurant in 300yd. Takeaway 3m. Open countryside. Nearby fishing, tennis, golf, riding, etc. Open March 1-Nov 14.

KESWICK

(3m). Burns Farm Caravan & Camping Site, St Johns-in-the-Vale, Keswick, Cumbria CA12 4RR. *01768 779225*. www.burnsfarm@btconnect.com. Owner: Mrs Linda Lamb. Small, quiet site with beautiful views 15m from M6 j40, take A66 Keswick, second L past Threlkeld village, SP Castlerigg-Stone Circle and Burns Farm caravan site. Quiet family run site. Beautiful views. Perfect walking country. Faclities block. 3 cottages for hire. AA 3 pennants. Open March-Nov.

(0.5m). Camping & Caravanning Club Site – Derwentwater, Derwentwater Caravan Park, Crow Park Road, Keswick, Cumbria CA12 5EN. *01768 772579*. www.campingandcaravanningclub.co.uk. Owner: Camping & Caravanning Club. From M6 J40 follow A66 for 13m, SP Keswick/Workington. At roundabout SP Keswick turn L. At T junction turn L to Keswick town centre. At mini roundabout turn R. Take road to R of church. Site on L. In the heart of the Lake District National Park, beside the peace of Lake Derwentwater. Non-members welcome. Caravans and motorcaravans only (No tents). All service pitches available. No awnings permitted. Golf, pony trekking, rock climbing, paragliding and swimming are all available in the area. Deals for families and backpackers. David Bellamy Gold Conservation Award. Open March – Nov.

(0.5m). Camping & Caravanning Club Site – Keswick, Crow Park Road, Keswick, Cumbria CA12 5EP. *01768 772392*. www.campingandcaravanningclub.co.uk. Owner: Camping & Caravanning Club. Off A66, follow signs for Keswick. Turn L at roundabout, turn L at T-junction. At mini-roundabout turn R, take road to R of church. Turn R up narrow lane, after rugby club. Beautiful woodland park with lake frontage and jetty. Some hardstanding. Non-members welcome. All units accepted. Deals for families and backpackers. David Bellamy Gold Conservation Award. Open Feb-Nov.

(1.5m). Castlerigg Hall Caravan &

CUMBRIA

**Camping Park, Castlerigg Hall,
Keswick, Cumbria CA12 4TE.** *017687 74499.* www.castlerigg.co.uk. Owner: Mrs B & Mr DD Jackson. Turn R off A591 Keswick to Ambleside. Spectacular views of lakes and mountains. Tea room. Fully serviced pitches available. Fees on application. Open mid March-mid Nov.

■ **(2m) Dalebottom Farm Caravan & Camping Park, Naddle, Keswick, Cumbria CA12 4TF.** *01687 72276.* Owner: Messrs Kitching. 2m S of Keswick on A591 Windermere road. The heart of Lakeland. Open March 1-Nov 1.

(4m). Low Manesty Caravan Club Site, Manesty, Keswick, Cumbria CA12 5UG. *01768 777275.* www.caravanclub.co.uk. Owner: The Caravan Club. See website for directions. 2m from Borrowdale. Set in National Trust woodland, close to Derwentwater with views over fells. Ideal location for lakes and walking. Own sanitation required. Advance booking advised and essential Bank Holidays, June to end Sept and late Oct. Non-members admitted. No tents. MV service point. Fishing and watersports. Some hardstanding, steel awning pegs required. Gas and Gaz, dog walk nearby, quiet and peaceful off peak. NCN cycle route in 5m. Recycling facilities. Open March-Nov.

(8.5m). North Lakes Caravan Park, Bewaldeth, Bassenthwaite Lake, Keswick, Cumbria CA13 9SY. *01768 776510.* www.northlakesholidays.co.uk. Owner: Messrs J A & P R Frew. On A591. N of Keswick. 30-acre park for people who enjoy peace and quiet in the less commercialised northern end of the Lake District. Bar. Laundry. Facilities block. TV area. Coarse fishing lake. Open March 1-Nov 14.

(2.5m). Scotgate Holiday Park, Braithwaite, Keswick, Cumbria CA12 5TF. *01768 778343.* www.scotgateholidaypark.co.uk. Owner: Mr Stuart. W of Keswick, just off A66 on B592 entrance to Braithwaite village. Licensed shop and restaurant. 7 chalets for hire also available. Open March-Oct.

Stonethwaite Farm, Borrowdale, Keswick, Cumbria. *01768 777234.* Owner: VB Brownlee. In Stonethwaite village. Through village, along track for 0.5m. Campsite alongside stream on L. Open March-Apr.

KIRKBY LONSDALE

Cragside, Hutton Roof, Kirkby Lonsdale, Cumbria. *01524 271415.* Owner: Mr Dixon. 6m from M6 at Carnforth, turn off A6 for Burton. Hutton Roof is 3m W of Kirkby Lonsdale, off A65 or W off B6254 at Whittington. Quiet site in countryside. Shops and buses 3m away. Fees on application. Advance booking advised.

(0.5m). Woodclose Caravan Park, Casterton, Kirkby Lonsdale, Cumbria LA6 2SE. *01524 271597.* www.woodclosepark.com. Owner: Lake District Estates Co Ltd. M6, J36 then A65, 0.5m SE of Kirkby Lonsdale. Quiet, rural site in easy driving distance of the Lake District, Yorkshire Dales and seaside. The park is well established, spreading over 9 acres and in a priviledged location in an area of outstanding natural beauty. Children's play area on site. Private and secluded yet only a short stroll from one of the most delightful market towns one could wish to find – Kirkby Lonsdale. Golf, fishing, horse riding, leisure club. Internet café and cycle hire. David Bellamy Gold Conservation Award. Open March 1-Oct 31.

KIRKBY STEPHEN

(4m). Bowber Head Caravan Site, Ravenstonedale, Kirkby Stephen, Cumbria CA17 4NL. *01539 623254.* www.bowberhead.co.uk. Owner: Mr W & Mrs C Hamer. 4.5m S of Kirkby Stephen, SP off the A683. Excellent centre for both the Lakes and the Dales. Beautiful views of Wildboar and the Howgill Fells. TV hook-ups. Bottled gas available. Payphone. Dogs allowed under control. Camping and Caravanning Club listed. Classic coach service operated from site.

(1m). Pennine View Caravan & Camping Park, Station Road, Kirkby Stephen, Cumbria CA17 4SZ. *01768 371717.* Owner: Mr & Mrs C Sim. M6, J38 follow A685 for 11m, site on R. A66 or

Brough follow A685 for 5m site on L. Open early March-end Oct.

LAMPLUGH

Dockray Meadow Caravan Club Site, Lamplugh, Cumbria CA14 4SH. *01946 861357.* www.caravanclub.co.uk. Owner: The Caravan Club. See website for directions. 4m from Ennerdale Bridge. Conveniently set on N edge of Lake District with mountain walks off site. All hardstanding. Gas. Advance booking essential Bank Holidays. No sanitation. MV service point. Non-members welcome. No tents. Fishing nearby. Good for walking. Part sloping, steel awning pegs required, gas ad gaz. Information room, dog walk nearby, quiet and peaceful off peak, NCN cycle route in 5m. Open March-Nov.

Inglenook Caravan Park, Lamplugh, Cumbria CA14 4SH. *01946 861240.* www.inglenookcaravanpark.co.uk. Owner: Mr & Mrs John Hoey. Leave A66 at Cockermouth on to A5086 to Lamplugh. L past 'Lamplugh Tip' pub. Site 0.5m on R. 7m from Cockermouth/Workington. Flat site with tarmac and gravel roads in beautiful surroundings. Fishing and horseriding nearby. Beach 10m. Play area. Rose Award.

MARYPORT

(6m). Manor House Caravan Park, Edderside Road, Allonby, Maryport, Cumbria CA15 6RA. *01900 881236.* www.manorhousepark.co.uk. Owner: Simon Brooks. From Maryport, take A596, pick up the B5300 to Allonby. 1m after Allonby take a R turn to Edderside. Licensed club. Sauna and fitness room. Open March 1-Nov 15.

(5m). Spring Lea Caravan Park, Allonby, Maryport, Cumbria CA15 6QF. *01900 881331.* www.springlea.co.uk. Owner: Mr J Williamson. Situated midway between Maryport and Silloth on B5300. Open March-Oct.

MILLOM

(1m). Butterflowers Holiday Homes, Port Haverigg, Millom, Cumbria LA18

DALEBOTTOM FARM CARAVAN & CAMPING PARK
NADDLE KESWICK, CUMBRIA CA12 4TF Tel: 017687 72176
"HEART OF LAKELAND"

Peacefully situated in the picturesque Naddle Valley two miles south of Keswick on A591 Windermere road. Touring & Tenting pitches. Electric hook ups. Toilet & Shower Facilities. Static Caravans & Country Cottages to let. Colour TV Toilet & Shower Facilities in all units. Static Caravans Tourers Tents March 1st to November 1st. Country Cottages available all year. S.A.E. for brochure to: Proprietors: Messrs Kitching

www.motorcaravanmagazine.co.uk   MOTOR CARAVAN & CAMPING PARKS 2009 **9**

CUMBRIA

4HB. *01229 772880.* www.butterflowers.net. Follow signs from Harbour Hotel past the Beach Café, the entrance is on the R before the Inshore Rescue. Indoor swimming pool.

MILNTHORPE

(4m). Fell End Caravan Park, Slackhead Road, Hale, Milnthorpe, Cumbria LA7 7BS. *01539 562122.* www.fellendcaravanpark.co.uk. Owner: Pure Leisure Group. Off M6 junction 35, off A6 at sign marked 'Sites'. Next to wildlife oasis just past Cumbria border sign. Follow brown signs. Close to Silverdale/Arnside area of outstanding natural beauty. Beautifully developed and landscaped park incorporating natural features including woodlands and limestone pavements. Shop, bar, restaurant. Shops 2m, Golf course 3m. Cinema 15m. David Bellamy Gold Conservation Award. Open March 1-Jan 14.

(2.5m). Hall More Caravan Park, Hale, Milnthorpe, Cumbria LA7 7BP. *01524 781453.* www.hallmorecaravanpark.co.uk. Owner: Pure Leisure Group. M6, J35. Follow A6 towards Milnthorpe for 4m. Take the first L marked Arnside with tourism signs for sites. Follow the unclassified road and the park is less than 1m. Three-acre trout lake on premises. Close to Silverdale/Arnside area of outstanding natural beauty. Good base for walking and exploring. Shops 2m, golf course 3m, cycle hire 5m, cinema 15m. David Bellamy Silver Conservation Award. Open March-Dec (statics), March-Nov (tourers).

Hazelslack Caravan Site, Carr Bank House, Carr Bank, Milnthorpe, Cumbria LA7 7LG. *01524 761974.* Owner: Mr Alf Barber. 3m SW of Milnthorpe. From Milnthorpe follow Arnside road. Go almost to Arnside then SP for Carr Bank and bear R along this road, turning L after 0.5m along narrow lane. Site 200yd on R. Edge of Lake District and near coast. Open March-Oct.

Millness Hill Holiday Park, Crooklands, Milnthorpe, Cumbria LA7 7NU. *01539 567306.* www.millness.co.uk. Owner: Mr C Ellis. Situated 0.5m from J36 on M6. Take A65 towards Kirkby Lonsdale and turn L at the next roundabout towards Endmoor. Park is a further 100yd on the L. Coarse fishing available on site and use of rowing boats. Free videos and paperbacks available from the lending library. Visitors renting self-catering homes can also make the most of the reduced cost membership fees at Kendal Leisure Centre and its swimming pool, sauna, sunbed, badminton, squash, table tennis, bowls and fitness centre.

PENRITH

(7m). Beckses Caravan Park, Penruddock, Penrith, Cumbria CA11 0RX. *01768 483224.* Owner: Mr John Teasdale. M6, J40 take A66 (SP Keswick). Continue for about 6m, then turn R on to B5288 (SP Greystoke). Beckses Park is 150yd on the R. Small, pleasant site on the edge of Lake District National Park. AA 3-pennants. English Lakes member. Open Easter-Oct 31.

Camping & Caravanning Club site – Troutbeck, Hutton Moor End, Troutbeck, Penrith, Cumbria CA11 0SX. *01768 779615.* www.campingandcaravanningclub.co.uk. Owner: Camping & Caravanning Club. From M6, Penrith, turn on to A66 towards Keswick. Sharp L turn at SP Wallthwaite. Continue and site is on L. Superb location in unbeatable walking country. Keswick and Penrith readily accessible. Local facilities for archery, horseriding. Coast to coast cycleway passes directly opposite the site. Close to Whinlatter Forest, England's only true mountain forest. Deals for family. Open June-Nov.

(7m). Cove Caravan Park, Ullswater, Watermillock, Penrith, Cumbria CA11 0LS. *01768 486549.* www.cove-park.co.uk. Owner: Mr L Wride. From M6 J40, A66 Keswick, roundabout A592 to Ullswater. T Junction, R, Brackenrigg Inn – R. Cove Park is 1.5m on L. RAC appointed. Clean & superb location. Peaceful park sheltered by nearby fells and overlooking Lake Ullswater. Excellent facilities, well maintained. Shop next door, lake 1.5m. David Bellamy Gold Conservation Award. Open March-Nov.

(9m). Cross Fell Caravan & Camping Park, The Fox Inn, Ousby, Penrith, Cumbria CA10 1QA. *01768 881374.* www.crossfell.biz. Owner: Mr & Mrs RG Thomas. 9m NE of Penrith. Leave M6, J40 on to A686 alston road. Take second R, 1.5m after Langwathby. site is 2m at Ousby. Flat, well-drained site. Behind village Inn. Beautiful countryside. Open March 1-Jan 10.

(7m). Dunroamin, Cross Dormont, Howtown, Penrith, Cumbria CA10 2NA. *017684 86537.* www.crossdormont.com. Owner: Mr AK & Mrs AC Bell. 2m from Pooley Bridge on the Howtown road, SP. Best view of the lake on the Howtown road. Small quiet family run site. Hot showers and clean toilets. PO 1.5m. Doctor 7m. Lake side access for boats, fishing, etc. Open March-end Oct.

(8m). Eden Valley Holidays, Newby End Farm, Newby, Penrith, Cumbria CA10 3EX. *01931 714 338.* www.newbyendfarm.co.uk. Owner: Jenny & David Jones. Midway between J39 & J40 on M6. In middle of triangle made by Penrith, Appleby and Shap. 1m S of Morland. 12 pitches for any kind of units. Open April 1-Oct 31.

(9m). Gill Head Caravan & Camping Park, Gill Head Farm, Troutbeck, Penrith, Cumbria CA11 0ST. *01768 779652.* Owner: Mrs J Wilson. Midway between Penrith and Keswick on A66, take A5091 (Ullswater Road). First R 200yd from junction we are first on R. AA 4 pennants. A beautiful maintained site with panoramic views of Northern Fells with modern facilities in ideal location for lakes. Open April-Nov.

(14m). Gillside Caravan & Camping Site, Gillside, Glenridding, Penrith, Cumbria CA11 0QQ. *01768 482346.* www.gillsidecaravanandcampingsite.co.uk. Owner: Messrs Lightfoot. Take the A592 to Glenridding, SP for Gillside Camping first L after Travellers Rest. Situated at the foot of Helvellyn and 5mins walk from Lake Ullswater. Bunkhouse accommodation. Open March 1-Nov 15.

(0.5m). Hillcroft Park, Roe Head Lane, Pooley Bridge, Penrith, Cumbria CA10 2LT. *01768 486363.* www.northdales.co.uk. Owner: North Dales LLP. Off M6 follow Northlakes, then Pooley Bridge, through village to crossroad, straight on. Elevated location with magnificent views. Ideal for fell walking, sailing, windsurfing and canoeing. Boat hire nearby. Dogs allowed if kept on a lead. Pooley Bridge 250yd, shops, PO etc. Open March 3-Jan 6.

Low Moor, Kirkby Thore, Penrith, Cumbria CA10 1XG. *01768 361231.* www.lowmoorpark.co.uk. Owner: Mrs M Farrell. On A66 Appleby (5m) to Penrith – trans Pennine route. Open country and all round views. Local authority approved criteria. Open April/Easter-Oct.

(6m). Park Foot Caravan & Camping Park, Howtown Road, Pooley Bridge, Penrith, Cumbria CA10 2NA. *01768 486309.* www.parkfootullswater.co.uk. Owner: Mrs Bell & Miss Allen. M6 J40 –

CUMBRIA

A66 Keswick/Ullswater, take A592 Ullswater, L at junction. In Pooley Bridge take Howtown road R at church. R at crossroads 1m on L. Views of Lake Ullswater with access. Licensed bar, restaurant and take away, entertainment. Laundry, car wash, public telephone, children's club during summer school holidays. Sailing, windsurfing, canoeing, fishing, walking, ponytrekking, tennis, bike hire, shop and two play areas. Calor Gas. 6m golf, cinema, shopping centre. RAC 3 pennants. Open 15 March-15 Nov.

(2m). Stonefold Caravan Park, Newbiggin, Stainton, Penrith, Cumbria CA11 0HP. 01768 866383. www.stonefold.co.uk. Owner: Graham & Gill Harrington. Leave M6 J40 and take A66 Keswick road, turn R at sign for Newbiggin and Stonefold is 1min drive on the L. No tents. Quiet small level peaceful touring site set in a beautiful panoramic position overlooking the Eden Valley with the majestic Pennine Hills in the background. Golf, swimming, fishing, quad biking, horse riding, sailing, tennis, bowls all in 4m. Pub 1m. Farm shop 1m. Lovely walks. Open March 1-Jan 7/East-Oct for touring park.

(8m). Thanet Well Park, Greystoke, Penrith, Cumbria CA11 0XX. 01768 484262. Owner: North Dales LLP. Off M6 junction 41, B5305. 6m towards Wigton turn L for Lamonby, follow caravan signs. Nearest town 20mins. Good walking. Golf, cinema, shopping 20mins. Open March 3-Oct 31 (camping & touring), March 3-Jan 6 (lodges).

(6m). The Quiet Caravan & Camping Site, Watermillock, Ullswater, Penrith, Cumbria CA11 0LS. 01768 486337. www.thequietsite.co.uk. Owner: Daniel Holder. M6, J40. A66 to Keswick. A592 to Ullswater. Turn R at lake, turn R at Brackerrigg Inn. Site on R after 1.5m. Family run site in idyllic location. Large adventure playground. Caravan and motorcaravan storage available. Open March 1-Nov 14.

(9m). Troutbeck Camping & Caravanning Club Site, Troutbeck, Penrith, Cumbria CA11 0SX. 01768 779149. www.campingandcaravanningclub.co.uk. Owner: Susan & Fraser Smith. On A66 9.5m W of M6 J40, turn L for Wallthwaite, site SP. 8m from Keswick. Quiet site for family and walkers. Licensed shop. Golf course just down the road. Rookin House activity centre 2m Open March-Nov plus Xmas and New Year.

(9m). Troutbeck Head Caravan Club Site, Troutbeck, Penrith, Cumbria CA11 0SS. 01768 483521. www.caravanclub.co.uk. Owner: The Caravan Club. See website for directions. Fabulous for nature lovers and walkers. The site sits in a valley alongside a babbling brook, below Great Mell Fell. Toilet blocks, baby and toddler washroom and laundry facilities. MV service point. Games room and play area. Dog walk on site. Fishing, golf, watersports and NCN route nearby. Good area for walking. Facilities for disabled. Ideal for families. Non-members welcome. Open March-Jan.

(7m). Ullswater Caravan Camping & Marine Park, Watermillock, Penrith, Cumbria CA11 0LR. 01768 486666. www.uccmp.co.uk. Owner: Messrs Dobinson. M6, J40, on A592 turn R SP Longthwaite & Watermillock Church. At telephone box. Playground. Bar. Games and TV room. Shop. Lake access 1m. Fishing, boating. Ideal for touring the lakes. Open March 1-Nov 14.

(5m). Waterfoot Caravan Park, Ullswater, Pooley Bridge, Penrith, Cumbria CA11 0JF. 01768 486302. www.waterfootpark.co.uk. Owner: Lake District Estates Co Ltd. Take J40, M6, join A66 for about 1m then take A592, park is on RH side. Sat Nav not compatible. Parkland site in grounds of a Georgian mansion. Site is well laid out with serviced static caravan pitches and an excellent touring area with a mix of hardstanding for ease of siting and lawn areas for awnings or recreation. Children's play area on site. Walking distance of Ullswater 'Steamers' Pier for cruises on Lake Ullswater. Private boat launch and dinghy storage facilities. Water sports, pony trekking nearby. Fishing, golf, cinema, shopping, lake cruises. David Bellamy Gold Conservation Award. Open March 1-Nov 14.

Waterside House Campsite, Howtown Road, Pooley Bridge, Penrith, Cumbria CA10 2NA. 01768 486332. www.watersidefarm-campsite.co.uk. Owner: Messrs Lowis. M6, J40. A66 1m then A592 to Ullswater, L a the lake for Pooley Bridge then R at church and R again. 2nd campsite on R. Waterside Campsite is situated on the shores of Lake Ullswater. It is an ideal base for sailing, canoeing, walking and biking. Pooley Bridge village is 1m away and can be reached by lakeside footpath or road. Penrith town is just a further 6m. Open March-Oct.

RAVENGLASS

(0.25m). Camping & Caravanning Club Site – Ravenglass, Ravenglass, Cumbria CA18 1SR. 01229 717250. www.campingandcaravanningclub.co.uk. Owner: Camping & Caravanning Club. Leave A595 SP to Ravenglass. Turn L at 30mph sign into private road. Site entrance is 25yd on L. The site is set in 5 acres of mature woodland which was once part of the Muncaster Castle Estate. This is walkers' paradise on Cumbria's western coast, where the Lake District National Park meets the sea. On site facilities include toilet, showers, laundry, CDP, washing up sinks and a play area. All unit types accepted. Non-members welcome. Special deals for families and backpackers. Open March-mid Nov.

SEASCALE

(6m). Church Stile Camp Site, Wasdale, Seascale, Cumbria CA20 1ET. 01946 726252. www.churchsite.com. Owner: Mr Alan John & Mrs Ruth Knight. Off A595. 4m E of Gosforth to Nether Wasdale site by church. Excellent climbing. Beautiful views, pretty little village. Good for families and couples. Fell walking near lake, sheltered, well run family site. Two inns serving bar meals. Sorry no touring caravans. Shower block newly refurbished. Open Mid March-Oct 31.

National Trust Camp Site, Wasdale Head, Wasdale, Seascale, Cumbria CA20 1EX. 01946 726220. wasdale.campsite@nationaltrust.org.uk. www.wasdalecampsite.org.uk. Owner: National Trust. At the head of Wasdale, 9m E of Gosforth. Access from unclassified road on the W shore of Wast Water. Base for fell walking and rock climbing. Fees on application. No bookings. Head Warden: R Jenkinson.

SEDBERGH

(5m). Conder Farm, Dent, Sedbergh, Cumbria LA10 5QT. 01539 625377. Owner: M J W Hodgkinson. Turn in Sedbergh (J37, M6) Dent 5.5m. From Sedbergh turn R at George and Dragon (Dent), from Hawes turn L at George and Dragon. Small, family site of 1.5 acres. Quiet with beautiful views. Shop 500yd. Open March-Nov.

(2.5m). Cross Hall Farm Caravan Site, Cautley, Sedbergh, Cumbria LA10 5LY. 015396 20668. crosshall@btopenworld.com. www.cautleycaravans.co.uk. Owner: Mr T R Harper. Off A683 to Kirkby Stephen and Brough overlooking the Howgill Fells and 1.5m to Cautley Spout. Quiet, family

www.motorcaravanmagazine.co.uk   MOTOR CARAVAN & CAMPING PARKS 2009 **11**

CUMBRIA

park nestling at the foot of the Howgill fells. Abundance of walking, flora and fauna. Shopping 2.5m, golf course 4m. Fell walking from site. Lake District nearby. Open April-Oct.

Yore House Farm Caravan & Camping Park, Yore House, Lunds, Sedbergh, Cumbria LA10 5PX. *01969 667358.* Owner: Jim & Liz Pedley. 6m Hawes, 10m Sedbergh on A684 near Moorcock pub. Quiet, farm site beside river Ure. Close to N Yorkshire border. Open April-Oct.

SILLOTH

(3m). Rowanbank Caravan Park, Beckfoot, Silloth, Cumbria CA7 4LA. *01697 331653.* Owner: Terry & Kay Watson. On B5300 Silloth to Maryport coast road. SP in village of Beckfoot. Small, family run site with all modern facilities. Set in beautfiul quiet countryside next to unspoilt Solway beaches. Open March-Nov.

(0.5m). Solway Holiday Village, Skinburness Drive, Silloth, Cumbria CA7 4QQ. *01697 331236/01697 3.* solway@ haganslesiure.co.uk. www. haganslesiure.co.uk. Owner: Hagans Leisure Group. Carlisle M6, J44 to Wigton on A595/596, follow Silloth sign, take B5302 end of Wigton bypass – park is 10yd on R. Open space, fresh air and spectacular views of some of England's most breathtaking scenery – all this can be yours with a visit to Solway Holiday Village. Located in the unspoiled seaside Victorian town of Silloth-on-Solway, this 120 acre family park has something for everyone. Facilities include indoor heated pool, kid's club, licensed bars with live entertainment, indoor & outdoor play areas, tennis, golf and much more. Open March-Nov 15.

■ **(1m). Stanwix Park Holiday Centre, Greenrow, Silloth, Cumbria CA7 4HH.** *01697 332666.* enquiries@stanwix.com. www.stanwix.com. Owner: E & R H Stanwix. On A596 at Wigton take B5302 To Silloth. Entering Silloth follow signs to Stanwix Park, about 1m. Large holiday centre – caravans for hire, tents and touring caravans welcome. Indoor leisure centre, pools, gym etc. Tenpin bowling, family entertainment, bars, disco and cabaret. Golf, fishing, bowling, tennis and shops. Ideal base to explore Lakes and historic Carlisle. Open all year except Xmas Day.

(1m). Tanglewood Caravan Park, Causeway Head, Silloth, Cumbria CA7 4PE. *01697 331253.* michael-tanglewood@hotmail.com. www.tanglewoodcaravanpark.co.uk. Owner: N M & G E Bowman. On B5302. 4m on from Abbeytown, on L before Silloth. Play area. Off-licence. Bottled gas. Pets allowed (free of charge). Club house. Modern, fully-serviced caravans with colour TV. Brochure with tariff available. Golf course, shops, PO, doctor available in 2m. Open Easter-Oct.

ST BEES

(0.5m). Seacote Park, The Beach, St Bees, Cumbria CA27 OET. *01946 822777.* reception@seacote.com. www.seacote.com. Owner: Milburns. From M6 J40. A66 W then A595 to Whitehaven (4m) then B5345 to St Bees. Adjoining lovely mile-long beach. Restaurant and bar. Cliff top walks, golf course close by. Children welcome. Fishing. PO and shops in St Bees village. Fringe of Lake District.

ULVERSTON

(0.25m). Bardsea Leisure Park, Priory Road, Ulverston, Cumbria LA12 9QE. *01229 584712.* reception@bardsealeisure.co.uk. Owner: Mr & Mrs T & G Varley. M6, J36, take A591 Kendal, A590 Barrow and A5087 coast road. Sheltered, select site in disused quarry. Extensively landscaped. Free hot showers. Dog exercise area. Fishing on site. Golf course, beach 1m.

(7m). Birch Bank Farm, Blawith, Ulverston, Cumbria LA12 8EW. *01229 885277.* birchbank@btinternet.com. www.birchbank.co.uk. Owner: Mrs L Nicholson. 3m SW of Coniston Water. On A5092, 0.5m W of Gawthwaite turn for Woodland, site 1.7m on R. Small farm site alongside stream and next to open fell. Ideal for walking or touring south lakes. Ulverston for shops etc 7m Open May-Oct.

WHICHAM

Silecroft Camping & Caravan Park, Silecroft, Whicham, Cumbria LA18 4NX. *01229 772659.* silecroftpark@aol.com. www.caravanholidayhomes.com. Owner: Mr & Mrs A Vaughan. A591 to Greenodd, take A5092 to coast road, follow signs. 3m from Millom. Golf course 100yd from beach. 1m from mountains. Indoor swimming pool. Open March 1-Oct 31.

WIGTON

Clea Hall Holiday Park, Westward, Wigton, Cumbria CA7 8NQ. *01697 342880.* Owner: Mr & Mrs G Kennedy. From M6 S leave motorway at J41, B5305 Wigton. Through Hutton in the Forest, Unthank, past L turning for Hesket Newmarket and through Sebergham. L turning B5299, Caldbeck, second crossroads turn R for 1.5m SP Westward Wigton.

EAST ANGLIA

See page 5 for key to symbols and abbreviations

(6m). Larches Caravan Park, Mealsgate, Wigton, Cumbria CA7 1LQ. *01697 371379.* melarches@btinternet. com. www.larchescaravanpark.com. Owner: Mr M & Mrs E Elliott. A595, 0.5m SW Mealsgate village on near side of road. Quiet park, ideal for couples. No ball games allowed. Superb facilities. Adults only. Open March 1-Oct 31.

WINDERMERE

(0.5m). Braithwaite Fold Caravan Club Site, Glebe Road, Bowness-on-Windermere, Windermere, Cumbria LA23 3HB. *01539 442177.* www.caravanclub.co.uk. Owner: The Caravan Club. See website for directions. Managed by The Club on behalf of South Lakeland District Council, this is an attractively laid out site, close to the shores of Lake Windermere and in easy walking distance of the town. Windermere has an excellent sailing centre from which to enjoy sailing, windsurfing and canoeing and you can hire equipment and take instruction. All hardstanding pitches, toilet block, laundry facilities, MV waste point, vegetable preparation area and dog walk. Non-members welcome. No tents. Open March 27 -Nov 9.

Hill of Oaks & Blakeholme Caravan Estate, Windermere, Cumbria LA12 8NR. *01539 531578.* enquiries@hillofoaks.co.uk. www.hillofoaks.co.uk. Owner: Lake District Estates Co Ltd. M6, J36, travel towards Newby Bridge A590, turn R at roundabout A591 towards Bowness for 3m. 0.75m private lake frontage. Boat launching. One of the most beautiful secluded lakeside caravan estates, the park welcomes touring caravans, motor homes and static caravan holidays. Fully stocked shop and information on site. Children's play area. Fishing from the shores (appropriate licence available locally). Fishing, golf, watersports (sailing, windsurfing, canoeing). David Bellamy Gold Conservation Award. Open March 1-Nov 14.

(2.5m). Limefitt Park, Patterdale Road, Windermere, Cumbria LA23 1PA. *01539 432564.* enquiries@southlakelandparks.co.uk. www.southlakelandparks.co.uk. Owner: South Lakeland Parks Ltd. M6, J36 follow signs 'South Lakes', then 'Windermere'. 0.5m beyond Windermere turn R at mini roundabout taking A592. Patterdale Road, SP 'Ullswater' Limefitt is 2m on R. Spectacular lakeland valley location. 10mins drive Lake Windermere. Tourers and family campers welcome, friendly Lakeland pub with bar meals, 'Do-it-Yourself' camper's kitchen plus full range of award winning facilities. Shops, cinema 3m. Sailing, fishing, swimming, boat launch nearby. Open March-Oct (tourers), March-Jan (statics).

(5m). Park Cliffe Camping and Caravan Estate, Birks Road, Tower Wood, Windermere, Cumbria LA23 3PG. *01539 531344.* info@parkcliffe.co.uk. www.parkcliffe.co.uk. Owner: S J Dickson. M6, J36. A590 to Barrow. At Newby Bridge, turn R on to A592. 4m turn R into Birks Road. Park is 0.3m on R. Playground. Café, bar and takeaway. Off licence. Windermere, cinema, golf course 4m. Kendal 15m. David Bellamy Gold Conservation Award. Open March 1-mid Nov.

BEDFORDSHIRE

LEIGHTON BUZZARD

The Silver Birch Café, Ivinghoe, Leighton Buzzard, Bedfordshire. *01296 668348.* Owner: Mr S J Newman & Mrs J M Rance. Off A41 at Tring to B488 Tring/Luton road. Site is on B488. Easy reach of Whipsnade Zoo, Woburn Abbey and Chiltern Hills. Fees on application.

RIDGMONT

Rose and Crown, 89 High Street, Ridgmont, Bedfordshire MK43 0TY. *01525 280245.* Owner: N C McGregor. 3km NE of Woburn on A507, 3m from J13 on M1. Flat, well-drained site close to Woburn Abbey and Safari Park. 5m from Milton Keynes.

CAMBRIDGESHIRE

CAMBRIDGE

(3m). Camping & Caravanning Club Site – Cambridge, 19 Cabbage Moor, Great Shelford, Cambridge, Cambridgeshire CB2 5NB. *01223 841185.* www.campingandcaravanningclub.co.uk. Owner: Camping & Caravanning Club. M11, J11 on to A1309 SP Cambridge. At first set of lights turn R, SP 'Skelford'. After 0.5m follow sign on L, pointing down the lane. Ideal for exploring the city and surrounding attractions. Plenty of space for children's ball games, play area. All units accepted. Non-members welcome. Deals for families and backpackers. Open March-Oct.

(2.5m). Cherry Hinton Caravan Club Site, Lime Kiln Road, Cherry Hinton, Cambridge, Cambridgeshire CB1 8NQ. *01223 244088.* www.caravanclub.co.uk. Owner: The Caravan Club. See website for directions. Imaginatively landscaped site ideally located for exploring Cambridge. Dog walk on site. Non-members and tent campers welcome. Advance booking essential Bank Holidays and weekends June-Aug. Some pitches limited in size and shape. MV service point. Shops, garage, PO, Doctor etc in one mile. Fishing, golf in 10m.

(5m). Highfield Farm Touring Park, Long Road, Comberton, Cambridge, Cambridgeshire CB23 7DG. *01223 262308.* enquiries@highfieldfarmtouringpark.co.uk. www.highfieldfarmtouringpark.co.uk. Owner: Mr & Mrs B H Chapman. From Cambridge take A428 (Bedford) and A1303 for 3m then follow signs for Comberton. From M11 leave J12 take A603 (Sandy) then B1046 to Comberton. Iron. Hairdryers. Razor points. Baby changing facilities. Washing up sinks. Public telephone. Postbox. Hardstandings. Golf course, PO, shops, doctor available nearby. Open April 1-Oct 31.

(8m). Roseberry Tourist Park, Earith Road, Willingham, Cambridge, Cambridgeshire CB4 5LT. *01954 260346.* Owner: Mrs Isobel Cuthbert. From A14 take B1050 at Bar Hill. Site 1m N of Willingham on L of B1050. 9-acre orchard site amid pear trees. Ideal for touring Cambridge, Ely or St Ives en route to Felixstowe or Harwich Ferry. Hardstandings. Golf/fishing nearby. Shops 1m.

(8m). Stanford Park, Weirs Road, Burwell, Cambridge, Cambridgeshire CB5 0BP. *01638 741547.* enquiries@stanfordcaravanpark.co.uk. www.stanfordcaravanpark.co.uk. Owner: Mr J Stanford. Caravan site signs at main junctions in village. Quiet adult only site. Ideally situated for exploring Cambridge and Newmarket. Shaver points. Hairdryers. Playground. Shops, restaurants only 15mins walk. RAC appointed. AA 4 pennant.

FENSTANTON

(0.5m). Crystal Lakes Touring Caravan & Rally Park, Low Road, Fenstanton, Cambridgeshire PE18 9HU. *01480 497728.* crystalleisure@msn.com. Owner: Scenic Estates Ltd. Fenstanton is situated just off A14 between Cambridge and Huntingdon, 8m from the top of M11-S and 8m from the A1 at A14 junction-N. 8m from A45. Picturesque, secluded site just outside village of Fenstanton. Spacious

www.motorcaravanmagazine.co.uk MOTOR CARAVAN & CAMPING PARKS 2009 **13**

EAST ANGLIA

shower facilities. Fishing on site, car boot fair Sundays. Children's indoor and outdoor activity centre available in Winter 2005. Open March-Oct.

HUNTINGDON

(5.25m). Grafham Water Caravan Club Site, Church Road, Grafham, Huntingdon, Cambridgeshire PE28 0BB. *01480 810264.* www.caravanclub.co.uk. Owner: The Caravan Club. Turn L off A1, at roundabout in Buckden on to B661. In 0.75m, turn R then follow signs. No tents. An attractive site situated W of picturesque Grafham village. A great place to relax and rewind. The site has a heated swimming pool as well as a children's play area. Ideal for nature lovers. Open Nov-Oct.

((2m). Houghton Mill Caravan Club Site, Mill Street, Houghton, Huntingdon, Cambridgeshire PE17 2AZ. *01480 466716.* www.caravanclub.co.uk. Owner: The Caravan Club. See website for directions. Set on the bank of the river Great Ouse with spectacular views across the river to the National Trust's Houghton Mill. Non-members and tent campers welcome. Toilet blocks with privacy cubicles and laundry facilities. Dog walk nearby, fishing and with 5m of National Cycle network. Open March-Oct.

(6m). Old Manor Caravan Park, Church Road, Grafham, Huntingdon, Cambridgeshire PE28 0BB. *01480 810264.* camping@old-manor.co.uk. www.old-manor.co.uk. Owner: DP & CG Howes. From A14 turn off at Ellington, 5m W of Huntingdon, and follow camping and caravan signs for 2.5m to Grafham. From A1 turn off at Buckden, 4m S of Huntingdon, and follow camping and caravan signs for 2.5m to Grafham. 7 hardstanding pitches. Heated outdoor swimming pool (end May-Sept). Dogs welcome. Gas. Laundry room. Deep freezer. Solar heated shower block with shaver points. Dishwashing room. Open all year except Xmas/New Year.

(5m). Quiet Waters Caravan Park, Hemingford Abbots, Huntingdon, Cambridgeshire PE28 9AJ. *01480 463405.* quietwaters.park@btopenworld.com. www.quietwaterscaravanpark.co.uk. Owner: W H Hutson & Son Ltd. A14, J25. 1m off A14, 13m from Cambridge. Riverside park. Angling on site. Golf, shop 1m. Open April-Oct.

Stroud Hill Park, Fen Road, Pidley, Huntingdon, Cambridgeshire PE28 3D. *01487 741333.* stroudhillpark@btconnect.com. www.stroudhillpark.co.uk. CARAVAN CLUB AFFILIATED SITE. Adults only. This quiet, attractive and rural site provides a five star location. Toilet blocks and launderette. Shop, café, bar and restaurant on site. Good area for walking. Fishing and golf nearby. Quiet and peaceful off peak.

(2m). The Willows Caravan Park, Bromholme Lane, Brampton, Huntingdon, Cambridgeshire PE28 4NE. *01480 437566.* willows@willows33.freeserve.co.uk. www.willowscaravanpark.com. Owner: Stephen A Carter. Leave A1 N join B1514, SP Brampton, follow signs for Huntingdon. Leave A1 S join A14 then B1514 follow signs for Huntingdon. Park on R turn opposite country park. Pub-restaurant, boating, fishing and attractive walks, historical Huntingdon town, Country Park and Grafham Water nearby. Dogs allowed under strict supervision. Shop nearby. Tents welcome. Children's playground (under 7's). Washing machine. AA 3 pennants.

(2m). Wyton Lakes Holiday Park, Wyton Lakes, Banks End Wyton, Huntingdon, Cambridgeshire PE28 2AA. *01480 412715.* loupeter@supanet.com. www.wytonlakes.com. Owner: Louise & Peter Bates. A14, exit 23, follow A141 to March. At fourth roundabout take A1123 to St Ives. 1m down pass Hartford Marina. Wyton Lakes is on R. Adults Only Park. Quality fishing on site. Boating, golfing, riding all nearby. Restaurants, shops, pubs in 1m. Doctor, PO in 2m. Marina next door, rural retreat in delightful scenery, river frontage, woodland and lakes. Each pitch with electric and water. Free showers, some hardstandings. Open April 1-Oct 31.

MARCH

(5m). Floods Ferry Marina Park, Staffurths Bridge, March, Cambridgeshire PE15 0YP. *01354 677302.* Owner: Mr T Quinn, Mr J Quinn and Mrs A Quinn. A141 bypass of March town, turn for Floods Ferry for 3m. Look for brown signs. Tranquil park in the heart of Fenland, on site marina, fishing, lisenced club house with bar food and occasional live music, all touring pitches, located on river bank.

PETERBOROUGH

(2m). Ferry Meadows Caravan Club Site, Ham Lane, Peterborough, **Cambridgeshire PE2 5UU.** *01733 233526.* www.caravanclub.co.uk. Owner: The Caravan Club. See website for directions. Ideal family site, level and open, located in country park with watersports, golf, fishing and cycling facilities. Non-members and tent campers welcome. Dogs must be exercised off site. Advance booking essential Bank holidays. MV service point. Grass and hardstanding pitches.

Northey Lodge Touring Park & Storage, North Bank, Whittlesey Road, Peterborough, Cambridgeshire PE6 7YZ. *01733 223918.* enquiries@northeylodge.co.uk. www.northeylodge.co.uk. Adjacent to the river Nene and in easy reach of Peterborough. Well-behaved dogs welcome but must be kept on a lead when on site.

(8m). Sacrewell Farm and Country Centre, Thornhaugh, Peterborough, Cambridgeshire PE8 6HJ. *01780 782254.* info@sacrewell.org.uk. www.sacrewell.org.uk. Owner: William Scott Abbott Trust. Located off A47 just E of A1/A47 junction near Wansford, Peterborough. The farm and country centre admission included in caravan fees: working watermill, bygones, animals. Children's play area. Farm trail. Nearest village with pubs, PO, doctor in 1m. Open March 1-Oct 31.

(8m). Yarwell Mill Caravan Park, Mill Lane, Yarwell, Peterborough, Cambridgeshire PE8 6PS. *01780 782344.* info@yarwellmill.co.uk. www.yarwellmill.co.uk. Owner: Paul & Company. Off A1 and A47 intersection. At Wansford church follow Yarwell signs. Boating and fishing on site. River Nene flows through site. Old stone town of Stamford 6m. Nene Way walks lead from site. Local shop, PO, doctor, medical centre in 1m. Open March 1-Oct 31.

ST NEOTS

(0.5m). Camping & Caravanning Club Site – St Neots, Hardwick Road, Eynesbury, St Neots, Cambridgeshire PE19 2PR. *01480 474404.* www.campingandcaravanningclub.co.uk. Owner: Camping & Caravanning Club. From A1 take A428 to Cambridge, 2nd roundabout L to Tesco's, past sport centre, site SP. On the banks of the Great Ouse. Ideal for boating and fishing. St Neots in easy reach. Non-members welcome and may join at site. All units accepted. Some all-weather pitches available. All facilities nearby eg shops, pubs, restaurants, doctors, dentist in St Neots. Fishing is available from this site. Paxton Pits Nature Reserve, just 2m away is a paradise for birdwatchers. Deals for families and backpackers. Open March-Oct.

14 MOTOR CARAVAN & CAMPING PARKS 2009

EAST ANGLIA

ESSEX

BRENTWOOD

(5m). Camping & Caravanning Club Site – Kelvedon Hatch, Warren Lane, Doddinghurst, Brentwood, Essex CM15 0JG. *01277 372773.* www.campingandcaravanningclub.co.uk. Owner: Camping & Caravanning Club. M25 J28 Brentwood 2m L on A128 SP Ongar. 3m turn R, SP. Between London and Chelmsford with plenty of sporting activities in easy reach. The site is peaceful and quiet surrounded by trees with 90 pitches. Caravans, motorcaravans and tents accepted. Non-members welcome. Area for ball games available with volleyball net. Deals for families and backpackers. Open March – Oct.

CLACTON-ON-SEA

((2m). Highfield Grange Holiday Park, London Road, Clacton-on-Sea, Essex CO16 9QY. *0871 6649746.* highfield@park-resorts.com. www.park-resorts.com. Owner: Park Resorts Ltd. Follow A12 to Colchester and take A120 Harwich road, leading to A133 then follow signs to Sea. Highfield is situated on B1441 on L. Water resorts programme, FREE kids club, FREE family evening entertainment. All weather sports court, adventure playground, amusements, shop on site, indoor and outdoor swimming pool complex, launderette, café and takeaway, pool, darts. New arcades in 2008! Clacton pier: amusements, stalls and shops. Open April-Oct.

(1m). Sacketts Grove, Jaywick Lane, Clacton-on-Sea, Essex CO16 7BD. *01255 427765.* Owner: TST (Parks) Ltd. From Colchester A133 turn R at Clacton roundabout. After 0.75m turn L at Jaywick Lane. Large level site. Tents separate from caravans. Fees on application. Riding school on site. Club. Swimming pool. Takeaway. Golf course nearby. PO, doctors, etc under 1m. Open Easter-Oct.

COLCHESTER

(0.75m). Colchester Camping & Caravan Park, Cymbeline Way, Lexden, Colchester, Essex CO3 4AG. *01206 545551.* enquiries@colchestercamping.co.uk. www.colchestercamping.co.uk. Owner: D M & S G Thorp. At junction of A12 and A133 Colchester Central, follow tourist signs. Colchester 5mins by car, 30mins walk Colchester. CARAVAN CLUB AFFILIATED SITE. Non members and tent campers welcome. Ideal for visiting Britain's oldest town or base for East Anglia and Constable country. Stop-over for ferry ports. Heated shower block. Secure storage available. Shop on site, golf course nearby.

(8m). Fen Farm, East Mersea, Colchester, Essex CO5 8FE. *01206 383275.* fenfarm@talk21.com. mersea-island.com/fenfarm. Owner: Mr & Mrs R Lord. Off B1025, take L fork over causeway, follow road to Dog and Pheasant PH -1st turning R. Quiet, rural site, close to beach and country park. Village shop & PO 1m. Supermarket, doctor 4m. Showers. Shaver points. Play area. Shower for people with disability. Family shower room. Laundry room + iron. Mobile shop calls. Safe swimming. David Bellamy Gold Conservation Award. Open March 15-Oct 31.

(6m). Mill Farm Camp Site, Harwich Road, Great Bromley, Colchester, Essex CO7 7JQ. *01206 250485.* Owner: Dean Bros. From A120 to Harwich, E of Colchester. Follow signs to Mill Farm. Quiet, peaceful site on No 1 cycle route from Harwich. Open May-Sept.

(10m). Seaview Holiday Park, Seaview Avenue, W Mersea, Colchester, Essex CO5 8DA. *01206 382534.* info@westmersea.com. www.westmersea.com. B1025 Colchester to Mersea. Open March 15-Jan 14.

(8m). The Grange Country Park, East Bergholt, Colchester, Essex CO7 6UX. *01206 298567.* Owner: Mr & Mrs P J Arnold. Off B1070 from A12 & A137. Club. Restaurant. Swimming pool. BBQ. Sauna. Rose Award. Closed Jan 3-Feb 1.

(10m). Waldegraves Holiday Park, Mersea Island, Colchester, Essex CO5 8SE. *01206 382898.* holidays@waldegraves.co.uk. www.waldegraves.co.uk. Owner: Mr D Lord. Off B1025 from Colchester, follow tourist signs on island. Rose Award. Private beach, golf, pitch & putt, fishing. Family entertainment. All weather sports area, swimming pool, children's play area. Shop & restaurant on site and nearby. David Bellamy Gold Conservation Award. Open March 1 – Nov 30.

HALSTEAD

(3m). Gosfield Lake Mobile Home Park, Church Road, Gosfield, Halstead, Essex CO9 1UG. *01787 475655.* turps@gosfieldlake.co.uk. www.gosfieldlake.co.uk. Owner: C W Turp. M11 Turn off for Stansted A120 towards Braintree A120. Follow to High Garrett then 1017 to Gosfield. Flat, sheltered site with picnic area and adjacent to large lake. Waterskiing and fishing on site.

LOUGHTON

Debden House Camp Site, Debden Green, Loughton, Essex IG10 2NZ. *020 8508 3008.* debben.

Ideal family park, grass park surrounded by trees and lakes. Safe private south facing beach. 65 miles from London.
- Licensed bar & restaurant
- Heated swimming pool
- Undercover Golf driving range, Pitch & putt
- Family Entertainment
- Children's play area & games room
- Fishing & Boating lakes
- Luxury Holiday Homes for Hire & Sale
- All inclusive Midweek and Weekend breaks
- Caravans, Motorhomes, trailer tents & tents all welcome.

Mersea Island, Colchester Essex CO5 8SE
Tel: (01206) 382898
Web: www.waldegraves.co.uk

EAST ANGLIA

house@newham.gov.uk. www.debben.house.com. Off A121. M25 exit J26, A121 to Loughton, L A1168, second L Pyrles Lane, T-junction R then second L. M11, 2m. London Tube 1.5m. Central line to Debden. Access from site into Epping Forest. Bottled gas sales. Laundry and café on site. Shop on site, PO 10mins walk. Golf nearby. No bottle gas sale. Prices Adult £7 per night, child from 3016yes £3.50 per night. Electric hook-up £3.50 per night. Open May 1-end Sept.

ROCHFORD

(4m). Riverside Village Holiday Park, Creeksea Ferry Road, Wallasea Island, Rochford, Essex SS4 2EY. *01702 258297.* Owner: K Parkes. A127, Rochford, Ashington to Wallasea or A130, Hullbridge, Ashingdon, Canewdon and Wallasea. Flat, well cut parkland with trees and lakes, ideal for walking, birdwatching, windsurfing and boating. Ferry to Burnham. Pub and restaurant adjoining. Open March 1-Nov 1.

SOUTHEND-ON-SEA

East Beach Caravan Park, East Beach, Shoeburyness, Southend-On-Sea, Essex SS3 9SG. *01702 292466.* Owner: Tingdene Parks Ltd. A127 or A13 to Shoebury then follow camp signs. Open mid March-Oct 31.

SOUTHMINSTER

Beacon Hill Holiday Village, St Lawrence Bay, Southminster, Essex CM0 7LS. *01621 779248.* 8m E of Maldon via B1018 and B1010 to Latchington. L at T-junc. and after Latchington take minor roads to Mayland, Steeple and St Lawrence. Farmland setting. Boat launching into adjoining river Blackwater Open April-Oct.

Saint Lawrence Holiday Home Park, 10 Main Road, St Lawrence Bay, Southminster, Essex CM0 7LY. *01621 779434.* A127 take A132 turn-off leading to Latchingdon, follow Bradwell road and tourism signs to 'The Stone' at St Lawrence Bay. Quiet, luxury, family, holiday park adjacent to the river Blackwater. Launching facilities for sailing and waterskiing. Welcome Host. David Bellamy Silver Conservation Award.

(5m). Steeple Bay Holiday Park, Steeple, Southminster, Essex CM0 7RS. *01621 773991.* www.ParkHolidaysUK.com. Owner: Park Holidays UK. Turn off A12 on to A414 on to B1010-1012 to Latchingdon follow signs through Mayland, then Steeple Village, turn L after Steeple sign. 1m down lane. Situated next to river Blackwater with slipway. Outdoor swimming pool. Crazy golf. Loopy Club for kids. Village store. Free evening entertainment for the family. Maldon, bars, restaurants, shopping. GS. David Bellamy Bronze Conservation Award. Open March-Nov.

(6m). Waterside at St Lawrence Bay, Main Road, St Lawrence Bay, Southminster, Essex CM0 7LY. *0871 6649794.* www.park-resorts.com. Owner: Park Resorts Ltd. A12 towards Chelmsford take the A414 to Maldon. Follow signs to Latchingdon on B1010. Drive through village and follow signs for St Lawrence. Pick up signs for Waterside Holiday Park. Indoor swimming pool, sauna and spa pool, café, fast food takeaway, outdoor play area, amusements, pub, FREE kids entertainment, FREE family evening entertainment. David Bellamy Gold Conservation Award. Open April-Oct.

WALTON-ON-THE-NAZE

(0.25m). Naze Marine Holiday Park, Hall Lane, Walton-on-the-Naze, Essex C014 8HL. *0871 6649755.* www.park-resorts.com. Owner: Park Resorts Ltd. Take A12 to Colchester – follow A120 Harwich Road as far as A133. On the A133 take the B1033 all the way to Walton Seafront. Park is on L. Water resorts programme, FREE kids clubs, FREE family entertainment, amusements, adventure playground, café, takeaway, shop. Indoor swimming pool. Launderette, bar, darts, pool tables. David Bellamy Gold Conservation Award. Open April-Oct.

HERTFORDSHIRE

BALDOCK

Ashridge Farm Caravan Club Site, Ashwell Street, Ashwell, Baldock, Hertfordshire SG7 5QF. *01462 742527.* www.caravanclub.co.uk. Owner: The Caravan Club. See website for directions. Caravan Club members only. No tents. This small and pretty site with its many trees and shrubs is the perfect place to relax and unwind. Toilet blocks, laundry facilities and MV service point. Good area for walking and in 5m of NCN route. Facilities for disabled. Quiet and peaceful off-peak.

Radwell Lake Caravan Site, Radwell Mill, Radwell, Baldock, Hertfordshire SG7 5ET. *01462 730242.* mmh@flymicro.com. Owner: Michael F Meredith-Hardy. A507 from Baldock and A507 from Shefford. Turning marked Radwell only on A507. Exit 10 A1 (M). Small site with lake and bird reserve. Takeaway meals, shop, café/restaurant available nearby at Motorway Services 0.5m. Open Easter-Oct 31.

HEMEL HEMPSTEAD

(2m). Breakspear Way Caravan Club Site, Buncefield Lane, Breakspear Way, Hemel Hempstead, Hertfordshire HP2 4TZ. *01442 268466.* www.caravanclub.co.uk. Owner: The Caravan Club. See website for directions. Caravan Club members only. No tents. Quiet, peaceful site yet convenient for London and M1. Advance booking advised. Some hardstanding, gas and gaz, play equipment. Toilet blocks. MV service point. Restaurant, golf and fishing nearby. Ideal for families. NCN cycle route in 5m.

HERTFORD

(1m). Camping & Caravanning Club Site – Hertford, Mangrove Road, Hertford, Hertfordshire SG13 8AJ. *01992 586696.* www.campingandcaravanningclub.co.uk. Owner: Camping & Caravanning Club. From the A1, avoid town centre signs at Hertford and follow A414. From A10 take A414 to Hertford, cross first roundabout, then first L into Mangrove Road. Site on L. Sports field. Non-members welcome. Local attractions include Lea Valley Park, Paradise Wildlife Park and the gardens of Benington Lordship. Deals for families and backpackers. All units accepted. Loo Of The Year (3 stars). David Bellamy Gold Conservation Award.

HODDESDON

(1m). Lee Valley Caravan Park, Essex Road, Dobbs Weir, Hoddesdon, Hertfordshire EN11 0AS. *01992 462090.* www.leevalleypark.com. Owner: Lee Valley Regional Park. 1.75m E of A10. Take Hoddesdon exit from A10. Follow Dinant Link Road and Essex Road. Attractive riverside setting; good fishing and walking. Boating and shop nearby. Open Easter-Oct 31.

WALTHAM CROSS

(2m). Camping & Caravanning Club Site – Theobalds Pk, Theobalds Park, Bulls Cross Ride, Waltham Cross, Hertfordshire EN7 5HS. *01992 620604.* www.campingandcaravanningclub.co.uk. Owner: Camping & Caravanning Club. Park is in Hertfordshire just 13m from Central London, 10mins drive from M25, leaving at

16 MOTOR CARAVAN & CAMPING PARKS 2009

EAST ANGLIA

J25. A10 towards London keep in R lane, R at first lights, R at T-junction, R behind dog kennels. Site 250yd towards top of lane on R. Plenty of open space for childrens games. All units accepted. Non-members welcome. Site is tree screened and there is plenty of wildlife to see from the site. Recreation hall and play area on site. There is boating, sailing, swimming pools and sports in nearby Lee Valley. Deals for families and backpackers. Open March-Oct.

WELWYN GARDEN CITY

(2m). Commons Wood Caravan Club Site, Ascots Lane, Welwyn Garden City, Hertfordshire AL7 4HJ. *01707 260786.* www.caravanclub.co.uk. Owner: The Caravan Club. See website for directions. Caravan Club members only. No tents. Pleasantly green, flat and rural site in easy reach of London by public transport. Toilet blocks. Privacy cubicles. Laundry facilities. Veg prep. MV service point. Golf, fishing and watersports nearby.

NORFOLK

ATTLEBOROUGH

(0.5m). Oak Tree Park, Norwich Road, Attleborough, Norfolk NR17 2JX. *01953 455565.* oaktree.cp@virgin.net. www.oaktree-caravan-park.co.uk. Owner: Mr & Mrs D A M Birkinshaw. Turn R off A11 (Thetford-Norwich) SP Attleborough, in 2m continue through Attleborough passing Sainsbury's, fork L immediately past church at T junction, site on R in 0.5m. Open March-Dec.

CROMER

(3m). Camping & Caravanning Club Site – W Runton, Holgate Lane, W Runton, Cromer, Norfolk NR27 9NW. *01263 837544.* www.campingandcaravanningclub.co.uk. Owner: Camping & Caravanning Club.

From King's Lynn on A148 towards Cromer, turn L at Roman Camp Inn. Site track on R at Crest of Hill, 0.5m to site. 1m from sea and sandy beaches, 3m to Cromer where golf and fishing are available. All units accepted. Non-members welcome. Visit nearby Cromer with its church tower and lighthouse. Kids will love the Seal Reserve at Blakeney Point and the Shire Horse Centre at W Runton. Panoramic views of the surrounding countryside can be enjoyed from the site. Deals for families and backpackers. Loo Of The Year (4 stars). Open March-Oct.

(1m). Forest Park Caravan Site, Northrepps Road, Cromer, Norfolk NR27 0JR. *01263 513290.* www.forestpark.co.uk. Owner: Forest Park Caravan Site Ltd. Off B1159. Indoor heated pool. Launderette. Clubhouse. Children's play area. Well stocked shop. Adjacent to Cromer Golf Course. Award winning Touring and Holiday Home haven. Golf course 0.5m. Cinema, shopping centre 1m. David Bellamy Gold Conservation Award. Open March 15-Jan 15.

(2m). Incleboro Fields Caravan Club Site, Station Close, W Runton, Cromer, Norfolk NR27 9QG. *01263 837419.* www.caravanclub.co.uk. Owner: The Caravan Club. See website for directions. Caravan Club members only. No tents. Located in a hillside area of 21 acres with sea views, woodlands, walks and wild flowers. 1m from sea. 9-hole golf course adjacent. Play area. Dog walk. Toilet blocks. Privacy cubicles. Laundry facilities. Baby/toddler washroom. Veg prep. MV service point. Ideal for families. Open March-Oct.

(1m). Manor Farm Caravan and Camping Site, East Runton, Cromer, Norfolk NR27 9PR. *01263 512858.* www.manorfarmcaravansite.co.uk. Owner: Mr S T Holliday. 1m W of Cromer turn off

A148 at brown and white Manor Farm signs. Secluded, family-run site situated on traditional mixed farm. Showers, washbasins, razor points. Hairdryer points. Laundry and washing-up sinks. Calor Gas. Two supermarkets in 0.25m. No motorcycles. Open Easter-Sept 30.

(0.5m). Seacroft Caravan Club Site, Runton Road, Cromer, Norfolk NR27 9NH. *01263 514938.* www.caravanclub.co.uk. Owner: The Caravan Club. See website for directions. Seacroft has a great location in walking distance of Cromer's sandy beaches. Ideal for a family holiday with so much to do on site and nearby. Non members and tent campers welcome. Open March-Jan.

■ **(1m). Woodhill Park, East Runton, Cromer, Norfolk NR27 9PX.** *01263 512242.* www.woodhill-park.com. Owner: Blue Sky Leisure, Timewell Properties Ltd. Clifftop location with sandy beach below between Cromer and Sheringham on A149. High quality park offering peace and tranquility. Magnificent views of the coastline and countryside. Rose Award. David Bellamy Gold Conservation Award. Open March 19-Oct 31.

DISS

(1.5m). The Willows Caravan & Camping Park, Diss Road, Scole, Diss, Norfolk IP21 4DH. *01379 740271.* www.thewillowspark.co.uk. Owner: M Shaw. 1.50m E of diss on A1066, 250yd from Scole A140 roundabout. On Norfolk/Suffolk county boundary. Level, peaceful site on the banks of the river Waveney, surrounded by conservation area. Walking distance to historical Saxon village of Scole. Fishing, golf driving range and golf course nearby. Open Easter-Oct.

NORTH NORFOLK... *naturally*

Woodhill Park

Relax in your touring caravan or tent enjoying peace and tranquillity with magnificent views of the sea and surrounding North Norfolk countryside. Multi-service, electric pitches and amenity buildings available. Luxurious centrally heated holiday homes for hire.

Bookings or brochure **01263 512242**
or online **www.woodhill-park.com**
Cromer Road, East Runton, Cromer, Norfolk NR27 9PX

EAST ANGLIA

FAKENHAM

(0.75m). Fakenham Racecourse Caravan & Camping Site, (Caravan Club affiliated site), The Racecourse, Fakenham, Norfolk NR21 7NY. 01328 862388. www.fakenhamracecourse.co.uk. Owner: Manager: David Hunter. From Norwich A1067. At roundabout follow brown signs to Racecourse Caravan/ Camping. From A1065 and A148 on approach to Fakenham follow signs as above. Set in beautiful countryside. Ideally located for visiting Norfolk's coastal resorts, stately homes, wildlife and many other attractions. Sports centre adjacent. Dog walk. Free access to racing for caravan/camping guests. Non Caravan Club members and tents welcome. Toilet blocks with showers and privacy cubicles. Laundry facilities. Veg prep. MV service point. Bar & restaurant at sports centre on site. Golf, fishing, tennis. Ideal for families.

(7m). Old Brick Kilns Caravan & Camping Park, Little Barney Lane, Barney, Fakenham, Norfolk NR21 0NL. 01328 878305. www.old-brick-kilns.co.uk. Owner: Alison & John Strahan. Off A148, at B1354 to Melton Constable follow brown Tourist Board signs to Barney. Turn L down Little Barney Lane. Park at end of lane (0.75m). Quiet, family park for the discerning caravanner or camper. Mostly flat, open or shaded all weather pitches. Clean modern facilities. Family games areas. Licensed restaurant. Fishing pond. AA 4-pennants. David Bellamy Gold Conservation Award. Open March 1 – Jan 4.

GREAT YARMOUTH

(4m). Beach Estate Caravan Park, Estate Office, Long Beach, Hemsby-on-Sea, Great Yarmouth, Norfolk NR29 4JD. 01493 730023. info@long-beach.co.uk. www.long-beach.co.uk. Owner: J M Groat. At the end of Beach Road Hemsby off B1159. Close to sandy beach. Well lit. Mains electrics, showers, deep sinks. Licensed club. Open end March- early Nov.

Broadlands Caravan Club Site, Johnson Street, Ludham, Great Yarmouth, Norfolk NR29 5NY. 01692 630457. www.caravanclub.co.uk. Owner: The Caravan Club. See website for directions. Caravan Club members only. No tents. A tranquil open site in the midst of the Broads. Toilet blocks, laundry facilities, baby and toddler washroom and MV service point. Playground and boules pitch. Fishing and watersports nearby. Ideal for families. Quiet and peaceful off-peak. Facilities for disabled. Open March 27-Nov 9.

(5m). Burgh Castle Marina, Butt Lane, Burgh Castle, Great Yarmouth, Norfolk NR31 9PZ. 01493 780331. info@burghcastlemarina.co.uk. www.burghcastlemarina.co.uk. Owner: Mr R D Wright. Off A143 Yarmouth to Beccles 3m W of Gorleston on Sea. Follow signs for marina to Betton. Turn R after 1m for Burgh Castle. Park entrance on L, another 0.75m. Pontoon moorings. Slipway. Generous space, quiet, rural setting. Spectacular views and walks to Roman ruins and bird reserves. Riverside pub and restaurant. Swimming pool. Information and exhibition centre with permanent displays of Roman ruins and marshland heritage. Visiting displays throughout season. Golf course 3m. Accessibility category 1 award. Green Tourism Business Scheme Silver award. David Bellamy Gold Conservation Award. Open Easter-Oct 31.

■ **(9m). Clippesby Hall, Hall Lane, Clippesby, Great Yarmouth, Norfolk NR29 3BL.** 01493 367800. holidays@clippesby.com. www.clippesby.com. Owner: Lindsay Family. In Norfolk Broads National Park between Acle and Potter Heigham off B1152, turning opposite Clippesby Village sign. Permineter parking. Woodland and parkland setting in 6 different areas. Quiet, family owned. Grassy, sheltered. Surrounded by rivers, Broads, nature reserves and tourist attractions. Lots to do. Colour brochure. Norfolk Broads 2m. Norwich 8m. Great Yarmouth 9m. David Bellamy Gold Conservation Award. Open Easter-Oct 31.

(1.5m). Great Yarmouth Racecourse Caravan Club Site, Jellicoe Road, Great Yarmouth, Norfolk NR30 4AU. 01493 855223. www.caravanclub.co.uk. Owner: The Caravan Club. See website for directions. An open site in excellent position next to racecourse and golf course. 300yd from seafront, at its quieter, northern end. Dogs must be exercised off site. Advance booking essential BH. Non-members welcome. No tents. Toilet blocks. Privacy cubicles. Laundry facilities. Veg prep. MV service point. Play area. Golf, fishing and watersports nearby. Ideal for families. In 5m of new cycle route. Open March-Nov.

(4m). Liffens Welcome Holiday Centre, Butt Lane, Burgh Castle, Great Yarmouth, Norfolk NR31 9PU. 01493 780481. www.liffens.co.uk. Owner: Mr Liffen. From Great Yarmouth to Beccles A143 road turn R for Burgh Castle. 0.5m turn R we are 0.5m on R. Family run holiday centre close Great Yarmouth, great facilities. Gym, solarium, indoor pool, bar, play area. Open March 31-Oct 30.

■ **(5m). Long Beach Caravan Park, Estate Office, Long Beach, Hemsby, Great Yarmouth, Norfolk NR29 4JD.** 01493 730023. info@long-beach.co.uk. www.long-beach.co.uk. Owner: Long Beach Estates. Turn E off B1159 Hemsby

www.clippesby.com

Clippesby Hall

The ideal base for exploring Norfolk.
From the Broads to the coast.
Perfect for a holiday of walking, cycling, fishing, eating, drinking
or just putting your feet up!

A wooded country setting with spacious perimeter pitching, mini-golf, cafe, family pub, swimming pool and much more

CALL NOW FOR YOUR FREE BROCHURE
(01493) 367800

18 MOTOR CARAVAN & CAMPING PARKS 2009

EAST ANGLIA

See page 5 for key to symbols and abbreviations

on Beach Road. Then 2nd L (Kings Lake), SP Long Beach. Club. Launderette. Café. Supermarket. Private sandy beach. PO 1m, doctor 0.75m. Open mid March-Nov.

(4m). Rose Farm Touring and Camping Park, Stepshort, Belton, Great Yarmouth, Norfolk NR31 9JS. *01493 780896*. www.rosefarmtouringpark.co.uk. Owner: Sue & Tore Myhra. From the A143 turn into new road, SP Belton and Burgh Castle first R at Stepshort, site first on R. Great Yarmouth 4m, Gorleston 2m. Swings. AA Tourist Board approved 4 pennant. GS. Local transport.

(5m). Scratby Hall Caravan Park, Scratby, Great Yarmouth, Norfolk NR29 3PH. *01493 730283*. Owner: Mrs B Rawnsley. 2m N of Caister via A149 and B1159. Site is about 1m from junction. Rural location, level and grassy. Children's play area. Gas supplies. Washing-up and food preparation room. Open Easter-mid Oct.

■ **(4m). The Grange Touring Park, Ormesby St Margaret, Great Yarmouth, Norfolk NR29 3QC.** *01493 730306*. info@grangetouring.co.uk. www.grangetouring.co.uk. Owner: John Groat. On B1159 N of Caister-on-Sea. 1m to beach; golf course, riding nearby and close to Norfolk Broads. Telephone bookings can be taken with a credit, debit or switch card. Internet reception & Wi Fi to all pitches. PO, doctor, shop and garage in Ormesby Village. Open mid March-end Sept.

(1m). Vauxhall Holiday Park, 2 Acle New Road, Great Yarmouth, Norfolk NR30 1TB. *01493 857231*. vauxhall.holidays@virgin.net. www.vauxhall-holiday-park.co.uk. Owner: Mr S G Biss. On A47 Norwich to Gt Yarmouth. Free entertainment. Heated indoor pool. Disco. Club. Adventure playground. Restaurant. Arcade. Supermarket. Multi-sport arena. Open May-Sept.

(12m). Waxham Sands Holiday Park, Warren Farm, Horsey, Great Yarmouth, Norfolk NR29 4EJ. *01692 598325*. Owner: CL Associates (Inc). On B1159 coast road between Sea Palling and Winterton. 12m up coast from Great Yarmouth, 22m from Cromer and 22m E of Norwich. Quiet, farm site bordering National Trust and farmland. Own beach. Freshwater fishing 1m, nearest bus 2m. Open May 20-Sept 30.

(4m). Wild Duck Holiday Park, Howard's Common, Belton, Great Yarmouth, Norfolk NR31 9NE. *01493 780268*. www.wildduck-park.co.uk. Owner: Bourne Leisure Ltd. A47 to Great Yarmouth then pick up A143 for Beccles. 2-3m turn R, SP Belton & Burgh Castle. Follow this road to a T-junction and turn L. The park is a further 200yd on the R. Park set in 98 acres of woodland. Heated indoor pool. Bar and café. New Jamboree club with visiting cabarets, games room, amusement arcade, takeaway. Children's clubs, playground, crazy golf, bike hire, mini bowling. Golf courses nearby. Family entertainment. David Bellamy Gold Conservation Award. Open March-Oct.

HARLESTON

(2m). Little Lakeland Caravan Park, Wortwell, Harleston, Norfolk IP20 0EL. *01986 788646*. information@littlelakeland.co.uk. www.littlelakeland.co.uk. Owner: Jean & Peter Leatherbarrow. Turn off A143 (Diss to Bungay) at roundabout SP Wortwell. In village turn R 350yd past Bell pub. Quiet, family touring park with fishing lake and library. Modern toilet block. AA Award for Environment. Open March 15-Oct 31.

HOLT

■ **(3m). Kelling Heath Holiday Park, Weybourne, Holt, Norfolk NR25 7HW.** *01263 588181*. info@kellingheath.co.uk. www.kellingheath.co.uk. Owner: Blue Sky Leisure. From A148 turn N at site sign at Bodham. From A149 turn S at Weybourne Church. A 250 acre estate of woodland and heathland. Nature trails and woodland walks. Health club. Bars and restaurants. Rose award. David Bellamy Gold Conservation Award. Open Feb 2-Dec 14.

HUNSTANTON

(0.5m). Searles Leisure Resort, South Beach, Hunstanton, Norfolk PE36 5BB. *01485 534211*. bookings@searles.co.uk. www.searles.co.uk. Owner: Searles Ltd. On B1161 off A149, 14m N of Kings Lynn. 200yd from Award beach. Indoor & outdoor pools. Air-conditioned club and health club. Tennis courts. Hire shop. Environmental award park. 9 hole golf course and driving range, fishing lake, hair and beauty salon. New kids soft play area. Colour brochure on request. Open all year excluding Christmas day.

KING'S LYNN

Diglea Caravan & Camping Park, Beach Road, Snettisham, King's Lynn, Norfolk PE31 7RA. *01485 541367*. 10.5m N of King's Lynn on A149 Hunstanton Road. Turn L at sign marked 'Snettisham Beach'. Park 1.5m on L. 0.25m from beach and RSPB Reserve. Friendly family-run park in rural setting. Children's playground. Café/restaurant and takeaway

---

Acres of private sandy beach.
Self service shop.
Licensed bar with childrens room.
Laundry. Electric Hook-ups.
First-class toilets.

A FAMILY-RUN SITE FOR ALL THE FAMILY

LONG BEACH CARAVAN PARK
Hemsby, Great Yarmouth, NR29 4JD
Tel: 01493 730023 Fax: 01493 730188
email: info@long-beach.co.uk
www.long-beach.co.uk
internet service

The Grange Touring Park
Ormesby St Margaret, Great Yarmouth, Norfolk, NR29 3QG
Tel: Gt.Yarmouth (std. 01493) 730 306 Fax: 01493 730188
E-mail: info@grangetouring.co.uk Web: www.grangetouring.co.uk

A lovely and carefully run Park, just 5 minutes from Great Yarmouth and an ideal touring centre for the Norfolk Broads with first class toilet and shower facilities. Laundromat, electric hook-ups, children's play area etc. WIFI to all pitches and small internet reception
Please write or telephone for free brochure and booking form.

EAST ANGLIA

available a few yards away. Rally field available. Dogs on leads welcome. Fees on application.

(4m). Greenwood Campsite, Manor Farm, Tattersett, King's Lynn, Norfolk PE31 8RS. *01485 529269.* mike@greenwoodscampsite.co.uk. www.greenwoodscampsite.co.uk. From King's Lynn A148 Fakenham (14m). 2m from East Rudham on A148 with PO, shops, butcher, PH. Doctors 5m to Fakenham or Massingham. Open March-Oct.

Heacham Beach Holiday Park, South Beach Road, Heacham, King's Lynn, Norfolk PE31 7BD. *0871 6649743.* heacham.beach@park-resorts.com. www.park-resorts.com. Owner: Park Resorts Ltd. Off A149 from Kings Lynn to Hunstanton (3m). Heacham first village after Snettisham. Turn L at sign for Heacham beach and fork L about 1m along this road. Sports resorts programme court. Free kids club. Children's adventure playground. Tavern with family entertainment. Shops, PO, doctors 0.5m. David Bellamy Bronze Conservation Award. Open March-Oct.

(2.5m). King's Lynn Caravan & Camping Park, Parkside House, New Road, North Runcton, King's Lynn, Norfolk PE33 0QR. *01553 840004.* klcc@btconnect.com. www.kl-cc.co.uk. Owner: Paul & Clare Yallop. 1.5m from the A17, A10, A47, A149 main King's Lynn Hardwick roundabout, on the R of the A47 going towards Swaffham. Well situated for King's Lynn, inland market towns and the north Norfolk coast. Park is in 3.5 acres of pleasant parkland. Good local pubs, Tescos (1.5m). Site is used and recommended by most of the caravan clubs. Clubs welcome. Fishing, golf course nearby. PO & shop 1m, doctor 3m.

(9m). Pentney Park, Main Road, Pentney, King's Lynn, Norfolk PE32 1HU. *01760 337479.* holidays@pentney.demon.co.uk. www.pentney-park.co.uk. Owner: Bryan and Hilary Webster. On A47 Swaffham to King's Lynn. At junction with B1153. 2 Heated swimming pools (indoor/outdoor), gym, spa and sauna. Spar shop, café/ bar. Play area. Fishing in 1m. Golf 8m, shopping & cinema 9m. Open all year (except for 4 weeks from Jan 15th for holiday homes only).

(16m). Rickels Caravan & Camping Park, Bircham Road, Stanhoe, King's Lynn, Norfolk PE31 8PU. *01485 518671.* Owner: Heather Crown. From Kings Lynn take A148 to Hillington L on to B1153, fork R on to B1155 site on L 100yd over crossroads. Adults only. Quiet, friendly, high quality, family-run offering a peaceful and relaxed atmosphere. Fishing, shop, PO, doctor 2m, golf course 6m. Open April-Oct.

NORTH WALSHAM

(1m). Two MillsTouring Park, Yarmouth Road, North Walsham, Norfolk NR28 9NA. *01692 405829.* enquiries@twomills.co.uk. www.twomills.co.uk. Owner: Barbara & Ray Barnes. From N Walsham follow old Yarmouth road 1m SE past police station and hospital to park on L opposite Scarborough Hill hotel. Adults only. 2 dogs per pitch. Shops, doctors, PO etc in 1m. AA 4 pennants. David Bellamy Gold Conservation Award. Open March 1-Jan 3.

NORWICH

(18m). Applewood Camping and Caravan Park, The Grove, Banham, Norwich, Norfolk NR16 2HB. *01953 887771.* info@banhamzoo.co.uk. www.banhamzoo.co.uk. Owner: Mr M Goymour. Between Attleborough and Diss. Choice of restaurants. Hairdressing. Craft courtyard and access to Banham Zoo. Clothes washing and drying. Caravan accessories shop. Freezer service. Local pub and PO. Open March-Oct/special events Nov/Dec.

(0.5m). Camping & Caravanning Club Site – Norwich, Martineau Lane, Norwich, Norfolk NR1 2HX. *01603 620060.* www.campingandcaravanningclub.co.uk. Owner: Camping & Caravanning Club. From A47, join the A146 towards city centre. L at lights to next lights, under Low Bridge to the Cock Pub, turn L. Site 150yd on R. A 2.5-acre site overlooking beautiful open countryside with some shade. In easy reach of the Norfolk Broads, perfect for boating, birdwatching and walking. Non-members welcome. All units accepted. 2mins to Pub/restaurant. 5mins walk to local shops and bus into city every 20mins. Norwich city 30mins walk away. Fishing in season. Deals for families and backpackers. Open March-Oct.

Deer's Glade Caravan & Camping Park, White Post Road, Hanworth, Norwich, Norfolk NR11 7HN. *01263 768633.* info@deersglade.co.uk. www.deersglade.co.uk. Owner: Heather & David Attew. From Norwich, take the A140 towards Cromer. 5m beyond Aylsham, turn R towards Suffield Green SP White Post Road. The site is 0.5m on the R. Fishing on site. Pitch and store facilities. Also offer a free run to the pub.

(9m). Haveringland Hall Park, Cawston, Norwich, Norfolk NR10 4PN. *08700 444444.* info@lifestylelivinguk.com. www.haveringlandhall.co.uk. Owner: Blue Acorn Ltd. Take B1149 N from Norwich to Holt. 2m after Horsford, turn L SP Eastgate. At the Ratcatcher public house turn L for 800yd until Lodge gates of the Park on your L. Follow concrete road for

KELLING HEATH
THE NATURAL ESCAPE

Enjoy the beauty of Kelling Heath from your touring pitch set amongst rare open heathland with backdrops of pine and native woodland. A magnificent range of facilities and environmental activities await you. Lodges and holiday homes available for hire.

Bookings or brochure 01263 588 181
or online www.kellingheath.co.uk
Kelling Heath, Weybourne, Holt,
Norfolk NR25 7HW

EAST ANGLIA

800yd to reception on L. In 120-acre estate with woods and parkland with 12-acre fishing lake. In different areas of the estate are 2 permanent residential parks and a holiday park for tourers, tents and privately owned static caravans. Static Caravan Hire. New development of timber clad holiday lodges for sale amongst the arboretum area of the holiday park. Open mid March-end Oct.

(4m). Norfolk Showground Caravan Club Site, Long Lane, Bawburgh, Norwich, Norfolk NR9 3LX. *01603 742708*. www.caravanclub.co.uk. Owner: The Caravan Club. See website for directions. A charming and secluded site adjacent to extensive country parkland and in easy travelling distance of Norwich. Toilet blocks with privacy cubicles and laundry facilities. MV service point. Golf and fishing nearby. Non-members are welcome. No tents. Facilities for disabled. Open March-Nov.

Pampas Lodge Holiday Park, The Street, Haddiscoe, Norwich, Norfolk NR14 6AA. *01502 677265*. colinshirley@internet.com. Owner: CJC & VJ Shirley. 5m N of Beccles and 10m SW of Great Yarmouth on A143. Site behind Haddiscoe Tavern PH. Broads holiday centre. Fishing, golf nearby. Shops, PO 2m. Doctor 5m. 8m from Great Yarmouth & Gorleston. Open March-Oct.

(15m). Reedham Ferry Touring Park, Reedham Ferry, Acle, Norwich, Norfolk NR13 3HA. *01493 700429*. reedhamferry@aol.com. www.archerstouringpark.co.uk. Owner: Mr D Archer. A47 to Acle. Reedham is well-signposted from Acle 7m S. Flat, landscaped site adjacent to 17th century pub. Modern toilet facilities. Tumble dryer. Barbecue. Fishing close by. Moorings and slipway for trailed boats. Open Easter-Oct.

(7m). Swans Harbour, Barford Road, Marlingford, Norwich, Norfolk NR9 5HU. *01603 759658*. info@swansharbour.co.uk. www.swansharbour.co.uk. Owner: Mr & Mrs Morter. Turn R off B1108 (Norwich-Watton) in Barford SP Marlingford. After 350yd turn R at T-junction. Site on L after 0.75m (immediately past river bridge). Modern under floor, heated toilet block. Designated as unspoilt area of river valley. Park & Ride 1m. PO 2m. Fishing on site. Golf course, golf driving range, supermarket in 1-2m.

(20m). The Dower House Touring Park, East Harling, Norwich, Norfolk NR16 2SE. *01953 717314*. info@dowerhouse.co.uk. www.dowerhouse.co.uk. Owner: D Bushell. From Thetford take A1066 E for 5m fork L at Camping and East Harling sign, site on L after 2m, set in Thetford Forest. Family run touring park set deep in Thetford forest. Heated swimming pool. Large pitches. David Bellamy Gold Conservation Award. Open March 18-Oct 31.

REPPS WITH BASTWICK

Willowcroft Camping & Caravan Park, Staithe Road, Repps with Bastwick, Norfolk NR29 5JU. *01692 670380*. willo wcroftsite@btinternet.com. www.willowcroft.net. Owner: Mrs Kandy Trigg-Dudley. Off A149 into Church Road at Repps then R into Staithe Road. About 10/15m from Norwich/Great Yarmouth/Wroxham. In 2m walk of river, with access for fishing and safe walk along riverbank into Potter Heigham. Flat site with good amenities, boasting peace and tranquility in abundance. Open from 1 March-31 Oct.

SANDRINGHAM

(2m). Camping & Caravanning Club Site – Sandringham, The Sandringham Estate, Double Lodges, Sandringham, Norfolk PE35 6EA. *01485 542555*. www.campingandcaravanningclub.co.uk. Owner: Camping & Caravanning Club. From A148 turn L on to B1440 signed W Newton. Follow signs to site or take A149 turning L and follow signs to site. 7.5m from Kings Lynn. Site nestles among trees of the Royal Sandringham Estate. A few m to beach. All units accepted. Non-members welcome. Sandringham House, grounds and museum are well worth a visit. The historic port of Kings Lynn is in easy reach. The area has some of the most unspoilt country in the UK. Ideal for families and backpackers. Visit Britain Caravan Holiday Park of the Year, East England winner. Loo Of The Year (5 stars). David Bellamy Gold Conservation Award. Open Feb-Nov.

(1.5m). The Sandringham Estate Caravan Club Site, Glucksburg Woods, Sandringham, Norfolk PE35 6EZ. *01553 631614*. www.caravanclub.co.uk. Owner: The Caravan Club. See website for directions. Re-developed to offer full facilities, while retaining its rural charm. Surrounded by 600-acre Sandringham Estate Country Park. Play area. Dog walk. Restricted use of barbecues. Advance booking essential Bank Holidays and July and Aug. Non-members admitted. No

tents. Toilet blocks. Privacy cubicles. Hardstandings. Laundry facilities. Baby & toddler washroom. Veg prep. MV service point. Playground. Good area for walking. Ideal for families. Shop 150yd from site in the estate. Open March-Jan.

SHERINGHAM

(0.75m). Beeston Regis Caravan and Camping Park, Cromer Road, W Runton, Cromer, Sheringham, Norfolk NR27 9NG. *01263 823614*. info@beestonregis.co.uk. www.beestonregis.co.uk. Owner: The Beeston Group. On A149 Cromer to Sheringham road, from Sheringham proceed to W Runton. The entrance is on L after 0.75m of a touring caravans and motorhomes. Need to proceed over the railway line, please follow directions. Tourers must proceed over the railway line to our main entrance. Open March 20-Oct 31 touring & camping season.

STALHAM

(4m). Golden Beach Holiday Centre, Beach Road, Sea Palling, Stalham, Norfolk NR12 0AL. *01692 598269*. goldenbeach@keme.co.uk. www.goldenbeachpark.co.uk. Owner: J Gillard. On B1159 Stalham to Sea Palling, turn L down beach road. Site is on L. Quiet family park in peaceful village 200yds from golden sandy beaches, cafés, village store, PO and pubs. Ideal location for exploring the Norfolk Broads, Norwich and Great Yarmouth. Open from 20/3/09 to 30/10/09.

SWAFFHAM

(0.5m). Breckland Meadows Touring Park (Adults only), Lynn Road, Swaffham, Norfolk PE37 7PT. *01760 721246*. info@brecklandmeadows.co.uk. www.brecklandmeadows.co.uk. Owner: Andy and Denise Bull. Take Swaffam turn-off from the A47 between King's Lynn and Norwich. Adults only. Small, friendly and clean. Three-acre site about 0.5m W of Swaffham with walkway adjacent linking with Peddars Way. Central for touring Norfolk. Heated amenity block with free showers. Hardstandings if required. 3 AA pennants.

THETFORD

(6m). Camping & Caravanning Club Site – Thetford Forest, Puddledock Farm, Great Hockham, Thetford, Norfolk IP24 1PA. *01953 498455*. www.campingandcaravanningcl

EAST ANGLIA

ub.co.uk. Owner: Camping and Caravanning Club. Accessible via the A134, the A11 when you reach the A1075, look out for the pinic spot, the site is adjacent. Our new club site at Thetford Forest is surrounded by natural history. R next to the site, the forest itself is home to rare butterfies and plants and you might spot red, roe or muntjac deer.

The Covert Caravan Club Site, High Ash, Hillborough, Thetford, Norfolk IP26 5BZ. *01842 878356.* Owner: The Caravan Club. See website for directions. 7.5m from Swaffham. Set in Forestry Commission woodland, a quiet, secluded site with pitching areas in little open glades-ideal for the wildlife observer. Dog walk. Own sanitation required. Restricted use of barbecues. Advance booking essential Bank Holidays. Non-members welcome. No toilet block. MV service point. No tents. Open March 14-Nov 2.

(5m). Thorpe Woodland Caravan & Camping Site, Forest Holidays, Shadwell, Thetford, Norfolk IP24 2RX. *01842 751042.* www.forestholidays.co.uk. Owner: Forest Holidays. Off A1066 Thetford to Diss. After 5m bear L to East Harling. The site is 0.25m on the L. A secluded site in Thetford Forest Park ideal for visiting the Norfolk Broads. No shower or toilet facilties at this site. Bookings and brochure requests on 0845 1308224. Open March-Nov.

WELLS-NEXT-THE-SEA

(0.75m). Pinewoods Holiday Park, Beach Road, Wells-next-the-Sea, Norfolk NR23 1DR. *01328 710439.* holiday@pinewoods.co.uk. www.pinewoods.co.uk. Owner: Pinewoods Partnership. Off A149 and B1105 at Wells Quay. Good facilities on north Norfolk coast beside national nature reserve. Ideally placed to explore. Boating, pitch and putt, launderette, and coffee shop/takeaway. 2mins to the safe sandy beach. Cinema, golf courses 10m, shopping centre 30m. Open March 15- Oct 31. Till Jan 2 for winterised homes.

SUFFOLK

BECCLES

(7.5m). Ilkestshall Camp Site, The Grange, Ilkestshall, St Lawrence, Beccles, Suffolk NR34 8LB. *01986 781241.* Owner: WJ, KJ & VJ Gowing. On A144, 4m N of Hawesworth, 5m S of Bungay. Level grass, surrounded by trees. Ideal touring area, 20m S of Norwich. Open Easter-Oct.

(6m). Waveney River Centre, Staithe Road, Burgh St Peter, Beccles, Suffolk NR34 OBT. *01502 677343.* info@waveneyrivercentre.co.uk. www.waveneyrivercentre.co.uk. Owner: Manager: Mr James Knight. Follow brown signs from A143 at Haddiscoe. Turn down Wiggs Road. After 2.3m turn L into Burgh Road, site is another 2m. (Site is 4m from A143). Indoor leisure centre with swimming pool and spa, restaurant and PH. Adjacent to River Waveney, fishing during open season, rowing boats and day cruisers for hire. Play area, well stocked shop. Golf course 6m. Open March-Nov.

BUNGAY

(0.3m). Outney Meadow Caravan Park, Outney Meadow, Bungay, Suffolk NR35 1HG. *01986 892338.* www.outneymeadow.co.uk. Owner: C R Hancy. Off A143 between Bungay golf course and river Waveney. Canoe trail. Bike hire, fishing and golf. Open March-Oct.

BURY ST EDMUNDS

(1m). Round Plantation Caravan Club Site, Brandon Road, Mildenhall, Bury St Edmunds, Suffolk IP28 7JE. *01638 713089.* www.caravanclub.co.uk. Owner: The Caravan Club. See website for directions. A pleasant carefully landscaped site in woodland setting. The woodland attracts all kinds of birds so good for bird watchers. Own sanitation required. Good area for walking, dog walk on site. Quiet and peaceful off-peak. Non-members welcome. No tents. Open March-Oct.

(5m). The Dell Caravan & Camping Park, Beyton Road, Thurston, Bury St Edmunds, Suffolk IP31 3RB. *01359 270121.* thedellcaravanpark@btinternet. com. Owner: Mr Andrew Leathley. Follow A14 take J46 for Beyton/Thurston, follow signs for caravan park. Less than 1hr from coast. Excellent clean toilet blocks. Ideal for touring East Anglia. Dogs welcome.

EYE

(5m). Honeypot Camp & Caravan Park, Wortham, Eye, Suffolk IP22 1PW. *01379 783312.* honeypotcamping@talk21.com. www.honeypotcamping.co.uk. Owner: C M P Smith. Off A143. South side of road, 17m E from Bury St Edmunds, 4m W of Diss.

Quiet, rural site (Established 1970). Well grassed and free draining. Under personal supervision of the owner for over 30 years. Free hot water, showers, playground. Bressingham steam museum 1m. Landscaped country park with lakeside pitches with fishing on site. Highly recommended. Peace & quiet given the highest priority. Open May day weekend-Sept 22.

HADLEIGH

(4m). Polstead Caravan & Camping Park, Holt Road, Polstead Heath, Hadleigh, Suffolk CO6 5BZ. *01787 211969.* polsteadtouringpark@hotmail.co.uk. www.polsteadtouring.com. Owner: K & N McMinn. Between Boxford and Hadleigh on A1071, opposite 'The Brewers Arms' Inn. 3.5 acres, level landscaped grounds. Hardstandings, dog walk area. Ideal for touring Constable country. Golf, fishing nearby. Now adults only. Open Jan 14-Feb 14.

IPSWICH

(3m). Low House Touring Caravan Centre, Bucklesham Road, Foxhall, Ipswich, Suffolk IP10 0AU. *01473 659437.* low.house@btinternet.com. www.travelengland.org.uk. Owner: Mr J E Booth. Turn off A14 Ipswich ring road S via slip road onto A1156 go over bridge second R and site is on L now, SP. 3.5 acres of lawns and trees. Situated between Felixistowe and Ipswich. Pets corner, play area. Tourist Board member.

(4m). Orwell Meadows Leisure Park, Priory Lane, Nacton, Ipswich, Suffolk IP10 0JS. *01473 726666.* recept@orwellmeadows.co.uk. Owner: Mr & Mrs D Miles. 1m from A14 Ipswich bypass follow sign for Ransomes Europark and Orwell Country Park. Luxury caravans for hire. Modern showers. Swimming pool. Clubhouse. Family run site adjacent to country park.

(4m). Priory Park, Ipswich, Suffolk IP10 0JT. *01473 727393.* whathc@priory-park.com. www.priory-park.com. Owner: Priory Park Ltd. Leave A14 Ipswich southern bypass at Nacton interchange. Follow signs towards Ipswich Town Centre. After 300yd turn L and follow road into Priory Park. Set in 100-acres of landscaped parkland with panoramic estuary views. 9-hole golf course, tennis courts, heated outdoor swimming pool, bar and restaurant. Doctor, dentist, hospital, shops 2m. Sainsbury's 1.5m. Open from 1/4/09 to 31/10/09.

22 MOTOR CARAVAN & CAMPING PARKS 2009

EAST ANGLIA

(4.5m). The Oaks Caravan Park, Chapel Road, Bucklesham, Ipswich, Suffolk IP10 0BJ. *01394 448837.* oakscaravanpark@aol.com. www. oakscaravanpark.co.uk. Owner: Lee Brown. A14 E towards Felixstowe exit L, SP Bucklesham/Brightwell continue for about 1m turn R to Kirton, site on R. Age 18 years and over. Quiet countryside. Free use of following: BBQs, on site quoits, boules, hot & cold wash up sinks. Patio area, local fishing lake, pay & display golf, on site cycle hire, local restaurants and pubs nearby. Open April-Oct.

LOWESTOFT

(2m). Azure Seas Caravan Park, The Street, Corton, Lowestoft, Suffolk NR32 5HN. *01502 731403.* azureseas@aol.com. www. azureseas2005@aol.com. Owner: Airstream Leisure Ltd. Off A12 2m N of Lowestoft on to Corton Long Lane, L then immediately R. Luxury caravan holiday homes for sale with sea views. Near Pleasurewood Hills American theme park. Adjoining beach. Gas. Shops near. Booking advisable July and Aug. Open March 8-Nov 8.

(4m). Camping & Caravanning Club Site – Kessingland, Suffolk Wildlife Park, Whites Lane, Kessingland, Lowestoft, Suffolk NR33 7TF. *01502 742040.* www.campingandcaravanningclub.co.uk. Camping & Caravanning Club. Follow Wildlife Park signs off A12 from Lowestoft towards London. After leaving A12 at roundabout SP Kessingland, turn R to site entrance. Adjacent to Suffolk Wildlife Park and in easy reach of east coast resorts. All units accepted. Non-members welcome. Great Yarmouth and Lowestoft are close by and boast excellent beaches. Deals for families and backpackers. Loo Of The Year (5 stars). Open March-Oct.

(3.5m). Chestnut Farm Caravan Site, Gisleham, Lowestoft, Suffolk NR33 8EE. *01502 740227.* Owner: Mr N D Collen. W off A12 at southern roundabout on Kessingland bypass (opposite Suffolk Wildlife Park) SP Rushmere, Mutford and Gisleham, then 2nd turning on L, then 1st drive on L. 3 acres, level grassy site.

Private fishing. AA 2-pennant. Open Easter-Oct.

(4m). Heathland Beach Caravan Park, London Road, Kessingland, Lowestoft, Suffolk NR33 7PJ. *01502 740337.* heat hlandbeach@btinternet.com. www. heathlandbeach.co.uk. Owner: Reader Family. On A12. Three heated outdoor pools. Tennis. Play are for children. Private beach access. Play area. Bar. Fishing. Open April 1-Oct 31.

(4m). Kessingland Beach Holiday Park, Kessingland Beach, Beach Road, Lowestoft, Suffolk NR33 7RN. *0871 6649749.* kessingland.beach@park-resorts.com. www.park-resorts.com. Owner: Park Resorts Ltd. Kessingland is on A12 Ipswich to Lowestoft Road. About 4m S of Lowestoft, take the Kessingland beach exit from the roundabout near the Wildlife Park on Whites Lane. Follow road for about 1.5m to the beach. Park is 400yd further on. Indoor and outdoor heated pools. Launderette. On site store. Tennis courts. Free kids club. Free evening entertainment for all the family. Amusements. Takeaway and restaurant. Bar. Mini ten pin bowling. Soft play area. Adventure playground. New all weather sports court for 2008. David Bellamy Gold Conservation Award. Open Easter-Oct.

(5m). White House Beach Caravan Club Site, Beach Road, Kessingland, Lowestoft, Suffolk NR33 7RW. *01502 740278.* www.caravanclub.co.uk. Owner: The Caravan Club. See website for directions. See website for standard directions. Caravan Club members only. No tents. Adjacent to beach and ideally located for touring the Norfolk Broads. Dog walk. No awnings on sea front pitches. Shop in village. Toilet blocks. Privacy cubicles. Laundry facilities. Veg Prep. MV Service point. Gas. Playframe. Watersports. Ideal for families. Open March 27-Nov 10.

(3m). White House Farm Caravan Site, Gisleham, Lowestoft, Suffolk NR33 8DX. *01502 740248.* Owner: Mr B G Collen. From London-1st exit off roundabout at Kessingland, SP Gisleham, follow road bearing R at junction, site

200yd on R From Lowestoft-exit to Gisleham at Morrisons roundabout 1.5m L at church, site 300yd on L. Calor Gas. Farm walks, play area, fishing close by. Shops, PO 0.75m away. Open April 1-Oct 31.

NAYLAND

(7m). Rushbanks Farm, Wiston, Nayland, Suffolk CO6 4NA. *01206 262350.* Owner: Mr G F Bates. 2m off A134 from Nayland and 7m from Colchester. A beautiful unspoilt riverside campsite on north bank of River Stour suitable for fishing and boating (no engines). Open May-Oct.

SAXMUNDHAM

(0.5m). Carlton Park Caravan Site, Saxmundham, Suffolk IP17 1AT. *01728 604413.* Owner: Saxmundham & District Sports & Recreational Club. On B1121 signed in both directions from the A12. Showers/toilets on site. 0.5m to shops, supermarket, doctors and PO. Open April 1-Oct 31.

(8m). Cliff House Holiday Park, Minsmere Road, Dunwich, Saxmundham, Suffolk IP17 3DQ. *01728 648282.* info@cliffhouseholidays.co.uk. www.cliffhouseholidays.co.uk. Owner: Beeston Group. From A12 at Yoxford turn off to Westleton. Turning L at T junction. Turn R to Dunwich Heath and after 1.5m turn R again. The park is 0.75m on the L. 6m from Southwold. Country house in 30-acres of woodland, beach frontage between Southwold (8m) and Aldeburgh adjoining National Trust and RSPB – Free House bar and informal restaurant. Games room and playground. Open March 1-Oct 31 for tourers. GS. Open March 1-Oct 31.

■ **(6m). Haw-Wood Farm Caravan Park, Haw-Wood Farm, Hinton, Saxmundham, Suffolk IP17 3QT.** *01986 784248.* bookings@hawwoodfarm.co.uk. www. hawwoodfarm.co.uk. Owner: Mr A Blois. Off A12. Turn R off A12 1.5m N of Darsham level crossing at Little Chef. Park 0.5m on R. 8m from Southwold. The perfect site for discovering the Suffolk coast and countryside. Quiet site with showers and play area. Managers: Tony

---

HAW WOOD FARM
CARAVAN PARK

Haw Wood Farm is the perfect site for discovering the beautiful Suffolk Coast and countryside including Southwold, Dunwich, Aldeburgh and the RSPB Nature Reserve at Minsmere. Static Caravan and Seasonal Pitches are available.

Tel: 01986 784248
www.hawwoodfarm.co.uk

www.motorcaravanmagazine.co.uk   MOTOR CARAVAN & CAMPING PARKS 2009   **23**

EAST ANGLIA

& Mavis Wiggins. Fishing and golf nearby. Little Chef 0.5m, nearest pub about 1.5m. Darsham station 2m. Open March 1-Jan 14.

(1m). Whitearch Touring Caravan Park, Main Road, Benhall, Saxmundham, Suffolk IP17 1NA. 01728 604646. Owner: Mr & Mrs Rowe. J A12 and B1121. Play area. One-acre coarse fishing lake. Tennis court. 50 pitches electric hook-ups, TV points Open April-end Sept.

SOUTHWOLD

(1m). Southwold Camping and Caravan Site, Ferry Road, Southwold, Suffolk IP18 6ND. 01502 722486. Owner: Waveney District Council. Off A12. Turn towards Southwold at Wrentham. Go through towards harbour mouth. Inquiries to the manager. No booking necessary. Open from 1/4/08 to 31/10/08.

STOWMARKET

Orchard View Caravan Park, Stowupland Service Station, Thorney Green, Stowmarket, Suffolk IP14 4BJ. 01449 612326. Owner: I D & B G Leeks. 1m off A14 on A1120, situated at rear of service station. Quiet, level, grassy site, close to orchard. Good touring centre. Dogs allowed under control. Open April-Oct inclusive.

SUDBURY

(2m). Willowmere Caravan & Camping Park, Bures Road, Little Cornard, Sudbury, Suffolk CO10 0NN. 01787 375559. Owner: Mrs A Wilson. Situated on the B1508, Sudbury to Bures road. Swimming, sports centre 0.5m. Sudbury 1m. Fishing on site. Golf, horse-riding 2m. Small quiet park in Suffolk countryside. Open Easter-Oct.

THEBERTON

■ **(1m). Cakes & Ale Caravan Park, Abbey Lane, Theberton, Suffolk IP16 4TE.** 01728 831655. cakesandalepark@gmail.com. www.cakesandale.net. Owner: Mr Fergus Little. Leave A12 turn on to B1121 to Saxmundham. Turn E on to B1119 towards Leiston. After 3m turn N to Theberton and follow camping park signs. 2m W of Minsmere bird sanctuary. Convenient Aldeburgh, Dunwich, Southwood. Quiet low key well maintained grounds and facilities. Most sites hardstanding supa pitch. Club. Tennis courts. Play area. Recreation area with golf driving range and practice nets. Volley ball, petanque. AA 3-pennant. Open April 1-Oct 31.

WOODBRIDGE

(6m). Forest Camping, in Rendlesham Forest, Tangham Campsite, Butley, Woodbridge, Suffolk IP12 3NF. 01394 450707. admin@forestcamping.co.uk. www.forestcamping.co.uk. Owner: Mrs C M Lummis. Off B1084 between Woodbridge and Orford. Follow Rendlesham Forest Centre tourist brown signs. Shower block. Spacious site in centre of Forestry Commission forest. Riding cycle trail. Miles of walks in the forest. Space for children to play. AA, EATB. Open April 1-Oct 31.

(4m). Moon and Sixpence, Newbourn Road, Waldringfield, Woodbridge, Suffolk IP12 4PP. 01473 736650. info@moonandsixpence.eu. www.moonandsixpence.eu. Turn off Ipswich eastern bypass A12 taking minor road towards Waldringfield. Park is SP. AA 5 pennant premier park. Superb loos and bathrooms, lounge bar and restaurant. 2-acre deep water lake with private fishing mid Sept and mid Oct, golden sand beach. Adventure play area. 3 hard tennis courts, volley & basket ball, petanque. 9 hole compact golf course. Quietness essential from 9pm – 8am. 18 hole golf 0.5m away. Sailing, watersports 2m. Indoor pool 4m. No Groups. Open April 1-Oct 31.

St Margaret's Caravan & Camping Park, Shottisham, Woodbridge, Suffolk IP12 3HD. 01394 411247. ken.norton@virgin.net. On B1083, from A12 SP Bawdsey, L at Shottisham T-junction. Site on L past Sorrel Horse Inn. In 5m of sea. Bird sanctuary 6m. Open April (Easter if earlier) – Oct.

GLOUCESTERSHIRE

BOURTON-ON-THE-WATER

(2.5m). Folly Farm, Notgrove, Bourton-on-the-Water, Gloucestershire GL54 3BY. 01451 820285. follyfarm@cotswoldcamping.net. www.cotswoldcamping.net. Owner: S A Kenwright. 2.5m from Bourton on the Water on the A436. Ideal for walkers and cyclists. Our site is in an area of 'outstanding natural beauty' and is deliberately basic with its facilities; ie: no floodlights, playgrounds, shops but do have showers, toilets, chemical disposal points. We are ideally situated close to Bourton on the Water and Stow on the Wold. Open March-Oct.

(4.5m). Notgrove Caravan Club Site, Cheltenham Road, Bourton-on-the-Water, Gloucestershire GL54 3BU. 01451 850249. www.caravanclub.co.uk. Owner: The Caravan Club. See website for directions. Caravan Club members only. No tents. Delightful site high up in the Cotswolds surrounded by open countryside and superb views. Chemical toilet disposal point. No toilet block. MV service point. Some hardstandings, gas dog walk on site, storage pitches, quiet and peaceful off peak. Open March-Oct.

CAKES AND ALE
The Centre for Coastal Suffolk

Set amongst the beautiful Suffolk scenery between Aldeburgh and Southwold, Cakes and Ale is an oasis of tranquillity and quality. Just minutes from Minsmere bird sanctuary and the ancient monument of Leiston Abbey. Cakes and Ale the ideal place to explore the Suffolk Heritage Coast (or just relax and put your feet up).
New holiday homes available from £30,000
Open 1st March to 15th January
For a free brochure call **01728831655** or email
cakesandalepark@gmail.com alternatively try
www.cakesandale.net
or just come and visit us
CAKES AND ALE   ABBEY LANE   THEBERTON   SUFFOLK   IP16 4TE

HEART OF ENGLAND

See page 5 for key to symbols and abbreviations

CAMBRIDGE

Riverside Caravan Park, The George, Cambridge, Gloucestershire GL2 7AL. 01453 890270. A38 Bristol to Gloucester. Exit M5, J13 or 14. Pub/restaurant on site. Summer barbecues. Children's play area. Pets corner. Storage available. Open all year – according to ground conditions.

CHELTENHAM

Briarfields Touring Park, Gloucester Road, Cheltenham, Gloucestershire GL51 0SX. 01242 235324. briarfields@hotmail.co.uk. www.briarfields.net. Owner: Mr Alan Aplin. Leave M5, J11, follow A40 Cheltenham, take first L at roundabout on to B4063. Entrance is 200 metres on L. AA 3 pennants.

(1.25m). Cheltenham Racecourse Caravan Club Site, Prestbury Park, Cheltenham, Gloucestershire GL50 4SH. 01242 523102. www.caravanclub.co.uk. Owner: The Caravan Club. See website for directions. A sophisticated location on the edge of Cheltenham with panoramic views of the Cleeve Hills. Dog walk. Non-members welcome. No tents. Toilet block. Laundry facilities. Veg prep. MV service point. Open April-Nov.

CIRENCESTER

(1m). Cirencester Park Caravan Club Site, Stroud Road, Cirencester, Gloucestershire GL7 1UT. 01285 651546. www.thecaravanclub.co.uk. Owner: The Caravan Club. See website for directions. Caravan Club members only. No tents. Set in beautiful grade 1 listed parkland, and forming part of the Bathurst Estate, this site is peaceful, level, with many mature trees and in walking distance of Cirencester. Toilet blocks, laundry facilities, baby and toddler washroom and MV service point. Playground, boules pitch and dog walk on site. Fishing, golf, watersports and NCN route nearby. Facilities for the disabled. Open March-Jan.

Cotswold Hoburne, Broadway Lane, South Cerney, Cirencester, Gloucestershire GL7 5UQ. 01285 860216. Owner: Hoburne Ltd. From J15 of M4, take A419, SP Cirencester to 4m S of Cirencester. SP to Cotswold Water Parks. Seventy acre park with two fishing lakes, Lakeside club house, indoor leisure pool, outdoor pool etc. Open April-Oct.

(2m). Mayfield Park, Cheltenham Road, Perrotts Brook, Cirencester, Gloucestershire GL7 7BH. 01285 831301. mayfield-park@cirencester.fsbusiness.co.uk. www.mayfieldpark.co.uk. Owner: Jan & Adrian Yates & June & Peter Rathbone. On A435, 2m from Cirencester and 13m Cheltenham. Leave new bypass at Burford Road junction. Turn towards Cirencester and follow brown camping and caravan signs. A mixture of grass and hardstanding pitches. Small shop with off sales and a selection of take away meals. Laundry room, tumble and spin dryers. Calor & Gaz stocked. New gravel area for winter use. Credit and debit card facilities available. Dogs allowed with caravans but not on camping field.

COLEFORD

Braceland Caravan & Camping – Forest of Dean, Forestry Holidays, Christchurch, Bracelands Drive, Coleford, Gloucestershire GL16 7NN. 01594 837258. www.forestholidays.co.uk. Owner: Forest Holidays. N of Coleford on minor road towards Symonds Yat Rock. Beautiful spacious site, great for families. Baby changing facilities. Booking and brochure requests on 0845 1308224. Open March-Nov.

(2m). Christchurch Caravan & Camping Site, Forest Holidays, Christchurch, Bracelands Drive, Coleford, Gloucestershire GL16 7NN. 01594 837258. www.forestholidays.co.uk. Owner: Forest Holidays. N of Coleford on the minor road to Symonds Yat. Set in the heart of the Forest of Dean, ideal for Symonds Yat. New wifi connection. Bookings and brochure requests on 0845 1308224. Open March-Jan.

Woodland Caravan & Camping Site – Forest of Dean, Forestry Holidays, Christchurch, Bracelands Drive, Coleford, Gloucestershire GL16 7NN. 01594 837258. www.forestholidays.co.uk. Owner: Forest Holidays. 1m N of Coleford, at A4136 crossroads, go N for 0.5m. Site SP. Each pitch is set back in its own stand of trees at this quiet site. No toilet or shower facilities. No tents of sleeping in awnings. Reception at Christchurch. Booking and brochure requests on 0845 1308224 Open early March-Nov.

DURSLEY

(5m). Hogsdown Farm Caravan & Camping Site, Lower Wick, Dursley, Gloucestershire GL11 6DS. 01453 810224. Owner: Mrs Jenny Smith. Off A38, between jcts 13 & 14, M5. Half way between Bristol & Gloucester, SP Lower Wick. Excellent walking and touring country on edge of Cotswold Hills. Fishing and golf nearby.

GLOUCESTER

(6m). Gables Farm, Moreton Valence, Gloucester, Gloucestershire GL2 7ND. 01452 720331. Owner: Mrs D M Dickenson. M5, J12 then 1.5m S on A38 and J13 then 1.5m N on A38. Overnight stop or local touring site. No shop but essentials are available in 3m. Slimbridge Wildfowl and Wetlands 6m. Open March-Nov.

(2m). Riverside Caravan Park, The George Inn, Nr Dursley, Gloucester, Gloucestershire GL2 7AL. 01453 890270. stay@theriverside.caravanpark.co.uk. www.theriversidecaravanpark.co.uk. Owner: Mr & Mrs E Hogben. A38 Bristol to Gloucester, exit M5 J13 or J14. From J13 travel S on the A38, from J14 travel N on A38. Pub/restaurant on site. Children's play area. Birds and animals pets corner. Toilet/shower block. Storage available. The nearest shop, PO, doctors are less than 3m away, there is an on site pub/restaurant, children play area. Storage available.

 **(5m). The Red LionCaravan Site, Wainlode Hill, Norton, Gloucester, Gloucestershire GL2 9LW.** 01452 730251. www.redlioninn-caravancampingpark.co.uk. Owner: G A Skilton. From Tewkesbury travel 3m S on A38, then turn R on to B4213. About 3m turn L to Wainlode Hill. On the banks of the river Severn. Shaver points. Hairdryers. Fishing. Central for touring Cotswolds and Severn valley. AA & RAC approved. Open all year if ground suitable.

LECHLADE

(0.25m). Bridge House Campsite, Bridge House, Thames Street, Lechlade, Gloucestershire GL7 3AG. 01367 252348. Owner: R Cooper. On A361, 0.25m S of Lechlade. Shops, PO, doctor, restaurants and pubs all in 0.25m. Fishing nearby. Golf 5m. Open March 1-Oct 31.

(0.5m). St Johns Priory Park, Faringdon Road, Lechlade, Gloucestershire GL7 3EZ. 07795 490521. info@britanniaparks.com. www.britanniaparks.com. Owner: Britannia Parks Ltd. 0.5m on L Lechlade to Faringdon A417. Bank of Thames adjoining famous Trout Inn. Pets welcome. Children allowed in residential homes. GS. Open March 1-Oct 31 for holiday homes.

www.motorcaravanmagazine.co.uk MOTOR CARAVAN & CAMPING PARKS 2009 **25**

HEART OF ENGLAND

LYDNEY

(3m). Whitemead Forest Park, Parkend, Lydney, Gloucestershire GL15 4LA. 0845 3453425. whitemead@csma.uk.com. www.whitemead.co.uk. Owner: CSMA Motoring & Leisure Services Ltd. Off the A48. 32 apartment for self catering also available. Shop, indoor heated swimming pool, with sauna, gym, steam room, jacuzzis. Heated shower and toilet blocks. Laundry x2. Daytime café, evening restaurant. Bar, entertainment venue with live entertainment at weekends and all school holidays. Family activities in school holidays. Beauty salon, play park, indoor soft play.

MORETON-IN-MARSH

(0.5m). Moreton-In-Marsh Caravan Club Site, Bourton Road, Moreton-in-Marsh, Gloucestershire GL56 0BT. 01608 650519. www.caravanclub.co.uk. Owner: The Caravan Club. See website for directions. This attractive site is in walking distance of Moreton-in-the-Marsh. Surrounded by picturesque Cotswold villages. Advance booking essential. Dog walk on site. Non-members welcome. No tents. Toilet blocks. Privacy cubicles. Laundry facilities. Baby/toddler washroom. Veg prep. MV service point. Hardstandings. Play equipment. Boules pitch. Fishing locally. Ideal for families. Shops in 0.25m.

SLIMBRIDGE

(0.5m). Tudor Caravan Park, Shepherds Patch, Slimbridge, Gloucestershire GL2 7BP. 01453 890483. info@tudorcaravanpark.co.uk. www.tudorcaravanpark.com. Owner: Keith, Joan and Robin Fairall. M5 J13, on to A38, follow signs for Slimbridge WWT Wetlands Centre. 1.5m off A38 at rear of Tudor Arms Pub. Quiet, family run park adjacent to bird sanctuary and Gloucester to Sharpness Canal. Separate area for adults only. Pub & restaurant adjoining. Fishing. Tearoom & small convenience shop adjacent. Golf course nearby. AA 3 pennants park. David Bellamy Gold Conservation Award.

TEWKESBURY

(6m). Camping & Caravanning Club Site – Winchcombe, Brooklands Farm, Alderton, Tewkesbury, Gloucestershire GL20 8NX. 01242 620259. www.campingandcaravanningclub.co.uk. Owner: Camping & Caravanning Club. On A46 from Tewkesbury keep straight on at roundabout and take B4077 to Stow on the Wold, site on R in 3m. Set amidst the lovely Cotswold countryside with its own fishing lake. Non-members welcome. All units accepted. 80 pitches set in 20 acres. A visit to nearby Cheltenham with its fine shopping is worthwhile. The village of Winchcombe with its pretty antique shops and tea rooms is close to the site. Plenty of room for childrens' ball games. Deals for families and backpackers. David Bellamy Gold Conservation Award. Open March – Jan.

(1.5m). Croft Farm Leisure & Water Park, Bredons Hardwick, Tewkesbury, Gloucestershire GL20 7EE. 01684 772321. alan@croftfarmleisure.com. www.croftfarmleisure.co.uk. Owner: Alan Newell. Take Bredon Road out of Tewkesbury on B4080. 1.5m on L. Touring caravan and camping site with own watersports lake and fitness centre. Luxury facilities. Bar and café. Winter storage. Tuition available in windsurfing, sailing and canoeing. Open March 1-Nov 30.

(2m). Dawleys Caravan Park, Owls Lane, Shuthonger, Tewkesbury, Gloucestershire GL20 6EQ. 01684 292622. enquiries@dawleyscaravanpark.co.uk. www.ukparks.co.uk/dawleys. Owner: Richard Harrison (Park Manager). M50 J1, take A38 S towards Tewkesbury-turn R after 1m. Quiet site in rural surroundings. Good walk and fishing nearby. Ideal for touring the Cotswolds, Malvern and Vale of Evesham. Special offers for 7 nights. Golf, fishing, cinema, swimming pool, shopping all in 2m. Park Manager: Richard Harrison. Open Easter-end of Sept.

(2m). Sunset View Touring Tent & Caravan Park & Ostrich Farm, Church Lane End, Twyning, Tewkesbury, Gloucestershire GL20 6EH. 01684 292145. cherylgoulstone@hotmail.com. Owner: Mr & Mrs A B Goulstone. 2m N of Tewkesbury on A38, almost opposite Crown Inn turn R. Site 200yd on R. Two level acres. A quiet family run site. Horse riding, fishing and golf nearby; pub with restaurant in 5mins walk. Ostrich eggs on sale at site.

(Tewkesbury Abbey Caravan Club Site, Gander Lane, Tewkesbury, Gloucestershire GL20 5PG. 01684 294035. www.caravanclub.co.uk. Owner: The Caravan Club. M5, leave at J9 on to A438 SP Tewkesbury at traffic lights keep R and continue straight. In town centre at mini roundabout keep L, in 200yd turn L into Gander Lane, site on L. Impressive site almost in the shadow of the ancient abbey and a short walk from town centre. Dog walk. Tents welcome. Advance booking advisable. Non-members welcome. Toilet blocks, privacy cubicles. Laundry facilities. MV service

---

THE RED LION
Caravan & Camping Park and Riverside Inn
WAINLODE HILL, NORTON, GLOUCESTER GL2 9LW Tel: 01452 730251 or 01299 400787

From Tewkesbury, travel 3 miles south on A38 then turn right on to B4213. Approx 3 miles turn left to Wainlode Hill. 109 pitches - some electric. Open all year round. Toilet/Shower Block. Beautiful River Severn bank location with oldie worldie pub serving great meals. Nearby towns: Gloucester, Cheltenham and Tewkesbury.

26 MOTOR CARAVAN & CAMPING PARKS 2009

See page 5 for key to symbols and abbreviations

HEART OF ENGLAND

point. Veg prep. Golf and fishing nearby. Ideal for families. Shop 0.25m away. Good walking, cycling nearby. Open mid March-early Nov.

HEREFORDSHIRE

CRASWALL

Old Mill Camp Site, Craswall, Herefordshire HR2 OPN. *01981 510226.* Owner: Mr J Watkins. 8m off the A465 at Pandy. Quiet camping site near river and the Offa's Dyke path. At the foot of the Black Mountains Open Easter-Oct 31.

HEREFORD

(4m). Cuckoos Corner, Moreton-on-Lugg, Hereford, Herefordshire HR4 8AH. *01432 760234.* cuckoos.corner@lc24.net. www.caravancampsites.co.uk. Owner: Adrian Spong. Easily accessible off A49. 4m N of Hereford. Ideal family site. 10 hardstandings of which 5 are 45feet long. Free wireless broadband. Archery, croquet. (Take away food and shop 0.5m). Fishing on Lugg and Wye.

(5m). Lucksall Caravan & Camping Park, Mordiford, Hereford, Herefordshire HR1 4LP. *01432 870213.* karen@lucksallpark.co.uk. www.lucksallpark.co.uk. Owner: Orleton Rise Park Ltd. Off B4224. Between Hereford and Ross on Wye. Bordered by river Wye. Level, non-commercialised. Fishing, walking, shop on site. Canoeing (hire). New static caravans for sale. Open March 1-Nov 30.

(7m). Millpond, Little Tarrington, Hereford, Herefordshire HR1 4JA. *01432 890243.* enquiries@millpond.co.uk. www.millpond.co.uk. Owner: Philip & Angela Stock. M50, J2, Ledbury A438 SP Tarrington (about 7m). Second turning R. Site 200yd on R. Coarse fishing on site. Golf nearby. Basics shopping (bread, milk, fruit, veg) 2.5m. PO 4m. Doctor 10mins by car. Rural setting, peaceful and quiet. David Bellamy Gold Conservation Award. Open March 1-Oct 31.

(11m). Poston Mill Park, Peterchurch, Golden Valley, Hereford, Herefordshire HR2 0SF. *01981 550225.* info@poston-mill.co.uk. www.bestparks.co.uk. Owner: Wayne & Sarah Jones. On B4348 mid-way Hereford and Hay-on-Wye. Caravan Holiday Park, Gold in England for excellence awards 2008, Gold Servicemark award for Quality at Heart. Highly recommended, well kept, quality park ideal for touring, walking and fishing.

Licensed restaurant on site. 1m to shops, PO, doctor. David Bellamy Gold Conservation Award. Open March 15-Jan 5.

(15m). Upper Gilvach Farm, St Margarets, Vowchurch, Hereford, Herefordshire HR2 0QY. *01981 510618.* Owner: A Watkins. S off B4348 Hay to Hereford road at Vowchurch. Peaceful farm site with ample space and many walks. Close to many churches and castles. Dogs allowed on leads. Telephone. Open April-Sept.

MOORHAMPTON

(10m). Moorhampton Caravan Club Site, The Old Station, Moorhampton, Herefordshire HR4 7BE. *01544 318594.* www.caravanclub.co.uk. Owner: The Caravan Club. See website for directions. 10m from Hereford. Caravan Club members only. No tents. Hereford 10m. A quiet little site in heart of Herefordshire countryside. Dog walk on site. Toilet blocks. Privacy cubicles. Laundry facilities. Veg prep. MV service point. Golf nearby. Open March-Oct.

ROSS-ON-WYE

(5m). Lower Ruxton Farm, Kings Caple, Ross-on-Wye, Herefordshire HR1 4TX. *01432 840223.* Owner: Mr H D Jenkins. Off A49 Ross/Hereford signs to King's Caple. Turn R at sign to Ruxton. Second farm on R. Level, riverside site, easily accessible. Disposal pit for chemical toilets. Mains water taps only. Open mid-July to end-Aug.

SHROPSHIRE

BISHOP'S CASTLE

(7m). Cwnd House Farm, Wentnor, Bishop's Castle, Shropshire. *01588 650237.* Owner: R E B Jones. Take A489 at Craven Arms. R off A489 at Lydham Heath signed Wentnor. Past Inn on the Green. Site on R after 1m. Peaceful farm site (10 pitches in total). Ideal touring site. Shop in 1m. Open May-Oct.

(5m). The Green Caravan Park, Wentnor, Bishop's Castle, Shropshire SY9 5EF. *01588 650605.* karen@greencaravanpark.co.uk. www.greencaravanpark.co.uk. Owner: Mr & Mrs J H Turley & Family. Follow brown tourist signs from A488 and A489. Long Mynd is unsuitable for caravans. Peaceful riverside park set in the Shropshire hills, an area of outstanding natural beauty. Superb walks. Excellent birdlife. Dog walk on site. Pub at site

entrance. In easy reach of Shrewsbury, Ludlow and Ironbridge. David Bellamy Gold Conservation Award. Open Easter-Oct 31.

BRIDGNORTH

(2m). Stanmore Hall Touring Park, Stourbridge Road, Bridgnorth, Shropshire WV15 6DT. *01746 761761.* stanmore@morris-leisure.co.uk. www.morris-leisure.co.uk. Owner: Morris Leisure. From Bridgnorth on A458 to Stourbridge. CARAVAN CLUB AFFILIATED SITE. Set in beautiful grounds, the park takes full advantage of the mature trees and two-acre lake with its water lilies and resident peacocks. Toilet blocks, laundry facilities and MV service point. Play area, shop and dog walk on site. Fishing and golf nearby. Facilities for disabled. Ideal for families. Quiet and peaceful off-peak.

(11m). Three Horse Shoes Caravan Park, Wheathill, Burwarton, Bridgnorth, Shropshire WV16 6QT. *01584 823206.* Owner: Mr C J Pritchard. 7m from Ludlow. On B4364 road. Adjoining the country inn. Bar snacks available during inn's opening hours. Excellent views and ideal for touring and walking. Many places of interest nearby. Open April-Oct.

CHURCH STRETTON

(2m). Small Batch, Little Stretton, Church Stretton, Shropshire SY6 6PW. *01694 723358.* Owner: Mrs P R Prince. N to S turn R of A49 for Little Stretton A49-B5477 second L. Then R through stream to site. 2 pubs nearby. Shop, PO, doctor 2m. Open Easter-end Sept.

CRAVEN ARMS

(7m). Bush Farm, Clunton, Craven Arms, Shropshire SY7 0HU. *01588 660330.* Owner: Mr & Mrs M Adams. From A49 at Craven Arms. 7m W on B4368. SP from Crown Inn at Clunton. Open March-Jan.

Kevindale Camping Site, Kevindale Broome, Craven Arms, Shropshire SY7 0NT. *01588 660199.* Owner: Mr Keith Rudd. From Craven Arms on A49. Take B4368 Clun/Bishops Castle. 2m L on B4367 to Knighton. 1.5m to Broome village on R. Close to village inn. Good food. Scenic views in Clun Valley. Close to mid-Wales border. Good walking. Open from 1/4/08 to 1/10/08.

HEART OF ENGLAND

MUCH WENLOCK

(2.5m). Presthope Caravan Club Site, Stretton Road, Much Wenlock, Shropshire TF13 6DQ. *01746 785234.* www.caravanclub.co.uk. Owner: The Caravan Club. See website for directions. Set in beautiful countryside ideal for naturalist with abundant wildlife on site. Own sanitation required. Chemical toilet disposal point. Advance booking essential all Bank Holidays. Non-members welcome. No tents. Hardstandings. Steel awning pegs required. Gas and Gaz. Fishing nearby. Good area for walking. Open April-Sept.

OSWESTRY

(19m). Camping & Caravanning Club Site – Oswestry, Cranberry Moss, Kinnerly, Oswestry, Shropshire SY10 8OY. *01743 741118.* www.caravanandcaravanningclub.co.uk. Owner: Camping & Caravanning Club. Turn off the A5 at the roundabout at the north end of the dual carriageway, signed B4396 (Knocklin). Once a vital frontier between England and Wales Oswestry is now a vibrant market town local attractions include Whittington Castle, Shrewsbury Abbey and Wroxeter Roman city.

PONTESBURY

Middle Darnford, Ratlinghope, Pontesbury, Shropshire SY5 0SR. *01694 751320.* Owner: Mr R H Hamer. 4m NW of Church Stretton. Opposite Long Mynd hills. On A49 turn W at Leebotwood 3m N of Church Stretton through Woolstaston. Quiet, country site, attractive to children. Open later than Oct if weather permits. Pets welcome. Washbasins.

SHREWSBURY

(1.5m). Beaconsfield Farm, Upper Battlefield, Shrewsbury, Shropshire SY4 4AA. *01939 210370/01939 2.* mail@beaconsfield-farm.co.uk. www.beaconsfield-farm.co.uk. Owner: PW & J Poole. 0.5m N of Shrewsbury on A49. Adults only. Traditional A La Carte restaurant. Indoor swimming pool, fly & coarse fishing pool. Bowling green. AA 5 pennant, Best of British Park, Loo of the Year. Golf 3m. Open Feb-Jan 3.

(6m). Cartref Caravan Park, Ford Heath, Shrewsbury, Shropshire SY5 9GD. *01743 821688.* www.caravancampingsites.co.uk/shropshire/cartref. Owner: A D & P Edwards. From Shrewsbury bypass A5, take A458 Welshpool for 2m. SP from Ford village or take B4386 Montgomery road for 2m to Cruckton crossroads (site signposted). Now SP from A5 Shrewsbury by-pass on Montgomery junction B4386. Small, level site Peaceful countryside. Dogs allowed on leads. Dish washing area. Free showers. Hot water in basins. AA 2 pennants. Café/restaurant, shop available nearby. Open Easter-Oct.

Mill Farm Holiday Park, Hughley, Shrewsbury, Shropshire SY5 6NT. *01746 785208/255.* mail@millfarmcaravanpark.co.uk. www.millfarmcaravanpark.co.uk. Owner: Mr M D Bosworth. A458 Much Wenloch to Shrewsbury road. 3.5m from Harley. Turn L, after 2m at SP for Harley, site SP. Attractive, sheltered site skirted by a trout stream. Pony-trekking available. Bus service 2 days a week. Open all year except month of Feb.

(2m). Oxon Hall Touring Park, Welshpool Road, Shrewsbury, Shropshire SY3 5FB. *01743 340868.* oxon@morris-leisure.co.uk. www.morris-leisure.co.uk. Owner: Morris Leisure. 2m from Shrewsbury Town Centre on A458 Welshpool Road. 1m from A5. Access to Park and Ride. Children welcome. Pubs in walking distance. Close to hospital and doctors. Golf, fishing in 3m. Adjacent to park & ride bus service. Open all year.

TELFORD

Camping & Caravanning Club Site – Ebury Hill, Ring Bank, Haughton, Telford, Shropshire TF6 6BU. *01743 709334.* www.campingandcaravanningclub.co.uk. Owner: Camping & Caravanning Club. 2.5m through Shrewsbury on A53. Turn R signed Haughton and Upton Magna. Continue 1.5m site on R. Non-members welcome and may join at site. All units accepted. Own sanitation required. Some all weather pitches available. Site is set upon an ancient Iron Age Hill Fort. Fishing is available from site which is close to Telford Park. Site is 6m from Shrewsbury and well situated for the Severn Valley and Welsh Borders. Nearby is the Shropshire Way Footpath. Deals for families and backpackers. David Bellamy Gold Conservation Award. Open March-Oct.

(3m). Severn Gorge Park, Bridgnorth Road, Tweedale, Telford, Shropshire TF7 4JB. *01952 684789.* info@severngorgepark.co.uk. www.severngorgepark.co.uk. Owner: Webb Park Home Estates Ltd. From M54 J4, take A442 for 1m, then A442 SP Kidderminster for 1.6m. Follow SP for Madeley then Tweedale. Level, sheltered site set amongst woodland. All modern facilities. Ideal for exploring Ironbridge and the rest of Shropshire.

WEM

(1m). Lower Lacon Caravan Park, Wem, Shropshire SY4 5RP. *01939 232376.* info@llcp.co.uk. www.lowerlaconcaravanpark.co.uk. Owner: Mr C H Shingler. Off A49. On to B5065. AA 3 pennants. Quiet rural site. Heated outdoor swimming pool. Licensed lounge. Food. Golf course 3m. Cinema, shopping centre 10m. Open April-Nov.

WHITCHURCH

(4m). Green Lane Farm, Green Lane, Prees, Whitchurch, Shropshire SY13 2AH. *01948 840460.* greenlanefarm@tiscali.co.uk. www.greenlanefarm.northshropshire.biz. Owner: Gerry & Pauline Quinn. Whitchurch-Newport A41. 4m S of Whitchurch turn R to Hodnet (park SP), after 150yd turn R for Prees. Site is first farm house on R. 3 spacious acres full of flowers. Games green. Children's play area. One mile to local PO, shop and doctor. 4m to swimming pool, 2m to fishing. Golf & horseriding nearby. Central for all local attractions. Open March 1-Oct 31.

STAFFORDSHIRE

CHEADLE

(0.5m). Hales Hall Caravan & Camping Park, Oakamoor Road, Cheadle, Staffordshire ST10 4BQ. *01538 753305.* Owner: Mr & Mrs R Clare. From Cheadle take B5417 to Alton Towers & Oakamoor. Site on L about 0.5m. Swimming pool. Games room. Bar and bar meals. Free showers. Limited facilites in off peak period. Rally field. Open March-Nov.

LEEK

(2.75m). Blackshaw Moor Caravan Club Site, Leek, Staffordshire ST13 8TW. *01538 300203.* www.caravanclub.co.uk. Owner: The Caravan Club. See website for directions. Attractive site with tempting views of the Staffordshire Climbs. Ideal site for families. All hardstandings. Play equipment. Dog walk. Toilet blocks. Privacy cubicles. Laundry facilities. Baby toddler washroom. Veg prep. MV service point. Gas and Gaz. Golf, fishing and watersports nearby. Advance booking required Bank Holidays and weekends. Non-members welcome. No

HEART OF ENGLAND

tents. No late night arrivals. Open March-Jan. 🚐♿🐕🏪🎣♪🔌📼🚿🚻

(2m). Camping & Caravanning Club Site – Leek, Blackshaw Grange, Blackshaw Moor, Leek, Staffordshire ST13 8TL. 01538 300285. www.campingandcaravanningclub.co.uk. Owner: Camping & Caravanning Club. On the main A53 Leek to Buxton Road. The site is located 200yd past the sign for 'Blackshaw Moor' on the L. An ideal site to enjoy the beautiful Peak District, visit Alton Towers. Leek town centre is full of interesting shops and markets. The potteries of Staffordshire are close to the site. Fly and coarse fishing available locally. The Tissington Trail is easy reach for walkers and cyclists. Caravans, motorcaravans and tents accepted. Non-members welcome. Deals for families and backpackers. Visit Heart of England Bronze Award. 🚐⛺☼♿🐕🏪🎣♪🔌📼🚿🚻

(3.5m). Glencote Caravan Park, Churnet Valley, Station Road, Leek, Staffordshire ST13 7EE. 01538 360745. canistay@glencote.co.uk. www.glencote.co.uk. Owner: Tom Burnside & Family. Sign off A520 Leek to Stone road. Small family run park adjacent to Heritage Steam Railway in the beautiful Churnet Valley. Canalside pub nearby. Winner of the Middle England 2007. David Bellamy Gold Conservation Award. Open from 1/2/09 to 31/12/09. 🚐⛺♿🐕🏪🎣♪🔌📼🚿🚻

RUGELEY

(3m). Camping & Caravanning Club Site – Cannock Chase, Old Youth Hostel, Wandon, Rugeley, Staffordshire WS15 1QW. 01889 582166. www.campingandcaravanningclub.co.uk. Owner: Camping & Caravanning Club. From Rugeley take A460, turn L at 'Hazelslade' SP and R in 1m for site. Non-members welcome. All units welcome. Loo Of The Year (5 stars). Site is a peaceful haven of heath and forest. The site is ideal for the avid walker with 17,000 acres of Chase to explore. Cannock boasts many shops, a leisure centre and an attractive market place. Deals for families and backpackers. Open March-Oct. 🚐⛺♿🐕🏪🎣♪🔌📼🚿🚻

STAFFORD

(7.75m). High Onn Caravan Club Site, Church Eaton, Stafford, Staffordshire ST20 0AX. 01785 840141. www.caravanclub.co.uk. Owner: The Caravan Club. See website for directions. Caravan Club members only. No tents. Peaceful and rural site with views into Shropshire and towards Wales. Own sanitation required. Chemical closet emptying points. Dog walk adjacent. Part hardstanding. Steel awning pegs required. Gas. MV service point. Local attractions include Ironbridge. Open March-Oct. 🚐🐕♪🔌🚻

Park View Farm Caravan & Camping Club Site, Park View Farm, Little Haywood, Stafford, Staffordshire ST18 0TR. 01889 808194. Owner: Mrs Christine Hill. Turn off A51 for villages of Great Haywood, Little Haywood and Colwich. Farm is at top of hill between Great and Little Haywood. In walking distance of Shugborough Hall. Restaurant and pub food nearby. Friendly working farm atmosphere. Open March 1-Oct 31. 🚐🐕🚿🚻

(12m). White Pump Farm, Ivetsey Bank, Wheaton Aston, Stafford, Staffordshire ST19 9QU. 01785 841153. janetash10@aol.com. www.whitepumpfarm.com. Owner: Peter Cambridge. Situated alongside the A5 road, from M6, J12, 5m E. From W, 3m from Weston-under-Lizard. This is a 5 van site situated on a small working farm. Ideally located for Weston Park, RAF, Cosford. Equal distance from Telford, Stafford, Cannock and Wolverhampton 🚐⛺🐕🔌🚻

STOKE-ON-TRENT

(10m). The Cross Inn Caravan Park, Cauldon Low, Stoke-on-Trent, Staffordshire ST10 3EX. 01538 308338. adrian_weaver@hotmail.com. www.crossinn.co.uk. Owner: A B Weaver & P Wilkinson. On A52 Stoke-Ashbourne road. Alton Towers 3m, Peak Park 5mins. Pub/restaurant on site. Carvery on Sundays. Families welcome. Family room with pool and football tables. Alton Towers 3m. Open March-Nov. 🚐♿🐕🏪✕🎣♪🔌📼🚿🚻

 ■ **(4m). The Star Caravan and Camping Park, Cotton, Nr Alton Towers, Stoke-on-Trent, Staffordshire ST10 3DW.** 01538 702219. www.starcaravanpark.co.uk. Owner: Mark & Margaret Mellor. Situated 1.25m from Alton Towers (closest site) in easy reach of Peak Park and Matlock Bath. 15m from the Potteries, about 9m from market town of Ashbourne, Leek and Uttoxeter. 200yd from Old Star Inn. 3.5m from Cheadle. We are on Star Road B5417. Static caravans to hire. Calor Gas. Facilities for disabled. Fishing in 2m, golf course in 1m. Extra shops, PO, doctor all in 2-3m. Central location to Alton Towers, market towns of Cheadle, Leek, Uttoxeter, Ashbourne; the Potteries and the Peak District. AA 4 pennants. Rose Award. Family Welcome Award. David Bellamy Silver Conservation Award. Open 11th March-5th Nov. 🚐⛺♿🐕🏪🎣♪🔌📼🚿🚻

TAMWORTH

(3m). Drayton Manor Park, Fazeley, Tamworth, Staffordshire B78 3TW. 08708 725252. info@draytonmanor.co.uk. www.draytonmanor.co.uk. On A4091, near J9 & 10, M42, exit T2, M6 toll. Theme park camping & caravan site for families only. Over 100 rides and attractions. Telephone or e-mail for more information. Open Easter-Oct. 🚐♿🐕🏪✕🎣♪🔌📼🚿🚻

(5m). Tameview Caravan Site, Cliff, Kingsbury, Tamworth, Staffordshire B78 2DR. 01827 873853. Owner: Mr & Mrs P Hollis. M42, J9. A4097 Kingsbury. A51 Tamworth, through Kingsbury. Opposite pub, first L, Cliff Hall Lane. Site at end of lane. 1m PO, doctors, shops, fish and chip shop. Kinsbury water park. 3m to Belfrey Golf course. Drayton Manor Park. 5m to Tamworth castle and NEC Twycross Zoo. 🚐⛺☼♿♪🔌🚿

UTTOXETER

 **(0.5m). Uttoxeter Racecourse Caravan Club Site, Wood Lane, Uttoxeter, Staffordshire ST14 8BD.** 01889 564172. www.caravanclub.co.uk. Owner: The Caravan Club. See website for directions. Situated on the National Hunt Racecourse with beautiful views over open countryside and golf course adjacent. Racing free to site users. Dog exercise area. Advance booking advised Bank Holidays, weekends and race days. Non-members and tent campers welcome. Toilet blocks. Privacy cubicles. Laundry facilities. Baby/toddler washroom. Veg prep. MV service point. Gas. Play area. Ideal for families. Local attractions include Alton Towers. Open March-Nov. 🚐⛺♿🐕🏪🎣♪🔌📼🚿🚻

WARWICKSHIRE

BIDFORD-ON-AVON

Cottage of Content, Welford Road, Barton, Bidford-on-Avon, Warwickshire B50 4NP. 01789 772279. Owner: John F Gash. Open March 1-Oct 31. 🚐🎣✕♪🔌🚿🚻

HENLEY-IN-ARDEN

 **(4m). Island Meadow Caravan Park, The Mill House, Aston Cantlow, Henley-in-Arden, Warwickshire B95 6JP.** 01789 488273. holiday@islandmeadowcaravanpark.co.uk. www.

HEART OF ENGLAND

islandmeadowcaravanpark.co.uk. Owner: PH & CA Lewis-Jones, KE Hudson. Off A3400 and A46 NW of Stratford (6m) in the village of Aston Cantlow. 3m from Alcester. Quiet, rural park on the river Alne in historic and picturesque village close to Stratford. Fishing free to guests. Booking essential at peak periods. David Bellamy Gold Conservation Award. Open March 1-Oct 31.

MARSTON

■ (1m). Marston Caravan, Touring & Camping Park, **Old Kingsbury Road, Marston, Warwickshire B76 0DP**. *01675 470902*. Owner: A I Loveridge. J9 Off M42, take A4097 towards Kingsbury. Marston Caravan Park is 0.75m on L. Park is 5m from Sutton Coldfield.

MERIDEN

(0.6m). Somers Wood Caravan Park, **Somers Road, Meriden, Warwickshire CV7 7PL**. *01676 522978*. enquiries@somerswood. co.uk. www.somerswood.co.uk. Owner: Marc & Angela Fowler. From A45 take 452, SP Meriden/Leamington. 1m at next roundabout turn L on to B4102 (Hampton Lane) site 0.5m on L. 4m from Solihull. Exclusively adults only. Adjacent to golf course with clubhouse and coarse fishery. Shops 0.5m, 3m from the National Exhibition Centre. 7 nights for the price of 5 on selected weeks, 4 nights for the price of 3. Please enquire for further details. Open Feb 1- Jan 3.

RUGBY

(5m). Sherwood Farm, Stretton-on-Dunsmore, **Rugby, Warwickshire**. *01788 810325*. Owner: Mr B S Chandler. W of Rugby on A45. Appeals more to short-stay campers. Convenient for tours to Coventry Cathedral and Warwick Castle.

SHIPSTON-ON-STOUR

Mill Farm, Long Compton Mill, Shipston-on-Stour, Warwickshire CV36 5NZ. *01608 684663*. herricksalmon @vodafonemail.co.uk. Owner: J H Salmon. Turn W off A3400 in Long Compton towards Barton for 0.5m. Site on R. Shipston-on-Stour, Moreton-in-Marsh and Chipping Norton all 6m. Local shops and PO 0.5m. Open April 1-Sept 30.

SOUTHAM

(3m). Holt Farm, **Southam, Warwickshire CV47 1NJ**. *01926 812225*. neil@holtfarm.fslife.co.uk. www. holtfarm.fslife.co.uk. Owner: N G & A C Adkins. From Southam bypass follow camping and caravan signs. Site 3m from Southam off Priors Marston Road. Quiet site on family farm, ideal for exploring Warwickshire. Dogs allowed on leads. Calor Gas. Free fishing. Open March 1-Oct 31.

STRATFORD-UPON-AVON

■ (2m). Dodwell Park, **Evesham Road, B439, Stratford-upon-Avon, Warwickshire CV37 9SR**. *01789 204957*. enquiries@dodwellpark.co.uk. www.dodwellpark.co.uk. Owner: Mr M J R & Mrs S B Bennett. From Stratford-upon-Avon take the B439 towards Bidford-on-Avon for 2m. The park is on the L and is SP. Country walks to Luddington village and river Avon. Ideal for visiting the Cotswolds and Warwick Castle.

(4m). Newlands Caravan Park, **Loxley Lane, Wellesbourne, Stratford-upon-Avon, Warwickshire CV35 9EN**. *01789 841096*. www.newlandscaravans.co.uk. Owner: Mr & Mrs C Warr. From M40/A46 Junction take A429 through Barford. Turn R go through Charlcote to crossroads. Straight over past all flying schools. Newlands is second bungalow on R, opposite helicopter school. The site has hardstanding, electric hook ups and a shower & toilet block. 5mins walk to a licensed café. Ideally situated to explore the Cotswolds, Warwick Castle, and the many National Trust properties in the area. Theatres, restaurants, shopping and Shakespeare properties can be enjoyed at nearby Stratford upon Avon.

(1m). Riverside Caravan Park, **Tiddington Road, Stratford-upon-Avon, Warwickshire CV37 7AB**. *01789 292312*. riverside@stratfordcaravans. co.uk. www.stratfordcaravans.co.uk. Owner: Avon Estates Ltd. Take B4086 Tiddington Road from the bridge in Stratford. As you enter the village of Tiddington the park entrance is on the L opposite the NFU. No tents or trailer tents. Riverside location with river taxi service to Stratford town centre. Bar, clubhouse on adjacent park, offers entertainment on Saturday nights throughout the season. Children's play area and coffee shop on site. 1.5m of free fishing. Golf course, cinema, leisure centre, restaurants all nearby. David Bellamy Gold Conservation Award. Open April 1-Oct 31.

WARWICK

(0.5m). Warwick Racecourse Caravan Club Site, **Hampton Street, Warwick, Warwickshire CV34 6HN**. *01926 495448*. www.caravanclub.co.uk. Owner: The Caravan Club. See website for directions. The site is set on grass and tarmac in the racecourse enclosure, and is only a 6mins walk from the centre of Warwick. Free access to racing. Non-members welcomed. No tents. Toilet

---

MARSTON CARAVAN AND CAMPING PARK
Kingsbury Road, Marston B76 0DP Near Sutton Coldfield and Birmingham Tel: 01675 470902 or 01299 400787

1 mile off Junction 9 of M42 towards Kingsbury on left hand side. Brand new park for 120 caravan/tents/motorhomes. Site (open all year around). All pitches have electricity and full hard standings. Brand new toilet/shower block. Pets allowed. Local attractions: Kingsbury Water Parks, Drayton Manor Park, Belfry Golf Course.
HAMS HALL – NATIONAL EXHIBITION CENTRE – LEE MANOR LEISURE COMPLEX

DODWELL PARK
Evesham Road, Stratford-upon-Avon, Warwickshire CV37 9SR
Telephone: 01789 204957

e-mail: enquiries@dodwellpark.co.uk web: www.dodwellpark.co.uk

A family run, clean, quiet touring park in the countryside, two miles south-west of Stratford-upon-Avon. An ideal location for visiting Shakespeare's birthplace, Warwick Castle and the Cotswolds. We have a well-provisioned shop and off-licence, free showers, and country walks to the river Avon. Open all year. Free brochure on request.

30 MOTOR CARAVAN & CAMPING PARKS 2009

HEART OF ENGLAND

See page 5 for key to symbols and abbreviations

blocks. Privacy cubicles. Laundry facilities. Veg Prep. MV Service point. Gas. No late nights arrivals area. Open March 27-Jan 5.

WEST MIDLANDS
BIRMINGHAM

(1m). Chapel Lane Caravan Club Site, Chapel Lane, Wythall, Birmingham, W Midlands B47 6JX. *01564 826483.* www.caravanclub.co.uk. Owner: The Caravan Club. See website for directions. Non-members welcome. No tents. Convenient for the NEC. All hardstandings. Toilet blocks. Privacy cubicles. Laundry facilities. Veg prep. MV Service point. Gas & gaz. Playframe. Local attractions include Cadbury World. Storage pitches. Fishing, golf and NCN cycle path in 5m. Quiet and peaceful off peak.

HALESOWEN

(1m). Camping & Caravanning Club Site – Clent Hills, Fieldhouse Lane, Romsley, Halesowen, W Midlands B62 0NH. *01562 710015.* www.campingandcaravanningclub.co.uk. Owner: Camping & Caravanning Club. M5, J3, take A456 then L on B4551 to Romsley, turn R past Sun Hotel take 5th L, SP Bell End and Broughton. Site is 330yd on L. Hidden away site has peaceful, tranquil atmosphere with 7.5 acres suitable for all units. In the heart of the country. Close to the Welsh Borders and Birmingham. Play area. Birmingham and attractions such as the National Sealife Centre, Millenium Point and the Botanical Gardens are only 15m away. Local attractions include Black Country Museum in Dudley. Steam trains enthusiasts will enjoy the nearby Seven Valley Railway. Non-members welcome. Deals for families and backpackers. Open March-Oct.

SUTTON COLDFIELD

(7m). Camping & Caravanning Club Site – Kingsbury Water Park, Bodymoor Heath Lane, Sutton Coldfield, W Midlands B76 ODY. *01827 874101.* www.campingandcaravanningclub.co.uk. Owner: Camping & Caravanning Club. Leave M6 at J4 and follow A446 N, turn R at junction with A4097. After 1.5m turn L at Water Park sign, continue for 0.5m then turn R at C&C sign. Surrounding the site are 600 acres of Kingsbury Water Park with lakes and countryside to explore. The park is ideal for walking, cycling, birdwatching and fishing. Gold award for excellence in tourism by the Heart of England Tourist Board. All units accepted. Non-members welcome. Watersports available at the Water Park complex. Nearby attractions include Drayton Manor Family Theme Park, Twycross Zoo, National Sea Life Centre, Cadbury World and the city museum art gallery. Try skiing and snowboarding on real snow at Snowdrome at nearby Tamworth. Deals for families and backpackers. Attained Silver Visit Britain Tourism in Excellence Award. Loo Of The Year (5 stars).

WORCESTERSHIRE
BROADWAY

(0.5m). Broadway Caravan Club Site, Station Road, Broadway, Worcestershire WR12 7DH. *01386 858786.* www.caravanclub.co.uk. Owner: The Caravan Club. See website for directions. Caravan Club members only. No tents. Landscaped on two levels, the site is on the edge of one of the loveliest of the golden-stoned villages of the Cotswolds. Toilet blocks, laundry facilities, baby and toddler washroom and MV service point. Good area for walking, dog walk on site and golf nearby. Facilities for the disabled. Ideal for families.

HANLEY SWAN

(1m). Camping & Caravanning Club Site – Blackmore, Blackmore Camp Site No 2, Hanley Swan, Worcestershire WR8 0EE. *01684 310280.* www.campingandcaravanningclub.co.uk. Owner: Camping & Caravanning Club. From J7, M5. Watch for Blackmore Camp sign at junction of B4211. All approaches to the site are well signposted. 4m from Malvern. Splendid centre for touring the countryside of the Malvern Hills and Severn Valley, 40sq m of walking around the site. All units accepted. Loo Of The Year (5 stars). Non-members welcome. Ball games area available. The site is conveniently situated for Tewkesbury and Great Malvern. Deals for families and backpackers.

HARTLEBURY

Shorthill Caravan & Camping Centre, Worcester Road, Crossway Green, Hartlebury, Worcestershire DY13 9SH. *01299 250571.* Owner: Mr P R George. Mid-way between Kidderminster & Worcester on A449, next to Little Chef. Small family site in heart of beautiful Worcestershire countryside. Ideal base for sightseeing. New rally site available. Fees on application.

KIDDERMINSTER

(2m). Camping & Caravanning Club Site – Wolverley, Brown Westhead Park, Wolverley, Kidderminster, Worcestershire DY10 3PX. *01562 850909.* www.campingandcaravanningclub.co.uk. Owner: Camping & Caravanning Club. From Kidderminster A449 to Wolverhampton, turn L at lights on to B4189 signed Wolverley. Follow brown camping signs, turn R. Site on L. A quiet and secluded site with peaceful ambience. Children's play area. Close to Severn Valley Railway. All units accepted. Non-members welcome. The site is adjacent to the Staffordshire and Worcestershire Canal, ideal for walking or cycling. Golf and horseriding available locally. Birmingham and its attractions are just a short drive away. Deals for families and backpackers. Open March-Oct.

The Old Vicarage Activity Centre (Camp-Easy), Stottesdon, Cleobury Mortimer, Kidderminster, Worcestershire DY14 8UH. *01746 718436.* Owner: Mr B G & A B Eddies-Davies. Off Bridgnorth/Cleobury Mortimer road. B4363, follow signs for Stottesdon. Our equipment on site if required. Set in 27 acres of nature reserve. Group activities through Act. Centre by arrangement. Hill boarding, archery, bike hire. Dogs on lead.

MALVERN

Kingsgreen Caravan Park, Kingsgreen, Berrow, Malvern, Worcestershire WR13 6AQ. *01531 650272.* Owner: Keith & Jill Davis. From M50 heading S exit J2 turn L on A417 towards Gloucester. Take 1st turn R, sign to Malvern. Keep straight for 1m, sit on R. 7m from Ledbury. Small family run site on a working farm situated at the foot of the Malvern Hills. Complete level site. Storage available. Fishing on site. We do accept dogs but have no dog walk. Open March 1-Oct 31.

(3.5m). Riverside Caravan Park, Little Clevelode, Malvern, Worcestershire WR13 6PE. *01684 310475.* www.ukparks.co.uk/riversidecp8. Owner: S & A Linnon & R Roberts. Halfway between Worcester and Upton-on-Severn on B4424. Club. Fishing. Tennis. Play area. AA 3 pennants. Newly developed riverside plots available. Open March 1 – Dec 31.

www.motorcaravanmagazine.co.uk   MOTOR CARAVAN & CAMPING PARKS 2009 **31**

HEART OF ENGLAND

(6m). Three Counties Park, Sledge Green, Berrow, Malvern, Worcestershire WR13 6JW. 01684 833439. Owner: J & E Fury Park Homes. On A438 Tewkesbury to Ledbury Road. Separate touring park with showers and chemical toilet disposal. David Bellamy conservation award winner. Open Easter-Oct 31 for tourers.

PERSHORE

Comberton Golf Club, Pershore Road, Great Comberton, Pershore, Worcestershire WR10 3DY. 07774 813381. gerryhickey@hotmail.co.uk. www.combertongolfclub.com. Adjacent to river Avon free fishing (licence needed). Beautiful country pubs and walks over Bredon Hill. 18-hole, starter golf course adjacent to site plus club room. Club house opened 2002. Fully licensed.

(3m). Eckington Riverside Park, Eckington, Pershore, Worcestershire WR10 3DD. 01386 750985. Off A440. By the river Avon with its own fishing. Level ground in pear orchard. Open March 1-Oct 31.

STOURPORT-ON-SEVERN

(1m). Lickhill Manor Caravan Park, Stourport-on-Severn, Worcestershire DY13 8RL. 01299 871041. excellent@lickhillmanor.co.uk. www.lickhillmanor.co.uk. Owner: Denis Lloyd Jones. SP at crossroads with traffic lights on the B4195 Bewdley to Stourport road, then R at park signs. Riverside position, level ground, superb washrooms. Fishing, many attractions in the area to suit all ages. Town centre, leisure centre 1m. Golf 2m. W Midlands Safari park and Severn Valley Railway 3m. David Bellamy Gold Conservation Award.

TENBURY WELLS

(2m). Orchard Holiday Park, New House Farm, St Michaels, Tenbury Wells, Worcestershire WR15 8TW. 01568 750245. www.orchardholidaypark.co.uk. Owner: Bill & Margaret Jones. On A4112 between Leominster and Tenbury Wells. Caravan Club site. Idyllic location, amongst beautiful countryside and pools, ideal for the fishing or walking enthusiast. 9 & 18 holes golf courses nearby. Village pubs and restaurants. Severn Steam railway, Bewdley Safari Park. Open from 1/3/08 to 31/12/08.

WORCESTER

Blackmore Caravan Club Site, Blackmore End, Hanley Swan, Worcester, Worcestershire WR8 0EE. 01684 310505. www.caravanclub.co.uk. Owner: The Caravan Club. See website for directions. 2.5m from Great Malvern. Caravan Club members only. No tents. The Malvern Hills overlook the site which is level, open, blissfully quiet and recommended for a peaceful holiday. Toilet blocks. Privacy cubicles. Laundry facilities. Veg prep. MV Service point. Gas & gaz. Play equipment. Dog walk. Good area for walking. Ideal family site. Mums and Toddlers room, small football pitch.

Bromyard Downs Caravan Club Site, Brockhampton, Bringsty, Worcester, Worcestershire WR6 5TE. 01885 482607. www.caravanclub.co.uk. Owner: The Caravan Club. See website for directions. This woodland site is well in the beautiful countryside between the cathedral cities of Worcester and Hereford. The site is arranged in two linked areas and is ideal for those seeking a rural holiday. Walking is a pleasure from the site, over Bromyard Downs, Bringsty Common or in the National Trust estate at Brockhampton with its lovely timbered moated manor house. Some hardstandings and dog walk nearby. No toilet block. Non-members welcome. No tents. Open April 3-Oct 5.

(5m). Coppice Leisure Park, Ockeridge Wood, Worcester, Worcestershire WR6 6YP. 01886 888305. info@hillandale.co.uk. www.hillandale.co.uk. Owner: D & D Lloyd Jones Securities Ltd. A443 N from Worcester, through Holt Heath, 0.5m L at caravan sign,1m on L. Set in 200 acres of woodland. Heated swimming pool. Exclusive woodland glade overlooking wildlife pools, positions for lodges. Open March-Jan.

(7m). Lenchford Meadow Park, Shrawley, Worcester, Worcestershire WR6 6TB. 01905 620246. info@lenchford.co.uk. www.lenchford.co.uk. Owner: Mrs M Bendall. On A443, B4196 Worcester-Holt Heath-Stourport, 1m from Holt Heath (Red Lion) R. NO FACILITIES FOR TOURERS. Boat slipway. Fishing. Shops & PO 5mins; doctor, golf course 10mins. Country walks nearby. Open Feb 7-Jan 6.

(3m). Mill House Caravan & Camping Site, Mill House, Hawford, Worcester, Worcestershire WR3 7SE. 01905 451283. millhousecaravansite@yahoo.co.uk. Owner: Mr F Ellaway. On A449 N from centre of Worcester. Quiet, level, grassy site. Dogs to be exercised off site, kept on leads and cleaned up after. Coarse fishing (small river). Open April-Oct.

DERBYSHIRE
ALFRETON

Golden Valley Caravan Park, Coach Road, Golden Valley, Alfreton, Derbyshire DE55 4ES. 01773 513881. e nquiries@goldenvalleycaravanpark.co.uk. www.goldenvalleycaravanpark.co.uk. Owner: Mr Fretnell. M1, J26 A610 bypass to Codnor, turn R R again on to Alfreton Road, follow for 1.5m, sign on L on to Coach road, L on to park. Gym, fishing. Bar, café shop. Pool table. Kids games indoor and outdoor. Bike hire and Fort adventure. New for 2008: disco room, new showers block. Golf course 1m. Shopping centre 5m. Cinema 10m. Butterley Railway free and half price on train. David Bellamy Gold Conservation Award.

AMBERGATE

(1m). The Firs Farm Caravan & Camping Park, Crich Lane, Nether Heage, Ambergate, Derbyshire DE56 2JH. 01773 852913. thefirsfarmcaravanpark@btinternet.com. www.thefirstfarmcaravanpark.btinternet.com. Owner: Stella Ragsdale. 1.5m S of Ambergate, turn L off A6 and follow signs for 1m. Exclusively for adults. Friendly, quiet, well-maintained, landscaped park with panoramic views. Quality heated facilities. Many local attractions to visit. Friendly local pubs and restaurants. Tourist Board member.

ASHBOURNE

(2m). Bank Top Farm, Fenny Bentley, Ashbourne, Derbyshire DE6 1LF. 01335 350250. Owner: Mr & Mrs Cotterell. Leave Ashbourne on the A515 road, Buxton in 2m take R-hand fork on to B5056, Bakewell road – we are 200yd along on R opposite to Bentley Brook Hotel. Dogs on leads allowed. Fees on application. AA 3 pennants. Open April 1-Sept 30.

(6m). Blackwall Plantation Caravan Club Site, Kirk Ireton, Ashbourne, Derbyshire DE6 3JL. 01335 370903. www.caravanclub.co.uk. Owner: The Caravan Club. See website for directions. No tents. Set in a pine plantation, convenient base for walkers with beautiful scenery of Dovedale and surrounding countryside. Carsington water 15mins walk away. Advance booking essential. Dog walk. Non-members welcome. Toilet block with privacy cubicles, laundry facilities and baby/toddler washroom. MV service point. Play equipment. Ideal for families. Open March-Nov.

32 MOTOR CARAVAN & CAMPING PARKS 2009

See page 5 for key to symbols and abbreviations

MIDDLE ENGLAND

(0.5m). Callow Top Holiday Park, Buxton Road, Ashbourne, Derbyshire DE6 2AQ. 01335 344020. enquiries@callowtop.co.uk. www.callowtop.co.uk. Owner: Mr & Mrs Palmer. On A515 Buxton road, 0.5m from Ashbourne town centre. Full facilities including heated pool, games room, restaurant and pub etc. Flat pitches. Adjacent to Tissington Trail cycle path. Family site in beautiful countryside. Alton Towers 20mins. Fishing on site. Open Easter-Nov.

(5m). Carsington Fields Caravan Park, Millfields Lane, Nr Carsington Water, Ashbourne, Derbyshire DE6 3JS. 01335 372872. www.carsingtoncaravanning.co.uk. Owner: Judy & Peter Booth. Turn R off A517 Belper to Ashbourne in 0.25m past Hulland Ward into Dog Lane in 0.75m turn R SP Carsington. The site is on the R in 0.75m o/s 119251493. 400yd from Carsington water. 1.5m from nearest shop/PO/pub. Fishing, watersports, boats for hire 1m. Open end March-end Sept.

(1m). Gateway Caravan Park, Osmaston, Ashbourne, Derbyshire DE6 1NA. 01335 344643. karen@gatewaypark.fsnet.co.uk. www.ashbourne-accommodation.co.uk. Owner: Mr P Cranstone & Miss K H Peach. S of Ashbourne off A52. Set amidst beautiful countryside. Flat site. Licensed bar open weekends, March-Nov, daily during school holidays. Entertainment Saturday nights during school holidays. Games room, laundry. Nearby fishing, golf, tennis, swimming, climbing. Close to Alton Towers. Ideal base for touring Park District. 2 AA pennants.

(4m). Peakland Caravan & Camping Park, Belper Road (A517), Bradley, Ashbourne, Derbyshire DE6 3EN. 01629 815703. holidays@peaklandcaravanandcampingpark.co.uk. www.peaklandcaravanandcampingpark.co.uk. Owner: James & Jill Green. E of Ashbourne on A517. Find us on OS landranger map 119. Exclusively for Adults family-run park. Dogs on a lead at all times. Open Feb 1-Nov 30.

(5m). Redhurst Farm, Wetton, Ashbourne, Derbyshire. 01335 27227. N of Ashbourne, off A515. Close to Dovedale and Manifold Valley.

(6m). Rivendale Caravan & Leisure Park, Buxton Road, Alsop-en-le-Dale, Ashbourne, Derbyshire DE6 1QU. 01335 310311. caravan@rivendalecaravanpark.co.uk. www.rivendalecaravanpark.co.uk. Owner: Alsop Rivendale Ltd. Heading N from Ashbourne, take the A515 towards Buxton. Find Rivendale after 6m on R. 25 acres of pasture and woodland. Close Tissington Trail. Hardstanding with 16amp supplies. New underfloor heated toilet and shower block. Warden: Vicky Bonsall. Café & bar now open. Static holiday homes for sale. Alan Rogers recommended. David Bellamy Gold Conservation Award. Open Feb 1-Jan 6.

The Closes Farm, Atlow, Ashbourne, Derbyshire DE6 1PW. 01335 370763. Owner: Mr Ian & Mary Webster. Own sanitation essential.

BAKEWELL

(3m). Camping & Caravanning Club Site – Bakewell, c/o Hopping Farm, Youlgreave, Bakewell, Derbyshire DE45 1NA. 01629 636555. www.campingandcaravanningclub.co.uk. Owner: Camping & Caravanning Club. A6/B5056 after 0.5m turn R to Youlgreave, turn sharp L after church down Bradford lane, opposite George Hotel. 0.5m to sign turn R. In the heart of the Peak National Park. 100 pitches in 14 acres. Local attractions include Speedwell Cavem in Castleton and Chatsworth House. Accepts all units. Non-members welcome. Own sanitation essential. Deals for families and backpackers. Open March-Oct.

(4m). Chatsworth Park Caravan Club Site, Baslow, Bakewell, Derbyshire DE45 1PN. 01246 582226. www.caravanclub.co.uk. Owner: The Caravan Club. See website for directions. Set in an old walled garden on 1000-acre Chatsworth Estate with views of surrounding countryside. No entrance through Chatsworth Estate. Please arrive after 1pm due to congestion and bottleneck in area. Playground. Advance booking essential. Dog walk. Non-members welcome. Toilet block with privacy cubicles and laundry facilities. Bab/toddler washroom. MV service point. Service pitches available at a supplement. Non-members welcome. No tents. Open March-Jan.

(1m). Greenhills Holiday Park, Crowhill Lane, Bakewell, Derbyshire DE45 1PX. 01629 813052. info@greenhillsholidaypark.co.uk. www.greenhillsholidaypark.co.uk. Owner: Mr J A Green. From A6 (Buxton-Matlock), 0.25m E at Ashfour-in-the-Water, turn S into Crowhill Lane, SP. Club house. Shop. Golf course 1m, shopping centre 1m, cinema 15m. Open Feb 1-Nov 30.

(4m). Haddon Grove, Bakewell, Derbyshire DE45 1JF. 01629 812343. Owner: W J D Finney. SW of Bakewell. B5055 road S about 2m from Monyash. Fees on application. Open March 1-Oct 31.

BUXTON

(0.75m). Cold Springs Farm, Manchester Road, Buxton, Derbyshire SK17 6ST. 01298 22762. Owner: Mr S Booth Millward. Take the A5004 from town centre.

(6m). Cottage Farm Caravan Park, Beech Croft, Blackwell in the Peak, Taddington, Buxton, Derbyshire SK17 9TQ. 01298 85330. mail@cottagefarmsite.co.uk. www.cottagefarmsite.co.uk. Owner: Ms Julie Gregory. Off A6 midway between Buxton and Bakewell. SP. Small quiet family run park located between Buxton and Bakewell in Derbyshire. Ideal base for exploring the Peak District National Park. Open March-Oct.

(10m). Endon Cottage, Hulme End, Sheen, Buxton, Derbyshire SK17 0HG.

MIDDLE ENGLAND

01298 84617. Owner: Mrs J Naylor. In Beresford Lane off Beresford Dale. Mains water. Eggs available. Dogs on lead.

(2m). Grin Low Caravan Club Site, Grin Low Road, Ladmanlow, Buxton, Derbyshire SK17 6UJ. 01298 77735. www.caravanclub.co.uk. Owner: The Caravan Club. See website for directions. Landscaped site set in heart of Peak District National Park. Advance booking advised. Play area and playframe. Tents accepted. Most pitches are hardstanding. Dog walk nearby. Non-members welcome. Toilet block, laundry facilities, baby/toddler washroom. MV service point. Golf nearby. Open March-Nov.

(0.5m). Lime Tree Park, Dukes Drive, Buxton, Derbyshire SK17 9RP. 01298 22988. info@limetreeparkbuxton.co.uk. www.limetreeparkbuxton.co.uk. Owner: Mr R & A Hidderley. Off A515, 1m S of Buxton. Duke's Drive links A515 to A6. In a rural valley setting, though in 20mins walk of Buxton. Ideal walking and cycling in the heart of the Peak District. Open from 1/3/09 to 31/10/09.

(7m). Longnor Wood Caravan & Camping Park, Newtown, Longnor, Buxton, Derbyshire SK17 0NG. 01298 83648. info@longnorwood.co.uk. www.longnorwood.co.uk. Owner: John & Debbie O'Neill. On reaching Longnor crossroads follow site signs for 1.25m to site. Adults only. Peaceful site in the heart of the country and central for many Peak District attractions including Chatsworth House, Hartington, Bakewell and the beautiful dales. Putting green, boules court and croquet. Adults only. AA 4 pennants. Pubs, café/restaurants/takaways nearby. David Bellamy Gold Conservation Award. Open March 1-Jan 10.

(9m). Newhaven Caravan & Camping Park, Newhaven, Buxton, Derbyshire SK17 0DT. 01298 84300. www.newhavencaravanpark.co.uk. Owner: R & K Macara. At junction A5012 and A515 halfway between Ashbourne and Buxton. Modern, 30-acre site in the heart of the Peak National Park. Restaurant adjacent. Phone on site. Playroom. AA 3 pennant. Close to the High Peak Trial and Tissinoton Trial, historic house and the Derbyshire Dales. Open March 1-Oct 31.

(5m). The Pomeroy Caravan and Camping Park, Street House Farm, Pomeroy, Flagg, Buxton, Derbyshire SK17 9QG. 01298 83259. Owner: Mr & Mrs J Melland. On A515 adjoining High Peak Trail central site for Peak National Park. Ashbourne 16m. H&C to wash basins and showers. Hand and hairdryers and shaver points. Site fully lit. Adjoins 'High Peak Trail'. Central for Peak Districk National Park. The Caravan Club and The Camping & Caravanning club members are welcome. Open April 1-Oct 31.

CASTLETON

(0.5m). Losehill Caravan Club Site, Hope Valley, Castleton, Derbyshire S33 8WB. 01433 620636. www.caravanclub.co.uk. Owner: The Caravan Club. See website for directions. A refurbished quiet and peaceful off peak site, ideal for all kinds of outdoor activities. New facilities block with family and baby wash room. Laundry facilities. Veg prep. MV service point. Gas and Gaz. Play equipment. Dog walk on site. Non-members and tent campers welcome. Fishing and golf nearby. Good area for walking. Ideal for families. Some hardstanding, shop 50yd from site. Fishing, golf 5m.

(2.5m). Rowter Farm, Hope Valley, Castleton, Derbyshire S33 8WA. 01433 620271. www.peakdistrict-nationalpark.com. Owner: Sarah Hall. W of Castleton off B6061. Flat field, partly sheltered overlooking Man Tor. Excellent for walkers and touring the Peak District. In Castleton (2.5m) 6 hotels, good range of shops and tearooms. Parking alongside units, reasonable rates. Open Easter-Oct.

DERBY

Cavendish Caravan & Camping Site, Derby Road, Doveridge, Derby, Derbyshire DE6 5JR. 01889 562092. Owner: G Wood. On A50 in Doveridge midway between Derby and Stoke-on-Trent. 1.5m E of Uttoxeter. Pub and food 100yd. Entrance to site is through double open gates across a closed garage forecourt. Dogs allowed on leads.

(4m). Elvaston Castle Country Park Caravan Club Site, Borrowash Road, Elvaston, Derby, Derbyshire DE72 3EP. 01332 573735. www.caravanclub.co.uk. Owner: The Caravan Club. See website for directions. Attractive site in well-kept 200-acre country park. Families will enjoy the castle, lake and large play area in the castle grounds. Advance booking essential. Non-members welcome. Toilet block. Non members and tent campers welcome. Fishing and golf nearby. Ideal for walkers. Local attractions include Alton Towers, American Adventure, Tales of Robin Hood and Denby Pottery. Battery charging, gas, dog walk nearby. Ideal for families. Open March-Oct.

HIGH PEAK

Camping & Caravanning Club Site – Hayfield, Kinder Road, Hayfield, High Peak, Derbyshire SK22 2LE. 01663 745394. www.campingandcaravanningclub.co.uk. Owner: Camping & Caravanning Club. A624 – Glossop to Chapel en le Frith. Hayfield by-pass, follow wooden carved signs to site. 4m N of Chapel en Le Firth. 12m from Stockport. 5m from Glossop. Site set on the banks of the River Sett, ideal for fell and moorland walkers. The National Trust Kinder Roundwalk is ideal for the bird watcher and botanist. NO TOWED CARAVANS permitted. Non-members welcome. Deals for families and backpackers. Open March-Oct.

Ringstones Caravan Park, Yeardsley Lane, Furness Vale, High Peak, Derbyshire SK23 7EB. 01663 747042. ringstonescp@aol.com. Owner: Mrs M A Hallworth. From Whaley Bridge, A6 to Furness Vale. Turn off A6 at Cantonese restaurant by pelican crossing then 0.75m up Yeardsley Lane. 10m from Buxton. 2m from Whaley Bridge. Beautifully situated, quiet site with lovely views of the Peak District. Small shop, PO, train station and bus stop all in 0.75m. Tennis, bowling, football pitch, 3 pubs in walking distance. 2m to supermarket, swimming pool, leisure centre. Golf, rock climbing nearby. Open March 1-Oct 31.

HOPE VALLEY

Eden Tree Caravan Park, Eccles Lane, Bradwell, Hope Valley, Derbyshire S33 9JT. 01433 623444. Owner: Mr M Allcroft. Off B6049 at New Bath Inn in Bradwell. 9m from Bakewell and 8m Buxton. Electric hook-ups. Free hot showers. All grass site. In easy walking distance of shops. Booking advisable. Dogs on leads allowed on touring field only. Shops & PO 0.5m. Doctors 2m. Fishing, golf course 3m. Static caravans are privately owned and are not let out. Open March-Oct.

Fieldhead Camp Site, Edale, Hope Valley, Derbyshire S33 7ZA. 01433 670386. bookings@fieldhead-campsite.co.uk. www.fieldhead-campsite.co.uk. Owner: Peak Planning Board. 5m from A625 at Hope. Site is midway between village and Edale railway station. SP 'Peak National Park Information Centre'. Heart of Peak District. Café/restaurant in 400yd.

34 motor caravan & camping parks 2009

MIDDLE ENGLAND

See page 5 for key to symbols and abbreviations

Highfield Farm, Nr Upper Booth, Edale, Hope Valley, Derbyshire S33 7ZJ. 01433 670245. Owner: C R Cooper. Turn off A6187 (previously A625) at Hope Church. Take minor road to Edale, past turn for Edale Village. At bottom of hill turn R under viaduct and past picnic area. Convenient site for hill walking. Fees on application. Shops, PO, café & restaurant in 2m. Doctor 7m Open Easter-Oct.

Laneside Caravan Site, Laneside, Hope, Hope Valley, Derbyshire S33 6RR. 01433 620215. laneside@lineone. net. www.lanesidecaravanpark.co.uk. Owner: Mrs D Neary. On A6187 Hathersage to Castleton. On Eastern border of Hope Village (200yd). 11m from Buxton. 8m from Bakewell. Level, riverside, site surrounded by hills bordering Hope village with late shopping and 3 pubs. Central heated shower block. Chemical toilet disposal point and motor van service area. Golf courses, horse riding and rock climbing all close by. Open March-Nov.

(12m). Stocking Farm Caravan Site, Calver, Hope Valley, Derbyshire S32 3XA. 01433 630516. Owner: Mrs O Harvey & Mrs M Newton. 5m from Bakewell. On A623. Follow the first two signs to Calver Mill then straight ahead. Shop, PO: 0.5m. Doctors: 2m. Dogs on leads allowed. Golf courses, Co-op Bakewell 5m. Morrison's Chesterfield 10m. Open April 1-Oct 31.

(0.5m). Swallowholme Caravan Park, Station Road, Bamford, Hope Valley, Derbyshire S33 0BN. 01433 650981. Owner: Mr John Frogatt. On A6013. 2m S of Ladybower Reservoir. Fishing and golf nearby. Shop 0.25m. Site unsuitable for children. Open April 1-Oct 31.

Upper Booth Farm, Edale, Hope Valley, Derbyshire S33 7ZJ. 01433 670250. Owner: The National Trust. Leave A625 at Hope, up valley to Edale, turn L by public car park-follow road W to Barber Booth, R turn to Upper Booth and Jacob's Ladder. Heart of Peak District, on Pennine Way. Dogs to be kept on leads at all times. Open Feb 1-Oct 31.

(5m). Waterside Farm, Barber Booth Road, Edale, Hope Valley, Derbyshire S33 7ZL. 01433 670215. Owner: Mrs J M Cooper. Off the A6 bypass at Chapel, SP Rushop Edge, Edale. Small quiet site, family run. Located in the Peak District with wonderful views. Café, shop, pub and PO in 1m. Open April 1-Sept 30.

MATLOCK

(6m). Haytop Country Park, Whatstandwell, Matlock, Derbyshire DE4 5HP. 01773 852063. Owner: Mrs E George and Mr H George. Entrance at Whatstandwell Bridge off A6. 65-acre country park with river and woodland. 1m of river frontage. Fishing, boating and canoeing. Long stay sites available. Near train station. 2.5m to PO, general stores and garage.

(2.5m). Lickpenny Touring Park, Lickpenny Lane, Tansley, Matlock, Derbyshire DE4 5GF. 01629 583040. lickpenny@btinternet.com. www. lickpennycaravanpark.co.uk. Owner: A & J Reynolds. M1, J28. A38 SP Derby, take Alfreton exit and immediately L turn to A615 for 8m, turn R on to Lickpenny Lane SP on R. Fishing nearby. Café/garden centre 500yd. Local shops, doctor, PO 3m. Bus service at end of lane. Train station in Matlock.

SWADLINCOTE

(5m). Camping & Caravanning Club Site – Conkers Club Site, Both Lane, Moira, Swadlincote, Derbyshire DE12 6BD. 0845 1307633. www.campingandcaravanningclub.co.uk. Owner: Camping & Caravanning Club. Located just off the A444 Conkers is accessible from the M42, A50 and also the M1. Our new club site at Conkers is in the heart of the country's youngest forest. The site is under development and will eventually become a full facility site which is open all year round.

THULSTON

(0.25m). Beechwood Park, Main Road, Elvaston, Thulston, Derbyshire DE72 3EQ. 07973 562689. colinbeech@btconnect.com. www. beechwoodparkleisure.co.uk. Owner: Mr C Beech. Follow signs for Elvaston Castle, on B5010. Beechwood Park is 300yd from Castle entrance on opposite side of road. In 30 acres of idyllic green belt. 6 coarse fishing lakes. Children's go kart track. Shop on site and just 1m to village shops.

LEICESTERSHIRE

HINCKLEY

(5m). Villa Farm Caravan Park, Wolvey, Hinckley, Leicestershire LE10 3HF. 01455 220493. www. wolveycaravanpark.itgo.com. Owner: Mr H & PM Rusted. A46 Coventry to Leicester then B4065 (old A46). 0.5m W of Wolvey, M6 exit 2, M69 exit 1. AA 3 pennants. Fishing on site, putting green.

LINCOLNSHIRE

ALFORD

(3m). Woodthorpe Hall Leisure Park, Woodthorpe, Alford, Lincolnshire LN13 0DD. 01507 450294. enquiries@woodthorpehallleisure.co.uk. www. woodthorpehallleisure.co.uk. Access via Louth to Mablethorpe A157 or Alford, A1104 then B1373. Affiliated 18-hole golf course and fishing lake, garden centre and aquatic centre in the grounds. Woodys bar and restaurant with family room serving food. Snooker & pool tables. Open from 1/3/09 to 3/1/10.

BARTON-ON-HUMBER

(0.5m). Silver Birches Tourist Park, Waterside Road, Barton-on-Humber, Lincolnshire DN18 5BA. 01652 632509. Owner: Mr & Mrs T Prior. On A15 or 1077. Follow signs for Humber Bridge Viewing Area. Site just past the Sloop Public House. Follow viewing area signs to Waterside Road. Site situated next to Humber Bridge only 250yd from viewing area and nature reserves. AA 4 pennants recommended. Open April 1-Oct 31.

BOSTON

(1.5m). Pilgrim's Way Caravan & Camping Park, Church Green Road, Fishtoft, Boston, Lincolnshire PE21 0QY. 01205 366646. pilgrimsway@caravanandcampingpark.com. Owner: Mr & Mrs Peter and Jacqueline Jenkin. Take A52 out of Boston towards Skegness there are two signs first on Bargate Bridge. Second on Wainfleet Road or take any road to Fishtoft. A relaxing and peaceful site in the heart of the Lincolnshire countryside. Your home from home. Family park. Pilgrims Way is only 1.5m from Boston Centre, 20mins drive to Skegness and Spalding, nice quiet park with pubs lots to do just up the road. AA 4 pennants De luxe. Open Easter-End Sept.

(8m). White Cat Caravan Park, Shaw Lane, Old Leake, Boston, Lincolnshire PE22 9LQ. 01205 870121. kevin@klannen.freeserve. co.uk. www.whitecatpark.com. Owner: Mr & Mrs Lannen. On A52 Boston to Skegness Road. Turn R opposite B1184 Sibsey road. Free showers. Swings. PO & pub nearby. Restaurant. Ideal base for Skegness and touring the Fens. Seasonal pitches for tourers. Limited

MOTOR CARAVAN & CAMPING PARKS 2009 **35**

MIDDLE ENGLAND

facilities for disabled. Childrens' play area. Restaurant/pub nearby. AA 3 pennant. Equestrian centre 2m. Golf, cinema, swimming, shopping 6m. Open April 1-Oct 31.

CAISTOR

(1m). Caistor Fisheries Ltd, 99a Brigg Road, Caistor, Lincolnshire LN7 6RX. 01472 852032. info@caistorfisheries. co.uk. www.caistorfisheries.co.uk. Owner: Margaret Rybakowski. 12m from Grimsby. Caistor is situated off the A46 and the site is on the A1084 to Brigg Road. Other routes include the M180 to Brigg and then the A1084 to Caistor Road. Three fishing lakes on site. 10mins walk to town centre which offers shops and takeaways. Viking Way 500yd away. Humberside airport 5m. Caistor is situated on the edge of the Lincolnshire Wolds with breathtaking scenery.

CLEETHORPES

(2m). Thorpe Park Holiday Centre, Cleethorpes, Lincolnshire DN35 0PW. 01472 813395. www.thorpepark-park.co.uk. Owner: Bourne Leisure Ltd. From M180 take A180 and follow signs for Grimsby and Cleethorpes town centre. Follow signs for Holiday Parks and Pleasure Island. Heated indoor pool, adventure splashzone family entertainment, kid's clubs, multi sports court, fishing & golf. Two mini markets, bakery. Investor in People. Outdoor family funzone with bouncy castle, trampolines, adventure crazy golf, orbiters and much more. David Bellamy Gold Conservation Award. Open March-end Oct.

GRANTHAM

(8m). Woodland Waters, Willoughby Road, Ancaster, Grantham, Lincolnshire NG32 3RT. 01400 230888. info@woodlandwaters.co.uk. www.woodlandwaters.co.uk. Owner: Mr & Mrs M Corradine. On A153 between Grantham and Sleaford, from S leave A1 at Colsterworth to B6403 to Ancaster. From N leave A1 at Newark to A17 to Sleaford, leave just before RAF Cranwell R to B6403 to Ancaster. 72 acre picturesque park set in a beautiful wooded valley with five fishing lakes on site. AA 3 pennant. 4 golf courses nearby. The historic city of Lincoln close by and the local market towns of Grantham, Newark and Sleaford a short drive away. Go-karting, golf, paint balling and horse riding venues close by. Bar/restaurant on site, garage with shop at entrance of park.

HORNCASTLE

(1.5m). Ashby Park, West Ashby, Horncastle, Lincolnshire LN9 5PP. 01507 527966. ashbypark@btconnect. com. www.ukparks.co.uk/ashby. Owner: Margaret & Robin Francis. 1.5m N of Horncastle between the A153 and A158. Touring site of 70 acres with 7 fishing lakes. The site has been awarded a David Bellamy Conservation Gold award for the last eight years. Lincolnshire environmental trophy. Golf 1m, Horncastle and shops 1.5m. Holiday statics for sale. Open March 1-Jan 6.

IMMINGHAM

(5m). Killingholme Caravan Site, Church End, East Halton, Immingham, Lincolnshire DN40 3NX. 01469 540594. Owner: Mrs T J Chapman. From A180 take A160 towards Killingholme. Turn L at roundabout, site 1.5m on R, opposite church. Semi-rural location. Short drive to beaches/holiday resort. Improved facilities planned for 2005. 1m to shop, PO, pub.

LINCOLN

(3m). Hartsholme Country Park, Skellingthorpe Road, Lincoln, Lincolnshire LN6 0EY. 01522 873578. SP from A46, 3m S of Lincoln. Sheltered, level site beautifully in a country park with woods, meadows and lakes. Perfect for exploring the historic City of Lincoln. Open for Lincoln's Christmas market. Open March 1-Oct 31.

(18m). Tattershall Park Country Club, Tattershall, Lincoln, Lincolnshire LN4 4LR. 01526 343193. www.tattershallpark. co.uk. On the A153 Sleaford to Skegness. 365-acre leisure park with bars. Horseriding, jet skiing, water skiing, canoeing, fishing & boating. Restaurants. Gymnasium, saunas, squash & snooker. Limited facilities for the disabled. RAC recommended. Open March-Oct.

(12m). White Horse Inn Holiday Park, Dunston Fen, Metheringham, Lincoln, Lincolnshire LN4 3AP. 01526 398341. B1188 Lincoln/Sleaford road, turn into Dunston village. Follow signs in village to Dunston Fen and River Witham. 5m down Fen Road to rive. Small, family run site adjacent to river Witham. 12m from Lincoln. Booking advisable. Open Feb 1-Dec 31.

LOUTH

(7m). Saltfleetby Fisheries, Main Road Saltfleetby, Louth, Lincolnshire LN11 7SS. 01507 338272. saltfleetbyfish@btint ernet.com. www.saltfleetbyfisheries.co.uk. Owner: Mr & Mrs Musgrave. B1200, E of Louth. Quiet, peaceful, adult only site. Fishing lakes, well stocked. Shop on site. Close to Mablethorpe and Skegness. Open March-Nov.

(10m). Sunnydale Holiday Park, Sea Lane, Saltfleet, Louth, Lincolnshire LN11 7RP. 0871 6649776. sunnydale@park-resorts.com. www.park-resorts.com. Owner: Park Resorts Ltd. Head towards Louth on the B1200 through Manby & Saltfleet. Sea Lane is on R in Saltfleet. The park is about 400yd on the L. Indoor heated pool, on site store, bar, cabaret bar, play zone for kids. Outdoor play area, FREE kids clubs, FREE family evening entertainment. Sandy beach 2m, 18 hole golf course 9m. Fishing pond. Amusements. Darts. Pool table. David Bellamy Bronze Conservation Award. Open April-Oct.

MABLETHORPE

(1m). Camping & Caravanning Club Site – Mablethorpe, Highfield, 120 Church Lane, Mablethorpe, Lincolnshire LN12 2NU. 01507 472374. www.campingandcaravanningclub.co.uk. Owner: Camping & Caravanning Club. Take A157 from Louth to Mablethorpe, then A1104 N and follow the sign to site is on the R just 1m from beach. All units accepted. Non-members welcome. Located in a flat surrounding area, perfect for cyclists. The site is conveniently situated 10-15mins walk from both town and shore. Skegness is not far away, this pretty seaside resort area is always winning awards for its beaches. The Lincolnshire Wolds are a haven for birds and animals. Deals for families and backpackers. Open March-Oct.

(1m). Denehurst Touring Site, Alford Road, Mablethorpe, Lincolnshire LN12 1PX. 01507 472951. Owner: Mr & Mrs J Birks. On A1104 Alford-Louth-Mablethorpe road. Small, family-run site in a country setting close to town centre of Mablethorpe and 1m to beach. Fishing and golf nearby. Open March 1-Nov 30.

(1m). Golden Sands Holiday Park, Quebec Road, Mablethorpe, Lincolnshire LN12 1QJ. 01507 477871. www.goldensands-park.co.uk. Owner: Bourne Leisure Ltd. Head towards Mablethorpe located between Cleethorpes

36 MOTOR CARAVAN & CAMPING PARKS 2009

MIDDLE ENGLAND

See page 5 for key to symbols and abbreviations

and Skegness on the Lincolnshire coast. From Mablethorpe town centre, turn L on to the seafront road towards the North End. Golden Sands is situated along this road on the L. Indoor and outdoor pools, go karts, crazy golf, playground. Supermarket. Bakery. Coffee shop. Fish & Chip shop. Children's Funzone. Free kid's club. Daytime and evening entertainment. Multi sports court, fishing lake, amusements. Touring site 10-15mins from main facilities. David Bellamy Gold Conservation Award. Open mid March-end Oct.

Hawthorn Farm Caravan Club Site, Crabtree Lane, Sutton-On-Sea, Mablethorpe, Lincolnshire LN12 2RS. 01507 441503. www.caravanclub.co.uk. Owner: The Caravan Club. See website for directions. 1.25m from Sutton-On-Sea. Caravan Club members only. No tents. Sutton-on-sea 1.25m. An ideal base for family holidays with excellent facilities, only 0.75m from safe bathing beach. Dog walk. Advance booking advised Bank Holidays, July and Aug. Toilet blocks. Privacy cubicles. Laundry facilities. Veg prep. MV service point. Golf, fishing and watersports nearby. Open: March-Nov.

MARKET DEEPING

(2.5m). Deepings Caravan Park, Outgang Road, Towngate East, Market Deeping, Lincolnshire PE6 8LQ. 01778 344275. info@thedeepings.com. www.thedeepings.com. Owner: Mr D M & Mrs B J Young. Take A16 towards Spalding. After 2.5m take R turn on to B1525 SP Deeping St James. After 1m turn R (following brown signs). Site is 400yd on R. Calor Gas sales. Fishing on site. Childrens' play area, on site shop, caravan accessory shop. Club house. Fully licensed bar weekly entertainment. Darts & pool table. Static caravans to let.

MARKET RASEN

(1m). Market Rasen Racecourse Caravan Club Site, Legsby Road, Market Rasen, Lincolnshire LN8 3EA. 01673 842307. See website for directions. Caravan Club affiliated site. Set on the edge of the lovely, rolling Lincolnshire Wolds. There's a pay and play golf course adjacent to the site, and in a short distance another golf course. Non-members and tent campers welcome. Good area for walking. Open March-Oct.

(1.5m). The Rother Camp Site, Gainsborough Road, Middle Rasen, Market Rasen, Lincolnshire LN8 3JU.

01673 842433. Owner: Mr & Mrs K A Steed. W of Market Rasen and 200yd E of junction A46 and A631. In easy access of Lincoln city and coatal restors. An ideal touring base.

Viking Way Walesby, Mill House Farm, Walesby, Market Rasen, Lincolnshire LN8 3UR. 01673 838333. Owner: Mr A J & Mrs K Burton. On Viking Way footpath or at cross roads. A46 and A1103. 1.5m NW Market Rasen. Follow sign Walesby. A quiet, secluded site at the foot of the Lincolnshire Wolds. Excellent yet non-demanding circular walks. Open March 1-Dec 31.

Walesby Woodlands Caravan Park, Walesby Road, Walesby, Lincolnshire LN8 3UN. 01673 843285. Owner: R H & B Papworth. Take B1203 from Market Rasen. In 0.75m turn L to Walesby. Site is 0.25m on L (SP). High-quality site on edge of Lincolnshire Wolds, bordered by forest. Woodland walks, peace and fresh air. AA 3-pennant. RAC appointed. Open March 1-Nov 1.

NORTON DISNEY

(1.5m). Oakhill Leisure, Oakhill Farm, Butt Lane, Thurlby Moor, Norton Disney, Lincolnshire LN6 9QG. 01522 868771. ron@oakhill-leisure.co.uk. www.oakhill-leisure.co.uk. Owner: Mr Ron De Raad. A46 Newark to Lincoln – signed Thurlby, at roundabout, R at t-junction, round S-bend, straight in front sign for Oakhill Leisure. Turn R then L into park. 6m from Newark. Children's play area, fishing lake, woodland, country walks. Pub 1m, shops 4m.

SKEGNESS

(3m). Conifer Park Touring Site, Walls Lane, Ingoldmells, Skegness, Lincolnshire PE25 1JH. 01754 762494. Owner: Chris & Marian Brookes. Take A52 from Skegness towards Ingoldmells, upon reaching Butlins, turn L down Walls Lane, Conifer Park Site is about 0.5m on R. Conifer park site is appreciated by the more mature campers who like a clean peaceful site with a country environment. 5 acre field where you can exercise your dog. Only 0.75m from the sea front. Garage, fishing, golf, PO, doctor, vet, shops, swimming, bingo, theatre, Butlins, waterskiing, café all nearby. Large market. Open March 16-Oct 31.

(4m). Countrymeadows Holiday Park, Anchor Lane, Ingoldmells, Skegness, Lincolnshire PE25 1LZ. 01754 874455. mail@countrymeadows.co.uk. www.countrymeadows.co.uk. Owner: J G & G D

Hardy. 4m N of Skegness on A52 to Ingoldmells, follow A52 through Ingoldmells and take first R on leaving village down Anchor Lane. Park 0.5m on L follow signs to Animal Farm. 300yd past animal farm. Play area. Fishing available. Families only. Close to beach, Hordys Animal farm and 10mins to Fantasy Island. Open Easter-end Oct.

(6m). Riverside Caravan Park, Wainfleet Bank, Wainfleet, Skegness, Lincolnshire PE24 4ND. 01754 880205. Owner: Mr J W & Mrs J Bingham. Leave bypass on to B1195, follow signs. A52 Boston to Skegness. Secluded caravan site with limited space for tents. Hot & Cold to washbasins. Fishing nearby. Shops, PO, doctor, rail, bus all in 1m. Golf 1m. Open March 15-Oct 31.

(2m). Skegness Water Leisure Park, Walls Lane, Skegness, Lincolnshire PE25 1JF. 01754 899400. enquiries@skegnesswaterleisurepark.co.uk. www.skegnesswaterleisurepark.co.uk. A52, turn L on to Walls Lane, opposite Butlins. SP 'Water Leisure Park". On site facilities: fishing, cable tow water skiing, coffee shop, the Barn Inn (pub). Children's play area. Open first Saturday March – last Saturday Oct.

Twit Twoo's, Holme Field Lane, Orby, Skegness, Lincolnshire PE24 5TB. 01754 811025. sarahtaylor601@btinternet.com. www.twittwoos.uk.campsite.co.uk. Owner: SJ Taylor. From A158 to A16 to Gunby roundabout follow Fantasy Island signs through Orby, turn L info Holmefield Lane. Quiet location 3m to Fantasy Island and Skegness. Lovely walks. Local town is Burghle Marsh. Doctor, PO, hairdresser, fishing, pubs 3m S to Burgh le Marsh. Hard standing site, super pitches, no charge for awnings.

SLEAFORD

(9m). Low Farm Touring & Camping Park, Spring Lane, Folkingham, Sleaford, Lincolnshire NG34 0SJ. 01529 497322. www.ukparks.co.uk/lowfarm. Owner: Mr & Mrs N R Stevens. Situated just off A15, midway between Bourne and Sleaford. Quiet family-run park in walking distance of conservation village with all amenities, ie shop, PO and public house. Fishing available nearby. Open Easter- end Sept.

SPALDING

(9m). Delph Bank Touring Park, Old Main Road, Fleet Hargate, Spalding,

www.motorcaravanmagazine.co.uk MOTOR CARAVAN & CAMPING PARKS 2009 **37**

MIDDLE ENGLAND

Lincolnshire PE12 8LL. *01406 422910.* enquiries@delphbank.co.uk. www.delphbank.co.uk. Owner: Mr M Watts & Miss J Lawton. 550yd off A17 between Kings Lynn and Sleaford. Quiet site in centre of village. Adults only. Pubs, shop and eating places all in easy walking distance. David Bellamy Gold Conservation Award.

(12m). Foremans Bridge Caravan Park, Sutton St James, Spalding, Lincolnshire PE12 0HU. *01945 440346.* foremansbridge@btconnect.com. www.foremans-bridge.co.uk. Owner: John Hoey. From A17 take B1390 to Sutton St James Park on L after 2m. Rural location adjacent to tranquil Fen waterway. 2 holiday cottages open all year. Fishing on site. Static holiday homes for sale. Prices starting from £10,250. David Bellamy Gold Conservation Award. Open March-Jan.

(15m). Orchard View Caravan and Camping Park, Broadgate, Sutton St Edmund, Spalding, Lincolnshire PE12 0LT. *01945 700482.* orchardview@hotmail.com. Owner: Ray & Ria Oddy. A47 Peterborough to Wisbech. At Guyhirn take B1187 to Murrow pass through Parson Drove. Over double bridge, 2nd R then 0.5m on the R. 9m from Crowland/Wisbech/Holbeach or telephone for help. Rural site close to fishing, horse riding, golf and Hull to Harwich cycle route. Licensed clubhouse. Peaceful location. Excellent escape from the madness! Just wildlife to enjoy. Campfire facility. Open March-Nov.

SUTTON-ON-SEA

(1.5m). Cherry Tree Site, Huttoft Road, Sutton-on-Sea, Lincolnshire LN12 2RU. *01507 441626.* info@cherrytreesite.co.uk. www.cherrytreesite.co.uk. Owner: Geoff & Margaret Murray. 1.5m S of Sutton on Sea on L of A52. Entrance via lay-by. Now adults only. Family run site close to safe, sandy beaches and delightful Wolds villages. Perfect for touring Lincolnshire. Golf and horse riding nearby. All hardstanding pitches. 10 fully serviced. Café/restaurant nearby. Open March-end Oct.

TATTERSHALL

(1.5m). Willow Holt Caravan and Camping Park, Lodge Road, Tattershall, Lincolnshire LN4 4JS. *01526 343111.* enquiries@willowholt.co.uk. www.willowholt.co.uk. Owner: B & R Stevenson. Leave A153 road at Tattershall market place SP Woodhall Spa. Site on L in 1.5m. Well-drained, family run parkland with woods, lakes and abundant wildlife. New facilities block. Fishing on

site. Golf, Swimming, horse-riding, tennis, bowls and water-skiing nearby. Dogs on leads allowed. Open March 15-Oct 31 (tourers) – March 1-Jan 5 (static holiday homes).

WOODHALL SPA

(1.5m). Bainland Country Park, Horncastle Road, Woodhall Spa, Lincolnshire LN10 6UX. *01526 352903.* bookings@bainland.co.uk. www.bainland.co.uk. Owner: Mr & Mrs Craddock. From Woodhall Spa travel E towards Horncastle on the B1191, 1.5m on R next to petrol station. The park of over 40 acres is classified as one of the top parks in Lincolnshire. 18 hole, par 3 golf course. All weather bowling green, indoor/outdoor tennis, heated indoor swimming pool, sauna, jacuzzi, children's adventure playground, trampoline and many more facilities on site, including bar and restaurant. Open Bungalow all year, Caravans March 21-Nov 6.

(3m). Camping & Caravanning Club Site – Woodhall Spa, Wellsyke Lane, Kirkby-on-Bain, Woodhall Spa, Lincolnshire LN10 6YU. *01526 352911.* www.campingandcaravanningclub.co.uk. Owner: Camping & Caravanning Club. From Sleaford or Horncastle take A153 to Hailsham. At garage turn on to side road, over bridge, L towards Kirkby on Bain. First turn R signed. Non-members welcome. All units accepted. Parent and baby room. A nature lovers dream with woodpeckers, kestrels and kingfishers often seen from the site. The lake on site is not for fishing. The town of Woodhall Spa set in a magnificent pine and birch wood is just 3m away. The site is peaceful and relaxing with a friendly atmosphere. Lincoln is not far away and is well worth a visit. Deals for families and backpackers. David Bellamy Gold Conservation Award. Open March-Oct.

(1m). Jubilee Park, Stixwould Road, Woodhall Spa, Lincolnshire LN10 6QH. *01526 352448.* Owner: East Lindsey District Council. Near centre of town junction B1191 and B1192. Park overlooking woods, with all amenities close by. Fees on application to Park Manager. On site facilities include a heated outdoor swimming pool (May-Sept), bowls, putting, tennis and cycle hire. Open April 1-Oct 31.

NORTHAMPTONSHIRE

BRACKLEY

(4m). Bungalow Farm, Greatworth, Banbury, Brackley, Northamptonshire OX17 2DJ. *01295 760503.* Owner: Baylis

& Sons. N of Brackley. Quiet rural site. Fees on application. Open Easter-Oct.

CORBY

(Top Lodge Caravan Club Site, Fineshade, Corby, Northamptonshire NN17 3BB. *01780 444617.* www.caravanclub.co.uk. Owner: The Caravan Club. See website for directions. Tranquil, open meadowland site surrounded by woodland. Good walks, ideal for wildlife enthusiasts. Dog walk adjacent. Advance booking essential Bank Holidays and weekends. No toilet block. MV waste. Non-members welcome. No tents. Fishing and golf nearby. Open March-Nov.

KETTERING

Wicksteed Park, Barton Road, Kettering, Northamptonshire NN15 6NJ. *01536 512475.* information@wicksteedpark.co.uk. www.wicksteedpark.co.uk. From N: leave M1, J9 and join the A14. Exit at J10 and follow brown signs. From S: leave M1, J15 and join A43 then take A14 (J8) E to J10. Set in 147 acres of lakes and parklands, with facilities that include 45 rides and attractions including fishing, pitch N putt, year round events programme, narrow gauge railway, daytime entertainment shows and much much more. Open March-Oct.

NORTHAMPTON

(3m). Billing Aquadrome, Crow Lane, Great Billing, Northampton, Northamptonshire NN3 9DA. *01604 408181.* brochures@aquadrome.co.uk. www.billingaquadrome.com. Owner: Pure Leisure Group. Off A45, 3m from Northampton, 7m from M1 exit 15. Set in 235 acres of beautiful parkland with nine lakes. Excellent facilities include: jet ski lake, fishing, licensed bars, supermarket, funfair, dining and take away food and full events programme. Open March 12-Nov 14.

NOTTINGHAMSHIRE

MANSFIELD

(5m). Sherwood Forest Caravan Park, Nr Edwinstowe, Mansfield, Nottinghamshire NG21 9HW. *01623 823132.* Owner: Torksey Caravans Ltd. 4m NE of Mansfield via B6030 and N to Warsop. A quiet retreat in the heart of Robin Hood country. Good facilities. Special area for dog exercising on leads.

MIDDLE ENGLAND

Close to many places of interest. Privately owned and managed with a resident warden.

NEWARK

(6m). Carlton Manor Caravan Park, Ossington Road, Carlton on Trent, Newark, Nottinghamshire NG23 6NU. 01530 835662. Owner: Mr & Mrs A S Goodman. 6m Newark North & South. Signed site Carlton-on Trent. A1 London Yorkshire. 8m Lincoln. Retford 10m, Nottingham 15m, Doncaster 35m. Fly and coarse fishing nearby. Clean, quiet park. Showers. Hot and cold water. Clean toilets. Level grass. Warden on site (01636 821347). Hotel restaurant opposite park. Shops and doctors in village. Fishing 0.5m, 3 lakes 2m. Dogs allowed on leads. Also tents on touring park. In the heart of Robin Hood country. Open March-Nov.

(16m). Greenacres Caravan & Touring Park, Lincoln Road, Tuxford, Newark, Nottinghamshire NG22 0JN. 01777 870264. stay@greenacres-tuxford.co.uk. www.greenacres-tuxford.co.uk. Owner: S & M Bailey. A1(N) leave at Tuxford sign. At village centre turn R (church opposite). After Fountain PH, site on L in 50yd. (A6075). A1(S) leave at Tuxford local services sign follow slip road to 'T' junction, turn R, SP Lincoln (A57). After Fountain PH site on L in 50yd (A6075). Retford 6m. Ideal for night halts and for touring Robin Hood country. Tourist info centre. Euro payments accepted. Local shops, pubs etc. (nearest pub 100yd). Static holiday homes for sale and hire. Open mid March-end Oct (owner), April-Sept (hire).

(5m). Milestone Caravan Park, Great North Road, Cromwell, Newark, Nottinghamshire NG23 6JE. 01636 821244. enquiries@milestone-park.co.uk. www.milestonepark.co.uk. CARAVAN CLUB AFFILIATED SITE. Small pretty and level site with a coarse fishing lake and picnic area. This is an ideal site for walkers and anglers. Toilet blocks, laundry facilities and MV service point. Golf and NCN route nearby. Facilities for disabled.

((12m). Orchard Park Touring Caravan & Camping Park, Marnham Road, Tuxford, Newark, Nottinghamshire NG22 0PY. 01777 870228. info@orchardcaravanpark.co.uk. www.orchardcaravanpark.co.uk. Owner: John & Dorothy Anderson. 1.25m SE of A1, off A6075 Lincoln road. Turn R in 0.75m on to Marnham Road. Site on R in 0.75m. Quiet, sheltered, level site. Ideal for Sherwood Forest. Modern amenities block with facilities for disabled. AA 3 pennants. Open March-Nov.

(1m). Smeaton's Lakes Caravan and Fishing Park, Great North Road, Newark, Nottinghamshire NG23 6ED. 01636 605088. lesley@smeatonslakes.co.uk. www.smeatonslakes.co.uk. Owner: Mrs C Price. On A616 close to A46 to A1. 90 acres parkland. 1m to nearest town for PO, doctor, restaurant etc. Takeaway meals delivered to site.

The Shannon Caravan & Camping, Wellow Road, Ollerton, Newark, Nottinghamshire NG22 9AP. 01623 869002. buxts@aol.com. www.caravan-sitefinder.co.uk. Owner: Mrs Buxton. Leave A1 on to A614 SP Nottingham. In 6.5m at roundabout, take A616 SP Ollerton. At next roundabout turn R on A616 SP Newark. Park in 1m on L. Fishing, golf, horse riding, small town, village pub, shop all in 1m. AA 3 pennants. We also rent tourers on site. New laundry facilities. Open from 1/1/08 to 31/12/08.

NOTTINGHAM

(3.5m). Holme Pierrepont Caravan & Camping Park, National Water Sports Centre, Adbolton Lane, Holme Pierrepont, Nottingham, Nottinghamshire NG12 2LU. 0115 9824721. holme.pierrpont@leisureconnection.co.uk. www.nationalwatersportsevents.co.uk. Owner: The Sports Council. 3.5m SE of Nottingham via A52 Grantham road. Site SP National Water Sports Centre. 270 acres country park, water sports available if pre-booked; site is 28 acres of flat grass. Rallies welcome. Close to river, fishing in river and ponds. Open April-Oct.

(5m). Thornton's Holt Camping Park, Stragglethorpe, Radcliffe-on-Trent, Nottingham, Nottinghamshire NG12 2JZ. 01159 332125. camping@thorntons-holt.co.uk. www.thorntons-holt.co.uk. Owner: Mr P G Taylor. SP from A46 and A52. Hot and cold water to basins. Washing-up room. Information room. Indoor heated swimming pool. Play area. 18 hardstandings. 100yd to pub and restaurant. 0.5m to golf driving range and course.

RETFORD

(0.75m). Hallcroft Fishery & Caravan Park, Hallcroft Road, Retford, Nottinghamshire DN22 7RA. 01777 710448. www.hallcroftfishery.co.uk. Owner: Messrs T A N J & L A Sears. M1, J30 take Worksop Road, then to Retford, Retford centre. A638 to Bawtry. Pass Honda garage on L and King/Miller PH on R. Turn R Hallcroft Industrial Estate. The park is 80 acres. There are 5 lakes for coarse fishing totalling 380+ pegs. A fully equipped and stocked tackle shop on site. Café/restaurant and license bar. A fully equipped and stocked tackle shop on site. Café/restaurant and license bar. Match bookings for clubs. We also cater for larger corporate events including large rallies. Open all year for tourers, 11 months for statics.

TEVERSAL

(3m). Camping & Caravanning Club site – Teversal, Shardaraba, Silverhall Lane, Teversal, Nottinghamshire NG17 3JJ. 01623 551838. www.campingandcaravanningclub.co.uk. Owner: Camping & Caravanning Club. M1, J29 follow A6175 L on to B6039, on to 36014, then L at Carnarvon Arms. Set in 6 acres of glorious countryside Teversal gives you the chance to explore both Nottinghamshire and neighbouring Derbyshire. The Silverwood Country Park is opposite the site, wireless internet is available and car hire.

WORKSOP

(4.5m). Clumber Park Caravan Club Site, Lime Tree Avenue, Clumber Park, Worksop, Nottinghamshire S80 3AE. 01909 484758. www.caravanclub.co.uk. Owner: The Caravan Club. See website for directions. 20-acre site set in 4000 acres of parkland where you can walk, cycle or ride. Barbecues with permission only. Dog walk. Advance booking essential Bank Holidays and weekends. MV waste. Play equipment. Non-members welcome. No tents. Toilet blocks. Laundry facilities. Baby/toddler washroom. Veg prep. Ideal for families, quiet and peaceful off peak. Significant interest nearby. Golf, fishing and NCN cycle path all in 5m. Good area for walking.

(0.25m). Riverside Caravan Park, Central Avenue, Worksop, Nottinghamshire S80 1ER. 01909 474118. Owner: Mrs G McPhail. At roundabout JA57/A60 Mansfield, follow international site signs to town centre onto Newcastle Ave. !st L onto Stubbing Lane, R onto Central Avenue, next L to site. A level site with waterside walks. Secluded yet adjacent to town centre. Everything in walking distance up to 0.5m. Dogs allowed on short lead only.

RUTLAND

OAKHAM

(4m). Greendale Farm Park, Pickwell Lane, Whissendine, Oakham, Rutland LE15 7LB. 01664 474516.

MIDDLE ENGLAND

enq@rutlandgreendale.co.uk. www.rutlandgreendale.co.uk. Owner: Sue & Ian Barron. Caravans must approach from A606. Take the 3rd turning to Whissendine from Melton Mowbray or the 2nd from Oakham or bypass opposite brown signs, then 0.5m on R. Small, quiet adults only site, set in rolling countryside. 6m from Rutland Water and 0.5m from village of Whissendine with 2 pubs and bistro. Ideal for walking, cycling, birdwatching. Wi-fi. Amazing facilities for such a small park! England in Excellence awards 1006/2007. David Bellamy Gold Conservation Award. Open from 15/4/08 to 30/9/08.

(2m). Ranksborough Hall, Langham, Oakham, Rutland LE15 7ER. *01572 722984.* sales@ranksboroughhall.com. www.ranksboroughhall.com. Owner: Edward James & Anthony White. On A606 Melton to Oakham. In village of Langham. PO, picnic area on site. Free bus to local supermarket. Medical practice/hospital/pharmacy 2m. Bowling green 2m. 3 golf courses nearby. Fishing, birdwatching, sailing, cycling 4m.

(5m). Rutland Caravan & Camping, Park Lane, Greetham, Oakham, Rutland LE15 7FN. *01572 813 520.* info@rutlandcaravanandcamping.co.uk. www.rutlandcaravanandcamping.co.uk. Owner: Mr Hinch. From A1 N or S bound turn off on to B668 towards Greetham village. Turn R at crossroads before the village and take 2nd L to site. Wireless internet site coverage. Site next to Greetham village with 3 pubs all serving food, shop, garage, garden centre, walk to from site and Viking Way foot path. Golf course, fishing, horse riding all in 1m; Rutland water 4m with fishing, cycling, rock climbing, butterflies. AA graded 3 pennants.

Wing Caravan & Camping Park, Wing Hall, Wing Village, Oakham, Rutland LE15 8RY. *01572 737709.* winghall1891@aol.com. www.winghall-rutnet/wing. Owner: Wing Estates. From A1 Wansford, A47 to Leicester, 12m to Morcott, turn R then first L to Wing 2.5m outside village by 400yd. Parkland setting. Fishing on site. Pubs with meals. Rutland Water 2m. Eye Booke 8m. Dogs allowed.

CHESHIRE
CHESTER

(3m). Birch Bank Farm, Stamford Lane, Christleton, Chester, Cheshire CH3 7QD. *01244 335233.* www.birchbankfarm.co.uk. Owner: Mr A W Mitchell. Turn R off A51 Chester to Nantwich road, opposite Vicars Cross golf club, Christleton-Waverton road. A small site on a working farm in the green Cheshire countryside and free of traffic noise. Open May 1-Oct 31.

(4m). Chester Fairoaks Caravan Club Site, Rake Lane, Little Stanney, Chester, Cheshire CH2 4HS. *01513 551600.* www.caravanclub.co.uk. Owner: The Caravan Club. See website for directions. Pleasant, open and level site with oak trees on the boundary, conveniently located just off the M53. Some hardstandings, toilet block, laundry facilities, baby/toddler washroom, MV point, play equipment and dog walk on site. Golf, fishing and NCN route in 5m. Non-members and tent campers admitted.

(3m). Chester Southerly Caravan Park, Balderton Lane, Marlston-cum-Lache, Chester, Cheshire CH4 9LF. *01244 671308.* Owner: Tony & Ann McArdle. Off A55 and A483. All pitches are level and attractively situated. Sports and shopping facilties etc. in Chester. Play area, public telephone. Calor Gas. Ideal touring base. Rallies by arrangement.

(7m). Northwood Hall Country Touring Park, Dog Lane, Kelsall, Chester, Cheshire CW6 0RP. *01829 752569.* enquiries@northwood-hall.co.uk. www.northwood-hall.co.uk. Owner: Mr & Mrs Nock. Off the A556, E of Chester. An idyllic setting, this attractive family run park is set amongst oak and chestnut trees. Adjacent Delamere Forest. Seasonal pitches available. Fishing, tennis 1m. Golf courses 3-5m. Cinema/shopping 7m. Open March 1-Nov 30.

GLOSSOP

Camping & Caravanning Club Site – Crowden, Woodhead Road, Crowden, Glossop, Cheshire SK13 1HZ. *01457 866050.* www.campingandcaravanningclub.co.uk. Owner: Camping & Caravanning Club. A628 Manchester to Barnsley Road, At Crowden follow sign for Youth Hostel car park. Campsite is 300yd from main road. In the heart of the Peak National Park, on the Pennine way and adjacent to the Langdale trail. NO CARAVANS OR MOTORHOMES. TENT CAMPERS ONLY. Non-members welcome. VB grade: 3 stars.

NORTHWICH

Camping & Caravanning Club Site – Delamere Forest, Station Road, Delamere, Northwich, Cheshire CW8 2HZ. *01606 889231.* www.campingandcaravanningclub.co.uk. Owner: Camping & Caravanning Club. Located on the B5152 is accessible from the A556, the B5152 and close to the M6. The wonderful new club site at Delamere Forest has many environmentally friendly features to complement the beauty of the forest and is a stone's throw from the Go Ape theme park.

(4.5m). Woodbine Cottage, Warrington Road, Acton Bridge, Northwich, Cheshire CW8 3QB. *01606 852319.* Owner: Mr Done. 9m SE of Warrington and 4m W of Northwich on A49. A beautiful country site on the banks of the river Weaver at the heart of Cheshire. Convenient for many places of interest around Cheshire. Open March-Oct.

WARRINGTON

(5m). Holly Bank Caravan Park, Warburton Bridge Road, Rixton, Warrington, Cheshire WA3 6HL. *01617 752842.* Owner: Mr James O Walsh. 2m E of M6 J21. On A57 (Irlam). Turn R at lights into Warburton Bridge Road. Entry on L. Chemical toilet disposal point. Shaver points. Gas. Laundry facilities. Games room. Free showers. Public telephone. AA 3 pennants. 440yd to 3 pubs, shop (village).

WINSFORD

(3m). Elm Cottage Touring Park, Chester Lane, Winsford, Cheshire CW7 2QJ. *01829 760544.* chris@elmcottagecp.co.uk. www.elmcottagecp.co.uk. Owner: Mr & Mrs C J Buss. W of Winsford on A54. The Shrewsbury Arms is only 400yd away. Supermarkets, doctors, dentists and vets in a 5m radius. Good fishing and golf courses nearby. Free tyre inflation facility on site. Open Feb 15-Jan 31.

GREATER MANCHESTER
ROCHDALE

(4m). Hollingworth Lake Caravan Park, Rakewood, Littleborough, Rochdale, Greater Manchester OL15 0AT. *01706 378651.* Owner: F Mills. J21, M62. Follow Hollingworth Lake Country Park sign to Fisherman's Inn/Wine Press. Take Rakewood road then second R. Rural area. Overlooking lake, restaurant and bar 1m. Showers. Laundry. Dryer. Golf, shops, PO, doctors in 1.5m. Pony trekking. Large fishing and boating lake nearby.

40 MOTOR CARAVAN & CAMPING PARKS 2009

NORTH-WEST ENGLAND

See page 5 for key to symbols and abbreviations

WIGAN

Gathurst Hall Farm Camp Site, Shevington, Wigan, Greater Manchester WN6 8JA. *01257 253464.* 5m NW of Wigan halfway between M6 J26 and 27. Off B5206 at Shevington. Site is alongside Leeds & Liverpool Canal. Near to the Navigation public house. About 4.5m from Wigan Pier. Advance booking advisable.

LANCASHIRE

ACCRINGTON

(0.5m). Harwood Bar Caravan Park, Mill Lane, Great Harwood, Accrington, Lancashire BB6 7UQ. *01254 884853.* A59 towards Clitheroe, then A680 to Great Harwood, 0.5m before Great Harwood on L, first road on L past Nightingale garage. Quiet park on edge of Ribble Valley. Open 11 months. Open Feb-Jan.

BLACKPOOL

(3m). Blackpool South Caravan Club Site, Cropper Road, Marton, Blackpool, Lancashire FY4 5LB. *01253 762051.* www.caravanclub.co.uk. Owner: The Caravan Club. See website for directions. Caravan Club members only. No tents. Probably the nearest site to Blackpool. Ideal location for the family holiday. Toilet blocks. Laundry facilities. Baby/toddler washroom. Veg prep. MV service point. Information room. Golf, fishing and watersports nearby. Good area for walking. Open March-Jan.

(3m). Gillett Farm Caravan Park, Peel Road, Peel, Blackpool, Lancashire FY4 5JU. *01253 761676.* Travelling on M55 take exit 4 turn L on to A583 to Kirkham. At roundabout go straight across to traffic lights. At lights turn R and immediately L on to Peel Road, 2nd caravan park on R. Washhouse. Launderette and ironing room. Telephone. TV and games room. Action time play centre. Hardstandings for tourers. Chemical disposal. Calor Gas exchange. Golf course, cinema, shopping centre available in 3m. Open March-Oct.

(7m). Kneps Farm Holiday Park, River Road, Thornton-Cleveleys, Blackpool, Lancashire FY5 5LR. *01253 823632.* enquiries@knepsfarm.co.uk. www.knepsfarm.co.uk. Owner: Mr Jonathan Porter. From A585 Kirkham to Fleetwood take B5412 at roundabout signed Little Thornton. Turn R at mini roundabout after school on to Stanah Road, straight over second mini roundabout leading to River Road. Quiet, family run park with luxurious amenities, family bathrooms and facilities for the disabled. A rural retreat close to Blackpool and Wyre countryside. Open March 1-Nov 15.

(4m). Mariclough-Hampsfield Touring Site, Preston New Road, Peel, Blackpool, Lancashire FY4 5JR. *01253 761034.* tony@mariclough.fsnet.co.uk. www.maricloughhampsfieldcamping.com. Owner: R A & J Cookson – retiring. Off the M55 J4, L on to the A583 straight through lights, 300yd on L. Adults only. Mid week offer/seasonal pitches. Dogs welcome. Brochure booking form available. Sheltered well maintained level site. Open Easter-Oct.

(3m). Marton Mere Holiday Village, Mythop Road, Blackpool, Lancashire FY4 4XN. *01253 767544.* www.martonmere-park.co.uk. Owner: Bourne Leisure Ltd. M55, J4. Turn R at the roundabout and take the A583 towards Blackpool. Pass the Windmill and turn R at the Clifton Arms traffic lights, on to Mythop Road. The park is 150yd on the L. Investor in People. Bowling green, Indoor heated pool with water chute. Bowlingo bowling. Outdoor splashzone, multi sports court. Fencing, table tennis, family entertainment. Adventure golf. Café. Showbar. Bike hire, trampolines, kids mini go karts. Marton Mere nature reserve. David Bellamy Gold Conservation Award. Open March-end Oct.

(3m). Pipers Height Caravan & Camping Park, Peel, Blackpool, Lancashire FY4 5JT. *01253 763767.* sales@pipersheight.co.uk. www.pipersheight.co.uk. Owner: Mr Rawcliffe. S of Blackpool from M55, J4. 40yd to Peel Corner turn into Peel Road, site is 50yd on R. Families only. Fees by arrangement. Licensed club house with entertainment high season – restaurant. Open Mar 1-Oct 31 for tourers, Mar 1-Jan 14 for statics.

(5m). Stanah House Caravan Park, River Road, Thornton, Blackpool, Lancashire FY5 5LR. *01253 824000.* stanahhouse@talk21.com. Exit 3 M55, A585 Fleetwood R at roundabout, sign to river turn R. A small, select, touring caravan site overlooking the river Wyre with good views of the Fells and Lake District mountains. Modern, fully-tiled toilet block with shower rooms and all amenities including laundry room. Adventure play-area for children. Open March-Oct.

(3.5m). Underhill Caravan & Camping Site, Preston New Road, Peel, Blackpool, Lancashire FY4 5JS. *01253 763107.* lesleys@ilph.org. www.underhill.biz. Site is E of Blackpool on the A583 road and only 0.5m from M55 off jct 4, M55, first L on to A583, site on R through traffic lights. Wardens: Brian & Jacqui Buddle. Open Easter-Nov 1.

(6m). Windy Harbour Holiday Centre, Little Singleton, Blackpool, Lancashire FY6 8NB. *01253 883064.* info@windyharbour.net. www.windyharbour.net. Owner: Partington's Holiday Centre Ltd. J3, M55. Take third exit off roundabout, SP A585 Fleetwood, and follow road for about 3m until set of traffic lights. Go straight on, park entrance is about 300m straight ahead. Fully serviced pitches. Hardstanding for vehicles. Toilet and amenity facilities with free hot water and showers, washing up facilities. Rally rates for group bookings on request. Indoor heated swimming pool, junior and teen club, children's play area. Coarse fishing ponds, amusement arcade. Fish and Chip shop, snack bar café. Open March 1-Nov 15.

BURY

(1.25m). Burrs Country Park Caravan Club Site, Burrs, Bury, Lancashire BL8 1DA. *0161 7610489.* www.caravanclub.co.uk. Owner: The Caravan Club. See website for directions. Using Satnav include 'Woodhill Road'. Burrs has much to offer: relaxing river and countryside walks. Handy for trips into Manchester. Ideal for families. Non-members welcome. No tents. Double barrier system – arrivals before 8pm.

CARNFORTH

(2m). Bolton Holmes & Detrongate Holiday Park, Off Mill Lane, Bolton-le-Sands, Carnforth, Lancashire LA5 8ES. *01524 732854.* info@holgatesleisureparks.co.uk. www.holgatesleisureparks.co.uk. Owner: Holgates Caravan Parks. Situated on W side of A6. 2m S of Carnforth. 7m N of Lancaster. Down Mill Lane. On shore front. Extensive views over Morecambe Bay. 0.75m to nearest shops, PO and doctors, etc. Open March 1-Oct 31.

(1m). Detron Gate Farm, Bolton-le-Sands, Carnforth, Lancashire LA5 9TN. *01524 732842/733617.* Owner: Mr E Makinson. Exit 35 from M6 – 2m S on A6. Electric shower point, hot water supply, children's play area. Boating, fishing, golf all nearby. Open Easter-Oct 1.

www.motorcaravanmagazine.co.uk · MOTOR CARAVAN & CAMPING PARKS 2009 **41**

NORTH-WEST ENGLAND

(5m). Gibraltar Farm, Silverdale, Carnforth, Lancashire. 01524 701736. Owner: Mr F W Burrow. SP Silverdale N out of Carnforth. At Silverdale turn W on road SP to hospital and Gibraltar, to T-junction in Lindeth Road; farm entrance opposite. Peaceful situation near beach and woodland. Open March 1-Nov 30.

(4.5m). Hollins Farm, Far Arnside, Silverdale, Carnforth, Lancashire LA5 0SL. 01524 701767. Owner: M Holgate. From M6 join M6 at J35. 1m towards Carnforth turn R at traffic lights on to minor road Warton and Silverdale sign. In Warton turn sharp L by gardens. R after level crossing. Fork L past phone box, R into Cove Road second L after children's home into farmyard. In Area of Natural Outstanding Beauty, 5mins walk to shore of Morecambe Bay. Open Easter-Oct.

(3m). Red Bank Farm, Bolton-le-Sands, Carnforth, Lancashire LA5 8JR. 01524 823196. archer_mark@lycos.co.uk. www.redbankfarm.co.uk. Owner: Mr M Archer. From A6 at Bolton-le-Sands take A5015 to Morecambe, after 500yd turn sharp R, signed shore. R again over railway bridge, turn L along the shore. Café on site. Working farm. Pets corner. On the shore. Pubs, restaurants, shop, PO: 1m. Golf: 3m. Open Easter-Oct 1.

(2m). Sandside Caravan & Camping Park, The Shore, Bolton-le-Sands, Carnforth, Lancashire LA5 8JS. 01524 822311. From J35, M6 follow signs for Morecambe about 3m, turn R after Far Pavillion Indian restaurant. Small, quiet site close to beach. Modern facilities block. Laundry Room. AA 3 pennants. Open March 1-4 Jan.

Woodclose Caravan Park, Casterton, Kirkby Lonsdale, Carnforth, Lancashire LA6 2SE. 01524 271597. michaelhodgkins@woodclosecaravanpark.fsnet.co.uk. www.woodclosepark.com. Owner: Mr F Hodgkins. 0.5m SE of Kirkby Lonsdale off A65. Small, quiet, family site with Lake district and Yorkshire Dales a short drive away. AA 4 pennants. Open March 1-Nov 1.

CLITHEROE

(1.5m). Camping & Caravanning Club Site – Clitheroe, Edisford Road, Clitheroe, Lancashire BB7 3LA. 01200 425294. www.campingandcaravanningclub.co.uk. Owner: Camping & Caravanning Club. A671 to Clitheroe. L at sports centre. Turn into Greenacre Road L at Edisford Road T Jct. Sports Centre on R, site 50yd on L. 6 acre site accepting all units types. On the banks of the river Ribble in the Ribble Valley, in sheltered wooded setting. Adjacent to site are a pitch and putt and, miniature steam railway. The Yorkshire Dales are a popular destination with site visitors. Two ancient hunting forests encompass Clitheroe, those of Pendle and Bowland. The charming ancient market town of Clitheroe is 20mins walk from the site. Non-members welcome. Deals for families and backpackers. Open March-Oct.

(2m). Three Rivers Mobile Park, Eaves Hall Lane, West Bradford, Clitheroe, Lancashire BB7 3JG. 01200 423523. enquiries@threeriverspark.co.uk. www.threeriverspark.co.uk. Owner: Ribble Motels Ltd. Turn off A59 at 'Clitheroe North' sign. Continue into West Bradford village. Turn L at T-junction. Take next R, Eaves Hall Lane. Indoor heated swimming pool. Club open all year. Weekend entertainment. Woodland nature trails. New luxury amenities block open. Launderette. Play area. No children in residential homes. GS. Open March 1-Nov 1.

LANCASTER

(6m). Mosswood Caravan Park, Crimbles Lane, Cockerham, Lancaster, Lancashire LA2 0ES. 01524 791041. info@mosswood.co.uk. www.mosswood.co.uk. Owner: S Wild. M6, J33 turn L on to A6, after about 1m turn R at front of white house onto Cockerham Road, continue to T junction. Turn R. At next T junction (Manor Pub) turn L. After 1m turn L into Crimbles Lane. Park is 1m down on R. BEWARE OF HORSES ON CRIMBLES LANE. Fishing 400yd. Parachuting, microlights 2m Golf, horse riding 3m. David Bellamy Gold Conservation Award. Open March 1-Oct 31.

MORECAMBE

(5m). Hawthorne Caravan Park, Carr Lane, Middleton Sands, Morecambe, Lancashire LA3 3LL. 01524 852074. enquiries@southlakelandparks.co.uk. www.southlakelandparks.co.uk. Owner: South Lakeland Parks Ltd. M6, J34, follow A683 SP Morecambe, then follow signs Heysham then Middleton road, turn R into Carr Lane. Quiet park located near Morecambe. Bar facilities and children's area.

(3m). Melbreak Caravan Site, Carr Lane, Middleton, Morecambe, Lancashire LA3 3LH. 01524 852430. Owner: Mr A E & G A Syson. A589 out of Morecambe SP to Middleton. 1m from sandy beach. Open March 1-Oct 31.

(3m). Ocean Edge Caravan Park, Moneyclose Lane, Heysham, Morecambe, Lancashire LA3 2XA. 01524 855657. enquiries@southlakelandparks.co.uk. www.southlakelandparks.co.uk. Owner: South Lakeland Parks Ltd. Follow M6, A589, B5273 to Lancaster, Morecambe and Port of Heysham at traffic lights at Moneyclose Inn, turn L access road to the park. GS. Indoor heated pool and sauna, boat launch, bowling green. Indoor childrens play area, cabaret lounge, 10mins drive from Morecambe. Golf 2m, shops 3m, cinema 5m. Open Feb-Nov (statics), March-Nov (tourers).

(0.75m). Venture Caravan Park, Langridge Way, Westgate, Morecambe, Lancashire LA4 4TQ. 01524 412986. www.venturecaravanpark.co.uk. Owner: Mahdeen Leisure Ltd. 1m from seafront, off A589, 6m from J34, M6. Play area. Public phone. Off-licence. Specially adapted holiday caravans for the disabled. Indoor heated swimming pool. Bar with entertainment and bar meals eat in or take away. Award winning en-suite toilet facilities. GS. Cinema, shopping centre 1.25m; golf course, leisure centre 1.5m. Open all year (tourers) – Feb 22-Jan 6 (statics).

ORMSKIRK

(1.5m). Abbey Farm Caravan Park, Dark Lane, Ormskirk, Lancashire L40 5TX. 01695 572686. abbeyfarm@yahoo.com. www.abbeyfarmcaravanpark.com. Owner: Joan & Alan Bridge. M6, J27-A2509 SP Parbold Island, L B5240 immediate R. Quiet, peaceful park 1.5m on R, entrance alongside white cottage. First class facilities. Playground. Library. Off licence shop. David Bellamy Silver Conservation Award.

(5m). Shaw Hall Caravan Park, Smithy Lane, Scarisbrick, Ormskirk, Lancashire L40 8HJ. 01704 840298. shawhall@btconnect.com. www.shawhall.com. Owner: Barley Mow Ltd. 4m E of Southport off A570. Situated on Leeds/Liverpool canal 6m from Southport. Clubhouse with entertainment. Open March 1-Jan 7.

PRESTON

(15m). Beacon Fell View Holiday Park, Higher Road, Longridge, Preston, Lancashire PR3 2TY. 01772 785434/783233.

42 MOTOR CARAVAN & CAMPING PARKS 2009

NORTHUMBRIA

beaconfell@haganasleisure.co.uk. www.haganasleisure.co.uk. Owner: Hagans Leisure Group. Leave M6 J32 to Garstang A6. Follow sign to Longridge (not Beacon Fell). At Longridge, straight across roundabout then L at White Bull. Park 1m on R. Commanding breathtaking views over the Ribble Valley, Beacon Fell View Holiday Park is set in 30 acres of beautiful landscaped parkland, and is sure to offer you and your family a holiday to remember. Facilities include an indoor heated pool, a family clubhouse with live entertainment, indoor & outdoor play areas and kid's club. Gym and sauna adults only bar. Open March – Nov.

(10m). Claylands Caravan Park, Cabus, Garstang, Preston, Lancashire PR3 1AJ. 01524 791242. alan@claylands.com. www.claylands.com. Owner: Mr F Robinson. Off A6 S of Little Chef. 14 acres of woodland alongside the river Wyre with excellent coarse fishing available on site also bar and restaurant. Ring for free brochure. Open March 1-Nov 31.

(4m). Primrose Bank Caravan Park, Singleton Road, Weeton, Preston, Lancashire PR4 3JJ. 01253 836273. info@primrosecaravanpark.co.uk. Owner: Primrose Bank Caravan Park Ltd (Manager: Michael Greaves). 1.5m S of Singleton on B5260 and 5m E of Blackpool. Leave M55 towards Fleetwood on A585 then B5260 is third on L. L at T junction the park is 1m on L. Hardstanding, easy access. All touring pitches are fully furnished with electric, water, drainage. AA listed. Fishing, golf, shops, PO all closeby. Open March-Jan.

(7m). Royal Umpire Caravan Park, Southport Road (A581), Croston, Preston, Lancashire PR5 7JB. 01772 600257. info@royalumpire.co.uk. www.royalumpire.co.uk. Owner: G & E Harrison & Sons. On A581 midway between A59 and A49. Relax in the NW, within 1 hour of tourist attractions. 10m E of Southport, 5m W of Chorley, 1m E of Croston village.

ROCHDALE

Gelder Wood Country Park, Ashworth Road, Heywood, Rochdale, Lancashire OL10 4BD. 01706 364858. gelderwood@alo.com. Owner: Joyce, Peter and Paul Chadwick. J18, M62 to M66 (SP Bury) at second exit L, J2 leave M66 turn R on a A58 (SP Heywood) at Morrison's supermarket turn L into Bamford Road B6222 to T-junction. Turn L after 100yd turn R into Ashworth Road, park on R.

SOUTHPORT

(4m). Riverside Holiday Park, Southport New Road, Banks, Southport, Lancashire PR9 8DF. 01704 228886. reception@harrisonleisureuk.com. www.riversideleisurecentre.co.uk. Owner: Harrison Leisure UK Ltd. 2.5m W of Tarleton Cross Roads on S of A565, E Southport. Set in acres of pleasant meadow. Fishing on site. Play area, disco, launderette, showers. Calor Gas and Camping Gaz stockist. Excellent entertainment for adults and children. Café. Country & Western and 60s. Indoor heated swimming pool. AA holiday centre. David Bellamy Bronze Conservation Award. Open March 1-Jan 7.

Southport Caravan Club Site, The Esplanade, Southport, Lancashire PR8 1RX. 01704 565214. www.caravanclub.co.uk. Owner: The Caravan Club. See website for directions. Caravan Club members only. No tents. Situated on the Esplanade of traditional seaside resort, close to famous sands. Dog walk, off site. Gas. Toilet blocks. Privacy cubicles. Laundry facilities. Baby washroom. Veg prep. MV service point. Information room. Play area. Golf, fishing and watersports nearby. Ideal for families. Open March-Jan.

MERSEYSIDE

WIRRAL

Wirral Country Park Caravan Club Site, Station Road, Thurstaston, Wirral, Merseyside CH61 0HN. 01516 485228. wirralcountrypark@caravanclub.co.uk. www.caravanclub.co.uk. Owner: The Caravan Club. See website for directions. The site has several flat grassy pitching areas separated by trees and shrubs, some overlooking the Dee estuary which is easily accessible. Toilet blocks, laundry facilities and MV service point. Play equipment. Golf, fishing and NCN route nearby. Good area for walking. Facilities for disabled. Ideal for families. Quiet and peaceful off-peak. Non-members welcome. No tents. Open March 27-Nov 16.

DURHAM

BARNARD CASTLE

(2m). Camping & Caravanning Club Site – Barnard Castle, Dockenflatts Lane, Lartington, Barnard Castle, Durham DL12 9DG. 01833 630228. www.campingandcaravanningclub.co.uk.

Owner: Camping & Caravanning Club. From Barnard Castle take B6277 towards Middleton-in-Teesdale, after 1m at Club sign turn L, site 500yd on L. Well placed for exploring the Pennines and the city of Durham. In easy walking distance of Barnard Castle. 90 pitches set in 10 acres. Non-members welcome. Caravans, motorcaravans and tents accepted. 11,000 trees have been planted at this beautiful site. Visit Britain Tourism in Excellence Award – Caravan Holiday Park of the Year. NE England runner up. Loo Of The Year (5 stars). Fishing, golf, horse riding, swimming pool and tennis all nearby. Deals for families and backpackers. Open March – Oct.

(3m). Hetherick Caravan Park, Kinninvie, Barnard Castle, Durham DL12 8QX. 01833 631173. info@hetherickcaravanpark.co.uk. www.hetherickcaravanpark.co.uk. Owner: Janet Embleton, Christopher & Ernest Holmes. Located just off B6279 from Staindrop and B6278 from Barnard Castle. Pleasant park located on a working farm in the heart of beautiful Teesdale. Pretty market town of Barnard Castle 3m. Ideally situated for all local attractions. Golf course and sports centre (including swimming pool) in 2m. Open March 1-Oct 31.

BISHOP AUCKLAND

(7m). Westgate Camping Site, Westgate-in-Weardale, Stanhope, Bishop Auckland, Durham DL13 1LN. 01388 517309. Owner: Mr M G Pears. On A689 Alston to Stanhope. Flat, well-drained site close to river Wear. Open March-Oct.

(4m). Witton Castle, Witton-le-Wear, Bishop Auckland, Durham DL14 0DE. 01388 488230. www.wittoncastle.com. Owner: The Lambton Estates. Off A68 and between Toft Hill and Witton-le-Wear. Caravan storage. Bars. Fly fishing. Swimming pool. Padling pool, children's playground. Bar meals. Special facilities for rallies. Periodic special events. Shopping 2m. Golf 4m. Cinema 10m. Open March 1-Jan10.

CONSETT

(3m). Manor Park, Broadmeadows, Castleside, Consett, Durham DH8 9HD. 01207 501000. Owner: Manor Park Ltd. 2.5m S of Castleside (A68). A quiet, family-run and owned country park centrally situated for touring Durham and Northumberland. Supermarkets in 5m radius. Golf range and fishing 2.5m. Open May 1-Sept 30.

NORTHUMBRIA

DARLINGTON

(10m). Winston Caravan Park, The Old Forge, Winston, Darlington, Durham DL2 3RH. *01325 730228.* m.willetts@ic24.net. www.touristnetuk.com/ne/winston. Owner: Mrs M J Willetts. On A67,10m W of Darlington, turn L into Winston Village follow road for 400yd then turn R into site. 5.5m from Barnard Castle. Disabled person's holiday home for hire. Golf course 5.5m. Shops and doctor 2m. PO 200yd. Pub 400yd. Shop/takeaway/café/restaurant in 2m. Open March 1-Oct 31.

DURHAM

(4.5m). Finchale Abbey Farm, Finchale, Durham, Durham DH1 5SH. *01913 866528.* godricawatson@hotmail.com. www.finchaleabbey.co.uk. Owner: Mr E Welsh & Mrs A Watson. Off A1 at Chester-Le-Street, on A167 (S) follow signs for Arnison Centre. Then signs for Finchale Priory. Café on site, bar at golf range. 24h security river walks. Hardstandings, credit cards accepted. Play area for children on holiday park. Shops 1.5m, fishing, golf course in 15mns walk. Beautiful countryside park. David Bellamy Silver Conservation Award.

(2.5m). Grange Caravan Club Site, Meadow Lane, Durham, Durham DH1 1TL. *01913 844778.* www.caravanclub.co.uk. Owner: The Caravan Club. See website for directions. An open and level site in easy reach of the historic city of Durham. Advance bookings essential. Non-members and tent campers are welcome. Hardstandings. Dog walk. Toilet blocks with privacy cubicles and laundry facilities. Fishing and golf nearby. Ideal for families.

STOCKTON-ON-TEES

(1.25m). White Water Park Caravan Club Site, Tees Barrage, Stockton-on-Tees, Durham TS18 2QW. *01642 634080.* www.caravanclub.co.uk. Owner: The Caravan Club. See website for directions. This pleasantly landscaped site is adjacent to the largest white water canoeing and rafting course built to international standard in Britain. Toilet blocks, baby and toddler washroom and laundry facilities. MV service point. TV, games and information rooms and play equipment. Fishing, golf and NCN route nearby. Good area for walking. Facilities for disabled. Ideal for families. Non-members and tent campers welcome.

HARTLEPOOL

HARTLEPOOL

Ash Vale Holiday Park, Easington Road, Hartlepool, Hartlepool TS24 9RF. *01429 862111.* Owner: Tony & Joy Pinto. Take A179 (off A19) to Hartlepool at 3rd roundabout turn L on to A1086 coast road. Over next roundabout, 400yd on L. A picturesque, quiet, rural park, 1m from long, sandy beach. Dogs allowed.

NORTHUMBERLAND

ALNWICK

(1m). Camping & Caravanning Club Site – Dunstan Hill, Dunstan, Alnwick, Northumberland NE66 3TQ. *01665 576310.* www.campingandcaravanningclub.co.uk. Owner: Camping & Caravanning Club. From A1 take B1340 signed Seahouses. R at T junction at Christon Bank. Take 2nd R SP Embleton, 3rd L on to B1339 coastal route, site 2m on L. The site is set in 14 acres in the shadow of Dunstan Borough Castle and 1m from coast with a footpath to beach from site. Non-members welcome and may join at the site. All units accepted. One of the park's major attractions is Kielder Water, Europe's largest man-made lake is nearby. Close to Alnwick Castle, a location used in the recent Harry Potter films. Deals for families and backpackers. Loo Of The Year (4 stars). Open March-Oct.

River Breamish Caravan Club Site, Powburn, Alnwick, Northumberland NE66 4HY. *01665 578320.* www.caravanclub.co.uk. Owner: The Caravan Club. See website for directions. Set amid the Cheviot Hills, with excellent walking and cycling in the immediate area. Toilet blocks with privacy cubicles and laundry facilities. Baby and dog walk on site. Non members and tent campers welcome. Facilities for the disabled. Open March-Nov.

ASHINGTON

(6m). Sandy Bay Holiday Park, North Seaton, Ashington, Northumberland NE63 9YD. *0871 6649764.* sandy.bay@park-resorts.com. www.park-resorts.com. Owner: Park Resorts Ltd. From A1 at Seaton Burn, go on A19, at roundabout go on to A189 to Ashington, head N. At first roundabout on A189 turn R on to B1334 towards Newbiggin by Sea. Park is on R handside. Indoor pool, water resorts programme, adventure playground, sports court, shop, launderette, amusements, takeway, free kids clubs, free family evening entertainment. Restaurant, Koi carp lake. Darts. Pool table. Alnwick Castle. David Bellamy Silver Conservation Award. Open April-Oct.

(2m). Wansbeck Riverside Caravan & Camping Site, Ashington, Northumberland NE63 8TX. *01670 812323.* wansbeckcaravan@aol.com. www.wansbeck.gov.uk. Owner: Wansbeck District Council. SP off the A1068, guide post to Ashington Road (brown sign). Touring site set in picturesque Wansbeck Riverside Park. On the banks of the river Wansbeck, and an ideal touring base. A warden lives on the site and runs a well-stocked shop. Children's play area & paddling pool.

BAMBURGH

(3m). Waren Caravan & Camping Park, Waren Mill, Bamburgh, Northumberland NE70 7EE. *01668 214366.* waren@meadowhead.co.uk. www.meadowhead.co.uk. Owner: Meadowhead Ltd. Follow B1342 from A1 to Waren Mill towards Bamburgh. By Budle Bay turn R and follow signs to park. Restaurant with children's licence. Shop, games room, laundry. Wigwams. Children's play area. Internet access on park. Heated outdoor splash pool (May-Sept). Golf 2m, fishing 5m, PO & doctor 6m,cinema 17m. David Bellamy Gold Conservation Award. Open mid March-End Oct.

BELLINGHAM

(0.5m). Bellingham Camping & Caravanning Club Site, Brown Rigg, Bellingham, Northumberland NE48 2JY. *01434 220175.* bellingham.site@thefriendlyclub.co.uk. www.thefriendlyclub.co.uk. Owner: Barry & Carole Howard. Fishing, golf, canoe launch, swimming 0.5m from site. Pennine way adjacent to site. Village 0.5m, shops, pubs and restaurant. Dog walk on site. 8m Kielder Water. 10m Hadrians Wall. Walks straight from site. Open: March-mid Nov.

Berwick-upon-Tweed Beachcomber Campsite, Goswick, Berwick-upon-Tweed, Northumberland TD15 2RW. *01289 381217.* johngregson@microplus.web.net. Owner: John & Sheila Gregson. 4m S of Berwick on A1. 4m past Holy Island turn off. From S, SP Goswick, follow road to end through golf club, about 4m from A1. Small site in remote spot on sandunes

44 MOTOR CARAVAN & CAMPING PARKS 2009

NORTHUMBRIA

overlooking Goswick Sands. Excellent facilities with glorious views over Cheviot Hills. Horse riding on site. Open March-End Sept.

(7m). Haggerston Castle Holiday Park, Beal, Berwick-upon-Tweed, Northumberland TD15 2PA. *01289 381333.* www.haggerstoncastle-park. co.uk. Owner: Bourne Leisure Ltd. Park SP from A1. Heated indoor and outdoor swimming pools. New luxury SPA treatment rooms. Club. Bars. Entertainment. Horse riding. Boating lake. Chinese restaurant. Burger King. Tennis courts. 9-hole golf course. Mini market. Bike hire. Crazy golf. Rose award. Welcome Host Award, Investor in People. Golf courses nearby. Beach 5m. David Bellamy Gold Conservation Award. Open March-end Oct.

(1.5m). Ord House Country Park, East Ord, Berwick-upon-Tweed, Northumberland TD15 2NS. *01289 305288.* enquiries@ordhouse.co.uk. www. ordhouse.co.uk. Owner: W Maguire. Off Berwick bypass (A1) at East Ord. Licensed club. Silver Award Green Tourism Business Scheme. Pride of Northumbria Caravan Park of the Year 1997-2003. AA 5 pennants. Award winner Toilet and Amenity Building & Disabled Suite. North East Tourism Holiday Park of the Year 2006. Members of the Best of British. Licensed club in the 18th century manor house. Mini golf and children's play area. Golf and sports centre in 1.5m. GS. David Bellamy Gold Conservation Award.

(0.5m). Seaview Caravan Club Site, Billendean Road, Spittal, Berwick-upon-Tweed, Northumberland TD15 1QU. *01289 305198.* www.caravanclub. co.uk. Owner: The Caravan Club. See website for directions. Excellent views of the Tweed and old town. Good site for children with safe bathing and play facilities at Spittal beach. Tent campers and non-members welcome. Hardstandings available. Advance booking advised BH and July and Aug. Toilet blocks. Privacy cubicles. Laundry facilities. Baby/toddler washroom. Veg prep. MV service point. Golf, fishing, cycling and watersports nearby. Open March-Nov.

CHATHILL

Camping & Caravanning Club Site – Beadnell Bay, Beadnell, Chathill, Northumberland NE67 5BX. *01665 720586.* www.campingandcaravanningclu b.co.uk. Owner: Camping & Caravanning Club. Site is on L after Beadnell Village, just beyond L hand bend. 10m from Alnwick. Follow 'Seahouses' SP. 20m from Berwick-upon-Tweed. 6-acre site with 150 pitches with full facilities next to the beach. Ideal for exploring Northumberland coastline and in easy reach of A1. NO TOWED CARAVANS PERMITTED. Non-members accepted. Motorhomes & tents welcome. A superb site for walkers and cyclists. Deals for families and backpackers. Open April-Oct.

HALTWHISTLE

(1.5m). Camping & Caravanning Club Site – Haltwhistle, Burnfoot Park Village, Haltwhistle, Northumberland NE49 0JP. *01434 320106.* www.campingandc aravanningclub.co.uk. Owner: Camping & Caravanning Club . From A69, take Alston road S (A689). Coanwood and Halton Lea Gate. Follow site signs. Site is in the National Trust Bellister Castle Estate on south bank of South Tyne river and 4m from Hadrian's Wall. Close to the Pennine Way on the banks of river South Tyne. All units accepted. Non-members welcome. Fishing available on site. Deals for families and backpackers. Open March-Oct.

(3m). Hadrian's Wall Camping and Caravan Site, Melkridge Tilery, Haltwhistle, Northumberland NE49 9PG. *01434 320495.* info@romanwallcamping.co.uk. www. romanwallcamping.co.uk. Owner: Graham & Pat Reed. 300yd S of B6318, 1m W of Once Brewed. 2m due N of Melkridge (A69). 0.5m from Hadrian's Wall world heritage site.

(1m). Seldom Seen Caravan Park, Seldom Seen, Haltwhistle, Northumberland NE49 0NE. *01434 320571.* www.seldomseencaravanpark. co.uk. Owner: Mr W & Mrs J E Dale. Off A69. SP Haltwhistle. Quiet, riverside park. Birdwatching, peaceful walks. 2m Hadrian's Wall World Heritage site. Nr Northumberland National Park, Historical Borders, High Pennines AONB. Golf 5m. David Bellamy Gold Conservation Award. Open March 1-Jan 31.

(5m). Yont the Cleugh Caravan Park, Coanwood, Haltwhistle, Northumberland NE49 0QN. *01434 320274.* yontthecleugh@yahoo.co.uk. www.yontthecleugh.co.uk. Owner: Ian & Desley Whitaker. SP 4.5m off A69 and 3.5m off A689. A quiet park in outstanding unspoilt location. Near main Roman wall sites. Bar. Children's play area. Open March 1-Jan 31 (statics), March-Nov (tourers).

HEXHAM

(10m). Barrasford Park, 1 Front Drive, Hexham, Northumberland NE48 4BE. *01434 681210.* Owner: Mr T & M Smith. 8m N of Corbridge off A68. 60 acres of woodland. Laundry. Licensed clubhouse. Salmon fishing in 2m. Open April 1-Oct 31.

(17m). Camping & Caravanning Club Site – Bellingham Brown Rigg, Brown Rigg, Bellingham, Hexham, Northumberland NE48 2JY. *01434 220175.* Owner: Camping & Caravanning Club. Located on the B6320 Bellingham is accessible from the A68 driving S or the A6079 driving N from Newcastle. Located in the most tranquil area of England Bellingham is close to the Pennine, also offers access to Hadrian's Wall just a bus ride away. Wireless internet access available. Open March 17-Oct 31.

(1.5m). Causey Hill Caravan Park, Causey Hill, Hexham, Northumberland NE46 2JN. *01434 602834.* causeyhillcp@aol.com. www. causeyhill.co.uk. Owner: Mary Scott and Linda Ogle. 1.5m SW Hexham. Follow B6306 or signs for Hexham racecourse and then Causey Hill. Quiet Country Park, woodland walks, wildlife pond. Fishing, golf courses nearby. Many hardstandings, all electric. Stunning views. Unique park, static caravans for sale. Open March 1-Oct 31.

(2m). Fallowfield Dene, Acomb, Hexham, Northumberland NE46 4RP. *01434 603553.* den@fallowfielddene. co.uk. www.fallowfielddene.co.uk. Owner: Mr P Straker. 2m N of Hexham via A69 bypass (N of river Tyne) for 0.5m W. Turn N on to A6079. Site is 1m beyond village of Acomb. 10 tent pitches also available. Roman wall nearby. Manager: Dennis & Jen Burnell. Open March-Oct inclusive.

(2m). Hexham Racecourse, High Yarridge, Hexham, Northumberland NE46 2JP. *01434 605814.* hexrace@aol. com. www.hexham-racecourse.co.uk. Owner: Hexham Steeplechase Co Ltd. Off A69 on B6306, turn L after 3m. 1.5m to site. Situated on second highest racecourse in Britain with dramatic views across large area of Northumberland. Dog walk. Advance booking not essential. Shops, doctor, dentist, golf course all in 2m. Open May-Sept.

NORTHUMBRIA

Kielder Water Caravan Club Site, Leaplish Waterside Park, Falstone, Hexham, Northumberland NE48 1AX. 01434 250278. www.caravanclub.co.uk. Owner: The Caravan Club. See website for directions. 4m from Kielder. A fabulous site for an active holiday, with some pitches overlooking Kielder Water, the largest man-made lake in Western Europe. Ideal family site with watersports, ponytrekking, horse riding, orienteering, birdwatching, cycling and crazy golf. All pitches on hardstanding but awnings possible. Dog walk. Non members and tent campers welcome. Toilet blocks and laundry facilities. MV service point. Open March-Nov.

(6m). **Poplars Riverside Caravan Park, East Lands End, Haydon Bridge, Hexham, Northumberland NE47 6BY.** 01434 684427. Owner: Mrs N Pattison. Near the A69 Newcastle-upon-Tyne to Carlisle road. Look for caravan sign on bridge in village. A secluded riverside site at Haydon Bridge. Fishing on site. Near village and convenient for Hadrian's Wall. Railway station in village. Open March 1-Oct 31.

(7m). **Springhouse Caravan Park, Slaley, Hexham, Northumberland NE47 0AW.** 01434 673241. enquire@springhousecaravanpark.co.uk. www.springhousecaravanpark.co.uk. Owner: Mr C Phillips. SP from A68 at Kiln Pit Hill. Quiet park surrounded by forest and magnificent views. Slaley golf complex nearby. David Bellamy Silver Conservation Award. Open March 1-Oct 31.

MORPETH

Nunnykirk Caravan Club Site, Nunnykirk, Morpeth, Northumberland NE61 4PZ. 01669 620762. www.caravanclub.co.uk. Owner: The Caravan Club. See website for directions. 5.5m from Rothbury. Peace and tranquility reign at this attractive site, making it a haven for wildlife, and a bird watcher's paradise. Own sanitation required. Good area for walking, dog walk nearby. Fishing in 5m. Non-members welcome. No tents. Open April-Oct.

OTTERBURN

(8m). **Border Forest Caravan Park, Cottonshopeburnfoot, Otterburn, Northumberland NE19 1TF.** 01830 520259. borderforest@btinternet.com. www.borderforest.com. Owner: Mrs A Flanagan. Adjacent A68. 6m S of Scottish border (Carter bar). 8m N of Otterburn. Family run park in beautiful Northumberland Border country. Directly onto Pennine Way and Kielder Forest. Free hot showers. Timber lodge hire. Bed and breakfast. Ensuite rooms. Restaurant nearby. David Bellamy Gold Conservation Award. Open March 1-Oct 31.

PRUDHOE

(1.4m). **The High Hermitage Caravan Park, Ovingham, Prudhoe, Northumberland NE42 6HH.** 01661 832250. highhermitage@onetel.com. www.highermitagecaravanpark.co.uk. Owner: Mr & Mrs W S Lee. Off A69. SP 'Wylam' and follow main road to apparent T-junction SP R to Ovingham, continue on main road 1.5 m towards Ovingham along riverside. Just after paved and railed-in water extraction point, turn R into drive entrance (concealed). Can also accommodate up to 10 tents. Communal BBQ, giant draught/chess board. Distance to shops, PO, doctor 1m. In 1.5m: chemists, garage, playgrounds, rail station, restaurants, Pubs. Fishing rights on boundary river bank. Cinema, theatre, museum, towns of Newcastle and Hexham 12m. Metro shopping centre 10m. Golf course 4m. Open March 1-Jan 7.

STOCKSFIELD

(4m). **Wellhouse Caravan & Camping Park, Wellhouse Farm, Newton, Stocksfield, Northumberland NE43 7UY.** 01661 842193. www.wellhousefarm.co.uk. Owner: K J Richardson & Sons. 1m from A69 on B6309 to Matfen & Stamfordham. 9m from Hexham. 1m from B6318, Hadrians Wall. 2m from Corbridge fishing and golf. Quiet family site. Ideal for visiting Northumberland and surrounding areas. Open April-Oct.

WOOLER

(0.25m). **Highburn House Caravan and Camping Park, Wooler, Northumberland NE71 6EE.** 01668 281344. relax@highburn-house.co.uk. www.highburn-house.co.uk. Owner: Mr R DTait. From A1 take A697 to Wooler, turn L to High Street at the top turn L into Burnhouse road, park is on L. Farm park with good views over the Cheviot Hills. Shops, pubs, doctors, dentist etc. 0.25m from park. Takeaway meals, café/restaurant, diary produce available nearby. Castles, light railway, wild cattle. Scottish border all in 7m of park. Golf course 2m. Open March-Nov.

(2m). **Riverside Holiday Park, South Road, Wooler, Northumberland NE71 6NU.** 01668 281447. riversidepark@northdales.co.uk. www.northdales.co.uk. Owner: North Dales LLP. From South take A697 off A1, SP Coldstream to Wooler about 35m. Park on L on outskirts of village. Situated on edge of Northumbria National Park. Indoor pool. Family lounge bar and clubroom. Open March-Jan.

TYNE & WEAR

ROWLANDS GILL

Derwent Park Caravan & Camping Park, Mr & Mrs I Jeavons, The Bungalow, Derwent Park, Rowlands Gill, Tyne & Wear NE39 1LG. 01207 543383. Owner: Gateshead Metropolitan District Council. At junction of A694 and B6314 in Rowlands Gill, 7m SW of Newcastle-upon-Tyne. Flat, sheltered site by river. Hot showers, laundry, playground, tennis, bowls, crazy golf and trout fishing. Near Beamish and Gateshead Metro Centre. 2m from shops, clubs, restaurants. Open March 1-Oct 31.

SOUTH SHIELDS

Lizard Lane Camping & Caravan Park, Marsden, South Shields, Tyne & Wear NE34 7AB. 01914 544982. Owner: Community Services. 2m SE of South Shields town centre via A183. 9 hole put on site. Children's play area up to 8 years. Close to museums, leisure centre and Roman remains. Fees on request (advance bookings only for weekly stays). Sea 100yd.

WHITLEY BAY

(2m). **Old Hartley Caravan Club Site, Whitley Bay, Tyne & Wear NE26 4RL.** 01912 370256. www.caravanclub.co.uk. Owner: The Caravan Club. See website for directions. Caravan Club members only. No tents. Slightly sloping site with views overlooking the sea. Beach 1m. Hardstandings. Toilet blocks. Privacy cubicles. Laundry facilities. Veg Prep. Gas & Gaz. MV Service point. Late night arrivals area. Ideal for families. Open March-Nov.

(1.5m). **Whitley Bay Holiday Park, Blyth Road, The Links, Whitley Bay, Tyne & Wear NE26 4BR.** 0871 6649800. whitley.bay@park-resorts.com. www.park-resorts.com. Owner: Park Resorts Ltd. From S: A1 N to Washington, then A19 through the Tyne tunnel (toll payable). Take the signed coast road. Follow the A1058 to Tynemouth seafront, turn L. From N: A1 S to A19 SP to the Tyne tunnel. Take slip road to Whitley Bay, follow signs to park. Indoor pool, water resorts programme, FREE kids clubs, FREE family evening entertainment, takeaway, amusements, village shop, launderette. Restaurant, entertainment centre. Pool table. Darts. Adventure playground. Metro centre, Millennium Bridge. Open April-Oct.

SOUTH-EAST ENGLAND

See page 5 for key to symbols and abbreviations

KENT

ASHFORD

(3m). Broadhembury Camping & Caravan Park, Steeds Lane, Kingsnorth, Ashford, Kent TN26 1N. 01233 620859. holidaypark@broadhembury.co.uk. www.broadhembury.co.uk. Owner: Mr Keith & Jenny Taylor. From M20, exit 10 take A2070 to 2nd roundabout, SP following signs for Kingsnorth L at second crossroad in village. Lovely Kentish park with first class facilities (65 mixed units). Plenty to do regardless of weather. Central to 100s of interesting places, Channel Ports and Eurotunnel. Ideal location for walking and cycling. Good fishing and golf course with driving range only 5mins away.

Dunn Street Farm, Westwell, Ashford, Kent TN25 4NJ. 01233 712537. www.caravancampingsites.co.uk. Owner: Joe Stuart-Smith. On North Downs Way, 4m NW of M20 J19, 2m N of A20 at Hothfield. Quiet farm site in easy reach of Canterbury, Chilham, Sissinghurst etc. Dishwashing facilities. Café/restaurant nearby. Open March 1-Oct 31.

Spill Land Farm Holiday Caravan Park, Benenden Road, Biddenden, Ashford, Kent TN27 8BX. 01580 291379. www.spilllandfarm.co.uk. Owner: Mr DS Waite & Mr AK Waite. Turn off A262 Biddenden to Tenterden road at Vineyard and Hospital sign, after 0.25m R behind white farm house. 5m from Tenterden. 1.25m from Biddenden. NO MOTORCARAVANS. Park is central to the Kent and Sussex Weald with many local attractions. Ideally suited to the 50+ age group looking for a quiet, peaceful and more relaxed atmosphere with no clubs or swimming pools. Pitch & putt 1m. Golf course, food shops 5m. Cinema, shopping centre 12m. Static holiday caravans for sale. No persons under 18 years old permitted in any touring caravan or tent. Open March 1-Sept.

BIDDENDEN

(3m). Woodlands Park, Tenterden Road, Biddenden, Kent TN27 8BT. 01580 291216. woodlandsp@aol.com. www.campingsite.co.uk. Owner: Mr R Jessop. Travel along A28 from Ashford to Tenterden. About 3m before Tenterden take R turn onto A262. Site is about 0.5m on R. New toilet/shower block. Gas and accessories. Central to Kent and E. Sussex attractions. Dogs allowed under control in touring park. Level park with bus stop at entrance. Open March-Oct for tourists, weather permitting.

BIRCHINGTON

(1.5m). Two Chimneys Caravan Park, Shottendane Road, Birchington, Kent CT7 OHD. 01843 841068/843157. info@twochimneys.co.uk. www.twochimneys.co.uk. Owner: Mrs L Sullivan. From A299, turn R into Park Lane (B2048) at Birchington Church. L fork B2050 'RAF Manston'. 1st L on to B2049. Site 0.5m on R. Licensed bar. Heated enclosed pool. Tennis court. Children's play area, amusement arcade. Golf, cinema, beaches, sea, horse riding, sports centre, watersports, fishing, theme park all in 3m. Near lovely sandy beaches of Margate, Ramsgate and Broadstairs. Open Easter-Oct 31. March 1-Jan 17 for owner occupied.

CANTERBURY

(7m). Ashfield Farm, Waddenhall, Petham, Canterbury, Kent CT4 5PX. 01227 700624. mpatterson@ashfieldfarm.freeserve.co.uk. Owner: M C Patterson. Situated on B2068 about 6m from Canterbury. Level, well-screened site with modern facilities. 9-hole putting course on site. Kennelling available. Open April 1-Oct 31.

(1m). Camping & Caravanning Club Site – Canterbury, Bekesbourne Lane, Canterbury, Kent CT3 4AB. 01227 463216. www.campingandcaravanningclub.co.uk. Owner: Camping & Caravanning Club. From Canterbury follow A257 signs (Sandwich), turn R opposite golf course. Canterbury Cathedral and many other places of interest in easy reach from site. Ideal location for day trips to France or as a stopover for the Continent. All units accepted. Non-members welcome. Take a trip to nearby Herne Bay for beautiful beaches. Deals for families and backpackers. David Bellamy Gold Conservation Award.

Royal Oak, 114 Sweechgate, Broad Oak, Canterbury, Kent. 01227 710448. 2.5m NE of Canterbury via A28 to Sturry. Then A291 towards Herne Bay and first turn L to Broad Oak. Site is behind inn. Small orchard site. Fees on application Open April-Oct.

(5m). South View, Maypole Lane, Hoath, Canterbury, Kent CT3 4LL. 01227 860280. southviewcamping@aol.com. Owner: Mr K R Underdown & Mrs U J Underdown. Off A28. Off A299. Quiet rural flat situation. Good food and drink country pub 100yd. Laundry facilities. Shop 1m. 3m from beaches of Thanet. 5m from cathedral city. Open April-Oct.

(4m). Yew Tree Park, Stone Street, Petham, Canterbury, Kent CT4 5PL. 01227 700306. info@yewtreepark.com. www.yewtreepark.com. Owner: Mr & Mrs

---

stay in Kent with Keat Farm — Beautiful Parks in Kent

3 BEAUTIFUL TOURING PARKS
HAWTHORN FARM - DOVER
LITTLE SATMAR - FOLKESTONE
QUEX PARK - BIRCHINGTON

FREEPHONE 0800 305070
KEAT FARM PARKS
RECULVER ROAD   HERNE BAY   KENT CT6 6SR
TEL: 01227 374581   FAX: 01227 740785
E.MAIL: info@keatfarm.co.uk

www.keatfarm.co.uk

www.motorcaravanmagazine.co.uk   MOTOR CARAVAN & CAMPING PARKS 2009   **47**

SOUTH-EAST ENGLAND

D Zanders. On B2068 4m from Canterbury and 9 m from J11 of M20. Small, picturesque country park overlooking beautiful Chartham Downs. Ideally situated for exploring local heritage and Kent. Large open-air swimming pool. Canterbury 4m. Open March 1-Nov 1.

CHATHAM

(3m). **Woolmans Wood, Bridgewood, Rochester Road, Chatham, Kent ME5 9SB.** *01634 867685.* woolmans.wood@currantbun.com. www.woolmans-wood.co.uk. Owner: John Western. M2, J3, take A229 to Bridgewood roundabout then B2097. Park 0.25m rhs. M20, J6 same as above. Adults only. Shops (Asda), PO in 10mins walk. Doctor 2m, Golf course 2m. Garage 3-4m.

DOVER

■ (3m). **Hawthorn Farm, Martin Mill, Dover, Kent CT15 5LA.** *01304 852658.* info@keatfarm.co.uk. www.keatfarm.co.uk. Owner: Keat Farm (Caravans) Ltd. Situated off main road between Deal and Dover A258. Well SP. Showers, toilets, laundry, washing up facilities. Disabled toilet and shower room. Mother/toddler room. Shop. Café. Take away food. Wifi internet. Fishing and Golf nearby. David Bellamy Gold Conservation Award. Open March 1-Nov 30.

(3m). **St Margaret's Bay, Reach Road, St Margaret's-at-Cliffe, Dover, Kent CT15 6AG.** *0871 6649773.* stmargarets.bay@park-resorts.com. www.park-resorts.com. Owner: Park Resorts Ltd. From London take M20 or A2 to Dover. Take the A258 and follow signs for St Margarets Cliffe. Turn R on Reach Road. The park is then on R. Indoor pool, restaurant, bar, outdoor play area, FREE kids club, FREE family entertainment, amusements, on site store. Sauna, solarium, gym. Darts, pool table. David Bellamy Gold Conservation Award. Open April-Oct.

DYMCHURCH

(1m). **New Beach Holiday Park, Hythe Road, Dymchurch, Kent TN29 0JX.** *01303 872234.* newbeach@ParkHolidaysUK.com. www.ParkHolidaysUK.com. Owner: Park Holidays UK. On the coastal road A259 between Hythe and Dymchurch. Indoor pool, children's facilities, restaurant, shops, entertainment. Visit Britain Holiday Park (4 stars). David Bellamy Silver Conservation Award. Open: Jan – Nov.

FOLKESTONE

(4m). **Black Horse Farm Caravan Club Site, 385 Canterbury Road, Densole, Folkestone, Kent CT18 7BG.** *01303 892665.* www.caravanclub.co.uk. Owner: The Caravan Club. See website for directions. Set in the heart of farming country in the Kentish village of Densole on the Downs. Quiet and relaxed country site, ideally suited for families wishing to visit the many interesting local attractions. Non-members and tent campers welcome. Toilet blocks. Hardstandings. Privacy cubicles. Laundry facilities. Veg prep. MV service point. Playground. Golf, fishing nearby. Good area for walking. Baby/toddler washroom. Dog walk.

(4m). **Camping & Caravanning Club Site – Folkestone, The Warren, Folkestone, Kent CT19 6NQ.** *01303 255093.* www.campingandcaravanningclub.co.uk. Owner: The Camping & Caravanning Club. From M2 and Canterbury join A260, take L at island into Folkestone, Hill Road, straight on over crossroads into Wear Bay Road and second L turn before Martello Tower, site 0.5m on R. This cliff site is in an Area of Outstanding Beauty, adjacent to a pebble beach. On a clear day you can see France from this club site. Non-members welcome. NO TOWED CARAVANS permitted. Folkestone harbour is picturesque with its own cliff top promenade. Sea fishing is available from the beach. Deals for families and backpackers. Loo Of The Year (5 stars). Visit Britain Tourism in Excellence Award – SE runner up. Open March-Oct.

■ (2.5m). **Little Satmar Holiday Park, Winehouse Lane, Capel-le-Ferne, Folkestone, Kent CT18 7JF.** *01303 251188.* info@keatfarm.co.uk. www.keatfarm.co.uk. Owner: Keat Farm Caravans Ltd. Inland off B2011 Folkestone to Dover. Quiet, well-maintained park convenient for ferries and Channel Tunnel. Wifi internet on whole park. David Bellamy Gold Conservation Award. Open March-Nov 30.

(1.5m). **Little Switzerland Caravan and Camping Park, Wear Bay Road, Folkestone, Kent CT19 6PS.** *01303 252168.* btony328@aol.com. www.caravancampingsites.co.uk/littleswitzerland. Owner: D Gasson. Off A20. Follow signs Country Park. Small family run site. Shop 0.25m. Licensed restaurant. Booking advisable. Open March 1-Oct 31.

HYTHE

(4m). **Daleacres Caravan Club Site, Lower Wall Road, W Hythe, Hythe, Kent CT21 4NW.** *01303 267679.* www.caravanclub.co.uk. Owner: The Caravan Club. See website for directions. Caravan Club members only. No tents. Attractive, level site. Play area. Dog walk. Toilet blocks. Privacy cubicles. Laundry facilities. Veg prep. MV service point. Play equipment. Golf, fishing and watersports nearby. Good for walking. Ideal for families. Open: March-Nov.

Folkestone Racecourse Caravan Club Site, Folkestone Racecourse, Westenhanger, Hythe, Kent CT21 4HX. *01303 261761.* 6.5m from Folkestone. About 2m from M20 en route to or from the ferries and Channel Tunnel, with easy rail access to London. Toilet blocks with privacy cubicles, laundry facilities, vegetable preparation area and gas/gaz exchange. Fishing and golf in 5m, watersports, dog walk on site. Good area for walking. Open March-Sept.

ISLE OF SHEPPEY

(6m). **Warden Springs Holiday Park, Thorn Hill Road, East Church, Isle of Sheppey, Kent ME12 4HF.** *0871 6649791.* warden.springs@park-resorts.com. www.park-resorts.com. Owner: Park Resorts Ltd. From M25 take A2, J2. Then take M2, till J5. Follow A249 for 8m then R, on to B2231 to Eastchurch. Turn L following signs for park. Outdoor, heated swimming pool, club house, FREE kids clubs, FREE family evening entertainment. Restaurant, bar, playground. David Bellamy Gold Conservation Award. Open April-Oct.

LEYSDOWN-ON-SEA

(0.5m). **Priory Hill Holiday Park, Wing Road, Leysdown-on-Sea, Kent ME12 4QT.** *01795 510267.* info@prioryhill.co.uk. www.prioryhill.co.uk. M2/M20-A249 to Isle of Sheppey, B2231 to Leysdown follow brown signs to Priory Hill. Clubhouse entertainment, swimming pool (indoor heated) and lots more. See our website. Open March-Oct.

MAIDSTONE

Coldblow Farm, Coldblow Lane, Thurnham, Maidstone, Kent ME14 3LR. *01622 735038.* coldblowcamping@btconnect.com. www.coldblow-camping.co.uk. Owner: Jeffrey Pilkington. From J7 on M20 take A249 towards Detling. Turn into Detling village, R into Pilgrims Way, at 2nd crossroads turn L towards Hucking.

48 MOTOR CARAVAN & CAMPING PARKS 2009

SOUTH-EAST ENGLAND

Site 0.5m on R. Camping barn 200yd from North Downs Way.

(3m). Pine Lodge Touring Park, A20 Ashford Road, Bearsted, Maidstone, Kent ME17 1XH. *01622 730018.* booking@pinelodgetouringpark.co.uk. www.pinelodgetouringpark.co.uk. Owner: Janet & Stan Hollingsworth. From J8, M20 (Leeds Castle exit), park 1m towards Bearsted and Maidstone. Sheltered site with rural views. Ideal for Continental ports and touring Kent. Centrally heated facilities block. Easy access. Play area. Shop. Gas. Laundry-dishwashing room. No dogs.

Riverside Caravan Park, Farleigh Bridge, East Farleigh, Maidstone, Kent ME16 9ND. *01622 726647.* From M20 J5 turn R at traffic lights turn L (Hermatage Lane) Straight across two sets of traffic lights and down hill, over level crossing immediately turn R into park entrance. Open March 1-Oct 31.

NEW ROMNEY

(0.25m). Marlie Farm Holiday Park, Dymchurch Road (A259), New Romney, Kent TN28 8UE. *01797 363060.* marliefarm@ParkHolidaysUK.com. www.ParkHolidaysUK.com. Owner: Park Holidays UK. On A259 coast road. Close to beach. Club house, indoor leisure complex with pool. Jacuzzi/play area and café. Horses, donkeys, ducks and rabbits. New Romney: bars. David Bellamy Silver Conservation Award. Open Easter-Oct (tourers), March-Jan (statics).

(3m). Romney Sands Holiday Park, The Parade, Greatstone-on-Sea, New Romney, Kent TN28 8RN. *0871 6649761.* romney.sands@park-resorts.com. www.park-resorts.com. Owner: Park Resorts. From London, take M20 to Ashford. Exit at J10, and follow signs to Brenzett. Follow signs to New Romney taking 1st R past Shell garage to the seafront. Turn R on coast road. Indoor heated pool, FREE kids club, FREE family entertainment, adventure playground, amusements, launderette, diner, takeaway, tennis courts. Bar, family club room, pool, darts. Southbeach Club for 2008. David Bellamy Silver Conservation Award. Open April-Oct.

RAMSGATE

(2.5m). Manston Caravan & Camping Park, Manston Court Road, Manston, Ramsgate, Kent CT12 5AU. *01843 823442.* enquiries@manston-park.co.uk. www.manston-park.co.uk. Owner: Mrs M Neale & Mr B Austen. M2 motorway follow A299 to Monkton roundabout, follow Kent International Airport signs to join B2050. 1st L after airport first L, park 400yd on R. Play area. Golf in 1m; supermarket, PO in 2m. Ramsgate, Margate and Broadstairs 3m away. Open April 1-Oct 31.

Nethercourt Park Camp Site, Nethercourt Hill, Ramsgate, Kent CT11 0RZ. *01843 595485.* Owner: P Barrowcliffe. Follow A253 into Ramsgate. At Nethercourt Circus roundabout. Bear L to site entrance 150yd on L. 0.5m from beach and 1m to yacht marina and ferry. Limited facilites for the disabled. Fees on application.

SANDWICH

(0.2m). Sandwich Leisure Park, Woodnesborough Road, Sandwich, Kent CT13 0AA. *01304 612681.* Follow A257 to Sandwich then follow caravan park brown signs. Relaxed park with excellent shower and WC facilities. Town 5mins on foot. Laundry, phone, playground. Open March-Oct. W/E Nov, Dec and X-mas.

SEVENOAKS

(4m). Camping & Caravanning Club Site – Oldbury Hill, Styants Bottom, Seal, Sevenoaks, Kent TN15 0ET. *01732 762728.* www.campingandcaravanningclub.co.uk. Owner: Camping & Caravanning Club. 0.5m off the A25 between Sevenoaks and Borough Green. Turn L just after Crown Point Inn. Down narrow lane to Styants Bottom, site on L. A 4-acre site. Levelling ramps required. Ideal site for exploring the delights of the Garden of England. All units accepted. Non-members welcome. Site is located in National Trust land surrounded by woodland walks. Convenient for Channel Ports at Dover and Folkestone. Deals for families and backpackers. Open March-Oct.

(9m). Gate House Wood Touring Park, Ford Lane, Wrotham Heath, Sevenoaks, Kent TN15 7SD. *01732 843062.* gatehousewood@btinternet.com. www.gatehousewoodtouring.co.uk. Owner: Mr & Mrs Long and Mr & Mrs Storey. M26, J2A take A20 S towards Maidstone, through traffic lights at Wrotham Heath take first L, SP Trottiscliffe, L at next junction. Gate House Wood is 100yd on L. 12 month licence for winter rallies, etc. American RVs welcome. Open March 1-End Nov (all year by arrangement only).

(0.5m). To The Woods Caravan & Camping Park, Botsom Lane, W Kingsdown, Sevenoaks, Kent TN15 6BN. *01322 863751.* Owner: Mrs E Helsdon. 4m NW of Wrotham. Turn L at Botsom Lane off A20. Site (800yd). Small, quiet park with limited facilities. Idyllic setting close to mainline to London (19m from Central London).The site is high on the North Downs, but sheltered by trees and well-drained. Brands Hatch circuit 1m Shops 5m, pub 7m. Site Manager: Mr M J Firman

SHEERNESS

(1.5m). Sheerness Holiday Park, Halfway Road, Minster-on-Sea, Sheerness, Kent ME12 3AA. *01795 662638.* sheerness@ParkHolidaysUK.com. www.ParkHolidaysUK.com. Owner: Park Holidays UK. Off M2 and A2 following signs to Sheerness, 0.5m from town on R. Club. Indoor pool. Children's club. Amusements, sports & leisure facilities, playground, on site shop, takeaway & café. David Bellamy Silver Conservation Award. Open March-Oct.

TONBRIDGE

(10m). Tanner Farm Touring Caravan & Camping Park, Goudhurst Road, Marden, Tonbridge, Kent TN12 9ND. *01622 832399.* enquiries@tannerfarmpark.co.uk. www.tannerfarmpark.co.uk. Owner: S Mannington & Son Ltd. 3m from Marden, 10m Maidstone from either A229 or A262 on to B2079, midway between Goudhurst & Marden. CARAVAN CLUB AFFILIATED SITE. Extremely peaceful setting in centre of attractive family farm. Mainly flat and grass. Farm animals. B&B also available in Tudor farmhouse. Green Business Tourism Scheme Silver. David Bellamy Gold Conservation Award.

(5m). The Hop Farm Country Park, Beltring, Paddock Wood, Tonbridge, Kent TN12 6PY. *01622 872068.* Owner: The Hop Farm Ltd. Situated on A228 Paddock Wood, 30mins from J5, M25, 10mins from J4, M20. Secluded site in the grounds of the largest collection of oast houses in the world. Open March-Oct.

WHITSTABLE

(1m). Primrose Cottage Caravan Park, Golden Hill, Whitstable, Kent CT5 3AR. *01227 273694.* campbell_brian@btconnect.com. Owner: Mr Brian Campbell. 1m E of Whitstable roundabout on A2990 (Thanet Way), next to Tesco supermarket. A quiet park with no clubhouse. Tesco superstore nearby. 1m to Whitstable town and 7m to Canterbury. Open March 1-Oct 31.

SOUTH-EAST ENGLAND

■ **(1.5m). Seaview Holiday Park,** St John's Road, Swalecliffe, Whitstable, Kent CT5 2RY. 01227 792246. seaview@ParkHolidaysUK.com. www.ParkHolidaysUK.com. Owner: Park Holidays UK. Off A299, at double roundabout L under railway bridge, mini roundabout turn R 600yd on L, lane down to park (SP). AA 3 pennants. Leisure pool, bar, bar snacks. Canterbury: shopping, restaurants. David Bellamy Silver Conservation Award. Open March 1-Oct 31.

WROTHAM

Thriftwood Caravan & Camping Park, Plaxdale Green Road, Stansted, Wrotham, Kent TN15 7PB. 01732 822261. booking@thriftwoodleisure.co.uk. www.thriftwoodleisure.co.uk. Owner: Mr & Mrs K Hollingsworth. From M25, take M20 towards Dover, J2. Follow A2 Northbound and Thriftwood signs. M26 J2A follow A20 Northbound towards W Kingsdown. Gas supplies & refills. Bar. Shaver points. tennis nearby. Play area. Outdoor swimming pool. Licensed club house. Open March 1-Jan 31.

LONDON

ABBEY WOOD

Abbey Wood Caravan Club Site, Federation Road, Abbey Wood, London SE2 0LS. 020 83117708. www.caravanclub.co.uk. Owner: The Caravan Club. See website for directions. Only 35mins by train to central London yet retaining a rural atmosphere. Playframe. Advance booking essential Bank holidays, July and Aug. Hardstandings. Heated toilet blocks. Privacy cubicles. Laundry facilities. Baby changing facilities. Veg prep. MV service point. Golf, watersports and cycling all in 5m. Non-members welcome. Tent campers admitted.

CHINGFORD

(2m). Lee Valley Campsite, Sewardstone Road, Chingford, London E4 7RA. 020 8529 5689. scs@leevalleypark.org.uk. www.leevalleypark.org.uk. Owner: Lee Valley Regional Park Authority. Site is on A112 between Chingford and Waltham Abbey to the S of M25, leave M25 at J26. Close to M25 and Epping Forest. Play area. Bus stops on site for connection to London. Open April-Oct.

CRYSTAL PALACE

Crystal Palace Caravan Club Site, Crystal Palace Parade, Crystal Palace, London SE19 1UF. 020 87787155. www.caravanclub.co.uk. Owner: The Caravan Club. See website for directions. Adjacent to pleasant park with many attractions for children. Next to National Sports Centre. Excellent facilities. Mainline railway stations to central London in walking distance. Non-members and tent campers welcome (66 pitches). Hardstandings. Advance booking necessary. Toilet blocks. Privacy cubicles. Laundry facilities. Veg prep. MV service point.

Edmonton
(1m). Lee Valley Camping & Caravan Park, Meridian Way, Edmonton, London N9 0AS. 020 8803 6900. leisure complex@leevalleypark.org.uk. www.leevalleypark.org.uk. Owner: Lee Valley Regional Park. M25 J25, follow signs for A10 (City). At first set of traffic lights turn L, continue on this road for 6m. At Odeon cinema turn L into leisure centre complex, camping is SP. Golf and driving range on site. 0.5m to nearest shops. Open all year except Christmas, Boxing Day & New Years Day.

LONDON

Lee Valley Cycle Circuit & Campsite, Quartermile Lane, Leyton, London, London E10 5PD. 020 8534 6085. www.leevalleypark.org.uk. Owner: Lee Valley Regional Park. Off A102M East Way Route. 4m from central London. Open April-Oct.

SURREY

CHERTSEY

(1m). Camping & Caravanning Club Site – Chertsey, Bridge Road, Chertsey, Surrey KT16 8JX. 01932 562405. www.campingandcaravanningclub.co.uk. Owner: Camping & Caravanning Club. Leave M25 exit 11. Follow signs (A317) to Chertsey. At roundabout take first exit to lights. Straight over at next lights. Turn R 400yd turn L into site. Picturesque site on banks of the Thames. Good access to London and surrounding areas. Fishing is permitted from the riverbank with the holiday site managers' permission. (Local attractions include Thorpe Park, Windsor Castle and Legoland). Non-members welcome. All units accepted. Deals for families and backpackers.

EAST HORSLEY

(2m). Camping & Caravanning Club Site – Horsley, Ockham Road North, East Horsley, Surrey KT24 6PE. 01483 283973. www.campingandcaravanningclub.co.uk. Owner: Camping & Caravanning Club. M25, J10 on to A3. Take B2039, exit marked Ockham, East Horsley, look for post box on R at Green Lane, access road to site SP on R. Recreation hall and play area. Next to Horsley Lake, ideal for fishing. Non-members welcome. The site has an abundance of wildlife, with foxes, deer, rabbits and ducks often spotted. Deals for families and backpackers. All units accepted. Open March-Oct.

GODALMING

(3m). The Merry Harriers, Hambledon, Godalming, Surrey GU8 4DR. 01428 682883. merry.harriers@virgin.net. Owner: Mr Colin Beasley. Off A3 on to A283, L to Hambledon after Wormley. 2m S of Milford. Milford or Whitley station 1.5m. Shower and shaver point. Fishing nearby.

LINGFIELD

(1.5m). Long Acres Caravan & Camping, Newchapel Road, Lingfield, Surrey RH7 6LE. 01342 833205. Owner: Mr Jeffrey Pilkington. Off J6, M25 S on A22 towards East Grinstead turn L on B2028 towards Lingfield. Clean site, ideal for visiting London, Surrey, Kent and Sussex. Set in 40 acres. Plenty to see and do. 1hr from London by train, 1hr from South Coast. Many local attractions, Hever, Chartwell, Chessington, various gardens. Local fishing and golf.

MYTCHETT

Canal Visitor Centre, Mytchett Place Road, Mytchett, Surrey GU16 6DD. 01252 370073. info@basingstoke-canal.co.uk. www.basingstoke-canal.co.uk. Owner: Basingstoke Canal Authority. M3, J4, follow A331 S and turn L to Mytchett. 2.5m from Farnborough. 3m from Camberley. Beautiful canalside setting. 45mins away from London.

REDHILL

(4m). Alderstead Heath Caravan Club Site, Dean Lane, Merstham, Redhill, Surrey RH1 3AH. 01737 644629. www.caravanclub.co.uk. Owner: The Caravan Club. See website for directions. Non-members admitted. A quiet site surrounded by rolling, wooded countryside with marvellous views. Dog walk on site. Shops 3m. Toilet blocks. Privacy cubicles. Laundry facilities. Veg Prep. MV Service point. Gas & Gaz. Playframe. Fishing and Golf nearby. Ideal for families. Local attractions include Chessington World of Adventure. Thorpe Park. Bluebell Line Steam Railway. Some hardstanding. Baby and toddler washroom. Quiet and peaceful off peak. Good area for walking. NCN

50 MOTOR CARAVAN & CAMPING PARKS 2009

SOUTH-EAST ENGLAND

See page 5 for key to symbols and abbreviations

cycle path in 5m.

STAINES

Laleham Park Camping Site, Thameside, Laleham, Staines, Surrey TW18 1SH. *01932 564149.* Owner: Spelthorne Borough Council. From Staines or Shepperton (B376 and B377). Take turning opposite Three Horseshoes Inn to riverside. Site is 500yd down river along tow path road. From Chertsey, cross Chertsey Bridge (B375), on to tow path road. Riverside site.

WALTON-ON-THAMES

(3m). Camping & Caravanning Club Site – Walton-on-Thames, Fieldcommon Lane, Walton-on-Thames, Surrey KT12 3QG. *01932 220392.* www.campingandcaravanningclub.co.uk. Owner: Camping & Caravanning Club. From M25 J13 to Staines and then to Walton, turn L at traffic lights, SP Molesey at the end of Rydens Road, turn L and turn sharp R into Fieldcommon Lane. Camped beside the river Mole under a weeping willow – it's hard to believe London is just 15m away! Club members only. Own san essential. Fishing is available from this site. Caravans, motorcaravans and tents accepted. Golf, horseriding and swimming close by, also Kempton Park Racecourse and Hampton Court. Deals for families and backpackers. Open March – Oct.

EAST SUSSEX

BATTLE

(2.5m). Crazy Lane Tourist Park, Whydown Farm, Sedlescombe, Battle, East Sussex TN33 0QT. *01424 870147.* info@crazylane.co.uk. www.crazylane.co.uk. Owner: G C & R J Morgan. S on A21 turn L 100yd past junction B2244 opposite Blackbrooks Garden Centre. A small, secluded park in a suntrap valley in the heart of 1066 country. In easy reach of beaches and historical sites. Open March-Nov.

(3m). Normanhurst Court Caravan Club Site, Stevens Crouch, Battle, East Sussex TN33 9LR. *01424 773808.* www.caravanclub.co.uk. Owner: The Caravan Club. See website for directions. Located in a former garden with specimen trees and shrubs. Views of distant downs. Dog walk. Advance booking essential Bank Holidays, July, Aug and weekends. Toilet blocks with privacy cubicles and laundry facilities. MV service point. Hardstandings. Playground. Fishing and golf nearby. Ideal for families. Shops in 3m away. Non-members welcome. No tents. Open arch-Nov.

(2m). Senlac Park Caravan Site, Main Road, Catsfield, Battle, East Sussex TN33 9DU. *01424 773969.* www.senlacpark.co.uk. Owner: Mr Wray, Mr Gibbs and Miss Harris. On B2204 formerly the A269. Can be approached from A271. 5mins drive from Battle, 15mins Hastings. 20 acres of woodland walks and all the usual facilities on quiet site. Riding, golf and fishing nearby. Historic sites and walks. Open March 1-Oct 31.

BEXHILL-ON-SEA

(1m). Cobbs Hill Farm Caravan & Camping Park, Watermill Lane, Bexhill-on-Sea, East Sussex TN39 5JA. *01424 213460.* cobbshillfarmuk@hotmail.com. www.cobbshillfarm.co.uk. Owner: Mr B & L Claxton. From Bexhill take A269, turn R into Watermill Lane. Site 1m on L, SP. Quiet, farm site with level sheltered pitches and in easy reach of Battle, Hastings and Eastbourne. Rally field and tent field available. Open April-Oct.

(4m). Kloofs Caravan Park, Sandhurst Lane, Whydown, Bexhill-on-Sea, East Sussex TN39 4RG. *01424 842839.* camping@kloofs.com. www.kloofs.com. Owner: Helen & Terry Griggs. From Bexhill take A259 W to Little Common roundabout, turn R into Peartree Lane, 1m turn L to Whydown, signs to site. Quiet country site about 2m from sea. Ultra modern all year pitches. Facilities, play area.

BRIGHTON

Sheepcote Valley Caravan Club Site, East Brighton Park, Brighton, East Sussex BN2 5TS. *01273 626546.* www.caravanclub.co.uk. Owner: The Caravan Club. See website for directions. Ideally located 2m E of Brighton, snuggled into a fold in the South Downs, a short distance inland from the marina and adjacent to extensive recreation grounds. Baby/toddler washroom. MV service point, gas/gaz and vegetable preparation area. Golf, watersports and NCN route nearby. Facilities for disabled. Playground, ideal site for families. Non-members and tent campers welcome.

CROWBOROUGH

(0.5m). Camping & Caravanning Club Site – Crowborough, Goldsmith Recreation Ground, Crowborough, East Sussex TN6 2TN. *01892 664827.* www.campingandcaravanningclub.co.uk. Owner: Camping & Caravanning Club. Leave M25 at exit 5 take A21 to Tonbridge, then A26 through Tunbridge Wells to the northern outskirts of Crowborough. Turn L off A26 into entrance to Goldsmiths Grand signed Leisure Centre. At top of road turn R into site lane. A great view from the site across the Weald to the North Downs. Indoor swimming pool nearby with concession rates for campers. A peaceful relaxing atmosphere. Non-members welcome. All units accepted. Deals for families and backpackers. Open March-Dec.

CROWHURST

(0.5m). Brakes Coppice Park, Forewood Lane, Crowhurst, East Sussex TN33 9AB. *01424 830322.* brakesco@btinternet.com. www.brakescoppicepark.co.uk. Owner: Mr P & Mrs J C Dudley. Off A2100. 2m from Battle. A small, quiet, secluded park in a beautiful, sheltered position. Close to the beaches of Bexhill and Hastings. Washing up and laundry facilities. Coarse fishing on site. AA 3 pennant. Open March 1-Oct 31.

KLOOFS CARAVAN PARK Bexhill on Sea, East Sussex

Hooray! All Weather, All Year, Fully Serviced, hard standings for RV/Motor Homes. Ultra modern facilities, Private Washing Wells, central heated, Cat 1 Disabled facilities. Kloof's has a quiet, rural and tranquil setting, 2km from sea. Family run, living on site.

Sandhurst Lane, Whydown Bexhill on Sea, East Sussex TN39 4RG
Tel: 01424 842839 E-mail: camping@kloofs.com www.kloofs.com

---

www.motorcaravanmagazine.co.uk   MOTOR CARAVAN & CAMPING PARKS 2009 **51**

SOUTH-EAST ENGLAND

HASSOCKS

(5m). **Sandown Caravan Park, Streat Lane, Streat, Hassocks, East Sussex BN6 8RS.** *01273 890035.* Owner: Mr J Johnson & Ms E Olsson. Off B2116, 0.5m W of Plumpton. NO TOURERS. Dogs must be under control. Peaceful, rural site at the foot of the South Downs. No music – only the sound of the birds. Space for camping (max 20 tents).

HASTINGS

(6m). **Fairlight Wood Caravan Club Site, Watermill Lane, Pett, Hastings, East Sussex TN35 4HY.** *01424 812333.* www.caravanclub.co.uk. Owner: The Caravan Club. See website for directions. Caravan Club members only. No tents. A small and intimate site in flower-rich woodland. Dog walk. Shop 0.5m. Toilet blocks with privacy cubicles and laundry facilities. MV service point. Ideal for families. Open: March-Jan.

Shearbarn Holiday Park, Barley Lane, Hastings, East Sussex TN35 5DX. *01424 423583.* shearbarn@haulfryn.co.uk. www.haulfryn.co.uk. Owner: Haulfryn Group Ltd. M25, J5 and follow A21 to Hastings. Follow signs to the seafront and turn L. Follow road round to the Stables Theatre and turn R onto Harold Road. Turn R on to Gurth Road, carry on up the hill on to Barley Lane, the park reception if on the R. Bar and clubhouse, café, shop, children's play area, local golf and fishing, in easy reach of London.

(2.5m). **Stalkhurst Caravan Park, Ivyhouse Lane, Hastings, East Sussex TN35 4NN.** *01424 439015.* stalkhurstpark@yahoo.co.uk. Owner: Mr & Mrs D and Mr & Mrs C P Young. A259 from seafront towards Rye. Turn L on to B2093. After about 0.5m Ivyhouse Lane is on R. From A21 at the boundary take road SP A259 Folkestone. After 2.5m turn L into Ivyhouse Lane. Sites available for owner-occupied holiday static caravans. Good access. Gently sloping, well sheltered. Indoor heated swimming pool. New and used caravans for sale. Golf and fishing nearby. 2.5m to Hastings town centre and beach. 1m to nearest shops and PO. Open March 1- Jan 15.

HORAM

(0.25m). **Horam Manor Touring Park, Horam, East Sussex TN21 0YD.** *01435 813662.* camp@horam-manor.co.uk. www.horam-manor.co.uk. Owner: M T Harmer. On A267 3m S of Heathfield and 10m N of Eastbourne. A tranquil, rural setting in an Area of Outstanding Natural Beauty. Mother and toddler room. Nature trails, farm museum, craft workshops and fishing on estate. Golf course in 0.5m. Shops, PO, doctor in 0.25m. Open March 1-Oct 31.

LEWES

(7m). **Broomfield Farm Caravan Club Site, Stalkers Lane, East Hoathly, Lewes, East Sussex BN8 6QS.** *01825 872242.* www.caravanclub.co.uk. Owner: The Caravan Club. See website for directions. 1.5m from East Haothly. Caravan Club members only. No tents. A peaceful, rural site set in Sussex countryside. Own sanitation required. Dog walk. MV service point. Boules pitch. Golf and fishing nearby. Open: April 3-Oct 26.

PEVENSEY

Bay View Caravan & Camping Park, Old Martello Road, Pevensey, East Sussex BN24 6DX. *01323 768688.* holidays@bay-view.co.uk. www.bay-view.co.uk. Owner: Michael & Diana Adams. On A259 Eastbourne to Pevensey Bay. 1m to Pevensey Bay Village. Award winning park next to beach. Open April 1-Oct 6.

Camping & Caravanning Club Site – Normans Bay, Pevensey, East Sussex BN24 6PR. *01323 761190.* www.campingandcaravanningclub.co.uk. Owner: Camping & Caravanning Club. Head E on A259 from Eastbourne to Pevensey, site SP. From roundabout at junction of A27/A259 follow A259 SP Eastbourne. In Pevensey Bay village take 1st L SP Beachlands only. After 1.25m site is on L. 11m from Eastbourne. Ideally placed for visiting Eastbourne and adjacent to its own private beach. All units accepted. Non-members welcome. Fishing is available from the beach. Walkers will enjoy 80m of walks on the South Downs way. Deals for families and backpackers. Open March-Oct.

ROBERTSBRIDGE

Park Farm Caravan Site, Bodiam, Robertsbridge, East Sussex TN32 5XA. *01580 830514.* bodiam@hotmail.co.uk. www.parkfarmcamping.co.uk. Owner: Mr Richard Bailey. 3m S of Hawkhurst on B2244. Beautiful rural site near river and Bodiam Castle. Children's play area. Free fishing in river Rother. Barbecues allowed. Many walks around farm. Open April 1-Oct 31.

RYE

(4m). **Camber Sands Holiday Park, New Lydd Road, Camber, Rye, East Sussex TN31 7RT.** *01797 222497.* camber.sands@park-resorts.com. www.park-resorts.com. Owner: Park Resorts Ltd. From M25 take M20 come off at J10. Come on to A2070, follow signs to Hastings and Rye, staying on A259, take a L before Rye, SP Camber. The park is 3m along on this road. 4 indoor pools, spa bath, adventure playground, multi-sports court, amusements, FREE kids clubs, FREE family evening entertainment. Sauna, solarium. David Bellamy Gold Conservation Award. Open from 1/3/08 to 31/12/08.

UCKFIELD

(8m). **Heaven Farm, Furners Green, Uckfield, East Sussex TN22 3RG.** *01825 790226.* heavenfarmleisure@btinternet.com. www.heavenfarm.co.uk. Owner: John & Margaret Butler. On A275 1m S of Danehill. 1m N of Sheffield park, Bluebell Railway. A 1.5m nature trail with wallabies, ponds and parkland which surrounds this ancient farm with many surprises. Fishing on site. Shop, PO 1m. Golf courses nearby. Doctor 5m. Hospital 8m. AA 2 pennant.

(4m). **Honeys Green Caravan Park, Easons Green, Halland, Uckfield, East Sussex TN22 5GJ.** *01732 860205.* honeysgreenpark@tiscali.co.uk. Owner: Mrs S Lavender. At Halland roundabout (A22) turn on to B2192 Heathfield road. Site is 0.25m on L. Small friendly privately owned site in stunning rural location surrounded by farmland. Modern facilities block. Telephone. Walks. Own coarse fishing lake. Open Easter or April 1-Sept.

WEST SUSSEX

ARUNDEL

(6m). **Camping & Caravanning Club Site – Slindon, Slindon Park, Arundel, W Sussex BN18 0RG.** *01243 814387.* www.campingandcaravanningclub.co.uk. Owner: Camping & Caravanning Club. From A27 Fontwell to Chichester turn R at SP Brittons Lane and second R to Slindon, site is on this road. In the National Trust property of Slindon Park. Own sanitation essential. Non-members welcome. Caravans, motorcaravans and tents accepted. The site is set in an orchard in 3500 acres of Slindon park with 40 pitches. Nearby is Goodwood Racecourse. Fishing, swimming and golf closeby at Chichester. The area is a walkers' paradise with many footpaths and bridleways. Deals for families and backpackers. Campers must provide their own chemical toilets. Open March – Oct.

(0.75m). **Maynards Caravan and Camping Park, Crossbush, Arundel,**

52 MOTOR CARAVAN & CAMPING PARKS 2009

SOUTH-EAST ENGLAND

See page 5 for key to symbols and abbreviations

W Sussex BN18 9PQ. *01903 882075.* Owner: Mr R Hewitt. A27 Arundel to Worthing after 0.75m turn L into Beefeater pub and restaurant. Places to visit include Arundel Castle, bird sanctuary and large Sunday market. Also scenic walks on the downs at Burpham, Warnicamp and Wepham.

(2m). Ship & Anchor Marina, Ford, Arundel, W Sussex BN18 0BJ. *01243 551262.* enquiries@shipandanchormarina.co.uk. Owner: Heywood & Bryett Ltd. On road W of river Arun, S off A27 in Arundel or N off A259 at Climping. PH and restaurant. Shaver points. Boating. David Bellamy Gold Conservation Award. Open March 1-Oct 31.

BILLINGSHURST

(1m). Bat & Ball, New Pound, Wisborough Green, Billingshurst, W Sussex RH14 0EH. *01403 700313.* Owner: Mr K W Turrill. Off A272 on B2133 from south to north. Quiet, uncrowded site. Dogs on leads. Pub and restaurant. Calor Gas.

(1.5m). Limeburners Camping Ltd, Newbridge, Billingshurst, W Sussex RH14 9JA. *01403 782311.* chippy.sawyer@virgin.net. Owner: Mr R C Sawyer. 1.5m W of Billingshurst on A272, turn L on to B2133, site 300yd on the L. Showers. Chemical toilet disposal point. Licensed bar. Toilets H & C water to basins. AA 2 pennants. Open April-Oct.

BOGNOR REGIS

(1.25m). Rowan Park Caravan Club Site, Rowan Way, Bognor Regis, W Sussex PO22 9RP. *01243 828515.* www.caravanclub.co.uk. Owner: The Caravan Club. See website for directions. An attractive site screened by trees and with views of downs. 1m from beach. Shops 0.5m. Advance booking advised Bank Holidays, July and Aug. Non-members and tent campers welcome. Toilet blocks. Privacy cubicles. Laundry facilities. Veg Prep. MV Service point. Gas & Gaz. Playframe. Dog walk, some hardstanding, shop 50yd, fishing, golf, and NCN cyclepath in 5m. Watersports nearby. Open: March-Nov.

CHICHESTER

(4m). Ellscott Park, Sidlesham Lane, Birdham, Chichester, W Sussex PO20 7QL. *01243 512003.* camping@ellscottpark.co.uk. www.ellscottpark.co.uk. Owner: M S Parks. From Chichester take the A286 to Bracklesham and Wittering, turn L, SP to Butterfly Gardens. Quiet country site. Café and bus service nearby. Nearest shop, PO 0.75m. Booking essential July and Aug. AA 3 pennants. Open April 1-Oct 31.

Goodwood Racecourse, Chichester, W Sussex PO18 0PS. *01243 755033.* www.goodwood.co.uk. Owner: Goodwood Racecourse Ltd. A286 at Singleton, follow signs. Via Petworth on the A285. 1.25m E of Singleton. 6m S of Midhurst, 7m N of Chichester. Not open race days. Open April-Sept.

(3m). Lakeside Holiday Park, Vinnetrow Road, Chichester, W Sussex PO20 1QH. *01243 787715.* lakeside@ParkHolidaysUK.com. www.ParkHolidaysUK.com. Owner: Park Holidays UK. Take A27 to Chichester until Bognor road roundabout take Pagham exit which leads to Lakeside. Set in 220 acres of scenic parkland and a nature reserve with over 150 acres of water covering 12 lakes. Outdoor heated leisure pool, fishing. Bar, bistro. Chichester: shopping, restaurants. David Bellamy Silver Conservation Award. Open all year.

(7m). Red House Farm, Bookers Lane, Earnley, Chichester, W Sussex PO20 7JG. *01243 512959.* bookings@rhfcamping.co.uk. www.rhfcamping.co.uk. Owner: Clay & Son. Take road A286 to Witterings from Chichester, 5m fork L at Total garage towards Bracksham on B2198, 0.5m at sharp bend turn L into Bookers Lane, site 500yd on L. Flat, level. Site 1m from sea and village, car recommended. Takeaways, shops and café/restaurant available nearby. Ideal for Marina, 8m to Goodwood. Booking advised at peak periods. No single sex groups (4 and over). Open Easter-Oct.

The Gees Camp, 127 Stocks Lane, East Wittering, Chichester, W Sussex PO20 8NY. *01243 670223.* Owner: Mrs L Grigg. A286 S from Chichester and B2198 to Bracklesham Bay. Site is in lane opposite British Legion headquarters. 7m S of Chichester. Close to sea. Dogs welcome if kept on lead. Open March-Oct.

(6m). Wicks Farm Holiday Park, Redlands Lane, W Wittering, Chichester, W Sussex PO20 8QE. *01243 513116.* wicks.farm@virgin.net. www.wicksfarm.co.uk. Owner: Mr R C Shrubb. Off A27 at Chichester, take A286/B2179 from Chichester for 6m towards W Wittering, turn R into Redlands Lane. 1m before W Wittering village. Children's play areas. Tennis court. Table tennis, basket ball, shop. Beach 2m, shopping 3m, cinema/bowling 6m. David Bellamy Gold Conservation Award. Open from 1 March-31 Oct.

CRAWLEY

(2m). Amberley Fields Caravan Club Site, Charlwood Road, Lowfield Heath, Crawley, W Sussex RH11 0QA. *01293 524834.* www.caravanclub.co.uk. Owner: The Caravan Club. See website for directions. Caravan Club members only. No tents. Marvellous for plane spotters, also a storage site. Toilet blocks. Privacy cubicles. Laundry facilities. MV Service point. Gas. Dog walk. Local attractions include Thorpe Park and Bluebell Line Steam Railway.

HENFIELD

(2.5m). Downsview Park, Bramlands Lane, Woodmancote, Henfield, W Sussex BN5 9TG. *01273 492801.* phr.peter@lineone.net. www.downsviewpark.co.uk. Owner: Mr & Mrs P Harries-Rees. Signed on the A281 in the village of Woodmancote, 2.5m E of Henfield, 9m N W of Brighton Seafront. A small secluded site in peaceful countryside, close to the South Downs yet in easy reach of Brighton. Good walking and cycling routes. Privately owned static holiday homes and lodges. No facilities for children. Doctor 3m. Pub 1m, golf 1.5m, shops 2.5m, horseriding 3m, fishing 5m. Open Feb1 – Dec 31.

(2m). Farmhouse Caravan & Camping, Tottington Drive, Small Dole, Henfield, W Sussex BN5 9XZ. *01273 493157.* Owner: Mrs R Griffiths. Turn off A2037 in Small Dole. Site SP in village. Small, quiet, farm site near South Downs and 10m from Brighton. Peaceful setting with panoramic views and well away from the main roads. Ideal for families and walkers. Shop and pub nearby. Open March-Nov.

HORSHAM

(10m). Honeybridge Park, Honeybridge Lane, Dial Post, Horsham, W Sussex RH13 8NX. *01403 710923.* www.honeybridgepark.co.uk. Owner: Harvey Pratt. S of Horsham on A24. Turn at the 'Old Barn Nurseries'. Park 300yd on R. Spacious park set on the outskirts of woodlands and beautiful countryside. On the edge of the South Downs and in an Area of Outstanding Natural Beauty. An ideal touring base convenient to Brighton, Chichester and ports. 1hr from theme parks and London by train. Hardstanding and grass pitches, heated amenity blocks, facilities for disabled visitors, licensed shop.

SOUTH-EAST ENGLAND

(4.5m). Slinfold Caravan Club Site, Spring Lane, Slinfold, Horsham, W Sussex RH13 0RT. 01403 790269. www.caravanclub.co.uk. Owner: The Caravan Club. See website for directions. Caravan Club members only. No tents. Imaginatively landscaped site with silver birch, rowan and flowering cherry at the end of a country lane, close to a pretty village. No sanitation. Dog walk. Shop 0.5m. Hardstandings. Steel awning pegs advised. MV Service point. Gas & Gaz. Open March-Sept.

LITTLEHAMPTON

(1.5m). Daisyfields Touring Park, Cornfield Close, Worthing Road, Littlehampton, W Sussex BN17 6LD. 01903 714240. daisyfields@f2s.com. www.camping-caravaning.co.uk. Owner: L S Rutherford. On A259 Worthing to Bognor Regis road. Free showers and hairdryers. Gas. Ball game area and badminton courts. Nature areas. Level, well-drained site. Fishing, golf, horse riding, boating all nearby.

(1m). White Rose Touring Park, Mill Lane, Wick, Littlehampton, W Sussex BN17 7PH. 01903 716176. snowdondavid@hotmail.com. www.whiterosetouringpark.co.uk. Owner: Mr & Mrs D Snowdon. Between Arundel and Littlehampton on A284. Turn LH after 6 Bells Pub. Award winning quiet family site close to sandy beaches and south downs. Mixture of hedged and open pitches, heated shower block, play area, dog area, seasonal pitches. Concrete roads. Shops, PO 0.5m. Fishing, golf nearby. Open March 15-Dec 15.

PETWORTH

(2m). Camping & Caravanning Club Site – Graffham, Great Bury, Graffham, Petworth, W Sussex GU28 0QJ. 01798 867476. www.campingandcaravanningclub.co.uk. Owner: Camping & Caravanning Club. 2m from Petworth off the A285. Take a L at sign for Selham Graffham. 1m turn L, SP Graffham. 400yd, site entrance on L, just past house. The site is set in 20 acres with secluded pitches dispersed in trees and rhododendrons. In the heart of the South Downs, an Area Of Outstanding Natural Beauty. Excellent for walkers and bird watchers will find many varieties of bird living around the site. Non-members welcome. Caravans, motorcaravans and tents accepted. Deals for families and backpackers. Open March-Oct.

SELSEY

(1m). Warner Farm Touring Park, Warner Lane, Selsey, W Sussex PO20 9EL. 01243 604499. touring@bunnleisure.co.uk. www.bunnleisure.co.uk. Owner: White Horse Caravan Co Ltd. A27 to Chichester, take B2145 to Selsey SP from Chichester. Use of 3 club houses, heated swimming pools included with your booking when staying on the touring park. Open March-Oct.

WASHINGTON

Washington Caravan & Camping Park, London Road, Washington, W Sussex RH20 4AT. 01903 892869. washcamp@amserve.com. www.washcamp.com. Owner: Mr M F Edlin. N of Washington on A283 E of roundabout with A24, SP. Halfway stop on South Downs Way below Chanctonbury Ring. Walking, cycling. Close to many points of interest.

WEST WITTERING

Nunnington Camping Site, Rookwood Road, West Wittering, W Sussex PO20 8LZ. 01243 514013. nunningtonfarm@hotmail.com. www.camping-in-sussex.com. Owner: Mr & Mrs G Jacobs. From Chichester A286 on to B2179. Flat site 1m from sea and 1.5m from Itchenor for sailing. 125 units in total (tourers, motorcaravans, tents). Shop in village 300yd. Friendly, family site. Small animal park free for our customers. Open Easter-2nd week Oct.

WORTHING

(2.5m). Northbrook Farm Caravan Club Site, Titnore Way, Worthing, W Sussex BN13 3RT. 01903 502962. www.caravanclub.co.uk. Owner: The Caravan Club. See website for directions. An attractive, grassy site in open countryside with good trees and only 2m from the coast. Non-members welcome. No tents. Storage pitches and hardstandings, shops 0.25m. Toilet blocks. Privacy cubicles. Laundry facilities. Veg Prep. MV Service point. Gas & Gaz. Playground. Dog walk. Watersports and golf nearby. Ideal for families. Quiet and peaceful off peak. Good area for walking. Open March-Nov.

BERKSHIRE

MAIDENHEAD

(3m). Amerden Caravan and Camp Site, Old Marsh Lane, Dorney Reach, Maidenhead, Berkshire SL6 0EE. 01628 627461. beverly@amerdencaravanpark.co.uk. www.freewebs.com/amerdencaravanpark. Owner: Mrs B Hakesley. Leave M4 J7 (Slough West) turn L along A4 towards Maidenhead, 3rd turn L Marsh Lane,1st turn R Old Marsh Lane. Small riverside site. River fishing in season. Supermarket 1.5m. Train station to London 1.25m Open April 1-Oct 31.

■ **(4m). Hurley Riverside Park, Park Office, Hurley, Maidenhead, Berkshire SL6 5NE.** 01628 823501/824493. info@hurleyriversidepark.co.uk. www.hurleyriversidepark.co.uk. Owner: Hurley Riverside Park Ltd. A4130 midway between Henley on Thames and Maidenhead. Entrance via Shepherds Lane. 1m W of Hurley Village. Follow signs. 3m from Marlow. Family run park on the river Thames. Slipway. Fishing in season. Holiday homes with all mains facilities. Own gardens. No sub-letting. Shopping centre, cinema 4m. David Bellamy Gold Conservation Award. Open March 1-Oct 31.

NEWBURY

(2m). Oakley Farm Caravan Park, Wash Water, Newbury, Berkshire RG20 0LP. 01635 36581. info@oakleyfarm.co.uk. www.oakleyfarm.co.uk. Owner: Mr W Hall. 2.5m S of Newbury off A343. From A34 Newbury bypass, take exit marked Highclere/Wash Common. Turn L towards Newbury on A343. After 400yd turn R into Penwood Road. Not suitable for caravans over 22 foot long or motorcaravans over 24 foot long. Open March 1-Oct 31.

READING

(6m). Wellington Country Park, Riseley, Reading, Berkshire RG7 1SP. 01189 326444. info@wellington-country-park.co.uk. www.wellington-country-park.co.uk. Off A33 between Reading and Basingstoke, 4m S of M4, J11. Beautiful campsite set in woodland glades located in the country park. Park attractions include miniature railway, crazy golf, sandpit and play areas. Café and gift/toy shop. All amenities in 3m. Open March-Nov.

BUCKINGHAMSHIRE

BEACONSFIELD

(3m). Highclere Farm Country Touring Park, Newbarn Lane, Seer Green, Beaconsfield, Buckinghamshire HP9 2QZ. 01494 874505. highclerepark@aol.com. www.highclerepark.co.uk. Owner: M F Penfold Ltd. A355 Beaconsfield to

54 MOTOR CARAVAN & CAMPING PARKS 2009

SOUTHERN ENGLAND

See page 5 for key to symbols and abbreviations

Amersham, R to Seer Green then follow tourist signs. Only 20m from London. Local train service to Marylebone 35mins. Station 1m. Windsor 10m. A peaceful site well situated for touring Buckinghamshire. Open March-Jan.

OLNEY

(0.5m). Emberton Country Park, Emberton, Olney, Buckinghamshire MK46 5FJ. *01234 711575.* embertonpark@milton-keynes.gov.uk. www.mkweb.co.uk/embertonpark. Owner: Milton Keynes Council. On A509 Newport Pagnell to Olney. 200 acres of beautiful parkland. 5 all year fishing lakes and river Ouse (closed season observed on river). Visitor's information centre. Rallies welcome, special rates. Open April 1-Oct 31.

UXBRIDGE

(1m). Wyatts Covert Caravan Club Site, Tilehouse Lane, Denham, Uxbridge, Buckinghamshire UB9 5DH. *01895 832729.* www.caravanclub.co.uk. Owner: The Caravan Club. See website for directions. 1m from Denham. Caravan Club members only. No tents. Conveniently placed not far from both the M25 and M40, but surprisingly green, and screened by good trees. Toilet blocks, laundry facilities and MV service point. Fishing, golf and NCN route nearby. Facilities for disabled.

DORSET

BERE REGIS

(0.75m). Rowlands Wait Touring Park, Rye Hill, Bere Regis, Dorset BH20 7LP. *01929 472727.* info@rowlandswait.co.uk. www.rowlandswait.co.uk. Owner: Mr Cargill. From Bere Regis take Wool-Bovington road. Site 0.75m up Rye Hill on R. Private, quiet and select in an area of outstanding natural beauty. Ideal for nature lovers, birdwatchers and quiet family holidays. Modern facilities. AA Award. Open in winter by arrangement. Telephone for free brochure. David Bellamy Gold Conservation Award. Open March-Oct + winter by arrangement.

BLANDFORD FORUM

(5m). Lady Bailey Residential Park, Winterborne Whitechurch, Blandford Forum, Dorset DT11 0HS. *01458 272266.* Owner: J & K Penfold. On A354 Dorchester to Blandford. In the heart of this beautiful Dorset countryside. Excellent touring centre for exploring. 6 beaches all nearby. Award winning local pub/restaurant. Children welcome. GS. Open March 16-Oct 31.

(2m). The Inside Park, Blandford Forum, Dorset DT11 9AD. *01258 453719.* inspark@aol.com. http://members.aol.com/inspark. Owner: Mr & Mrs J Cooper. 2m SW of Blandford on road to Winterborne Stickland, clearly signed from bypass.

Parkland site surrounded by woodland. Play area. AA 3 pennants. RAC appointed. Open April 1-Oct 31.

BRIDPORT

(1.5m). Binghams Grange Touring & Camping Park, Melplash, Bridport, Dorset DT6 3TT. *01308 488234.* enquiries@binghamgrange.co.uk. www.binghamgrange.co.uk. Owner: Totemplant Ltd. Turn off A35 in Bridport, at roundabout on to A3066 (SP Beaminster) after 1.5m turn L into farm road. Adult only award winning family run park. Excellent heated modern facilities. Bar/restaurant. Views over Dorset's Brit Valley yet only 4.5m from the coast. Pets welcome – great walking. Open March-Nov.

(3.5m). Coastal Caravan Park, Annings Lane, Burton Bradstock, Bridport, Dorset DT6 4QP. *01308 897361.* Owner: West Dorset Leisure Holidays. In village of Burton Bradstock turn at Anchor Hotel, 2nd R into Annings Lane – park 1m on R. Flat, well-drained country site. Quiet rural park, near (about 1m) coast. Golf nearby and the pubs and shop in Burton Bradstock. David Bellamy Silver Conservation Award. Open March 16-Nov 4.

(1m). Cummins Farm, Penn Cross, Charmouth, Bridport, Dorset DT6 6BX. Owner: Mr B P Lugg. 1m W of Charmouth, W on A35 through Charmouth. Turn L on to A3052 after 0.5m (SP Lyme Regis). At top of hill turn R into lane. Penn Cross is next

---

Hurley, Maidenhead, Berkshire SL6 5NE
Tel: 01628 824493/823501
email: info@hurleyriversidepark.co.uk Website: www.hurleyriversidepark.co.uk

- Family-run Park on the River Thames in the village of Hurley • Ideal for visiting Windsor Legoland, London and Thames Valley • 200 level pitches for touring caravans, motorhomes & tents
- Free individual and family showers • Rallies welcome in low season • Open March 1 - 31 October

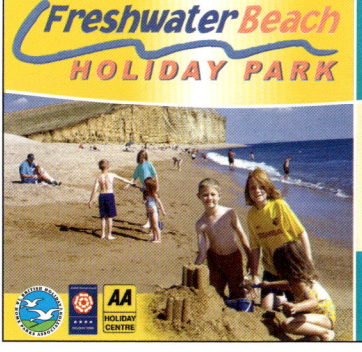

---

family seaside fun!

Freshwater Beach HOLIDAY PARK

Family-owned park with large touring and camping field. Own private beach on Dorset's world renowned Jurassic Coast. Nightly family entertainment and children's activities

- **Free entertainment** (Spring BH - Mid Sept)
- **Free Club Membership**

www.freshwaterbeach.co.uk
01308 897317
Freshwater Beach Holiday Park, Burton Bradstock, Bridport, DT6 4PT

SOUTHERN ENGLAND

crossroad after 200yd. Sheltered site with good views. 1m from coast. Open mid March-end Oct.

(1.5m). Eype House Caravan & Camping Site, Eype, Bridport, Dorset DT6 6AL. *01308 424903.* enquiries@eypehouse.co.uk. www.eypehouse.co.uk. Owner: Sue & Graham Dannan & Keith Mundy. Off A35 to Honiton take turning to Eype, then the turning to the sea. Follow lane to the bottom, entrance to park on R. 200yd to beach, on the Dorset Coastal Path. Open Easter-Oct.

■ **(2m). Freshwater Beach Holiday Park,** Burton Bradstock, Bridport, **Dorset DT6 4PT.** *01308 897317.* info@freshwaterbeach.co.uk. www.freshwaterbeach.co.uk. Owner: R Condliffe. On B3157. Bridport to Weymouth Coast Road. Private beach. Amusements. Club. Entertainment. Takeaway food. Swimming pools. Riding. Launderette. Dogs allowed except in hired vans. Golf course adjoining site. Licensed restaurant, 3 bars. Play area. Coastal walks. David Bellamy Bronze Conservation Award. Open mid March 15-mid Nov.

(3m). Golden Cap Holiday Park, Seatown, Chideock, Bridport, Dorset DT6 6JX. *01308 422139.* holidays@wdlh.co.uk. www.wdlh.co.uk. Owner: West Dorset Leisure Holidays Ltd. Off A35 Lyme Regis to Bridport. Turn off to Seatown from Chideock, follow this road and Golden Cap can be found at the end on the L. Overlooked by the famous Golden Cap clifftop and surrounded by National Trust countryside on Heritage coastline. Ideal location for walking the coastal path. Fishing lake on site, leisure facilities available at Highlands End (sister park) about 2m away. Golf course 3m. David Bellamy Gold Conservation Award. Open March-Nov.

(1.5m). Highlands End Holiday Park, Eype, Bridport, Dorset DT6 6AR. *01308 422139.* holidays@wdlh.co.uk. www.wdlh.co.uk. Owner: West Dorset Leisure Holidays Ltd. Off A35,1m W of Bridport,

take sp to Eype, follow the road round and take the brown sign, turning on R, SP to Highlands End. Select, family park with exceptional views of Lyme Bay and the Heritage coastline. Indoor heated swimming pool and leisure complex, lounge bar with meals. Tennis court. Pitch & Putt course. Golf course 2m. David Bellamy Gold Conservation Award. Open March 18-Nov 4.

(6m). Manor Farm Holiday Centre, Charmouth, Bridport, Dorset DT6 6QL. *01297 560226.* enq@manorfarmholidaycentre.co.uk. www.manorfarmholidaycentre.co.uk. Owner: R C Loosmore & Son. In centre of Charmouth off Charmouth bypass (A35). Licensed bar. Family room. Bar with entertainment. Swimming pool. Fish and chip takeaway. Play area. Riding. Golf and fishing nearby. 10mins level walk to beach. Golf course, cinema 3m. Shopping centre 6m. Open all year – statics Mid March-Oct only.

(3m). Uploders Farm, Dorchester Road, Bridport, Dorset DT6 4NZ. *01308 423380.* Owner: S R Sheppard. E of Bridport on A35. Open July & Aug.

(1.5m). West Bay Holiday Park, West Bay, Bridport, Dorset DT6 4HB. *01308 422424.* enquiries@parkdeanholidays.co.uk. www.parkdeanholidays.com. Owner: Parkdean Holidays Plc. Off A35 Dorchester to Bridport. Follow 'West Bay' to harbour and roundabout. Shops in Bay include groceries, butchers, fish, newsagents, electrical. On site store, Costa Coffee shop, family entertainment, kids club, cabaret, arcade, pool. David Bellamy Silver Conservation Award. Open March 24-Nov 7.

CHARMOUTH

■ **Camping & Caravanning Club Site – Charmouth,** Monkton Wylde Farm, **Charmouth, Dorset DT6 6DB.** *01297 32965.* www.campingandcaravanningclub.co.uk. Owner: Camping & Caravanning Club. On A35 from Dorchester, turn R 0.5m past end of dual carriageway, SP 'Marskwood, B3165'. Site on L. 3m from Axminster. Situated on the Dorset and

Devon border amongst rolling countryside down to the sea. A walker's paradise with a 20m coastal parth nearby. Non-members welcome. All units accepted. Visitors travel for miles around to hunt for fossils along Charmouth coast. Local attractions include the undercliffe Nature Reserve near the site and Cobb Harbour. Deals for families and backpackers. David Bellamy Gold Conservation Award. Open March-Oct.

(0.5m). Seadown Holiday Park, Bridge Road, Charmouth, Dorset DT6 6QS. *01297 560154.* bookings@seadowncaravanpark.co.uk. www.seadownholidaypark.co.uk. Owner: L Aburrow. A35 Bridport to Axminster, SP to Charmouth main street L into Bridge road. Open March-Oct.

(1m). Wood Farm Caravan Park, Axminster Road, Charmouth, Dorset DT6 6BT. *01297 560697.* holidays@woodfarm.co.uk. www.woodfarm.co.uk. Owner: MacBennet Ltd. Off A35, to Western side of village of Charmouth. CARAVAN CLUB AFFILIATED SITE. Non members and tent campers welcome. Manager: J Bremmer. Best of British Park. World Heritage Coast and spectacular rural scenery.. the area is famous for its rugged coastline littered with fossils from the Jurassic age. Walkers are spoilt for choice. Open March-Nov.

CHRISTCHURCH

(8m). Holmsley Caravan & Camping Site, Forest Holidays, Forest Road, Thorneyhill, Bransgore, Christchurch, Dorset BH23 7EQ. *01425 674502.* www.forestholidays.co.uk. Owner: Forest Holidays. Located off A35 Lyndhurst-Christchurch road, 8m SW of Lyndhurst. Ideally situated for a seaside break, just a short drive from beaches at Bournemouth and Christchurch. Mainly grassland site. Great for children. Bookings and brochure requests on 0845 1308224. Open March-Nov.

(3m). Mount Pleasant Touring Park, Matchams Lane, Hurn, Christchurch, Dorset BH23 6AW. *01202 475474.* enq@mount-pleasant-cc.co.uk. www.

MONKTON WYLD
Charmouth
Dorset DT6 6DB
For free brochure
phone 01297 631 131

We are ideally suited to enjoy both the countryside and small resorts of Devon & Dorset. We offer spacious level pitches with plenty of room for families to relax and children to play. Two shower blocks, each with family rooms, launderette and dishwashing facilities and two play areas ensure that facilities remain uncrowded. We are only 3 miles from Lyme Regis and Charmouth's safe sandy beach. There are ,many and varied tourist attractions nearby. Also holiday flat, yurt, caravan storage and caravan holiday homes for sale.

www.monktonwyld.co.uk   e-mail: holidays@monktonwyld.co.uk

56 MOTOR CARAVAN & CAMPING PARKS 2009

SOUTHERN ENGLAND

See page 5 for key to symbols and abbreviations

mount-pleasant-cc.co.uk. Owner: Peter Dunn. Take A338 from Bournemouth or Ringwood, turn off at Christchurch-Hurn exit and turn R towards Hurn, at first roundabout take second exit on roundabout L into Matchams Lane, park is 1m on R. Manager: Peter Dunn. 4 AA pennants. Fishing, golf, swimming. Pony trekking, stock car racing, dry ski slope, New Forest, all nearby also closest park to Bournemouth PO 1m. Playground area. Excellent facilities, shop, café. Open March 1-Oct 31. Winter by arrangement.

CORFE CASTLE

Knitson Farm Tourers Site, Knitson Farm, Corfe Castle, Dorset BH20 5JB. *01929 425121.* tourers@knitson.co.uk. www.knitsonfarm.co.uk. Owner: Mrs J Helfer. L off A351 just after entering Swanage, Washpond Lane, then L at T-junction. Proceed for 0.5m, site on L and further on on R. Quiet family site on working farm for s/c units. Own sanitation necessary 1.5m to Swanage Beach, 3m Studland beach, excellent walking area. Near to World Heritage coast. Golf course, tennis, horseriding all nearby. Great mountain biking area. Open Easter-Oct.

Woody Hyde Camp Site, Valley Road, Corfe Castle, Dorset BH20 5HT. *01929 480274.* camp@woodyhyde.fsnet.co.uk. www.woodyhyde.co.uk. Owner: Laurence Jahn. On the A351 between Corfe and Swanage on the R about 1m from Corfe. In the heart of Purbeck country and Swanage Steam Railway nearby. Open Easter-end Sept.

DORCHESTER

(7m). Camping & Caravanning Club Site – Moreton, Station Road, Moreton, Dorchester, Dorset DT2 8BB. *01305 853801.* www.campingandcaravanningclub.co.uk. Owner: Camping & Caravanning Club. From Poole on A35, continue past Bere Regis, turn L B3390 SP Alfpuddle. After about 2m site on L before Moreton Station and next to Frampton Arms Pub. In a popular holiday area, 7m from Weymouth and Dorchester. 2 holiday bungalows available to let. Local leisure centre has large indoor pool with wave machine. Other local attractions include dry ski slope and cider museum. Visit Dorchester on Wednesday for market day. Deals for families and backpackers. Non-members welcome. All units accepted. Open March-Nov.

■ (8m). Clay Pigeon Caravan Park, Wardon Hill, Dorchester, Dorset DT2 9PB. *01935 83492.* southerncountiesleisure.com. Owner: Southern Counties Leisure. On A37 midway between Yeovil and Dorchester. Ideal centre for touring 'Hardy' country. Level, gently sloping mature site. Café, bar and restaurant open 7 days/week. Heated toilet block with showers. Fishing, shooting, karting, golf and riding nearby. Rally field available.

(5.5m). Crossways Caravan Club Site, Crossways, Dorchester, Dorset DT2 8BE. *01305 852032.* www.caravanclub.co.uk. Owner: The Caravan Club. See website for directions. 8.5m from Weymouth. Weymouth 8.5m. Imaginatively landscaped site, ideal for touring Dorset. Non-members welcome. No tents. Dog walk. Advance booking essential BH and July and Aug. Hardstandings. Shower blocks and laundry facilities, with privacy cubicles. MV service point. Open March-Oct.

(8m). Giants Head Camping & Caravan Park, Old Sherborne Road, Dorchester, Dorset DT2 7TR. *01300 341242.* holidays@giantshead.co.uk. www.giantshead.co.uk. Owner: Mr R Paul. From Dorchester, into town avoiding bypass, from top of town roundabout, take Sherborne road after about 500yd, fork R at Loders Garage, SP. From Cerne Abbas take Buckland Newton road. Cottage and chalet available. Shops, PO, doctor, fishing, golf all in 2-3m. Good walking and views. Open Easter-Oct.

(3m). Morn Gate Caravan Park, Bridport Road, Dorchester, Dorset DT2 8PS. *01305 889284.* morngate@ukonline.co.uk. www.morngate.co.uk. Owner: A&M Properties (Dorset) Ltd. W of Dorchester on main A35. Luxury Scandanavian style chalets, lodges and modern caravans. Small exclusive park set in heart of Thomas Hardy countryside. Children's play area and recreation ground. Cummunal BBQ areas. Ideal base to tour area. Open March 12-Jan 12.

(6m). Sandyholme Holiday Park, Moreton Road, Owermoigne, Dorchester, Dorset DT2 8HZ. *01305 852677.* smeatons@sandyholme.co.uk. www.sandyholme.co.uk. Owner: West Dorset Leisure Holidays Ltd. Minor road N of A352 6m SE of Dorchester. Site is 1m N of turning. Quiet family park in Hardy countryside with all amenities. Holiday vans for hire/sale. Games room, play park and licensed bar with food available (open peak times). Central for Weymouth, Dorchester and Lulworth Cove. Golf, cinema, shopping centre in 5m. David Bellamy Gold Conservation Award. Open March 16-Nov 5.

FERNDOWN

St Leonards Farm Caravan and Camping Park, Ringwood Road, A31, West Moors, Ferndown, Dorset BH22 0AQ. *01202 872637.* www.stleonardsfarm.biz. Owner: W E Love & Son. On A31 Ringwood to Ferndown, 5m W of Ringwood opposite Texaco Garage. Ideal for Bournemouth & Poole. Play area. 3AA pennants. Open April-Sept 30.

GILLINGHAM

(1m). Thorngrove Camping & Caravan Park, Common Mead Lane, Gillingham, Dorset SP8 4RE. *01747 821221.* Owner: P Richardson. Quiet, fishing, nearby shops and PO.

LYME REGIS

(3m). Newlands Holiday Park, Charmouth, Lyme Regis, Dorset DT6 6RB. *01297 560259.* enq@newlandsholidays.co.uk. www.newlandsholidays.co.uk. Owner: Newlands Ltd. On A35 Bridport to Lyme Regis. Two swimming pools. Delightful Dorset views. Heritage coast village near Lyme Regis. Short stroll to beach. Ideal for touring walking and all the family. Golf course 2.5m. Cinema 3m. Open all year except Xmas and Boxing Day.

BOURNEMOUTH ST LEONARDS FARM
Ringwood Road, West Moors, Ferndown, Dorset BH22 0AQ
Quiet level site near Bournemouth, Poole
Cross-Channel Ferries and New Forest. Easy access off A31. Electric hook-ups, modern shower and toilet block including room for disabled, launderette, play area with picnic tables. Shops, bars, restaurant, takeaways, swimming, golf, riding and windsurfing all nearby.
Open April-September. Booking advisable July and August
Bookings: W. E. Love and Son
Tel: 01202 872 637   www.stleonardsfarm.biz

MOTOR CARAVAN & CAMPING PARKS 2009

SOUTHERN ENGLAND

■ **(3m). Shrubbery Touring Park, Rousdon, Lyme Regis, Dorset DT7 3XW.** *01297 442227.* info@shrubberypark.co.uk. www.shrubberypark.co.uk. Owner: Mr J Godfrey. W of picturesque Lyme Regis on the A3052 coast road. The Shrubbery is a level site in an unspoilt and uncommercialised part of the world heritage coastline of outstanding natural beauty. Ideal base for fossil hunters. AA 4 stars. Open mid March-Oct 31.

POOLE

■ **(3m). Beacon Hill Touring Park, Blandford Road North, Poole, Dorset BH16 6AB.** *01202 631631.* www.beaconhilltouringpark.co.uk. Owner: Mrs Rosemary Bond. Situated 0.25m N from jct. of A35 on A350 towards Blandford, approx 3m N of Poole to Cherbourg and Poole to St Malo and Channel Island Ferries. Heated swimming pool. Fully licensed bar with entertainment and takeaway in high season. All-weather tennis court. Coarse fishing lake on site. Children's play area. Open Easter-end Sept.

(4m). Huntick Farm, Lytchett Matravers, Poole, Dorset BH16 6BB. *01202 622222.* huntickcaravans@btconnect.com. Owner: Mr & Mrs Studley. Just off A350 on Poole-Blandford, take sign to L Matravers. First L and L at Rose & Crown pub. Site 1m on R. Small, level grass site in wooded surroundings. 10% discount for OAPs. Rallies welcome. Convenient for ferry crossings from Poole. Storage for caravans and boats now available. Dogs allowed on leads. Fees according to season. AA 3 pennants. Open Easter-Oct 31.

■ **(5m). Merley Court Touring Park, Merley, Wimborne, Poole, Dorset BH21 3AA.** *01590 648331.* holidays@shorefield.co.uk. www.shorefield.co.uk. Owner: Mr K J Wright. Direct access off A31 roundabout. David Bellamy Gold Conservation Award. Open Feb 8 – Jan 2.

(3m). Pear Tree Touring Park, Organford Road, Holton Heath, Poole, Dorset BH16 6LA. *01202 622434.* info@visitpeartree.co.uk. www.visitpeartree.co.uk. Owner: Callum Allison. From A35 take A351 to Wareham, then 1st R to Organford. Centrally situated for Poole, Bournemouth, Swanage, Wareham and the New Forest. 24hr supervision. Open from 1/5/08 to 30/9/08.

(3m). Rockley Park Holiday Park, Hamworthy, Poole, Dorset BH15 4LZ. *01202 679393.* rockley.holidays@bourne-leisure.co.uk. www.rockley-park.co.uk. Owner: Bourne Leisure Ltd. Leave M27 and join A31. Follow signs for Poole town centre. In town centre SP for Rockley Park. Alternatively take Dorchester bypass leading to Poole and follow the signs for Rockley Park. Heated outdoor & indoor pool. Spa experience & treatment rooms for 2008. Restaurants & takeaway. Club, bar and family entertainment. Sailing. Windsurfing. Diving. Nature reserve, bowling green, amusements, tennis courts. New outdoor family funzone, new multi sports courts, play areas, roller blades, crazy golf. No dogs allowed Bank Holidays or school holidays (Touring). Welcome host. David Bellamy Gold Conservation Award. Open March-Nov.

(3m). Sandford Holiday Park, Organford Road, Holton Heath, Poole, Dorset BH16 6JZ. *0870 4440080.* bookings@weststarholidays.co.uk. www.weststarholidays.co.uk/ec. Owner: Weststar Holidays Ltd. On the A351 to Wareham which branches off A35 5m W of Pool. Turn off at Holton Heath traffic lights. Set in acres of peaceful Dorset woodland, close to the Jurassic coastline and busting centres of Poole and Bournemouth. Award winning entertainment, childrens' clubs, choice of pitches and holiday homes, heated indoor and outdoor pools, restaurants, and plenty of family attractions near to the park. David Bellamy Gold Conservation Award. Open Feb-Jan.

YOUR TOP 101 SITES 2009

(3m). South Lytchett Manor Caravan & Camping Park, Lytchett Minster, Poole, Dorset BH16 6JB. *01202 622577.* info@southlytchettmanor.co.uk. www.southlytchettmanor.co.uk. Owner: David & Joanne Bridgen. On B3067 off A35 follow A350 S from junction with A31 turn R, first sign to Lytchett Minster, follow road downhill for 1m, park on R at T-junction with B3067. AA 4 pennants. Set in 20 acres of stunning parkland of the former Lytchett Manor. Exceptional brand new amenities block. Superb dog walking area around our pond and woods. TV hook ups available. Open Easter-Mid Oct.

SHAFTESBURY

(2m). Blackmore Vale Caravan & Camping Park, Sherborne Causeway, Shaftesbury, Dorset SP7 9PX. *01747 852573/851523.* bmvgroup@ukf.net. www.caravancampingsites.co.uk/dorset/. Owner: Mr & M rs F Farrow. A30, W of Shaftesbury. Scenic views and ideal for touring. Close to famous Gold Hill, Saxon abbey ruins and hilltop market town of Shaftesbury. 2 AA Pennants.

SWANAGE

(2.5m). Downshay Farm, Haycrafts Lane, Swanage, Dorset BH19 3EB.

SOUTHERN ENGLAND

01929 480316. downshayfarm@tiscali.co.uk. www.downshayfarm.co.uk. Owner: Mr M Pike. A351 Swanage then turn R at Harmans Cross. 0.5m up Haycrafts Lane. Family site with spectacular views. Stunning views of Corfe Castle – working dairy farm, small friendly site, family run. Open Easter-Oct 31.

(3m). Flower Meadow Caravan Site, Flower Meadow, Haycrafts Lane, Harmans Cross, Swanage, Dorset BH19 3EB. 01929 480035. Owner: Mrs N A Mitchell & Mrs B Hobbs. Midway between Corfe Castle and Swanage. Turn S off the A351 in Harmans Cross towards steam railway. Site 200yd on L. Small, quiet site in heart of Purbeck Hills. Good walking and touring. Sea 3.5m. No dogs July/Aug. Open April 1-Oct 31.

(3m). Haycraft Caravan Club Site, Haycrafts Lane, Swanage, Dorset BH19 3EB. 01929 480572. www.caravanclub.co.uk. Owner: The Caravan Club. See website for directions. A delightfully situated site in the heart of the Purbeck countryside and in easy reach of Dorset's beautiful coastline. Toilet blocks with privacy cubicles and laundry facilities. Baby and toddler washroom. Fishing and golf in 5m, dog walk on site. Ideal for families and good area for walking. Non-members welcome. No tents. Open March-Nov.

(1m). Swanage Coastal Park (Formerly Priestway Holiday Park), Priestway, Swanage, Dorset BH19 2RS. 01590 648331. holidays@shorefield.co.uk. www.shorefield.co.uk. Owner: Shorefield Holidays Ltd. A351 through Wareham and Corfe Castle, past 'Welcome to Swanage' sign with Herston. Turn R into Bell Street. First L into Priests Road, firs R into Swanage Coastal Park. Now under new ownership – part of the Shorefield Group. The park has lovely views of sea and Purbeck Hills. 1m to beach and town with shops and cinema. Bottled gas. Pool, gym, shop and restaurant available at next door council-owned holiday park. David Bellamy Bronze Conservation Award. Open March 14-Oct 30.

(2.5m). Tom's Field Camping, Tom's Field Road, Langton Matravers, Swanage, Dorset BH19 3HN. 01929 427110. tomsfield@hotmail.com. www.tomsfieldcamping.co.uk. Owner: John & Sarah Wootton. W of Swanage, on B3069 looped A351 Tom's field Road in Langton Matravers. Area of Outstanding Natural Beauty. Access to coastal path. Dogs on leads. SAE for details. World Heritage Coastline David Bellamy Gold Conservation Award. Open from 15/3/08 to 31/10/08.

(1.5m). Ulwell Cottage Caravan Park, Ulwell, Swanage, Dorset BH19 3DG. 01929 422823. enq@ulwellcottagepark.co.uk. www.ulwellcottagepark.co.uk. Owner: Mr J Orchard & Mrs J Scadden. In the lovely Isle of Purbeck, 2m from Studland beach, on Swanage road. Family run park located near sandy beaches, coastal walks and golf. 'Village Inn', heated indoor pool. General shop. Open March 1-Jan 7.

(1.5m). Ulwell Farm Caravan Park, Ulwell, Swanage, Dorset BH19 3DG. 01929 422825. ulwell.farm@virgin.net. www.ukparks.co.uk/ulwellfarm. Owner: Mr R J Verge & Mrs C P Knowles. On Swanage to Studland and Sandbanks Ferry road, entrance 150yd beyond end 30mph limit on R. Fishing, riding, golf and watersports nearby. Easy access to good country and coastal walking. Open April-Sept 30th.

WAREHAM

■ **(3m). Birchwood Tourist Park, Bere Road, Cold Harbour, Wareham, Dorset BH20 7PA.** 01929 554763. www.birchwoodtouristpark.co.uk. Owner: John & Linda Orford. W on A351 at Wareham Railway Station Roundabout, turn R into Bere Road (unclassified) in a N.W. direction toward Bere Regis through Wareham Forest. Hardstanding barrier system.

Burnbake Campsite, Rempstone, Corfe Castle, Wareham, Dorset BH20 5JH. 01929 480570. info@burnbake.com. www.burnbake.com. Owner: Mrs P M Ryder & T Bircham. Take 3rd L on Corfe-Studland road B3351, for Rempstone. Site SP from there. Sheltered wooded site for tent campers and camper vans, 4m from Studland beaches and 4m from Swanage. Walkers paradise. No bookings.

(8m). Durdle Door Holiday Park, Lulworth Cove, Wareham, Dorset BH20 5PU. 01929 400200. durdle.door@lulworth.com. www.lulworth.com. Owner: Weld Enterprises Ltd. SW of Wareham via A352 and road S at Wood. Local road W in W Lulworth to site. Open March 1-Oct 31.

(3m). East Creech Farm, Wareham, Dorset BH20 5AP. 01929 480519. east.creech@virgin.net. www.eastcreechfarm.co.uk. Owner: Mr P F Best. Take by-pass at Wareham, on third roundabout take Furzebrook-Blue Pool road, site 2m on R. Fishing. 3m to shop, doctor and PO. AA 3 pennants. Open April 1-Oct 31.

(3m). Luckford Wood Caravan & Camping Park, Holme Lane, East Stoke, Wareham, Dorset BH20 6AW. 01929 463098. info@luckfordleisure.co.uk. www.luckfordleisure.co.uk. Owner: J Barnes, L Barnes. From Wareham take A352 towards Wool for 1m then take B3070 to Lulworth for 1m at W Holme, crossroad turn R along Holme Lane site

---

BIRCHWOOD TOURIST PARK

Family-run park, ideally situated for exploring Dorset. Well stocked shop. Off licence. Free hot showers. Children's paddling pool. Bike hire. Fully serviced pitches. Hard standings.

We accept: VISA Delta MasterCard

BIRCHWOOD TOURIST PARK
Cold Harbour, Wareham, Dorset, BH20 7PA
Tel: 01929 554763 Fax: 01929 556635
Web: www.birchwoodtouristpark.co.uk

SOUTHERN ENGLAND

entrance 1m on R. Storage facilities for caravans, boats, motorhomes vans etc. Camp fires and Hog Roast by arrangement. Open wooded and shaded areas. Close to Heritage Coast Tank Museum Monkey World. Fully serviced luxury Lodge Hire. Pets welcome on site, dog walking lane. Bike hire. Classical farmhouse B&B available. Rally site. Modest showers and toilets, free hot water. Open March 1-Oct 31.

(3m). Manor Farm Caravan Park, East Stoke, Wareham, Dorset BH20 6AW. 01929 462870. info@manorfarmcp.co.uk. www.manorfarmcp.co.uk. Owner: David & Gillian Topp. From Wareham take A352 turn L at Eaststoke redundant church, over railway crossing. Park 0.75m on R. Or A352 T L on to B3070 T R 1st SP East Stoke, crossroad T R SP MFCP – or from WOOL, SP. Family run, flat, grass touring park surrounded by countryside in an area of 2.5 acres, long and short stay plus winter/summer storage. Small, clean and secluded with showers, toilets and play area. Telephone on site. Resident proprietors. Golf course nearby. Seasonal pitches available. RAC appointed. SAE for brochure. Close to Jurassic coast, Monkey world and beaches, walking and bike. David Bellamy Bronze Conservation Award. Open from 15/3/09 to 15/10/09.

(1.2m). Ridge Farm Camping & Caravan Park, Barnhill Road, Wareham, Dorset BH20 5BG. 01929 556444. info@ridgefarm.co.uk. www.ridgefarm.co.uk. Owner: Mrs J L Pollock. B3075 from Wareham turn L in Stoborough down 'New Road' to village of Ridge. Site is at end of Barnhill Road on L. Quiet, secluded family run site. Level pitches. Hot showers and launderette. Shop in high season. Ideal centre for birdwatching, walking, cycling and boating (slipway nearby). Dogs welcome except in July & Aug. AA 3 pennants. Open Easter-end Sept.

(1.3m). The Lookout Holiday Park, Corfe Road, Stoborough, Wareham, Dorset BH20 5AZ. 01929 552546. enquiries@caravan-sites.co.uk. www.caravan-sites.co.uk. Owner: Frampton Leisure. From Wareham take A351 to Corfe Castle. Park is on the L. All amenities in Wareham. Games room. Adventure playground. Laundry. Showers. Crazy golf. Rose Award Park. Open March-end Dec for holiday homes and tourers.

(4m). The Woodland Caravan & Camping Park, Glebe Farm, Bucknowle, Wareham, Dorset BH20 5NS. 01929 480280. hazelparker@btconnect.com. Owner: Mr & Mrs R H Parker. Off A351, R at Corfe Castle, about 0.75m on Church Knowle Rd. No advance bookings. About 4m from beaches. Direct access by public footpath to Purbeck Hills and 0.75m from Corfe Castle. An uncommercialised family site with all essential facilities. AA 3 pennants Award. Open Easter-Oct 31.

■ **(3m). Wareham Forest Tourist Park, Bere Road, North Trigon, Wareham, Dorset BH20 7NZ.** 01929 551393. holiday@warehamforest.co.uk. www.warehamforest.co.uk. Owner: Tony & Sarah Birch. Off A35 midway between Wareham & Bere Regis. Spacious, level pitches in secluded woodland setting, with direct access into Wareham Forest, and a friendly, relaxing, family atmosphere. Shop and pool (high season), play area, seasonal pitches and storage. Central location. David Bellamy Silver Conservation Award.

(5m). Whitemead Caravan Park, East Burton Road, Wool, Wareham, Dorset BH20 6HG. 01929 462241. whitemead@aol.com. whitemeadcaravanpark.co.uk. Owner: Mr & Mrs C Church. Off A352 Wareham to Dorchester road, N of level crossing in Wool, 200yd on R. 4.5m W of Wareham, 300yd off A352 before Wool level crossing. Play area. Lake fishing 4m. Takeaways on site. Breakfast available at weekends. Shop and games room with pool table and darts. Open Mid March-Oct 31.

■ **WEYMOUTH**

Bagwell Farm Touring Park, Chickerell, Weymouth, Dorset DT3 4EA. 01305 782575. enquirebb@bagwellfarm.co.uk. www.bagwellfarm.co.uk. Owner: Mrs K Kennedy. 4m W of Weymouth on B3157. Tranquil rural setting near Dorset's Jurassic Coastline. Sea views from some pitches. Fully stocked shop. Bar open mid/high season. Green Tourism Business Award. Nearby activities include sailing, horse riding, fishing, watersports, diving, rock climbing and swimming pool.

(2m). East Fleet Farm Touring Park, Fleet Lane, Chickerell, Weymouth, Dorset DT3 4DW. 01305 785768. enquiries@eastfleet.co.uk. www.eastfleet.co.uk. Owner: Mr J Whitfield. B3157 from Weymouth, L at Chickerell TA Camp. Peaceful and spacious park. On working organic farm overlooking Fleet and Chesil Bank. 400 mixed pitches. Open mid March-end Oct.

(1.5m). Littlesea Holiday Park, Lynch Lane, Weymouth, Dorset DT4 9DT. 01305 774414. www.littlesea-park.co.uk. Owner: Bourne Leisure Ltd. Ring for directions. Welcome Host Award. Holiday Park of the Year 2007. Fun indoor and outdoor pools. March & Barrel café bar, family entertainment centre, amusements. 2 playgrounds. Mini golf. Bouncy castle and trampolines. Free kids clubs.10mins drive from town centre. Park is on bus route. David Bellamy Gold Conservation Award. Open March-end Oct.

(5m). Osmington Mills Holidays Ltd, Ranch House, Osmington Mills, Weymouth, Dorset DT3 6HB. 01305 832311. holidays@osmingtonmillsfsnet.co.uk. www.osmington-mills-holidays.co.uk. Owner: Osmington Mills Holidays Ltd. From Weymouth take A353 E for 5m. Turn R to Osmington Mills. SP. Heated outdoor swimming pool. Club house. Children's room. Horse riding nearby. Fishing on site. Dogs allowed by arrangement. 8m to Dorchester. 5m to Weymouth. Open Easter-Oct 31.

(1.5m). Pebble Bank Holiday Park, Wyke Regis, Weymouth, Dorset DT4 9HF. 01305 774844. info@pebblebank.co.uk. www.pebblebank.co.uk. Owner: Ian & Dot Harrey. From harbour roundabout in Weymouth, follow road for Portland, at mini roundabout turn R on to Wyke road (B3156). Camp Road 1m. Play area. Licensed bar. Freephone 0500 242656. Open April 1-early Oct.

(6m). Portesham Dairy Farm Camp Site, Bramdon Lane, Portesham, Weymouth, Dorset DT3 4HG. 01305 871297. info@porteshamdairyfarm.co.uk. www.porteshamdairyfarm.co.uk. Owner: Mr J M & Mrs S J Doble. B3157 Weymouth to Bridport coast road. Calor Gas and Camping Gaz from farmhouse. Play area. Fishing and horse riding nearby. Abbotsbury 2m away with Swannery Thithe barn and sub tropical gardens. Garage, PO, Pub serving food and doctor all nearby. Open March 15-Oct 31.

(3m). Sea Barn Farm, Fleet, Weymouth, Dorset DT3 4ED. 01305 782218. enquire@seabarnfarm.co.uk. www.seabarnfarm.co.uk. Owner: Mr J Coombe. On the road B3157 to Bridport. Turn S at the sign of Fleet and Moonfleet Manor Hotel, then next turn L to Sea Barn Farm. Amazing coastal and inland

Wareham Forest Tourist Park

Family run landscaped park set in 40 acres of delightful woodlands with open grassy spaces and direct access to Forest walks. Central location for lovely Dorset World Heritage Coastlines and developed to a high standard.

- ☆ Heated Swimming Pool (High Season)
- ☆ Wi Fi Available
- ☆ Table Tennis
- ☆ Children's Adventure Playground
- ☆ Long or Short Term Storage
- ☆ Individual Cubicles in the toilet block for ladies
- ☆ Toilet block heated during winter period
- ☆ Fully Serviced Luxury Pitches
- ☆ Launderette
- ☆ Shop/Off Licence
- ☆ Disabled Facilities & Family bathrooms
- ☆ Owners Tony & Sarah Birch previously from Carnon Downs
- ☆ Woodland Dog Walks

OPEN ALL YEAR

For further details and free colour brochure write or phone:
Wareham Forest Tourist Park
North Trigon Wareham Dorset BH20 7NZ
Tel/Fax: 01929 551393
e-mail address: holiday@warehamforest.co.uk
Please visit our website: www.warehamforest.co.uk

SOUTHERN ENGLAND

views. Ideally located for discovering Dorset. Open March-Nov.

(3m). Seaview Holiday Park, Preston, Weymouth, Dorset DT3 6DZ. *01305 832271.* www.seaview-park.co.uk. Owner: Bourne Leisure Ltd. Take A353 from centre of Weymouth to Preston. Seaview is 0.25m beyond village, uphill on R. Indoor and outdoor pools. Kids club. Daytime and evening entertainment for all the family. All the facilities at neighbouring Weymouth Bay to enjoy. Café bar and takeaway. David Bellamy Silver Conservation Award. Open March-end Oct.

(3m). West Fleet Holiday Farm, Fleet, Weymouth, Dorset DT3 4EF. *01305 782218.* enquire@seabarnfarm.co.uk. www.westfleetholidays.co.uk. Owner: N M & M J Coombe. On the B3157 towards Bridport. L at mini roundabout to Fleet. Kids love camping at West Fleet Farm. Rural location, play area, outdoor pool and family clubhouse. Open Easter-Sept.

WIMBORNE

Camping & Caravanning Club Site – Verwood, Sutton Hill, Woodlands, Wimborne, Dorset BH21 8NQ. *01202 822763.* www.campingandcaravanningclub.co.uk. Owner: Camping & Caravanning Club. From A31 Ringwood by-pass near Texaco Filling Station. Turn L on to B3081 to Verwood. Site on R 1.5m past Verwood and golf club. A 12.75 acre site for all types of units. Set on the borders of Dorset, Wiltshire and Hampshire this site offers a varied holiday. Non-members welcome. Play area and recreational hall on site. The site is beautifully situated next to Ringwood Forest. Golf course opposite site. Shops, doctors, vets, PO all in 1m. Deals for families and backpackers. Open March-Oct.

(1m). Charris Camping & Caravan Park, Candy's Lane, Corfe Mullen, Wimborne, Dorset BH21 3EF. *01202 885970.* bookings@charris.co.uk. www.charris.co.uk. Owner: Jane Watson & Judith Chapman. On A31, 1m W of Wimborne. Hot & cold facilities block. Calor Gas supplied. Camping & Caravanning Club listed. Personal service. Open March 1-Jan 31.

(1.5m). Springfield Touring Park, Candys Lane, Corfe Mullen, Wimborne, Dorset BH21 3EF. *01202 881719.* Owner: Sheila & John Clark. Turn L off A31 Ringwood to Dorchester, at roundabout W end of Wimborne bypass after 400yd turn R into Candys Lane. Family run park. Convenient for New Forest and coastal resorts. Free showers and awnings. Special offers low season. Fishing, golf, horse riding, swimming, leisure activities, boating on the river Stour – all available in 2-3m. Open April-Oct.

(1m). Wilksworth Farm Caravan Park, Cranborne Road, Furzehill, Wimborne, Dorset BH21 4HW. *01202 885467.* raya ndwendy@wilksworthfarmcaravanpark.co. www.wilksworthfarmcaravanpark.co.uk. Owner: Mr & Mrs R Lovell. N of Wimborne on the B3078. Heated swimming pool. Games room. Tennis court. Large play area. Open March-Oct.

(7m). Woolsbridge Manor Farm Caravan Park, Ringwood Road, Three Legged Cross, Wimborne, Dorset BH21 6RA. *01202 826369.* woolsbridge@btconnect.com. www.woolsbridgemanorcaravanpark.co.uk. Owner: Mrs L K Johnson. Take A31 W, 1m past Ringwood take filter and follow signs for Three Legged Cross and Moors Valley Country Park. Park is 2m along on R. Easy access to south coast. Level, semi-sheltered park with good facilities. Open March-Oct.

HAMPSHIRE

ALRESFORD

Spinney Caravan Site, Martlets, Haig Road, Alresford, Hampshire SO24 9LP. *01962 732829.* Owner: Mary Hide. Quiet and secluded licensed site in the heart of rural Hampshire. Excellent road links. Perfect starting point for exploring Hampshire. Level site in walking distance of the town. Open April 1 – Oct 31.

ANDOVER

(3m). Wyke Down Touring Caravan and Camping Park, Picket Piece, Andover, Hampshire SP11 6LX. *01264 352048.* info@wykedown.co.uk. www.wykedown.co.uk. Owner: Mr W Read. Camping Park signs from A303 trunk road, follow signs to Wyke Down. Swimming pool. Country pub and restaurant. Golf driving range. Supermarket 2.5m, Town 3m.

ASHURST

(5m). Ashurst Caravan & Camping Site, Forest Holidays, Lyndhurst Road, Ashurst, Hampshire SO40 7RA. *02380 292097.* www.forestholidays.co.uk. Owner: Forest Holidays. SW of Southampton on A35 sp. 2m from Ashurst. Attractive site set in woodland glade. Level campsite in mainly open ground with some shaded areas of oakwood. Dog free site. Bookings and brochure request on 0845 1308224. Open March-Sept.

BROCKENHURST

(1m). Aldridge Hill Caravan & Camping Site, Forest Holidays, Brockenhurst, Hampshire SO42 7QD. *01590 623152.* www.forestholidays.co.uk. Owner: Forest Holidays. Off A337, 1m NW of Brockenhurst village. An attractive level site on the edge of Blackwater stream, close to Brockenhurst village. No toilet facilities. Booking and brochure request on 0845 1308224. Open May-Sept.

(1m). Black Knowl Caravan Club Site, Aldridge Hill, Brockenhurst, Hampshire SO42 7QD. *01590 623600.* www.caravanclub.co.uk. Owner: The Caravan Club. See website for directions. Caravan Club members only. No tents. Located in the midst of the ancient royal hunting forest of William the Conqueror and in walking distance of Brockenhurst. Toilet blocks, laundry facilities and MV service point. Good area for walking, golf and NCN route nearby. Facilities for disabled. Ideal for families. Open March-Nov.

Decoy Pond Farm, Beaulieu Road, Beaulieu, Brockenhurst, Hampshire SO42 7YQ. *023 80292652.* Owner: D N Horton. Lyndhurst to Beaulieu B3056, over railway bridge, immediately L opposite Beaulieu Hotel. Small site in the heart of the New Forest. Easter-Oct.

(0.5m). Hollands Wood Caravan & Camping Site, Forest Holidays, Lyndhurst Road, Brockenhurst, Hampshire SO42 7QH. *01509 622967.* www.forestholidays.co.uk. Owner: Forest Holidays. 0.5m N of Brockenhurst on A337, SP. Nestling in oak woods, this peaceful site has generous pitches and level ground. Toilets and showers fully refurbished for 2008. No premium pitches available. booking and brochure requests 0845 1308224. David Bellamy Silver Conservation Award. Open March-Sept.

(2m). Roundhill Caravan & Camping Site, Forest Holidays, Beaulieu Road, Brockenhurst, Hampshire SO42 7QL. *01590 624344.* www.forestholidays.co.uk. Owner: Forest Holidays. B3055, SE of Brockenhurst, off A337 SP. A spacious site with plenty of room and lots to do. Minimum stay of 2 nights. Refurbished

62 MOTOR CARAVAN & CAMPING PARKS 2009

SOUTHERN ENGLAND

See page 5 for key to symbols and abbreviations

toilets and showers. Booking and brochure requests on 0845 1308224. Open March-Sept.

FAREHAM

(4m). Rookesbury Park Caravan Club Site, Hundred Acres Road, Wickham, Fareham, Hampshire PO17 6JR. *01329 834085.* www.caravanclub.co.uk. Owner: The Caravan Club. See website for directions. Caravan Club members only. No tents. Splendid setting in parkland on edge of the Forest of Bere. Good walking from site and convenient for Portsmouth and Isle of Wight. Toilet blocks. Privacy cubicles. Laundry facilities. Baby washroom. Veg prep. MV service point. Play equipment. Good area for walking. Ideal for families. Open March-Oct.

FORDINGBRIDGE

(1.5m). Sandy Balls Holiday Centre, Sandy Balls Estate, Godshill, Fordingbridge, Hampshire SP6 2JZ. *0845 2702248.* post@sandy-balls.co.uk. www.sandy-balls.co.uk. Owner: Sandy Balls Estate Ltd. From Salisbury A338 to Fordingbridge, turn off on to B3078 SP Godshill, situated at the W end of Godshill village. Fishing on site and nearby, own stables, full Leisure Club with pools, gym tempus, beauty therapy. 120 acre site with wood and parkland to explore and enjoy. Cycle Centre, Gift Shop, tourist info, Woodside Inn and Bistro. Seasonal tent pitches (120-240). Silver Award Winners 2006 Caravan Holiday Park of the Year. Waterpark 3m. Golf 7m. Beach 15m. David Bellamy Gold Conservation Award.

GOSPORT

(3m). Kingfisher Park, Browndown Road, Gosport, Hampshire PO13 9BE. *023 9250 2611.* info@kingfisher-caravan-park.co.uk. Owner: Mr Sargeant. M27 motorway junction 9 or 11 to Gosport. Open all year for tourers. March-Jan for hire & owners.

HAMBLE

(1m). Riverside Holidays, Satchell Lane, Hamble, Hampshire SO31 4HR. *02380 453220.* enquiries@riversideholidays.co.uk. www.riversideholidays.co.uk. Owner: Davidson Leisure Resorts Ltd. J8, M27 (Southampton East) then B3397 to Hamble, turn L into Satchell Lane. Site is adjacent to marina with restaurant and bar and overlooks the river. Set in the countryside, excellent walking, cycling and sailing. Close New Forest, Portsmouth and Winchester. AA 3 pennant award. Cycle hire on site. Oyster quay bar and restaurant on Hamble Marina (2mins walk). Shopping centre (Southampton 8m). Fishing, horse riding, beach (Netley 3m). Boat hire, tennis, sports centre, swimming pool, shop, supermarket, pubs/restaurants (Hamble 1m). Golf (Wickham 5m). Dogs welcome when touring. David Bellamy Bronze Conservation Award. Open March-Oct (camping/touring caravans), all year (for lodges/statics).

HAYLING ISLAND

(0.25m). Fishery Creek Park, 100 Fishery Lane, Hayling Island, Hampshire PO11 9NR. *02392 462164.* camping@fisherycreek.co.uk. www.keyparks.co.uk. Owner: Mr D Emersic. From A27 cross bridge to Hayling Island and follow signs. Delightful, peaceful park on flat grassland adjoining a tidal creek (own slipway) fishing from bank. 5mins walk to beach. Free showers. Open March 1-Oct 31.

DISCOVER RELAX EXPLORE UNWIND ENJOY

Have you heard about Shorefield Holidays?

All three of our holiday parks are set in peaceful, unspoilt parkland in the beautiful South Coast area.

There are comprehensive leisure facilities available and great entertainment for the whole family.

Pamper yourself in our 'Reflections' Day Spa at Shorefield Country Park, explore Britain's latest National Park - the New Forest, or relax on Bournemouth's sandy beaches.

For full details, ask for our brochure or browse online.

SHOREFIELD HOLIDAYS LIMITED

Tel 01590 648331
Ref: MCCP
holidays@shorefield.co.uk
www.shorefield.co.uk

HAMPSHIRE
Lytton Lawn Touring Park
Milford on Sea, SO41 0TX

Forest Edge Holiday Park
St. Leonards, BH24 2SD

DORSET
Merley Court Touring Park
Wimborne, BH21 3AA

SOUTHERN ENGLAND

(2m). Fleet Farm Caravan & Camping Park, Yew Tree Road, Hayling Island, Hampshire PO11 0QF. 023 9246 3684. www.haylingcampsites.co.uk. Owner: Colin Good. Exit A3M or M27 at Havant. Follow A3023 over road bridge onto island. About 1.5m on island then turn L into Copse Lane, then R into Yew Tree Road, site on L. Storage and rallies catered for. Long term parking on site. Site on creak. Handy touring area for Portsmouth, New Forest. Near a family pub close, fishing, tennis, nice beach. 3 golf courses in 2m; one is a famous Links course. Open March 1-Nov 1.

(0.5m). The Oven, Manor Road, Hayling Island, Hampshire PO11 0QX. 023 9246 4695. theovencampsite@talktalk.net. www.haylingcampsites.co.uk. Owner: Mrs Z Good. On A3023 about 3m from bridge, bear R at Mill by the roundabout, site is 450yd on the L. Blue Flag beach. Heated pool on site. Long term caravan parking. Rallies welcome. Manager: J Macallum. Open March 1-Nov 1.

LYMINGTON

(3m). Lytton Lawn Touring Park, Lymore Lane, Milford on Sea, Lymington, Hampshire SO41 0TX. 01590 648331. holidays@shorefield.co.uk. Owner: Shorefield Holidays Ltd. S of Lymington via A337 to Everton, then B3058 to site. Second turning on L. Well-drained site, 1m from beach and close to New Forest. Shop. Full access to the facilities of sister park 2.5m away: indoor & outdoor pool, gym, bars and eateries, day spa. David Bellamy Bronze Conservation Award. Open Feb 8-Jan 2.

LYNDHURST

Denny Wood Caravan & Camping Site, Forest Holidays, Beaulieu Road, Lyndhurst, Hampshire SO32 7FZ. 02380 293144. www.forestholidays.co.uk. Owner: Forest Holidays. On B3056, 3m SE of Lyndhurst. Peaceful grassland site among scattered oaks. Dog free site. No toilet or shower facilities. Booking and brochure request on 0845 1308224. Open March-Sept.

(2m). Matley Wood Caravan & Camping Site, Forestry Commission (Forest Holidays), Beaulieu Road, Lyndhurst, Hampshire SO43 7FZ. 02380 293144. www.forestholidays.co.uk. Owner: Forest Holidays. On B3056, 2m SE of Lyndhurst. Small scluded site in a beautiful woodland setting. No toilet or shower facilities. Permits from nearby DennyWood campsite. Booking and brochure requests on 0845 1308224 Open March-Sept.

Ocknell & Longbeech Caravan & Camping Site, Forest Holidays, Lyndhurst, Hampshire SO43 7HH. 02380 812740. www.forestholidays.co.uk. Owner: Forest Holidays. B3079 off A31 at Cadnam, then B3078 via Brook and Fritham. Ocknell is a heathland site whilst Lonbeech is in an ancient beechwood. Longbeech: temporary WC facilities, no hot water. Both sites: no showers, no premium pitches. Booking and brochure requests on 0845 1308224. Open March-Sept.

NEW MILTON

(6m). Setthorns Caravan & Camping Site, Forest Holidays, Wootton, New Milton, Hampshire BH25 5WA. 01590 681020. www.forestholidays.co.uk. Owner: Forest Holidays. SP from A35 Lyndhurst – Christchurch road, 7m SW of Lyndhurst. Pitch amongst the pines and oaks in a beautiful forest setting. Select pitches available. Refurbished for 2008. No toilet or shower facilities. Bookings and brochure requests on 0845 1308224.

RINGWOOD

(3.5m). Back of Beyond Touring Park, 234 Ringwood Road, St Leonards, Ringwood, Hampshire BH24 2SB. 01202 876968. melandsuepike@aol.com. www.backofbeyondtouringpark.co.uk. Owner: M J B & S Pike. 3.5m W of Ringwood, 2m E of Ferndown on A31. Adults only. 28 acres of peaceful, unspoilt countryside – well off the beaten track. Easy access to local amenities, coast and New Forest. Adults only. Fishing and golf on site. Open March-Oct.

Camping International, Athol Lodge, 229 Ringwood Road, St Leonards, Ringwood, Hampshire BH24 2SD. 01202 872817. Owner: Pegville Ltd. On southern side of A31, 3m Wof Ringwood. Popular family touring park for Bournemouth, New Forest, country and sea. AA 4 Pennant.

(3m). Forest Edge Holiday Park, Boundary Lane, St Leonards, Ringwood, Hampshire BH24 2SD. 01590 648331. holidays@shorefield.co.uk. www.shorefield.co.uk. Owner: Shorefield Holidays Ltd. Access off A31, turn L at 2nd roundabout, W of Ringwood into Boundary Lane. Park is on L. Open Febuary 1 – Jan 2.

(4m). Red Shoot Camping Site, Linwood, Ringwood, Hampshire BH24 3QT. 01425 473789. enquiries@redshoot-campingpark.com. www.redshoot-campingpark.com. Owner: Mrs S J Foulds. Off A31 (M27) at exit 1. Follow signs for New Forest and Linwood or minor road off A338 2m N of Ringwood, SP Linwood. Owner

---

RED SHOOT CAMPING PARK

Small, quiet family site. Beautifully situated in the NEW FOREST, ideal centre for walking, touring and for the nature lover — yet only half hour's drive from Bournemouth and the sea.
Facilities recently refurbished to an excellent standard

- ★ Approved site for tents, caravans and Motor Caravans.   ★ Excellent toilet and shower block.
- ★ Well-stocked shop and off-licence.   ★ Children's play area.   ★ Well equipped laundry room.
- ★ Electric hook-ups.   ★ Mountain bikes for hire.
- ★ Forest inn adjacent, serving good food, families welcome.
- ★ Facilities for the disabled.   ★ Owner supervised to a high standard.
- ★ Open 1st March to 31st October

Please send SAE for brochure **Linwood, Near Ringwood, Hants BH24 3QT**
Tel: Ringwood (01425) 473789   Fax: (01425) 471558
E-mail: enquiries@redshoot-campingpark.com   Internet: www.redshoot-campingpark.com

SOUTHERN ENGLAND

See page 5 for key to symbols and abbreviations

supervised to a high standard. Open March 1-Oct 31.

(2m). Shamba Holidays, 230 Ringwood Road, St Leonards, Ringwood, Hampshire BH24 2SB. 01202 873302. enquiries@shambaholidays.co.uk. www.shambaholidays.co.uk. Owner: Shamba Holidays Ltd. W of Ringwood on the A31 (sign on roadside). Family run park which is always friendly and clean, set in pleasant countryside. Clubhouse (inc a bar, and a large screen TV). Heated, indoor & outdoor swimming pool, play area. Modern toilet/shower facilities. Winter storage. Seasonal pitches. David Bellamy Silver Conservation Award. Open March-Oct.

ROMSEY

(4m). Green Pastures Farm, Ower, Romsey, Hampshire SO51 6AJ. 023 8081 4444. enquiries@greenpasturesfarm.com. www.greenpasturesfarm.com. Owner: Mr & Mrs A Pitt. SP from J2 off M27 (Salisbury direction) and A36 and A3090 at Ower. Family run site on working farm in New Forest National Park. Convenient ferries for Europe and Isle of Wight. Space for children to play safely. Local pub with good food and real ales. Fishing, golf and swimming pool nearby. Day kennelling available. Open March 15-Oct 31.

(3.5m). Hill Farm Caravan Park, Branches Lane, Sherfield English, Romsey, Hampshire SO51 6FN. 01794 340402. gjb@hillfarmpark.com. www.hillfarmpark.com. Owner: Geoff & Suzy Billett. 4m W of Romsey on A27 towards Salisbury. Turn N at second crossroads marked 'Branches Lane'. Site is 0.5m on R. 9 hole pitch and putt golf course on site. Our licensed shop offers freshly cooked bread, croissant and pasties daily as well as snack meals to take away or eat on our patio. Open March-Oct tourers, Feb-Dec statics.

SOUTHAMPTON

(5m). Dibles Park, Dibles Road, Warsash, Southampton, Hampshire SO31 9SA. 01489 575232. dibles.park@btconnect.com. www.diblespark.co.uk. Owner: Dibles Park Co Ltd. J8, M27 L on to A27 turn R at Sarisbury Green R at T junction L at mini roundabout, turn R into Fleet End Road, 2nd turning on R on to Dibles Road. Shops, PO, doctor available in 0.5m. Fishing and golf courses nearby. Warsash (a yachting centre) lies on the East bank of the river Hamble. Close by are the Hook Nature Reserve, Brownwich

Country Park and Solent Way. Excellent location for walking and cycling. Ideal for cross-channel ferries.

SOUTHBOURNE

(0.5m). Camping & Caravanning Club Site – Chichester, Main Road, Southbourne, Hampshire PO10 8JH. 01243 373202. www.campingandcaravanningclub.co.uk. Owner: Camping & Caravanning Club. 6m W of Chichester, 3m E of Havant, site is well marked on north side of A259, off A27. Follow signs Nutbourne or Southbourne. Site on R past Inlands Road. Ideally located for Chichester, South Downs, Bosham and Portsmouth. Close to sea and shops. The site is set in an ancient orchard. Attractions in nearby Portsmouth include HMS Victory and the huge maritime museum. The area is full of history with Iron Age Hillforts, Roman remains and Norman castles. Non-members welcome. All units accepted. Deals for families and backpackers. Open Feb-Nov.

SOUTHSEA

(5m). Southsea Leisure Park, Melville Road, Southsea, Hampshire PO4 9TB. 023 9273 5070. info@southsealeisurepark.com. www.southsealeisurepark.com. Owner: PG Estates Ltd. From M27, A27 and, A3M take Southsea exit (A2030 south) and follow signs along Eastern Road. Playground and room, organised activities in season. Heated outdoor swimming pool, free hot showers. Restaurant and bar. Direct access to beach. 10mins from cross-channel ferries.

WINCHESTER

(3m). Morn Hill Caravan Club Site, Morn Hill, Winchester, Hampshire SO21 1HL. 01962 869877. www.caravanclub.co.uk. Owner: The Caravan Club. See website for directions. Set on the outskirts of Winchester, convenient for ferries and exploring the New Forest. Advance booking essential Bank Holidays and July and Aug. Non-members and tent campers welcome. MV service point, playframe, laundry facilities. Toilet/shower block with privacy cubicles. Veg prep area. Shop 3m away. Fishing, golf and cycling routes all in 5m. Open March-Nov.

ISLE OF WIGHT

ADGESTONE

(1.5m). Camping & Caravanning Club site – Adgestone, Lower Road, Adgestone, Isle of Wight PO36 0HL.

01983 403432. www.campingandcaravanningclub.co.uk. Owner: Camping & Caravanning Club. Turn off A3055 at The Fairway by Manor House pub in Lake, which is between Sandown and Shanklin, past golf course on L, turn R at T-junction, park 200yd on R. 1m from Sandown. Site is adjacent to River Yar, beneath the Brading Downs in an area of natural beauty close to Sandown. Non-members welcome. Caravans, motorcaravans and tents accepted. Fishing on site at river and lake. Adventure playground. Outdoor heated swimming pool and take away on site. 270 pitches set in 22 acres. Golf course, Blackgang Chine theme park nearby and the marine heritage museum. Deals for families and backpackers. Formerly listed as one of Caravan Magazine 101 top sites. Open April-Oct.

BEMBRIDGE

■ **(1.5m). Whitecliff Bay Holiday Park, Hillway, Bembridge, Isle of Wight PO35 5PL.** 01983 872671. www.whitecliff-bay.com. Owner: Whitecliff Bay Holiday Park Ltd. Off the A3055 Ryde to Sandown on to B3395 to Bembridge and Whitecliff Bay. Heated swimming pools. Licensed clubs. Entertainment. Restaurant. Leisure centre. Snack bar with take-away, Humphrays play zone, coffee shop, fitness studio. David Bellamy Gold Conservation Award. Open Easter-Oct 31.

BRIGHSTONE BAY

(0.75m). Grange Farm Caravan & Camping Site, Military Road, Brighstone Bay, Isle of Wight PO30 4DA. 01983 740296. grangefarm@brighstonebay.fsnet.co.uk. www.brighstonebay.fsnet.co.uk. Owner: James & Chris Dungey. A3055 coast road midway between Freshwater Bay and Chale. 2-acre level site on small family run farm having many unusual friendly animals including llamas, kune-kune pigs, goats, pony, horse, water buffalos etc. Ideal for children. Easy access to our sandy beach (1min). Safe swimming. Walkers paradise, fossil hunting. An ideal family holiday for camping or self catering in our static caravans or converted barns. Open March-Oct 31.

CHALE

(7m). Chine Farm Camping Site, Military Road, Atherfield Bay, Chale, Isle of Wight PO38 2JH. 01983 740901. www.chine-farm.co.uk. Owner: Mr Jeffrey and Mrs Jill Goody. Situated on the south side of the Isle of Wight at Cowleaze Chine which is midway between the villages of Chale (3m) and

www.motorcaravanmagazine.co.uk   MOTOR CARAVAN & CAMPING PARKS 2009 **65**

SOUTHERN ENGLAND

Brighstone (2.5 m) on the A3055 crossroad. Friendly family run site. Outstanding scenery. Fishing, sea at site, coarse 2m away. Good walking area. Large spacious pitches including electric hook ups. Local amenities in village 2m. Open Easter-Oct 31.

COWES

(1m). Comforts Farm Camping Park, Comforts Farm, Pallance Road, Northwood, Cowes, Isle of Wight PO31 8LS. 01983 293888. www.comfortsfarm.co.uk. Owner: Mrs Annett. Off A3020. Open May-Oct 31.

(4m). Thorness Bay Holiday Park, Thorness Bay, Thorness, Cowes, Isle of Wight PO31 8NJ. 0871 664 9779. thorness.bay@park-resorts.com. www.park-resorts.com. Owner: Park Resorts Ltd. From East Cowes and Newport, follow signs to Newport and take A3054 towards Yarmouth. After 1m take first turning on R and follow signs to Thorness Bay. From Yarmouth, take A3054 towards Newport. After Shalfleet take first L and follow signs to Cowes. After about 5m, Thorness Bay will be on the L. New boathouse bar and restaurant in 208. Showbars. Food court/takeaway. Indoor pool. Excellent for all round fun and entertainment absolutely free. Free kids club. Multi sports court, playground, darts, pool table. David Bellamy Gold Conservation Award. Open March-Jan (owners),March-Oct (hire).

Waverley Park Holiday Centre, Old Road, Cowes, Isle of Wight PO32 6AW. 01983 293452. sue@waverley-park.co.uk. www.waverleypark.co.uk. Owner: Peter & Susan Adams. SP from Red Funnel Terminal, East Cowes. Friendly family run site, open air heated pool, entertainment, bar and evening meals in high season (Spring Bank Holiday – Early Sept). Open March 23-Nov 2.

FRESHWATER

(0.5m). Heathfield Farm Camping Site, Heathfield Road, Freshwater, Isle of Wight PO40 9SH. 01983 756306. web@heathfieldcamping.co.uk. www.heathfieldcamping.co.uk. Owner: Mr & Mrs Osman. 2m from Yarmouth ferry port off A3054 road at Freshwater. Family camping on level field with sea and downland views. Excellent modern shower facilities. Ideal walking area. David Bellamy Gold Conservation Award. Open May 1-Sept 30.

RYDE

(2.5m). Beaper Farm Camping & Caravan Park, Ryde, Isle of Wight PO33 1QJ. 01983 615210. beaper@btinternet.com. www.beaperfarm.com. Owner: Mrs H Harvey & Mrs S Lovegrove. 3mS of Ryde on A3055 towards Sandown. 150 mix units (tourers, motorcaravans, tents). Family site with play area in 13 acres of countryside. Phone for brochure. Two large closely mown camping fields offering plenty of space for children to play. No regimental marked pitches, 2 toilet blocks with toilet for disabled. Shower block laundry room, dishwashing, room chemical, toilet point. Open May 1-Sept 30.

(3m). Carpenters Farm Campsite, St Helens, Ryde, Isle of Wight PO33 1YL. 01983 874557. info@carpentersfarm.co.uk. www.carpentersfarm.co.uk. Owner: Mrs V Lovegrove. Off B3330. Small on site shop, milk, eggs, bread, ice creams, bottle gas, newspapers, etc. Open Easter (April)-Oct.

(3.25m). Kite Hill Farm Caravan & Camping Park, Kite Hill Farm, Wootton Bridge, Ryde, Isle of Wight PO33 4LE. 01983 882543. barry@kitehillfarm.freeserve.co.uk. www.campingparkisleofwight.com. Owner: J M Abraham. Village shops 10mins walk away including doctor. 3 pennant AA site.

(3m). Nodes Point Holiday Park, Nodes Road, St Helens, Ryde, Isle of Wight PO33 1YA. 0871 664 9758. nodes.point@park-resorts.com. www.park-resorts.com. Owner: Park Resorts Ltd. From fishbourne on A3054 E towards Ryde. At junction with A3055, then L on to B3330 to St Helens. Nodes Point is on the L. From Cowes on A3021, then as above. Indoor fun-pool with waterslide. Freek kids clubs. Sports resorts programme. Launderette. Evening entertainment for all the family. Amusements. Diner and take-away. Playground. Darts. Pool tables. Horseriding nearby. David Bellamy Gold Conservation Award. Open April-Oct.

(2m). Pondwell Camping Site, Pondwell Hill, Ryde, Isle of Wight PO34 5AQ. 01983 612330. info@isleofwightselfcatering.co.uk. www.isleofwightselfcatering.co.uk. Owner: I.W. Self Catering. On B3340. TV lounge. Walking distance to sea. Open April-Oct 31.

SANDOWN

(2m). Cheverton Copse Holiday Park, Scotchells Brook Lane, Sandown, Isle of Wight PO36 0JP. 01983 403161. holidays@cheverton-copse.co.uk. www.cheverton-copse.co.uk. Owner: Mr & Mrs M Berry. 1.5m W of town on A3056. Family park in delightful, wooded parkland. Licensed club and games room, entertainment in high season. Play area. Bus 300yd. Supermarket near. Lovely walking area 1.5m to beach. Open April-Sept.

(1m). Fairway Holiday Park, The Fairway, Sandown, Isle of Wight PO36 9PS. 01983 403462. www.fairwayholidaypark.co.uk. Off A3055. Picturesque camping and caravanning area. Modern caravans with showers. Snack Bar. Licensed club. Launderette. Arcade. Play area. Open March-Oct.

(1.5m). Old Barn Touring Park, Cheverton Farm, Newport Road, Apse Heath, Sandown, Isle of Wight PO36 9PJ. 01983 866414. oldbarn@weltinet.com. www.oldbarntouring.co.uk. Owner: Mr & Mrs A F Welti. 500yd S of Apse Heath on A3056 Newport to Sandown. 2m to sandy beaches of Shanklin and Sandown. Lovely downland views. Super pitches available. David Bellamy Gold Conservation Award. Open from 1/5/09 to 30/9/09.

(3m). Queen Bower Dairy Caravan Park, Alverstone Road, Queen Bower, Sandown, Isle of Wight PO36 0NZ. 01983 403840. queenbowerdairy@aol.com. www.queenbowerdairy.co.uk. Owner: Mr M J Reed. Off A3056 Sandown to Newport turn in to Alverstone Road at Apse Heath, entrance 1m on L. 60-acre National Trust copse nearby. Dogs must be exercised off site. PO 1m, Superstore 2m. Open May 1-Oct 31.

(3m). Southland Camping Park, Newchurch, Sandown, Isle of Wight PO36 0LZ. 01983 865385. info@southland.co.uk. www.southland.co.uk. Owner: Viv & Vanessa McGuinness. W of Sandown off A3055/6 on outskirts Newchurch village. SP from A3056 Newport to Sandown Road. Quiet rural setting. Flat, generous pitches. Easy access. Ideal location for exploring the Isle of Wight. Ferry bookings service available. 2003 winner of Calor Best Touring Park England award. David Bellamy Gold Conservation Award. Open from 5/4/09 to 30/9/09.

YOUR TOP 101 SITES 2009

SOUTHERN ENGLAND

See page 5 for key to symbols and abbreviations

(1.5m). Village Way, Newport Road, Apse Heath, Sandown, Isle of Wight PO36 9PJ. 01983 863279. normasmith@btconnect.com. www.villagewaypark.co.uk. Owner: Norma & Dennis. On A3056, follow Sandown sign from Newport. Hot water and showers. Power points in toilet block. Free carp fishing on site.

SHANKLIN

(0.5m). Landguard Holidays, Landguard Manor Road, Shanklin, Isle of Wight PO37 7PH. 01983 863100. enquiries@landguardholidays.co.uk. www.landguardholidays.co.uk. Owner: Davidson Leisure Resorts Ltd. From Cowes – take A3021 and then the A3054 to Ryde. Take the A3055 SP Brading and Sandown and continue on this road to lake. Turn R at the traffic lights SP to Newport and then turn L after 0.75m into Whitecross Lane. After 0.5m turn R into Landguard Holidays. Bookings from non-family parties will be at the discretion of the management. Large outdoor pool and paddling pool, indoor fun pool and slide, oasis pool bar, licensed club, entertainment for all ages, restaurant, takeaway meals, amusement and games room, shop, children's play area, launderette, corkies kids club. Beach 0.5m, fishing and boat hire 1.5m, supermarket, swimming pool, sports centre, tennis 1m. Golf 3m, horseriding 8m. Shopping centre 0.5m. Open all year.

(0.3m). Lower Hyde Holiday Park, Landguard Road, Shanklin, Isle of Wight PO37 7LL. 0871 664 9752. lower.hyde@park-resorts.com. www.park-resorts.com. Owner: Park Resorts Ltd. From Ryde follow A3055 to Shanklin via Sandown and Lake. At Lake turn R at the traffic lights towards Newport (A3056). After about 1m turn L into Whitecross Lane. Lower Hyde is 1m down on the R. In walking distance of Shanklin. Outdoor fun pool. Adventure playground. Multi sports court. Launderette. Amusements. Takeaway and restaurant. Free kids clubs. Free family entertainment. Advance booking advisable. Darts. Pool table. Spa pool. David Bellamy Gold Conservation Award. Open April-Oct.

(1m). Ninham Country Holidays, Ninham, Shanklin, Isle of Wight PO37 7PL. 01983 864243/866040. info@ninham.fsnet.co.uk. www.ninham-holidays.co.uk. Owner: D H Harvey & Mrs V J Harvey. Off A3056, W of Lake. Country park setting overlooking wooded valley with small lakes. Coarse fishing. Play areas. Launderette. Leisure centre 1m. Water sport school 1m. Advance booking advisable. Outdoor heated swimming pool. Games room. Ideal base for cycling. Open April-Sept.

VENTNOR

(2m). Appuldurcombe Gardens Holiday Park, Appuldurcombe Road, Wroxall, Ventnor, Isle of Wight PO38 3EP. 01983 852597. info@appuldurcombegardens.co.uk. www.appuldurcombegardens.co.uk. Owner: Mr P Saunders. Situated just slightly inland- between Shanklin and Ventnor, in the village of Wroxall. Pretty family holiday site in tranquil unspoilt countryside, a few minutes by car from beaches of Shanklin, Sandown and Ventnor. Ideal for walkers and cyclists. One of the Island's most beautiful holiday hideaways!

YARMOUTH

■ **(4m). Orchards Holiday Caravan & Camping Park, Main Road, Newbridge, Yarmouth, Isle of Wight PO41 0TS.** 01983 531331. info@orchards-holiday-park.co.uk. www.orchards-holiday-park.co.uk. Owner: Mr T Gray. E of Yarmouth and 6m W of Newport on B3401. Entrance opposite Newbridge PO. Beautiful rural situation with excellent views all round. Indoor and outdoor heated pools with poolside coffee shop. Takeaway food, shop, table tennis, play areas and dog walk. Excellent cycling and walking from the park. Bird watching area nearby. Green Island Gold award adn Best of British member. Complete car ferry booking service available. Nearest town Yarmouth. David Bellamy Gold Conservation Award. Open mid Feb – Jan.

OXFORDSHIRE
ABINGDON

(4m). Bridges House Caravan Site, Clifton Hampden, Abingdon, Oxfordshire OX14 3EH. 01865 407725. Owner: Elizabeth Gower. Fishing on site. Shops, PO, doctor in 0.25m. Open April 1-Oct 30.

BANBURY

(4m). Anita's Touring Caravan Park (formerly 'Mollington'), Church Farm, The Yews, Mollington, Banbury, Oxfordshire OX17 1AZ. 01295 750731. anitagail@btopenworld.com. Owner: Darrel Jeffries & Anita Gail. Leave M40, J11 on to A422 then A423 Southam road, park 4m on L, just past Mollington village turn. A family run site on a working farm. All pitches with electric hook-ups. Luxurious toilet and shower facilities. Central to many places of interest, Warwick, Stratford, Cotswolds, Blenheim etc. Good fishing close by and nice walks even to our village pub! Come for a relaxing holiday. A large play area for ball games etc. Large area for rallies.

(3.5m). Bo Peep Farm Caravan Park, Aynho Road, Adderbury, Banbury, Oxfordshire OX17 3NP. 01295 810605. warden@bo.peep.co.uk. www.bo.peep.co.uk. Owner: Mr A J Hodge. Situated on B4100 0.5m E of Adderbury and 3m S of Banbury. Access via M40, J10. Tranquil 13 acre touring site set in 85 acres of farmland. River frontage and woodland walks. Excellent facilities. Central for Oxford, Blenheim, Stratford-on-Avon and Warwick Castle. Year round caravan storage available. Open March 14-Oct 27.

BICESTER

(5m). Godwin's (Oxford) Ice Cream Farm Caravan Park, Northampton Road, Weston-on-the-Green, Bicester, Oxfordshire OX25 3QL. 01869 351647. neil@goodwins.biz. Owner: Neil & Lorna Godwin. Situated 2mins from J9M40, midway Oxford and Bicester. Homemade ice cream made on the farm. Café, bar/restaurant and shop. Golf course nearby. Nationwide cycle track linking Oxford to Milton Keynes (route 51). Oxfordshire way

SOUTHERN ENGLAND

footpath. PO, shops, pub/restaurants 10mins walk away. Open March-Oct.

Leys Farm Caravan Site, Upper Heyford, Bicester, Oxfordshire OX6 3LU. *01869 232048*. Off B4030 Chipping Norton to Bicester. 2m from M40. Children's play area.

BLETCHINGDON

(1m). Greenhill Leisure Park, Greenhill Farm, Station Road, Bletchingdon, Oxfordshire OX5 3BQ. *01869 351600*. info@greenhill-leisure-park.co.uk. www.greenhill-leisure-park.co.uk. Owner: Mr & Mrs P Bagnall. From Oxford on to A34 N, turn on to B4027. Bletchingdon site 0.5m after village. 3m from Woodstock. Quiet and spacious farm site. Pets corner, farm animals. Riverside walks, fishing on site. Rally field. Heated toilet block. Games room and playground. Ideal for touring the Cotswolds, 3m from Bleinheim Place.

BURFORD

(2m). Burford Caravan Club Site, Bradwell Grove, Burford, Oxfordshire OX18 4JJ. *01993 823080*. www.caravanclub.co.uk. Owner: The Caravan Club. See website for directions. An attractive and spacious site opposite Cotswold Wildlife Park. Some hardstanding pitches, toilet block with privacy cubicles and laundry facilities. MV service point, playground, shops in 2m and dog walk on site. Non-members welcome. No tents. Open: July 3 – Nov 9.

CHARLBURY

(1m). Cotswold View Caravan & Camping Site, Enstone Road, Charlbury, Oxfordshire OX7 3JH. *0800 0853474*. Owner: Mr & Mrs G F Widdows. Situated on the B4022, 1m N of Charlbury on the road to Enstone. High standard. Children's recreation area. Site is on a working farm. Open Easter-Oct 31.

CHIPPING NORTON

(2.5m). Camping & Caravanning Club Site – Chipping Norton, Chipping Norton Road, Chadlington, Chipping Norton, Oxfordshire OX7 3PE. *01608 641993*. www.campingandcaravanningclub.co.uk. Owner: Camping & Caravanning Club. Take Oxford ring road the A3400 to Stratford-upon-Avon, then A44 in Chipping Norton take A361 for Burford. In 1.5m bear L at fork SP Chadlington. Set in lovely spot in Cotswolds countryside. Site has childrens' play area and a woodland walk adjacent to the site. Local villages such as Stow-on-the-Wold and Bourton-on-the-Water are well worth a visit. Oxford and Stratford are both only 20m away. Non-members welcome. Deals for families and backpackers. Open March-Oct.

(10m). The New Inn, Nether Westcote, Chipping Norton, Oxfordshire OX7 6SD. *01993 830827*. Owner: Mr Steve Rix. L off A424, Stow-on-the-Wold to Burford road. Secluded site forming centre for touring Cotswolds. Pub food. Dogs allowed on leads.

HENLEY-ON-THAMES

YOUR TOP 101 SITES 2009

(0.75m). Four Oaks Caravan Club Site, Marlow Road, Henley-on-Thames, Oxfordshire RG9 2HY. *01491 572312*. www.caravanclub.co.uk. Owner: The Caravan Club. See website for directions. Caravan Club members only. No tents. Shops 0.5m. Pleasantly green and level site with mature trees. In walking distance of Henley. Hardstandings. Toilet blocks. Privacy cubicles. Laundry facilities. Baby/toddler washroom. Veg prep. MV service point. Dog walk on site. Playground. Ideal for families. Open March-Nov.

KIDLINGTON

(4m). Lince Copse Waterside Touring Caravan & Camping Park, Enslow, Nr Bletchingdon, Kidlington, Oxfordshire OX5 3AY. *01869 351321*. sales@kingsground.co.uk. Owner: R Haynes. On A4095 near junction with B4027, 6m from M40 J9 and 1m east of A4260. In the heart of the Cherwell Valley alongside Oxford Canal. Canal trips available locally. Fishing and golf nearby. Restaurant and pub five minutes from park entrance. Close to Blenheim Palace. Open April-Nov.

OXFORD

(0.5m). Benson Waterfront Holiday Park, Benson Cruiser Station, Benson, Oxford, Oxfordshire OX10 6SJ. *01491 838304*. subs@bensonwaterfront.co.uk. www.bensonwaterfront.com. Owner: B North & Sons (WW) Ltd. On A4074 Oxford to Henley at T-junction B4009. On river Thames. Close to Benson village and its facilities. Restaurant. Children allowed. Boat hire available. Open March 1-Jan 31.

(1m). Camping & Caravanning Club Site – Oxford, 426 Abingdon Road, Oxford, Oxfordshire OX1 4XG. *01865 244088*. www.campingandcaravanningclub.co.uk. Owner: Camping & Caravanning Club. South side of Oxford take A4144 to city centre from ring road, SP from A34. This site is 1.5m from the historic city centre makes an ideal touring base. Good access to M4/M40. Non-members welcome. All units accepted. This university city offers more than 650 listed buildings. Deals for families and backpackers.

(7m). Diamond Farm Caravan & Camping Park, Islip Road, Bletchingdon, Oxford, Oxfordshire OX5 3DR. *01869 350909*. warden@diamondpark.co.uk. www.diamondpark.co.uk. Owner: Mr Roger Hodge. Site is 7m N of Oxford on the B4027 from M40 J9 on to the A34 S for 3m follow signs for Bletchingdon. Heated swimming pool, club house, games room, snooker table and play field. New toilet block, family bathroom, launderette, dog walk next to site. AA 4 pennants. Open Feb-Nov.

WALLINGFORD

YOUR TOP 101 SITES 2009

(0.25m). Bridge Villa Camping & Caravan Park, Crowmarsh Gifford, Wallingford, Oxfordshire OX10 8HB. *01491 836860*. bridge.villa@btinternet.com. www.tiscover.co.uk/bridge.villa. Owner: Messrs E L Townsend and Son. Off A4130 in the village of Crowmarsh Gifford, nr Wallingford Bridge. Disabled facilities. Washroom. Hot showers and wash basins. Electric shaver & hairdryer points. Gas supplies. Launderette in 220yd. Ironing room available. Many sporting facilities in 2m of site. Information on request. Perfect location for visiting Oxford, Henely and Windsor. Open Feb 1-Dec 31.

(400m). Riverside Park, The Street, Wallingford, Oxfordshire OX11 8EB. *01491 835232*. Owner: Soll Leisure. Approach from E on A4130 as access is difficult at end of Wallingford Bridge. Wallingford is on the A4074 Oxford to Reading road. Lights control a single-file traffic flow. Fishing. 5mins walk to shops. Outdoor heated swimming pool. Small shop selling ice creams and drinks. Open May-Sept.

WITNEY

(4.5m). Hardwick Parks, Downs Road, Standlake, Witney, Oxfordshire OX29 7PZ. *01865 300501*. info@hardwickparks.co.uk. www.hardwickparks.co.uk. Owner: Hardwick

SOUTHERN ENGLAND

See page 5 for key to symbols and abbreviations

Parks Ltd. Off A415, S of Witney. Fishing. Golf course 4m. Horse riding 0.5m. Air conditioned shower and toilets. Air conditioned clubhouse. Wfi access. Open from 1/4/09 to 31/10/09.

(5.5m). Lincoln Farm Park, Oxfordshire, High Street, Standlake, Witney, Oxfordshire OX29 7RH. 01865 300239. info@lincolnfarm.touristnet.uk.com. www.lincolnfarm.touristnet.uk.com. Owner: Mr & Mrs Stephen & April Wilders. From A40 take Witney exit, follow signs for Standlake 4m, turn by Village Petrol Station, park is 300yds. In village, 2 pubs serving food, village PO, shop. 2 indoor swimming pools, Spa pools and saunas on site, kids pool all indoors. Fitness centre. Fishing nearby in private lake. GS. Open Feb 1-mid Nov.

WOODSTOCK

(0.75m). Bladon Chains Caravan Club Site, Bladon Road, Woodstock, Oxfordshire OX20 1PT. 01993 812390. www.caravanclub.co.uk. Owner: Caravan Club. See website for directions. Caravan Club members only. No tents. Level site surrounded by magnificent trees. Toilet blocks, laundry facilities and MV service point. Significant areas of interest and NCN route nearby. Facilities for disabled. Open: March-Nov.

WILTSHIRE

CHIPPENHAM

(4m). Piccadilly Caravan Site, Folly Lane West, Lacock, Chippenham, Wiltshire SN15 2LP. 01249 730260. piccadillylacock@aol.com. Owner: Peter Williams. Turn R off A350 Chippenham to Melksham road SP to Gastard from caravan symbol. Set in open countryside 0.5m from historic National Trust village of Lacock. Ideal touring centre. Open April-Oct.

MALMESBURY

(0.25m). Burton Hill Caravan & Camping Park, Arches Lane, Malmesbury, Wiltshire SN16 0EH. 01666 826880. stay@burtonhill.co.uk. www.burtonhill.co.uk. Owner: W & A Hateley. Off A429 Chippenham to Malmesbury Road, turn into Arches Lane, by 30/40mph sign. 5m N of M4, J7. Relaxed and friendly, Burton Hill is a level, grassy site overlooking the town and farmland. 5-10mins walk along part of the town's river walk into Malmesbury with pubs, shops, supermarket, restaurants, swimming pool. There are many walks and cycle ways, and shopping at the Outlet Centre, Swindon. Open April 1-Sept 30.

MARLBOROUGH

(6m). Hillview Park, Oare, Marlborough, Wiltshire SN8 4JG. 01672 563151. Owner: R A Harriman. S of Marlborough on A345. Level site. Free hot showers. SAE for brochure. Advance booking advisable. Shops and station in 2m. Open April 1-Sept 30.

(1m). Postern Hill – Savernake Forest, Forestry Commission (Forest Holidays), Postern Hill, Marlborough, Wiltshire SN8 4ND. 01672 515 195. www.forestholidays.co.uk. Owner: Forest Holidays. S of Marlborough on the A346 towards Tidworth. Set in woodland with sheltered pitches and plenty of wild life to enjoy. Toilets but no shower facilities. Refurbished in 2007. Bookings and brochure requests on 0845 1308224. Open early March-Nov.

MARSTON MEYSEY

Second Chance Touring Park, Marston Meysey, Wiltshire SN6 6SZ. 01285 810675/810939. Owner: B Stroud. Midway between cirencester and Swindon along A419. turn off at Fairford/Latton, SP. Proceed until Castle Eaton SP. Turn R, park 150yd on R. 3.5m from Fairford. Upper Thames riverside location on the edge of the Cotswolds. Fishing on site. Explore the Isis with your own canoe. Golf course nearby. 3.5m to shops, doctor, PO. Close to Roman town Cirencester, capital of Cotswolds. Open March 1-Nov 30.

MELKSHAM

(2m). Camping & Caravanning Club Site – Devizes, Spout Lane, Nr Seend, Melksham, Wiltshire SN12 6RN. 01380 828839. www.campingandcaravanningclub.co.uk. Owner: Camping & Caravanning Club. On A361 from Devizes turn R on to A365 over canal and next L down the lane beside '3 Magpies' PH, site on R. Bordering the Kennett and Avon Canal, 4m from Devizes. Non-members welcome. Caravans, motorcaravans and tents accepted. Fishing is available all year round in canal adjacent to site. Deals for families and backpackers. Loo of the Year (5 stars). SW Tourism Highly Commended: runner up. David Bellamy Silver Conservation Award.

SALISBURY

(3m). Alderbury Caravan & Camping Park, Old Southampton Road, Whaddon, Salisbury, Wiltshire SP5 3HB. 01722 710125. alderbury@aol.com. www.alderburycaravanpark.co.uk. Owner: Mr & Mrs N Campbell. Take A36 to Southampton and follow signs for Alderbury and Whaddon. Clean, pleasant site on the edge of village, opposite the Three Crowns inn with excellent food. Free showers, utility room. Excellent location for Stonehenge and New Forest.

(1.5m). Camping & Caravanning Club Site – Salisbury, Hudson's Field, Castle Road, Salisbury, Wiltshire SP1 3RR. 01722 320713. www.campingandcaravanningclub.co.uk. Owner: Camping & Caravanning Club. 1.5m from Salisbury on the A345. Large open field next to Old Sarum. The site is 30mins walk along river Avon from Salisbury. A visit to the city is a must, with its shops and spectacular cathedral. The Iron Age Settlement of Old Sarum, preserved by English Heritage is nearby. Gliding, fishing, horse riding and cycling are all in easy reach of the site. Non-members welcome. All units accepted. Deals for families and backpackers. Open March-Oct.

(11m). Church Farm Caravan & Camping Park, The Bungalow, High Street, Sixpenny Handley, Salisbury, Wiltshire SP5 5ND. 01725 552563. churchfarmcandcpark@yahoo.co.uk. www.churchfarmcandcpark.co.uk. Owner: Mr S Judd. 1m S of Handley Hill roundabout on A354 turn off for Sixpenny Handley. R by school. Site 300yd by church. Quiet family farm site, in the Cranborne Chase, central position for touring. Ideal for walking and mountain biking. Heated amenities block, free showers. Brochure available.

(4m). Coombe Touring Caravan Park, Race Plain, Netherhampton, Salisbury, Wiltshire SP2 8PN. 01722 328451. Owner: Brian & Margaret Hayter. Take A36 Salisbury to Warminster, 2m from Salisbury outskirts, turn at traffic lights on to A3094. Next to Salisbury racecourse. Launderette. Gas supplies. Shop open May to Sept. SAE for brochure. 2.5m to shops, PO. 4m to doctors. Adjacent to race course (flat). Golf course nearby. AA 4 pennants. Open from 5/1/08 to 30/11/08.

(10m). Green Hill Farm Camping & Caravan Park, New Road, Landford, Salisbury, Wiltshire SP5 2AZ. 01794 324117. greenhillcamping@btconnect.com. Owner: Mrs J Osman. M27 south bound exit J2. A36 Salisbury road 3m BP garage on L take next L into new road SP Nomansland, site on L 1m along new

SOUTHERN ENGLAND

road. Adults only site (over 18 years). On Hants/Wilts border in New Forest Heritage area. Two lakes, fishing on site. Shops, PO 1m, Doctors 2.5m. Ideal base for walking or cycling – direct access to New Forest at rear of site. Pubs and eating-houses in easy reach. Dogs must be kept on leads whilst on site and farm areas. Stock calor gas. AA 3 pennants. Open Jan 5-Dec 19.

(9m). Hillside Caravan Club Site, Andover Road, Lopcombe Corner, Salisbury, Wiltshire SP5 1BY. 01980 862527. www.caravanclub.co.uk. Owner: The Caravan Club. See website for directions. Caravan Club members only. No tents. Set in rolling countryside, most pitches in woodland glades in an Area of Outstanding Natural Beauty. Toilet blocks. Veg prep. Gas. MV service shop S/N. Local attractions include Salisbury Cathedral and Sherbourne Castle. Open March-Oct.

(11m). Stonehenge Park, Orcheston, Salisbury, Wiltshire SP3 4SH. 01980 620304. stay@stonehengetouringpark.com. www.stonehengetouringpark.com. Owner: Mrs J Young. Off A360 Devizes to Salisbury. Quiet, level, country site. Close to Stonehenge. Booking advisable. Dogs on leads for touring site. Children allowed.

TILSHEAD

Brades Acre Caravan Site, The Bungalow, Tilshead, Wiltshire SP3 4RX. 01980 620402. Owner: Mr G Brades. A360 Salisbury to Devizes. Close to places of interest. Salisbury 14m. Devizes 10m. Open March-Oct.

WARMINSTER

(5m). Longleat Caravan Club Site, Longleat, Warminster, Wiltshire BA12 7NL. 01985 844663. www.caravanclub.co.uk. Owner: The Caravan Club. See website for directions. The only Club site where you can hear lions roar at night – in a beautiful parkland site. Non-members welcome. No tents. Advance booking advised B H and July and Aug. Toilet block. Privacy cubicle. Laundry facilities. Baby/toddler washroom. Veg prep. MV service point. Gas & gaz. Play equipment. Childrens' room (music and videos). Watersports. Ideal for families. Some hardstanding, dog walk, good area for walking, fishing and NCN cyclepath in 5m. Open March-Nov.

WESTBURY

(3.5m). Brokerswood Country Park, Brokerswood, Westbury, Wiltshire

BA13 4EH. 01373 822238. woodland.park@virgin.net. www.brokerswood.co.uk. Owner: Mrs S H Capon. Follow brown tourist signs from A36 or A361. 3.5m N of Westbury. 5m from Trowbridge. Site set in 80 acres woodlands with lake and Heritage centre. Adventure playground. Narrow gauge railway. Toddlers undercover play area. Coarse fishing. David Bellamy Gold award winners. David Bellamy Gold Conservation Award.

BATH
BATH

Bury View Farm, Corston Fields, Bath, Bath BA2 9HD. 01225 873672. salbowd@btinternet.com. Owner: Mr & Mrs J A Bowden. On A39 Wells to Bath midway between Wheatsheaf Inn and Corston Car Sales Garage. 3m from Keynsham and 2.5m from Saltford. Dogs allowed on leads with tourers. Fishing, golf nearby. 2m to PO and shop, 3m to doctor.

■ (2m). Newton Mill Caravan & Camping Park (Bath), Newton Road, Bath, Bath BA2 9JF. 01225 333909. newtonmill@hotmail.com. www.campinginbath.co.uk. Owner: Mr & Mrs K W Davies. A4 towards Bristol. At roundabout by Globe PH take exit SP Newton St Loe, park is 1m on L. OPEN ALL YEAR and lying in a beautiful setting in a hidden valley CLOSE TO THE CENTRE OF BATH the park is an ideal touring centre with a nearby frequent bus service and level traffic-free cycle path to the centre. A feature is the Old Mill Bar, Restaurants and gardens which lie beside the millstream. Separate tent and caravan park meadows. Heated amenities of the highest standard including bathrooms. 5 star Loo of the Year award 2006. AA 4 Pennant. David Bellamy Gold Conservation Award.

BRISTOL
BRISTOL

(2m). Baltic Wharf Caravan Club Site, Cumberland Road, Bristol, Bristol BS1 6XG. 01179 268030. www.caravanclub.co.uk. Owner: The Caravan Club. See website for directions. A waterside site in the heart of the Bristol's beautifully redeveloped dockland. Non-members welcome. No tents. Advance booking essential BH and weeks either side, also July and Aug. MV service point. Heated toilet block with

laundry facilities. Golf nearby.

Bath Chew Valley Caravan Park, Ham Lane, Bishop Sutton, Bristol, Bristol BS39 5TZ. 01275 332127. enquiries@bathchewvalley.co.uk. www.bathchewvalley.co.uk. Owner: Keith Belton. On A368 Bath to Weston-super-Mare road. At Bishop Sutton turn opposite Red Lion pub. Approach from A38 or A37. Set amongst flowers and shrubs. 800yd from Chew Valley lake, famous for its trout fishing and birdlife. Adults only. One of Practical Caravan's Top 100 parks. Winner for 'Loo of the Year'. Ideal base for exploring Bath and Mendip Hills. David Bellamy Gold Conservation Award.

CORNWALL
BODMIN

(1m). Camping & Caravanning Club Site – Bodmin, Old Callywith Road, Bodmin, Cornwall PL31 2DZ. 01208 73834. www.campingandcaravanningclub.co.uk. Owner: Camping & Caravanning Club. On A30 at Bodmin, turn off dual carriageway at A389 and follow signs to site. Site is on L down 'Old Callywith Road'. In easy reach of all the attractions of the Cornish Riviera. Take advantage of attractions such as Eden Project, The Lost Gardens of Heligan and the Wheal Martyn China Clay museum near to the site. Non-members welcome. All units accepted. Deals for families and backpackers. Open March-Oct.

(4.5m). Croft Farm Holiday Park, Luxulyan, Bodmin, Cornwall PL30 5EQ. 01726 850228. lynpick@ukonline.co.uk. www.croftfarm.co.uk. Owner: Mr E & Mrs J Ager, Park Manager: Mrs J Howe. Follow directions to Eden Project from Tywardreath Highway, then follow road signs to Luxulyan village. Park is on the L, 0.75m from village. Quiet, sheltered park conveniently located close to St Austell Bay with its spectacular coastline and the beautiful Luxulyan Valley. Children allowed. 1m from the Eden Project. GS. David Bellamy Gold Conservation Award. Open April-Oct.

(9m). Lanarth Inn Caravan Park, St Kew Highway, Bodmin, Cornwall PL30 3EE. 01208 841215. Owner: Mrs J Buckley. On A39 4m E Wade Bridge. Set in 10 acres of landscaped gardens. Ideal location for touring. PO, doctor, supermarket 2mins away. Licensed bar, outdoor swimming pool. Family camping and B&B available. Golf 300yd. Caravan

WEST COUNTRY

storage available. Open Easter/April 1-Oct 31.

(4m). Ruthern Valley Holidays, Ruthern Bridge, Bodmin, Cornwall PL30 5LU. 01208 831395. holidays@ruthernvalley.com. www.ruthernvalley.com. Owner: Andrew & Nicola Johnston. From Bodmin, leave on A391 (St Austell). Take 2nd R for Nanstallon. By Pressingol Pottery, second L turn to Ruthern Bridge. L at bridge. Site 400yd on L. Quiet site in unspoilt valley. Touring centre or overnight stop. No dogs July/Aug period. Close to Camel trail. Eden Project 10m. David Bellamy Gold Conservation Award. Open April-New Year (Jan 2).

BOSCASTLE

(2.5m). Lower Pennycrocker Farm, St Juliot, Boscastle, Cornwall PL35 0BY. 01840 250257. www.pennycrocker.com. Owner: Mr Brian Heard. 2.5m N of Boscastle on B3263 SP Pennycrocker. Own farm produce available. Open Easter-Oct.

BUDE

(3m). Budemeadows Touring Park, Poundstock, Bude, Cornwall EX23 0NA. 01288 361646. holiday@budemeadows.com. www.budemeadows.com. Owner: Mr & Mrs Martin & Mr & Mrs Murphy. A39 S from Bude for 3m. Site on L after Widemouth turn off. Heated outdoor swimming pool. TV lounge and games room. Licensed bar. Private ladies' suites. Washing-up sinks. Free hairdryers. Free hot showers. Playground. Telephone. Internet access. Bathroom (baby bath and changing room).

(9m). Camping & Caravanning Club Site – Bude, Gillards Moor, St Gennys, Bude, Cornwall EX23 0BG. 01288 230650. www.campingandcaravanningclub.co.uk. Owner: Camping & Caravanning Club. From Wadebridge heading N on the A39 towards Bude. Site on L, SP. 10m from Camelford. Excellent position for touring the region. Near coastal paths in the heart of King Arthur's country. Cyclists are well catered for, with 42m of signposted traffic-free routes stretching from Bude to Bodmin. All units accepted. Non-members welcome. The site has some of the best surfing beaches nearby. Special deals for families and backpackers. Open April-Oct.

(5m). Cornish Coasts Caravan & Camping Park, Middle Penlean, Poundstock, Bude, Cornwall EX23 0EE. 01288 361380. info.1@cornishcoasts.co.uk. www.cornishcoasts.co.uk. Owner: Gary & Sue Cummings. On A39 5m S of Bude. Peaceful, friendly site with wonderful views and level terrraced pitches. Close to beaches and SW coastal path, ideal touring location. Play area. Open Easter-Oct.

Coxford Meadow, Crackington Haven, Bude, Cornwall EX23 0NS. 01840 230707. Owner: Mrs J Onions. 1m from Crackington Haven. 1-acre field with easy access. Shops, café 1m away. Above quiet wooded valley leading to sea. Open Easter-Sept 30.

(5m). East Thorne Touring Park, Kilkhampton, Bude, Cornwall EX23 9RY. 01288 321654. keith.ovenden@btinternet.com. Owner: Mr & Mrs Ovenden. 5m N of Bude on A39. Take B3254 0.5m to site. Family-run site set in quiet farmland. Games room. Playground. Open March-Oct 31.

(10m). Hentervene Caravan & Camping Park, Crackington Haven, Bude, Cornwall EX23 0LF. 01840 230365. contact@hentervene.co.uk. www.hentervene.co.uk. Owner: Mr & Mrs D R Turner & Mr & Mrs S A Turner. Off A39. Bude-Camelford road at Otterham station. Quiet meadow park near sandy beach. Entertainment facilities for children. Games room and baby bathroom. Pets welcome. TV lounge. Water sports, fishing, horseriding nearby. Ideal touring base. Caravan sales. (OS grid SX155944). Open March-Oct for camping – all year for statics.

(3m). Ivyleaf Camping Sites, Ivyleaf Hill, Bush, Bude, Cornwall EX23 9LD. 01288 321442. Owner: N A Butcher's. N of Bude on A39, turn R at Willow campsite up Ivyleaf Hill site halfway up hill on the R. Quiet, family owned site. Sheltered site with beautiful views; one of the cheapest sites in Bude.

(5m). Penhalt Farm Holiday Park, Widemouth Bay, Bude, Cornwall EX23 0DG. 01288 361210. denandjennie@penhaltfarm.fsnet.co.uk. www.penhaltfarm.co.uk. Owner: Mr D J Marks. 4m S of Bude on A39, take 2nd turn R for Widemouth Bay, turn L at the bottom by W B Hotel. Family site 2/3m along on R. Splendid sea views. Close to coastal path, 1.5m from sandy beach. Laundry. Play area. Telephone, Gas. Spectacular sea views from site. Widemouth Bay well known surfing beach. Garage and PO in Widemouth Bay. All amenities in Bude. Open Easter-Oct.

(4m). Penstowe Caravan and Camping Park, Stibb Road, Kilkhampton, Bude, Cornwall EX23 9QY. 01288 321601. info@penstoweholidays.co.uk. www.penstoweholidays.co.uk. Situated on A39, N of Bude. Family owned park in a peaceful countryside location with views to the sea. Walking distance to Kilkhampton village with shops. PO and pub nearby. Sandymouth beach 2m. Bude about 4m. Six local beaches in 6m.

(4m). Red Post Inn, Launcells, Bude, Cornwall EX23 9NW. 01288 381305. gsharp@redpostinn1.wanadoo.co.uk. www.redpostinn.co.uk. Owner: Mr & Mrs Sharp. E of Bude off A3072. Level, well sheltered, good family site, an ideal base for touring N. Devon and Cornwall. Bar and restaurant. Sporting facilities nearby. Children's playground. Open Easter-Oct.

(3m). Red Post Meadows, Launcells, Bude, Cornwall EX23 9NW. 01288 381306. Owner: Mr & Mrs Parnell. E of Bude off A3072. Good, level well sheltered family site. An ideal base for touring North Devon and Cornwall. Sporting facilities nearby. Open Easter-Oct.

(4m). Sandymouth Holiday Park, Sandymouth Bay, Bude, Cornwall EX23 9HW. 01288 352563. reception@sandymouthbay.co.uk. www.sandymouthbay.co.uk. Owner: M & G Luxon. On the Bude to Kilkhampton road (A39), 3m from Bude. Extensive coastal and countryside views. Licensed clubhouse with entertainment. Shower block, play area, Launderette. Gas sales. Indoor swimming pool. Crazy golf. Café/diner. Sauna. Open March-Nov. AA 3 pennants; 5-star.

(0.5m). Upper Lynstone Camping & Caravan Park, Bude, Cornwall EX23 0LP. 01288 352017. reception@upperlynstone.co.uk. www.upperlynstone.co.uk. Owner: Mr & Mrs J Cloke. S of Bude on coastal road to Widemouth Bay. Quiet, family site in walking distance of town, sandy beach, bars and restaurants. Coastal footpath from park along beautiful Cornish coast. Fishing available nearby. Open Easter or April 1-Oct.

Widemouth Fields Caravan & Camping Park, Park Farm, Poundstock, Bude, Cornwall EX23 0NA. 01288 361351. www.

WEST COUNTRY

widemouthbaytouring.co.uk. Located 1m from the beach at Widemouth Bay. Open May-.

(2m). Willow Valley Holiday Park, Dye House, Bush, Bude, Cornwall EX23 9LB. 01288 353104. willowvalley@talk21.com. www.caravansitecornwall.co.uk. Owner: Mr & Mrs Lewis. N of Bude on A39. 3m S of Kilkhampton. Small, sheltered site in beautiful Strat valley. Friendly atmosphere. Modern facilities block with laundry. Write or telephone for colour brochure. Open March-Jan.

(2m). Wooda Farm Park, Poughill, Bude, Cornwall EX23 9HJ. 01288 352069. enquiries@wooda.co.uk. www.wooda.co.uk. Owner: Mr G Colwill. From A39 North of Stratton, take Poughill/Coombe Valley Road for 1m. Through crossroads Wooda is 200yd on your R. Family run park 1.25m from sandy beaches. Adventure playground, woodland walks, well-stocked coarse fishing lake, licensed restaurant, off licence, takeaway, farmyard friends, fun golf course. Splash indoor pool is nearby. David Bellamy Gold Conservation Award. Open April 1-Oct 31.

CAMBORNE

(2m). Magor Farm Caravan Site, Tehidy, Camborne, Cornwall TR14 0JF. 01209 713367. www.magorfarm.co.uk. Owner: H Williams and Son. Take Camborne (W) exit off A30. Turn R over A30 bridge in approx. 0.5m go straight across, blind L hand corner. Site is 1.5m further on down over hill. Sheltered site with wooded surroundings in easy reach of all Cornwall's famous beauty spots and beaches. SP from cliff Portreath road near Hells Mouth café. Play area. Launderette, free showers. Electric shaving points. Country park nearby. RAC and Caravan Club. Tehidy golf club 2m, leisure centre, local coarse fishing, Camborne, Redruth, Mining Heritage Centres. Open Easter-Oct.

CAMELFORD

(1m). Juliot's Well Holiday Park, Camelford, Cornwall PL32 9RF. 01840 213302. juliot.well@holidaysincornwall.net. Owner: Kim & Phil Bolindy. Through Camelford on A39, take second turning R, then first L. Site 400yd down lane on R. Swimming pool. Tennis court. Pub garden, play area. Badminton. Licensed bar. Restaurant. Also available 10 pine lodges and 5 cottages. Open March 1-Oct 31.

(1m). Lakefield Caravan Park & Equestrian Centre, Lower Pendavey Farm, Camelford, Cornwall PL32 9TX. 01840 213279. Owner: Mr & Mrs D E Perring. A30 from Exeter to Launceston and shortly after A395 to join the A39 to Camelford. In 2m turn R on to B3314 and the L on to B3266 park is 100yd on the R. We now run a full riding school alongside park. Open April 1-Oct 31.

Valley Truckle Caravan Club Site, Camelford, Cornwall PL32 9RF. 01840 212206. www.caravanclub.co.uk. Owner: The Caravan Club. See website for directions. Caravan Club members only. No tents. A small, attractive site, quiet and peaceful off-peak. An adjacent tennis course and a championship golf course in easy walking distance. Toilet blocks, laundry facilities and MV service point. Dog walk nearby. Good area for walking, fishing and NCN route nearby. Facilities for disabled. Ideal for families. Open March-Oct.

DELABOLE

(0.2m). Planet Caravan Park, Delabole, Cornwall PL33 9BG. 01840 213361. Owner: Mr & Mrs R W Round. 4m W of Camelford and 6m S of Tintagel. SW end of village on B3314 off A39 road. Quiet park, wonderful views. Touring centre. Shop 300yd. Fees on application. Open Easter-Oct.

FALMOUTH

(5m). Goonreath, Broads Lane, Mylor Downs, Falmouth, Cornwall TR11 5UL. 01872 863670. Owner: Mr & Mrs D J Mawby. From Truro towards Falmouth turn E about 1m beyond Norway Inn, follow sign to Comfort, then 2nd lane on R, 0.5m to site. Last 400yd of lane is rough. Quiet and sheltered in beautiful area. No sanitation.

(3.5m). Menallack Farm, Treverva, Falmouth, Cornwall TR10 9BP. 01326 340333. menallack@fsbdial.co.uk. Owner: Mr & Mrs J Minson. Off Falmouth to Gweek road, 0.75m beyond Treverva village on L. Doctor in Constantine 3m. PO, fishing, golf, sailing, Asda supermarket all nearby in 3m. Our main bonus point and warmly enjoyed by 20 year returnees(!) is our peace, beauty but all in notable Cornish interesting places. Open Easter-Oct 31.

Pennance Mill Chalet and Camping Park, Maenporth, Falmouth, Cornwall TR11 5HJ. 01326 317431. pennancemill@amserve.com. www.pennancemill.co.uk. Owner: Mr A J Jewell. Approach Falmouth via A39 continue to Hillhead roundabout. Turn R towards Maenporth. Along road for 2m. Pennance Mill is on your L at bottom of hill. Open April-Oct.

FOWEY

(1.5m). Penhale Caravan and Camping Park, Fowey, Cornwall PL23 1JU. 01726 833425. info@penhale-fowey.co.uk. www.penhale-fowey.co.uk. Owner: Mr J and W J Berryman. On A3082 Par to Fowey road. Close to lovely walks and sandy beaches. Splendid views. No overcrowding. David Bellamy Bronze Conservation Award. Open Easter-Oct.

■ (1m). Penmarlam Caravan & Camping Park, Bodinnick-by-Fowey, Fowey, Cornwall PL23 1LZ. 01726 870088. info@penmarlampark.co.uk. www.penmarlampark.co.uk. Owner: Marcus Wallace. From Liskeard take A38, then A390 turn L on to B3359. Follow signs to Bodinnick. Level, grassy site with outstanding views. Quay, slipway and storage for small boats. Modern amenities block, shop and off licence on site, WIFI and internet access. Open Easter-Oct.

(0.5m). Polruan Holidays – Camping & Caravanning, Polruan-by-Fowey, Fowey, Cornwall PL23 1QH. 01726 870263. polholiday@aol.com. Owner: Mr & Mrs Cox. 12m SE of St Austell off the A390 between Fowey and Polperro. Select park in an area of outstanding natural beauty surrounded by sea. National Trust farmland, coastal path and beautiful Fowey estuary. Personal service guaranteed. David Bellamy Gold Conservation Award. Open Easter-Nov 1.

HAYLE

(1.5m). Atlantic Coast Caravan Park, Upton Towans, Hayle, Cornwall TR27 5BL. 01736 752071. enquiries@atlanticcoast-caravanpark.co.uk. www.atlanticcoast-caravanpark.co.uk. Owner: P S & M Smith. Take B3301 off A30 at double roundabout. Site is on L after about 1m. Situated on the edge of St Ives Bay, nestling in the sand dunes. Small bar. Licensed shop. Dogs allowed at a small charge. Open April 1-Oct 31.

(0.75m). Beachside Holiday Park, Hayle, Cornwall TR27 5AW. 01736 753080. www.beachside.co.uk. Owner: Beachside Leisure Holidays Ltd. Leave A30 at Hayle. Beside the sea, amidst sand dunes in St Ives Bay. Heated swimming and paddling pool. 100 chalets also available for hire. Open Easter-Oct 1.

72 MOTOR CARAVAN & CAMPING PARKS 2009

WEST COUNTRY

See page 5 for key to symbols and abbreviations

(3m). Godrevy Park Caravan Club Site, Upton Towans, Hayle, Cornwall TR27 5BL. *01736 753100.* www.caravanclub.co.uk. Owner: The Caravan Club. See website for directions. Caravan Club members only. No tents. Quiet and peaceful off peak. A spacious site surrounded by gorse-covered sand dune and only 1m from beautiful sandy beach. Dog walk adjacent. Shop 200yd. Advance booking advised in June and essential July and Aug. Toilet block with privacy cubicles and laundry facilities plus baby and toddler washroom. MV service point. Boules pitch. Fishing nearby. Good area for walking. Ideal for families. Veg prep area, gas and gaz. NCN cycle route in 5m. Open March-Nov.

(3m). Higher Trevaskis Caravan & Camping Park, Gwinear Road, Connor Downs, Hayle, Cornwall TR27 5JQ. *01209 831736.* Owner: Johanna & Duncan Leech. Leave A30 dual carriageway at Camborne W exit. Follow signs to Connor Downs (A3047), L at crossroads entering village. Park is 0.75m on R. Friendly secluded family run countryside park in a great location. Ideally situated for visiting local beaches and attractions of W Cornwall. Touring only. Spacious level pitches in small enclosures. Designated play areas & our renowned spotlessly clean facilities. 'Big enough to cope – Small enough to care'. Open mid April-end Sept.

(3m). Parbola Holiday Park, Wall Gwinear, Hayle, Cornwall TR27 5LE. *01209 831503.* bookings@parbola.co.uk. www.parbola.co.uk. Owner: Mr & Mrs Norman. Off A30. At Hayle roundabout take first exit to Connor Downs, at end of village turn R to Carnhell Green. Go over railway crossing and continue to T Junction, turn R. Park is located 1m on L. Large well-spaced pitches in woodland or parkland. Showers. Swimming pool. Adventure playground. Crazy golf. Games room. Table tennis. TV room. Launderette. Washing up facilities. Mother and baby room. Under fives play area. Local pub providing meals lunchtime and evening. PO, shop in nearby village. Comprehensive tourist information available for all visitors. Short driving distance to glorious sandy beaches. Open Easter-Sept.

(1m). St Ives Bay Holiday Park, 73 Loggans Road, Upton Towans, Hayle, Cornwall TR27 5BH. *01736 752274.* stivesbay@btconnect.com. www.stivesbay.co.uk. Take Hayle exit off A30 at mini-roundabouts turn R on to B3301, SP 'Portreath'. 600yd along B3301. In sand dunes running down to huge sandy beach.

Good offers for couples and young families. Many sea views. Huge choice of accommodation and pitches. Indoor heated swimming pool. Takeaway. Hire shop. Brochure on application. Open May-Sept.

HELSTON

(6m). Boscrege Caravan & Camping Park, Ashton, Helston, Cornwall TR13 9TG. *01736 762231.* enquiries@caravanparkcornwall.com. www.caravanparkcornwall.com. Owner: T Armstrong. Off A394 Penzance to Helston. 0.5 m along lane at side of PO in Ashton. Flat and sheltered park. Washing up room and laundry. TV, microwave. Top 100 parks GB. Most facilities available in Helston and Penzance. Centrally situated for visiting W Cornwall. Open March 31-Nov 1.

(5m). Franchis Holidays, Cury Cross Lanes, Mullion, Helston, Cornwall TR12 7AZ. *01326 240301.* enquiries@franchis.co.uk. www.franchis.co.uk. Owner: Phil Wilson and Kate D'Arcy. On A3083 Helston to Lizard. Quiet, family run park in an area of outstanding beauty. Close mown grass and woodland. Beaches, Helford river and Flambards theme park close by. Local to Glendurgan, Trebar and Trevano gardens. 3 AA pennants. Open Easter-Oct.

(3m). Gunwalloe Caravan Park, Helston, Cornwall TR12 7QP. *01326 572668.* Owner: Mr K M Wallis. S of Helston via A3083 to Lizard. 2m from Helston road for Gunwalloe. Site is SP. Holiday site. Café/restaurant nearby. Open April-Oct.

(10m). Henry's Camp Site, Caerthillian Farm, The Lizard, Helston, Cornwall TR12 7NX. *01326 290596.* henryscampsite@tiscali.co.uk. Owner: Mr R Lyne & Mrs J C Lyne. Take B3083 from Helston. Enter village take first R across village green then second R. Sea views. Beaches closeby. Near amenities in village centre but secluded.

(10m). Little Trevothan Caravan Park, Coverack, Helston, Cornwall TR12 6SD. *01326 280260.* sales@littletrevothan.co.uk. www.littletrevothan.com. Owner: S & R Flynn and A Holloway. SP from B3293 to Zoar garage. 0.75m from picturesque fishing village of Coverack. spacious family site with level, grassy pitches. Free hot showers. Children's playground. Beautiful walks. No noisy club. Modern holiday caravans for sale and for hire. AA 3

pennant. Colour brochure available. Open from 1/3/08 to 31/12/08.

(3m). Lower Polladras Touring Park, Carleen, Helston, Cornwall TR13 9NX. *01736 762220.* lowerpolladras@btinternet.co.uk. www.lower-polladras.co.uk. Owner: R J Bell. Take B3302 off A394 Helston to Penzance. Turn L to Carleen village, after 0.75m from A30 take B3303 after junction with B3302 take 1st R to Carleen. Tranquil and beautiful surroundings set in a small hamlet. Quiet family run site. AA 3 pennant. Open March 26-Oct 31.

(1.5m). Mullion Holiday Park, Ruan Minor, Helston, Cornwall TR12 7LJ. *0870 444 0080.* bookings@weststarholidays.co.uk. www.weststarholidays.co.uk/eb. Owner: Weststar Holidays Ltd. Follow the road to The Lizard from Helston, A3083. After about 7m we are on the L. Close to golden sandy beaches and secret coves, spectacular cliffs and coastline and family attractions. Free all weather facilities including indoor swimming pool, award winning live entertainment and children's clubs. Choose your accommodation from our wide range of fully equipped holiday homes and bungalows. Touring & camping facilities also available. Golf course, fishing all in 3m. David Bellamy Silver Conservation Award. Open from 5/4/08 to 25/10/08.

(3m). Penmarth Farm, Coverack, St Keverne, Helston, Cornwall TR12 6SB. *01326 280389.* Owner: Mr B Roskilly. Off B3293. Woodland walk and pond. Picnic area. Short walk to Coverack village – shops, PO and doctor. Open March 31-Oct 31.

(2.5m). Poldown Caravan Park, Carleen, Helston, Cornwall TR13 9NN. *01326 574560.* stay@poldown.com. www.poldown.co.uk. Owner: G & N Peyrin. Follow Penzance road from Helston (A394) for about 1m. Turn R at Hilltop garage on to B3302 to Hayle. Take 2nd L, site 0.75m down lane. Secluded site ideal for exploring W Cornwall. 3m to superb sandy coves and beaches. Shopping centre, attraction park, fishing trips 2m, golf 2.5m, surfing 3m. Open April-Sept.

(10m). Silver Sands Holiday Park, Gwendreath, Ruan Minor, Helston, Cornwall TR12 7LZ. *01326 290631.* enquiries@silversandsholidaypark.co.uk. www.silversandsholidaypark.co.uk. Owner: Mrs F M Pullinger. Take A3083 from Helston, then B3293. After Goonhilly turn R. In 1.50m turn L, signed 'Gwendreath'.

WEST COUNTRY

800yd walk to award winning sandy beach. On edge of The Lizard National Nature Reserve. Open April-Sept.

(10m). Teneriffe Farm, Predannack, Mullion, Helston, Cornwall TR12 7EZ. 01326 240293. teneriffefarm@aol.com. Owner: Mr A B Thomas. Off A3083, turn R on to B3296, through Mullion Village. At Mullion Meadows turn L, SP Predannack, camping site 1.5m away. Public telephone. SAE for bookings and details. Site has small play park, in walking distance of the coastal path and some pitches with sea views. 1m from Mullion village, PO, shops and pubs. AA 2 pennants. Open March 1-Jan 31.

(7m). The Friendly Camp Caravan Park, Tregullas Farm, Ruan Minor, Helston, Cornwall TR12 7LJ. 01326 240387. Owner: Mr J Bennetts. On A3083 Lizard to Helston road near junction with B3296 Mullion road. Open April 1-Oct 31.

LAND'S END

(4.5m). Cardinney Caravan and Camping Park, Crows-an-Wra, Land's End, Cornwall TR19 6HX. 01736 810880. cardinney@btinternet.com. www.cardinney-camping-park.co.uk. Owner: Liz & Kevin Lindley. On A30 between Penzance and Lands End. 4.5m from Penzance. Quiet family-run site in peaceful surroundings. Off licence. Spacious pitches. Hardstandings. Serviced pitches ie: electric hook up, water hook up and grey water soak-a-way. Cliff top walks, sandy coves, ancient monuments. Golf, beaches 3.5m. Penzance 5m. Open Feb 1-Nov 30.

LAUNCESTON

(7m). Chapmanswell Caravan Park, Chapmanswell Well, St-Giles-on-the-Heath, Launceston, Cornwall PL15 9SG. 01409 211382. george@chapmanswellcaravanpark.co.uk. www.chapmanswellcaravanpark.co.uk. Owner: Mr G Avery. Off A388, Launceston to Holsworthy road, at Chapmanswell take L turning to Boyton-200yd along on L. Quiet, country park supervised by the owner. Hardstanding and grass pitches. Central for touring Devon and Cornwall. Caravan storage available. Fishing, golf, watersports on reservoir in 7m.

LISKEARD

Colliford Tavern Campsite, Colliford Lake, St Neot, Liskeard, Cornwall PL14 6PZ. 01208 821335. info@colliford.com. www.colliford.com. Owner: Peter & Marian Mortimer. Off A30 2m W of Bolventor on Bodmin Moor. 10m from Bodmin. Quiet, family-run, sheltered site near Colliford Lake. Tavern and restaurant. Modern hot showers. Dishwashing. Laundry and baby care facilities. AA-4 pennant. Please ring for brochure.

(4m). Pine Green Caravan and Camping Park, Doublebois, Liskeard, Cornwall PL14 6LE. 01579 320183. mary.ruhleman@btinternet.com. www.pinegreenpark.co.uk. Owner: Pine Green Developments. 4m W of Liskeard via A38 through Dobwalls towards Bodmin, turn L on to the B3360 at Doublebois, peaceful, wooded park 150yd on the R. Manager on site. Golf course nearby. Shop, PO 2m. Doctor 3m. Open Jan-Dec.

(6m). Trenant Chapel House, Trenant Caravan Park, St Neot, Liskeard, Cornwall PL14 6RZ. 01579 320896. Owner: Mrs Parry. Off A38 at Dobwalls Theme Park follow signs to St Neot then Trenant Caravan Park signs. A small, quiet country park bounded by a tributary of the river Fowey. Flat, well-drained site in good walking and fishing area. Close to Bodmin Moor. Open April 1-Oct 31.

LOOE

(2m). Camping Caradon, Trelawne, Looe, Cornwall PL13 2NA. 01503 272388. enquiries@campingcaradon.co.uk. www.campingcaradon.co.uk. Owner: Stephen & Lene Cox. 2m W of Looe via A387 to Polperro, park is off B3359. Quiet rural locations. Hardstandings available. 3 acres with level pitches. Sea 2m. Club. Open all year – Nov till April by booking only.

(4m). Killigarth Manor Holiday Park, Polperro, Looe, Cornwall PL13 2JQ. 01503 272216. www.johnfowlerholidays.com. Owner: John Fowler Holidays. Cross Tama bridge A38, turn L at roundabout signed Looe. R A387, cross over bridge in Looe. 3.5m out turn L, SP Killigarth. In an area of outstanding beauty. Indoor pool. Entertainment daily. Adventure playground. Tennis court. Club. Takeaway. Fishing, golf course and Eden project nearby. Open Feb 4 – Jan 4.

(1.5m). Looe Caravan Club Site, St Martin, Looe, Cornwall PL13 1PB. 01503 264006. www.caravanclub.co.uk. Owner: The Caravan Club. See website for directions. Caravan Club members only. No tents. Calor Gas sales. Open air heated swimming pool. Mini-golf. Tennis courts. Play area. Public phone. Dog walk. Some hardstandings, part sloping, levelling blocks required. Storage pitches. MV service point. Toilet blocks and laundry facilities. Volleyball area. Golf and watersports nearby. Good area for walking. Ideal for families. NCN Cycle route in 5m.

(2.5m). Polborder House Caravan & Camping Park, Bucklawren Road, St Martins, Looe, Cornwall PL13 1NZ. 01503 240265. reception@peaceful-polborder.co.uk. www.peaceful-polborder.co.uk. Owner: Mr D Byers. 2.5m E of Looe off B3253, follow signs for Polborder and Monkey Sanctuary. Small select and peaceful caravan and camping park nestling in the sleepy hamlet of Bucklawren, set in beautiful countyside surroundings with stunning views. Open March-Oct.

(2m). Talland Caravan Park, Looe, Cornwall PL13 2JA. 01503 272715. www.tallandcaravanpark.co.uk. Owner: Mr & Mrs R S Haywood. Cross Looe bridge, at top of hill in about 1m turn L for Talland Bay park 1m on L. Adjadent to coast path and beaches. 3 stars AA. Open April 1-Oct 31.

(1.25m). Tencreek Caravan & Camping Park, Polperro Road, Looe, Cornwall PL13 2JR. 01503 262447. reception@tencreek.co.uk. www.dolphinholidays.co.uk. Owner: Dolphin Holidays. On A387, Looe to Polperro road. Family park overlooking sea. Public telephone. Heated indoor swimming pool with 45m water flume. Play area, amusement arcade. Takeaway meals. Licensed club with entertainment.

(3m). Trelay Farmpark, Pelynt, Looe, Cornwall PL13 2JX. 01503 220900. stay@trelay.co.uk. www.trelay.co.uk. Owner: Mr & Mrs B Doidge. 0.5m S of Pelynt on B3359. Small, uncommercialised, famil-run park surrounded by farmland. Superb washing facilities/Laundry/disabled suite. New children's play area. Shops/restaurants etc. in Pelynt (10mins walk). Amazing Eden Project 12m W. Looe and Polperro 3m. Fishing, golf, diving all nearby. Open Jan 1-Nov 30.

LOSTWITHIEL

(1m). Downend Camp Site, Lostwithiel, Cornwall PL22 0RB. 01208 872363. Owner: Mr J Hawke. On A390. Open March 1-Oct 31.

WEST COUNTRY

(1.5m). Powderham Castle Tourist Park, Lanlivery, Nr Fowey, Lostwithiel, Cornwall PL30 5BU. *01208 872277.* Owner: J Buckley Evans. Off A390,1.5m SW of Lostwithiel, turn R at SP Powderham Castle N 400m. Quiet uncommercialised select park. Ideal location for touring all Cornwall and near to the Eden Project. Children's activity centre, indoor badminton, soft tennis. TV room. Launderette. Seasonal pitches and storage. Holiday homes for sale on site – private use only. David Bellamy Silver Conservation Award. Open Easter-Oct.

MARAZION

(0.5m). Wheal Rodney, Gwallon Lane, Marazion, Cornwall TR17 0HL. *01736 710605.* reception@whealrodney.co.uk. www.whealrodney.co.uk. Owner: Mr & Mrs S P Lugg. Off A394. At Crowlas take road SP Rospeath, we are 1.5m on R. Showers. Sauna. Heated indoor swimming pool. Holiday bungalows for hire. Fishing, horse riding nearby. 0.5m to St Michaels mount and beaches. AA 3 pennants. Open April-Oct.

MEVAGISSEY

(4m). Pentewan Sands Holiday Park, Pentewan, Mevagissey, Cornwall PL26 6BT. *01726 843485.* info@pentewan.co.uk. www.pentewan.co.uk. Owner: Pentewan Sands Ltd. On B3273. 4m S of St Austell towards Mevagissey. Look for the large site beside the beach on your L. You are there. Large, safe, sandy private beach, boat launching facilities. Clubhouse, shop, restaurant and takeaway. Free showers. Launderette. Large level pitches. No jet skis. Traditional family site (no single sex bookings). Caravan and boat storage. Open March 21-Nov 1.

NEWQUAY

(5m). Camping & Caravanning Club Site – Tregurrian, Newquay, Cornwall TR8 4AE. *01637 860448.* www.campingandcaravanningclub.co.uk. Owner: Camping & Caravanning Club. From A3059 to Newquay. 1.5m on after service station, R to Newquay airport, continue to J, then L at Tregurrian. Follow Watergate Bay signs. The nearby beach at Watergate Bay is always popular with youngsters and excellent for surfers. Non-members welcome. All units welcome. Fishing, horse riding, golf, PO, shops, cycle routes, doctor, hospital, swimming pool, zoo, Eden project etc all in easy reach by car or public transport. Deals for families and backpackers. Ideal base for exploring North Cornwall. Loo Of The Year (4 stars). Open April-Oct.

(4m). Cottage Farm Touring Park, Treworgans, Cubert, Newquay, Cornwall TR8 5HH. *01637 831083.* info@cottagefarmpark.co.uk. www.cottagefarmpark.co.uk. Owner: Robert & Kath Harrison. 5m SW of Newquay. S from Newquay on A3075. At Rejerrah crossroads, turn W for Cubert, then turn N towards Crantock for 0.75m. Small, quiet family site. Families and couples only. Open April 1-end Oct.

(3.5m). Crantock Beach Holiday Park, Crantock, Newquay, Cornwall TR8 5RH. *01637 831005.* enquiries@parkdeanholidays.co.uk. www.parkdeanholidays.co.uk. Owner: Parkdean Holidays Plc. 3m W of Newquay off the A3075 SP Crantock. Quiet, peaceful park with magnificent views across a sandy, family beach which is a short walk away. Light evening entertainment, bar, children welcome, play areas, pitch and putt, takeway food, Launderette. Open April-Oct 30.

(3m). Crantock Plains Touring Park, Crantock, Newquay, Cornwall TR8 5PH. *01637 830955.* matthew-milburn@btconnect.com. www.crantock-plains.co.uk. Owner: J & K Gibbes M & E Milburn. S of Newquay via A3075 Redruth road. After lake on R, garage on L. Continue over mini roundabout. Site is 0.5m down second SP lane to Crantock on R, 1.5m from beach. Families & couples only. Swings. Recreation area. AA 3 pennants. Storage facilities available all year. Crantock beach 5mins by car. Golf 3m. Open Easter-Sept 30.

■ **(2m). Hendra Holiday Park, Newquay, Cornwall TR8 4NY.** *01637 875778.* enquiries@hendra-holidays.com. www.hendra-holidays.com. Owner: Mr & Mrs R Hyatt. From M5 at Exeter, take A30 to the Highgate Hill junction, follow the sign for the A392 to Newquay. At Quintrell Downs go straight across the roundabout and on for 0.5m. Hendra Holiday Park is on the L (1.5m from Newquay town centre). A family run park for couples and families. Heated outdoor pool and indoor fun pools with waterslide. Food bar. Sauna. Bars. Children's complex and club. Entertainment. Restaurant. (Riding, fishing and golf in 2m). Freephone brochure line: 0500 242523. David Bellamy Gold Conservation Award. Open March-Oct.

(3m). Holywell Bay Holiday Park, Holywell Bay, Newquay, Cornwall TR8 5PR. *01637 830227.* enquiries@parkdeanholidays.co.uk. www.parkdeanholidays.co.uk. Owner: Parkdean Holidays Plc. 6m W of Newquay off A3075 SP Cubert and Holywell Bay. 39 mixed pitches. Peaceful valley with a sandy, family beach a short walk away. Children club, free nightly entertainment, heated pool with 300ft slide, amusements. Pool open between May 19-Sept 25 only. David Bellamy Silver Conservation Award. Open mid March-early Nov.

(6m). Magic Cove Touring Park, Mawgan Porth, Newquay, Cornwall TR8 4BZ. *01637 860263.* magic@magiccove.co.uk. www.magiccove.co.uk. Owner: Lesley Lightfoot. Situated halfway between Newquay and Padstow on the north Cornish coast. Level site 300yd from the beach, shops and pub. Water and drain adjacent to each pitch. TV, hook up points. Well maintained facilities. Open Easter-End Sept.

Marver Holiday Park, Mawgan Porth, Newquay, Cornwall TR8 4BB. *01637 860493.* familyholidays@aol.com. www.marverholidaypark.co.uk. Owner: Mr & Mrs Rodding. Small level quiet family run site. Families and couples only. 200yd level walk to sandy beach. Dogs allowed on beach and nearby beach. Takeaway meals, shop, café/restaurant all available nearby. Open April-Oct.

(4m). Monkey Tree Holiday Park, Scotland Road, Rejerrah, Newquay, Cornwall TR8 5QR. *01872 572032.* enquiries@monkeytreeholidaypark.co.uk. www.monkeytreeholidaypark.co.uk. Owner: Walker Leisure. From M5, A30 to Exeter, Bodmin, Redruth off at Boxheater junction B3285, after 0.5m turn R, after 1m turn L to Monkey Tree. Set in ideal surroundings only a short distance from Cornwall's popular surfing beaches. Lounge bar. Café. Heated swimming pools. Sauna and solarium. Excellent disabled facilities. Clubhouse with entertainment, restaurant, shop.

■ **(4m). Newperran Holiday Park, Rejerrah, Newquay, Cornwall TR8 5QJ.** *0845 1668407.* www.newperran.co.uk. Owner: Keith & Christine Brewer. 5m S of Newquay via A3075 towards Redruth. Turn R to Newperran, 1m after garage. Ideal touring site made up of several small meadows enclosed by Cornish fences. Fees on application. Crazy golf. Off-licence. Cottage Inn and café. Open Easter-Oct 31.

www.motorcaravanmagazine.co.uk   MOTOR CARAVAN & CAMPING PARKS 2009 **75**

WEST COUNTRY

(2m). Newquay Holiday Park, Newquay, Cornwall TR8 4HS. 01637 871111. enquiries@parkdeanholidays.co.uk. www.parkdeanholidays.co.uk. Owner: Parkdean Holidays Plc. Off A3059. Direction Newquay – after 4m- park is SP at bottom of the hill. 2m from Newquay and its fabulous beaches. Children's club, free nightly entertainment, 3 heated swimming pools, water slide, amusements, pool, snooker, pitch & putt, crazy golf, playground, restaurant, takeaway food. Open March-Oct.

(3m). Perran Quay Tourist Park, Hendra Croft, Rejerrah, Newquay, Cornwall TR8 5QP. 01872 572561. rose@perran-quay.co.uk. www.cornwall-online.co.uk/perran-quay. On A3075 midway between Newquay & Perranporth. Bar and restaurant. Play area. Outdoor heated swimming pool. Quality shower and toilet facilities, modern launderette. Open Easter-Oct 31.

(1.5m). Porth Beach Tourist Park, Porth, Newquay, Cornwall TR7 3NH. 01637 876531. info@porthbeach.co.uk. www.porthbeach.co.uk. Owner: Mr & Mrs J Kase. Turn R off A30 at Indian Queens on to A392 to Quintrell Downs roundabout. A3058 to Newquay. At Porth, Four Turnings turn R on to B3276, coast road to Padstow. Close to beach. Playground. Shops near. Riding, fishing and boating 1m. Open April-Oct.

(2.5m). Riverside Holiday Park, Newquay, Cornwall TR8 4PE. 01637 873617. info@riversideholidaypark.co.uk. www.riversideholidaypark.co.uk. Off A392 at Quintrell Downs go straight across at roundabout, then take second turning on L, SP 'Gwills' past Lane Theatre and follow signs. On site: river fishing, games room, bar, café/takeway, swimming pool, showers, laundry. Short drive: amusements and other amenities. Newquay town centre, pony trekking 2m. Golf course, beaches 3m. Open Easter to end-Oct.

(5m). Summer Lodge Holiday Resort, Whitecross, Newquay, Cornwall TR8 4LW. 01726 860415. info@snootyfoxresorts.co.uk. www.snootyfoxresorts.co.uk. Owner: Snooty Fox Resorts Ltd. From M5 take A30 then turn on to A392 to Newquay. SP at Whitecross. Ideally situated for touring. Facilities include heated swimming pool, café, takeaway, club with live entertainment. Golf. Horse riding, full range of watersports. Open March-Oct 31.

(5.5m). Sun Haven Valley Caravan & Camping Park, Mawgan Porth, Newquay, Cornwall TR8 4BQ. 01637 860373. sunhaven@sunhavenvalley.com. www.sunhavenvalley.com. Owner: Steve & Helen Tavener. Turn R off B3276 Newquay to Padstow coast road, park on L 0.75m from coast. Dogs allowed on touring field. Families/couples only. Fishing, golf nearby. Open May 1-Oct 31.

(3m). Sunnyside Holiday Park, Quintrel Downs, Newquay, Cornwall TR8 4PD. 01637 873338. info@sunnyside.co.uk. www.sunnyside.co.uk. Owner: Mr D A Gamble. Situated off A392 Newquay road. Only 18-30's type holiday park. Nightclub. Swimming pool. Restaurant etc. Not suitable for families with children. Open March-Jan.

(5m). Treago Farm Caravan and Camping Site, Crantock, Newquay, Cornwall TR8 5QS. 01637 830277. treagofarm@aol.com. www.treagofarm.co.uk. Owner: Mr J A & P A Eastlake. Off A3075 2m S of Newquay follow signs to Crantock and the Treago, W Pentire signs. Site is in sheltered valley 0.5m from the sea and surrounded by National Trust land. Footpath to two sandy beaches. Open April 1-Nov 1.

(3m). Trebarber Farm Camping Park, St Columb Minor, Newquay, Cornwall TR8 4JT. 01637 873007. trebarberfarm@talktalk.net. www.trebarberfarmholidays.com. Owner: Mr & Mrs Shipton. Off A3059 Newquay to St Columb road. Level site 3m from beach. Coarse fishing & golf nearby. Open May-Oct.

(6.5m). Trekenning Tourist Park, Trekenning, Newquay, Cornwall TR8 4JF. 01637 880462. holidays@trekenning.co.uk. www.trekenning.co.uk. Just off A39 0.5m S of St Columb. 10mins Newquay, 4m Watergate and Mawgan Porth beaches. Swimming pool. Licensed bar. Family bathrooms and free showers. Hot and cold washing up basins. Dogs by arrangement.

(3m). Treloy Touring Park, Newquay, Cornwall TR8 4JN. 01637 872063. treloy.tp@btconnect.com. www.treloy.co.uk. Owner: Mr RJ Paull. Just off A3059 Newquay road. Heated swimming pool, licensed bar, family room, entertainment. Free showers. Adventure playground. Coarse fishing nearby. Own golf course concessionary green fees. David Bellamy Silver Conservation Award. Open April-end Sept.

(1m). Trencreek Holiday Park, Trencreek, Newquay, Cornwall TR8 4NS. 01637 874210. trencreek@btconnect.com. www.trencreekholidaypark.co.uk. Owner: Mr J Hautot. A392 to Quintrell Downs, turn R Newquay, E to Porth – four turnings, turn L into Trevenson Road. Licensed bar with entertainment. Children's room. Playfield. Coarse fishing. AA listed 4 pennants. Beach, golf, horseriding, tennis, doctor, Newquay town centre all in 1m. Open Easter-mid Sept.

(2m). Trethiggey Touring Park, Quintrell Downs, Newquay, Cornwall TR8 4QR. 01637 877672. enquiries@trethiggey.co.uk. www.trethiggey.co.uk. Off A3058. Family site with excellent facilities and wonderful country views. Level pitches. Adventure playground. Caravan storage. Dog walk area. Fishing and local pub a few minutes walk. 15m from Eden project. David Bellamy Silver Conservation Award. Open March 1st-Jan 1st inc Xmas and New Year.

(4.5m). Trevarrian Holiday Park, Mawgan Porth, Newquay, Cornwall TR8 4AQ. 01637 860381. holidays@trevarrian.co.uk. Owner: Dave & Tish Phillips. N of Newquay via B276 Padstow road. Flat, well-drained site with fine views; about 1m from beach. Level grassy site. Heated pool. Bar. Tennis court. Pitch and putt. Sports field. Special offers. Open Easter-end Sept.

(1.5m). Trevella Caravan Park, Crantock, Newquay, Cornwall TR8 5EW. 01637 830308. holidays@trevella.co.uk. www.trevella.co.uk. Off A3075, on the road to Crantock. Heated swimming pool, crazy golf, adventure playground, café, own fishing lake. Ideally situated to visit the Eden Project. David Bellamy Gold Conservation Award. Open Easter-Oct 31.

(4m). Trevornick Holiday Park, Holywell Bay, Newquay, Cornwall TR8 5PW. 0845 3455531. bookings@trevornick.co.uk. www.trevornick.co.uk. Off A3075 Newquay to Perranporth road. Large level pitches most with electric hook-ups. Heated pool, 18-hole golf course and 18-hole pitch and putt course, and fishing ponds.

76 MOTOR CARAVAN & CAMPING PARKS 2009

choose a great holiday from cornwall's finest quality parks... **cornwall's finest parks**

independent, top star graded parks, offering fabulous facilities, superb locations and superior service - especially for families and couples

NEWQUAY'S FAMILY FUN HOLIDAY PARK

Cornwall's Holiday Park of the Year!
Family run for families and couples, with top quality touring, camping and luxury holiday homes.

Care free days ....
Enjoy the Oasis indoor and outdoor fun pools, free children's club and acres of beautiful landscaped park with Newquay's golden beaches only minutes away.

.... and laid back evenings
Choose high energy cabaret, a quiet drink or supper by the pools, a takeaway or an evening stroll, entertainment is included!

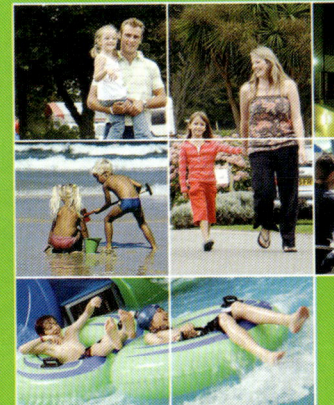

Hendra
HOLIDAY PARK

Click and explore
www.hendra-holidays.com
for your best holiday ever!
For a brochure call FREE on **0500 242 523**
or click enquiries@hendra-holidays.com

Hendra Holidays, NEWQUAY, Cornwall TR8 4NY. Telephone: 01637 875778

Looking for five star smiles this summer?

"Best in the West!"
Proud to be a family park with a friendly relaxed atmosphere, specialising in touring and camping for families and couples only. Also Eurotents for hire.

You want to surf, swim, relax, play golf and go fishing?
Here at Trevornick Holiday Park we have on-site coarse fishing, golf, fun park, stunning pool, free full entertainment programme, children's club and a beautiful beach within walking distance.

Recent Additions Stunning Club House, Restaurant and Takeaway.

Check out our website and book online at
www.trevornick.co.uk
Call for brochure (local rate)
0845 345 5531
bookings@trevornick.co.uk

trevornick
the five star holiday park
HOLYWELL BAY, NEWQUAY, CORNWALL TR8 5PW

cornwall's finest parks

choose a great holiday from cornwall's finest quality parks

NEWPERRAN Holiday Park

Peaceful family holiday park, renowed for its spacious, flat perimeter pitching, with breathtaking open countryside and sea views.

- New luxury toilet blocks
- free showers
- family rooms
- disabled facilities
- launderette
- cafe/takeaway
- premium all-service pitches
- shop/off licence
- entertainments
- TV/games room
- Cottage Inn
- aviary
- adventure playground
- toddlers play area
- outdoor heated swimming pool with sunbathing terraces

Call for a Brochure
Tel: 0845 1668407
Fax: 01872 571254
Rejerrah, Newquay, Cornwall TR8 5QJ

www.newperran.co.uk

Trevella Park
CARAVAN AND CAMPING PARK
CRANTOCK NEWQUAY CORNWALL TR8 5EW

One of Cornwall's Finest Parks

★ Set in beautiful parkland surroundings
★ Modern facilities including heated swimming & paddling pools
★ Ninth year David Bellamy Gold Award
★ Nature reserve and two fishing lakes
★ Luxury Rose Award caravans
★ Online booking available

01637 830308
www.trevella.co.uk
Email holidays@trevella.co.uk

TEHIDY HOLIDAY PARK

"..a green champion"
David Bellamy

Nestled in a wooded valley near broad, sandy beaches, hidden coves and the crystal clear ocean. Safe, quiet, natural surroundings. Central Cornwall. Famous attractions and breathtaking scenery.

COTTAGES, PARK HOMES CARAVANS & TOURERS

01209 216489
holiday@tehidy.co.uk
www.tehidy.co.uk

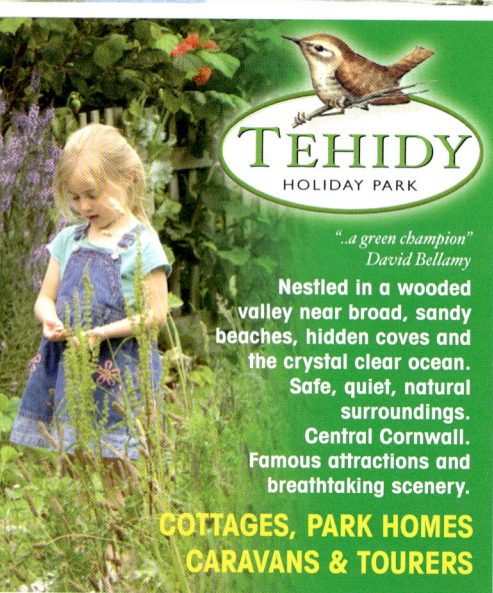

Holiday Park of the Year 2008 - Shires Magazine

Treloy Touring Park

The friendly park in beautiful Cornwall - for touring caravans, tents and motorhomes

- Heated swimming pool & paddling pool
- Licensed family bar
- Free entertainment
- Café / takeaway
- Adventure playground
- Disabled wc/shower
- Laundry / baby baths
- Free showers
- Shop
- Recreation Area
- Hook-ups
- TV & games room
- Indoor dishwashing
- Treloy golf course nearby
- Driving range nearby
- Coarse fishing nearby

Tel/Fax: 01637 872063
www.treloy.co.uk
Newquay, Cornwall TR8 4JN

Cornwall's finest parks

choose a great holiday from cornwall's finest quality parks...

Porth Beach
Tourist Park • Newquay

a superb family and couples park only 100m from the beach

Porth, Newquay,
Cornwall, TR7 3NH
t: 01637 876531
e: info@porthbeach.co.uk
www.porthbeach.co.uk

Trethiggey Touring Park

Set in beautiful countryside, our award winning park is on the edge of Newquay and close to some of the finest beaches in Europe.

Whether you are camping, touring or staying in one of our luxury holiday homes, you'll find Trethiggey is a great base for exploring all that Cornwall has to offer.

The park is well landscaped and many of the pitches are surrounded by trees and shrubs.

We have a bistro café, shop, off licence, games rooms, internet access and high standard amenities to make sure you enjoy your stay. We're proud that many families come back to us year after year.

Why not join them? For more information –
check out our website at **www.trethiggey.co.uk**

Trethiggey Touring Park, Quintrell Downs, Newquay
Phone: **01637 877672**
Email: enquiries@trethiggey.co.uk

www.cornwallfinestparks.co.uk

Full programme of free entertainment with disco and cabaret. Children's club. Great places to eat and Holywell Bay Fun Park and wonderful beach R next door. Also 68 euro tents. David Bellamy Gold Conservation Award. Open mid May-mid Sept.

(4m). Watergate Bay Tourist Park, Trequrrian, Watergate Bay, Newquay, Cornwall TR8 4AD. *01637 860387.* e.mail@watergatebaytouringpark.co.uk. www.watergatebaytouringpark.co.uk. Owner: Mr B & Mrs C M Jennings. 4m N of Newquay on B3276 coast road to Padstow at Watergate Bay. Heated pool, licensed bar, evening entertainment, cafétéria, adventure playground, sports field, dog exercise area, free minibus to beach and access to coastal footpath. David Bellamy Bronze Conservation Award. Open March 1-Oct 31.

(6m). White Acres Holiday Park, Whitecross, Newquay, Cornwall TR8 4LW. *01726 862100.* enquiries@parkdeanholidays.co.uk. www.parkdeanholidays.co.uk. Owner: Parkdean Holidays Plc. A392 to Newquay, travel over first roundabout. Park entrance on R. Heated indoor pool, Fun Factory and amusements. Bar, restaurant and live family entertainment. Fifteen fishing lakes. David Bellamy Gold Conservation Award. Open from 20/3/09 to 7/11/09.

PADSTOW

(4m). Carnevas Farm Holiday Park, St Merryn, Padstow, Cornwall PL28 8PN. *01841 520230.* carnevascampsite@aol.com. www.carnevasholidaypark.co.uk. Owner: The Brewer Family. From St Merryn take B3276 towards Porthcothan Bay (about 2m), turn R opposite Tredrea Inn. Beach 0.5m. Family run site. Showers, family bathrooms, laundry, children's play area, games room, club wifi, bar. Rose Award Park 2008. Beach 0.5m, fishing, golf course nearby. Open April 1-Oct 31.

(0.25m). Dennis Cove Camping Ltd, Dennis Lane, Padstow, Cornwall PL28 8DR. *01841 532349.* denniscove@freeuk.com. www.denniscove.co.uk. Owner: Simon Zeal. At S side of town. Approaching A389, turn R at Tesco supermarket. Quiet family site. Advance booking necessary. Adjacent to Camel estuary and Camel trail cycle track. 10mins walk to Padstow harbour. Supermarket, cafés and restaurants nearby. Open April-end Sept.

(3m). Harlyn Sands Caravan Park, Lighthouse Road, Trevose Head, St Merryn, Padstow, Cornwall PL28 8SQ. *01841 520720.* harlyn@freenet.co.uk. www.harlynsands.free-online.co.uk. Owner: Mr Richards. Licensed bar. Reception area. Play park. Holiday caravans for hire. 300yd from superb beaches. Families only. Shop, restaurant, childrens' games room. Open April-Oct.

(3m). Higher Harlyn Park, St Merryn, Padstow, Cornwall PL28 8SG. *01841 520022.* pbharlyn@aol.com. www.cornwall-online.co.uk. Owner: Mr P H, C A & M H Bennett. Off B3276. Licensed bar. Outdoor heated swimming pool. Children's play area. Launderette. Diner. St Merryn village is only a 5mins flat walk away. No under 25's permitted

WEST COUNTRY

unless with their families. No groups. Open Good Friday Easter-Oct.

(4m). Mother Ivey's Bay Caravan Park, Trevose Head, Padstow, Cornwall PL28 8SL. *01841 520990.* info@motheriveysbay.com. www.motheriveysbay.com. Owner: Patrick Langmaid. 4m from Padstow signed off the B3276 Padstow to Newquay coast road (Trevose Head). Outstanding coastal location. Private beach. Golf, fishing and watersports nearby. Perfect for traditional family holidays with beautiful landscape grounds and immaculate facilities. David Bellamy Gold Conservation Award. Open April 1-Oct 31.

(5m). Old MacDonald's Farm, Porthcothan Bay, Padstow, Cornwall PL28 8LW. *01841 540829.* enquiry@oldmacdonalds.co.uk. www.oldmacdonals.co.uk. Owner: John & Karen Nederpel. On B3276 coast road between Padstow and Newquay, look for signs. Quiet park ideal for families. Free entrance to farm park during stay. Showers. Play area. Pony rides on site. Sporting facilities nearby. Half mile from beach, ideal for surfing and swimming. Advance booking accepted. Colour brochure.

(1m). Padstow Touring Park, Padstow, Cornwall PL28 8LE. *01841 532061.* mail@padstowtouringpark.co.uk. www.padstowtouringpark.co.uk. Owner: Mr Barnes. On A389 1m S, SW of Padstow. If towing or large motorhonme, avoid A389 through St Issey, take B3274. Quiet family park. Easy access. Panoramic views with public footpath to Padstow. Storage available. Some en suite pitches. Colour brochure available. Motorvan pumpout. David Bellamy Silver Conservation Award.

(4m). Seagull Tourist Park, St Merryn, Padstow, Cornwall PL28 8PT. *01841 520117.* Owner: Mrs Wendy Pollard. B3274 via St Columb bypass to Padstow. Signs to St Merryn, past Maribu – Point Curlew. Seagull park 100yd turn L, follow road through farm. Quiet, family site with easy access. Coastal views and sandy beaches nearby. All year storage facilities. Booking essential. Quaint fishing port of Padstow with famous seafood restaurant. Golf, surfing, cliff walks, bike trails, endless activities and interests nearby. Open Easter-Oct.

(2m). Tregavone Touring Park, Tregavone Farm, St Merryn, Padstow, Cornwall PL28 8JZ. *01841 520148.* www.tregavonefarm.co.uk. Owner: Mr &

Mrs J Dennis. SW of Padstow on A389. 4-acres, 40 mixed pitches, quiet, family-run site with unspoilt country views. Kept to a high standard of cleanliness, ideal for sandy beaches and touring Cornwall. 2m to picturesque Padstow, fishing and golf course. AA 2 pennants. Open March-Oct.

(3.75m). Tregidier Caravan Park, Trevean Lane, St Merryn, Padstow, Cornwall PL28 8PR. *01841 520264.* Owner: Brian & Jean Parker. Situated 1.75m from Treyarnon Bay, which has one of the finest surfing beaches in the country and a natural swimming pool. Other beaches in easy distance. 11m from Newquay. Small friendly site with sea views.

(4m). Trethias Farm Caravan Site, Treyarnon Bay, St Merryn, Padstow, Cornwall PL28 8PL. *01841 520323.* Owner: David & Sandi Chandler. Off B3276 from St Merryn past Farmers Arms, 3rd turning R, park SP from here. Shop and beach nearby. Golf course 2m, PO, doctor 1.5m. David Bellamy Gold Conservation Award. Open April 1-Sept 30.

(4m). Trevean Caravan and Camping Park, St Merryn, Padstow, Cornwall PL28 8PR. *01841 520772.* trevean.info@virgin.net. Owner: Mrs J Raymont. From St Merryn village take the B3276 Newquay road for 1m, turn L for Rumford, site 0.25m on R. An ideal family site, situated near sandy surfing beaches. Coastal footpaths with spectacular scenery of the north Cornish coast. Open Easter-Oct 31.

(4m). Treyarnon Bay Caravan & Camping Park, Treyarnon Bay, Padstow, Cornwall PL28 8JR. *01841 520681.* www.treyarnonbay.co.uk. Owner: Old & Partridge. Off B3276 Newquay to Padstow road, turn off for Treyarnon Bay follow lane into beach car park. Holiday park adjacent. Ideal family site 200yd from beach overlooking Treyarnon Bay. Coastal walks and surfing. Site wardens: Warren & Lin Dentith. Dogs not allowed on touring site main Summer weeks. Open April 1-Sept 30.

PENRYN

(2.5m). Calamankey Farm, Longdowns, Penryn, Cornwall TR10 9DL. *01209 860314.* chrisdavidson@calamankey.com. www.calamankey.boltblue.net. Owner: Mr C C Davidson. On A394 opposite Gulf filling station in Longdowns village. Working farm campsite (45 pitches) in open

countryside with views to St Mawes and Roseland Peninsula beyond. Centrally situated (Truro 10m, Helston 9m, Redruth 9m, Falmouth 4m) ideal for exploring Lizard and Helford river. Many family attractions nearby (Flambards Theme Park, Seal Sanctuary, Poldark Mine). Local shop/PO and PH 20yd from drive entrance, large ASDA just 1.5m away. Golf, boating, fishing, tennis, scuba diving, riding, sailing & swimming all available nearby. Open Easter-Nov.

PENZANCE

(5m). Boleigh Farm, Lamorna Cove, Penzance, Cornwall TR19 6BN. *01736 810305.* Owner: Mr D Eddy. 5m from Penzance on B3315, pass the cove and take first R. Friendly, small farm site. On site of ancient battle and in easy reach of beaches and places of interest in the Land's end peninsula. Open Easter-Oct.

(1m). Bone Valley Caravan & Camping Park, Heamoor, Penzance, Cornwall TR20 8UJ. *01736 360313.* enquiries@bonevalleycandcpark.com. www.cornwalltouristboard.co.uk/bonevalley. Owner: Margaret & Bob Maddock. Follow A30 Penzance bypass, turn off at Heamoor roundabout, continue through Heamoor to caravan and camping sign on R. Continue down hill to next sign on L sp Bone Valley, site is 200yd on L. Quiet family run park. Sheltered, clean and friendly. Supervised 24hrs. Limited disabled facilities in holiday caravans. TV room, laundry facilities, kitchen with microwave and electric kettle, shower/toilet block. Baby changing facilities. Bottled gas calor/camping gaz, battery charging. AA 3 pennants. Cornwall Tourist Board quality member. All amenities in local village.

(7m). Camping & Caravanning Club Site – Sennen Cove, Higher Tregiffian Farm, St Buryan, Penzance, Cornwall TR19 6JB. *01736 871588.* www.campingandcaravanningclub.co.uk. Owner: Camping & Caravanning Club. Follow A30 towards Lands End. Turn R on to the A3306 St Just/Pendeen Road. Site 200yd on L. A 4-acre site with 75 pitches accepting all units. Sennen Cove Blue Flag beach in easy reach. Non-members welcome. Ball game area and playing field available. Situated on a farm in peaceful countryside in an area of spectacular coastline. Deals for families and backpackers. Open April-Oct.

(2.5m). Garris Farm, Gulval, Penzance, Cornwall TR20 8XD. *01736 365806.* Owner: Mr I A Phillips. Leave A30

80 MOTOR CARAVAN & CAMPING PARKS 2009

WEST COUNTRY

at Crowlas on B3309 to Ludgvan and Gastlegate. On road to Chysanster, ancient village. Quiet, farm site established 1920. Takeaway meals nearby. Shops, PO 2m, fishing, golf 7m. Open April-Oct.

(7m). Kelynack Caravan and Camping Park, St Just, Penzance, Cornwall TR19 7RE. *01736 787633.* francis&wendy@kelynackholidays.co.uk. www.kelynackholidays.co.uk. Owner: Mr & Mrs W Grose. On B3306 St Ives to Land's End. 1m S of St Just alongside stream in secluded valley. Close to the coast. 1m from shops, pubs, PO, doctors. 2m from golf course. David Bellamy Gold Conservation Award. Open April 1-31 Oct.

(6m). Kenneggy Cove Holiday Park, Higher Kenneggy, Rosudgeon, Penzance, Cornwall TR20 9AU. *01736 763453.* enquiries@kenneggycove.co.uk. www.kenneggycove.co.uk. Owner: Linda Garthwaite. Off A394 Helston to Penzance, 3m E of Marazion on the south coast. Set in an area of Outstanding Natural Beauty with the Rose Award for excellence, this immaculate park offers spacious lawned pitches in a beautiful garden setting with panoramic sea views. Freshly baked bread and home made meals to take away. 15mins walk to SW coast path and safe secluded beach. NB: this is a quiet site operating a policy of no noise after 10pm or before 8am. Open April 1-Oct 31.

(7m). Levant House, Levant Road, Pendeen, Penzance, Cornwall TR19 7SX. *01736 788795.* Owner: Mr J H A Boyns. On B3306 3m N of St Just-in-Penwith. Fishing, golf, cliff climbing nearby. Shop, PO, doctors 4mins drive. Coastal path 5-7mins walk. Open April 1-Oct 31.

(6m). Lower Treave Caravan Park, Crows-an-Wra, St Buryan, Penzance, Cornwall TR19 6HZ. *01736 810559.* camping@lowertreave.co.uk. www.lowertreave.co.uk. Owner: Mr & Mrs N A Bliss. 6m W of Penzance on A30. Quiet, family site at the heart of the Land's End peninsula. Panoramic rural views to the sea. Sheltered grass terraces. Internet and free wi-fi. Sennen Blue Flag beach 2.5m. David Bellamy Gold Conservation Award. Open April-Oct.

River Valley Country Park, Relubbus, Penzance, Cornwall TR20 9ER. *01736 763398.* rivervalley@surfbay.dircon.co.uk. www.rivervalley.co.uk. Owner: Mr & Mrs Milsom. From A30 at St Michaels Mount roundabout, take A394 Helston. At the next roundabout turn L on to B3280 SP Relubbus. Travel for about 3m, then just over a small bridge, River Valley Country Park is on L. Quiet, rural, family park on banks of clear shallow stream. Short or long stays welcome. Large level pitches. Open March-Jan (statics), March-Jan (touring).

(4.5m). Roseland's Caravan & Camping Park, Dowran, St Just, Penzance, Cornwall TR19 7RS. *01736 788571.* camping@roseland84freeserve.co.uk. www.roselands.co.uk. Owner: Peter & Jane Hall. From Penzance on A3071 to St Just – 6m, SP on R 800yd. Play area. Breakfast and evening meals served in our new conservatory. Seaviews, level pitches. Ideal base for walking, water activities and local attractions including golf course. Eden project 75mins drive, Maritime Museum 30mins drive. Open Jan 1-Oct 31.

(8m). Seaview Holiday Park, Sennen, Penzance, Cornwall TR19 7AD. *01736 871266.* seaview.landsend@btopenworld.com. www.seaview.org.uk. Owner: Mrs Brownbridge. On A30 Penzance to Lands End. Family park. Outdoor swimming pool, café and BBQ area on site. Bike hire. Crazy golf, extended play area, playtrain, table tennis. Cinema in Penzance. 2-lane 10 pin bowling alley, space maze, bar, restaurant, play zone. Minack open air threatre. Golf 3m. Tennis court on site, trampolines, pizza take-away. Dogs welcome by agreement only.

Threeways Caravan Club Site, St Hilary, Goldsithney, Penzance, Cornwall TR20 9DU. *01736 710723.* www.caravanclub.co.uk. Owner: The Caravan Club. See website for directions. 2m from Marazion. Caravan Club members only. No tents. Attractive site in parkland setting with beautiful views. Quiet and peaceful off peak. Levelling blocks required, steel awning pegs required. Gas. No sanitation. Dog walk. MV service point. Fishing, golf and watersports nearby. Ideal for families. NCN cycle route in 5m. Open March-Oct.

(5m). Tower Park Caravans & Camping, St Buryan, Penzance, Cornwall TR19 6BZ. *01736 810286.* enquiries@towerparkcamping.co.uk. www.towerparkcamping.co.uk. Owner: Jerry & Jude Gasson. From A30 Lands End road turn L on B3283 SP St Buryan. 300yd from village on St Just road. Peaceful, family run campsite with level grass and sheltering hedges. Short walk to village pub and shop. Near unspoilt beaches and coves, ideal for Minack Theatre. Open March-Nov.

(6m). Trevair Caravan Park, South Treveneague, St Hilary, Penzance, Cornwall TR20 9BY. *01736 740647.* philandval@trevair.freeserve.co.uk. www.trevairtouringpark.co.uk. Owner: Mr & Mrs Luxford. 2m NE Marazion B3280. Set in 3 secluded acres surrounded by fields and woodland. A well maintained friendly family site. Clean facilities. Caravans to let. AA 3 pennants. Open Easter-Oct 31.

(7m). Trevedra Farm Caravan Club Site, Sennen, Lands End, Penzance, Cornwall TR19 7BE. *01736 871835.* trevedra@btconnect.com. www.sennen-cove.com/trevedra. Owner: Mr & Mrs J M Nicholas. Turn R off A30 just after B3306 junction. 2.5m from Lands End. CARAVAN CLUB AFFILIATED SITE. AA 3 pennants. Non members and tent campers welcome. Certain areas for members only. Takeaway meals available in peak season only. Public telephone. Calor and Camping Gaz. Shower block. Laudrette. Footpath to Gwenver Beach and coastal path. Brochure available (with SAE). Open April-Oct 31.

(6m). Treverven Touring Caravan & Camping Park, St Buryan, Penzance, Cornwall TR19 6DL. *01736 810200.* skewjack@aol.com. www.chycor.co.uk/camping. Owner: Mrs H M Gwennap. On B3315 coastal road. Quiet, farm site with excellent sea views. Easy access to coves and beaches. Well situated for touring W Cornwall. Shaver points. Hair dryer units. Deep freeze. Children's play area, lovely walks. AA 3 pennant site. Rock fishing, course fishing nearby, golf course about 6m away. Open Easter-Oct 31.

(5m). Wayfarers Caravan & Camping Park, Relubbus Lane, St Hilary, Penzance, Cornwall TR20 9EF. *01736 763326.* elaine@wayfarerspark.co.uk. www.wayfarerspark.co.uk. Owner: Steve & Elaine Holding. From Penzance A30 roundabout, L on to A394. First roundabout L on to B3280 proceed for 1.5m. Wayfarers on L. 2m from Marazion. Adult only park. Two village pubs in 1m. Tranquil award winning park beautifully landscaped, marked, level pitches. Excellent facilities. Graded excellent by English Tourist Council. Golf, horse riding. Coastal walks, water sports. Fishing 1m. Open April-Oct.

www.motorcaravanmagazine.co.uk

WEST COUNTRY

PERRANPORTH

(2.5m). Perran Springs Holiday Park, Goonhavern, Perranporth, Cornwall TR4 9QG. *01872 540568.* info@perransprings.co.uk. www.perransprings.co.uk. Owner: Natalie Lord, Michael Thomas, Andrew Thomas. Leave A30 turn R on to the B3285 'Perranporth'. Follow brown tourism signs marked 'Perran Springs' for 1.5m. Entrance to park on R. Award winning, friendly, quiet family park, 21 acres 120 units in total (for tourers or tents): Private stocked coarse fishing lakes, Nature Trail and Pond, licensed shop, caravan holiday homes to hire and buy, eurotents, spacious level pitches, hook-ups, play area, launderette, panoramic countryside views. Open Whitsun-Sept.

(1m). Perran-Sands Holiday Park, Perranporth, Cornwall TR6 0AQ. *01872 573742.* www.perransands-park.co.uk. Owner: Bourne Leisure Ltd. From Exeter take A30 through Devon and Cornwall. 1m beyond Wind Farm roundabout (Mitchell) turn R on to B3285 towards Perranporth. Perran Sands is on the R before going down hill into Perranporth. Heated indoor pool, daytime and evening entertainment for all the family. All-weather multi sports court. Adventure playground. Near beach, golf course, Eden Project. David Bellamy Gold Conservation Award. Open March-Oct, Apr-Oct (holidaymakers).

POLZEATH

Tristram Caravan & Camping Park, Polzeath, Cornwall PL27 6UG. *01208 862215.* info@tristramcampsite.co.uk. www.polzeathcamping.co.uk. Owner: Mr R R Harris. 7m N of Wadebridge via B3314 road signs to Polzeath. On clifftop overlooking beach with own private access. Site is fenced off for safety. Booking advisable in school holidays. Fishing, surfing, boating, skiing, golf, potholing, all nearby. AA 3 pennants. Open Easter-Oct.

PORTREATH

(1.5m). Tehidy Holiday Park, Harris Mill, Illogan, Portreath, Cornwall TR16 4JQ. *01209 216489.* holiday@tehidy.co.uk. www.tehidy.co.uk. Owner: Mr & Mrs J & G Williams. Take B3300 out of Redruth, L at fork, L again at Cornish Arms pub. Playground. Payphone. Off licence. Razor points. Gas sales. Ideal to explore coastlines. Dogs welcome by prior agreement. Open April-Oct.

REDRUTH

(2m). Cambrose Touring Park, Portreath Road, Redruth, Cornwall TR16 4HT. *01209 890747.* cambrosetouringpark@supanet.com. www.cambrosetouringpark.co.uk. Owner: Mr & Mrs R G Fitton. Off B3303 Redruth to Portreath. Pass Treasure Park, first R, SP Porthtowan 100yd on L. Small, family run park. Heated outdoor pool from May to Sept. Adventure playground, mini football pitch away from camping area. Wet weather room. Shops, doctor, golf in 2m. Open April-Oct.

(2m). Lanyon Holiday Park, Loscombe Lane, Four Lanes, Redruth, Cornwall TR16 6LP. *01209 313474.* info@lanyonholidaypark.co.uk. www.lanyonholidaypark.co.uk. Owner: Mr & Mrs J Rielly. On B3297 Redruth to Helston road in the confines of Four Lanes village. Lovely family fun park set in beautiful Cornish countryside looking out towards the sea. Heated covered pool, games room, bar and restaurant, play park, launderette, 3 modern toilet and shower blocks, pets welcome – large dog walking paddock. Village 10mins walk with pubs, shops and bus stop. In 2m fishing, watersports, horseriding, walking, cycling path. Cinema, market indoor/outdoor, leisure centre 3m. Beach 5m. Sorry no young groups. Open March-Oct 31.

(2m). St Day Holiday Park, St Day, Redruth, Cornwall TR16 5LE. *01209 820459.* holidays@stday.co.uk. www.stday.co.uk. Owner: Linda & Geoffrey Stewart. E of Redruth on B3298, site SP. Small, quiet site central for south Cornwall. Open close-mown meadow screened by hedging. Four chalets for hire. Open April 1-Oct 31.

SALTASH

■ (4m). Dolbeare Caravan and Camping Park, St Ive Road, Landrake, Saltash, Cornwall PL12 5AF. *01752 851332.* reception@dolbeare.co.uk. www.dolbeare.co.uk. Owner: Chris & Ian Cousens. 4m W of Saltash via A38 to Landrake. Then R just after footbridge. We are 1m on R. We are located in beautiful countryside but just 1m from A38. Flat and gently sloping. Hardstanding with electric. Plymouth, Looe, Eden project in 20mins. Children's play area. Dog walk.

(3.5m). Notter Bridge Park, Notter Bridge, Saltash, Cornwall PL12 4RW. *01752 842318.* info@notterbridge.co.uk. www.notterbridge.co.uk. Owner: Ian & Francesca James. On A38. 3.5m W of Tamar Bridge, Plymouth. Sheltered, level site in picturesque, wooded valley with river frontage. Pub/food opposite, good centre Plymouth/Cornwall/Devon. Fishing. Golf, sailing, supermarket, pool in 3m. Open March 1-Dec 31.

ST AGNES

(2m). Beacon Cottage Farm Touring Park, Beacon Drive, St Agnes, Cornwall TR5 0NU. *01872 552347.* beaconcottagefarm@lineone.net. www.beaconcottagefarmholidays.co.uk. Owner: Mr & Mrs J Sawle. Leave A30 at roundabout and follow B3277 to St Agnes at mini-roundabout turn L towards Chapel Porth and follow signs to park. Site is SP. Small secluded farm. 5mins walk to sandy beach. Spectacular coastal scenery. Ideal for touring Cornwall. Razor points. Telephone. Free showers and hot water. Laundry and dishwashing facilities. Gas available. Play area. Dog exercise field. Open April 1-Oct 1.

(1m). Presingoll Farm, St Agnes, Cornwall TR5 0PB. *01872 552333.* pam@presingollfarm.fsbusiness.co.uk. www.presingollfarm.fsbusiness.co.uk. Owner: Mrs P Williams. Off A30. At Chyverton Cross roundabout take B3277 for St Agnes. Park about 3m on R. The site is 2m from the north coast surfing beaches. The fully serviced village is only a walking distance of about 0.75m. Many leisure facilities are in 2-3m. Dairy produce available. AA 3 pennant. Open April 1/Easter-Oct 31.

(0.75m). St Agnes Beacon Caravan Club Site, Beacon Drive, St Agnes, Cornwall TR5 0NU. *01872 552543.* www.caravanclub.co.uk. Owner: The Caravan Club. See website for directions. Caravan Club members only. No tents. Panoramic views of Cornish coastline from this gently sloping site. Quiet and peaceful off peak. Conveniently located for some of the best beaches in Cornwall, good area for walking. Dog walk on site. Tradesman calls. Advance booking advised mid- June to Aug. No sanitation. Gas and gaz, laundry. Recycling facilities. MV service point. Bathing off this coastline can be dangerous, please note local notices. Open March-Oct.

ST AUSTELL

(3m). Carlyon Bay Camping & Caravan Park (Bethesda), Bethesda, Carlyon Bay, St Austell, Cornwall PL25 3RE. *01726 812735.* holidays@carlyonbay.net. www.carlyonbay.net. Owner: Mr J & Mrs S Taylor. SP off the A3082. Turn off A390 at Britannia Inn roundabout then first R to

82 MOTOR CARAVAN & CAMPING PARKS 2009

WEST COUNTRY

Cypress Avenue. Path to beach. 1.5m from the Eden Project. Open from 1/4/08 to 30/9/08.

Par Sands Holiday Park, Par Beach, St Austell, Cornwall PL24 2AS. 01726 812868. holidays@parsands.co.uk. www.parsands.co.uk. Owner: Mr S Dancey. 0.5m E of Par off A3082. Level site by large safe sandy beach. Crazy golf and children's playground. Indoor heated pool with aquaslide. Tennis. Bowls. Pets welcome. Takeaway meals, café/restaurant available nearby. Open Good Friday or April 1-Oct 31.

(1.5m). River Valley Holiday Park, London Apprentice, St Austell, Cornwall PL26 7AP. 01726 73533. mail@cornwall-holidays.co.uk. www.cornwall-holidays.co.uk. Owner: Mr & Mrs John Clemo. Just off B3273, 1.5m from St Austell in the small hamlet of London Apprentice. A quiet family park set in the Pentewan Valley with an off road cycle trail to the beach. Open March-Oct.

(10m). Sea View International Caravan Park, Boswinger, Gorran, St Austell, Cornwall PL26 6LL. 01726 843425. holidays@seaviewinternational.com. www.seaviewinternational.com. Owner: Mr & Mrs C J Royden. From St Austell, take B3273, signed Mevagissey. Prior to village, turn R following brown signs (avoids narrow streets). 3.5m from Mevagissey. Large, level pitches for tourers and tents overlooking bay with award winning beaches. Close to the Eden Project & Heligan. Views worth writing home about! Heated pools. All facilities centrally heated. Extensive play area. Three times 'Best in Britain' winners. Award-winning caravans. Write or phone for free brochure. Offers outside peak season. Open March-Oct.

(2m). Sun Valley Holiday Park, Pentewan Road, St Austell, Cornwall PL26 6DJ. 01726 843266. reception@sunvalleyholidays.co.uk. www.sunvalleyholidays.co.uk. Owner: Mr C Mynard. From St Austell take B3273 to Mevagissey. Park 2.5m on R. Ideal touring centre in wooded valley 1m from the sea. Licensed club and indoor swimming pool. Open Easter-Oct 31.

(7m). Tregarton Park, Gorran, Nr Mevagissey, St Austell, Cornwall PL26 6NF. 01726 843666. reception@tregarton.co.uk. www.tregarton.co.uk. Owner: The Hicks Family. Travel S on B3273. Turn R at top of Pentewan Hill, 3m on R. Large hedged pitches, either grass or hardstanding, in a beautiful sheltered park with glimpses of the sea through the valley. On site – shop, take-away, large heated swimming pool. 2mins from fabulous beaches and the 'Lost Gardens of Heligan', 20mins from the 'Eden Project'. Sports facilities nearby including golf and fishing. Open April 1-Oct 31.

(10m). Trelispen Caravan & Camping Park, Gorran Haven, St Austell, Cornwall PL26 6NT. 01726 843501. trelispen@care4free.net. www.trelispen.co.uk. Owner: Dr James Whetter. Take B3273 from St Austell, for Mevagissey then road for Gorran Haven. Level & sheltered park, near cliffs and sea with private nature reserve. Hot showers and hot water to basins. Shop, café/restaurant, bottled gas supply, dairy produce all available nearby. Open Easter or April 1-Oct 31.

(9m). Treveor Farm Caravan & Camping Park, Gorran, St Austell, Cornwall PL26 6LW. 01726 842387. info@treveorfarm.co.uk. www.treveorfarm.co.uk. Owner: Mrs M Parkhouse. Take B3273 from St Austell having passed Pentewan beach, go up hill and turn R to Gorran. After about 4m turn R at sign boards. Coarse fishing. Village shop, PO, pub, coastal path and beaches in 1m. Lost Gardens of Heligan – 3m, Mevagissey – 5m, Railway Station – 10m, Eden project is 12m. Open April-Oct.

(1.5m). Trewhiddle Holiday Estate, Pentewan Road, St Austell, Cornwall PL26 7AD. 01726 879420. holidays@trewhiddle.com. www.trewhiddle.co.uk. Owner: Mr W McIntosh. Take the B3273 Mevagissey road from St Austell. Estate is 0.75m on R. Gentle sloping park extending to 16.5acres. Excellent facilities. Ideally situated for touring Cornwall. 15mins from Eden Project. Open March 1-Jan 31.

ST COLUMB

(1m). Camping & Caravanning Club Site – Trewan Hall, St Columb, Cornwall TR9 6DB. 01637 880261. www.campingandcaravanningclub.co.uk. Owner: Camping & Caravanning Club. From intersection A3059 and A39 go N on A39 for 1.5m, turn L, site 0.5m on L. Camping and Caravanning Club members only. All units accepted. Showers, hot snacks available, telephone, chemical toilet disposal points, swimming pool. The site is set in the midst of 36 acres of woodland. The Eden project is just 13m away. David Bellamy Gold Conservation Award. Open May-Sept.

ST IVES

(0.5m). Ayr Holiday Park, Higher Ayr, St Ives, Cornwall TR26 1EJ. 01736 795855. recept@ayrholidaypark.co.uk. www.ayrholidaypark.co.uk. Owner: Mr R D Baragwanath. 0.5m from town centre turn off B3306 into Bullans Lane or Carnellis Road and then to Ayr Terrace. Dogs allowed with permission.

(2.5m). Balnoon Camping Site, Halsetown, St Ives, Cornwall TR26 3JA. 01736 795431. nat@balnoon.fsnet.co.uk. Owner: Mrs J M Long. From A30 take A3074 SP St Ives, L at second mini-roundabout. SP Tate St Ives (B3311) and second R SP (Balnoon) about 3m from A30. Sheltered site 2m from sea. Facilities nearby, public house, horse riding, golf course, fishing, coastal footpath. AA 2 pennants. Open Easter-Oct 31.

(2m). Little Trevarrack Touring Park, Laity Lane, Carbis Bay, St Ives, Cornwall TR26 3HW. 01736 797580. littletrevarrack@hotmail.com. www.littletrevarrack.co.uk. Owner: Neil Osborne. From A30 take A3074 to St Ives. SP L opposite turning for Carbis Bay Beach. Straight across at next crossroads. About 200yd on R. A well maintained and spacious landscaped park, ideal for family holidays with a range of superb modern facilities. Some pitches with sea views. About 1m from the stunning Carbis Bay beach and the coastal footpath into St Ives. High season bus service from the site into St Ives. Open Whitsun-Oct.

(2.5m). Penderleath Caravan & Camping Park, Towednack, St Ives, Cornwall TR26 3AF. 01736 798403. holidays@penderleath.co.uk. www.penderleath.co.uk. Owner: Miss M Harris & Mr C Maskell. Off B3311 from St Ives take 1st R turn after Halsetown. After 0.25m take L fork, second L. Set in classified area of outstanding natural beauty with unrivalled views. Peaceful, family run and supervised park. Quiet 'Olde Worlde' licensed bar on site. 2m to St Ives local bus service, shop. Open Easter-Oct.

(2m). Polmanter Tourist Park, Halsetown, St Ives, Cornwall TR26 3LX. 01736 795640. reception@polmanter.com. www.polmanter.com. Owner: Mr P J

WEST COUNTRY

Osborne. Off B3311, take HR route off the A30 to St Ives. Family park with lovely sea views, in walking distance of St Ives and beaches. Swimming pool. Tennis courts. Family lounge. Games room. Lounge bar. TV. Golf & fishing 2m. Open from 1/4/09 to 31/10/09.

(4.5m). Sunny Meadow Holiday Park, Lelant Downs, Hayle, St Ives, Cornwall TR27 6LL. 01736 752243. Owner: Mr & Mrs Renfree. Off A30 by-pass, sign for St Ives (B3311). Small family run site, quiet and ideally placed for touring Cornwall. Close to premier tourist attraction. Coach route.

ST JUST

(0.5m). Trevaylor Caravan and Camping Park, Botallack, St Just, Cornwall TR19 7PU. 01736 787016. bookings@trevaylor.com. www.trevaylor.com. Owner: Mr & Mrs W Sanderson. 0.5m from St Just on B3306 to St Ives. Graded AA 3 pennants. Trevaylor is in an Area of Outstanding Natural Beauty and only 500yd from the coastal path and the sea. The golf course is 3m away and horseriding is 200yd away from the site. The nearest swimming pool is at the golf course and the bus stops at the entrance to the site; regular service to Penzance, St Ives and Lands End. Open April-Nov.

TINTAGEL

(0.75m). Bossiney Farm Caravan Site, Bossiney Farm, Tintagel, Cornwall PL34 0AY. 01840 770481. www.bossineyfarm.co.uk. On B3263. From Tintagel to Boscastle brown signed. Near cliffs and beach. Sheltered and flat walking and touring centre. Pets welcome. Free colour brochure. Children allowed. Open April-Oct.

The Headland Caravan & Camping Site, Atlantic Road, Tintagel, Cornwall PL34 0DE. 01840 770239. headland.caravanp@btconnect.com. www.headlandcaravanpark.co.uk. Owner: Mr & Mrs M H Francis. From B3263 through village to site. 3mins walk to centre of Tintagel. 2mins walk from coastal paths and 15mins walk to swimming beach. Essential needs sold on site. Calor Gas and Camping Gaz supplies. Public telephone. Open Easter-Oct.

YOUR TOP 101 SITES 2009 (1.5m). Trewethett Farm Caravan Club Site, Trethevy, Tintagel, Cornwall PL34 0BQ. 01840 770222. www.caravanclub.co.uk. Owner: The Caravan Club. See website for

directions. The views from here are breathtaking as the site boasts a cliff top setting, overlooking Bossiney Cove with its safe sandy beach. Fishing, golf and NCN route nearby, good area for walking. Facilities for disabled. Non-members and tent campers admitted. Open March-Oct.

TORPOINT

(6m). Whitsand Bay Holiday Park Ltd, Millbrook, Torpoint, Cornwall PL10 1JZ. 01752 822597. enquiries@whitsandbaylodgepark.co.uk. www.whitsandbaylodgepark.co.uk. Owner: Mr R Wintle. Off B3247. 8m from Plymouth with panoramic views. South-east Cornwall's award winning park. Full range of facilities including heated pool. Club with entertainment. Free colour brochure. Open March 1-Dec 31.

TRURO

(10m). Camping & Caravanning Club Site – Veryan, Tretheake Manor, Veryan, Truro, Cornwall TR2 5PP. 01872 501658. www.campingandcaravanningclub.co.uk. Owner: The Camping & Caravanning Club. 2m S of Tregony on A3078 turn L for Veryan after petrol station and follow international signs. Site on L. Set in 9 acres with on site facilities include: launderette, coarse fishing, playground, games room, TV room, beach and coastal path 1.5m. Holiday lodge to let on site. Close by is the Eden Project. The cornish coast near the site is dotted with unspoilt beaches and tiny fishing villages. A little paradise on the Roseland Peninsula. All units accepted. Non-members welcome. Deals for families and backpackers. Open March-Oct.

YOUR TOP 101 SITES 2009 (2.5m). Carnon Downs Caravan & Camping Park, Carnon Downs, Truro, Cornwall TR3 6JJ. 01872 862283. info@carnon-downs-caravanpark.co.uk. www.carnon-downs-caravanpark.co.uk. Owner: Markrun Ltd. Between Truro and Falmouth off A39 at Carnon Downs roundabout. Easy access. Restaurant nearby. David Bellamy Gold Conservation Award.

(6m). Chacewater Park, Cox Hill, Chacewater, Truro, Cornwall TR4 8LY. 01209 820762. chacewaterpark@aol.com. www.chacewaterpark.co.uk. Owner: R A & D Peterken. From A30 take A3047 to Scorrier, L at Crossroads Hotel take B3298 1.25m, L to Chacewater 0.75m, SP to park. Flat, grassy, quiet caravan park central for touring W Cornwall. Exclusively for adults

over 30. Dogs allowed on touring pitches by prior agreement only. Open from 2/5/09 to 4/10/09.

(5m). Chiverton Caravan & Touring Park, Blackwater, Truro, Cornwall TR4 8HS. 01872 560667. chivertonpark@btopenworld.com. www.chivertonpark.co.uk. Owner: Mr & Mrs Ford-Dunn. From A30 Chiverton roundabout take B3277 to St Agnes, 0.5m turn L. Park 200yd on L. Limited facilities for the disabled. Dogs allowed. Quiet family run park. Shop, laundry room, children's Play area. PO and shop in Blackwater, doctors in St Agnes/Chacewater. Swimming, surfing, golf, fishing, horse riding in 5m. Sauna, steam room, gym. Fully heated toilet and shower block. Open March 1-Oct 30.

(6m). Cosawes Park Ltd, The Office, Perran-ar-Worthal, Truro, Cornwall TR3 7QS. 01872 863724. info@cosawes.com. www.cosawestouringandcamping.co.uk. Owner: AR Fraser & IK Fraser. Off A39 midway between Truro and Falmouth. 100 acres wooded valley between Truro and Falmouth. Safe, peaceful, friendly. WiFi, hardstandings. GS.

(3m). Liskey Holiday Park, Greenbottom, Chacelwater, Truro, Cornwall TR4 8QN. 01872 560274. info@liskey.co.uk. www.liskey.co.uk. Owner: Jason Masters. Off A390 between Chacewater and Threemilestone. Situated 3m W of Truro, Liskey is ideally situated whether you want to explore the North, South, East or West. Shops, golf courses, fishing lakes are only 3m away. Special offers are available for the over 50's. Wireless internet access on whole park.

(17m). Merrose Farm Caravan Club Site, Portscatho, Truro, Cornwall TR2 5EL. 01872 580380. www.caravanclub.co.uk. Owner: The Caravan Club. See website for directions. Caravan Club members only. No tents. Immaculate, well-landscaped parkland on Roseland Peninsula with good views of surrounding countryside. Some hardstandings, toilet block, privacy cubicles, laundry facilities, baby and toddler washroom. Gas, boules pitch, quiet and peaceful off peak. Dog walk on site. Advance booking essential June to Aug. MV service point. Playfield and equipment. Watersports. Ideal for families. Beach and NCN cycle route in 5m. Open March-Nov.

(9m). Penrose Farm Touring Park, Goonhavern, Truro, Cornwall TR4 9QF. 01872 573185. www.penrosefarmtouringpark.com. Owner:

84 MOTOR CARAVAN & CAMPING PARKS 2009

WEST COUNTRY

Welch, Salisbury & Moore Family. From the A30 turn R on to the B3285 Perranporth. Site 1.5m on L. 2.5m from Perranporth beach. Quiet, level, sheltered park with adventure playground. Award winning private 'Superloos'. No club or bar. Families and couples only. Toilets and showers brand new 2008. 2m from Perranporth. Open April 1-Oct 31.

(8m). Porthtowan Tourist Park, Mile Hill, Porthtowan, Truro, Cornwall TR4 8TY. *01209 890256.* admin@porthtowan touristpark.co.uk. www. porthtowantouristpark.co.uk. Owner: Mr & Mrs Jonas. Drive along A30 until you reach the exit 'Redruth to Porthtowan'. Cross the A30, and continue through North Country to 'T' junction, turn R up the hill. About 0.5m park entrance on L. Level, grassy family site. 1m from blue flag beach. Ideal for touring Cornwall as close to Coastal Path and cycle trail. David Bellamy Silver Conservation Award. Open Easter-Sept.

Rose Hill Touring Park, Rosehill, Porthtowan, Truro, Cornwall TR4 8AR. *01209 890802.* reception@rosehillcampin g.co.uk. www.rosehillcamping.co.uk. Owner: Mr & Mrs J E Barrow. From A30 follow B3277 SP Porthtowan, brown tourism signs to Rosehill. 50yd past Beach Road. 3m from Redruth. Sheltered woodland site 4mins level walk to beach, pubs, restaurants. Fresh crusty bread, croissants baked daily on the premises. 5 star immaculate toilet/shower block. Fully equiped launderette. Open April-Oct.

(2.5m). Silverbow Park, Goonhaven, Truro, Cornwall TR4 9NY. *01872 572347.* Owner: Mr & Mrs G A Taylor. 0.5m S Goonhavern Village. On A3075 Newquay to Redruth. No noisy clubs or bars. All weather & grass tennis & badminton courts, short mat bowls. Heated swimming pool. Playground. Open May-Oct 14.

(2m). Summer Valley Touring Park, Shortlanesend, Truro, Cornwall TR4 9DW. *01872 277878.* res@summervalley. co.uk. www.summervalley.co.uk. Owner: Mr & Mrs C R Simpkins. Site SP on B3284 2.5m from Truro, 1.5m from A30. Quiet, family run site with excellent facilities. Site bordered by mature trees but allowing rural views. Close to County Town and superb beaches. David Bellamy Silver Conservation Award. Open April 1-Oct 31.

Treamble Valley Caravan Club Site, Rose, Truro, Cornwall TR4 9PR. *01872 573675.* www.caravanclub.co.uk. Owner: The Caravan Club. See website for directions. 1.5m from Perranporth. Caravan Club members only. No tents. MV service point. Fishing, golf and watersports nearby. Facilities for walking disabled. Ideal for families. Some hardstanding, toilet block, privacy cubicles, laundry, gas and gaz, dog walk on site, storage pitches, quiet and peaceful off peak, good area for walking, beach and NCN cycle route in 5m. Open March-Nov.

(14m). Treloan Coastal Farm Holidays, Treloan Lane, Portscatho, Truro, Cornwall TR2 5EF. *01872 580899.* holidays@treloan.freeserve.co.uk. www. coastalfarmholidays.com. Owner: Mr V Barry. A30 take A3076 to Truro then A390 to St Austell. Take A3078 to St Mawes. At Trewithian turn to Gerrans/Portscatho until church where Treloan Lane runs alongside the 'Royal Standard' pub. A small traditional 1930's working farm overlooking a spectacular panorama of the south coast, Treloan provides classic touring facilities in peaceful surroundings. Three secluded coves, the coastal footpath and villages with shops all in few minutes walk. Also self catering new static vans. Working shire horses, Jersey cows, pigs and poultry. Mooring facilities, season pitches, super pitches, winter storage.

(6m). Trethem Mill Touring Park, St Just-in-Roseland, St Mawes, Truro, Cornwall TR2 5JF. *01872 580504.* reception@trethem.com. www.trethem.com. Owner: D & I Akeroyd. Follow brown signs on A3078 for Trethem Mill. 3m N pf St Mawes. Small, clean, family park. Ideal location for beaches, watersports, country walks and exploring Cornwall. Still the only 5 star park on the Roseland Peninsula. Open April 1-mid Oct.

(5m). Trevarth Holiday Park, Blackwater, Truro, Cornwall TR4 8HR. *01872 560266.* trevarth@lineone.net. www.trevarth.co.uk. Owner: Mr John Goldring. Leave A30 at Chiverton roundabout, on to B3277 SP St Agnes. At next roundabout, take road signed Blackwater, site on R in 200yd. A small, family- run park in an excellent location for N and S coast resorts. PO 0.5m, doctor, fishing 2.5m. Golf, cinema, leisure centre 5m. Open April-Oct.

WADEBRIDGE

■ **(0.5m). Little Bodieve Holiday Park, Bodieve Road, Wadebridge, Cornwall PL27 6EG.** *01208 812323.* be rry@littlebodieveholidaypark.fsnet.co.uk. www.littlebodieve.co.uk. Owner: Karen & Christopher Berry, Barbara Hills. 1m N of Wadebridge.Take A39 at Camelford turn N at second roundabout in Wadebridge on B3314. Site is SP 600yd R. 4m from beach. Heated outdoor swimming pool, waterslide. Club house with live entertainment in high season. Bar meals.

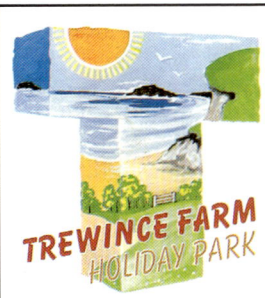

Rose Award Park overlooking a wooded valley only 4 miles from picturesque Padstow, The Camel Trail and many superb sandy beaches.
Luxury 6 berth Caravans, fully equipped to a high standard.
Excellent amenities on site: Heated Outdoor Pool, Children's Play Area, Games Room, Crazy Golf, also fishing lake & woodland walk, Launderette, Shop.
Superb facilities for Tents and Tourers, inc luxury Hook-ups, Showers/Toilets.

TREWINCE FARM HOLIDAY PARK
St. Issey, Wadebridge
Cornwall PL27 7RL

BOOKING LINE 01208 812830
Fax: 01208 812835
www.trewincefarm-holidaypark.co.uk

WEST COUNTRY

Nearest to Camel Trail. 25mins car drive to Eden project. Club rallies welcome. Luxury caravans for hire or sale. Open April-Oct.

(4m). Music Water Touring Park, Rumford, Wadebridge, Cornwall PL27 7SJ. *01841 540257.* www.caravancampingsites.co.uk. Owner: The Mabbley Family & Vercoe Family. 4m S of Padstow from A39 Wadebridge to St Columb road. Turn N on B3274 for 2m the W for 500yd to site. Fees on application. Pets corner inc donkeys. Beautiful views. 3m from sea, sailing, golf. Dogs allowed, swimming pool, games room, bar on site. Fishing, shops, riding available all nearby. Open April 1-Oct 31.

(1m). South Winds Touring Caravan & Camping Park, Polzeath, Wadebridge, Cornwall PL27 6QU. *01208 863267.* info@southwindscamping.co.uk. www.polzeathcamping.co.uk. Owner: Mr R Harris. N of Wadebridge via B3314 road signs to Polzeath. Quiet and peaceful with beautiful sea and panoramic rural views yet only 0.5m from the beach. Flat and well-drained with showers and laundry. Booking advisable in school holidays. AA 3 pennants. Open April-Sept.

(2m). The Laurels Holiday Park, Padstow Road, Whitecross, Wadebridge, Cornwall PL27 7JQ. *01209 313474.* info@thelaurelsholidaypark.co.uk. www.thelaurelsholidaypark.co.uk. Owner: Mr & Mrs J Rielly. Situated near junction of A39 and A389 Padstow (5m). W of Wadebridge. Ideal touring centre for Cornwall and North Devon. Designated Area of Outstanding Natural Beauty. Small, relaxing park in family run friendly atmosphere. Individual shrub lined pitches and excellent facilities. Supermarket 1m. Numerous pubs/restaurants in locality. Camel trail, Eden project and sandy beaches nearby. Padstow, Rock, Port Issac in short drive. St Ives, Falmouth, Newquay a little further. Open April-Oct.

(5m). Trenant Steading Touring Park, New Polzeath, St Minver, Wadebridge, Cornwall PL27 6SA. *01208 869091.* Owner: Robert Love. Off B3314 NW of Wadebridge. Close to safe, sandy beaches, surfing, water skiing and boating. Golf course nearby; also shops, PO, eating places. Open Easter-Oct.

■ **(3.5m). Trewince Farm Holiday Park, St Issey, Wadebridge, Cornwall PL27 7RL.** *01208 812830.* holidays@trewincefarm.fsnet.com. www.trewincefarmholidaypark.co.uk. Owner: M John & Betty Brewer. Off A389 Wadebridge to Padstow. Open Easter-Oct.

DEVON

ASHBURTON

(1.25m). Ashburton Caravan Park, Waterleat, Ashburton, Devon TQ13 7HU. *01364 652552.* info@ashburtoncaravanpark.co.uk. www.ashburtoncaravanpark.co.uk. Owner: Mr R Pummell & Mrs P Pummell. Off A38 to centre of Ashburton, turn into North Street, bear R before bridge SP Waterleat. Riverside location inside Dartmoor National Park. Rose Award Park. GS. Open Easter-Sept.

(2m). Parkers Farm Holiday Park, Higher Mead Farm, Ashburton, Devon TQ13 7LJ. *01364 654869.* parkersfarm@btconnect.com. www.parkersfarm.co.uk. Owner: Colin & Sam Parker. From Exeter, take the A38 to Plymouth. When SP 'Plymouth 26', take the second L at Alston Cross SP to Woodland and Denbury. Friendly family park. Set in beautiful countryside with spectacular open views. Children's and pets paradise. Regular farm walks to feed the animals. Dogs welcome. Short breaks available. 12m to coast. David Bellamy Silver Conservation Award. Open Easter-end Oct.

AXMINSTER

(3m). Andrewshayes Caravan Park, Dalwood, Axminster, Devon EX13 7DY. *01404 831225.* info@andrewshays.co.uk. www.andrewshayes.co.uk. Owner: Mr H K & Mrs S D Lawrence. Off A35, 6m Honiton, 3m Axminster. Turn N at Taunton Cross (by garage/Little Chef) signed Stockland/Dalwood. 150yd to park. Bar and restaurant. Heated outdoor swimming pool. Play park. Games room. Launderette. Take away open July/Aug. Rose award. Fishing 3m. Golf course, cinema 6-7m. Beach 6m. Open March-Dec.

BARNSTAPLE

(2m). Brightlycott Barton Caravan & Camping Site, Barnstaple, Devon EX31 4JJ. *01271 850330.* friend.brightlycott@virgin.net. Owner: Charles & Julia Friend. 2m NE of Barnstaple off A39. Road to farm site is SP Brightlycott and Roborough. Central touring site with panoramic views of moor and estuary. Leisure centre in Barnstaple. Fishing, golf, horse riding, swimming and tennis all available nearby. Games room, play area. Water heated via solar panels in ablution block. Open mid March-mid Nov.

(4m). Chivenor Caravan Park, Chivenor Cross, Barnstaple, Devon EX31 4BN. *01272 812217.* chivenorcp@lineone.net. www.chivenorcaravanpark.co.uk. Owner: Andy Bambridge. Easy access off A361 Barnstaple to Ilfracombe. Small family-run site. 100yd from Tarka Trail. All amenities either on site or in close proximity. Centrally located for touring. Open March 15-Jan 15.

(2m). Tarka Holiday Park (previously known as Midland Caravan Park), Ashford, Barnstaple, Devon EX31 4AU. *01271 343691.* info@tarkaholidaypark.co.uk. www.tarkaholidaypark.co.uk. Owner: Mr & Mrs Fry. Take A361 Barnstaple to Ilfracombe road. Site is on R from Barnstaple. Sheltered grass parkland site on A361. Quality graded by the West Country Tourist Board. AA 3 pennants. Close to Tarka Trail – bike hire available. David Bellamy Gold Conservation Award. Open Easter to mid Nov.

BIDEFORD

(9m). Dyke Green Farm Camp Site, Clovelly, Bideford, Devon EX39 5RU. *01237 431279.* Owner: Mrs J Johns. About 1.5m S of Clovelly at junction of B3237 & A39. Sheltered, level site just off roundabout at Clovelly Cross. Breakfast available at farm also bed and breakfast. Dogs under control welcome. Open Easter-Oct.

(13m). Hartland Caravan & Camping Park, Southlane, Hartland, Bideford, Devon EX39 6DG. *01237 441876.* Owner: L Allin. From A39 through Clovelly X roundabout, take first R. SP Hartland B3248. On entering village, site is on L. Quiet, family run site set in 6 acres of well maintained meadows, 4mins walk to shops/PH/takeaway meals, café/restaurant. New toilet/shower block. Baby changing/family/disabled room. Laundry facilities. Small fishing lake. Convenient for coastal footpath, beaches and woodland walks. 2 holiday homes 6/7 berth to let, set in own gardens. Caravan storage. Open March-Oct.

(5m). Steart Farm Touring Park, Horn's Cross, Bideford, Devon EX39 5DW. *01237 431836.* steartenquiries@btc

86 MOTOR CARAVAN & CAMPING PARKS 2009

WEST COUNTRY

onnect.com. www.steartfarmtouringpark.co.uk. Owner: R C & L F Croslegh. From Bideford follow A39 W (signed Bude). 2m after Horns Cross, site entrance on R. Set in 17 acres overlooking Bideford Bay. 1m from sea. Dog exercise field. Children's playing field. Open Easter-Setpember 30.

BRAUNTON

(5m). Bayview Farm Holidays, Croyde Bay, Braunton, Devon EX33 1PN. *01271 890501.* www.bayviewfarm.co.uk. Owner: George & Janet Hakin. M5, J27, take A361 then on to B3231 at Braunton. We are on RT approaching Croyde Village. A few minutes walk to sandy beach and olde worlde village. Dogs allowed by arrangement. One week only, Saturday to Saturday limited. Golf 2m. Open Easter-Oct.

(1m). Lobb Fields Caravan & Camping Park, Saunton Road, Braunton, Devon EX33 1EB. *01271 812090.* info@lobbfields.com. www.lobbfields.com. Owner: Mrs E Dodge, Mrs J Bury, Mrs J Smith-Bingham. From Barnstaple W on A361, 6m to Braunton. In Braunton take B3231 towards Croyde, park on R. Large grassy park 1.5m from Saunton beach faces S with panoramic views. Golf, all shops, doctor, garages, Tarka Trail for cycling and walking 1m. Fishing 3m. All water sports nearby. Open from 21/3/09 to 1/11/09.

YOUR TOP 101 SITES 2009

BRIXHAM

(0.5m). Centry Touring Caravan & Tent Site, Centry Road, Brixham, Devon TQ5 9EY. *01803 853215.* jlacentry.touring@talk21.com. www.english-riviera.co.uk. Owner: Mrs J Allen. Approaching Brixham on 3022 follow signs for Berry Head Country Park. Small site close to town and beaches. Showers. Milk & papers available. Shop nearby. Advance booking July and Aug. From Paignton follow signs for Berry Head. SAE for brochure. Open Easter-Oct.

(3m). Galmpton Touring Park, Greenway Road, Galmpton, Brixham, Devon TQ5 0EP. *01803 842066.* galmptontouringpark.co.uk. Owner: Chris & Pam Collins. A380 Torbay ring road then A379 towards Brixham, park SP on the R through Galmpton village. Family park with spectacular views of river Dart and close to beaches and all Torbay attractions. Immaculate facilities. Good access. No dogs in peak period. Two self-catering cottages and two studios available. Open from 3/4/09 to 30/9/09.

(2m). Hillhead Holiday Park, Hillhead, Brixham, Devon TQ5 0HH. *01803 853204.* www.caravanclub.co.uk. Owner: The Caravan Club. See website for directions. Set in 22 acres of Devon countryside this site offers some of the finest facilities on the Caravan Club network. Non members and tent campers welcome, part sloping, toilet blocks, privacy cubicles, baby and toddler washroom, baby changing facilities, laundry, MV service pt, veg prep area, battery charging, gas and gaz, games room. Information room, club, bar, restaurant, takeaway, playground, play area, play equipment, dog walk on site, swimming pool, fishing, golf and watersports nearby. Ideal for families, good area for walking. Open March-Jan.

BUCKFAST

(0.5m). Churchill Farm Camp Site, Churchill Farm, Buckfast, Devon TQ11 0EZ. *01364 642844.* apedrick04@btinternet.com. Owner: A Pedrick. From A38, follow signs for Buckfast Abbey, proceed up hill then L at crossroads, farm entrance opposite church. Panoramic views of Dartmoor overlooking Buckfast Abbey. Ideal base for exploring Dartmoor and south Devon. Shops, café/restaurant, takeaway meals available nearby. Open April-end of Sept.

BUCKFASTLEIGH

(1.5m). Beara Farm Caravan & Camping Site, Beara Farm, Colston Road, Buckfastleigh, Devon TQ11 0LW. *01364 642234.* Owner: Mr W J Thorn. From Exeter leave A38 at Dart Bridge. Follow signs to South Devon Steam Railway and Butterfly Farm. Take first L after passing entrance. SP Old Totnes road. After 0.5m turn R, site 1m. Also SP. Site is in an idyllic position, close by the River Dart. It is also in easy reach of the sea and Dartmoor. Fishing nearby. Steam railway and butterfly and otter park. Buckfast Abbey, Pennywell Farm all in short distance of site.

CHUDLEIGH

(1m). Holmans Wood Holiday Park, Harcombe Cross, Chudleigh, Devon TQ13 0DZ. *01626 853785.* enquiries@holmanswood.co.uk. www.holmanswood.co.uk. Owner: Mrs M Barzilay. Follow M5 to Exeter. A38 towards Plymouth. From top of Haldon Hill, past racecourse. Park is 100yd on L. Ideally situated for Dartmoor, Exeter and Torquay.

Seasonal pitches & storage available. Tents welcome in our meadow. Neat and level park in beautiful countryside setting. Excellent toilets/showers. David Bellamy Bronze Conservation Award. Open March-Oct.

COLYTON

(2m). Leacroft Touring Park, Colyton Hill, Colyton, Devon EX24 6HY. *01297 552823.* Owner: Anne & John Robinson. SP from A3052 Sidmouth to Lyme Regis, at Stafford Cross, do not go into Colyton. Quiet, peaceful site in open countryside with views to Lyme Bay. Picturesque villages and woodland walks nearby. Ideal for touring. Hardstandings. Storage facilities. Open Easter-Oct.

COMBE MARTIN

(0.25m). Newberry Valley Park, Newberry Farm, Woodlands, Combe Martin, Devon EX34 0AT. *01271 882334.* relax@newberryvalleypark.co.uk. www.newberryvalleypark.co.uk. Owner: Martin & Dawn Fletcher. On A399. NW edge of Combe Martin. Quiet and peaceful countryside location on North Devon Coast. Combe Martin village with beach, shops, café's, pubs in 5mins walk, just off SW coastal path. Small shop with essentials and delightful coarse fishing lake and woodland walks. David Bellamy Gold Conservation Award. Open from 21/3/08 to 30/9/08.

CROYDE BAY

Ruda Holiday Park, Croyde Bay, Devon EX33 1NY. *01271 890671.* enquiries@parkdeanholidays.co.uk. www.parkdeanholidays.co.uk. Owner: Parkdean Holidays Plc. Leave M5 at J27 for A361 to Barnstaple and Braunton then B3231 to Croyde. 4m from Braunton. Park is 100yd from own beach. Blue Flag and Quality Coast Award 2007. Fishing. Club with entertainment. Heated indoor fun pool. Organised children's activities. Phone for brochure. Rose Award caravans. England for Excellence 'Holiday Park of the Year' Silver award. Best Holiday Park in West Country 1998 and 1999. Open March-Nov, Lodges & Apartments: all year.

CULLOMPTON

(5m). Forest Glade Holiday Park, Cullompton, Devon EX15 2DT. *01404 841381.* enquiries@forest-glade.co.uk. www.forest-glade.co.uk. Owner: Mr N P Wellard. Please contact park for details. Flat, sheltered, secluded park in forest situated on the Blackdown Hills AONB. Free heated indoor pool. Adventure play area. All-weather tennis court. Free colour

WEST COUNTRY

brochure on request. Touring caravans must phone for access route. Golf 6m, cinema 11m, shopping centre 20m. Open March-end Oct.

DARTMOUTH

(2m). Deer Park Touring & Camping, Dartmouth Road, Stoke Fleming, Dartmouth, Devon TQ6 ORF. *01803 770253.* info@deerparkinn.co.uk. www.deerparkinn.co.uk. Owner: Peter & Sarah Keane. On A379 Kingsbridge to Dartmouth. At Eastern end of Stoke Fleming. Free House and restaurant. Adventure playground. Flats also for hire. 1m from Dartmouth or Blackpool sands. Open March 15-Nov 15.

■ **(2.5m). Leonards Cove, Stoke Fleming, Dartmouth, Devon TQ6 0NR.** *01803 770206.* enquiry@leonardscove.co.uk. www.leonardscove.co.uk. On A379 Dartmouth to Kingsbridge. In village of Stoke Fleming, walking distance Blackpool Sands. Sea views from the camping/touring field. Village PO/stores. Golf & Country Club 3m. Open March-Oct.

YOUR TOP 101 SITES 2009 **(2m). Little Cotton Caravan Park, Dartmouth, Devon TQ6 0LB.** *01803 832558.* enquiries@littlecotton.co.uk. littlecotton.co.uk. Owner: Paul & Dorothy White. Leave A38 at Buckfastleigh, A384 to Totnes, from Totnes to Halwell on A381, at Halwell take A3122 Dartmouth Road. Park on R of entrance to town. Seven acres, level and gently sloping, some sheltered with scenic outlook. Park and ride service adjacent. Ideal touring area. Luxurious toilet and shower facilities. Golf course nearby. Open mid March-Oct.

Sea View Campsite, Newlands Farm, Slapton, Dartmouth, Devon TQ7 2RB. *01548 580366.* seaview@camping-devon.com. www.camping-devon.com. Owner: Roger Bradford. From Totnes, take A381 towards Kingsbridge. After Halwell take 4th L SP Slapton, go 4m to Buckland Cross. Proceed 0.5m, site on L. Quiet site overlooking farmland and sea. Open May-Sept.

■ **(5m). Woodlands Leisure Park, Blackawton, Dartmouth, Devon TQ9 7DQ.** *01803 712598.* fun@woodlandspark.com. www.woodlands-caravanpark.com. Owner: Bendalls Leisure Ltd. SP from A38 and Totnes, on A3122. Alan Rogers 'Best Family Campsite in Europe'. Combining excellent facilities with personal supervision. Spacious pitches in beautiful countryside. Excellent bathrooms, laundry, free hot showers. Two nights stay gives FREE entrance to 80 Acre Leisure Park. 3 watercoasters, 500yd toboggan run and arctic gliders, commando course, action tracks and Master Blaster. Live entertainment days, excellent indoor falconry centre with flying displays. An ocean of undercover play. Guaranteed fun whatever the weather! 'Over '50's mid week' – enquire for special rates. Open Easter-Nov.

DAWLISH

■ **(2m). Cofton Country Holidays, Starcross, Dawlish, Devon EX6 8RP.** *01626 890111.* info@coftonholidays.co.uk. www.coftonholidays.co.uk. Owner: Mr & Mrs W G Jeffrey. On A379 Exeter to Dawlish road after Cockwood village. Heated swimming pool. Adventure playground and woodland trails. Takeaway. 'Swan' pub (two bars), family rooms. Coarse fishing. Woodland walks. Free showers. Launderette. Short drive to Dawlish Warren beach. Open March-Oct.

■ **(1m). Golden Sands Holiday Park, Week Lane, Dawlish, Devon EX7 0LZ.** *01626 863099.* info@goldensands.co.uk. www.goldensands.co.uk. Owner: Park Holidays UK. From M5 Exeter take A379 to Dawlish. 2m after Starcross the park is SP on the L. Week Lane is second L past garage on R. Heated indoor and outdoor pool. Licensed club and free entertainment. Small, select touring park. 0.5m to safe, sandy beach. Family run for families. Ideally located for touring South Devon. Open Easter-Oct 31.

(1m). Lady's Mile Touring Park, Exeter Road, Dawlish, Devon EX7 0LX. *01626 863411.* www.ladysmile.com. Owner: Mr A J Jeffery. On A379 Exeter to Dawlish

Clifftop Touring & Camping with magnificent unrestricted sea views.
Situated in an area of outstanding natural beauty, peace and quiet.
Coastal village, Stoke Fleming has: village stores, post office, pub serving food and a restaurant/take away. **Blackpool Sands, blue flag beach,** is 1/2 mile. Dartmouth is 3 miles away. Laundrette. Accommodation is also available.
Tel: **01803 770206**   www.leonardscove.co.uk or write
Leonards Cove, Stoke Fleming, Dartmouth, S. Devon.

Cofton Country HOLIDAYS

Superb family-run four star park
in a Glorious Corner of Devon

• swimming pools • Swan pub • play areas • shop
• fishing lakes • blue flag beach five minutes • take-away
• WiFi • David Bellamy gold awards for conservation

0800 085 8649   www.coftonholidays.co.uk

WEST COUNTRY

See page 5 for key to symbols and abbreviations

road. Easy access from J30, M5. Indoor and outdoors heated swimming pools with 100ft water chutes. Play area and games room. Takeaway food. Bar. Launderette. Showers. Short distance Dawlish Warren beach and town. Open mid-March to Oct 31.

■ **(2m). Leadstone Camping,** Warren Road, Dawlish, Devon EX7 0NG. *01626 864411.* info@leadstonecamping.co.uk. www.leadstonecamping.co.uk. Owner: Mr A C I Bulpin. M5, J30. Take A379 to Dawlish. On approaching Dawlish turn L on brow of hill signed Dawlish Warren. Site 0.5m on R. Rolling grassland in natural secluded bowl 0.5m from Dawlish Warren beach and nature reserve. One night stop-overs welcome. Ideal base for 'day-touring' Devon. The park is licensed for a total of 137 units (tourers, tents, motorhomes) Open from 12/6/09 to 6/9/09.

DAWLISH WARREN

■ **Peppermint Park,** Warren Road, Dawlish Warren, Devon EX7 0PQ. *01626 863436.* info@peppermintpark.co.uk. www.peppermintpark.co.uk. Owner: Park Holidays UK. Leave M5 at Exeter. A379 to Dawlish. Then follow signs to Dawlish Warren and continue down steep hill and follow road round to the L. Park is then 200yd on L. Dog exercise enclosure. Heated pool with water slide. Play area. Games room. Licensed club. Coarse fishing lake. Golf course 0.25m. David Bellamy Gold Conservation Award. Open all year. Hire vans & Lodges Easter-end Oct.

DREWSTEIGNTON

■ **(4m). Woodland Springs Touring Park,** Venton, Drewsteighton, Devon EX6 6PG. *01647 231695.* enquiries@woodlandsprings.co.uk. www.woodlandsprings.co.uk. Owner: Chris & Jan Patrick. From A30 Whiddon Down junction follow A382 Moretonhampstead. Then Brown Tourist signs. 8m from Okehampton. Adults only. Quiet, peaceful, natural site in Dartmoor National Park. Ideal for touring Devon, Cornwall and Southwest. Special offers available, seasonal pitches. Day kennels,

18m from cathedral city Exeter

EXETER

■ **(11m). Barley Meadow Caravan & Camping Park, Crockernwell, Exeter, Devon EX6 6NR.** *01647 281629.* welcome@barleymeadow.com. www.barleymeadow.com. Owner: Paul & Cath Chadney. Crockernwell turning off A30 Exeter to Okehampton road. Passing through Cheriton Bishop, park on L in Crockernwell. AA 4 pennants. Grassy site with good access. Refurbished heated shower block. Seasonal pitches available. Hardstanding pitches. Garage, shop, PO, doctors all 2m away. Okehampton 7m. Fishing, golf course nearby. In Dartmoor National Park. Walkers welcome. Children's play area. Open from 15/3/08 to 6/11/08.

■ **(6m). Castle Brake, Castle Lane, Woodbury, Exeter, Devon EX5 1HA.** *01395 232431.* reception@castlebrake.co.uk. www.castlebrake.co.uk. Owner: T Walker. M5, J30. Take A3052 to Halfway Inn. Turn R B3180 to Exmouth. Turn R after golf/caravan site sign. 4m from Exmouth. Grassy, level park between Exeter and Exmouth. Medium size park with lovely facilities. Centrally heated holiday caravans for hire. Shower blocks, sauna, steam, bar and restaurant. Hotel quality shower rooms. Adventure playground. Extensive heathland 500yd. Sandy beach 6m. Caravan storage and seasonal pitches available. Rose award for holiday caravans. Good area for walking and attractions. David Bellamy Gold Conservation Award. Open March-Oct.

■ **Culm Valley Camping Park, Rewe, Exeter, Devon EX5 4HB.** *01392 841349.* Owner: G Forrest-Jones. 6m N of Exeter via A396, take first turn R after Rewe. Camping sign at junction. M5 traffic take Sampford Peverell junction, via Tiverton 8m to site. Overnight stop Midlands to South Devon. Peaceful holiday centre.

■ **(6m). Exeter Racecourse Caravan Club Site, Kennford, Exeter, Devon EX6 7XS.** *01392 832107.* www.caravanclub.co.uk. Owner: The Caravan

Club. From Plymouth on A38 turn L immediately past Little Chef at top of Haldon Hill into underpass, SP Exeter racecourse. Follow R'course signs then caravan club signs. Located at top of Haldon Hill with superb views. An excellent base for exploring Exeter and Dartmoor. Advance booking essential Bank Holidays and advised June-Aug. Excellent site for dogs. Non-members and tent campers welcome. Free access to racing. Toilet block and laundry facilities. MV service point. Veg prep area, gas and gaz, fishing nearby. Quiet and peaceful off peak, good area for walking. Open March-Oct.

■ **(5m). Haldon Lodge Farm Caravan & Camping Site, Clapham, Nr Kennford, Exeter, Devon EX6 7YG.** *01392 832312.* Owner: Mr D L Salter. S of Exeter off A38 Kennford Services. Turn L through Kennford village past PO. Proceed to motor bridge turn L Dunchideock. 1m to caravan park. Peaceful, family site with excellent touring centre. 15mins from sea and Exeter. Forest nature trails, riding and trekking. Fishing, shop on site. PO, doctor's surgery, all a short distance from site.

■ **(4m). Kennford International Caravan Park, Kennford, Exeter, Devon EX6 7YN.** *01392 833046.* ian@kennfordint.fsbusiness.co.uk. www.kennfordinternational.co.uk. Owner: Mr & Mrs Hopkins. 1m from end of M5 alongside A38. Family run park. Individually marked pitches. 10% discount on holiday bookings for over 50's and Tamba members. Ideal touring centre for Dartmoor, Torquay and the benefits of south Devon. Full facility park near villages and country walks.

■ **(8m). Springfield Holiday Park, Tedburn St Mary, Exeter, Devon EX6 6EW.** *01647 24242.* enquires@springfieldholidaypark.co.uk. www.springfieldholidaypark.co.uk. Owner: Ros & Brodie McIntyre. From J31 of M5 travel W on A30. 2nd exit SP Cheriton Bishop – follow signs to park. Ideal for touring Dartmoor. Superb views. Excellent site facilities. Golf courses nearby, shops and PO close. Selection of pubs and restaurants 1m. Open March 15-Nov 15.

Leadstone Camping

7 acres of rolling grassland in a natural secluded bowl.

...a great little site!

Owned and managed by the same local family for 35 years. Friendly, quiet and uncomplicated. Half a mile from Dawlish Warren's Blue Flag Beach. One-night stop-overs welcome. Ideal base for 'day-touring' Devon.

Write or phone for a full colour brochure. Warren Road, Dawlish, South Devon EX7 0NG
Tel: 01626 864411   Fax: 01626 873873   www.leadstonecamping.co.uk

WEST COUNTRY

Webbers Caravan & Camping Park, Castle Lane, Woodbury, Exeter, Devon EX5 1EA. 01395 232276. reception@webberspark.co.uk. www.webberspark.co.uk. Owner: M & Mrs M Osborne. From M5 J30 take A376 then B3179 to Woodbury, then follow brown and white signs. A friendly, family park close to Woodbury village. Breathtaking countryside views. Lots of space to relax. Ideal for beaches, golf, fishing, walking, cycling and exploring East Devon. All year caravan storage. Please call for a brochure. Open mid March-end Oct.

EXMOUTH

(3m). Devon Cliffs Holiday Park, Sandy Bay, Exmouth, Devon EX8 5BT. 01395 226226. www.devoncliffs-park.co.uk. Owner: Bourne Leisure Ltd. M5 exit 30 after Exeter and take A376 for Exmouth. At Exmouth follow the brown tourism signs to Sandy Bay and this will bring you directly on to the park. Indoor and outdoor fun pools. Free kid's clubs. Adventure playground. All weather multi sports court. Daytime and evening entertainment. Spa complex. 3 family bars, great choice of eating areas, shopping arcade. Direct access to Blue Flag beach. Town 3m, golf courses 5m. Exeter 12m. David Bellamy Gold Conservation Award. Open March-end Oct.

Great Torrington (2m). Smytham Manor Leisure, Smytham Manor, Little Torrington, Great Torrington, Devon EX38 8PU. 01805 622110. info@smytham.co.uk. www.smytham.co.uk. Owner: Great Leisure Ltd. S of Torrington towards Okehampton on A386. 25-acres of beautiful gently undulating grounds with ponds. Heated facilities block with showers, shaver points. Play area. Heated outdoor swimming pool and sun terrace. Licensed bar. Putting green, direct access to Tarka Trail. Caravan Club. Booking advisable. Close to Moors and beaches. RHS Rosemoor and Dartington Crystal 1.5m. David Bellamy Gold Conservation Award. Open March-Oct.

HAWKCHURCH

(5m). Hunters Moon Country Estate, Wareham Road, Hawkchurch, Devon EX13 5UL. 01297 678402. enquiries@huntersmooncountryestate.co.uk. www.huntersmooncountryestate.co.uk. Owner: Totemplant Ltd. Turn off A35 on to B3165 SP Crewkerne follow signs 2.5m turn L. Shop, bar, restaurant and take-away at high season, free showers, play area. 5m from sea at Lyme Regis or Charmouth. Quiet park overlooking beautiful Axe Valley.

One field reserved for adults only. High quality park with the ambience of a traditional Devonshire country estate. Many sporting activities, sailing, diving and many tourist attractions. Swimming pool, beach nearby. Open March 15-Nov 15.

HOLSWORTHY

(5m). Hedley Wood Caravan & Camping Park, Bridgerule, Holsworthy, Devon EX22 7ED. 01288 381404. alan@hedleywood.co.uk. www.hedleywood.co.uk. Owner: Mr A Bryant. Take A3072 Holdsworth to Bude, midway turn S on to B3254 to Launceston. 2.5m turn R 500yd on R. Woodland, family run site with outstanding views and a laid-back atmosphere. Pets welcome, daily kennelling, dog walk and nature trail. Clubroom, bar, and all amenities. Adventure area. Open and sheltered areas. Caravan storage.

Newbuildings, Brandis Corner, Holsworthy, Devon EX22 7YQ. 01409 221305. Owner: Mr & Mrs B Lynds. A3072 Holsworthy/Hatherleigh road. 4m from Holsworthy towards Hatherleigh, turn L at Dunsland Cross (opposite R hand turn to Okehampton) site on L after 200yd. Working family farm. Open all year depending on ground condition. Off road walking on National Trust lane. Dogs allowed if kept under control.

(2.5m). Noteworthy Caravan & Camping Site, Bude Road, Holsworthy, Devon EX22 7JB. 01409 253731. enquiries@noteworthy-devon.co.uk. www.noteworthy-devon.co.uk. Owner: Mr & Mrs Snook-Bevis. W of Holsworthy on A3072. 1m past golf course. Touring centre for moors and beaches. Quiet family run site. Takeaway meals nearby. AA approved & Quality in Tourism on a working farm.

Penhallym Farm, Week St Mary, Holsworthy, Devon EX22 6XR. 01288 341274. Owner: Mrs A Brenton. Off A39 at Treskinnick Cross, SP Week St Mary. First R for Jacobstow to farm house and site on R. Midway between Bude & Boscastle. Quiet with sea views. No sanitation. Bottle gas supply in 2m.

HONITON

Fishpond House Campsite, Dunkeswell, Honiton, Devon EX14 0SH. 01404 891287. www.fishpondshotel.com. Owner: Mrs J Cole, Mr M Hartley. From A30 and A35 Honiton follow signs for Dunkeswell & Luppitt. 3m to Limers Cross and R to Luppitt and Smeathorpe. Open March-

Oct.

ILFRACOMBE

(2.5m). Brook Lea Caravan Club Site, West Down, Ilfracombe, Devon EX34 8NE. 01271 862848. www.caravanclub.co.uk. Owner: The Caravan Club. See website for directions. In elevated position 3m inland from Ilfracombe with superb views to two coasts and Dartmoor. Non-members welcome. No tents. No sanitation. Advance booking advised July and Aug. MV service point. Playfield. Golf, fishing and watersports nearby. Good area for walking. Ideal for families. Gas and Gaz, dog walk on site. Storage pitches, quiet and peaceful off peak. Volunteer run site. Recycling facilities, in 5m of NCN cycle route. Open mid March-early Oct.

(1m). Hele Valley Holiday Park, Hele Bay, Ilfracombe, Devon EX34 9RD. 01271 862460. holidays@helevalley.co.uk. www.helevalley.co.uk. Owner: Mr & Mrs D Dovey. Hele Valley is 1m E of Ilfracombe town centre. Follow brown signs on A399 to take a R turn to Hele Valley. Visit Hele Valley to experience peace and tranquility of this natural holiday park in walking distance of beach and town. Modern caravans, spacious lodges, luxury cottages and camping. On-site launderette, children's play area. Pets and short breaks welcome. Basic supply shop. Cinema, theatre, boat trips, fishing, golf, indoor heated pool and shopping in 0.5m. Horse riding and quads 3m.

(5m). Hidden Valley Park, West Down, Ilfracombe, Devon EX34 8NU. 01271 813837. relax@hiddenvalleypark.com. www.hiddenvalleypark.com. Owner: Martin & Dawn Fletcher. J27, M5 take A361 to Barnstaple, continue A361 towards Ilfracombe. 8m from Barnstaple, park entrance is on L side of A361. Secluded site in beautiful wooded valley with numerous birds and wildlife. Only a few minutes drive from coast and Exmoor National Park. Sheltered, level, grass and hardstandings. Free hot showers, laundry & dishwashing facilities. Fabulous restaurant & bar, with indoor games rooms. Two outdoor play area. Dog walking. Woodland walks. Gold award for wildlife & conservation, 4 pennant AA park. David Bellamy Gold Conservation Award.

YOUR TOP 101 SITES 2009

(2.5m). Little Meadow Camping Site, Lydford Farm, Watermouth, Ilfracombe, Devon EX34 9SJ. 01271

WEST COUNTRY

See page 5 for key to symbols and abbreviations

866862. info@littlemeadow.co.uk. www.littlemeadow.co.uk. Owner: Nick Barten. 2m E of Ilfracombe on A399. A small, tranquil, uncommercialised site with one of the most spectacular views of the Bristol Channel. Shop on site. Golf course, sea fishing, trips to Lundy Island, horse riding available. On the SW coastal footpath. Open Easter-Sept.

Little Shelfin Farm, Ilfracombe, Devon. 01271 862449. Owner: Mr & Mrs M Hale. 1.5m S of Ilfracombe via A361. Turn W along B3343 at Mullacott Cross for 500yd to site. Flat site in pleasant holiday country. Café/restaurant nearby. Fees and dates on application. Manager on site: Mr G W Ballard. Open Easter-Oct.

(3m). Mill Park Touring Site, Berrynarbor, Combe Martin, Ilfracombe, Devon EX34 9SH. 01271 882647. millpark@globalnet.co.uk. www.millpark.co.uk. Owner: Brian & Mary Malin. Between Ilfracombe and Combe Martin, take turning off A399, opposite Sawmills Restaurant for pretty Berrynarbor. Picturesque, level park in woodland setting with waterfall and stream-fed coarse fishing lake. Free hot water and showers. Well-stocked shop. Bar, hot meals. Off-licence. Phone. Laundry. Play area. Dog walks. Open March 15-Nov 15.

(2m). Mullacott Cross Caravan Park, Mullacott Cross, Ilfracombe, Devon EX34 8NB. 01271 862212. info@mullacottcaravans.co.uk. www.mullacottcaravans.co.uk. Owner: R E Donovan. On main A361 road, S of Ilfracombe. Gently sloping with views over Bristol Channel. Open Easter-end Oct.

(3.5m). Napps Touring Holidays, Old Coast Road, Berrynarbor, Ilfracombe,

Devon EX34 9SW. 01271 882557. info@napps.fsnet.co.uk. www.napps.co.uk. Owner: R M Richards. M5, J27 on to A391 for 20m, turn R at Aller Cross, follow signs to Combe Martin (about 17m), drive through Combe Martin, Napps is 1.5m past Combe Martin beach, SP on R. Modern amenity block. Tennis court. Heated swimming pool, paddling pool. Takeaway food. Family bar, beer garden. Adventure playground. Launderette. Beach. Winter and summer storage. Shop, off license, games room. Shops, PO, doctors, restaurants 1.5m. Fishing 0.5m; golf 2m; horse riding 3.5m. On the edge of Exmoor. Open March 3-Oct 31.

YOUR TOP 101 SITES 2009 ■ **(4m). Stowford Farm Meadows, Berry Down, Combe Martin, Ilfracombe, Devon EX34 0PW.** 01271 882476. enquiries@stowford.co.uk. www.stowford.co.uk. Owner: Mr W D Rice. Leave M5, exit 27, N Devon link road to Barnstaple. Take A39 for 1m then turn L on to B3230. Turn R at garage. At Lynton Cross, on to A3123. Stowford Farm Meadows is 1.5m on the R, down its own private road. AA 4 pennant site. Caravan service & accessories. Horse riding, mini zoo, crazy golf, indoor pool, bar. Cycle hire, shop, take-away, restaurant, awnings and tents. Award winning caravan centre supplying Elddis, Coachman, Fleetwood and Bailey.

YOUR TOP 101 SITES 2009 **(2.5m). Watermouth Cove Holiday Park, Berrynarbor, Ilfracombe, Devon EX34 9SJ.** 01271 862504. info@watermouthcoveholidays.co.uk. www.watermouthcoveholidays.co.uk. Owner: Mr

& Mrs Dave Fry. M5, J27 take A361 signs Barnstaple to Ilfracombe. Family management. Swimming pools. Club with entertainment. Bar meals, takeaway, outside play area, laundry, free hot water. Headland walks. Adjacent to harbour. Private beach and caves. Shop and arcade. Sea fishing. Luxury chalets. Open March-Oct.

(2.5m). Watermouth Valley Camping Park, Watermouth, Ilfracombe, Devon EX34 9SJ. 01271 862282. www.watermouthpark.co.uk. Owner: Mr D L Wassall. Situated on the coast road A399, between Ilfracombe and Combe Martin. Family site on the coastline between Combe Martin and Ilfracombe. Watermouth Harbour and beach 200yd. Children's play area. The Old Sawmill Inn and restaurant adjoins Watermouth Valley Camping Park. Open May-Oct.

IVYBRIDGE

(8m). Broad Park Caravan Club Site, Higher East Leigh, Modbury, Ivybridge, Devon PL21 0SH. 01548 830714. www.caravanclub.co.uk. Owner: The Caravan Club. See website for directions. Between moor and sea. Non-members welcome. No tents. Toilet blocks with privacy cubicles & laundry facilities. Some hardstanding, veg prep area, gas and gaz. Dog walk on site, quiet and peaceful off peak. Good area for walking. MV service point. Playfield and play equipment. Boules pitch. Ideal for families. Open: March 27-Nov 9.

(7m). Camping & Caravanning Club Site – California Cross, Modbury, Ivybridge, Devon PL21 0SG. 01548 821297. www.campingandcaravanningclub.co.uk. Owner: Camping & Caravanning Club. Leave A38 at Wranton Cross onto A3121. Over crossroads to B3196. Turn L

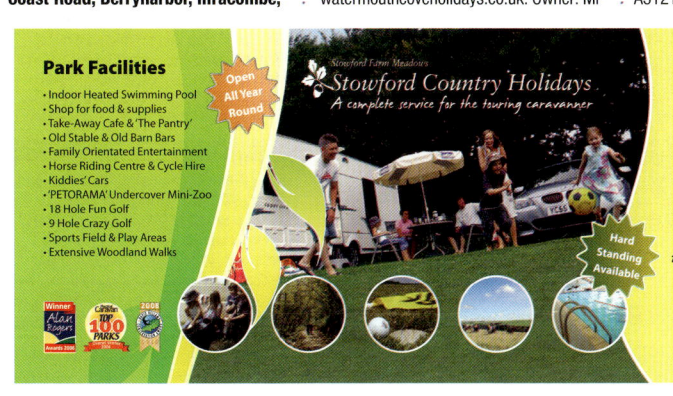

Park Facilities
- Indoor Heated Swimming Pool
- Shop for food & supplies
- Take-Away Cafe & 'The Pantry'
- Old Stable & Old Barn Bars
- Family Orientated Entertainment
- Horse Riding Centre & Cycle Hire
- Kiddies' Cars
- 'PETORAMA' Undercover Mini-Zoo
- 18 Hole Fun Golf
- 9 Hole Crazy Golf
- Sports Field & Play Areas
- Extensive Woodland Walks

Open All Year Round

Stowford Country Holidays
A complete service for the touring caravanner

Hard Standing Available

Stowford Farm Meadows is an award winning touring caravan and camping site close to Combe Martin in the beautiful surroundings of the North Devon countryside.

To book call us on
✆ **01271 882476**

Combe Martin Devon EX34 0PW
www.stowford.co.uk

www.motorcaravanmagazine.co.uk   MOTOR CARAVAN & CAMPING PARKS 2009 **91**

WEST COUNTRY

before filling station, SP Dartmouth, site on R. 8m from Bigbury-on-Sea with sandy beach and golf course. Salcombe 12m, centre for yachting. Near beautiful villages. All units accepted. Non-members welcome. Loo Of The Year (4 stars). Indoor and outdoor swimming pools situated 7m away. Special arrangements for early morning site departure for Plymouth ferries. Deals for families and backpackers. Open April-Oct.

KINGSBRIDGE

(8m). Camping & Caravanning Club Site – Slapton Sands, Middle Grounds, Slapton, Kingsbridge, Devon TQ7 2QW. *01548 580538.* www.campingandcaravanningclub.co.uk. Owner: Camping & Caravanning Club. On A379 from Kingsbridge, entrance on R 0.25m beyond brow of hill approaching Slapton Village. Motorhome and tents, Non-members welcome. Caravan owners must be members due to restrictions on numbers. Near wild bird sanctuary at Slapton Ley. Blackpool Sands, 4m away is also popular with families. Sea fishing from the beach near the site. Deals for families and backpackers. Loo Of The Year (4 stars). Open March-Oct.

(1m). Island Lodge Caravan & Camping Site, Stumpy Post Cross, Kingsbridge, Devon TQ7 4BL. *01548 852956.* www.islandlodgesite.co.uk. Owner: Kay Parker. Travelling S from Totnes on A381. Turn R at Stumpy Post Cross. Next turning L to site entrance. Unspoilt, rural site in easy reach of beaches and moors. Ideal for a quiet holiday for couples and families. Laundry facilities. Good clean modern facilities. Fridge, freezer and microwave facilities on site. Easy access. Childrens' play area. Sea glimpses. Licensed caravan/boat storage. Seasonal pitches.

■ **(6m). Karrageen Caravan & Camping Park, Bolberry, Malborough, Kingsbridge, Devon TQ7 3EN.** *01548 561230.* www.karrageen.co.uk. Owner: Phil & Nikki Higgin. Take A381 towards Salcombe. At Malborough turn R, after 0.6m turn R (sp Bolberry). After 0.9m park on R. 4m from Salcombe. Terraced, level, tree lined pitches with a view. NT cliff top walks. Hot takeaway and shop. Beach 1m. First class facilities. AA 3 pennants. See advertisement under Salcombe. Open 21 March-30 Sept.

(3m). Mounts Farm Touring Park, The Mounts, East Allington, Kingsbridge, **Devon TQ9 7QJ.** *01548 521591.* www.mountsfarm.co.uk. Owner: Karen Meacher & Mrs Peggy Wain. N of Kingsbridge on A381, family run site, ideal base for touring South Devon. Free showers and hot water. No overcrowding. No charge for awnings, pets and children. Shop with camping accessories. Near many beaches and attractions. Free brochure. Children's play field. AA 3 pennant. Open March 15-Nov 1.

(5m). Old Cotmore Farm Touring Caravan & Camping Park, Old Cotmore Farm, Stokenham, Kingsbridge, Devon TQ7 2LR. *01548 580240.* oldcotmorefarm@tiscali.co.uk. www.oldcotmorefarm.co.uk. Owner: Gwen Needham. From Kingsbridge, take A379 towards Dartmouth. At Stokenham village turn at mini roundabout to Beesands. Park 1m on R, SP. Picturesque park, 1m from sea and glorious beaches. Farm has holiday cottages. Dogs allowed. AA 3 pennants. Open March 15-Oct 31.

(1m). Parkland Caravan & Camping Site, Sorley Green Cross, Kingsbridge, Devon TQ7 4AF. *01548 852723.* www.parklandsite.co.uk. Owner: James K Parker. A38 S turn off at Totnes junction (A384). At Totnes take A381 for 10m to Stumpy Post Cross junction, follow A381 to the R and follow tourist board signs. High quality traditional site, set in three acres of level grounds. Free electric hook-ups. Seasonal pitches. Modern facilities, family/disabled suites. Views Salcombe, nearest site to Bantham beach. Storage.

(6m). Start Bay Caravan Club Site, Stokenham, Kingsbridge, Devon TQ7 2SE. *01548 580430.* www.caravanclub.co.uk. Owner: The Caravan Club. See website for directions. Caravan Club members only. No tents. A long, gently sloping meadow site screened with well kept shrubs and trees, with the sea only 0.75m away. Toilet blocks, laundry facilities and MV service point. Play equipment and dog walk on site. Fishing and watersports nearby. Good area for walking. Facilities for disabled. Ideal for families. Open May-Nov.

LYNTON

(2m). Camping & Caravanning Club Site – Lynton, Caffyn's Cross, Lynton, Devon EX35 6JS. *01598 752379.* www.campingandcaravanningclub.co.uk. Owner: Camping & Caravanning Club. M5, J27 on to A361 to 2nd South Molton roundabout. R on to A399 to Blackmoor gate. R on to A39 towards Lynton, L after 5m, signed Caffyns, immediately R to site in 1m. Set in 5.5 acres with pitches accepting all units, superbly situated on the cliff overlooking the Bristol Channel. Non-members welcome. Close to Exmoor National Park for walks in rugged countryside. Quiet site with stunning views of Lorna Doone countryside. Deals for families and backpackers. Open March-Oct.

(2m). Channel View Caravan and Camping Park, Manor Farm, Lynton, Devon EX35 6LD. *01598 753349.* www.channel-view.co.uk. Owner: Mr R C Wren. On A39 Barnstaple to Lynmouth. Licensed pub and restaurant nearby. Fully serviced pitches available, café on site. David Bellamy Gold Conservation Award. Open March 15-Nov 15.

(1m). Cloud Farm Riverside Camping, Cloud Farm, Oare, Lynton, Devon EX35 6NU. *01598 741234.* www.doonevalleyholidays.co.uk. Owner: C L Haman. 6 m W of Porlock. SP from A39 near county boundary of Devon and Somerset. Follow signs for Lorna Doone Farm, then see Cloud Farm on L before river. In heart of idyllic Doone Valley by side of river. Well behaved dogs allowed. Camp fires and barbeques allowed on site.

Hillsford Camping Site, Hillsford Bridge, Lynton, Devon. *01598 741256.* Owner: Mr & Mrs B Woollacott. 100yd off main A39. 3.5m from Lynton & Lynmouth. Level site 6m from Doone Valley. Open early March to end-Oct.

(0.25m). Sunny Lyn Holiday Park, Lynbridge, Lynton, Devon EX35 6NS. *01598 753384.* info@caravandevon.co.uk. www.caravandevon.co.uk. Owner: Mr & Mrs Oney. S of Lynton on B3234. Or 1m N of junction of this road with A39 at Barbrook, avoiding the steep hill out of Lynton. Holiday site, easy reach of coast on edge of Exmoor. On SW coastal path alongside village pub and river. Cooked breakfast available. Lodge and apartments open all year. Free hot showers. Open March-Oct 31.

MODBURY

(3m). Moor View Touring Park, California Cross, Modbury, Devon PL21 0SG. *01548 821485.* www.moorviewtouringpark.co.uk. Owner: Edward & Liz Corwood. From A38 westbound, leave at Wrangaton Cross (signed Modbury, Ermington) turn L, straight on at crossroads and follow park signs. Rural, adults only park backing onto woodland, with panoramic views towards Dartmoor, close to coastal walks and beaches. 68 individual level pitches all with electric hook-up of which 65

WEST COUNTRY

are fully serviced, hardstandings pitches. Centrally heated luxury showers, shop, laundry and information room. Dogs welcome.

(2m). Pennymoor Camping and Caravan Park, Higher Brocks Plantations, Modbury, Devon PL21 0SB. 01548 830542. www.pennymoor-camping.co.uk. Owner: RA & MD Blackler. From Exeter leave A38 at Wrangaton Cross turn L for 1m to crossroads, straight across and continue for about 4m to petrol garage then take second L and continue for 1m. Immaculately maintained, peaceful site with panoramic views. An ideal family park. Open March 15-Nov 15.

NEWTON ABBOT

(2.5m). Compass Caravans Touring Park, Higher Brocks Plantations, Teigngrace, Newton Abbot, Devon TQ12 6QZ. 01626 832792. www.compasscaravansdevon.com. Owner: John & Karen Lewis. Alongside A38 westbound, SP Teigngrace. Entrance 100yd on L. Accessory shop. Workshop, storage. Seasonal sites. Sales. Local shops and PO 1m. Country park 150yd.

(2.5m). Dornafield Touring Park, Two Mile Oak, Newton Abbot, Devon TQ12 6DD. 01803 812732. www.dornafield.com. Owner: JP, SL & JPA Dewhirst. Take A381 (Newton Abbot to Totnes) in 2m at Two Mile Oak Pub turn R in 0.5m first turn L. Park 100yd on R. Caravan Club affiliated site. Site is in a quiet valley close to an ancient farmhouse and surrounded by beautiful countryside. Toilet blocks, laundry facilities, baby and toddler washroom and MV service point. Games room, play equipment and dog walk on site. Golf and NCN route nearby. Facilities for disabled. Ideal for families. David Bellamy Gold Conservation Award. Open 14 March-3 Jan.

(3m). Lemonford Caravan Park, Bickington, Newton Abbot, Devon TQ12 6JR. 01626 821242/821263. www.lemonford.co.uk. Owner: Tim & Sam Ayres. From Exeter along A38 towards Plymouth take A382. Roundabout, 3rd exit to Bickington. AA 4 pennants. Excellent facilities for tourers and tents. Friendly, family run park, close to the coast and the moor. Holiday homes for hire. Golf course, cinema, shopping 3m in Newton Abbot. Horse riding 4m. Open March 15-Jan 15.

Manor Farm Campsite and B&B, Daccombe, Newton Abbot, Devon TQ12 4ST. 01803 328294. daccombe1@btopenworld.com. Owner: DJ Nicholls. A380 from Newton Abbot to Torquay to Kerswell Gardens. Over roundabout to traffic lights, turn L at lights up the hill. Follow campsite signs. B&B available. Open Easter-Oct 1.

(3m). Stover Caravan Club Site, Stover, Newton Abbot, Devon TQ12 6QG. 01626 361430. www.caravanclub.co.uk. Owner: The Caravan Club. See website for directions. Caravan Club members only. No tents. A quiet, open site in country park on edge of Dartmoor. Ideal for mature caravanners looking for peace and interesting walking. No sanitation. Some hardstandings. Gas and Gaz, dog walk on site. MV service point. Fishing and golf nearby. Open March-Nov.

(2m). Twelve Oaks Farm Caravan Park, Twelve Oaks Farm, Teigngrace, Newton Abbot, Devon TQ12 6QT. 01626 352769. www.twelveoaksfarm.co.uk. Owner: A W & A R Gale. From Exeter follow A38 Plymouth bound. Take turning off L SP Teigngrace (before Drumbridges roundabout), continue for about 1.5m through village and find Twelve Oaks on your L handside. Family run site on a working farm of nearly 250 acres. Bordered by the river Teign in the village of Teigngrace. Coarse fishing available. Heated outdoor swimming pool. Rallies welcome. Caravan storage. Self-catering holiday cottages.

NEWTON FERRERS

Briar Hill Farm Caravan & Camping Park, Briar Hill Farm, Newton Ferrers, Devon PL8 1AR. 01752 872252. Owner: Simon & Valerie Lister. 10m from Plymouth. A quiet picturesque caravan site in the centre of Newton Ferrers in 250yd to local shops (PO, grocery, butcher and chemist) and pub. Set on the opposite side of Newton Creek to Noss Mayo, which is a branch of the beautiful Yealm estuary. Open March-Nov.

OKEHAMPTON

(6m). Bridestowe Caravan Park, Glebe Park, Bridestowe, Okehampton, Devon EX20 4ER. 01837 861261. www.myoung.demon.co.uk. Owner: Mrs W A Young, Mr G W Young & Mr M S Young. From Okehampton, turn off A30 SP direction Bridestowe, in village follow caravan signs to park. Children allowed. Open March 1-Dec 30.

(3m). Bundu Camping & Caravan Park, Bundu, Sourton Down, Okehampton, Devon EX20 4HT. 01837 861611. www.bundu.co.uk. Owner: Mr M & Mrs F Sargent. From A30 take slip road A386 to Tavistock, L at T-junction then L again 100yd. Site 0.5m ahead. Access good. Level site in Dartmoor National Park. Direct access onto National Cycle Way. Adjacent Inn. Short walk to garage and shop. Near golf, fishing and horse riding.

(9m). Camping & Caravanning Club Site – Lydford, Okehampton, Devon EX20 4BE. 01822 820275. www.campingandcaravanningclub.co.uk. Owner: Camping & Caravanning Club. From A30 take A386 to Tavistock, continue to filling station on R. Turn R to Lydford. At War Memorial, turn R. Site signed 200yd. Site located in quiet rural setting, picturesque, plenty of space for children's games. Non-members welcome. All units accepted. Take a walk around the beautiful woodlands of Lydford Gorge. Walks along the ravine take you to the dramatic 27 metre White Lady waterfall and the Devil's Cauldron whirlpool. Dartmoor is in easy walking distance. Deals for families and backpackers. Open March-Oct.

PAIGNTON

(1m). Barton Pines, Blagdon Road, Paignton, Devon TQ3 3YG. 01803 553350. www.bartonpines.com. Owner: Mr McClarron. Turn R off A380 (Newton Abbot to Torquay) on to A380 (Torbay ring road to Paignton). In 2m turn R at Preston Down roundabout SP Berry Pomeroy and Barton Pines, 2m, crossroads is SP Barton Pines. Heated outdoor pool. Tennis. Open March 1-Oct 31.

WEST COUNTRY

■ **(1.5m). Beverley Park Holiday Centre, Goodrington Road, Paignton, Devon TQ4 7JE.** *01803 661968.* info@beverley-holidays.co.uk. www.beverley-holidays.co.uk. Off A379 Dartmouth to Paignton. Fabulous sea views overlooking Torbay. Lodges and touring open all year. Runner up Alan Rogers 2006. English Riviera 'Best Holiday Park' 2004. SW England Tourism Excellence 'Caravan Park of the Year' 2007/2008. Club. Bar. Heated indoor and outdoor pools. Tennis court. Sauna and fitness suite, playground. Beach, golf course 1m. Cinema, Paignton town 1.5m. David Bellamy Gold Conservation Award.

(3m). Byslades International Touring Park, Totnes Road, Paignton, Devon TQ4 7PY. *01803 555072.* info@byslades.co.uk. www.byslades.co.uk. Owner: Robert & Kay Wedd. 2m W of Paignton situated on A385. Friendly award winning park set in 23 acres of beautiful Devon countryside. Terraced pitches and excellent amenities. Sorry no dogs mid-July to end Aug. Nearby the historic town of Totnes, the South Hams and Dartmoor National Park. Open mid May-Sept.

■ **(1.5m). Whitehill Country Park, Stoke Road, Paignton, Devon TQ4 7PF.** *01803 782338.* info@whitehill-park.co.uk. www.whitehill-park.co.uk. Off A385 Totnes to Paignton. Countryside and woodland walking, bar, restaurant, takeaway, heated swimming pool, playgrounds, craft room, arcade, shop. Golf course and cinema 2m. 3m to nearest beach. David Bellamy Gold Conservation Award. Open April 9 – Oct 3.

(3m). Widend Touring Park, Berry Pomeroy Road, Marldon, Paignton, Devon TQ3 1RT. *01803 550116.* Owner: Roger & Heather Cowen & Family. Follow the A380 Torbay Ring road. Turn towards Marldon at the second roundabout. At the next roundabout turn second L into Five Lanes – Head towards Berry Pomeroy and Totnes through Marldon Village. Park on rh side 0.5m past Marldon. 4m to Torbay seafront, spacious, award-winning, family-run park with views of the sea, countryside and with superb facilities. Friendly atmosphere. Heated outdoor pool, adventure playground, family bar. Couples and families only. No dogs July and Aug. Seasonal pitches available. Static holiday homes for sale. Storage available. David Bellamy Gold Conservation Award. Open April – Sept.

PLYMOUTH

(6m). Pilgrim's Rest, 41 Knighton Road, Wembury, Plymouth, Devon PL9 0EA. *01752 863429.* Owner: Mrs D Manley. Certificated site for 5 caravans etc, and separate area for tents available at Pilgrim's Rest coastal village of Wembury in an Area of Outstanding Natural Beauty. Sea views. Beautiful walks. 5 mins drive from beach. On main bus route. Phone for more details and brochure. Open May-Sept.

(5m). Plymouth Sound Caravan Club Site, Bovisand Lane, Down Thomas, Plymouth, Devon PL9 0AE. *01752 862325.* www.caravanclub.co.uk. Owner: The Caravan Club. See website for directions. In easy reach of the historic port, set on a headland outside Plymouth with broad views over the sound and close to the South West Coastal footpath and lovely beaches. Own sanitation required. Good for walking, dog walk on site. Golf, watersports and NCN route nearby. Ideal for families. Non-members welcome. No tents. Open March-Oct.

(3.5m). Riverside Caravan Park, Liegham Manor Drive, Longbridge Road, Marsh Mills, Plymouth, Devon PL6 8LL. *01752 344122.* www.riversidecaravanpark.com. Owner: Ian Gray. Take Plymouth slip road from A38 to large roundabout, around roundabout, take road to Plymouth, 1st set traffic lights, turn L.

SALCOMBE

(2m). Alston Farm Camping & Caravan Site, Kingsbridge, Salcombe, Devon TQ7 3BJ. *01548 561260.* info@alstoncampsite.co.uk. www.alstoncampsite.co.uk. Owner: Mr P W Shepherd. Off A381. Level, sheltered site. RAC 3 pennants. Supermarket 1m, boating & fishing 2m, golf and cinema 3m. Lots of beaches in 5m. Open mid March-end Oct.

Bolberry House Farm Caravanning & Camping Park, Bolberry, Marlborough, Salcombe, Devon TQ7 3DY. *01548 561251.* www.bolberryparks.co.uk. Owner: Dudley & Jessie Stidston. Quiet, family-run park amidst outstanding coastal countryside, good access to superb cliff walks and all boating facilities with safe sandy beaches 1m. Children's play area and barn. Dogs welcome with separate exercising paddock. Low season discounts with special rates for over 50's. AA 3 pennants. Please book early. Open Easter-Oct.

(1m). Higher Rew Caravan & Camping Park, Malborough, Kingsbridge, Salcombe, Devon TQ7 3DW. *01548 842681.* www.higherrew.co.uk. Owner: Mrs V Squire. Follow A381 towards Salcombe. At Malborough turn R following signs for Soar. After 1m turn L towards Combe/South Sands. Rural situation. Good, clean facilities. Close to beaches, Salcombe Estuary and cliff walks.

Hope Cove

AA

KARRAGEEN
www.karrageen.co.uk

A Park with character and sea views.
Tree lined terraces, peaceful with plenty
of space. Hope Cove beach 1 mile.
Salcombe 4 miles. Licensed shop
with quality hot takeaway food.
First class toilet facilities.
Special rates for the over 50's
(not high season) from
£60.00 week incl ehu

Small fleet of luxury caravans for hire.

For colour brochure, please contact:
Phil & Nikki Higgin,
Karrageen Bolberry,
Malborough, Kingsbridge,
South Devon
Tel. 01540 501200   Fax. 01540 500192

---

94 MOTOR CARAVAN & CAMPING PARKS 2009

WEST COUNTRY

Brochure on application. Level pitches all with rural views. Tennis court for hire. Open from 21 March-31 Oct.

(3m). Sun Park, Soar Mill Cove, Malborough, Salcombe, Devon TQ7 3DS. *01548 561378*. www.sun-park.co.uk. Owner: Mrs B J Sweetman. On entering village of Malborough (on Kingsbridge to Salcombe road) turn sharp R, SP Soar. Park is 1.5 m down this road on R. Peaceful site, surrounded by National Trust land. Walking distance to beach. Playground. Indoor games and TV room. Open Easter-Sept.

SEATON

(0.5m). Manor Farm Caravan Site, Seaton Down Hill, Seaton, Devon EX12 2JA. *01297 21524*. www.manorfarmcaravansite.com. Owner: Mr M Salter. Off A3052 at Tower Cross, Seaton clearly signed. Glorious views of Lyme Bay and Axe Valley. Spacious, quiet, farm site with good facilities. Animals to see and feed. Good playground. Free showers. Beach 1m. Breakfasts served by the site shop, own lamb, pork and free range eggs sold in shop. Open March 15-Nov 15.

SIDMOUTH

(3m). Kingsdown Tail Caravan & Camping Park, Salcombe Regis, Sidmouth, Devon EX10 0PD. *01297 680313*. www.kingsdowntail.co.uk. Owner: Mr IJ Mckenzie-Edwards. Adjacent to A3052 3m E of Sidmouth. A family run quiet, five-acre park. Level and sheltered just inland from Devon's stunning heritage coastline. A variety of craft, animal and historic attractions close by. Open 15 March-15 Nov.

(3m). Oakdown Touring & Holiday Caravan Park, Gatedown Lane, Weston, Sidmouth, Devon EX10 0PH. *01297 680387*. www.oakdown.co.uk. Owner: Mr & Mrs R Franks. On the A3052, E of Sidmouth. Turn R at Oakdown International signs. Level landscaped park. Play area. Microwave. Deep freeze. Free hot water. Family bathrooms and dishwashing facilities all centrally heated. Field trail to donkey sanctuary. Serviced super pitches available. Alarmed caravan storage. Brochure available. Adjacent 9-hole, par 3 golf course now open, with new reception/café. Near Jurassic Coast. David Bellamy Gold Conservation Award. Open from 1 April to 7 Nov.

Beautiful South Devon

- 10 acres of woodland
- Modern touring facilities and holiday homes
- Outdoor heated pool
- David Bellamy Gold Award
- Hayloft Bar & family room
- Children's play areas
- Woodland walks
- Shop, café & takeaway

Whitehill Country Park
Stoke Road, Paignton, South Devon TQ4 7PF
info@whitehill-park.co.uk
01803 782 338
www.whitehill-park.co.uk

Beverley Holidays

Escape to the perfect seaside resort and rediscover the things that really matter.

- Family run 5 star holidays
- Playground & children's room
- Indoor & outdoor pools
- Great nightly entertainment
- Crazy golf, tennis & snooker tables
- On site bars, restaurants & takeaway

holidays to remember

01803 661970   HOLIDAY CARAVANS   TOURING   LODGES
www.beverley-holidays.co.uk

---

fun filled holidays
REGISTER ONLINE FOR LATEST OFFERS
woolacombe.com/ipc
WOOLACOMBE BAY

WEST COUNTRY

(5m). Putts Corner Caravan Club Site, Sidbury, Sidmouth, Devon EX10 0QQ. *01404 42875. www.caravanclub.co.uk.* Owner: The Caravan Club. See website for directions. Open site surrounded by trees, a good base from which to explore south Devon and Dorset. Toilet with privacy cubicles block and laundry facilities. MV service point. Dog walk nearby. Play equipment. Boules pitch. Non-members welcome. Open March-Nov.

(1.5m). Salcombe Regis Caravan & Camping Park, Salcombe Regis, Sidmouth, Devon EX10 0JH. *01395 514303. www.salcombe-regis.co.uk.* Owner: Mr Neil Hook. E of Sidmouth SP off A3052. Exeter to Lyme Regis coast road. Hardstandings for tourers and motor caravans. Nearest park to Sidmouth. In an area of outstanding natural beauty on the Heritage coast. Ideal base for exploring rural East Devon. Brochure available. 2m from Sidmouth golf club, cinema, shops. Open Easter-Nov.

SOUTH BRENT

(1.5m). Cheston Caravan Park, Wrangaton Road, South Brent, Devon TQ10 9HF. *01364 72586. www.chestoncaravanpark.co.uk.* Owner: E Gourley. A38 Exeter, exit SP Wrangaton Cross. Level site. Showers. Set in Dartmoor National Park. Fishing, golf, shop, PO, doctor, horse riding, leisure centre, all nearby. Holiday caravans to let. Open March-Oct.

SOUTH MOLTON

(4.5m). Romansleigh Holiday Park, Odam Hill, South Molton, Devon EX36 4NB. *01769 550259. www.romansleigh.com.* Owner: John & Heather Gazeley. On B3137 South Molton to Witheridge road. SP R 2m past Alswear. 5m to nearby facilities. 10m Exmoor, 20m coast. 14-acre secluded, rural site, ideal touring base for Devon. Heated pool. Games room. Licensed club and bar open all year. Snooker and pool, skittle alley. TV. Pet animals. Open 15 March-31 Oct.

(4m). Yeo Valley Holiday Park, Blackcock Inn, Molland, South Molton, Devon EX36 3NW. *01769 550297. www.yeovalleyholidays.com.* Owner: Mr M D Harris & Mrs Z R Harris. Follow Blackcock Inn sign on the A361 about 4m E of South Molton. Indoor swimming pool (Easter-Sept). Near country inn, fishing, clay pigeon shooting. Children and dogs welcome. Open March-Nov.

(4m). Yeo Valley Holiday Park, Molland, South Molton, Devon EX36 3NW. *01769 550297. www.yeovalleyholidays.com.* Owner: Mr & Mrs AW Bull. E of South Molton. 2m off A361. Take B3227 to Bampton. A361, follow The Black Cock Inn signs. Pub. Indoor heated swimming pool. Hot showers. About 4m from Exmoor. Open March-Nov.

TAVISTOCK

(2m). Harford Bridge Holiday Park, Peter Tavy, Tavistock, Devon PL19 9LS. *01822 810349. www.harfordbridge.co.uk.* Owner: Mr G Williamson. Off A386 Okehampton to Tavistock Road, take Peter Tavy turn. Level, sheltered park by the river Tavy in Dartmoor National Park. Self-catering caravan holiday homes. Rose Award. Fly fishing, tennis, walking – nearby golf, pony trekking, swimming pool. Cinema, shops, PO, doctor, garage all in 2m. David Bellamy Gold Conservation Award.

(2m). Higher Longford Caravan Park, Moorshop, Tavistock, Devon PL19 9LQ. *01822 613360. www.higherlongford.co.uk.* Owner: Higher Longford Ltd. From Tavistock take B3357 to Princetown, 2m on RHS before Moors. Deluxe toilet block, bathroom, disabled toilet. Campers lounge/games room, shop, off licence. Well maintained, level pitches, grass, tarmac and hardstanding. David Bellamy Gold Conservation Award.

(2.5m). Langstone Manor Camping and Caravan Park, Moortown, Tavistock, Devon PL19 9JZ. *01822 613371. web@langstone-manor.co.uk. www.langstone-manor.co.uk.* Owner: D & J Kellett. Off A386 near Tavistock, take B3357 to Princetown. Turn R at crossroads follow brown signs. Quiet secluded park with direct access to Dartmoor National Park. Clean facilities and warm welcome. Lounge bar, evening meals. Games room. Near National Trust properties, gardens, golf, fishing, horse-riding, climbing. Swimming pool, slide and cinema available nearby. Open March-end Oct.

(4m). Woodovis Park, Gulworthy, Tavistock, Devon PL19 8NY. *01822 832968. www.woodovis.com.* Owner: John & Dorothy Lewis. 3.5m W of Tavistock via A390 Callington and Gunnislake road. Turn R at roundabout SP Lamerton, Chipshop. Park sign 1.5m on L. Spacious, peaceful, quiet and rural with outstanding views. Sauna & jacuzzi, mini golf, games room. Play area. Bread/croissants baked on site. Tavistock: theatre, cinema, shops 4m. Golf 4m. Fishing 2m. Plymouth 15m. Open March 15-Nov 1.

TEIGNMOUTH

(1m). Coast View Holiday Park, Torquay Road, Shaldon, Teignmouth, Devon TQ14 0BG. *01626 872392. www.coastview.co.uk.* Owner: Mr M Collett. S of Teignmouth, 0.5m through Shaldon on A379. Shop, bar, indoor swimming pool, adventure playground. Holiday chalets and caravans. Superb views of Lyme Bay. Families and couples only. Fees on application. Open mid March-end Oct.

(3m). Wear Farm, Newton Road, Bishopsteignton, Teignmouth, Devon TQ14 9PT. *01626 779265. nigdavey@aol.com.* Owner: E S Coaker & Co. On A381 between Teignmouth and Newton Abbot. Pleasant site beside river Teign with unequalled views over the estuary. Showers. Play area. Free brochure. Open Easter-Oct.

TIVERTON

(5m). Minnows Caravan Club Site, Sampford Peverell, Tiverton, Devon EX16 7EN. *01884 821770. www.ukparks.co.uk/minnows.* Owner: Zig & Krystyna Grochala. Leave M5, J27. Take A361 SP Barnstaple. After 0.25m take slip road on L and follow brown signs. Caravan Club affiliated. Coarse fishing and canoeing on Grand Western Canal. 15mins walk to pub, shops, PO, doctor & tennis courts. Non-members welcome. Golf driving range 0.25m. Public transport. National Cycle Route 3 and walking on the canal paths. Open March 9-Nov 9.

(8.5m). West Middlewick Farm, Nomansland, Tiverton, Devon EX16 8NP. *01884 861235. www.westmiddlewick.co.uk.* Owner: Mr JH & Mrs JL Gibson, John & Jo Gibson. From Tiverton take B3137 towards Witheridge. 1m after Nomansland on N side of road. Small, informal site, in the family for 70 years. Hardstandings. B&B. Working farm with superb views and walks. Level 3 acre field with easy access. Central for touring Devon. Shops, pub and PO 1m.

(7m). Zeacombe House Caravan Park, East Anstey, Tiverton, Devon EX16 9JU. *01398 341279. www.zeacombeadultretreat.co.uk.* Owner: Peter

YOUR TOP 101 SITES 2009

96 MOTOR CARAVAN & CAMPING PARKS 2009

See page 5 for key to symbols and abbreviations

WEST COUNTRY

& Lin Keeble. Exit J27 to A361 Tiverton. Turn R next roundabout A396 Minehead Dulverton 5m, Exeter Inn L to B3227. SP S Molton 5m turn L. Level, lawned site. Hardstandings. Razor points, hairdryers. Home-cooked food available daily. Good for touring Exmoor, Taunton, Minehead and Exeter. Adults only. AA 4 pennants. Coarse and trout fishing 3m; golf 10m. Open March 15-Oct 31.

TORQUAY

(2.5m). Widdicombe Farm Touring Park, Compton, Torquay, Devon TQ3 1ST. *01803 558325.* www.widdicombefarm.co.uk. Owners: Gordon & Thelma Glynn. 2.5m from Torquay and Paignton. On the A380. Separate adults only sections. Lovely views; landscaped, spacious, level pitches. Easy access. Luxurious facilities, free hot water, ladies private washrooms, launderette and bathroom, shop. Entertainment bar and restaurant. Bargain breaks from £50 per week inc electric and awning. Discounts for over 60s. Separate family area and adults only areas. Fully services pitches available. Storage and seasonal welcome. Golf, cinema, shopping centre all in 2m.

Open March-mid Oct.

TOTNES

(5m). Higher Well Farm Holiday Park, Waddeton Road, Stoke Gabriel, Totnes, Devon TQ9 6RN. *01803 782289.* www.higherwellfarmholidaypark.co.uk. Owner: Mr & Mrs John & Liz Ball. A380 from Exeter to Torquay. Turn R on to the ring road, R for Totnes on A385. L at Collaton Carvery pub for Stoke Gabriel and follow SP. Park in 1.75m. 1m from village of Stoke Gabriel on River Dart, shops, PO. Golf course, leisure centre 3m. Cinema 4m. Open 4 April-31 Oct.

Ramslade Caravan Club Site, Stoke Road, Stoke Gabriel, Totnes, Devon TQ9 6QB. *01803 782575.* www.caravanclub.co.uk. Owner: The Caravan Club. See website for directions. 2.5m from Paignton. Caravan Club members only. A delightfully situated small park amid rural surroundings with beautiful hillside views from most pitches. Toilet blocks, laundry facilities and baby and toddler washroom. Games room, play area and dog walk on site. Fishing, golf, watersports and NCN route nearby. Facilities for disabled. Ideal for families. Quiet off-peak. Open March-Nov.

Steamer Quay Caravan Club Site, Steamer Quay Road, Totnes, Devon TQ9 5AL. *01803 862738.* www.caravanclub.co.uk. Owner: The Caravan Club. See website for directions. A surprisingly quiet, green and open site with rural views yet in a short walk of bustling Totnes. Advance booking essential Bank Holidays. Non-members welcome. Toilet block & laundry facilities. Battery charging available. Veg prep area, gas and Gaz, quiet off peak. Near beach, walks, recycling, NCN cycle route, fishing and golf. Ideal for families. Open March-Oct.

UMBERLEIGH

(0.25m). Camping & Caravanning Club Site – Umberleigh, Over Weir, Umberleigh, Devon EX37 9DU. *01769 560009.* www.campingandcaravanningclub.co.uk. Owner: Camping & Caravanning Club. On A377 from Barnstaple turn R, onto B3227 at Umberleigh sign, site on R in 0.25m. 8m from Barnstaple. In

---

HIGHER WELL FARM HOLIDAY PARK
TOURING & MOTOR CARAVANS & TENTS WELCOME

A quiet, secluded farm park, central for touring South Devon, within 4 miles Torbay beaches and 1 mile from River Dart. Facilities include toilet and shower block with dishwashing and family rooms. Launderette, shop and payphone. Electric hook-ups and hard standings.

ALSO HOLIDAY CARAVANS FOR HIRE

John & Liz Ball, Higher Well Farm Holiday Park, Stoke Gabriel TQ9 6RN
Tel: 01803 782289   www.higherwellfarmholidaypark.co.uk

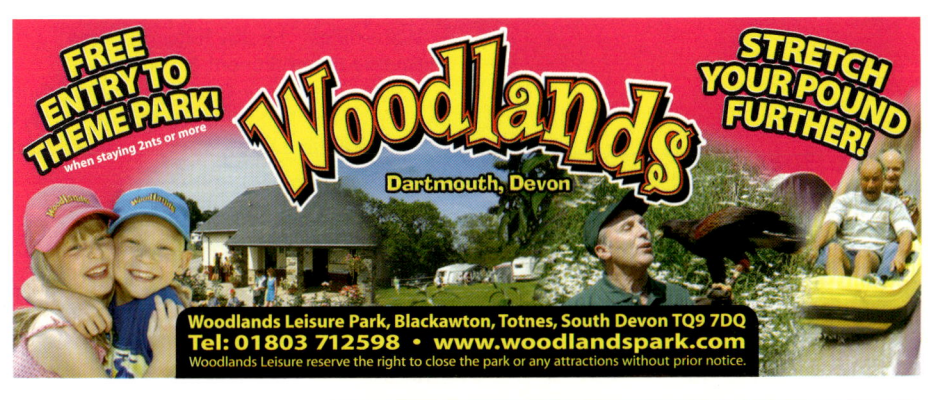

Woodlands
Dartmouth, Devon

FREE ENTRY TO THEME PARK! when staying 2nts or more

STRETCH YOUR POUND FURTHER!

Woodlands Leisure Park, Blackawton, Totnes, South Devon TQ9 7DQ
Tel: 01803 712598 • www.woodlandspark.com
Woodlands Leisure reserve the right to close the park or any attractions without prior notice.

---

fun filled holidays
REGISTER ONLINE FOR LATEST OFFERS
woolacombe.com/ipc   **WOOLACOMBE BAY**

---

www.motorcaravanmagazine.co.uk   MOTOR CARAVAN & CAMPING PARKS 2009   **97**

TOURING FROM ONLY £15 per van a night

CAMPING FROM ONLY £5 per person a night

fun
filled holidays

Four award winning Holiday Parks set in Devon's breathtaking countryside next to Woolacombe's 3 miles of golden Blue Flag sandy beach!

SEAVIEW Camping, Touring & Supersite Pitches plus Luxury Lodges & Holiday Homes

Over 40 FREE activities...

- 10 Heated Indoor & Outdoor Pools
- Waterslides • Health Suite • Cinema
- Nightly Entertainment & Star Cabaret
- Tennis • Snooker • Crazy Golf • Kid's Clubs
- Kid's Indoor & Outdoor Play Areas • Playzone
- Coarse Fishing Ponds ... Plus so much more!

...and for just a little more

- 10 Pin Bowling
- 17th Century Inn
- Waves Ceramic Studio
- Affiliated Golf Club
- Indoor Bowls Rinks
- WaterWalkerz
- Restaurants & Bars
- Activities Programme
- Kiddy Karts
- Sports Bar
- Amusement Arcade
- Electric Hook-ups
- Laundry Facilities
- On-site Shop
- Climbing Wall
- Swimming Lessons

REGISTER ONLINE FOR LATEST OFFERS!!
woolacombe.com/ipc
01271 870 343

WOOLACOMBE BAY

WEST COUNTRY

beautiful and sheltered Taw valley. In easy reach of beaches, surfing and swimming. Fishing, on-site also games room, skittle alley, pool table, table tennis, public phone, ice-pack freezing, launderette, tennis court with free tennis coaching for children in high season, non-members welcome. All units accepted. Deals for families and backpackers. Loo Of The Year (4 stars). Open April-Oct.

WOOLACOMBE

(2m). Damage Barton, Mortehoe, Woolacombe, Devon EX34 7EJ. *01271 870963.* info@damagebarton.co.uk. www.campingandcaravanningclub.co.uk. Owner: JP & M S Lethbridge. A361 turn L on to B3343 at Mullacott Cross roundabout. Follow Mortehoe signs. After Turnpike cross turn R then straight along minor road. Site 1m on R. Caravan Club Affiliated Club & CC Club site - members only. Site on 600-acre working family farm. Toilet blocks, laundry facilities and MV service point. Play area and dog walk on site. Near golf, watersports and NCN route. Facilities for disabled. Quiet and peaceful off-peak. Ideal for families. Good area for walking. Open mid-March-5 Nov.

■ **(1m). Easewell Farm Holiday Parc, Mortehoe, Woolacombe, Devon EX34 7HW.** *01271 870343.* www.woolacombe.com. Owner: Mr R Lancaster. M5, J27 take A361. Turn L at Mullacott Cross to Mortehoe village. Easewell SP on the R before the village. Indoor heated pool, bar, restaurant and takeaway. Bus to beach. Use of facilities at 3 other nearby holiday parks. Fishing nearby. Golf course on site. Doctor, shops 10mins by car. PO in 10mins walk. Open March-Oct.

Europa Park, Station Road, Woolacombe, Devon EX34 7AN. *01271 871425.* www.europapark.co.uk. Owner: Graham Toms & Sue Wallace. Full facilities with superb camping, surf cabins, luxury wooden lodges, static caravans, licensed club house, sauna, children's play area.

(1m). Golden Coast Holiday Village, Station Road, Woolacombe, Devon EX34 7HW. *01271 870343.* www.woolacombe.com. Owner: Woolacombe Bay Holiday Parcs. M5 J27, A361 Barnstaple to Mullacott Cross. First exit to Woolacombe. SP. Tennis, cabaret, kids' club. Hair & beauty salon. Near ten-pin bowling, fishing, golf course. Bus to beach. Heated indoor and outdoor pools, restaurant and take-away, bar, shop, cinema, sauna, solarium, amusements. Ceramic studio. Open Feb-Jan.

(1m). Little Roadway Farm Camping Park, Woolacombe, Devon EX34 7HL. *01271 870313.* Owner: Steve & Vanessa Malin. J27, M5, A361 Barnstaple towards Ilfracombe. Mullacott Cross roundabout L to Woolacombe B3343, first L B3231 to Georgeham, 2m on L. L/R camping park. Open March-Nov.

(1m). North Morte Farm Caravan Park, North Morte Road, Mortehoe, Woolacombe, Devon EX34 7EG. *01271 870381.* www.northmortefarm.co.uk. Owner: Mr & Mrs B W Gilbert. Off B3343. In Mortehoe village turn off at PO on to North Morte Road, park is 500yd on L. Quiet, family park in beautiful countryside. Play area. Payphone. Sea 500yd. Golf course, shop 0.5m. Open April 1-end Sept.

(1m). Twitchen Parc, Mortehoe, Woolacombe, Devon EX34 7ES. *01271 870343.* www.woolacombe.com. Owner:

Relax *you've earned it*

Easewell holiday park

Easewell is a family owned holiday park offering camping, touring and farm cottages, set amidst the beautiful & tranquil North Devon countryside with **STUNNING SEA VIEWS**.

Come and appreciate the meaning of relaxation.

Register online for latest offers

woolacombe.com/ipc 01271 870343

Great facilities
- Indoor Heated Pool
- Indoor Bowls
- Indoor Skittles
- Snooker
- Club House & Café
- 9 Hole Affiliated Golf Course
- Takeaway & Restaurant
- Adventure Playgrounds
- Indoor Games Room
- Dishwashing Area
- Electric Hook-ups
- Super Site Pitches
- Free Hot Showers
- Well Stocked Shop
- Launderette
- 1 Mile to Woolacombe Beach

GREAT NEW RATES FOR 2009

Part of **WOOLACOMBE BAY Holiday Parks**

WEST COUNTRY

Woolacombe Bay Holiday Parcs. M5, J27, A361 from Barnstaple L on B3343 1.75m. Keep R, SP Mortehoe for 1.5m. Park on L. Licensed club. Entertainment. Indoor and outdoor pool. Adventure playground. Children's club. Bus to beach. Sauna, sunshower, bar, restaurant and takeaway, fishing, golf course, crazy golf. Open March-Oct.

(1.5m). Warcombe Farm Camping Park, Station Road, Mortehoe, Woolacombe, Devon EX34 7EJ. 01271 870690. www.warcombefarm.co.uk. Owner: Martin & Christine Grafton. Turn R off B3343 towards Mortehoe, park on R in less than 1m. Beautiful sea views. Clean, excellent facilities. Play area. Fishing lake. Open March 15-Oct 31.

(2m). Willingcott Caravan Club Site, Woolacombe, Devon EX34 7HN. 01271 870554. www.caravanclub.co.uk. Owner: The Caravan Club. See website for directions. Caravan Club members only. No tents. Spacious site with lovely views over Lundy and only 2m from best sandy beach in the county. Toilet block with privacy cubicles & laundry facilities. Some hardstandings, MV service pt, veg prep area, gas and gaz, dog walk nearby. Quiet and peaceful off peak. NCN cycle route in 5m. Boules pitch. Play equipment. Fishing, golf and watersports nearby. Ideal for families. Open March 27-Nov 9.

■ **(0.75m). Woolacombe Bay Holiday Village, Sandy Lane, Woolacombe, Devon EX34 7AH.** 01271 870343. www.woolacombe.com. Owner: Woolacombe Bay Holiday Parcs. M5 J27, A361 from Barnstaple then first exit at Mullacott Cross, R turn to Mortehoe. No tourers. Indoor & outdoor heated pool, Romano health spa, tennis, golf, free cabaret and kids club. Bus between sites and beach. Shop, restaurant and take away, bar, solarium. Open March-Oct.

■ **Woolacombe Sands Holiday Park, Beach Road, Woolacombe, Devon EX34 7AF.** 01271 870569. www.woolacombe-sands.co.uk. Owner: Richards Holidays. Set in beautiful countryside overlooking fabulous golden sands. Indoor heated pool, club with entertainment. Children's club May-Sept. Open April-Oct.

SOMERSET
BREAN

(5m). Warren Farm Holiday Centre (Isis Park), Brean Sands, Brean, Somerset TA8 2RP. 01278 751227. www.warren-farm.co.uk. Owner: HG & J Harris. Leave M5, J22. Take B3140 to Berrow and Brean. 1.5m past Brean Leisure Park. Family run park in 100yd of sandy beach. Large indoor play area, shop, bar and restaurant. Dogs not allowed in hire caravans. Riding, swimming, golf available nearby. Open April-end Oct.

BRIDGWATER

Fairways International Touring Caravan & Camping Park, Bath Road, Bawdrip, Bridgwater, Somerset TA7 8PP. 01278 685569. www.fairwaysint.btinternet.co.uk. 2m off J23, M5 in Glastonbury direction. Park at junction of A39 and B3141. Purpose built park on drained land. Short stays, storage, seasonals, rallies, pensioners' weeks. 7-day booking in March, June, Sept, Oct (£55 a week). Accessory centre on site. Open March 1-Nov 16.

■ **(6m). Mill Farm Caravan & Camping Park, Fiddington, Bridgwater, Somerset TA5 1JQ.** 01278 732286. www.millfarm.biz. Owner: Mr M J Evans. M5 J23 or 24 to Bridgwater, take A39 (Minehead direction) for 6m. Turn R to Fiddington, follow caravan and camping signs. Beautiful, sheltered site. 3 heated swimming pools, riding centre, canoes and boating on shallow lake. Phone for brochure. See display advertisement.

(3m). The Fairways International Caravan & Camping Park, Bath Road, Bawdrip, Bridgwater, Somerset TA7 8PP. 01278 685569. www.fairwaysint.btinternet.co.uk. Owner: Mr & Mrs Walker. Access from A39 junction with B3141; 2m off junction 23 of M5. Free showers, shaver and drying points. Near sports and sandy beaches. Winner 'Loo of the Year' every year 1994-2002. Fishing 0.5m, boating 2m. 'Pensioners only' weeks in March, June, Sept and Oct, 7 days consecutive booking £55; daily £10. Open March 1-Nov 16.

BURNHAM-ON-SEA

(1m). Burnham Touring Park, Stoddens Road, Burnham-on-Sea, Somerset TA8 2NZ. 01278 788355. www.basc.co.uk. Owner: Burnham Association of Sports Clubs. M5, J22, head to Burnham-on-sea. Turn R at Tesco roundabout, 0.5m to sharp L hand bend. 100 yards on R. 30-acre, quiet, sheltered sports ground near beach and shops. Suits self-contained caravanner. Inc the use of clubhouse. Skittles and pool in club house. Booking advisable. Open March 1 – Dec 31.

(0.25m). Burnham-On-Sea Holiday Village, Marine Drive, Burnham-on-

WOOLACOMBE SANDS HOLIDAY PARK
IT'S FUN FOR ALL THE FAMILY
NEAREST HOLIDAY PARK TO THE BEACH

Heated Indoor & Outdoor Swimming Pools, Licensed Club, Nightly Entertainment, Amusement Arcade, Indoor & Outdoor Play Areas, Crazy Golf & Bowling.
• Touring & Camping • Chalets, Caravans & Cottages

Beach Rd, Woolacombe, N. Devon EX34 7AF
01271 870569
www.woolacombe-sands.co.uk

CAMPING FROM £5 pppn

WEST COUNTRY

See page 5 for key to symbols and abbreviations

Sea, Somerset TA8 1LA. *01278 783591.* www.burnhamonsea-park.co.uk. Owner: Bourne Leisure Ltd. From A38 take B3139 to Burnham. Turn L after garage to Marine Drive – the park is 400yd on the L. On Esplanade facing sea, near town. 95 acres of level park with indoor and outdoor swimming pools. Entertainment. Mini market. Bakery. Launderette. Children play area. Welcome Host Award. David Bellamy Gold Conservation Award. Open March-end Oct.

(4.5m). Diamond Farm Caravan Park, Weston Road, Brean, Burnham-on-Sea, Somerset TA8 2RL. *01278 751263.* www.diamondfarm.co.uk. Owner: Mr MHR Hicks Ltd. Off A370. From coast road take junction to Weston and Lympsham, Diamond Farm is 800yd from junction. Working farm. 0.5m to golf, beach. Open March-Oct.

■ **(3m). Holiday Resort Unity, Coast Road, Brean Sands, Burnham-on-Sea, Somerset TA8 2RB.** *01278 751235.* www.hru.co.uk. Off M5 J22. Follow signs for Brean Leisure Park for 4.5m. Bars, entertainment, food venues. Pool with slides, 18-hole golf course, riding, fishing, children's club. Fun park with 30 rides and attractions, cinema, bingo, play area. David Bellamy Silver Conservation Award. Open Feb – Nov.

(1m). Home Farm Holiday Park & Country Club, Edithmead, Burnham-on-Sea, Somerset TA9 4HD. *01278 788888.* www.homefarmholidaypark.com. Owner: Mr G Atkinson. M5 exit 22, to Burnham-on-Sea, Edithmead. Level site. Heated showers and bathrooms. Gift shop. Adventure playground. Fishing. Bars, live entertainment. Swimming pool. Caravan service and sales. Open Feb-Jan.

(3.5m). Hurn Lane Caravan Club Site, Berrow, Burnham-on-Sea, Somerset TA8 2QT. *01278 751412.* www.caravanclub.co.uk. Owner: The Caravan Club. See website for directions. Caravan Club members only. No tents. 15mins walk from safe, sandy beach. Play area. Arrive after 12 noon. Toilet blocks. Privacy cubicles. Laundry facilities. Veg prep. MV service point. Gas and Gaz. Late night arrivals area. Near golf, fishing and watersports. Open March-Nov.

(6m). Northam Farm Caravan Park, South Road, Brean, Burnham-on-Sea, Somerset TA8 2SE. *01278 751244.* www.northamfarm.co.uk. Owner: Mr MH Scott. Easy access from M5, J22. SP to Brean 0.5m past Leisure Park on R. Attractive family run park near 5m of sandy beach. 30-acre park. Children's play areas, fishing lake, café, shop, launderette and dog walks. Open March-Oct.

(3m). Rose Farm Touring Park, Red Road, Berrow, Burnham-on-Sea, Somerset TA8 2RW. *01278 785888.* Owner: Mr F L Forrest & Mr D Kruk. Open March 1-Oct 31.

(4m). Southfield Farm Caravan Park, Brean, Burnham-on-Sea, Somerset TA8 2RL. *01278 751233.* office. southfield@btinternet.com. Owner: A G Hicks Ltd. Off B3139, J22, M5, 4m N of Burnham. Near golf course and entertainment. Own access to beach. Open March-Oct.

CHARD

(1.5m). Alpine Grove Touring Park, Alpine Grove, Forton, Chard, Somerset TA20 4HD. *01460 63379.* www.alpinegrovetouringpark.com. Owner: Richard & Helen Gurd. A358 to B3162 and A30 then B3167. 8.5-acre park of oaks and rhododendrons. Hardstanding area. Free showers, laundry, swings, outdoor heated pool, trampoline, walking, cycling. New log cabin for hire. David Bellamy Silver Conservation Award. Open April 1-Oct 1.

(4m). Five Acres Caravan Club Site, Beetham, Chard, Somerset TA20 3QA. *01460 234519.* www.caravanclub.co.uk. Owner: The Caravan Club. See website for directions. Pleasant site, quiet off peak,

---

Mill Farm Caravan and Camping Park
Fiddington, Bridgwater, Somerset TA5 1JQ

Family friendly & sheltered country Park. Situated at the foot of the beautiful Quantock Hills and beside a picturesque stream. The Ideal family site, Free Boating & Swimming. Fully licenced Club & Bar with Entertainment and Hot Take-Away Food during high season. Well Stocked Shop, Off Licence, Tourist information. Electric Hook-ups, clean modern toilet blocks and FREE showers, Laundry room, Payphone. Good Local Pubs

Holiday Apartments to Let. Caravan Storage. Rallies Welcome. Separate Meadows Available

TEL: 01278 732286
WEB: www.millfarm.biz

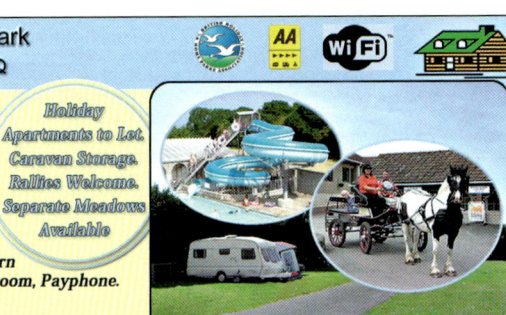

Holiday Resort UNITY — More than just a holiday! All the facilities you could want!

The South West's Leading Resort!
PITCHES FOR CARAVANS, TENTS & MOTORHOMES!
LODGES, CARAVANS, VILLAS AND TENTS FOR HIRE & SALE.
Book online www.hru.co.uk or call 0845 230 3350

www.motorcaravanmagazine.co.uk   MOTOR CARAVAN & CAMPING PARKS 2009 **101**

WEST COUNTRY

slightly sloping in lovely countryside. Non-members welcome. No tents. Advance bookings advised, bank holidays, July/Aug. Some hardstandings. Toilet blocks. Laundry facilities. Veg prep. MV service point. Gas and Gaz. Ideal for families. NCN cycle path in 5m. Open March-Oct.

(1m). Snowdown Hill Farm, Berleymow's Farm Shop, Chard, Somerset TA20 3PS. 01460 62130. Owner: Mrs R Burrough. From Chard take A30 W (to Honiton), 0.75m turn R into Farm Shop car park. Lovely views, peaceful. Children and dogs welcome. Farm park open July to Sept. Country walks.

(3m). South Somerset Holiday Park Ltd, The Turnpike, A30 Exeter Road, Chard, Somerset TA20 3EA. 01460 66036. sshpltd@btconnect.com. Owner: RM Weeks. W of Chard on A30 to Exeter. Newly refurbished toilet and shower facilities. Children's play area. 4-acre dog walk area. All-weather pitches. Many local attractions. GS. Open March 1-Jan 31.

CHEDDAR

(1m). Broadway House Caravan and Camping Park, Axbridge Road, Cheddar, Somerset BS27 3DB. 01934 742610. www.broadwayhouse.uk.com. Owner: Mr & Mrs DR Moore. On A371 between Cheddar and Axbridge. Heated pool. Licensed bar, family room. TV. Launderette. Showers, bathrooms. Playgrounds, archery, abseiling, caving canoeing. Crazy golf and skateboard park. Open March-Nov.

(3m). Bucklegrove Caravan Park, Wells Road, Rodney Stoke, Cheddar, Somerset BS27 3UZ. 01749 870261. www.bucklegrove.co.uk. Owner: Mr & Mrs D Clarke. On A371 between Wells and Cheddar. Beautifully, landscaped, family-run park with clean, modern facilities. Dogs off-peak only. Free indoor heated pool. Spacious pitches with parking beside caravan. Holiday homes for sale and hire. David Bellamy Silver Conservation Award. Open March 1-Jan 15.

Cheddar Bridge Touring Park, Draycott Road, Cheddar, Somerset BS27 3RJ. 01934 743048. www.cheddarbridge.co.uk. Owner: D Combe and T Combe. On A371 through Cheddar Village. Next to football club on R. Adults only. Walk to shops, village and gorge. Fishing, PO, doctors, quiet. Views of Mendips riverside setting. Open March-Nov.

Cheddar Caravan Club Site, Gas House Lane, Draycott Road, Cheddar, Somerset BS27 3RL. 01934 740207. www.caravanclub.co.uk. Owner: The Caravan Club. See website for directions. Caravan Club members only. No tents. This site situated on the edge of Cheddar village boasts magnificent views of the Mendips and surrounding countryside. Toilet blocks and laundry facilities. Fishing, golf and watersports nearby. Good area for walking. Quiet and peaceful off-peak. Facilities for the disabled. Open April-Nov.

(3m). Netherdale Caravan & Camping Park, Bridgwater Road (A38), Sidcot, Winscombe, Cheddar, Somerset BS25 1NH. 01934 843007. www.netherdale.net. Owner: Mr VJ Mortimer & Mrs Y A Mortimer. Easy to find on A38 road midway between Bristol and Bridgwater. Village shops/supermarket/takeaways 1m. Restaurant/pub next door. Pools, sports centres, activity centre, ski slopes 3m. Golf and fishing 4m. Mendip Hills adjoining. Excellent walking area. Dogs allowed on lead only. Open March 1-Oct 31.

(2m). Rodney Stoke Caravan Site, Rodney Stoke Inn, Wells Road, Cheddar, Somerset BS27 3XB. 01749 870209. Owner: Neil Sinclair. On A371 midway between Cheddar and Wells. Adults only site. Excellent for walkers, tourist attractions. Small quiet park behind pub. Open March 1-Oct 31.

CONGRESBURY

(4m). Oak Farm Touring Park, Weston Road, Congresbury, Somerset BS49 5EB. 01934 833246. ben@sweet.orangehome.co.uk. Owner: BA Sweet. On A370, 4m from J21, M5. Small dogs allowed with permission. Level orchard site, close to all amenities. Booking advised. Near golf course, Cheddar Valley Railway Walk, cycle way to Cheddar. Fishing. Village with shops close by. Next to Greek restaurant. Open April 1-Oct 1.

DULVERTON

(5m). Exe Valley Caravan Site, Bridgetown, Dulverton, Somerset TA22 9JR. 01643 851432. www.exevalleycamping.co.uk. Owners: Christine & Paul Matthews. On A396. Level site in beautiful wooded valley in Exmoor National Park. Hot water. Shaver points. Gas. Fly fishing – no charge. Adults only. Tents welcome. Pitches beside river or mill stream. Pub 500yd, good walking. Open mid March-mid Oct.

Exmoor House Caravan Club Site, Dulverton, Somerset TA22 9HL. 01398 323268. www.caravanclub.co.uk. Owner: The Caravan Club. See website for directions. Ideal for Exmoor. Pretty site overlooked by wooded hillsides. Shops 200yd. Dog walk. Gas and Gaz. MV waste. Non-members welcome. No tents. Advance booking necessary. Do not arrive before 1pm. Some hardstandings. Toilet blocks. Privacy cubicles. Laundry facilities. Veg prep. Fishing, NCN cycle path in 5m. Quiet off peak. Open March-Jan.

(3m). Lakeside Caravan Club Site, Higher Grants, Exebridge, Dulverton, Somerset TA22 9BE. 01398 324068. www.caravanclub.co.uk. Owner: The Caravan Club. See website for directions. In a quiet village with views to Exmoor. Toilet blocks and laundry facilities, gas/gaz exchange. Good for walking. Dog walk on site. Fishing and NCN route in 5m. Quiet off-peak. Non-members welcome. No tents. Open March-Nov.

GLASTONBURY

Isle of Avalon Touring Caravan Park, Godney Road, Glastonbury, Somerset BA6 9AF. 01458 833618. Owners: Mr & Mrs M Webb, Mr & Mrs A R Freeman. B3151 signed Godney. 500yd on R. Flat, level park in quiet location. Easy walk to Glastonbury. Excellent facilities. Free family-sized showers. Near restaurant, cycle hire.

(5m). Rose Farm, Westhay, Glastonbury, Somerset BA6 9TR. 01458 860256. Owner: Mrs P Willcox. B3151 to Westhay village. 4m S of Wedmore. Good overnight stop on way to Devon and Cornwall. Flat moors. Open May-Oct.

(3m). The Old Oaks Touring Park, Wick Farm, Wick, Glastonbury, Somerset BA6 8JS. 01458 831437. www.theoldoaks.co.uk. Owners: Mr & Mrs J White. L off A361. 2m from Glastonbury at Wick SP. Park on L in 1m. Small, friendly park, adults only, in unspoilt countryside with panoramic views. Spacious pitches, excellent facilities and coarse fishing. 20% low season discount for bookings of 1 week or more. David Bellamy Gold Conservation Award. Open March 1-Nov 20.

ILMINSTER

(2.5m). Thornleigh Caravan Park, Hanning Road, Horton, Ilminster, Somerset TA19 9QH. 01460 53450. thor

WEST COUNTRY

See page 5 for key to symbols and abbreviations

nleighsite@btinternet.com. Owner: Mr & Mrs KG White. W of Ilminster take A358 SP Chard for 0.25m and turn R, SP Horton & Broadway, site 0.75m on L. Flat grassy open field on edge of village with PO and pub nearby. 18m from coast, 6m Cricket St Thomas, Yeovilton Air Museum and National Trust properties nearby. Village location. Ideal for rallies and small village hall nearby. Open March 1-Oct 31.

LANGPORT

(1.5m). Bowdens Crest Caravan & Camping Park, Bowden's, Langport, Somerset TA10 0DD. *01458 250553*. www.bowdenscrest.co.uk. Owner: Mrs May. Off A372. Tranquil, level site. Disabled unit available. Licensed bar, laundry, washing up sinks and free showers. Near fishing, walking, cycling and local attractions. Walking route from park. Shop & meals available, children & pets welcome. Fishing 1m, cycling routes 2m, golf 4m.

(2m). Thorney Lakes Caravan & Camping Park, Thorney Lakes, Muchelney, Langport, Somerset TA10 0DW. *01458 250811*. www.thorneylakes.co.uk. Owner: R&A England. A372 to Langport. L at Huish Episcopi church, 100yd L to Muchelney. 2m to Thorney Lake Caravan Park. Fishing on site. Near golf course. 2m shops and doctor. David Bellamy Gold Conservation Award. Open Easter-end of Oct.

MARTOCK

(1m). Southfork Caravan Park, Parrett Works, Martock, Somerset TA12 6AE. *01935 825661*. www.southforkcaravans.co.uk. Owner: Mr & Mrs MA Broadley. 8m NW of Yeovil. 2m N of a A303. Small rural, level site near river. Clean, modern, heated amenities block (free showers). Play area. AA 4-pennant. Approved caravan workshop for repairs/servicing. Caravan accessories/spares. Fishing nearby. Village 1m.

MINEHEAD

Blue Anchor Park, Blue Anchor Bay, Minehead, Somerset TA24 6JT. *01643 821360*. www.hoburn.com. Owner: Hoburne Ltd. A39 then R on to B3191 at Carhampton Park. 1.5m on R. Level pitches, close to sea. Views of hills. Near Exmoor and Quantocks. No tents allowed. Rose Award. Open March-Oct.

■ **(5m). Burrowhayes Farm, Caravan & Camping Site, West Luccombe, Porlock, Minehead, Somerset TA24 8HT.** *01643 862463*. www.burrowhayes.co.uk. Owner: Mr & Mrs J C Dascombe. 5m W of Minehead turn L off A39 to West Luccombe site 0.25m on R. Between Minehead and Porlock in Exmoor National Park. Glorious National Trust site in Exmoor National Park. Riding stables on site. Telephone, launderette, free showers, well stocked shop. Cinema, golf course, swimming pool, supermarket all in 5m. Open March-Oct.

(2m). Camping & Caravanning Club Site – Minehead, Hill Road, North Hill, Minehead, Somerset TA24 5LB. *01643 704138*. www.campingandcaravanningclub.co.uk. Owner: Camping & Caravanning Club. From A39 to town centre. R on dual carriageway. Turn L into Blenheim Road; L into Martlett Road, L into St Michael's Road. Past church into Moor Road, then Hill Road, site on R. 3.75-acre site with 60 pitches. Non-members welcome. Hilltop site, spectacular views. Coastal path 0.5m from site, lakes, rivers, hills and valleys of the Exmoor national park. Deals for families and backpackers. No towed caravans allowed. Open April-Oct.

(16m). Halse Farm Caravan & Camping Park, Winsford, Minehead, Somerset TA24 7JL. *01643 851259*. www.halsefarm.co.uk. Owner: Mrs Laetitia Brown. SP from A396. In Winsford turn L in front of thatched pub. After 1m, L after cattle grid. In Exmoor National Park next to moor on working farm. Peaceful. Spectacular views. Quality toilet block. Shop, pub, garage in 1m. David Bellamy Gold Conservation Award. Open March 21-Oct 31.

(1m). Minehead & Exmoor Caravan Park, Porlock Road, Minehead, Somerset TA24 8SN. *01643 703074*. Owner: Mrs PM Jones. Off A39 W of Minehead centre, in open country. AONB, on edge of Exmoor. Calor Gas. Telephone. Clean first class toilet facilities. Open March-3rd week Oct.

Minehead Caravan Club Site, Hopcott Road, Minehead, Somerset TA24 6DJ. *01643 704345*. www.caravanclub.co.uk. Owner: The Caravan Club. See website for directions. Caravan Club members only. No tents. Small, hillside site, screened from the road, with lovely views of hills. Beach 0.5m. Bathing off the coast can be dangerous. Some hardstandings. Toilet blocks. Laundry facilities. Veg prep. MV service point. Gas and Gaz. No late night arrivals area. Near golf, walks. Suits families.

(6m). Porlock Caravan Park, Highbank, Porlock, Minehead, Somerset TA24 8ND. *01643 862269*. www.porlockcaravanpark.co.uk. Owner: Jan, Ray & Sue Macey. A39. In Porlock turn R B3225 Weir, park SP. Quiet, family run park. Excellent for touring, walking, riding on Exmoor. 2mins to village, near beach. Children allowed. Brochure. David Bellamy Gold Conservation Award. Open March 15-Oct 31.

BURROWHAYES FARM CARAVAN & CAMPING SITE & RIDING STABLES

www.burrowhayes.co.uk
01643 862463

- Popular family site in a delightful National Trust setting on Exmoor, just 2 miles from the Coast.
- Surrounding moors and woods provide a walkers paradise and children can play and explore safely.
- Riding stables offer pony trekking for all abilities. • Heated shower block with disabled and baby changing facilities, laundrette & pot wash.• Sites for Touring Caravans, Tents and Motorhomes with hook-ups. Caravan holiday homes for hire

Proprietors: Julian & Marion Dascombe
WEST LUCCOMBE, Nr PORLOCK, MINEHEAD, SOMERSET, TA24 8HT

---

www.motorcaravanmagazine.co.uk   MOTOR CARAVAN & CAMPING PARKS 2009 **103**

WEST COUNTRY

(8m). St Audries Bay Holiday Club, St Audries Bay, West Quantoxhead, Minehead, Somerset TA4 4DY. 01984 632515. www.staudriesbay.co.uk. Owner: M Randle. Off A39. Free family entertainment. Sports and leisure facilities. Licensed bar, restaurant, shop, indoor pool. Level site. David Bellamy Gold Conservation Award. Open May-Oct.

Westermill Farm, Exford, Exmoor, Minehead, Somerset TA24 7NJ. 01643 831238. www.westermill.com. Owner: Edwards family. Leave Exford on Porlock road. After 0.25m fork L. Go 2m along valley. Site on L. Beautiful, secluded site beside the river Exe in the heart of Exmoor. 4 waymarked walks over 300 acres. Log cabins for hire. David Bellamy Gold Conservation Award.

PRIDDY WELLS

Camping & Caravanning Club Site – Cheddar, Mendip Heights, Townsend, Priddy Wells, Somerset BA5 3BP. 01749 870241. www.campingandcaravanningclub.co.uk. Owner: The Camping and Caravanning Club. A39 N from Wells, turn L B3135 toward Cheddar for 4.5m, turn L for 200yd. Peaceful, rural park in an area of outstanding natural beauty. Close to Cheddar, Wookey Hole and Wells. Cycling, walking, abseiling and caving. Tents, caravans and motorhomes accepted. Non-members welcome. Deals for families and backpackers. Open March-Nov.

RADSTOCK

(4m). Old Down Touring Park, Emborough, Radstock, Somerset BA3 4SA. 01761 232355. www.olddowntouringpark.co.uk. Owner: Mrs T Small. From A37 turn R on B3139, entrance on R opposite Old Down Inn. AA 3 pennants. Convenient for Bath, Wells, The Mendips and Bath & West Showground, Longleat, Wookey Hole and Cheddar Caves. Opposite a 17th century coaching inn with good food. Open March-Nov.

SHEPTON MALLET

Greenacres Camping, Barrow Lane, North Wootton, Shepton Mallet, Somerset BA4 4HL. 01749 890497. Owner: Mr & Mrs D V Harvie. A39 follow campsite sign at Brown's Garden Centre, Wells. A361 follow campsite sign at Steanbow. Quiet 4.5 acre site near Glastonbury, B&W Showground. Free use of fridges and freezers. Open March-Oct.

(1m). Manleaze Caravan Park, Cannards Grave, Shepton Mallet, Somerset BA4 4LY. 01749 342404. Owner: Mr AA Manly. On A371, S of Shepton Mallet. Overnight stop London to South West.

(0.5m). Phippens Farm, Stoke St Michael, Oakhill, Shepton Mallet, Somerset BA3 5JH. 01749 840395. Owner: Mr & Mrs Francis. 4m NE of Shepton Mallet via A37 and A367 to Oakhill. Turn E to Stoke St Michael and site. Central for touring. Shepton Mallet 4-5m, Bath 12-14m. Reasonably level site. Open April-Oct.

STREET

(2m). Bramble Hill Caravan & Camping Park, Bramble Hill, Walton, Street, Somerset BA16 9RQ. 01458 442548. www.caravancampingsites.co.uk. Owner: Mrs Rogers. On the A39 SP. Quiet and relaxing site in the centre of the Polden Hills. Beautiful views and walks. Swimming, fishing and restaurants in easy reach. 'Clarks Village', Sainsbury's supermarket 1m. Dogs allowed on lead. Open April-Oct.

TAUNTON

(4m). Ashe Farm Caravan Site, Thornfalcon, Taunton, Somerset TA3 5NW. 01823 443764. camping@ashe-farm.fsnet.co.uk. Owner: Mrs S Small. From M5 at J25, SE. Take A358 for 2.5m, turn R at Nags Head. Peaceful, family farm site with lovely views. Washroom, play area, tennis court, dog walk. Golf course in 3m. Open April 1-Oct 31.

(2m). Cornish Farm Touring Park, Shoreditch, Taunton, Somerset TA3 7BS. 01823 327746. www.cornishfarm.com. Owner: Mr & Mrs E Jones. From M5 follow Taunton/Racecourse signs then brown signs. Level well drained site. Luxury fully tiled and heated toilets and showers. Family room/disabled facilities and laundry. Well lit site. AA 4 pennants.

(6m). Holly Bush Park, Culmhead, Taunton, Somerset TA3 7EA. 01823 421515. www.hollybushpark.com. Owner: Gary & Rachel Todd. M5 J25 towards Taunton. At lights turn L and follow signs for Corfe. 3.5m after Corfe turn R at crossroads then R again, park on L. Peaceful site in the beautiful Blackdown Hills with shop, telephone, gas and launderette. Near fishing, golf, swimming, forestry, ideal for walking, cycling etc. Country pub 100yd, with good food. Dogs & children under 3 years go free.

(2m). Home Farm Holiday Centre, St Audries Bay, Williton, Taunton, Somerset TA4 4DP. 01984 632487. www.homefarmholidaycentre.co.uk. Owner: Michael and Patricia Nethercott. A39 Bridgwater towards Minehead for 17m. At West Quantoxhead take B3191 SP Doniford, 1st R in 0.5m. Mile long drive with ramps. 2m from Watchet. Family run with private beach Indoor swimming pool (40 mixed pitches). Licensed bar. Play area and dog walk. Bungalows and caravans for hire. Shop and bar closed Nov-March, pool open all year. 3 AA pennants.

(10m). Quantock Orchard Caravan Park, Flaxpool, Crowcombe, Taunton, Somerset TA4 4AW. 01984 618618. www.flaxpool.freeserve.co.uk. Owners: Mr & Mrs M Barrett. Off A358 outside Crowcombe Village. Small, clean, family run park at foot of beautiful Quantock Hills. New fitness suite. Close to Exmoor and the coast. Ideal touring base with delightful rural attractions.

(12m). Waterrow Touring Park, Waterrow, Wiveliscombe, Taunton, Somerset TA4 2AZ. 01984 623464. www.waterrowpark.co.uk. Owner: Mr & Mrs A Taylor. 3m SW of Wiveliscombe via B3227. 300yd past The Rock pub at Waterrow. Gently sloping site in attractive river valley. Adults only. One holiday home for hire. Fly fishing on site. Dog walking field. Landscaped hardstandings all with views. Watercolour painting holidays and fly fishing tuition. Near pub. David Bellamy Gold Conservation Award.

WATCHET

(2m). Doniford Bay Holiday Park, Doniford, Watchet, Somerset TA23 0TJ. 01984 632423. www.donifordbay-park.co.uk. Owner: Bourne Leisure Ltd. A39 towards Minehead. After about 15m, in West Quantoxhead, R after garage. Doniford bay is on the R in 1m. Heated indoor pool. Kids' clubs, family entertainment. Convenience store. Bakery. All weather multi-sports court. Mini golf, go-karts, indoor fun palace. David Bellamy Gold Conservation Award. Open March-end Oct.

WEDMORE

Splott Farm, Blackford, Wedmore, Somerset BS28 4PD. 01278 641522. Owner: Mr S B G Duckett. On the B3139, 5m from Burnham on Sea. 7m from Cheddar. Peaceful site of 4.5 acres. Excellent views. Near golf course at Wedmore, fishing lakes 5mins drive. Seasonal pitches available. Open March-Nov.

104 MOTOR CARAVAN & CAMPING PARKS 2009

YORKSHIRE/HUMBERSIDE

See page 5 for key to symbols and abbreviations

WELLINGTON

(1m). Cadeside Caravan Club Site, Nynehead Road, Wellington, Somerset TA21 9HN. *01823 663103.* www.caravanclub.co.uk. Owner: The Caravan Club. See website for directions. Well screened rural site with distant views of hills,10mins walk to Wellington. No toilet block, dog walk on site and recycling facilities in 1m. All year secure storage area. Non-members welcome. No tents.

WELLS

Ebborlands Camping Grounds, Wookey Hole, Wells, Somerset BA5 1AY. *01749 672550.* After Wookey Hole Caves, site is 400yd on L, Priddy to Cheddar road. Small, friendly, non-commercial site with views of Mendip hills. Wells Cathedral 2.5m. Near Wookey Hole Caves and Ebbor Gorge.

(1.5m). Homestead Park, Wookey Hole, Wells, Somerset BA5 1BW. *01749 673022.* www.homesteadpark.co.uk. Owner: Ingledene Ltd. Leave Wells by A371 to Cheddar, turn R for Wookey Hole. Open Easter-Oct.

WESTON-SUPER-MARE

(2m). Camping & Caravanning Club Site – Weston Super Mare, West End Farm, Locking, Weston-super-Mare, Somerset BS24 8RH. *01934 822548.* www.campingandcaravanningclub.co.uk. Owner: Camping & Caravanning Club. A370 to WSM. SP Helicopter Museum signs, then turn R after museum. Enter West End Farm, turn R into site. Traditional seaside holiday resort. Club Members only. Near fishing, golf and riding, Bath, Bristol and Glastonbury. Deals for families and backpackers. All units accepted. Open March – Oct.

(3m). Country View Caravan & Touring Park, 29 Sand Road, Sand Bay, Weston-super-Mare, Somerset BS22 9UJ. *01934 627195.* www.cvhp.co.uk. Owner: Giles & Vicki Moroney. M5 exit 21, SP to Sand Bay, along Queen's Way, into Norton Lane then Sand Road. 200yd from beach. Outdoor heated swimming pool. Licensed club. Dogs allowed. Shop, children's play area. New shower/toilet block. Golf 1m. Open March 1-end Jan.

Dulhorn Farm Holiday Park, Weston Road, Lympsham, Weston-super-Mare, Somerset BS24 0JQ. *01934 750298.* gary@dulhornfarmholidaypark.co.uk. Owner: John & Gladys Bowden. A370 SP Weston-Super-Mare. After traffic lights 0.75m on L. Working farm in countryside near Mendip Hills, sea 4m. Open March 1-Oct 31.

(1.5m). Purn Holiday Park, Bridgwater Road (A370), Bleadon, Weston-Super-Mare, Somerset BS24 0AN. *01934 812342.* www.snootyfoxresorts.co.uk. Owner: Snooty Fox Resorts Ltd. M5 J21 SP Weston hospital, turn L to A370, park 1m on R. Licensed club with entertainment, dining and dancing, children allowed. Heated swimming pools, games room etc. Open March-Jan.

(4m). Weston Gateway Tourist Caravan Park, West Wick, Weston-super-Mare, Somerset BS24 7TF. *01934 510344.* Owner: Mr WJE Davies. A370, SP for Westwick. Supermarket 0.5m. Fishing, golf, horse riding, dry slope skiing all in 3m. No single parties or commercial vehicles allowed. Maximum 2 dogs per unit. Open March-Oct. Weekends only mid March-end April.

WINCANTON

(0.5m). Wincanton Racecourse Caravan Club Site, Wincanton, Somerset BA9 8BJ. *01963 34276.* www.caravanclub.co.uk. Owner: Caravan Club. See website for directions. Attractive location in open countryside with beautiful views to Bruton Forest and Downs. TV and information room. 9-hole golf course in the racecourse. Dog walk. Shops 1m. Shower for disabled. Non-members and tent campers welcome. Toilet blocks and laundry facilities. Gas. Open April 3 – Oct 5.

WINSCOMBE

Longbottom Farm, Shipham, Winscombe, Somerset BS25 1RW. *01934 743166.* Owner: Mr & Mrs RA Craggs. 1m N of Cheddar on unclassified road to Charterhouse. Quiet Mendip Hills. Outstanding views. Bring your horse and camping/B&B, Downland woodland.

YEOVIL

(3m). Halfway Caravan & Camping Park, Halfway, Ilchester Road, Yeovil, Somerset BA22 8RE. *01935 840342.* www.halfwaycaravanpark.com. Owner: Barrow family. Between Ilchester and Yeovil on A37. Next door to Halfway House Inn. Great food, drinks. Site overlooks the inn's fishing lake. AA 2 stars.

(7m). Long Hazel Park, High Street, Sparkford, Yeovil, Somerset BA22 7JH. *01963 440002.* lwww.sparkford.f9.co.uk/lhi.htm. Owner: Mr and Mrs AR Walton. A303/A359, Hazlegrove Services roundabout, brown and white tourist signs to village. Adults only. Level site 40 hardstandings. Holiday lodges for sale and hire. Walk to shop, garage, pub and McDonalds. Modern facilities. Public phone. Bus stop outside. Near Haynes International Motor Museum and Fleet Air Arm Museum. Open Feb 16-Jan 16.

EAST YORKSHIRE

BEVERLEY

(1m). Lakeminster Park Caravan Site, Hull Road, Beverley, E Yorkshire HU17 0PN. *01482 882655.* Owner: Mossways Ltd. Off A1174. Well-drained site close to woods, stream and lake. 30mins to coast. Fishing. Drinks licence. Food.

BRIDLINGTON

(6m). Barmston Beach Holiday Park, Sands Lane, Barmston, Bridlington, E Yorkshire YO25 8PJ. *0871 664 9704.* www.park-resorts.com. Owner: Park Resorts Ltd. 6m S of Bridlington on beautiful Yorkshire coast. Licensed club. Free kids' club. Shop, launderette, Takeaway and restaurant. Amusement. Outdoor play area, heated outdoor pool with splash area. Visiting entertainment cabaret. 4 golf courses in 10m. Yorkshire Moors, steam railway. Historic cities of Beverley and York. David Bellamy Bronze Conservation Award. Open April-Oct.

(1m). South Cliff Caravan Park, South Cliff, Wilsthorpe, Bridlington, E Yorkshire YO15 3QN. *01262 671051.* www.southcliff.co.uk. Owner: East Riding of Yorkshire Council. On A165 Hull to Bridlington. All touring pitches hardstanding. Play area, club, shop. Near golf course and boat launch. Open March 1-Nov 30.

(4m). Thornwick and Sea Farm Holiday Centre, North Marine Road, Flamborough, Bridlington, E Yorkshire YO15 1AN. *01262 850369.* www.thornwickbay.co.uk. Owner: Mr SH Gibbon. In Flamborough go to the 'North Landing'. The park is to your L. On Heritage Coast. Pool, gym, bars and entertainment on site. Near 2 golf courses. Super pitch facilities. New coarse fishing lake open. David Bellamy Silver Conservation Award. Open March 1-Oct 31.

www.motorcaravanmagazine.co.uk — MOTOR CARAVAN & CAMPING PARKS 2009 **105**

YORKSHIRE/HUMBERSIDE

DRIFFIELD

(10m). Dacre Lakeside Park, Brandesburton, Driffield, E Yorkshire YO25 8RT. 01964 543704. www.dacrepark.co.uk. Owner: Sandsfield Gravel Co Ltd. A165 Beverley-Bridlington. Follow road for 700yd and turn L to park. Lake for fishing, windsurfing, sailing, canoeing. Tennis court, clubhouse. Near golf, clay pigeon shooting and jet skiing. Hot tubs on lodge verandas. Walk to village pubs, Chinese and fish and chips. Open all year.

Seaside Caravan Park, Ulrome, Driffield, E Yorkshire YO25 8TT. 01262 468228. B1242 to Ulrome, turn L in village. On leaving village turn L to park. Good for beach holiday with views of Bridlington Bay.

(9m). Thorpe Hall Caravan & Camping Site, Thorpe Hall, Rudston, Driffield, E Yorkshire YO25 4JE. 01262 420393. www.thorpehall.co.uk. Owner: Sir Ian Macdonald of Sleat. 4m W from Bridlington on the B1253. 4.5 acres in former walled garden at Thorpe Hall. Own coarse fishery. Manager: Mrs Jayne Chatterton. Shops, golf course, sea fishing, PO, hospital minor injuries in 4m. David Bellamy Gold Conservation Award. Open March 1-Oct 31.

HORNSEA

(1m). Springfield Farm Caravan Park, Atwick Road, Hornsea, E Yorkshire HU18 1EJ. 01964 532253. N of Hornsea on B1242 SP Bridlington at top of hill on L. Open May – Oct.

HULL

(8m). Burton Constable Holiday Park & Arboretum, Old Lodges, Sproatley, Hull, E Yorkshire HU11 4LN. 01964 562508. www.burtonconstable.co.uk. Owner: JR Chichester Constable. On B1238 Hull to Aldborough. Modern facilities. Shaver points. Licensed club. Telephone. Snooker room. Golf nearby. Open March 1-Oct 31 (tourers), March 1-Feb 28 (statics).

(1m). Easington Beach Caravan Park, Seaside Road, Easington, Hull, E Yorkshire HU12 0TY. 01964 650293. www.easingtonbeach.com. Owner: Easington Caravan Sites Ltd. Head for Hull docks, then Withernsea. At Patrington, branch off towards Easington. Heated indoor swimming pool. Tennis & badminton courts. Bowling & putting greens. Club. Playground. Pets corner includes big Koi carp fish pond and over 150 foreign birds. Open March-Feb.

SKIPSEA

Low Skirlington, Skipsea, E Yorkshire YO25 8SY. 01262 468213. Owner: MB & J Goodwin Ltd. 3m N of Hornsea on B1242. Site SP on N of road. Holiday site 400yd from sandy beach. Dogs allowed on lead. Open March-Oct.

Mill Farm Country Park, Mill Lane, Skipsea, E Yorkshire YO25 8SS. 01262 468211. Owner: Judy Willmott. A165 Hull to Bridlington. At Beeford take B1249 to Skipsea. At cross roads turn R, then L up Cross Street, to Mill Lane and office in Mill Farm on R. Level site with mature hedges. Shaver points, showers, pot washing, free hot water. Sea 0.5m. Shop, café/restaurant, bottle gas supply, swimming pool. Near village shop and pub, fishing and golf. Open March 13-Sept 27.

WITHERNSEA

(0.5m). Withernsea Sands Holiday Park, North Road, Withernsea, E Yorkshire HU19 2BS. 0871 6649803. www.park-resorts.com. Owner: Park Resorts Ltd. A1033 to Withernsea then B1242. The park is 0.5m on R. Adventure playground, outdoor play area, shop, bar, indoor swimming pool. Sandy beach 200yd. David Bellamy Bronze Conservation Award. Open April-Oct.

NORTH YORKSHIRE

ACASTER MALBIS

Poplar Farm Caravan Park, Acaster Malbis, N Yorkshire YO23 2UH. 01904 706548. www.poplarfarmcaravans.co.uk. Owner: G Taylor. A64 to Copmanthorpe junction (A1237) follow signs. Family-run park on the banks of River Ouse, river-bus to York daily. Bar, restaurant. Open end March- end Oct.

BENTHAM

(3m). Goodenbergh Country Holiday Park, Low Bentham, Bentham, N Yorkshire LA2 7EU. 01524 262022. www.goodenberghleisure.co.uk. Owner: George Luscombe Builders Ltd. Off A65 to Low Bentham. Park 4m from Bentham. Beautiful woodland site, walks. Golf course, market town 4m. David Bellamy Gold Conservation Award. Open March 1-Jan 4.

BOROUGHBRIDGE

(1m). Blue Bell Caravan Park, Kirby Hill, Boroughbridge, N Yorkshire YO51 9DN. 07946 549529. Owner: Mr J Townend. Park on B6265 1m, N Boro'Bridge. Pub/restaurant 400yd. Fishing nearby. Leisure centre, superstore, shops, pubs & restaurant 1m. Open March-Jan.

(0.75m). Camping & Caravanning Club Site – Boroughbridge, Bar Lane, Roecliffe, Boroughbridge, N Yorkshire YO51 9LS. 01423 322683. www.campingandcaravanningclub.co.uk. Owner: Camping & Caravanning Club. From A1(M) J48 SP Bar Lane Industrial Estate and Roecliffe. Site 0.25m from roundabout. Near Moors and Dales on riverbank with fishing and boating. All units accepted. Non-members welcome. Recreation hall, pool table, colour TV. Deals for families and backpackers. Loo Of The Year (5 stars).

CONEYSTHORPE

(5m). Castle Howard Caravan & Camping Site, Coneysthorpe, N Yorkshire YO60 7DD. 01653 648366/648316. lakeside@castlehoward.co.uk. Owner: Castle Howard Estate Ltd. SP Castle Howard. Next to 70-acre lake. Well-drained site, woodland walks. Dogs allowed under strict control. Open March 1-Oct 31.

EASINGWOLD

(1.5m). Easingwold Caravan & Camping Park, White House Farm, Easingwold, N Yorkshire YO6 3NF. 01347 821479. Owner: Mr G & KM Hood. On old A19. Quiet site near York and Herriot country. Ideal stopover for Scotland. Open March 1-Oct 31.

FILEY

(6m). Blue Dolphin Holiday Park, Gristhorpe Bay, Filey, N Yorkshire YO14 9PU. 01723 515155. www.bluedolphin-park.co.uk. Owner: Bourne Leisure Ltd. Park on A165 2m N of Filey. Amusement arcade. Indoor and outdoor swimming pools. Supermarket. Bars. Indoor funzone. Adventure playgrounds. Mini ten-pin bowling. All-weather sports court. Kid's clubs. Family entertainment. David Bellamy Gold Conservation Award. Open March 20-Oct 30.

(2m). Crows Nest Caravan Park, Gristhorpe, Filey, N Yorkshire YO14 9PS. 01723 582206. www.crowsnestcaravanpark.com. Owner: Mr Ian

106 MOTOR CARAVAN & CAMPING PARKS 2009

YORKSHIRE/HUMBERSIDE

See page 5 for key to symbols and abbreviations

Palmer. 2m N of Filey, 5m S of Scarborough off A165. Rose Award park with full facilities, ideal for quiet, relaxing family holiday or weekend break. Shop, bar, indoor heated swimming pool, games room, play area, fish & chips. Open March 1-Nov 1.

(0.5m). Filey Brigg Camping & Caravan Park, North Cliff, Filey, N Yorkshire YO14 9ET. 01723 513852. Owner: Scarborough Borough Council. On the A165, on cliffs north of Filey. Well-equipped holiday site. Maximum stay 21 days. Path to beach. Laundry. AA 3 pennant site. Open Easter-Oct 31.

(3m). Orchard Farm Holiday Village, Stonegate, Hunmanby, Filey, N Yorkshire YO14 0PU. 01723 891582. www.orchardfarmholidayvillage.co.uk. Owner: Mr & Mrs D Dugdale. Turn W off A165 at Royal Oak railway crossing, SP Hunmanby Park 0.5m on R. 14 acres. Level, secluded site with full amenities. Indoor pool, bar, entertainment, play area, private fishing. Award winning beaches. Historical village. Open end March-Oct.

(3m). Primrose Valley Holiday Park, Primrose Valley, Filey, N Yorkshire YO14 9RF. 01723 513771. www.primrosevalley-park.co.uk. Owner: Bourne Leisure Ltd. Park is on A165 3m S of Filey. Blue Flag Award, Welcome Host Award. Large heated pool complex. Multi-sports court. Adventure playground, climbing wall, boating lake, funfair, abseiling, go-karts, shop, 2 cabaret bars, sports bar, restaurants, family entertainment. David Bellamy Gold Conservation Award. Open March-end Oct.

(5m). Reighton Sands Holiday Park, Reighton Gap, Filey, N Yorkshire YO14 9SH. 01723 890476. www.reightonsands-park.co.uk. Owner: Bourne Leisure Ltd. Park is on A165. Heated indoor swimming pool. Free kids' club. Family entertainment. Ten-pin bowling. Adventure playground. Convenience store. Outdoor sports. Soft play area. Golf course 3m. David Bellamy Gold Conservation Award. Open March – end Oct.

HARROGATE

(2m). Bilton Park, Village Farm, Bilton Lane, Harrogate, N Yorkshire HG1 4DL. 01423 863121. www.biltonpark.co.uk. Owner: Mrs A M Ashton. From A59 in Harrogate (between A661 & A61). Turn into Bilton Lane at Skipton Inn. Park 1.5m. Own fishing. Open March-End Oct.

(1.5m). Great Yorkshire Showground Caravan Club Site, Wetherby Road, Harrogate, N Yorkshire HG3 1TZ. 01423 560470. www.caravanclub.co.uk. Owner: The Caravan Club. See website for directions. Just off the A661, this flat and pleasantly open site is ideal for Harrogate. Non-members and (small) tent campers welcome. Some hardstanding, gas and gaz, play equipment, dog walk nearby. Toilet blocks. Laundry facilities. Veg prep. Ideal for families. Beach and golf in 5m. Open March-Nov.

(4m). High Moor Farm Park, High Moor Farm, Skipton Road, Harrogate, N Yorkshire HG3 2LZ. 01423 563637/564955. highmoorfarmpark@btconnect.com. Owner: Mr & Mrs P Kershaw. On A59 Harrogate to Skipton. Holiday site surrounded by trees, on the edge of Yorkshire Dales. Ideal touring base. Club. Golf on site. Bowling green. Open April-Oct.

(10m). Manor House Farm Caravan Site, Summerbridge, Harrogate, N Yorkshire HG3 4JS. 01423 780322. Owner: TJ Houseman & MJ Liddle. Off B6165, near river Nidd. Quiet and peaceful and near beauty spots Brinhan Rocks and Fountains Abbey. Hardstanding. No dogs. Good walking. Adjacent to Nidderdale Way. 2mins to village shops and doctor. Open March 1-Oct 31.

(3m). Ripley Caravan Park, Knaresborough Road, Ripley, Harrogate, N Yorkshire HG3 3AU. 01423 770050. Owner: Mr P & V House. A61 to Ripley roundabout, B6165 to Knaresborough, site 300yd on L. Level country park with indoor heated pool, launderette, playground, games and nursery play room, sauna and football pitch. Near golf course, PO. Maximum 2 dogs. David Bellamy Gold Conservation Award. Open Easter-Oct 31.

(14m). Riverside Caravan Park, Low Wath Road, Pateley Bridge, Harrogate, N Yorkshire HG3 5HL. 01423 711383. Owner: Mr DH & CA Weatherhead. From Pateley Bridge, about 0.25m along Low Wath Road on R. Shop, takeaway, café/restaurant near. Open April 1-Oct 31.

(3m). Rudding Holiday Park, Follifoot, Harrogate, N Yorkshire HG3 1JH. 01423 870439. www.ruddingpark.co.uk. Owner: Mr Simon Mackaness. 2m S of Harrogate between A661 and A658. Set in beautiful parkland. Heated outdoor swimming pool, playground, 18-hole golf course, 6-hole short course and driving range, shop, Deer House family pub. David Bellamy Gold Conservation Award. Open March-Jan.

(1m). Shaw's Trailer Park, Knaresborough Road, Harrogate, N Yorkshire HG2 7NE. 01423 884432. Owner: Mr J Shaw. On A59 between Harrogate and Knaresborough (2.5m). Entrance next to Johnson's cleaners. Walk to doctor, bus stop, pub PO. Shops, garages and hospital near. Fishing, golf course in 0.5m. SAE for brochure.

(20m). Studfold Farm, Lofthouse, Harrogate, N Yorkshire HG3 5SG. 01423 755210. www.studfoldfarm.co.uk. Owner: F&I and A Walker. 7m from Pately Bridge at head of Nidderdale. Ideal for walking the Dales. Level site on working farm, near Howstean Gorge. Village, PO 0.5m. Shopping, golf, fishing 7-10m. Open April 1 to Oct 31.

(15m). Westfield Farm, Heathfield, Pateley Bridge, Harrogate, N Yorkshire HG3 5BX. 01423 711880. Owner: E Simpson. Off B6265. At Pately Bridge take Ramsgill Road, 1m, turn L towards Heathfield, L again in 100yd, site is third on the L. Open April 1-Oct 31.

(7m). Yorkshire Hussar Inn Holiday Caravan Park, Markington, Harrogate, N Yorkshire HG3 3NR. 01765 677327. www.yorkshire-hussar-inn.co.uk. Owner: JS Brayshaw (Caravans) Ltd. A61, turn W at Wormald Green. 1m into village of Markington. Secluded family park behind Olde Worlde Village Inn, close to Fountain Abbey, Brimham Rocks, Emmerdale country. PO & Shop in village. Play area. Pub. 3AA pennants. Open April 1/Easter-Oct 31.

HAWES

(0.5m). Bainbridge Ings Caravan Site, Hawes, N Yorkshire DL8 3NU. 01969 667354. www.bainbridge-ings.co.uk. Owner: Mr & Mrs M Facer. A684 Bainbridge to Hawes, L at SP to Gayle 300yd. Near fishing. Good for walking and touring the Dales. Shops, bus service in 0.5m. Lovely views of hills. Launderette on site. Open April 1-Oct 31.

(0.25m). Brown Moor Caravan Club Site, Brunt Acres Road, Hawes, N Yorkshire DL8 3PS. 01969 667338. www.caravanclub.co.uk. Owner: The

YORKSHIRE/HUMBERSIDE

Caravan Club. See website for directions. Caravan Club members only. No tents. Site is in beautiful Wensleydale between the river Ure and the market town of Hawes. Toilet blocks, laundry facilities, baby and toddler washroom and MV service point. Dog walk and games room on site. Area for walking, fishing. Ideal for families, facilities for disabled. Quiet off-peak. Open March 27-Jan 4.

(2m). Shaw Ghyll, Simonstone, Hawes, N Yorkshire DL8 3LY. 01969 667359. rogerstott@aol.com. Owner: Mr & Mrs R Stott. Follow signs from Hawes to Muker, for 2m. The site is 400yd past Simonstone Hall guest house on L. A beautiful, secluded site by a trout stream with a magnificent backdrop of hills. New facilities block. Hot showers. Hair & hand dryers. River fishing, fell walking. Open March-Oct.

HELMSLEY

(4m). Foxholme Touring Caravan and Camping Park, Harome, Helmsley, N Yorkshire Y062 5JG. 01439 771696/771241. Owner: Mr KJR Binks. Leave Helmsley on A170 towards Scarborough, take 1st R SP Harome, in village turn L at church and follow signs. Adults only. Sheltered by trees. Use of indoor swimming pool (2m). Washbasins in private cubicles. Send stamp for brochure. Open March 1-Oct 31.

(2m). Golden Square Caravan & Camping Park, Golden Square, Oswaldkirk, Helmsley, N Yorkshire YO6 25YQ. 01439 788269. www.goldensquarecaravanpark.com. Owner: Mr & Mrs D Armstrong. Off B1257 Malton Road to Ampleforth. Secluded site in open countryside and woodland. Magnificent views. Award-winning facilities block with underflooring heating. Disabled/family bathroom. Launderette. Shop. Outdoor/indoor play areas. Sports centre, fishing and golf nearby. Service pitches, seasonal pitches and storage compound. Open March 1-Oct 31.

(4m). Wombleton Caravan Park, Moorfield Lane, Wombleton, Helmsley, N Yorkshire YO62 7RY. 01751 431684. www.europage.co.uk/wombletonpark. Owner: Brenda & David Willoughby. 4m E of Helmsley, stay on A170 until you see sign for Wombleton. Go straight through village, turn L for park. Quiet and level with excellent modern facilities. Seasonal/storage pitches available. Open 1 March-31 Oct.

(3m). Wrens of Ryedale Caravan Camp Site, Gale Lane, Nawton, Helmsley, N Yorkshire YO62 7SD. 01439 771260. www.wrensofryedale.co.uk. Owner: David & Maria Taylor. 3m E of Helmsley on the A170. At Beadlam turn R on to Gale Lane after the Spice Club restaurant. We are on the R 600yd from the village. A delightful, small, family run site in the heart of the Ryedale countryside. Ideal for N Yorkshire moors, dales, coast and York. In walking distance of village pub, restaurant, takeaway and major bus route Open from 31 March-31 Oct.

KNARESBOROUGH

(3m). Allerton Park Caravan Park, Allerton Mauleverer, Knaresborough, N Yorkshire HG5 0SE. 01423 330569. www.yorkshireholidayparks.co.uk. Owner: Mr & Mrs D Hind. From A1 take A59 1m towards York. Peaceful woodland park setting E of A1. Touring base for York area and Moors. Timber lodges, holiday homes for sale and hire. David Bellamy Gold Conservation Award. Open Feb 1-Jan 3.

(2m). Kingfisher Caravan Park, Low Moor Lane, Farnham, Knaresborough, N Yorkshire HG5 9JB. 01423 869411. Owner: Mr Richardson. From Knaresborough take A6055 SP Boroughbridge, from L for Farnham. Turn L Site 1m from church on the L. Sheltered area for touring caravans and level hardstandings for motor caravans. Facilities with free hot water, washing up area, showers, laundry, large playground. Most sporting facilities nearby. Fishing available. Open March 1-Oct 31.

(2m). Knaresborough Caravan Club Site, New Road, Scotton, Knaresborough, N Yorkshire HG5 9HH. 01423 860196. www.caravanclub.co.uk. Owner: The Caravan Club. See website for directions. The site offers a gateway to the Yorkshire Dales and the many attractions of the North of England. Toilet blocks with privacy cubicles, laundry facilities and baby/toddler washroom. MV service point and vegetable preparation area. Bar, restaurant and children's playroom. Fishing, golf and NCN in 5m. Dog walk nearby, good area for walking. Ideal for families. Non-members and tent campers admitted. Open March 1-Jan 14.

LANCASTER

(11m). Riverside Caravan Park, High Bentham, Lancaster, N Yorkshire LA2 7FJ. 01524 261272. www.riversidecaravanpark.co.uk. Owner: J Marshall & Son. M6 J34, turn on to A683 towards Kirkby Lonsdale. Turn R before Hornby on to B6480, SP to High Bentham. R turn by Black Bull Hotel. Park is 0.5m on R. Laundry room, indoor games room, outdoor adventure playground, fishing on private stretch of river. Market town of Bentham with shops, pubs and takeaways 5mins walk from park and golf course. David Bellamy Gold Conservation Award. Open March-Nov.

LEYBURN

(4m). Akebar Park (Wensleydale), Leyburn, N Yorkshire DL8 5LY. 01677 450201. www.akebarpark.com. On A684 SP from A1. 10-bay golf driving range, a challenging 18-hole golf course. Activities such as fishing, walking, golf, petanque, croquet and boules are all available, as well as our traditional pub situated at the entrance to the park. Open March 1-Dec 31.

Little Cote Farm, West Burton, Leyburn, N Yorkshire DL8 4JY. 01969 663450. 1m SE of Aysgarth. A684 from Leyburn. A6160 to West Burton to site 0.5m beyond on no through road. SP Walden. Quiet, remote Dale site. No sanitation, but emptying point provided.

(1m). Lower Wensleydale Caravan Club Site, Harmby, Leyburn, N Yorkshire DL8 5NU. 01969 623366. www.caravanclub.co.uk. Owner: The Caravan Club. See website for directions. Set in the hollow of a disused quarry, now overrun with wildflowers and mosses. Non-members welcome. Tents welcome in a separate area. No late arrivals area. Toilet blocks. Privacy cubicles. Laundry facilities. Veg prep. Waste disposal for motor caravans. Information room. Good area for walking. Open March-Nov.

(9m). Street Head Caravan Park, Newbiggin, Bishopdale, Leyburn, N Yorkshire DL8 3TE. 01969 663472. d.coop@btinternet.com. Owner: Mr D J Cooper. Off A684, on B6160 next to Street Head Inn. Small, quiet caravan & camping park in middle of Yorkshire Dales National Park. Open March 1-Oct 31.

(7m). Westholme Caravan & Camping Park, Aysgarth, Leyburn, N Yorkshire DL8 3SP. 01969 663268. Owner: A & I Woodhouse Ltd. Off A684 Leyburn to Hawes. 1m east of Aysgarth. An attractive, well maintained park with splendid views. Borders the Yorkshire Dales National Park. Play area. Dog walk. Fishing. Licensed

108 MOTOR CARAVAN & CAMPING PARKS 2009

YORKSHIRE/HUMBERSIDE

See page 5 for key to symbols and abbreviations

club with meals when open. TV room. 4 AA pennants. Open March-Oct.

MALTON

(8m). Flamingo Land Theme Park, Zoo & Holiday Village, Kirby Misperton, Malton, N Yorkshire YO17 6UX. *0870 7528000.* www.flamingoland.co.uk. Owner: Mrs M Gibb. Off A169. Leisure complex, golf course, evening venues in family fun park with over 100 free attractions, including rollercoaster, family rides, 6 shows and an extensive zoo. Open March-Oct.

(10m). The Snooty Fox, East Heslerton, Malton, N Yorkshire YO17 8EN. *01944 710 554.* Owner: S&J Butterworth. Ganton golf 10mins away. Wold Way, close to coast and Dales. Dogs on lead welcome (extra charge).

(4m). Wolds Way Caravan & Camping, Knapton Wold, West Knapton, Malton, N Yorkshire YO17 8JE. *01944 728 463.* www.ryedalesbest.co.uk. Owner: Derek and Carol Watson. Open March 1-Oct 31.

MASHAM

(2m). Fearby Caravan & Camping Site, Rear Black Swan Hotel, Fearby, Masham, N Yorkshire HG4 4NF. *01765 689477.* www.blackswanholiday.co.uk. Owner: Mr J McCourt. Turn L off A6108 NW of Masham. Site is 2m ot L at rear of Black Swan Inn in Fearby. Near Black Sheep and Theakstons breweries. Open March 1-Oct 31.

NORTHALLERTON

(6m). Cote Ghyll Caravan & Camping Park, Osmotherley, Northallerton, N Yorkshire DL6 3AH. *01609 883425.* www.coteghyll.com. Owner: Mr & Mrs J Hills. Exit A19 at A684 to Osmotherley village. Turn L in village. Park in 0.25m. Beautiful family site in peaceful valley of North York Moors National Park with Stream. New luxury heated shower block with bathroom. Superpitches, seasonals, caravan storage and Rose Award holiday caravans for hire and sale. Play area and stream. Village pubs/shops in 10mins walk. Next to Cleveland Way, coast to coast, Lyke Wake Walk and National Cycleway. Golf, fishing, horseriding, sportscentre and market towns all in 6m. Open March 1-Oct 31.

(4m). Hutton Bonville Caravan Park, Hutton Bonville, Northallerton, N Yorkshire DL7 0NR. *01609 881416.* Owner: Leisure Parks. On A167, 13m from Darlington. Privately owned statics, nice and quiet all with superb views. Retirement/ semi retirement. Shops, doctors, fishing, golf etc all close by. Open March 1-Jan 7.

(4m). Otterington Caravan Park, Station Farm, South Otterington, Northallerton, N Yorkshire DL7 9JB. *01609 780656.* www.otteringtonpark.com. Owner: Keith & Carol Bowe. Located on the A167 near South Otterington, N off the A61. Shops, PO, doctors, golf course available in Northallerton. Fishing on site. David Bellamy Gold Conservation Award. Open March-Oct.

(6m). Pembroke Caravan Park, Leeming Bar, Northallerton, N Yorkshire DL7 9BW. *01677 422652/422608.* Owner: G&S Liddell. 0.5m from A684, 1m from A1. Good A1 stopover. Good for touring the Yorkshire Dales, N Yorkshire Moors and the historic city of York. PO and pub with bar food in small village. Golf course 3m. Fishing 2m. Open March 1-Oct 31.

PICKERING

(1.5m). Black Bull Caravan & Camping Park, Malton Road, Pickering, N Yorkshire YO18 8EA. *01751 472528.* www. blackbullcaravanpark.co.uk. Owner: Mrs Louise Wright. S of Pickering on A169, behind Black Bull pub. Quiet family site. Toilet and shower block. Children's playground, play field, games room, takeaway, bar meals. Static holiday caravans for hire. Near swimming, fishing, tennis, golf, steam railway, theme park and zoo, shops, bars and restaurants. Open March 1-31 Oct.

(2m). Overbrook Caravan Park, Maltongate, Thornton-le-Dale, Pickering, N Yorkshire YO18 7SE. *01751 474417.* www. overbrookcaravanpark.co.uk. Owner: Darren & Natalie Ellis. Off A170, follow stream down Maltongate. Off A169 towards Thornton-le-Dale old railway station on R. Adults only, level well drained site, resident owners. 0.5m level walk to shops, PO, PHs, tea rooms and bus route. Centrally located for sight-seeing. David Bellamy Gold Conservation Award. Open March 1-Oct 31.

(10m). Rosedale Caravan Park, Rosedale Abbey, Pickering, N Yorkshire YO18 8SA. *01751 417272.* www.flowerofmay.com. Owner: Flower of May Holiday Parks Ltd. Off A170 to Rosedale. AA 4 pennants – nestling in beautiful valley, walking and touring country. Luxurious new toilet blocks. Dogs by arrangement. Open March-Oct.

(7m). Spiers House Caravan & Camping Site, Forest Holidays, Cropton, Pickering, N Yorkshire YO18 8ES. *01751 417591.* www.forestholidays. co.uk. Owner: Forest Holidays. A170 W from Pickering. 1m N of Cropton on the Rosedale road turn R to site. Refurbished 2008. Good for exploring the North York Moors National Park. Easy driving distance of York, Scarborough and Whitby. Bookings and brochure requests on 0845 1308224. Open May-Jan.

(8.75m). The Howard Rosedale Abbey Caravan Site, Rosedale Abbey, Pickering, N Yorkshire YO18 8SA. *01751 417842.* www.caravanclub.co.uk. Owner: The Caravan Club. Attractive riverside site in N Yorkshire Moors National Park. Easy driving distance to coast and Pickering for shops. Own sanitation required. Members only. No tents. Open March-Oct.

(1.5m). Upper Carr Touring Park, Upper Carr Lane, Malton Road, Pickering, N Yorkshire YO18 7JP. *01751 473115.* www.uppercarr.demon. co.uk. Owner: M&A Harker. Off A169. Level, family park with licensed shop, laundry, pets corner, play area, cycle hire, payphone. Golf, pub, swimming, walking, and fishing nearby. 30mins to York, Scarborough, Whitby and North Moors National Park. Brochure. Open March 1-Oct 31.

(6m). Vale of Pickering Caravan Park, Carr House Farm, Allerston, Pickering, N Yorkshire YO18 7PQ. *01723 859280.* www.valeofpickering. co.uk. Owner: Tony & Marjorie Stockdale. E of Pickering off A170 & B1415. Modern facilities, baths. Hairdryer. Gas supplies. Fishing 1m. Forestry walks 2m. Large play area. Microwave. Fully-lit. Spirit licence. Play and games area. David Bellamy Silver Conservation Award. Open March-Jan.

(2.5m). Wayside Caravan Park, Wrelton, Pickering, N Yorkshire YO18 8PG. *01751 472608.* www.waysideparks. co.uk. Owner: VR Goodson. Off A170 from Pickering 2.5m W at Wrelton. Touring centre for moors. South facing park with country views and modern facilities. Historic steam railway. Near fishing, gf course, service station, shop, PO. Pub/

MOTOR CARAVAN & CAMPING PARKS 2009 **109**

YORKSHIRE/HUMBERSIDE

restaurant 100yd. Open March-Oct.

RICHMOND

(3.5m). Hargill House Caravan Club Site, Gilling West, Richmond, N Yorkshire DL10 5LJ. *01748 822734.* www.caravanclub.co.uk. Owner: The Caravan Club. See website for directions. Part sloping site with views over Yorkshire Dales National Park. Great walking. Non-members welcome. No tents. Hardstandings. Toilet blocks. Privacy cubicles. Laundry. Veg prep. MV service point. Information room. Near golf, fishing. Dog walk. Open March-Nov.

Park Lodge Farm, Keld, Richmond, N Yorkshire DL11 6LJ. *01748 886274.* www.rukins-keld.co.uk. Owner: Mrs B Rukin. In Keld village on B6270. Good for touring the Dales. 1 hr drive to Lakes. Open April-Oct inclusive.

(3m). Scotch Corner Caravan Park, Scotch Corner, Richmond, N Yorkshire DL10 6NS. *01748 822530.* marshallleisure@aol.com. Owner: W&E Marshall. From Scotch Corner take A6108 Richmond road for 250yd. Cross to other carriageway and return 200yd to site. Bar & restaurant adjacent. 3m to fishing, golf. Good stopover, 0.25m from A1. Near leisure centre. Open Easter-Oct.

(7m). Tavern House Caravan Site, Newsham, Richmond, N Yorkshire DL11 7RA. *01833 621223.* Owner: Mr Stephen Thompson. 7m W from Scotch Corner in centre of village. Adults only. Quiet, enclosed site. Dogs on leads allowed. Good walking, bike riding. Open March 1-Oct 31.

(24m). Usha Gap Caravan & Camp Site, Usha Gap, Muker, Richmond, N Yorkshire DL11 6DW. *01748 886214.* www.ushagap.btinternet.co.uk. Owner: Mrs A Metcalfe. B6270. 20m W of Richmond along Swale Dale or over Butter Tubs Pass from Hawes. Small site on family farm. Washing up facilities. Dryer. 0.25m to village shop, PO, pub serving meals, fishing.

RIPON

(5m). Gold Coin Farm, Galphay, Ripon, N Yorks HG4 3NJ. *01765 658508.* Owner: Mrs C Weatherhead. W of Ripon via B6265 Pateley Bridge road. After 1m turn R to Galphay and site. Good for touring Dales. Flat and sloping well-drained and quiet site in unspoilt countryside. 6m from Fountains Abbey. Own sanitation required. Open April 1-Sept 30.

(9m). Old Station Holiday Park, Old Station, Low Burton, Masham, Ripon, N Yorkshire HG4 4DF. *01765 689569.* oldstation-masham.co.uk. Owner: The Grainger Family. From A1, B6267 to Masham. Secluded park, 0.5m footpath to town. Near garage for gas, shops, PO and doctor. Many nice walks by river. Near child's playground, brewery tours. AA 3 pennants. Open March 1-Nov 30.

(0.5m). Riverside Meadows Caravan Park, Ure Bank Top, Ripon, N Yorkshire HG4 1JD. *01765 602964.* www.flowerofmay.com. Owner: Flower of May Holiday Parks Ltd. Off A61 at Ripon. Tent and touring caravan park for families only. AA 3 pennants – tranquil setting in trees above river. Ideal for touring Dales or Yorkshire Moors. Open March-Oct.

(5.5m). Sleningford Watermill Caravan & Camping Park, North Stainley, Ripon, N Yorkshire HG4 3HQ. *01765 635201.* www.sleningfordwatermill.co.uk. Follow signs for Lightwater Valley, taking A6108 out of Ripon, site is clearly SP. Beautiful, quiet, riverside site. A holiday flatlet also available for hire. On-site fly fishing and white water canoeing on River Ure. Ideal for walking, bird and wild flower spotting. Central for Herriot country and the N Yorks Dales. PO & garage 1-2m. Doctor's surgery 4m. Golf courses, shops 5m. Small shop and canoe shop on site. David Bellamy Gold Conservation Award. Open April 1-Oct 31.

(5m). Woodhouse Farm Caravan and Camping Park, Winksley, Ripon, N Yorkshire HG4 3PG. *01765 658309.* www.woodhousewinkley.com. Owner: AM Hitchen. SP after 3.5m off B6265 Ripon to Pateley Bridge at Winksley and Grantley turn R. TV and games room. Play equipment. Touring base for Yorkshire Dales. Restaurant with home cooked food and real ale. Open March-Oct 31.

SCARBOROUGH

(4m). Arosa Caravan & Camping Park, Ratten Row, Seamer, Scarborough, N Yorkshire YO12 4QB. *01723 862166.* www.arosacamping.co.uk. Owner: NR Cherry. 4m S of Scarborough on A64. From York, 1st L in Seamer. Quiet, family site in picturesque countryside. Ideal for touring. Modern facilities. TV & games room. Play area. Launderette. Public phone. Club house. Entertainment in high season. Open March 1-Jan 4.

(1m). Camping & Caravanning Club Site – Scarborough, Field Lane, Burniston Road, Scarborough, N Yorkshire YO13 0DA. *01723 366 212.* www.campingandcaravanningclub.co.uk. Owner: Camping & Caravanning Club. On W side of A165, 1m N of Scarborough. 20 acre-site with stunning views of countryside. High on the hills N of Scarborough. All units welcome. Some all weather pitches available. Laundry, children's play area. Near swimming, fishing and tennis. Non-members welcome. Deals for families and backpackers. Visit Britain Caravan Holiday Park of the Year. Yorkshire finalist. Loo Of The Year (4 stars). Open April-Oct.

(3m). Cayton Village Caravan Park Ltd, Mill Lane, Cayton Bay, Scarborough, N Yorkshire YO11 3NN. *01723 583171.* www.caytontouring.co.uk. Owner: Mrs C Croft. From A165 S of Scarborough, turn inland at Cayton Bay, park 0.5m on R. From A64 take B1261 to Filey. In Cayton, take 2nd L after Blacksmiths Arms, park is 200yd on L. The best of coast and country. Luxurious facilities, adventure playground, site shop, dog walk. Seasonal pitches, supersites, hardstanding, storage. Supersaver and OAP discounts. 0.5m to beach, 3m to Scarborough, 4m to Filey, adjoining village with pubs, chip shop, PO, bus. Fishing nearby. David Bellamy Gold Conservation Award. Open March 1- Oct 31.

(5m). Flower of May Holiday Park, Lebberston Cliff, Scarborough, N Yorkshire YO11 3NU. *01723 584311.* www.flowerofmay.com. Owner: Mr JG Atkinson. On A165 Filey to Scarborough. Games room. Family room. Bar. Laundry. Supermarket. Play area. Indoor heated pool. One dog per pitch, by arrangement. Rose Award caravans. Golf, basketball, bowling. Open March-Oct. Hire: Easter-Sept.

(2m). Jacobs Mount Caravan Park and Camping Site, Stepney Road, Scarborough, N Yorkshire YO12 5NL. *01723 361178.* www.jacobsmount.co.uk. Owner: Mr G Dale. Manager: Mr P Benjamin. 2m W of town on A170. Level, all weather pitches. Tap, drain, electric etc. Licensed club. Bar meals. 2 play areas. Family room. Centrally heated showers. Laundry. Street lights. Rose Award. AA-4 flags. Open March-Jan.

YORKSHIRE/HUMBERSIDE

See page 5 for key to symbols and abbreviations

(8m). Jasmine Park, Cross Lane, Snainton, Scarborough, N Yorkshire YO13 9BE. *01723 859240.* www.jasminepark.co.uk. Owner: I Palmer. Turn S off A170 in Snainton (midway between Pickering and Scarborough), SP. Quiet picturesque park in the ideal location for exploring coast and countryside, with level pitches. Multi award-winning park. Brochure. David Bellamy Gold Conservation Award. Open from 1 March-31 Oct.

Lowfield Camping Park, Downdale Road, Staintondale, Scarborough, N Yorkshire YO13 0EZ. *01723 870574.* www.lowfieldcaravanandcamping.co.uk. Quiet and rural site in sylvian setting. Golf course, fishing, shop nearby. Horse riding, llama trekking. Open Feb-Dec.

(2m). Scalby Close Park, Burniston Road, Scarborough, N Yorkshire YO13 0DA. *01723 365908.* www.scalbyclosepark.co.uk. Owner: P F & M Bayes. Park signed 400yd on A165 N of Scarborough. Family owned and run with level, sheltered pitches. Insulated and heated holiday homes for hire. Touring base for N Yorkshire moors and coast. 2m from Scarborough's North Bay attractions pools, boating, etc. David Bellamy Gold Conservation Award. Open March-Dec.

(4m). Spring Willows Touring Caravan & Camping Park, Main Road, Staxton, Scarborough, N Yorkshire YO12 4SB. *01723 891505.* www.springwillows.co.uk. A64 Filey to Bridlington road to Staxton roundabout. Bar. Free hot showers. Swimming pool. Sauna. Bistro. Playground. Children's club. Free entertainment. AA 4 pennants. Open March-Jan.

(6m). St Helens in the Park, Wykeham, Scarborough, N Yorkshire YO13 9QD. *01723 862771.* www.sthelenscaravanpark.co.uk. Owner: St Helens in the Park Ltd. On A170. Hardstandings on adult only area. In N Yorkshire Moors National Park. New 'zip slide' on playground and bike hire on site. Unusual animals (alpacas and Jacob sheep) nearby. Pets welcome. David Bellamy Gold Conservation Award. Open mid Feb-mid Jan.

(4m). West Ayton Caravan Club Site, Cockrah Road, West Ayton, Scarborough, N Yorkshire YO13 9JD. *01723 862989.* www.caravanclub.co.uk. Owner: The Caravan Club. See website for directions. Club members only. No tents.

4m from Scarborough's safe beaches. Ideal family holiday site. Toilet blocks. Privacy cubicles. Laundry. Baby/toddler washroom. Veg prep. MV service point. Games room. Play field, play equipment. Near golf, fishing. Open March 27-Jan 4.

SELBY

(6m). Oakmere Caravan Park and Coarse Fishery, Hill Farm, Skipwith, Selby, N Yorkshire YO8 5SN. *01757 288910.* Owner: MG Patrick & Sons. A19 York to Escrick, L to Skipwith about 3m. Peaceful 300-acre working farm in Skipwith Nature Reserve with 9 acres of landscaped fisheries. Near historic York, pets welcome. Golf courses nearby. Local shops. Open March 1-Oct 31.

(4m). The Ranch Caravan Park, In the Vale of York, Cliffe Common, Selby, N Yorkshire YO8 6EF. *01757 638984.* www.theranchcaravanpark.co.uk. Owner: Lance & Madge Brownridge, Robert & Sue Macvean. A63 towards Selby. At Cliffe turn R, 1m, L at crossroads. Park on R. Set in 6 acres of woodland, family run site. Near shop and pub. Open Feb 5-Jan 5.

SETTLE

(2.5m). Knight Stainforth Hall, Little Stainforth, Settle, N Yorkshire BD24 0DP. *01729 822200.* www.knightstainforth.co.uk. Owner: Mrs S Maudsley. Turn off A65 into Settle, then turn opposite Settle community college on to Stack House lane, site is then 2m. Beside river in Dales National Park. Booking advised. Open March-Oct.

(1m). Langcliffe Caravan Park, Settle, N Yorkshire BD23 9LX. *01729 822387.* www.langcliffe.com. Owner: Mr & Mrs JT Smith. Off A65 on to B6480 continue on B6479 to Horton in Ribblesdale. Past Watersbed Mill, take first L. Park is at end of lane. Children's playground. 1m to golf course, fishing, swimming pool, restaurants, pubs, Settle. Beautiful surroundings. David Bellamy Gold Conservation Award. Open March – Jan.

SHERIFF HUTTON

(1.5m). Camping & Caravanning Club Site – Sheriff Hutton, Bracken Hill, Sheriff Hutton, N Yorkshire YO60 6QG. *01347 878660.* www.campingandcaravanningclub.co.uk. Owner: Camping & Caravanning Club. From York follow Earswick/Strensall signs. L at petrol station and Ship Inn. Site 2nd on R. 10-acre site with 90 pitches. Near York, N Yorkshire Moors National Park, east coast. All units accepted. Non-members welcome. Near seaside resorts Bridlington, Scarborough and Filey. Deals for families and backpackers. Open March-Oct.

SKIPTON

(4.5m). Eshton Road Caravan Site, Gargrave, Skipton, N Yorkshire BD23 3AN. *01756 749229.* Owner: F Green & Son Ltd. Off A65. Fishing on site. Golf course 4m. Shops, PO, doctor 5mins walk.

(12m). Gordale Scar Camping Site, Malham, Skipton, N Yorkshire BD23 4DL. *01729 830333.* Owner: Mr A Wilson. A65 to Gargrave. N (R) for 1m then to Airton and Kirkby Malham to Malham. In Malham turn R over bridge and keep R for site, 1m along no through road. Pleasant picturesque site in good walking country. Near restaurants, café, hotels. Ring afternoons and eves only.

(15m). Hawkswick Cote Caravan Park, Arncliffe, Skipton, N Yorkshire BD23 5PX. *01756 770226.* www.northdales.co.uk. Owner: North Dales LLP. B6265 from Skipton. At Threshfield take B6160, 0.25m past Kilnsey, L into Littondale, park 1.5m on L. 5m from Grassington. Manager: Mr E Carter. 5m to small town, doctors. Climbing available nearby. Fishing, local pub/restaurant 2.5m. Garage, pony treking 3m. Open March-mid-Nov.

(8m). Howgill Lodge Caravan Park, Barden, Skipton, N Yorkshire BD23 6DJ. *01756 720655.* www.howgill-lodge.co.uk. Owner: Mrs Ann Foster. Turn off B6160 at Barden Tower, park 1m on R, by phone box. Family-run park, B&B. Quiet with beautiful views over Wharfedale. Ideal walking area. Dogs allowed with tourers only. 1m pub. Skipton 7m. David Bellamy Gold Conservation Award. Open mid March- 31 Oct.

Strid Wood Caravan Club Site, Bolton Abbey, Skipton, N Yorkshire BD23 6AN. *01756 710433.* www.caravanclub.co.uk. Owner: The Caravan Club. See website for directions. Set in open glade surrounded by woodland and the Yorkshire Dales. Non-members welcome. No tents, booking essential. All hardstanding, steel awning pegs required, gas and gaz, dog walk on site. Toilet blocks. Privacy cubicles. Laundry, baby changing facilities, veg prep. MV service point. Information room. Near

YORKSHIRE/HUMBERSIDE

walks, fishing, watersports. Peaceful off peak. Open March-Jan.

(6m). Threaplands House Farm, Cracoe, Skipton, N Yorkshire BD23 6LD. 01756 730248. Owner: Mr J C Wade. Access via Skipton to Grassington B6265. Calor and Camping Gaz on site. Fishing, shops, Doctor, PO, shopping in 3m. Golf course, cinema 6m. Open March 1-Oct 31.

Wharfedale Caravan Club Site, Long Ashes, Threshfield, Skipton, N Yorkshire BD23 5PN. 01756 753340. www.caravanclub.co.uk. Owner: The Caravan Club. See website for directions. Club members only. No tents. Yorkshire Dales site screened with mature trees, in two fields divided by drystone walls. Toilet blocks, laundry, baby and toddler washroom. MV service point. Play equipment and dog walk on site. Near walks, fishing. Facilities for the disabled. Ideal for families. Open March 27-Jan 4.

(9m). Wood Nook Caravan Park, Skirethorns Lane, Threshfield, Skipton, N Yorkshire BD23 5NU. 01756 752412. www.woodnook.net. Owner: Mr Thompson. From Skipton take B6265 to Threshfield then B6160 for 100yd. L after garage. Site SP at 300yd and 600yd. Licensed shop. Play area. 9m golf, cinema, supermarkets. Fishing 2m. David Bellamy Gold Conservation Award. Open March 1-Oct 31.

SLINGSBY

(0.5m). Camping & Caravanning Club Site – Slingsby, Railway Street, Slingsby, N Yorkshire Y062 4AN. 01653 628335. www.campingandcaravanningclub.co.uk. Owner: Camping & Caravanning Club. At Slingsby on B1257 turn downhill to site on R at end of village. 3-acre site with 60 pitches, accepting all units, mainly grass, some hardstanding. Close to the N Yorkshire Moors and seaside resorts. Non-members welcome. Near Malton, attractive market village. Deals for families and backpackers. Open March-Oct.

Robin Hood Caravan & Camping Park, Green Dyke Lane, Slingsby, N Yorkshire Y062 4AP. 01653 628391. www.robinhoodcaravanpark.co.uk. Owner: Rebecca Palmer-Bunting. On B1257 Malton to Helmsley Road, in picturesque Ryedale. Peace and tranquility, near York, the Moors, Heartbeat country, and seaside resorts of Scarborough, Whitby and Filey. Open March 1-Oct 31.

SUTTON-ON-THE-FOREST

Ponderosa Caravan & Camping, Sutton-on-the-Forest, N Yorkshire Y061 1ET. 01347 810744/810706. Owner: WIS & J Whatnell. B1363 from York (7m), SP on B1363. Site 800yd. Country inn and restaurant. Children's play area. Children allowed.

TADCASTER

(5m). White Cote Caravan Park, Ryther Road, Ulleskelf, Tadcaster, N Yorkshire LS24 9DY. 01937 835231. www.whitecotecaravanpark.co.uk. Owner: Richard and Pauline Boyes. Off A162 S of Tadcaster, E on B1223 towards Selby. Sheltered, well maintained site. Licensed bar open weekends 0.5m to village PO and petrol station. Family room. Fresh milk and ice cream available. 0.5m to local shop, PO and petrol station selling gas and pub serving meals. River fishing 1m, golf 4m. Open March 1-Jan 31.

THIRSK

(3m). Thirkleby Hall Caravan Park, Thirkleby Hall, Thirsk, N Yorkshire Y07 3AR. 01845 501360. www.greenwoodparks.com. Owner: Pratt family. On A19 York to Thirsk. Lovely park built in grounds of a former stately home with lake and woods. Play area. Bar. Games room. Bottled gas. Fishing lake on park. Playground. Golf course 3m, weekly market in Thirsk 3m, York 16m. AA 2 pennant. Free brochure 01243 514433. Open March 1-Jan 5.

(0.25m). Thirsk Racecourse Caravan Club Site, Station Road, Thirsk, N Yorkshire Y07 1QL. 01845 525266. www.caravanclub.co.uk. Owner: The Caravan Club. See website for directions. Pitch near the main stand, with the famous turf before you, 5mins walk to the market town of Thirsk. Toilet blocks and laundry, veg prep and gas/gaz. Dog walk on site, golf and NCN route nearby. Facilities for disabled. Non-members and tent campers welcome. Suits families. Open March-Oct.

(2.6m). York House Holiday Park, Balk, Bagby, Thirsk, N Yorkshire Y07 2AQ. 01845 597495. www.yhlparks.co.uk. Owner: York House Leisure. Travelling from Thirsk on A19 take L turn signed Bagby, Balk, Kilburn. Go through Bagby to T Junction, turn R go 500yd down hill, park is on the L. Beautiful location on the edge of the North York Moors National Park. Local pub and meals nearby. Shopping and cinema 3m. Golf 6m. David Bellamy Gold Conservation Award. Open March-Nov.

WHITBY

(9m). Abbots House Farm, Camping & Caravan Site, Goathland, Whitby, N Yorkshire Y022 5NH. 01947 896270. www.abbotshouse.org.uk. Owner: Mr & Mrs Cox and Mr & Mrs Jenkinson. From Whitby S on A169, SP Goathland. Site 0.5m beside Goathland Hotel. Moorland scenery and N Yorkshire Moors Steam Railway. 'Heartbeat' country. Facilities include showers, toilets, freezer pack exchange. Under 5s, dogs, awnings, hot showers all free. Open Easter-Oct 31.

(9m). Brow House Farm, Goathland, Whitby, N Yorkshire Y022 5NP. 01947 896274. Owner: Mr J T Jackson. York-Pickering-Goathland or Middlesborough-Whitby-Goathland. Shops, PO in 0.5m. Doctor 4m. Fishing, golf 7-8m. Open March 1-Oct 31.

(7m). Burnt House Holiday Park, Ugthorpe, Whitby, N Yorkshire Y021 2BG. 01947 840448. www.caravancampingsites.co.uk. Owner: A&S Booth. A171 Whitby to Guisborough road SP Ugthorpe, 275yd on R. Free showers. Play area. Hardstanding or grass. Well-lit site, near pubs. Holiday cottage for hire. Open March-Oct 31.

(9m). Hollins Farm, Glaisdale, Whitby, N Yorkshire Y021 2PZ. 01947 897516. Owner: Mr & Mrs A Mortimer. A171, 4m to Glaisdale village. SP Glaisdale Dale for 1.5m. Small farm on edge of Moors, handy for coast, steam railway, lovely villages. Tents only. Dogs by arrangement. Good pub (with meals), shop & PO in village. Fishing nearby. Open Easter-End Oct.

(4.5m). Low Moor Caravan Club Site, Sneaton, Whitby, N Yorkshire Y022 5JE. 01947 810505. www.caravanclub.co.uk. Owner: The Caravan Club. See website for directions. Tranquil site in the N Yorkshire Moors National Park, in TV's Heartbeat country. No sanitation. Pitching areas are pleasantly open and spacious. Non-members welcome. No tents. Boules pitch, mini-golf. Information room. MV service point. Open March-Nov.

■ **(5.5m). Middlewood Farm Holiday Park, Middlewood Lane, Fylingthorpe, Robin Hood's Bay, Whitby, N Yorkshire Y022 4UF.** 01947 880414. www.middlewoodfarm.com. Owner: Mr & Mrs P Beeforth. Scarborough/Whitby A171 turn for Robin Hood's Bay; Fylingthorpe. At Fylingthorpe crossroads and PO turn on to

112 MOTOR CARAVAN & CAMPING PARKS 2009

YORKSHIRE/HUMBERSIDE

See page 5 for key to symbols and abbreviations

Middlewood Lane. Follow brown signs. Magnificent views and walking country. Fantastic new facilities, hardstandings. Adventure playground. 10mins walk to beach. Pub and shop 5mins walk. Gas/Gaz. Luxury caravans for hire. Rose Award. Near fishing, golf, sailing, tennis, bowls. David Bellamy Gold Conservation Award. Open March 1- Jan 4.

(3m). Northcliffe Holiday Park, Bottoms Lane, High Hawsker, Whitby, N Yorkshire YO22 4LL. *01947 880477.* www.northcliffe-seaview.com. Owner: S&S Martin. 3m S Whitby (A171) L on to (B1447), 0.5m L on to private road. Whitby's top award-winning park. Fabulous sea views. Seasonal touring park only. Luxury caravans for sale. David Bellamy Gold Conservation Award. Open March 1- Oct 31.

(4m). Rigg Farm Caravan Park, Stainsacre, Whitby, N Yorkshire YO22 4LP. *01947 880430.* www.riggfarmcaravanpark.co.uk. Owner: DA & AE Stuart. A171 before Whitby take B1416. 1.5m S of Ruswarp, turn SP Sneatonthorpe, Hawkser. Stainsacre (and Rigg Farm). Site 2m on L. Small, quiet site in National Park with scenic views. Separate site for tourers. Children allowed. Separate tent pitches. AA 3 pennants. Open March 1-Oct 31.

(8m). Serenity Touring Caravan & Camping Park, Hinderwell, Whitby, N Yorkshire TS13 5JH. *01947 841292.* www.serenitycaravanpark.co.uk. Owner: Nigel and Pat Little. 8m N of Whitby on A174, Cleveland Way 1m. Quiet, sheltered, secure predominately adult site with lovely country views. 0.5m from the sea. Refurbished facilities block. Marvellous coastal, country and moorland walks. Near village shops, pubs. Open March 1-Oct 31.

(8m). Ugthorpe Lodge Caravan & Camping Site, Guisborough Road, Whitby, N Yorkshire YO21 2BE. *01947 840518.* Owner: D Stainsby. On A171 Guisborough to Whitby. Quiet, family site with full services. Beautiful views. Pub and restaurant on site. Separate field for rallies. B&B. Play area. Fishing 2m. Golf, beach 5m. Open April 1-Oct 31.

YORK

Acomb Grange, Grange Lane, York, N Yorkshire YO23 3QZ. *0871 2884763.* www.acombgrange.co.uk. Owner: CA Brown. Important historical site, moated farmhouse. A residence of kings in the Middle Ages, and the last Royalist stand at the Battle of Marston. Please phone for directions as it is complicated!

(10m). Alders Caravan Park, Homefarm, Monk Green, Alne, York, N Yorkshire YO61 1RY. *01347 838722.* www.alderscaravanpark.co.uk. Owner: Mr JD Whiteley & Mrs RH Price. 3m S of Easingwold in centre of village. Near tennis courts, children's playground, PO, pub with restaurant. 3m to golf courses and fishing. Open March 1- Oct 31.

(3m). Beechwood Grange Caravan Club Site, Malton Road, York, N Yorkshire YO32 9TH. *01904 424637.* www.caravanclub.co.uk. Owner: The Caravan Club. See website for directions. In open countryside outside York, screened with trees and hedges. Ideal base for York and Yorkshire's attractions. Toilet block and baby/toddler washroom, laundry, veg prep area, MV service point, play area and dog walk on site. Non-members welcome. No tents. Open March-Nov.

(8m). Cawood Holiday Park, Ryther Road, Cawood, York, N Yorkshire YO8 3TT. *01757 268450.* www.cawoodpark.com. Owner: Andrew & Esther Pringle. On B1222 from A1 or York to Cawood traffic lights, and on B1223 signed Tadcaster 1m, park is on L. Selby 5m. Pool tables. Coarse fishing. Lakeside bar. Entertainment. AA 4 pennants and RAC Awards. 3 homes adapted for disabled. Seasonal pitches available for touring caravans.

(3.5m). Chestnut Farm Holiday Park, Acaster Malbis, York, N Yorkshire YO23 2UQ. *01904 704576.* www.chestnutfarmholidaypark.co.uk. Owner: SG & AJ Smith. Family run park in pretty village by river Ouse 3.5m from York. Ideal for touring Dales, coasts and moors. Modern facilities. Rose Award caravans. Open March-end Nov.

(8m). Fangfoss Park, Fangfoss, York, N Yorkshire YO41 5QB. *01759 380491.* www.fangfosspark.co.uk. Owner: Jo & Simon Bell. 2m from A1079 at Wilberfoss. Quiet park at the foot of the Wolds. Laundry facilities. Play area. AA 3-pennant. Near York, seasonal and touring pitches. Open March-Nov.

(8m). Goose Wood Caravan Park, Sutton-on-the-Forest, York, N Yorkshire YO61 1ET. *01347 810829.* www.goosewood.co.uk. Owner: Sue & Eddie Prince. From A1237 (York outer ring road) take B1363 N, pass Haxby-Wigginton junction, take next R, and follow signs. Or from N, take first L after 2nd Easingwold roundabout (A19) into Huby then Sutton-on-the-Forest. Quiet and peaceful country park, near York. All hardstanding pitches with patio and electric hook up. Fishing on site. Open Feb 1-Jan 14.

Holly Brook Caravan Park, Penny Carr Lane, Easingwold, York, N Yorkshire YO61 3EU. *01347 821906.* www.hollybrookpark.co.uk. Owner: Chris & Alice Cameron. Off A19 York to Thirsk road. Near Easingwold take first R, SP Stillington, in 0.5m turn R into Pennycarr Lane. Site on R after third of a mile. Pleasant well-equipped, secluded, level grass site. Regret no children. AA 3 Pennants. Fishing, golf nearby. Open March 1-Dec 31.

(8m). Lakeside Adult Touring Park and Coarse Fishery, Lakeside, Bielby, Nr Pocklington, York, N Yorkshire YO42 4JP. *01759 318100.* www.lakesidewebsite.com. Owner: Mr R Smith. SP off 1079. 6-acre fishing lake on site. Tradesmen call daily. Luxury log cabin for hire. Long or short breaks. Overlooking lake.

(4m). Moor End Farm, Acaster Malbis, York, N Yorkshire YO23 2UQ. *01904 706727.* www.moor-end-farm.co.uk. Owner: R & D Hall. Off A64 York (4m) to Tadcaster, turn off at Copmanthorpe, SP Acaster Malbis. Small well appointed park in nice location for York, Yorkshire and York/Selby cycle track. AA 2 pennants. RAC Approved. Open April-Oct.

(6m). Moorside Caravan Park, Lords Moor Lane, Strensall, York, N Yorkshire YO32 5XJ. *01904 491208.* www.moorsidecaravanpark.co.uk. Owner: Mr P Smith. Take Strensall turn off A1237 and head towards Flaxton. Opposite York golf course. Washing-up area and laundry. Free hot showers. Fishing on site. No children. Dogs must be kept on lead at all times. Golf course nearby. Open March-Oct.

(4m). Naburn Lock Caravan Park, Naburn, York, N Yorkshire YO19 4RU. *01904 728697.* www.naburnlock.co.uk. 4m S of York. From York take A19. Turn R on B1222, 2.5m. River fishing. Riding.

YORKSHIRE/HUMBERSIDE

Launderette. Well stocked shop inc papers. Dogs on lead welcome. Riverboat from park. Bus from park. Pub 10mins walk. Restaurants locally. Excellent cycle track in village. Please ring to book. Open March 1-Nov 6.

(3.5m). Rawcliffe Manor Caravan Park, Manor Lane, Shipton Road, York, N Yorkshire YO3 6TZ. *01904 640845.* www.lysanderarms.co.uk. Owner: Ms C Ellerby. Off A19 at junction with A1237 (new bypass). Adults only. 13 super pitches with water, drainage, foul waste, electric and sat TV. Club. Gas on site. Tesco Superstore. 12-screen cinema. Bowling alley and shopping complex next to site. Site pub, entertainment, restaurant, Sunday carvery.

(2m). Riverside Caravan & Camping Park, York Marine Services, Ferry Lane, Bishopthorpe, York, N Yorkshire YO23 2SB. *01904 704442.* www.yorkmarine.co.uk/camping. Owner: York Marine Services Ltd. A1036 at Bishopthorpe, go down main street then R on to Acaster Lane. L 2m into Ferry Lane, drive through car park to site, 400yd from Bishop's Palace. An attractive site alongside river Ouse with moorings and river bus for York. Open April 1-Oct 31.

Rowntree Park Caravan Club Site, Terry Avenue, York, N Yorkshire YO23 1JQ. *01904 658797.* www.caravanclub.co.uk. Owner: The Caravan Club. See website for directions. A Popular site, level and on the banks of the Ouse. MV waste. Advance booking essential. Non-members and tent campers welcome. Toilet blocks. Privacy cubicles. Laundry facilities. Veg prep. Information room. Ideal for families. Local attractions include Jorvik Viking centre and York Minster. Fishing, golf nearby.

(12m). South Lea Caravan Park, The Balk, Poklington, York, N Yorkshire YO42 2NX. *01759 303467.* www.south-lea.co.uk. Owner: Nick & Louise Woodward. A1079 (York-Hull) turn at the Yorkway Motel onto to B1247. Park is 400yd on L in 15 acres of flat grass. 1m from Pocklington. Luxury shower/toilet facilities, large play area, security barrier. Golf and fishing in 5m. Near York, the East Coast and Yorkshire moors. David Bellamy Silver Conservation Award. Open March 1-Oct 31.

(7m). The Old Gate House, Wheldrake Lane, Elvington, York, N Yorkshire YO41 4AZ. *01904 608225.* Owner: Mr & Mrs GL Gatenby. A64. Turn E on A1079, then on B1228 to Elvington. 3m about turn R opposite garage to Wheldrake. Site is 1m on L. Wheldrake Lane nature reserve, Yorkshire Air Museum (2m). Fishing, golf nearby. Garage with shop (1m). Open March 1-Oct 31.

(7m). The Sycamores Touring Caravan Park, Feoffe Common Lane, Barmby Moor, York, N Yorkshire YO4 5HS. *01759 388838.* Owner: Mr R A Wright. 3-acre site between Wilberfoss and Barmby Moor, at the foot of the picturesque Yorkshire Wolds, E of York.

Tollerton Holiday Park, Station Road, Tollerton, York, N Yorkshire YO6 2HD. *01347 838313.* www.greenwoodparks.com. Owner: Pratt Family. Off A19 between York and Easingwold, Tollerton and Linton-on-Ouse turn-off. Playground. Shop, PO in Tollerton 0.5m. Golf, fishing in 3m. Good shopping in York and Easingwold. Free brochure 01243 514433. AA 3 pennants. Open March 1-Nov 30.

(8m). Weir Caravan Park, Stamford Bridge, York, N Yorkshire YO41 1AN. *01759 371377.* www.yorkshireholidayparks.co.uk. Owner: Mr & Mrs D Hind. On A166 Bridlington to York. Peaceful site, 5mins walk to village, shops and pubs. Buses to York. Fishing on park. Open March 1-Oct 31.

Wigman Hall, Crockley Hill, York, N Yorkshire YO1 4SQ. *01904 448221.* Owner: Mrs G Duncan. Take the A19 from York turn off for Wheldrake and Thorganby about 4m out of York. 1.5m down this road site is on R. Adults only. Open March-Oct.

Willow House Caravan Park, Wigginton Road, Wigginton, York, N Yorkshire YO32 2RH. *01904 750060.* www.willowhouseyork.co.uk. Owner: Mr & Mrs J Pulleyn. From A1237 north side of York outer ring road, take B1363 SP Wigginton. 1m on R. Coarse fishing. Adults only.

(5m). York Touring Caravan Park, Greystones Farm, Towthorpe Moor Lane, York, N Yorkshire YO32 9ST. *01904 499275.* www.yorkcaravansite.co.uk. Owner: Graham & Mary Chapman. Take Strensall/Haxby, turn off the A64. Park is 1m on L. On-site golf range and 9-hole pay & play course. 3 golf courses in 5m. Strensall village 2m away (shops, PO,

doctor). All new park facilities (showers, toilets, laundry room).

SOUTH YORKSHIRE
BARNSLEY

(3m). Greensprings Touring Park, Rockley Abbey Farm, Rockley Lane, Worsbrough, Barnsley, S Yorkshire S75 3DS. *01226 288298.* Owner: JB & M Hodgson. Off M1 J36, A61 towards Barnsley L after 0.25m, park 1m down hill on L. Award-winning site in picturesque wood and farmland in the Pennine foothills. Suitable for a relaxing break on journeys north and south or for touring the Peak District and Pennine Yorkshire. Open April-Oct.

DONCASTER

(8m). Hatfield Water Park, Old Thorne Road, Hatfield, Doncaster, S Yorkshire DN7 6EQ. *01302 841572.* hatfield.waterpark@doncaster.gov.uk. Owner: Doncaster Metropolitan Borough Council. Between Doncaster and Thorne on the A18. From M18 take J5 to M180 then J1, for A18. SP Hatfield. Site has lake with watersports. Centre is recognised by RYA for sailing & windsurfing and BCU for canoeing & kayaking. Fishing by day ticket. Bunkhouse dormitories available for groups. Children's playground. Hot & cold drinks, snacks, ice creams available from visitor centre. Local shops 10 mins walk. Superstores 10mins by car. Open April-Oct.

SHEFFIELD

(4m). Fox Hagg Farm, Lodge Lane, Rivelin, Sheffield, S Yorkshire S6 5SN. *01142 305589.* Owner: Mrs M Dyson & Son. W of Sheffield on A57. Between Sheffield and Peak District. Wash room. Free showers. Near Rivelin PO, shops & doctor nearby in 0.25m. Near rock climbing, golf, 2m Peak District. Open April 1-Oct 31.

WEST YORKSHIRE
BINGLEY

(2.5m). Harden and Bingley Holiday Park, Goit Stock Lane, Harden, Bingley, W Yorkshire BD16 1DF. *01535 273810.* www.ukparks.co.uk/harden. Owner: Ms J Dunham & Mr P Davis. Take B6429 from A650 in Bingley towards Harden. In Harden village turn L toward Wilsden. At bottom of hill and before bridge turn R on to Goit Stock Lane. Ideal

114 MOTOR CARAVAN & CAMPING PARKS 2009

YORKSHIRE/HUMBERSIDE

See page 5 for key to symbols and abbreviations

for peaceful country lovers. Set in private woodlands with waterfalls. Local shops 0.5m. Fishing, horse riding, golf, courses close by. David Bellamy Gold Conservation Award. Open March 1-Jan 31.

HAWORTH

(1.5m). Upwood Park, Blackmoor Road, Oxenhope, Haworth, W Yorkshire BD22 9SS. *01535 644242.* www.upwoodpark.co.uk. Owner: F Towers. A629 to B6141 Denholme Oxenhope. Turn into Blackmoor Road. Site 0.5m. Near Yorkshire Dales National Park with panoramic views over Bronte country. Bar with family room/food, play area. David Bellamy Gold Conservation Award. Open March 1-Jan 4.

HEBDEN BRIDGE

(2.5m). Lower Clough Foot Caravan Club Site, Cragg Vale, Hebden Bridge, W Yorkshire HX7 5RU. *01422 882531.* www.caravanclub.co.uk. Owner: The Caravan Club. See website for directions. A site for the discerning, tucked away off the road, well screened and gently sloping. MV service point and gas/gaz exchange. Fishing, golf, watersports and NCN route nearby. Good area for walking. Quiet and peaceful off-peak. Own sanitation required. Non-members welcome. No tents. Open March-Nov.

(3m). Pennine Camp & Caravan Site, High Greenwood House, Heptonstall, Hebden Bridge, W Yorkshire HX7 7AZ. *01422 842287.* Owner: Mr G Sunderland. From Hebden Bridge take Heptonstall Road. Then follow camping and caravan signs. We are in the Camping and Caravan Club site. Golf course, shops, garages, doctor 3m. PO, fishing and climbing in 3m. Early bookings required. Open April-Oct.

HOLMFIRTH

(1.5m). Holme Valley Camping & Caravan Park, Thongsbridge, Holmfirth, W Yorkshire HD9 7TD. *01444 665819.* www.holmevalleycamping.com. Owner: Mr & Mrs Philip and Hazel Peaker. Halfway between Holmfirth & Honley In the valley bottom off the A6024 (turn off main road by the bottle banks). In delightful setting in the heart of the beautiful 'Last of the Summer Wine' country and on the fringe of the Peak District National Park. Laundry room. On-site angling. Enclosed play area. David Bellamy Gold Conservation Award.

KEIGHLEY

(2m). Bronte Caravan Park & Storage, Off Halifax Road, Keighley, W Yorkshire BD25 5QF. *01535 649111/222.* www.brontecaravanpark.co.uk. Owner: Marshall & Gregson Ltd. From Keighley, take Halifax Road A629 – the park is 1.5m on R. Peaceful and quiet park. Security barriers with access/exit key. Excellent on site fishing. Own deer park and lake with black swans and other wildlife. Open March 1-end Jan (closed Feb).

(5m). Brown Bank Caravan Park, Brown Bank Lane, Silsden, Keighley, WYorkshire BD20 0NN. *01535 653241.* timlaycock@btconnect.com. Owner: Mr TJ Laycock. Off A6034 from Silsden (2m) or Addingham. Peaceful site on edge of Ilkley Moor. Ideal for the Dales with many local walks. Golf courses 1-2m, pony trekking, cinema, swimming, shopping, all in 2-5m. Open April 1-Oct 31.

(1m). Dales Bank Holiday Park, Low Lane, Silsden, Keighley, W Yorkshire BD20 9JH. *01535 653321.* Owner: Mr R M Preston. Off A65, Bolton Road from Silsden tophill. L Cringles Lane, keep L for 2m. Licensed bar. Café. Games/function room. Lodge rooms. 6 B&B. Doctor 1m, hospital 3m. Golf 3m, 1m to Silsden. Horse riding 1m. Open April 1-Nov 7.

Lower Heights Farm, Silsden, Keighley, W Yorkshire. *01535 653035.* mmsrowling@aol.com. Owner: Mr F & Mrs K Rowling. 4m SE of Skipton on road N off A6034 at Cringles. Haworth, Bronte country, Bolton Abbey, Ilkley Moor and Skipton Castle all in 5m. Fees on application. Takeaway meals nearby.

LEEDS

(7m). Haighfield Caravan Site, Blackmoor Lane, Bardsey, Leeds, W Yorkshire LS17 9DY. *01937 574658.* www.haighfieldcaravanpark.co.uk. Owner: Mrs J Brown. Turn off at A58 Leeds to Wetherby, turn at Bardsey into Church Lane, past the Bingley Arms to the top of hill, park 50yd on L. Pretty immaculately kept park with holiday homes for sale and hire. 7m to Leeds. 28 day camping field and Loo Award Shower Block.

(7m). Moor Lodge Caravan Park, Blackmoor Lane, Bardsey, Leeds, W Yorkshire LS17 9DZ. *01937 572424.* www.ukparks.co.uk/moorlodge. Owner: Mr R Brown. Off A58, 7m from Leeds, L at Shadwell sign then follow caravan signs. 1.5m to shops.

(4m). Roundhay Caravan & Camping Park, Elmete Lane, Leeds, W Yorkshire LS8 2LG. *01132 652354.* Owner: Leeds City Council. In Roundhay 700-acre public park with its year round Tropical World, close by Royal Armouries, Medical Museum at Jimmy's. Near York, Bronte, Herriot country and Dales. Showers, launderette, play area and public telephone. Tourist information. Open March-Nov.

OTLEY

Stubbings Farm, Leeds Road, Otley, W Yorkshire LS21 1DN. *01943 464168.* Owner: Mr M Rimmer. On A660, 1m E of Otley to Leeds. Farm site in easy reach of Dales. A quiet, rural, old fashioned camping site with beautiful views of Wharfe Valley.

SHIPLEY

(4m). Dobrudden Caravan Park, Baildon Moor, Baildon, Shipley, W Yorkshire BD17 5EE. *01274 581016.* www.dobrudden.co.uk. Owner: Mrs ER Lawrence & Mr PA Lawrence. 3m N of Baildon. Close to Ilkley Moor and Haworth. Bronte country. Golf, shops 2m. Horse riding 3m. Open March 1-Dec 31.

WAKEFIELD

(5m). Nostell Priory Holiday Park, Doncaster Road, Nostell, Wakefield, W Yorkshire WF4 1QE. *01924 863938.* www.nostellprioryholidaypark.co.uk. Off A638 Wakefield to Doncaster. Tranquil, secluded, woodland park ideal for the country lover, in the estate of a stately home. A warm welcome for all. Holiday caravans to the highest standard. On-site fishing lakes. 5m to shopping centre, golf, swimming and boating. David Bellamy Gold Conservation Award. Open March 1-Oct 31.

WETHERBY

(4m). Maustin Caravan Park Ltd, Kearby with Netherby, Wetherby, W Yorkshire LS22 4DA. *01132 886234.* www.maustin.co.uk. Owner: Mr & Mrs W Webb. South facing, sheltered in Lower Wharfe Valley between Harrogate (5m) and Wetherby, close to Harewood House. Ring for directions or see website. Peaceful haven for people without family responsibilities. Flat green bowling. Restaurant/bar on the park. Brochure on request. Lots to do including Harewood House nearby. Open March 1-Jan 28.

SCOTLAND

ABERDEENSHIRE

ABERDEEN

(8m). Skene Caravan Park, Mains of Keir, Skene, Aberdeen, Aberdeenshire AB32 6YA. *01224 743282.* Owner: Thomas Mitchell. Take A944 road from Aberdeen for 7m, turn R, SP to Kirktown of Skene, and follow caravan signs. Shop 0.5m. PO and doctor 2.5m. Open April-Oct.

ABOYNE

Camping & Caravanning Club Site – Tarland, Aboyne, Aberdeenshire AB34 4UP. *01339 881388.* www.campingandcaravanningclub.co.uk. Owner: Camping & Caravanning Club. From Aberdeen on A93 turn R in Aboyne at Strua Hotel on to B9094. After 6m take next R and then fork L before bridge, 600yd, site on L. Paradise for walkers and anglers. In quiet, pretty village of Tarland, with Royal Deeside's spectacular mountain scenery. Non-members welcome. Special deals for families and backpackers. Some all weather pitches available. Near golf courses. Open April-Oct.

ALFORD

Haughton House Caravan Park, Montgarrie Road, Alford, Aberdeenshire AB33 8NA. *01975 562107.* www.aberdeenshire.gov.uk. Owner: Aberdeenshire Council. 25m W of Aberdeen. Beautiful country location. Ideal touring base. Fishing and golf on or adjacent to site. Dogs allowed but not in holiday hire caravans. 5 flats and 1 bungalow also for hire. Open late March-Sept.

BALLATER

(0.25m). Ballater Caravan Park, Anderson Road, Ballater, Aberdeenshire AB35 5QR. *01339 755727.* www.aberdeenshire.gov.uk. Owner: Aberdeenshire Council. Site is off A93 Aberdeen to Braemar situated by river Dee. Stunning scenery, rugged hills. Park is beside the River Dee. 30mins drive to Queen Victoria's 'Dear paradise' and Royal Deeside to the Cairngorm National Park. Bicycle hire from garage. Open April-Oct.

(0.5m). The Invercauld Caravan Club Site, Glenshee Road, Braemar, Ballater, Aberdeenshire AB35 5YQ. *01339 741373.* www.caravanclub.co.uk. Owner: The Caravan Club. See website for directions. Near village of Braemar, 1100 feet above sea level, the eastern gateway to the Cairngorms. Ideal for walkers and mountain bikers. Non-members welcome. Tent campers welcome. Some hardstandings. Facilities for skiers, ski rocks, boot store, drying room and community room. Toilet block, privacy cubicles, laundry, MV service point, veg prep area, gas, playground, dog walk. Ideal for families, quiet and peaceful off peak for walking, fishing and golf in 5m. Advance booking essential. Open Dec-Oct.

BANCHORY

(5m). Feughside Caravan Park, Strachan, Banchory, Aberdeenshire AB31 6NT. *01330 850669.* www.feughsidecaravanpark.co.uk. Owner: Mr G Hay. Take B974 from Banchory W to Strachan then B976 to Feughside Inn turn R, site is behind Inn. Quiet family run park. Caravan well spaced, good toilet facilities. Level, grassy, hotel adjacent. Fishing nearby, forest walks 1.5m, shops 2m. Several golf courses in area. Open April 1 to mid-Oct.

(2m). Silver Ladies Caravan Park, Strachan, Banchory, Aberdeenshire AB31 6NL. *01330 822800.* Owner: Normanhurst Enterprises Ltd. S of Banchory on L of B974 Fettercairn Road. Fishing nearby. Castles and Whiskey trails. 25m to Aberdeen. David Bellamy Gold Conservation Award. Open April 1-Oct 31.

(1.5m). Silverbank Caravan Club Site, North Deeside Road, Banchory, Aberdeenshire AB31 5PY. *01330 822477.* www.caravanclub.co.uk. Owner: The Caravan Club. See website for directions. Caravan Club members only. No tents. Close to river Dee. Convenient for walking, pony trekking, golf and fishing. Indoor pool at Banchory. All hardstandings, toilet block (privacy cubicles), laundry facilities, veg prep, MV service point, gas and gaz, shops 0.5m, dogwalk. Open March-Nov.

BANFF

(1m). Banff Links Caravan Park, Airnavaig, Boyndie Road, Banff, Aberdeenshire AB45 2JD. *01261 812228.* www.aberdeenshire.gov.uk. Owner: Aberdeenshire Council. Off A98 Cullen to Banff. 1m W of Banff, SP coastal route. Popular park near large sandy beach of Banff Bay, a great attraction to surfers, next door is a well equipped new children's play park. Open Late March-Oct 31.

FRASERBURGH

Esplanade Caravan Park, The Esplanade, Fraserburgh, Aberdeenshire AB43 5EU. *01346 510041.* www.aberdeenshire.gov.uk. Owner: Aberdeenshire Council. On the E side of Fraserburgh known locally as the Broch, overlooking Esplanade and large beach (in Marine Conservation Society's Good Beach Guide) golden sands that stretch round the bay to the Waters of Philorth and its Nature Reserve. Open April-Oct.

HUNTLY

(0.5m). Huntly Castle Caravan Park, The Meadow, Huntly, Aberdeenshire AB54 4UJ. *01466 794999.* www.huntlycastle.co.uk. Owner: Mr & Mrs Hugh Ballantyne. From Aberdeen on A96 (Huntly bypass), at roundabout outside Huntly take A96 (SP Inverness). In about 0.75m turn R then 2nd L (Riverside Dir). Caravan Club affiliated. Large indoor recreation facility including badminton, snooker, table tennis, large play area and refreshments. 5mins walk to town. Ideal touring base for Whisky castle and coastal trails. Golf course, river fishing, swimming, shops, all in 0.5m. Open April-Oct.

KINTORE

(1m). Hillhead Caravan Park, Kintore, Aberdeenshire AB51 0YX. *01467 632809.* www.hillheadcaravan.co.uk. Owner: Dennis & Mary Smith. From S leave A96 at Broomhill roundabout 3rd exit. From N stay on A96 past Kintore (Do not enter Kintore), leave at Broomhill roundabout 1st exit. Follow brown caravan signs on to B994. Then take second R, 3m along B994. Hillhead is 1m on R. AA 3-pennant and RAC approved. Well-equipped, high quality, quiet park. Fishing permit sold on park, golf, shop, PO, doctor nearby. Castle trail, whisky. Aberdeen city 12m, airport 6m.

LAURENCEKIRK

(4m). Brownmuir Caravan Park, Fordoun, Laurencekirk, Aberdeenshire AB30 1SJ. *01561 320786.* www.brownmuircaravanpark.co.uk. Owner: Mr M B Bowers. Off A90, 4m N of Laurencekirk, 10m S of Stonehaven. At Fordoun pass village, 1m on R. Park 1m from village of Fordoun. Fishing, golf course in village; cycling, hiking 1m to shops in village and bowls, tennis. Play area. Flat and grassy site. Open April 1-Oct 31.

(5m). Dovecot Caravan Park, Northwaterbridge, Laurencekirk, Aberdeenshire AB30 1QL. *01674 840630.* www.dovecotcaravanpark.co.uk. Owner: Mrs A Mowatt. Off A90 Dundee-Aberdeen road, 5m N of Brechin, turn off at Northwaterbridge at Edzell Woods sign 500yd on L. Map reference 045/648663.

See page 5 for key to symbols and abbreviations

SCOTLAND

Well maintained, sheltered park. Excellent base for touring. David Bellamy Silver Conservation Award. Open April to mid-Oct.

MONTROSE

(6m). East Bowstrips Caravan Park, St Cyrus, Montrose, Aberdeenshire DD10 0DE. 01674 850328. www.ukparks.com/eastbowstrips. Owner: P & G Tully. About 6m N of Montrose on A92. From S (Montrose) enter St Cyrus, pass hotel 1st L, 2nd R. From N (Aberdeen) enter St Cyrus 1st R, 2nd R. Delightful quiet park, set in attractively landscaped grounds, close to beach and nature reserve. Ideal touring centre. Facilities for disabled visitors. Fishing 1m, golf 6m. AA 4 pennants. Open April-Oct.

YOUR TOP 101 SITES 2009

PETERHEAD

(8m) Aden Caravan Park, Aden Country Park, Mintlaw, Peterhead, Aberdeenshire AB42 8FQ. 01771 623460. www.aberdeenshire.gov.uk. Owner: Aberdeenshire Council. On A950. Set in a woodland area with a heritage centre, working farm, restaurant and sensory garden. Open Late March-Oct.

Peterhead Lido Caravan Park, The Lido, Peterhead, Aberdeenshire AB42 2YP. 01779 473358. www.aberdeenshire.gov.uk. Owner: Aberdeenshire Council. Situated at the Peterhead Lido, the park is next to a busy road overlooking the Bay of Refuge, and marina close to the maritime heritage centre, gift shop, café and tea area. Open Late March-Oct.

PORTSOY

(0.25m). Portsoy Caravan Park, The Links, Portsoy, Aberdeenshire AB45 2RQ. 01261 842695. www.aberdeenshire.gov.uk. Owner: Aberdeenshire Council. Set overlooking Portsoy Bay near to the 17th century harbour and village shops. Open Late March-Oct.

(3m). Sandend Caravan Park, Sandend, Portsoy, Aberdeenshire AB4 2UA. 01261 842660. sandendholidays@aol.com. Owner: Mr B & Mrs J Winfield. Off A98 between Cullen and Portsoy. Beside sandy beach in conservation village. 200yds to village harbour. Open April-Oct.

ROSEHEARTY

Rosehearty Caravan Park, The Harbour, Rosehearty, Aberdeenshire

AB43 7JQ. 01346 510041. www.aberdeenshire.gov.uk. Owner: Aberdeenshire Council. Situated on the seashore in the village, close to shops, hotels and services. On-site laundry and toilet/shower facilities. Open Late March-Oct.

STONEHAVEN

Queen Elizabeth Caravan Park, Stonehaven, Aberdeenshire AB39 2RD. 01569 764041. www.aberdeenshire.gov.uk. Owner: Aberdeenshire Council. Off A92 Aberdeen to Stonehaven. The park is situated beside the village of Cowie, on the promenade next to the sports centre. Stonehaven is famous for its quaint little shops, tranquil restaurants and historic enclosed harbour. Open late March-Oct.

TURRIFF

(10m). East Balthangie Caravan Park, East Balthangie, Cuminestown, Turriff, Aberdeenshire AB53 5XY. 01888 544261. www.eastbalthangie.co.uk. Owner: John & Anna Burdon. From Ellon on A948 to New Deer, road becomes B9170 to Cuminestow. Continue straight on for 2m, then turn R at the junction SP New Byth. Park is 3.5m down this road on L. PO and shop 2m. Secure area for pet owners. Farm walk. Open March-Oct with CL site all year.

(0.5m). Turriff Caravan Park, Station Road, Turriff, Aberdeenshire AB53 7ER. 01888 562205. www.aberdeenshire.gov.uk. Owner: Aberdeenshire Council. From Turriff town centre off A947 Aberdeen to Banff road 9m S of Banff. Site is adjacent to attractive park with children's play area, crazy golf, bowling and boating pond. Sports centre. Dogs on leads allowed. Open Late March-Oct.

ANGUS
BRECHIN

(7m). Glenesk Caravan Park, Edzell, Brechin, Angus DD9 7YP. 01356 648565. www.angusglens.co.uk. From A90 Aberdeen-Dundee take B966 to Edzell, 1.5 m N of Edzell turn N, SP Glenesk. Park 1m from junction. An attractive woodland site featuring a small fishing lake. Many local attractions and outdoor activities. Manager: Ms NJ Morgan Open April-Oct.

FORFAR

(2m). Foresterseat Caravan Park, Burnside, Arbroath Road, Forfar, Angus DD8 2RY. 01307 818880. www.

foresterseat.co.uk. Owner: Emma Laird. This modern, peaceful family run park on the outskirts of Forfar has beautiful views from hardstanding pitches with water and electricity hook up. Kookaburras licensed restaurant next door.

KIRRIEMUIR

(2m). Drumshademuir Caravan Park, Kirriemuir, Angus DD8 1QT. 01575 573284. www.drumshademuir.com. Owner: I&P Easson. Midway between Glamis Castle and Kirriemuir on the A928. Well kept family-run site. Lunches, evening meals, pub. Putting. Laundry. Woodland walk. Caravan storage. AA 4 pennant.

MONTROSE

(10m). Wairds Park Caravan Site, Wairds Park, Beach Road, Johnshaven, Montrose, Angus DD10 0EP. 01561 362395. www.johnshaven.com. Owner: Wairds Park Committee. On A92. By the sea. Putting. Bowling. Play area. Multi-sports courts with floodlights. 0.25m to village shops and PO. Refreshments in park reception. 6 golf courses in 20m radius. Open April 1-Oct 15.

ARGYLL & BUTE
ALEXANDRIA

Camping & Caravanning Club Site – Luss, Loch Lomond, Alexandria, Argyll & Bute G83 8NT. 01436 860658. www.campingandcaravanningclub.co.uk. Owner: Camping & Caravanning Club. From Erskine Bridge take A82 N towards Tarbet. Turn R at lodge of Loch Lomond and International Camping Sign. Go S from Tarbet, take first L after site sign and lodge of Loch Lomond sign. Site 200yd. 11m from Dumbarton. Club members' caravans and motorcaravans only. Tents accepted. On the banks of Loch Lomond with views of Ben Lomond. 90 pitches set in 12 acres. Fishing on site. Near golf, riding, rock climbing and swimming. Deals for families and backpackers. Open March – Oct.

ARDLUI

Beinglas Campsite, Beinglas Farm, Inverarnan, Ardlui, Argyll & Bute G83 7DX. 01301 704281. www.beinglascampsite.co.uk. 20m from Balloch. Camping cabins on site. Bar and restaurant open all day. Campsite shelter with kitchen area and launderette. Open April-Oct.

SCOTLAND

ARGYLL

Glendaruel Caravan & Camping Park, Glendaruel, Argyll, Argyll & Bute PA22 3AB. 01369 820267. www.glendaruelcaravanpark.co.uk. Owner: Mrs A Craig & family. Off A886. Near Kyles of Bute. 17m from Dunoon. Small, peaceful family run park in a 22-acre country estate. Walking, cycling and bird/wildlife watching. Thistle Award. Well stocked shop on park including Loch Fyne Ales, range of wines, Orkney ice-cream, Venison, books, maps and much more. Good base for touring. Discounts arranged with various local attractions. Open April-Oct.

BALLACHULISH

(1.5m). Camping & Caravanning Club Site – Glencoe, Ballachulish, Argyll & Bute PH49 4LA. 01855 811397. www.campingandcaravanningclub.co.uk. Owner: Camping & Caravanning Club. On A82. Crianlarich to Glencoe road. SP Glencoe visitors' centre. 18m from Fort William. Site refurbished last year. All pitches enjoy breathtaking views of mountains. The woodlands around the site have streams tumbling over boulders. Open March 13-Nov 3.

BARCALDINE-BY-CONNEL

(0.5m). Camping & Caravanning Club Site – Oban, Barcaldine-by-Connel, Argyll & Bute PA37 1SG. 01631 720348. www.campingandcaravanningclub.co.uk. Owner: Camping & Caravanning Club. N from Connel Bridge on A828 site on R of village. Opposite the Marine Resource Centre go through large iron gates. 12m from Oban. Ideal for touring Highlands and Islands. Licensed bar on site, bar meals. All units accepted. Non-members welcome. Site in 4.5 acres of walled garden. Woodland walks 5 mins. Deals for families and backpackers. Open April-Oct.

CAMPBELTOWN

(15m). Carradale Bay Caravan Site, Carradale, Campbeltown, Argyll & Bute PA28 6QG. 01583 431665. www.carradalebay.com. Owner: Colin Burgess. Off B842. Caravan Club affiliated site on the wooded east coast of Kintyre, R on the sandy beach, facing the Isle of Arran. Toilet blocks, laundry, veg prep area. Near fishing, golf, watersports and NCN route. Good walking, dog walk nearby. Quiet and peaceful off-peak. Open March-Sept.

(10m). Machribeg, Southend, Campbeltown, Argyll & Bute PA28 6RW. 01586 830249. Owner: Mr J Barbour. A83 to Campbeltown. B843 for 10m to Southend. Site is on L 0.5m beyond village. Beside safe, sandy beach and 18-hole golf course. Showers and shaver points. Laundry. Payphone. Dogs allowed on leads only. No booking required. Shop and doctor's surgery 0.25m. Ideal for fishing and walking. Open April 1-Sept 30.

DUNOON

(7m). Stratheck Country Park, Inverchapel, Loch Eck, Dunoon, Argyll & Bute PA23 8SG. 01369 840472. www.stratheck.com. N of Dunoon on A815 next to Younger Botanic Gardens. Country club. Play area. Boating. Walking. Climbing etc. Superb location with magnificent Highland scenery. Open March 1-Jan 2.

GLENCOE

(0.25m). Invercoe Caravan and Camping Park, Glencoe, Argyll & Bute PH49 4HP. 01855 811210. www.invercoe.co.uk. Owner: Iain & Lynn Brown. On B863, beside loch. Holiday touring centre. Advance bookings for electric hook-ups. Thistle commendation.

Red Squirrel Camping Site, Glencoe, Argyll & Bute PA49 4HX. 01855 811256. www.redsquirrelcampsite.com. 12m S of Fort Williams. On the old Glencoe Road. 1.5m through Glencoe village over hump bridge. Parallel with 82. An easy going, hill farm site on the river Coe. Climbing, walking country. Appeals to naturalists.

INVERARAY

(2.5m). Argyll Caravan Park, Inveraray, Argyll & Bute PA32 8XT. 01499 302285. www.argyllcaravanpark.com. Owner: Duke of Argyll. 2.5m S of Inveraray. Ideal location for relaxing and touring. Many places of interest in easy reach and Oban and Iona ferry 1hr drive away. Open March-Oct.

ISLE OF COLL

Garden House, Isle of Coll, Argyll & Bute PA78 6TB. 01879 230374. www.visitcoll.co.uk. From Ferry, through village, take L fork W for 4m. Between two white cottages at Uig on L private road down to walled garden. Open May 1-Sept 1.

ISLE OF MULL

(0.5m). Shieling Holidays, Craignure, Isle of Mull, Argyll & Bute PA65 6AY. 01680 812496. www.shielingholidays.co.uk. Owner: David & Moira Gracie. From ferry pier at Craignure turn L, in 400yd L again, follow signs to reception by the sea. 0.5m from Craignure. On the sea with views of Ben Nevis. Hot showers, laundry. all spotlessly clean. Short stroll to shop, pub, bistro and buses. Visit Scotland '5 stars'. Open March-Nov.

Tobermory Campsite, Newdale, Dervaig Road, Tobermory, Isle of Mull, Argyll & Bute PA75 6QF. www.tobermorycampsite.co.uk. Owner: Mr & Mrs A Williams. Small, peaceful campsite only 1.5m from Tobermory on the road towards Dervaig. Ideal base for sightseeing, fishing, boat trips and visiting 'Balamory'. Open March-Oct.

LOCH LOMOND

Ardlui Hotel & Caravan Park, Ardlui, Loch Lomond, Argyll & Bute G83 7EB. 01301 704243. www.ardlui.co.uk. Owner: Mr D B & Mrs A E Squires. On A82, 43m N of Glasgow. 8m to Arrochar. Situated on the shores of Loch Lomond, in the centre of the Loch Lomond and Trossachs National Park. 16m to Loch Lomond international golf course.

LOCHGILPHEAD

(11m). Leachive Caravan Park, Leachive Farm, Tayvallich, Lochgilphead, Argyll & Bute PA31 8PL. 01546 870206. fiona@leachive.co.uk. Owner: Mr & Mrs R MacArthur. A816 N from Lochgilphead, fork L on B841 for 3m, turn L and join B8025 to Tayvallich, site on R in village. Open April-Oct.

(0.3m). Lochgilphead Caravan Park, Bank Park, Lochgilphead, Argyll & Bute PA31 8NX. 01546 602003. www.lochgilpheadcaravanpark.co.uk. At junction A83 and A816. Golf, swimming pool, heritage sites, fishing and beautiful walks close by. Clean heated toilets, laundry and all facilities. Open March-Oct.

MORVEN

Fiunary Caravan & Camping Park, Morven, Argyll & Bute PA34 5XX. 01967 421 225. www.caravancampingsites.co.uk. Owner: Philip & Joanne Henderson. Leave A82, 8m S of Fort William. Cross Corran-Ardgour car ferry. Follow sign posts to Lochaline (A884) 31m turnR on B849. 4.5m to site. Shop, doctor, PO 4.5m in Lochaline. Own beach. Ideal for launching small craft. Fishing and swimming locally. Forest walks from site. Convenient for Isle of Mull car ferry from Lochline 4.5m. Passenger ferry straight into Tobermory (6m). Open May-Sept.

SCOTLAND

See page 5 for key to symbols and abbreviations

MULL OF KINTYRE

(4.5m). The Machrihanish Caravan & Camping Park, East Trodigal, Machrihanish, Campbeltown, Mull of Kintyre, Argyll & Bute PA28 6PT. *01586 810266.* www.campkintyre.co.uk. Owner: Dave & Chris Gordon. In Campbeltown take B843, SP Machrihanish, site on R before village. Set in a little seaside village just 0.5m walk to a good sandy beach. Privately owned site in 0.5m of the Atlantic shore with its wildlife and seals Machrihanish Bay has 3m of golden sands and famous golf course. Cinema, shopping centre, swimming pool in 5m. Open Feb – end Oct.

OBAN

(2.5m). Oban Caravan & Camping Park, Gallanachmore Farm, Gallanach Road, Oban, Argyll & Bute PA34 4QH. *01631 562425.* www.obancaravanpark.com. Owner: Mr & Mrs H Jones. Follow signs to Gallanach from Oban centre roundabout. Family run farm on seafront overlooking the island of Kerrera, an area of outstanding scenic beauty. Showers. H&C basins. Launderette. Brochure available. Open April-end Sept.

(1.5m). Roseview Caravan Park, Rose View, Glenshellach Road, Oban, Argyll & Bute PA34 4QJ. *01631 562755.* www.rosevieweoban.co.uk. Owner: Mr AD Falconer. At traffic island by tourist office, take ferry terminal exit (Albany Street). Then 2nd L, 1st R, 1st L following 'Glenshellach' camping signs. A family park in a delightful and quiet setting. Golf course, fishing, supermarkets nearby.

(8m). Seaview Caravan & Camping Park, Seaview, Keil Croft, Benderloch, Oban, Argyll & Bute PA37 1QS. *01631 720360.* Owner: Violet MacKellar. A85 to Connel Cross Connel Ferry Bridge on to the A828 road, N. Seaview is 3m over bridge. Couples only. Shop, PO, garage under 1m. Doctor 2.5m. Open Easter – Sept 30.

TARBERT

Killegruer Caravan Park, Woodend, Glenbarr, Tarbert, Argyll & Bute PA29 6XB. *01583 421241.* anne@littlesan.fsnet.co.uk. Owner: Mr N Littleson. On R of A83, 12m N of Campbeltown, 24m S of Tarbert, Loch Fyne. Ideal for ferry routes to Arran and Inner Hebrides. Level, grassy park overlooking safe, sandy beach. Bottled gas delivery service. Park has now been upgraded to include showers, facilities for the disabled etc. Shop 1m of site. Restaurant, bar in 2m. Near walking, golf, riding. Open Easter or April 1-Oct 22.

(22m). Muasdale Holiday Park, Muasdale, Tarbert, Argyll & Bute PA29 6XD. *01583 421207.* www.muasdaleholidays.com. Owner: Adrian & Alison Clements. On main A83 southern end of Muasdale village. 15m from Campbeltown. Touring park next to beach. Shop 100yd. Caravan holiday homes and tourers have view of the Atlantic, islands and wildlife. Check our website for more details. Open April 4-Oct 10.

(17m). Point Sands Caravan Park, Tayinloan, Tarbert, Argyll & Bute PA29 6XG. *01583 441263.* www.pointsands.co.uk. Owner: Largie Estates. Off A83, S of Tarbert, Loch Fyne. Beautiful peaceful park. Safe sandy beach. Open April 1-Oct 31.

(15m). Port Ban Caravan Park, Port Ban, Kilberry, Tarbert, Argyll & Bute PA29 6YD. *01880 770224.* www.portban.com. Owner: Mrs J F Sheldrick & family. On B8024 off A83. 1m N of Kilberry. 15m S of Ardrishaig situated on the beach with a panoramic view of Islay and Jura. Family run park with cycling, tennis and other sports facilities available. Coffee bar and evening meals in busy season. Shop on site. Fishing, golf course nearby. Kilberry Inn 1m from park. Open April-Oct.

TAYNUILT

(2m). Crunachy Caravan Park, Bridge of Awe, Taynuilt, Argyll & Bute PA35 1HT. *01866 822612.* www.crunachy.co.uk. Owner: Angus Douglas. On A85 Oban to Clanlarich. 14m E of Oban. Shower, Launderette, phone, restaurant, games room and swings. Hotel/bar 300yd. Golf 2m. Fishing, walking, climbing nearby. Open March-Nov.

AYRSHIRE (EAST)

NEW CUMNOCK

(2m). Glen Afton Leisure Park, Afton Road, New Cumnock, East Ayrshire KA18 4PR. *01290 332228.* Owner: M&A Richardson. A76 Glasgow to Dumfries, midway. Follow sign from mini roundabout in village off New Cumnock. In picturesque valley, ideal for walkers, fishing and golf nearby. Family pub on site.

AYRSHIRE (NORTH)

ISLE OF ARRAN

Lochranza Golf Caravan and Camping Site, Lochranza, Isle of Arran, North Ayrshire KA27 8HL. *01770 830273.* www.lochranzagolf.com. Owner: IM Robertson. In the village at N end of island, beside our own superb golf course. Ideal site for golfers, birdwatchers and walkers. Climbing, hill walking, canoeing etc close by. Level, grass site. Best hot showers, clean facilities. Open 1 March-20 Oct.

KILMARNOCK

(2.5m). Cunninghamhead Estate, Stewarton Road, Irvine, Kilmarnock, North Ayrshire KA3 2PE. *01294 850510.* www.lairdestates.co.uk. Owner: Laird Estates Group. From Stancastle roundabout, Irvine take B769 Stewarton Road for 2.5m. Park is on L, SP at roundabout. 2m to all services. Secluded site in pleasant country. Good for touring Burns country and Clyde resorts. Open April 1-Sept 30 for holiday vans.

LAMLASH

Middleton Caravan & Camping Park, Lamlash, North Ayrshire KA27 8NN. *01770 600255/251.* Owner: Mr RJ Middleton. 0.25m from centre of Lamlash. Flat, grassy site. 5mins from beach. Night lighting.

LARGS

(2.25m). South Whittlieburn Farm, Brisbane Glen, Largs, North Ayrshire KA30 8SN. *01475 675881.* www.SouthHound.co.uk/hotels/whittlie.html. Owner: Tom & Mary Watson. Working sheep farm is situated NE of Largs – only 5mins from town centre. Go 0.5m along A78 shore road from town centre/pier, heading for Greenock, turn R at large SP for Brisbane Glen Road. Drive 2.25m – 2nd farm on L, beside road. Fishing, hillwalking, golf course, sailing, fishing, horse riding, diving. Ferries to Islands, shops, restaurants, doctor etc 2.5m. Near swimming pool, theatre, putting green. 4 star AA + STB 'B&B' in Farmhouse.

SKELMORLIE

(0.5m). Mains Caravan Park, Skelmorlie Mains, Skelmorlie, North Ayrshire PA17 5EU. *01475 520794.* www.skelmoriemainscaravanpark.co.uk. Owner: T A James Stirrat & Norman Stirrat. Off A78 Greenock to Largs. 4m N of Largs, SP. No tents. Tourers and motor caravans only. No bookings. Outstanding views with a quiet relaxed atmosphere. Open Easter-Oct.

AYRSHIRE (SOUTH)

AYR

(4m). Craig Tara Holiday Park, Dunure Road, Ayr, South Ayrshire KA7 4LB.

SCOTLAND

01292 265141. www.craigtara-park.co.uk. Owner: Bourne Leisure Ltd. A77 towards Stranraer. 2nd R after Bankfield roundabout, S of Ayr. From Doonholm Road take L at the junction and immediately R into Greenfield Avenue. L at junction, SP Craig Tara. Heated indoor fun pool, kids' clubs, entertainment, shop, bakery, sports court, play area. Go karts, mini bowling, crazy golf. 9-hole golf course. Climbing wall. David Bellamy Gold Conservation Award. Open March-end Oct.

(0.5m). Craigie Gardens Caravan Club Site, Craigie Road, Ayr, South Ayrshire KA8 0SS. 01292 264909. www.caravanclub.co.uk. Owner: The Caravan Club. See website for directions. Laundry. Baby and toddler washroom. Veg prep area. Motorvan waste point. Gas and Gaz. Information room. Play frame, play area, dog walks quiet and peaceful off peak. Toilet block with privacy cubicles. Advance booking essential. Non-members admitted. No tents. All hardstandings. Suits families. Beach, fishing, golf and NCN cycle route in 5m.

(2m). Crofthead Holiday Park, McNairston Road, Ayr, South Ayrshire KA6 6EN. 01292 263516. www.croftheadholidaypark.co.uk. SP off A70.

(4m). Sundrum Castle Holiday Park, Ayr, South Ayrshire KA6 5JH. 01292 570057. www.parkdeanholidays.co.uk. Owner: Parkdean Holidays Plc. M74, J12 to A70. Indoor pool with toddlers' pool and solarium. Kids' club, amusement and adventure play. Bar, food and live family entertainment. Open March-Oct.

GIRVAN

(10m). Queensland Holiday Park, Barrhill, Girvan, South Ayrshire KA26 0PZ. 01465 821364. www.queenslandholidaypark.co.uk. Owner: David & Joanne Russell. From Girvan take A714 heading SE, park on R 1m before Barrhill. Peaceful woodland park. Excellent local fishing and golf. Ideal location for walking in Southern Upland Mountains. Open March 1-Jan 31.

(9m). Windsor Holiday Park, Barrhill, Girvan, South Ayrshire KA26 0PZ. 01465 821355. www.windsorholidaypark.com. Owner: Mr & Mrs M Langford and Mr & Mrs A Cartwright. On A714 between Newton Stewart and Girvan, 1m N of Barrhill. Quiet, peaceful site set in rolling hills, sheltered by trees. Hardstanding and level grass pitches. Excellent outdoor activities. Ideal for exploring an unspoilt area. Golf, shops, swimming pool, beach in 10m. Open March 1-Oct 31, weekends and 2 weeks at Xmas.

MAYBOLE

(3m). Camping & Caravanning Club Site – Culzean Castle, Maybole, South Ayrshire KA19 8JX. 01655 760627. www.campingandcaravanningclub.co.uk. Owner: Camping & Caravanning Club. From S on A77 turn L on to A719. Site 4m on L. From N on A77 turn R on to B7023 in Maybole. After 100yd turn L, site 4m. Views and spectacular sunsets. Non-members welcome. All units accepted. Site next to historic castle and country park. 17m of country walks in easy access, sandy beaches, a deer park and an aviary. Deals for families and backpackers. Open March-Oct.

(4m). The Walled Garden Caravan & Camping Park, Kilkerran Estate, Crosshill, Maybole, South Ayrshire KA19 7SG. 01655 740323. www.walledgardencp.co.uk. Owner: Jim McCosh. From A77 (4m S of Ayr) pass through Minishant 200yd turn L at Hoggs Corner and follow brown and white tourist signs. From roundabout N of Girvan follow signs. Fishing in season on River Girvan on estate. Golf courses 3m & 5m. 3m supermarket. 3-4m doctors. PO 2m. Petrol station 5m. Open all year except Feb, Xmas/Boxing day.

BORDERS

DUNS

(6m). Greenlaw Caravan Park, Blackadder Touring Park, Greenlaw, Duns, Borders TD10 6XX. 01361 810341. www.greenlawcaravanpark.com. Owner: Mr C Gregg. 10m N of Coldstream and 37m S of Edinburgh on A697. SP in Greenlaw village at junction of A697 and A6105. Riverside park with free fishing. Licensed bowling club. Shops nearby. New children's play area with swings. Open 11.5 months, closed 15-31 Jan.

EYEMOUTH

(2m). Scoutscroft Holiday Centre, St Abbs Road, Coldingham, Eyemouth, Borders TD14 5NB. 01890 771338. www.scoutscroft.co.uk. Owner: David, Margaret, John & Mark Hamilton. Turn off A1 on to A1107 head for St Abbs, site SP. 5mins walk to nearest shop, 5-10 mins walk to Coldingham Beach. Fishing in village, 18-hole golf course, swimming pool in Eyemouth. Dive centre on site. Park is flat but site is slightly sloping and may not suit wheelchair users. Open March 1-Nov 30.

HAWICK

(2.5m). Hawick Riverside Caravan Park, Hornshole Bridge, Hawick, Borders TD9 8SY. 01450 373785. www.riversidehawick.co.uk. Owner: Mr & Mrs B Wetherley. On A698 Hawick to Jedburgh road. Quiet 8-acre site. Leisure centre near. Dogs allowed. Fees on application. Free fishing. Open April 1-Oct 31.

JEDBURGH

(1m). Camping & Caravanning Club Site – Jedburgh, Elliot Park, Jedburgh, Borders TD8 6EF. 01835 863393. www.campingandcaravanningclub.co.uk. Owner: Camping & Caravanning Club. Off the A68 N of the town; SP. Directly opposite the Edinburgh and Jedburgh Woollen Mills. All units accepted. Some all-weather pitches available. Non-members welcome. There is a picturesque 1m riverside walk to Jedburgh town with its good leisure centre, golf and fly fishing. Deals for families and backpackers. Open April-Oct.

(3m). Jedwater Caravan Park, Jedburgh, Borders TD8 6PJ. 01835 840219. www.jedwater.co.uk. Owner: Mr N Gibson. Off A68. S of Jedburgh. Quiet peaceful site on banks of River Ted, free fishing on site. Fishing, golf all nearby. Open Easter-Oct.

(5m). Lilliardsedge Park & Golf Course, Ancrum, Jedburgh, Borders TD8 6TZ. 01835 830271. www.lilliardsedgepark.co.uk. On A68, between Ancrum and St Boswells. Tourist information. 9 hole golf course surrounds park – new office/shop/reception for 2008. Newly enhanced/refurbished bar. Open March-Jan.

KELSO

(8m). Kirkfield Caravan Park, Grafton Road, Town Yetholm, Kelso, Borders TD5 8RU. 01573 420346. Owner: Frank Gibson. On B6352 from south on A697 turn L onto B6396 for Yetholm. 0.25m to village shop, butcher, garage and PO. Open April 1-Oct 31.

(1m). Springwood Caravan Park, Springwood Estate, Kelso, Borders TD5 8LS. 01573 224596. www.springwood.biz. Owner: Springwood

120 MOTOR CARAVAN & CAMPING PARKS 2009

SCOTLAND

See page 5 for key to symbols and abbreviations

Estate. On A699. On site: play area, table tennis. Nearby: golf, swimming, pony treking, tennis. Ideal for walking. David Bellamy Gold Conservation Award. Open March 31-Oct 9 for tourers, Feb 24-Nov 27 for holiday caravans.

LAUDER

(4m). Camping & Caravanning Club Site – Lauder, Carfraemill, Oxton, Lauder, Borders TD2 6RA. *01578 750697.* www.campingandcaravanningclub.co.uk. Owner: Camping & Caravanning Club. From Lauder, turn R at roundabout on to A697 then L at Lodge Hotel. Site on R behind Carfraemill Hotel. 24m S of Edinburgh, close to Thirlestane Castle and a good fishing area. 4 self-catering timber chalets to let. Non-members welcome. All units accepted. Valley site in the Scottish Borders, complete with its own river. Deals for families and backpackers. Open March – Oct.

(1m). Thirlestane Castle Caravan and Camping Park, Lauder, Borders TD2 6RU. *079762 31032.* maitland_carew@compuserve.com. Owner: Mr Edward Maitland-Carew. SP just off A68 and A697 28m S of Edinburgh. Outside Royal Burgh of Lauder which has excellent shops and pubs. Secluded site with glorious views across wooded countryside and near the river. Adjacent to the touring park, holiday homes (statics) area is being developed. Open April 1-Oct 1.

MELROSE

(1m). Gibson Caravan Club Site, Gibson Park, High Street, Melrose, Borders TD6 9RY. *01896 822969.* www.caravanclub.co.uk. Owner: The Caravan Club. See website for directions. This is a level and peaceful site in the edge of Melrose overlooked by the three hills. Non-members welcome. Shops adjacent. MV service pt. Toilet block with laundry. Tents welcome. Fishing and golf in 1m. Good walking, some hardstanding, gas, dog walk, ideal for families, quiet and peaceful off peak. NCN cycle path in 5m.

PEEBLES

(0.5m). Crossburn Caravan Park, Edinburgh Road, Peebles, Borders EH45 8ED. *01721 720501.* www.crossburncaravans.co.uk. Owner: The Chisholm Family. On A703. Laundry. Full on-site facilities. Games room. Play area. Open Easter or April 1-Oct 31.

Rosetta Caravan & Camping Park, Rosetta Road, Peebles, Borders EH45 8PG. *01721 720770.* Owner: The Clay family. Well SP from Peebles. Open April-end Oct.

SELKIRK

(16m). Honey Cottage Caravan Park, Hope House, Ettrick Valley, Selkirk, Borders TD7 5HU. *01750 62246.* www.honeycottagecaravanpark.co.uk. Owner: CA&S Woof. On B709 Langholm Road and B7009 from Selkirk. B711 from Hawick, L for 1m at Tushielaw on B709. Reduced facilities Oct to April. Shop on site. Fishing on site. Beautiful quiet site, ideal for walking, fishing, wild life or just relaxing.

(0.75m). Victoria Caravan Park, Buccleuch Road, Selkirk, Borders TD7 5DW. *01750 20897.* Owner: Scottish Borders Council. From S on A7, follow signs from Selkirk market place, from N on A7 turn R at entrance to town (SP A72 Peebles and A708 Moffat) and follow signs. Open April-Oct.

CLACKMANNAN

DOLLAR

(0.5m). Riverside Caravan Park, Dollarfield, Dollar, Clackmannan FK14 7LX. *01259 742896.* www.riverside-caravanpark.co.uk. Owner: Mr & Mrs A Small. On B913 Dollar to Dunfermline. Ideal base for hill walking, birdwatching, fishing and golf. Close to many places of interest and Knockhill racing circuit. Open April 1-Sept 30.

DUMFRIES & GALLOWAY

CASTLE DOUGLAS

Auchenlarie Holiday Park, Gatehouse-of-Fleet, Castle Douglas, Dumfries & Galloway DG7 2EX. *01557 840251.* www.auchenlarie.co.uk. Owner: Mr & Mrs J M Swalwell. On A 75. 5m W of Gatehouse-of-Fleet on S coast of Galloway with small sandy cove. Friendly park overlooking Wigtown Bay with several golf courses nearby and both sea and coarse fishing. Excellent touring and holiday home facilities. Entertainment, launderette, 3 bars with meals, games room, amusements, crazy golf and three play areas. AA 4 pennants. Indoor swimming pool & leisure suite including gym, sauna, solarium, sports hall. Open March 1-Oct 31.

(5m). Barlochan Caravan Park, Palnackie, Castle Douglas, Dumfries & Galloway DG7 1PF. *01556 600256/booking.* www.gillespie-leisure.co.uk. Owner: Gillespie Leisure Ltd. On A711, 2.5m SW of Dalbeattie. Friendly park overlooking Urr estuary with nearby coarse fishing loch (free). Exceptional facilities. Launderette, dishwashing, games and TV rooms, mini-golf and play area. Pub nearby. Open April 1-Oct 31.

■ **(7m). Loch Ken Holiday Park, Parton, Castle Douglas, Dumfries & Galloway DG7 3NE.** *01644 470282.* www.lochkenholidaypark.co.uk. Owner: Penny Bryson. A713 Castle Douglas to Ayr road. On the shores of the loch with sandy beach. Lovely natural park. Fishing. Cycle hire. Canoeing, boating & sailing on site. Waterskiing, sailing and golf nearby. Charge for dogs. David Bellamy Gold Conservation Award. Open March 1-Oct 31.

(0.25m). Lochside Caravan & Camping Site, Lochside Park, Castle Douglas, Dumfries & Galloway DG7 1EZ. *01556 502949.* www.dumgal.gov.uk/lochsidecs. Owner: Dumfries & Galloway Council. Just off A75 at Castle Douglas. Site is located by Carlingwark Loch, Castle Douglas. Dogs on lead. Nearby facilities include: Doctor, PO, shops, tennis, swimming pool, golf, fishing, sailing, play area and park, boating, putting, Threave Gardens. Castle Douglas has been designated as the region's "food town" – 3 pennant AA rating. Open Easter to end-Oct.

(15m). Mossyard Caravan Park, Gatehouse-of-Fleet, Castle Douglas, Dumfries & Galloway DG7 2ET. *01557 840226.* enquiry@mossyard.co.uk. www.mossyard.co.uk. Owner: McConchie Partnership. On A75 Dumfries to Stranraer 4m beyond Gatehouse-of-Fleet. SP. Family-run park on the shores of the Fleet estuary. Ideal location for swimming, boating. Coarse fishing, swimming pool in 0.25m – nearest village, golf, tennis 5m away. Open March 28-Oct 31.

DALBEATTIE

(6m). Castle Point Caravan Park, Rockcliffe, Dalbeattie, Dumfries & Galloway DG5 4QL. *01556 630248.* www.homepage.mac.com/castle-point-site/personalpage.html. Owner: Mr J Bigham. From Dalbeattie take A710. In 5m turn R to Rockcliffe, then L after 1m. Overlooking the sea with outstanding views. Close to two lovely beaches. Excellent walks. Fully serviced high quality hire caravans. Spacious camping area. Small quiet site! Open Early March-Late Oct.

www.motorcaravanmagazine.co.uk   MOTOR CARAVAN & CAMPING PARKS 2009   **121**

SCOTLAND

(1m). Glenearly Caravan Park, Dalbeattie, Dumfries & Galloway DG5 4NE. 01556 611393. Owner: Fred & Debbie Jardine. From Dumfries take the A711 to Dalbeattie. See park entrance on R just before you enter Dalbeattie. Walking distance to shops in Dalbeattie. 6m to nearest beach. Golf courses in 10mins drive. Near pony trekking, mountain biking, fishing, tennis, forest walks.

(3m). Kippford Holiday Park, Kippford, Dalbeattie, Dumfries & Galloway DG5 4LF. 01556 620636. www.kippfordholidaypark.co.uk. Owner: C R Aston. 3m S of Dalbeattie on A710 towards Kippford (beautiful seaside village). Touring and tent pitches in small groups attractively terraced and level with hardstand, screened, on sloping ground. Thistle award holiday caravan hire. 15mins stroll to Kippford, with pubs, and spectacular seaside walk to the beach. Shop, cycle hire, golf & fishing adjacent. David Bellamy Gold Conservation Award. Open all year (winter booking required).

(6m). Sandyhills Bay Leisure Park, Sandyhills Bay, Dalbeattie, Dumfries & Galloway DG5 4NY. 01387 780257. www.gillespie-leisure.co.uk. Owner: Gillespie Leisure Ltd. On A710 Dumfries to Dalbeattie. Award winning park only a few yards from the finest beach in the area. Spectacular coastal walks. Smugglers' cave. Excellent facilities. Showers, launderette, dishwashing and takeaways. 18-hole golf course adjacent. Fishing, riding and eating out in walking distance. Advance bookings: 015578 70267. Exceptional facilities at Brighouse Bay are available. Open April 1-Oct 31.

DUMFRIES

(6m). Barnsoul Farm and Wild Life Area, Barnsoul Farm, Shawhead, Dumfries, Dumfries & Galloway DG2 9SQ. 01387 730249. www.barnsoulfarm.co.uk. Owner: A J Wight & Co. From Dumfries take A75 (Stranraer) for 6m turn R for Shawhead. At T-junction turn R then bear L (Dunscore). Farm is 1m on L. Unspoilt site with ponds and woodlands set in well-known wild life area. Fishing close by. Mountain bikes, Mabie Forest, AE Forest all in 8m. AA 3 pennants. 6 Wigwam bothies to hire – timber one roomed bothies with electricity, sleep 4/6, based on Scandinavian mountain huts. David Bellamy Gold Conservation Award. Open April-Oct.

(8m). Mossband Caravan Park, Kirkgunzeon, Dumfries, Dumfries & Galloway DG2 8JP. 01387 760208. Owner: G & M Dempster. Off A711. Tennis court. Play area. Open March-Oct.

(9m). Park of Brandedleys, Crocketford, Dumfries, Dumfries & Galloway DG2 8RG. 0845 4561760. www.holgates.com. Owner: Arthur Holgate & Sons Ltd. Off A75. At W end of Crocketford. Indoor swimming pool, sauna, tennis and badminton courts, games room, recreational areas, bar and restaurant. Golfers will love no fewer than 25 challenging courses in a 20m radius of the park. Fishing – opportunity for sea fishing, trout and salmon as well as coarse fishing, in 20m radius. David Bellamy Gold Conservation Award.

(17m). Southerness Holiday Village, Southerness, Dumfries, Dumfries & Galloway DG2 8AZ. 01387 880256. www.parkdeanholidays.co.uk. Owner: Parkdean Holidays Plc. Off A710. Follow Solway Coast SP from Dumfries. Modern holiday village with separate touring park mainly for families. Licensed club, bar meals and indoor café with takeaway, heated indoor swimming pool, family entertainment, adventure play park. Brochure on request. Championship golf, Pay and Play golf. Local attractions. David Bellamy Gold Conservation Award. Open March 1-Oct 31.

GRETNA

(0.5m). Braids Caravan Park, Annan Road, Gretna, Dumfries & Galloway DG16 5DQ. 01461 337409. www.thebraidscaravanpark.com. Owner: John & Isabel Scott. B721 Gretna to Annan Road. Fishing information. Golf course nearby. PO, shops, doctor all in 0.75m. Bus service to Carlisle, Annan and Dumfries. 100m from Stranraer ferries. Calor Gas agency.

KIRKCUDBRIGHT

YOUR TOP 101 SITES 2009

(6m). Brighouse Bay Holiday Park, Borgue, Kirkcudbright, Dumfries & Galloway DG6 4TS. 01557 870267. www.gillespie-leisure.co.uk. Owner: Gillespie Leisure Ltd. Off B727 Kirkcudbright to Borgue or take A755 (Kirkcudbright) off A75 2m W of Twynholm. Clear SP for 8m. In 1200 acres next to beach and bluebell woods. Exceptional amenities and entertainment galore. Golf and leisure club with indoor pool, toddler pool, steam room, jacuzzi, family lounge, bar, bistro, bowling, golf, canoes, bike hire. Pony trekking. Quad bikes. Luxury caravans and lodges for sale and hire.

(2.5m). Seaward Caravan Park, Dhoon Bay, Kirkcudbright, Dumfries & Galloway DG6 4TJ. 01557 331079. www.gillespie-leisure.co.uk. Owner: Gillespie Leisure Ltd. A755 W, then B727 to Borgue. Panoramic views over bay. Award-winning park. Excellent facilities include heated outdoor pool, dishwashing, launderette and showers. Sea angling, Beach picnic area nearby. Advance bookings 01557 870267. Games and TV room, 9-hole pitch & putt. Exceptional facilities at Brighouse Bay available. Open March 1-Oct 31.

(0.5m). Silvercraigs Caravan and Camping Site, Silvercraigs Road, Kirkcudbright, Dumfries & Galloway DG6 4BT. 01557 330123. www.dumgal.gov.uk/silvercraigscs. Owner: Dumfries & Galloway Council. In Kirkcudbright off Silvercraigs road overlooking the town. No advance booking. Fees on application. Dogs on lead. Nearby facilities include: Shops, PO, doctor, tennis, swimming pool, golf, museum, wildlife park, fishing, sailing, beaches, play area and park. This elevated site overlooks the historical town of Kirkcudbright, providing panoramic views of the Solway coast – 3 pennants AA rating. Open Easter-late Oct.

LOCHMABEN

(0.25m). Kirkloch Caravan Site, Kirkloch Brae, Lochmaben, Dumfries & Galloway DG11 1PZ. 01556 503806. www.dumgal.gov.uk/kirklochcs. Owner: Dumfries & Galloway Council. B709 at Lochmaben, near Lockerbie, Dumfrieshire. Enter site by Kirkloch Brae. Near shops, PO, doctor, golf, fishing, play area. Site is on the picturesque Kirkloch in the small historical town of Lochmaben – 2 pennants AA rating. Open Easter-late Oct.

LOCKERBIE

(5m). Cressfield Caravan Park, Ecclefechan, Lockerbie, Dumfries & Galloway DG11 3DR. 01576 300702. www.cressfieldcaravanpark.co.uk. Leave A74 (M) at Ecclefechan J19. Follow B7076 for 0.5m to south side of village, SP. Peaceful country park with superb facilities. Sportsfield. Play area. Dog walk. Village amenities 0.25m. Good touring base or night halt. Golf, fishing 2m. Supermarket, cinema 5m. Holiday homes for sale.

(3m). Halleaths Caravan Park, Lochmaben, Lockerbie, Dumfries & Galloway DG11 1NA. 01387 810630. www.caravan-sitefinder.co.uk/sites/2436. Owner: Gordon Hoey. From Lockerbie

122 MOTOR CARAVAN & CAMPING PARKS 2009

SCOTLAND

See page 5 for key to symbols and abbreviations

(M74) take A709 Lockerbie to Dumfries road. Site 0.5m on R after crossing river Annan. Kitchen area with microwave. Winter storage available. Well sheltered site surrounded by trees. Game and coarse fishing in 1m. 5 golf courses in 9m. Open 15 March – 15 Nov for touring caravans.

(5m). Hoddom Castle Caravan Park, Hoddom, Lockerbie, Dumfries & Galloway DG11 1AS. 01576 300251. www.hoddomcastle.co.uk. Owner: Hoddom & Kinmount Estates. Exit A74 M, J19, follow signs. Peaceful site part of 10,000 acre estate. Bar, restaurant, golf, tennis, fishing, nature trails on site. AA 5 pennants, 5 stars Scottish Tourist Board. Cinema, shopping centre, 2x18 hole golf course in 5m. Open April 1-Oct 31.

(12m). King Robert The Bruce's Cave Camping & Caravan Site, Cove Farm, Kirkpatrick Fleming, Lockerbie, Dumfries & Galloway DG11 3AT. 01461 800285. www.brucescave.co.uk. Owner: Mr Andrew Ritchie, Mrs Jan Ritchie. A74 turn off at SP Kirkpatrick Fleming, then follow all signs to Bruce's Cave. Wooded site on 80-acre estate with coarse fishing on site in pond (small charge). Holiday suites available. Restricted facilities from Oct 31-March 1. Shop in summer. Quad riding, clay pigeon shooting, paintball available nearby. BMX bikes on site.

MOFFAT

**[101 LOGO]
(0.25m). Camping & Caravanning Club Site – Moffat, Hammerland's Farm, Moffat, Dumfries & Galloway DG10 9QL.** 01683 220436. www.campingandcaravanningclub.co.uk. Owner: Camping & Caravanning Club. A708 towards Selkirk, turn R at camping sign. L at nursery. SP to site. Near picturesque border country. All units accepted. Non-members welcome. Near superb golf and fishing, 300-year-old Drumlarig Castle. Moffat has won 'Best Kept Village in Scotland'. Deals for families and backpackers. Open March-Oct.

(2m). Craigielands Country Park, Beattock, Moffat, Dumfries & Galloway DG10 9RB. 01683 300591. www.craigielandsleisure.com. Owner: Darren Fowler. J15 off new M74, follow signs for Beattock, follow through village, we're at the end under the bridge. Set in lovely country estate of over 56 acres with own loch and woodland walks. Pony-trekking. 1 static van suitable for disabled.

Log cabins and holiday static caravans for sale. Yearly touring caravan plots. Public house and restaurant on site.

NEWTON STEWART

(22m). Burrowhead Holiday Village, Tonderghie Road, Isle of Whithorn, Newton Stewart, Dumfries & Galloway DG8 8JB. 01988 500252. www.burrowheadholidayvillage.co.uk. Owner: Stuart & Neil Fairclough. A714 and A746 S from Newton Stewart to Isle of Whithorn. Beautiful views of the Isle of Man. Indoor leisure complex. Play area, club house and entertainment. Soft ball play area. Open March 1-Oct 31.

(6m). Castle Cary Holiday Park, Creetown, Newton Stewart, Dumfries & Galloway DG8 7DQ. 01671 820264. www.castlecary-caravans.com. Owner: Caird Leisure Ltd. Off A75. Main euro route UK-Northern Ireland. Large heated outdoor swimming and paddling pool. Olde world inn with bar meals and takeaway. Sun patio. Playground. Coarse fishing lake. Super indoor pool. Adult snooker room. Woodland walks. Donkeys. Crazy golf. 0.25m to PO, village shops, garage. New timber lodges at Loch Murray. Holiday homes for sale. AA 5 pennants. David Bellamy Bronze Conservation Award.

(2m). Castlewigg Caravan Park, Castlewigg, Whithorn, Newton Stewart, Dumfries & Galloway DG8 8DP. 01988 500616. www.castlewiggcaravanpark.co.uk. Owner: York House Leisure. N of Whithorn on A746. Fantastic location. Beaches only 5mins drive away. Beautifully maintained quiet park. Open March 1-Jan 7.

(0.25m). Creebridge Caravan Park, Newton Stewart, Dumfries & Galloway DG8 6AJ. 01671 402324. www.creebridgecaravanpark.com. Owner: Mr & Mrs J M Sharples. Off A75, 1m E of Newton Stewart, head for Minnigaff. Site is 200yd before bridge over river. If in Newton Stewart go over old bridge to Minnigaff, site is 200yd on R. Quiet, secluded site next to town. 3m into Newton Stewart, shops, PO etc.

(12m). Drumroamin Farm Touring Site, 1 South Balfern, Kirkinner, Newton Stewart, Dumfries & Galloway DE8 9DB. 01988 840613. www.drumroamin.co.uk. Owner: Ralph & Lesley Shell. A746 through Kirkinner. B7004 Garlieston, 2nd L, campsite at end of lane. Rural location, 1.5m to village

shop and PO. Wigtown, book capital of Scotland, for golf, doctors, butchers and Co-op. Sea and river fishing all close by. Near cycle routes.

Garlieston Caravan Club Site, Garlieston, Newton Stewart, Dumfries & Galloway DG8 8BS. 01988 600636. www.caravanclub.co.uk. Owner: The Caravan Club. See website for directions. Club members only. No tents. deal location for an undemanding, relaxing holiday on the Machars Peninsular. Toilet blocks, laundry facilities and MV service point. Good area for walking, and cycling nearby. Facilities for disabled. Quiet and peaceful off-peak. 1min to beach. Open March-Nov.

(15m). Glenluce Caravan Park, Glenluce, Newton Stewart, Dumfries & Galloway DG8 0QR. 01581 300412. www.glenlucecaravan.co.uk. Owner: RH&RA Rankin. Leave A75 at Glenluce SP. Concealed entrance in centre of village opposite Brambles restaurant. Secluded suntrap park near village, sea, bowling, fishing, pony trekking, golf and superb walks within 1m. Luxury caravans. Thistle Award.

(9m). Glentrool Holiday Park, Bargrennan, Newton Stewart, Dumfries & Galloway DG8 6RN. 01671 840280. www.glentroolholidaypark.co.uk. Owner: Mr & Mrs M Moore. Off A714. N of Newton Stewart. A pleasant, peaceful park in an ideal situation for touring and exploring the Galloway forest and hills. Super scenery. Static caravans for hire. Near café, horse riding, bird watching, fishing, off-road cycle routes. Open March – Nov.

(18m). Knock School Caravan Park, Monreith, Newton Stewart, Dumfries & Galloway DG8 8NJ. 01988 700414. www.knockschool.co.uk. Owner: Mrs P R Heywood. On A747. 3m S of Port William. entrance by golf course and beaches. Small, peaceful touring park. Bird watching, archaeology and gardens locally. Golf, beaches and fishing all in 5mins. Hardstanding pitches available. Open Easter- end Sept.

(12m). Monreith Sands Holiday Park, Monreith, Port William, Newton Stewart, Dumfries & Galloway DG8 9LJ. 01988 700218. 2m E of Port William on the A747 and about 20mins drive from Newton Stewart on the A714. 300yds to sandy beach and 0.75m for golf. Open March-Oct.

www.motorcaravanmagazine.co.uk MOTOR CARAVAN & CAMPING PARKS 2009 **123**

SCOTLAND

(18m). West Barr Farm Caravan Site, Port William, Newton Stewart, Dumfries & Galloway DG8 9QS. 01988 700367. Owner: James Stewart. On A747 2m N of Port William. Small, privately owned site on Luce Bay, close to sea and 1m from Port William. Open April-Oct.

SANQUHAR

(0.25m). Castleview Caravan & Camping Site, Sanquhar, Dumfries & Galloway DG4 6AX. 01659 50291. On A76 at S (Dumfries) end of town. At Esso petrol station. Fishing, 9-hole golf course, shops, PO all nearby. Open Easter-Sept.

SOUTHERNESS-ON-SOLWAY

Lighthouse Leisure, Southerness-on-Solway, Dumfries & Galloway DG2 8AZ. 01387 880277. www.lighthouseleisure.co.uk. Owner: C Robertson. From Drumfries, follow A710 for 20mins turn off to Southerness on L – 5mins to site. Level, lawned family-owned park. Leisure complex with bar, restaurant, heated pool, sauna, gym, ten-pin bowling, amusements. Toytown. All facilities. Close to sweeping sandy beaches and championship golf course. Open March-Oct.

STRANRAER

(1m). Aird Donald Caravan Park, London Road, Stranraer, Dumfries & Galloway DG9 8RN. 01776 702025. www.aird-donald.co.uk. Owner: Mr HM Cassie. On A75 Newton Stewart to Stranraer. Small, sheltered site, level grass. Excellently situated for ferries to Ireland. 1m from town. Tarmac hardstandings for wet weather. Excellent facilities.

(6m). Cairnyan Caravan Park, Cairnryan, Stranraer, Dumfries & Galloway DG9 8QX. 01581 200231. Owner: Charles Dobson. On A77, opposite P&O ferry terminal, Cairnryan. Shop 500yd Open April-Oct.

(0.75m). Castle Bay Holiday & Residential Park, Portpatrick, Stranraer, Dumfries & Galloway DG9 9AA. 01776 810462. www.castlebaycaravanpark.co.uk. From N take A77 S from Glasgow, from S take A75 W from Dumfries onto A77 to Portpatrick. 22 acres overlooking Irish Sea and Dunskey Castle. 0.5m coastal walk to villae of Portpatrick. Open March 1-Oct 31.

(7m). Galloway Point Holiday Park, Portree Farm, Portpatrick, Stranraer, Dumfries & Galloway DG9 9AA. 01776 810561. www.gallowaypointholidaypark.co.uk. Owner: Mr & Mrs AJ Mackie. A75 W from Dumfries. 1st L after 30mph on R, office at house/pub on L. Sea view near golf, fishing and bowling. Lounge bar and meals. Caravan & Camping Club Listed Location. RAC. Shops, PO 0.75m. David Bellamy Silver Conservation Award. Open Easter-Sept 30.

(14m). New England Bay Caravan Club Site, Port Logan, Stranraer, Dumfries & Galloway DG9 9NX. 01776 860275. www.caravanclub.co.uk. Owner: The Caravan Club. See website for directions. Site on the edge of Luce Bay, landscaped into seven pitching areas with sea views. Non-members welcome. No tents. Advance booking essential BH and July-Aug. Toilet blocks with privacy cubicles and family rooms. Veg prep area, gas, dog walk nearby. MV service point. Games room. Play equipment. Ideal for families. Steel awning pegs required. Storage pitches, watersports and beach nearby. Quiet and peaceful off peak. Open March-Nov.

(6m). Sands of Luce Caravan Park, Sandhead, Stranraer, Dumfries & Galloway DG9 9JR. 01776 830456. At junction of B7084 and A716, S of Stranraer. Beside sandy beach. Beach walk to village of Sandhead. Open March 15-Oct 31.

(7m). Sunnymeade Caravan Park, Portpatrick, Stranraer, Dumfries & Galloway DG9 8LN. 01776 810293. info-sunnymeade@btconnect.com. Owner: Mr & Mrs E Gray. A75 to Portpatrick, turn L on entering Portpatrick. Site 0.5m on L. Near beach and golf. Private fishing pond. Open April-Sept.

(4m). Wig Bay Holiday Park, Loch Ryan, Stranraer, Dumfries & Galloway DG9 0PS. 01776 853233. On entering take A718 Kirkcolm road, R at roundabout, past garden centre. Park is on L. Heated indoor swimming pool. Play area. Bar. Telephone. Open March 1-Oct 31.

THORNHILL

(2m). Penpont Caravan & Camping Park, Penpont, Thornhill, Dumfries & Galloway DG3 4BH. 01848 330470. www.penpontleisure.com. Owner: Mr & Mrs Miller. At north end of Thornhill take the A702 to Penpont 2m. Park is on the L just before Penpont village. Quiet, riverside park in beautiful country. 5mins walk to shop, local pub and PO. Golf course 3m. River and loch fishing, mountain bike trails available. Good cycling area. Open end March-end Oct.

WIGTOWN

Whitecairn Caravan Park, Glenluce, Wigtown, Dumfries & Galloway DG8 0NZ. 01581 300267. www.whitecairncaravans.co.uk. Owner: Mr & Mrs Rankin. 1.5m N of Glenluce village and 2m from A75. 12m from Stranraer. SP from village, main street. Small, family run park in easy reach of many local attractions. Fully serviced pitches for touring caravans and campers. Caravans for sale or hire.

DUNBARTONSHIRE (WEST)

ARROCHAR

(2m). Ardgartan Caravan & Camping Site, Forest Holidays, Ardgartan, Arrochar, West Dunbartonshire G83 7AR. 01301 702293. www.forestholidays.co.uk. Owner: Forest Holidays. On A83 Inverary to Arrochar. W of Arrochar. On the shores of Loch Long surrounded by the magnificent scenery of the Argyll Forest Park. Bookings and brochure requests on 0845 1308224. Open March-Jan.

(2m). Camping & Caravanning Club Site – Ardgartan, Coilessan Road, Arrochar, West Dunbartonshire G83 7AR. 01301 702253. www.campingandcaravanningclub.co.uk. Owner: Camping & Caravanning Club. Turn off the A83 at the Forest Tourist Information Centre (TIC) and follow signs for site. Site is surrounded by Argyll Forest Park, with stunning scenery and fascinating wildlife, including seals, herons and eagles. Club members only. All units accepted. 55 pitches set in 3.5 acres with spectacular views over Loch Long and Arrochar Alps. Deals for families and backpackers. Open April – Oct.

LOCH LOMOND

(0.25m). Lomond Woods Holiday Park, Tullichewan, Balloch, Loch Lomond, West Dunbartonshire G83 8QP. 01389 755000. lomondwoods@holiday-parks.co.uk. www.holiday-parks.co.uk. Owner: Colin & Margaret Wood. Turn R off A82, 17m N of Glasgow at roundabout SP Balloch. At next roundabout take a L following signs. A811 for Lomond Woods. Play area, games room, TV lounge, launderette. Pine lodges and caravan holiday homes also for hire. Next to 'Lomond Shores' visitor attraction. Short walk to Loch Lomond and Balloch village

SCOTLAND

for Restaurants, Bars, and shops. Huge variety of activities locally including water sports, golf and fishing. At Gateway to Loch Lomond National Park and next to Loch Lomond Shores visitor experience. David Bellamy Gold Conservation Award. Open all year.

EDINBURGH
EDINBURGH

Edinburgh Caravan Club Site, 35 – 37 Marine Drive, Edinburgh, Edinburgh EH4 5EN. 0131 3126874. www.caravanclub.co.uk. Owner: The Caravan Club. See website for directions. This site is in an ideal location for a caravanning holiday. Situated to the N of the city on the Firth of Fourth, the site provides easy access to Edinburgh. Hardstandings; toilet block; laundry facilities and veg prep; play area; dog walk. Non-members and tent campers welcome. MV service point. Serviced pitches, gas and gaz, ideal for families, beach in 5m. Near golf, water sports, zoo, holy road. NCN cycle route in 5m.

Little France Caravan & Camping Park, Old Dalkeith Road, Edinburgh, Edinburgh EH16 4SE. Owner: Little France Caravan Co. On A7 (formerly A68). Dishwashing facilities. Period of opening and fees on application.

(4m). Mortonhall Caravan & Camping Park, Frogston Road East, 38 Mortonhall Gate, Edinburgh, Edinburgh EH16 6TJ. 0131 664 1533. www.meadowhead.co.uk. Owner: Meadowhead Parks. From city by-pass A720 leave at Lothianburn Junction A702 and follow signs for Mortonhall. Arboretum on park. Internet access/bar/restaurant, children's play areas. Golf, supermarket, dry ski slope all in 2m. Cinema/theatre 2.5m. Excellent access to Edinburgh City centre. David Bellamy Gold Conservation Award. Open March 14-Jan 4.

FIFE
ANSTRUTHER

Ashburn House Caravan Site, St Andrews Road, Crail, Anstruther, Fife KY10 3UL. 01333 450314. Owner: A & M Ireland & Sons. On A917 Crail to St Andrews (9m). Quiet, family run site close to town centre, harbour, golf and bowling. Excellent facilities. Open March 1-Oct 31.

(2m). Grangemuir Woodland Park, Pittenweem, Anstruther, Fife KY10 2RB. 01333 311213. Owner: A&M Ireland & Sons. Off A917. 1m from Pittenweem. Bar and games room. Shops, PO 1m, doctor 2m. Fishing, golf nearby. Open March 1-Oct 31.

(2m). St Monans Caravan Site, St Monans, Anstruther, Fife KY10 2DN. 01333 730778. Owner: Abbeyford Caravans Ltd (Scotland). Adjoining A917 E of St Monans. Small quiet park beside park, village and seaside. Open March 21-Oct 31.

CRAIL

Sauchope Links Caravan Park, Crail, Fife KY10 3XJ. 01333 450460. www.sauchope.co.uk. Owner: Largo Leisure Parks Ltd. On A917. On the seashore with heated outdoor swimming pool, games room, play area. Wash basins, shaver points. GS. David Bellamy Gold Conservation Award. Open March-Oct.

GLENROTHES

(2.25m). Balbirnie Park Caravan Club Site, Markinch, Glenrothes, Fife KY7 6NR. 01592 759130. www.caravanclub.co.uk. Owner: The Caravan Club. See website for directions. 0.5m from Markinch. An attractive site set in 400 acres of parkland. Laundry. Preparation area. Motorcaravan waste point. Toilet block. Non-members welcome. Tent camping limited. Part hardstandings, part sloping. Steel awning pegs required. Gas, information room, dog walk nearby. Ideal for families, quiet and peaceful off peak. Watersports nearby. NCN cycle route wihtin 5m. Advance booking advised all BH and July-Aug. Open March-Nov.

LUNDIN LINKS

(1m). Woodland Gardens Caravan & Camping Site, Blindwell Road, Lundin Links, Fife KY8 5QG. 01333 360319. www.woodland-gardens.co.uk. Owner: Mr & Mrs J D Anderson. Turn N off A915 at east end of Lundin Links. SP on A915 by international camping and caravanning signs. Ideal centre for St Andrews and East Neuk of Fife. Small quiet family run site. Not suitable for young children. Peace and tranquility in a beautiful rural setting overlooking the river Forth to Edinburgh. Fishing nearby. Open April-Oct.

ST ANDREWS

(1m). Cairnsmill Caravan Park, Largo Road, St Andrews, Fife KY16 8NN. 01334 473604. www.ukparks.co.uk/cairnsmill. Owner: Kirkcaldy family. On A915 Leven to St Andrews, SW of town centre. Ideal touring base, in close proximity to a choice of golf courses and the east Fife coast. Indoor heated swimming pool. Coffee bar. GS. Fly fishing, bunkhouse. David Bellamy Gold Conservation Award. Open April-Oct.

(1.5m). Craigtoun Meadows Holiday Park, Mount Melville, St Andrews, Fife KY16 8PQ. 01334 475959. www.craigtounmeadows.co.uk. Owner: Craigtoun Meadows Ltd. Off A91, at Guardbridge turn R for Strathkiness, follow signs for Craigtoun. Licensed restaurant. AA 5 pennant. Indoor/outdoor games room, shop, telephone, tennis court. 1.5m to golf, cinema, shops, restaurants, hotels and pubs. David Bellamy Gold Conservation Award. Open March 15-Nov 15.

GLASGOW
DRYMEN

(1.5m). Camping & Caravanning Club Site – Milarrochy Bay, Balmaha, Drymen, Glasgow G63 0AL. 01360 870236. www.campingandcaravanningclub.co.uk. Owner: Camping & Caravanning Club. A811 Balloch to Stirling then in Drymen take B837 to Balmaha. 5m up Steep Hill. Site 1.5m further. On East bank of Loch Lomond in the heart of Rob Roy country adjacent to the West Highland way. Boat hire and pleasure cruises. All units accepted. Non-members welcome. Near Queen Elizabeth Forest Park. The site has a peaceful and quiet atmosphere. Deals for families and backpackers. AA's Best Campsite in Scotland award. Visit Scotland Thistle Award finalist. Open March-Oct.

HIGHLAND
ACHARACLE

(4m). Resipole Farm Caravan & Camping Park, Loch Sunart, Acharacle, Highland PH36 4HX. 01967 431235. www.resipole.co.uk. Owner: Mr P Sinclair. On A861. 8m W of Strontian. Launderette. Pay-phone. Private slip-way. Art gallery and studios Open April 1-Oct 31.

ACHNASHEEN

(36m). Camping & Caravanning Club Site – Inverewe Gardens, Inverewe Gardens, Poolewe, Achnasheen,

SCOTLAND

Highland IV22 2LF. 01445 781249. www.campingandcaravanningclub.co.uk. Owner: Camping & Caravanning Club. On A832, just N of Poolewe, close to Inverewe Gardens and on shores of Loch Ewe. All units accepted. Non-members welcome. The site nestles in spectacular mountain scenery. The National Trust for Scotland organise some excellent walks led by a ranger. There is good sea and fly fishing close to the site. Wildlife includes seals, otters, and golden eagles. Deals for families and backpackers. Open April-Oct.

(8m). Kinlochewe Caravan Club Site, Kinlochewe, Achnasheen, Highland IV22 2PA. 01445 760239. www.caravanclub.co.uk. Owner: The Caravan Club. See website for directions. A small and intimate site in a peaceful position at the foot of the rugged slopes of Ben Eighe. Non-members welcome. No tents. Advance booking essential BH and June-Aug. Toilet blocks. Laundry facilities. MV service point. Good area for walking. All hardstandings, steel awning pegs required, dog walk, quiet and peaceful off peak. Open March-Oct.

ARISAIG

(2m). Gorton Farm Caravan Site, Gorton Farmhouse, Back of Keppoch, Arisaig, Highland PH39 4NS. 01687 450283. Owner: Mr A Macdonald. A830 to point 2m W of Arisaig, turn L at SP 'Back of Keppoch' 0.75m to end of road across cattle grid. Beach site with hot water, showers and shaver points, laundry, payphone, gas. Views to Skye. Abundant wildlife. Open April 1-Sept 30.

(1.5m). Invercaimbe Caravan Site, Invercaimbe, Arisaig, Highland PH39 4NT. 01687 450375. www.invercaimbecaravansite.co.uk. On the beach. Golf nearby. Fishing and boat trips locally.

BEAULY

(1m). Lovat Bridge Caravan and Camping Site, Lovat Bridge, Beauly, Highland IV4 7AY. 01463 782374. allanlymburn@beauly782.fsnet.co.uk. Owner: Allan S Lymburn. On A832 Inverness to Beauly. Set in the old Caledonian Forest next to the river Beauly. Licensed family lounge. Fishing on site. Open March-Oct.

BENBECULA

Shell Bay Holiday Park, Liniclate, Benbecula, Highland HS7 5PJ. 01870 602447. Owner: Allan & Katie Buchanan. Site 23m from Lochboisdale on A865/B892. 21m from Lochmaddy. Near beaches and community school. Near shop and restaurant. Open March 1-Oct 15.

BOAT OF GARTEN

Boat of Garten Caravan Park, Deshar Road, Boat of Garten, Highland PH24 3BN. 01479 831652. www.campgroundsofscotland.com. Owner: Brian & Maureen Gillies. Off A95 Grantown to Aviemore. In the centre of the village. Thistle Award Park. PO 300yd, fishing 500yd, golf and tennis 300yd, Railway 250yd. Beautiful forest walks all around. Osprey Hide 2m.

(1m). Loch Garten Lodges & Caravan Park, Loch Garten Road, Boat of Garten, Highland PH24 3BY. 01479 831769. www.lochgarten.co.uk. Leave A9 immediately N of Aviemore follow Boat of Garten signs, through village and cross river Spey, turn L on B970, first R to Tulloch, park on L overlooking river and Spey Valley. Aviemore 7m. 3 Golf courses, fishing in 1m. Bird watching at Osprey Centre 0.5m. Woodland walks in RSPB Nature Reserve next to site.

BRORA

(1.5m). Dalchalm Caravan Club Site, Brora, Highland KW9 6LP. 01408 621479. www.caravanclub.co.uk. Owner: The Caravan Club. See website for directions. A site on the east coast of Sutherland just 300yd from a safe, sandy beach. Tent campers admitted. Non-members welcome. Advance booking advised June-Aug. Toilet blocks. Privacy cubicles. Laundry. Veg prep. MV service point. Golf, fishing nearby. Good area for walking. Ideal for families. Some hardstandings, gas and gaz. Dog walk nearby, quiet and peaceful off peak. Open April-Nov.

YOUR TOP 101 SITES 2009

CAITHNESS

Dunnet Bay Caravan Club Site, Dunnet, Thurso, Caithness, Highland KW14 8XD. 01847 821319. www.caravanclub.co.uk. Owner: The Caravan Club. See website for directions. A good site for those who like to be solitary; you can look out to Dunnet Head, the northernmost point of mainland Britain. Toilet block, laundry and MV service point. Fishing and watersports in 5m, ideal for families. Non-members and tent campers welcome. Open April-Oct.

(0.25m). Inver Caravan Park, Houstry Road, Dunbeath, Caithness, Highland KW6 6EH. 01593 731441. www.inver-caravan-park.co.uk. Owner: Rhona Gwillim. Off A9 just N of Dunbeath. Park entrance 40yd up road SP 'Houstry 3'. Smooth grassy site: 8 hardstandings, dump station. Free showers, beautiful views over Dunbeath Bay. Friendly welcome. Luxury 6-berth holiday caravan for hire. Near shop and pub/restaurant. Near Orkney crossings.

DINGWALL

(5m). Black Rock Caravan Park, Evanton, Dingwall, Highland IV16 9UN. 01349 830917. www.blackrockscotland.co.uk. Owner: Mr & Mrs S C Macpherson. Off A9, 15m N from Inverness, turn L for Evanton B817, proceed for 0.75m. Set in wooded glen on the banks of river Glass. Level, grassy and sheltered park in easy reach of west and east coasts. Free showers. Play area. Telephone. Laundry. Shops nearby. Open April 15-Oct 31.

(0.5m). Camping & Caravanning Club Site – Dingwall, Jubilee Park Road, Dingwall, Highland IVI5 9QZ. 01349 862236. www.campingandcaravanningclub.co.uk. Owner: Camping & Caravanning Club. In Dingwall coming from S, take bypass and follow signs, first R down Hill Street, R at junction, L over railway bridge, then first L, SP. Ideal base for exploring the Western Highlands. All units accepted. Non-members welcome. Site set in 6.5 acres. Millbuie Forest in the nearby Black Isle. Trains go from Dingwall to the Kyle of Lochalsh. Deals for families and backpackers. Open April-Oct.

DORNOCH

(0.5m). Dornoch Caravan and Camping Park, The Links, Dornoch, Highland IV25 3LX. 01862 810423. www.dornochcaravans.co.uk. Owner: Mr W Macrae. A9, 6m N of Tain. Turn R on to A949 E for 2m, entry via River Street. Adjacent to beach and golf course. Town centre 5mins walk. Open April 1-Oct 24.

(2.5m). Grannie's Heilan Hame Holiday Park, Embo, Dornoch, Highland IV25 3QD. 01862 810383. www.parkdeanholidays.co.uk. Owner: Parkdean Holidays Plc. Take A9 from Inverness northwards to Dornoch and Embo. Follow the road for Embo. Park is at the end of this road. Free indoor pool and spa bath, solarium, sauna, bar, clubhouse, entertainment/meals, tennis court, playground, games room, bowleasy mini bowling and pool. Caravan sales. Open March-Oct.

126 MOTOR CARAVAN & CAMPING PARKS 2009

SCOTLAND

(1.25m). Seaview Farm Caravan Park, Hilton, Dornoch, Highland IV25 3PW. *01862 810294.* Owner: Mr TR Preston. From Dornoch turn L at square. After 1.25m turn R at road junction by telephone box. Caravanning & Camping Club member. Dogs allowed on leads. Flat site. Golf course nearby. Shops, PO, doctor in village. Open April-Oct.

FORT AUGUS

(0.5m). Fort Augus Caravan & Camping Park, Market Hill, Fort Augus, Highland PH32 4DS. *01320 366618.* info@campinglochness.co.uk. www.campinglochness.co.uk. Owner: Mr Brian Clark. On A82. 0.5m S from the southern end of Loch Ness on the outskirts of Fort Augus. Flat, well drained site. Camp kitchen. Takeaway meals, shop, café/restaurant available nearby. Adjacent to 9-hole golf course. Near canoeing, kayaking, speed boats, target sports, sailing, windsurfing and tennis. Good walking and cycling area. Open mid April-end Sept.

FORT WILLIAM

(8m). Bunree Caravan Club Site, Onich, Fort William, Highland PH33 6SE. *01855 821283.* www.caravanclub.co.uk. Owner: The Caravan Club. See website for directions. On safe, sandy beach. Quiet and peaceful off peak. Laundry room, drying room. Play area and playframe. Toilet block with privacy cubicles. Baby and toddler washroom. Motorvan waste point. Non-members welcome. No tents. Advance booking advised BH and June-Aug. Recreation and info rooms. Boat launch area. Fishing from site, PH/restaurant in walking distance. Good for walking. Ideal for families. Open March 27-Nov 9.

(5m). Linnhe Lochside Holidays, Corpach, Fort William, Highland PH33 7NL. *01397 772376.* www.linnhe-lochside-holidays.co.uk. Owner: Linnhe Lochside Holidays Ltd. On A830, 1m W of Corpach. 5m from Fort William. One of the best and most beautiful lochside parks in Scotland. Pets welcome. Free fishing. 18-hole golf, cinema 5m PO, shops 0.5m. Brochure on request.

(2.5m). Lochy Caravan Park, Camaghael, Fort William, Highland PH33 7NF. *01397 703446.* www.lochy-holiday-park.co.uk. Owner: Ian C Brown. On A830, off A82. Park is situated along the same road as the Medical centre/High School in the District of Camaghael. Laundry shop, play area, showers, toilets. Golf 0.5m, Fishing 1m. Town centre 2m. Open April-Oct.

FORTROSE

(0.5m). Camping & Caravanning Club Site – Rosemarkie, Ness Road East, Rosemarkie, Fortrose, Highland IV10 8SE. *01381 621117.* www.campingandcaravanningclub.co.uk. Owner: Camping & Caravanning Club. A832 then A9. Through Avoch, Fortrose turn R at police house Down Ness Road, first L, small turning sign Golf and Caravan Site. On the shore of the Black Isle in the small seaside village of Rosemarkie. Non-members welcome. All units accepted. Disabled facilities. Spectacular coastline is famous for its bottlenose dolphins. The area is a paradise for bird watchers, with many local nature reserves. Deals for families and backpackers. Loo Of The Year (4 stars). Open April-Oct.

GAIRLOCH

Gairloch Caravan and Camping Park, Strath, Gairloch, Highland IV21 2BX. *01445 712373.* www.gairlochcaravanpark.com. Owner: Mr Robert Forbes. Turn W off A832 (Gairloch) onto B8021, in 0.5m turn R immediately after Millcroft Hotel, site on R. Family-run site with shower block, launderette. Close to shops, café & restaurants. Chemical toilet disposal point if required. AA listed and graded. 70m from Inverness. Open April-Oct.

(3m). Sands Holiday Centre, Gairloch, Highland IV21 2DL. *01445 712152.* www.sandsholidaycentre.co.uk. Owner: W & M Cameron. Following A833 to Gairloch then take B8021 4m along this road will bring you to Sands Holiday centre. Play area. Public phone. Slipway for boats. Beach adjoining. Full facilities May 2 to mid-Sept. Underfloor heated toilet and shower rooms. Free Loch fishing to residents. Open April 1-Oct 15.

GRANTOWN-ON-SPEY

(0.5m). Grantown-on-Spey Caravan Park, Seafield Avenue, Grantown-on-Spey, Highland PH26 3JQ. *01479 872474.* www.caravanscotland.com. Owner: Sandra McKelvie & John Fleming. From town centre turn N at Bank of Scotland. Park 0.5m straight forward. Caravan Club affiliated site in the heart of the Highlands, quiet and peaceful off peak. Laundry, dishwashing and games room. Three chemical toilet disposal points. Motor caravan service point. Fully serviced pitches with Sky TV & internet Open Dec 21-Oct 30.

INVERGARRY

(1m). Faichemard Farm Touring Caravan & Camping Site, Invergarry, **Highland PH35 4HG.** *01809 501314.* www.faichemard-caravancamping.co.uk. Owner: A & D Grant. SP (green writing) from A87 1m W from junction with A82. Turn R and go past Ardgarry Farm, R at sign A&D Grant. Adults only. All pitches have picnic tables. Laundry. Some individual pitches, hardstanding and hook ups available. Open April 1-Oct 31.

INVERNESS

(10m). Auchnahillin Caravan and Camping Park, Daviot East, Inverness, Highland IV2 5XQ. *01463 772286.* www.auchnahillin.co.uk. Owner: The Gibson Family. 8m SE of Inverness off the A9 on B9154 (Moy/Daviot East). Scenic rural location with excellent facilities surrounded by hills and forest. Tranquil yet many destinations and attractions in an easy drive. Children's playpark. Small shop. All amenities available in Inverness (7-10m). Open March 15-Oct 31.

(16m). Borlum Farm Camping Park, Borlum Farm, Drumnadrochit, Inverness, Highland IV63 6XN. *01456 450220.* www.borlum.com. Owner: A D Macdonald-Haig. 1m S of Drumnadrochit on A82 Fort William road. Park 500yd on R after Lewiston. Fishing on Loch Ness. Riding centre on site. Shops 0.75m. Open March-Nov.

Bught Caravan & Camping Site, Bught Lane, Bught Park, Inverness, Highland IV3 5SR. *01463 236920.* www.invernesscaravanpark.com. Owner: John MacDonald. In Inverness on the A82 road, next to the Aquadene Leisure Park and ice rink, beside the river Ness and Caledonian Canal. Site is in S boundary of Inverness. 4m from the N shores of Loch Ness. Well-equipped site. Children's play area, sports facilities. Walk to town. Open Easter-Oct 10.

(3m). Bunchrew Caravan Park, Bunchrew, Inverness, Highland IV3 8TD. *01463 237802.* www.bunchrew-caravanpark.co.uk. Owner: Bunchrew Caravan Park Ltd. 3m from Inverness on A862 Beauly road. Bunchrew Caravan Park is in a beautiful, quiet setting on the southern shore of the Beauly Firth. In 20 acres of parkland. 14 Thistle Award caravans for hire (all sleep 6), licensed shop, childrens play area, 125 grassy pitches and 50 electric hook-ups. Dogs welcome but not all breeds allowed. Internet access. Open March 15-Nov 30.

(26m). Cannich Caravan & Camping, Cannich, Strathglass, Inverness, Highland IV4 7LN. *01456 415364.* www.

SCOTLAND

highlandcamping.co.uk. Owner: Matthew & Fay Jones. Out of Inverness on A82 at Drumnadrochit take A831 to Cannich. 16m from Beauly. Friendly site situated 0.5m from village centre where there is a shop, pub. Close to Glen Affric Nature Reserve. Highland and lowland trails for walkers and mountain bikers. Site has 24 hour public telephone, laundry, play area, TV/rec room, indoor washing up facilities. Open Dec 1-Oct 31.

Culloden Moor Caravan Club Site, Newlands, Culloden Moor, Inverness, Highland IV1 5EF. 01463 790625. www.caravanclub.co.uk. Owner: The Caravan Club. See website for directions. A gently sloping site facing a glorious view over the Nairn Valley. Vegetable preparation area. Motorvan waste point. Playframe. Toilet block with privacy cubicles. Tent campers admitted. Non-members and tent campers welcome. Advance booking advised June-Aug essential July and BH. Information room. Fishing. Good area for walking. Ideal for families. Significant area of interest nearby including Loch Ness. Hardstandings, part sloping, laundry, gas and gaz, dog walk nearby, quiet and peaceful off peak, beach in 5m. NCN cycle route in 5m. Open March-Jan.

(30m). Loch Ness Caravan and Camping Park, Easter Port Clair, Invermoriston, Loch Ness, Inverness, Highland IV63 7YE. 01320 351207. www.lochnesscaravancampingpark.co.uk. Owner: Bob & Liz Girvan. On A82 1.5m S of Invermoriston. The only park on Loch Ness. All vans have magnificent views, fishing allowed by off loch, permits for salmon fishing with charge. Play area and lounge bar/family room with hot meals available. Laundry. Mobile shop. Adjacent to Great Glen walk. 5mins to Fort Augas with 2 supermarkets. 1m to village, PO, shop and hotel. Golf course 5mins, indoor pool 9m. Open March 1-Oct 30.

(0.5m). McDonalds Bught Caravan & Camping Site, Bught Park, Bught Drive, Inverness, Highland IV3 5SR. 01463 236920. www.invernesscaravanpark.com. Owner: Mr J P MacDonald, Mrs P MacDonald. On A82. On outskirts of Inverness. Tents welcome. Well equipped site. Includes an internet café and small shop. Many sports facilities nearby. Walking distance to town. Open Easter-Nov.

ISLE OF SKYE

Glenbrittle Beach Site, Glenbrittle, Isle of Skye, Highland. 01478 640404. www.dunvegancastle.com. Owner: Macleod Estates. Leave A850 at Sligachan and take A863 W for 5m. B8009 2.5m to Merkadale. Turn S on to road for 8m to site. Safe swimming from a shallow sandy beach. Ideal for the outdoor activity lover and fans of wilderness camping. The centre for the Cuillins. Other email address: glenbrittleacampsite@yahoo.co.uk Open April 1-Sept 30.

Loch Greshornish Caravan & Camping Site, Borve, Arnisort, Edinbane, Isle of Skye, Highland IV51 9PS. 01470 582230. www.skyecamp.com. Owner: Camping & Caravanning Club. A9. Slight L at Millbank. At roundabout, 2nd exit, turn L, turn L and L again. Near attractions, boat trips, distillery, restaurants and pub. We are working croft, see the Highland cows, sheep, duck, and chickens. Open April 1-Oct 12.

Staffin Caravan Site, Staffin, Portree, Isle of Skye, Highland IV51 9JX. 01470 562213. www.staffincampsite.co.uk. Owner: Mr & Mrs Young. Off A855 Portree to Staffin on south side of village. 16m from Portree. Excellent fishing and hill walking available locally. Quiet location overlooking Western Isles. Restaurant and shops in village 0.25m from site. Open April-Oct.

(1m). Torvaig Caravan & Camping Site, Portree, Isle of Skye, Highland IV51 9HU. 01478 611849. www.portreecampsite.co.uk. Owner: Mr John Maclean. On A855 Staffin road on outskirts of village of Portree. Ideal for touring all parts of the island. Open April 1-Oct 20.

(16m). Uig Bay Caravan & Camping Site, 10 Idrigill, Uig, Isle of Skye, Highland IV51 9XU. 01470 542714. www.uig-camping-skye.co.uk. Owner: M & L Madigan. From Portree follow A87 to Uig, past PO on L, carry on for 1m passing Caledonian MacBrayne on the R. Campsite is 200yd away. Fishing from bottom of campsite, pub 100yd away. Fuel station, PO, doctors all close by. Walks. Beautiful place to mull away the time.

JOHN O'GROATS

John O'Groats Caravan Site, John O'Groats, Highland KW1 4YR. 01955 611329.www.johnogroatscampsite.co.uk. Owner: W & C J Steven. At end of A99 on sea front overlooking Orkney Islands. Magnificent cliff scenery 1.5m. Seal colony 4m. Harbour Hotel & snack bar in 200yd. Phone 100yd. PO, grocery store 600yd. Day trips by passenger ferry to Orkney. Open April 1-Sept 30.

KINLOCHLEVEN

(3m). Caolasnacon Caravan Site, Kinlochleven, Highland PH50 4RJ. 01855 831279. www.kinlochlevencaravans.com. Owner: Patsy Cameron. Off A82. On to B863 at Glencoe. Lochside location – free sea loch fishing; golf course 4m. Shops, PO, doctor 1m. Open April-Oct.

KYLE OF LOCHALSH

(8m). Ardelve Caravan Site, Dornie, Kyle of Lochalsh, Highland. 01599 555231. Owner: Mr M Macrae. On A87. Invergarry to Kyle of Lochalsh. 1m beyond Eilean Donau Castle. A short walk from the famous Eilean Donan Castle and the village of Domie where you will find a shop, PO, hotel and PH. Ideal location for touring: Skye Lochalsh, Outer Hebrides and Wester ross Open Easter-Oct.

(13m). Morvich Caravan Club Site, Inverinate, Kyle of Lochalsh, Highland IV40 8HQ. 01599 511354. www.caravanclub.co.uk. Owner: The Caravan Club. See website for directions. 3m Shielbridge. Morvich has all the amenities for an ideal family holiday base. The site is on the level valley floor, while all around there are hills and mountains. Tent campers and non-members welcome. Advance booking essential BH and June-Aug. Toilet blocks. Privacy cubicles. Laundry facilities. Baby washroom. Veg prep. MV service point. Games room. Info room. Public transport available. Fishing nearby. Good area for walking. Ideal for families. Part hardstandings, steel awning pegs required, gas and gaz, dog walk nearby. Quiet and peaceful off peak. Beach in 5m. Open March-Nov.

(16m). Shiel Bridge Campsite, Shiel Bridge, Glenshiel, Kyle of Lochalsh, Highland IV40 8HW. 01599 511221. Owner: John Metcalfe. On A87. Café and PO on site. (PO open 8 hours week only). Fishing: sea and sea lochs, rivers and inland lochs – subject to permit. Open March 16-Oct 16 (caravan), all year for tents.

LAIRG

(25m). Grummore Caravan Club Site, Altnaharra, Lairg, Highland IV27 1UA. 01549 411266. www.caravanclub.co.uk.

SCOTLAND

Owner: (leaseholder) The Caravan Club. See website for directions. 2.75m from Altnaharra. Caravan Club members only. No tents. This site is perfect for those wanting to get away from it all, and the nearest shops are 20m away! Own sanitation required. Fishing, watersports and NCN route nearby. Good area for walking. Quiet and peaceful off-peak. Open mid April-early Oct.

Scourie Caravan & Camping Park, Harbour Road, Scourie, Lairg, Highland IV27 4TG. 01971 502060. Near Scourie village. Overlooking Scourie Bay. At junction of Harbour Road and A894. 20m S of Cape Wrath. Holiday site. Hill walking. Handa Island birdwatching. No bookings taken. Fees on application SAE. Open Easter-Sept 30.

(5m) Woodend Caravan & Camping Site, Woodend, Achnairn, Lairg, Highland IV27 4DN. 01549 402248. Owner: Mrs C M Ross. A836 from Lairg on to A838 SP. AA 3 pennants. Campers kitchen. Gold award for quality and service from International Caravanning & Camping Guide. Shops, PO, doctor in 5m. Gof course 14m. Open April 1-Sept 30.

LOCHINVER

(7m) Clachtoll Beach Campsite, Clachtoll, Lochinver, Highland IV27 4JD. 01571 855377. www.clachtollbeachcampsite.co.uk. Off A837 0.5m before Lochinver on to B869 site about 6m. 40 pitches in total. Children welcome. 100yd from beautiful sandy beach. Breathtaking scenery. Open Easter-end Sept.

MELVICH

Halladale Inn Caravan Site, Halladale Inn, Melvich, Highland KW14 7YJ. 01641 531 282. mazfling@tinyworld.co.uk. Owner: Ian & Marilyn Fling. 16m W of Thurso along A836. Small quiet site, next door to Halladale Inn. Beautiful scenery and sandy beach. Ideal for surfers, walking, birdwatching. Village shop and PO 1m. Open April 1-Oct 31.

NAIRN

Camping & Caravanning Club Site – Nairn, Delnies Wood, Nairn, Highland IV12 5NX. 01667 455281. www.campingandcaravanningclub.co.uk. Owner: Camping & Caravanning Club. Off the main A96 Inverness to Aberdeen road, 2m W of the town of Nairn. Look out for 'Delnies Wood' SP. 13m from Inverness. In wooded setting, 2m from the beach and close to the town of Nairn. 75 pitches set in 14 acres. Non-members welcome. Caravans, motorcaravans and tents accepted. Fort George, Loch Ness and Cawdor are all worth a visit. Dolphins often seen in waters of Firth. Deals for families and backpackers. Open April – Oct.

(2m) Delnies Woods Caravan Park, Delnies Wood, Nairn, Highland IV12 5NX. 01667 455281. Owner: G M Munro. W of Nairn on A96 Aberdeen to Inverness road. Secluded site 3m from beach. Attractive scenery and historic countryside abounding in sporting activities. Dogs welcome. Open Easte-October.

(0.5m) Nairn Lochloy Holiday Park, East Beach, Nairn, Highland IV12 5DE. 01667 453764. www.parkdeanholidays.co.uk. Owner: Parkdean Holidays Plc. A1 to Edinburgh, then A9 to Inverness, A96 to Nairn. Indoor heated pool, adventure play and amusements. Kid's club and crazy golf. Restaurant, bar and live family entertainment. David Bellamy Silver Conservation Award. Open March-Nov.

NEWTONMORE

(3m) Invernahavon Caravan Site, Glentruim, Newtonmore, Highland PH20 1BE. 01540 673534. www.invernahavon.com. Owner: Mr & Mrs K W Knox. Off A9, S of Newtownmore 10m N of Dalwhinnie. Caravan Club affiliated site. Level site close to river Truim. Surrounded by woods and mountains. Non members and tent campers welcome. Ideal family site. Good area for walking. 2 golf courses in 8m, pets welcome. Fishing permits for sale from site office. Mountain bike track 8m. Open April-Oct.

ROY BRIDGE

(0.3m) Bunroy Camping & Caravanning Site, Roy Bridge, Highland PH31 4AG. 01397 712332. www.bunroycamping.co.uk. Owner: AD & G Markham. A82 from Fort William, on A86 at Spean Bridge then 3m to Roy Bridge. At Stronlossit Hotel, turn R past school, follow signs for 350yd to end of road. 12m from Fort William. Peaceful site surrounded by woodland on the banks of the river Spean. Two hotels/restaurants, shop and PO in a few mins walk. Good for touring, walking and outdoor activities. Open March 15-Oct 15.

STRATHCARRON

(23m) Applecross Camp Site, Applecross, Strathcarron, Highland IV54 8ND. 0845 1662681. www.applecross.uk.com. Owner: Mr AC Goldthorpe. 8m N of Lochcarron on A896, turn L onto Applecross Road. (Bealoch-na-Ba). Applecross 11m, road not suitable for caravans. Caravans proceed on A896 for 7m, turn L, SP Applecross, 24m. Instore bakery, licensed tea room in covered garden. Open Easter-Oct.

STRATHPEFFER

(2m) Riverside Chalets Caravan Park, Contin, Strathpeffer, Highland IV14 9ES. 01403 243766. www.riversidecontin.co.uk. Owner: Miss Finnie. On A835 junction of Ullapool to Strathpeffer to Maryburgh in Contin village. Quiet riverside site with mini market, PO next to site. Garage, golf, fishing, forest walks all available locally in 2m.

SUTHERLAND

(1m) Pitgrudy Caravan Park, Poles Road, Dornoch, Sutherland, Highland IV25 3HY. 01862 810001. www.pitgrudycaravanpark.co.uk. Owner: Mr GNR Sutherland. On B9168, off A9 turn L at War Memorial. Panoramic views of Dornoch Firth. Showers. Launderette. Telephone. Play area. Thistle Award. Caravans for hire. Holiday caravans for sale. Open April-Sept.

Sango Sands Caravan & Camping Site, Durness, Sutherland, Highland IV27 4PT. 01971 511262. keith.durness@btinternet.com. Owner: Mr Francis RM Keith. Adjacent A838 overlooking Sango Bay. Café and restaurant, lounge bar. Gift shop. No advance bookings except for electric hook-ups. Golf course 1m. Shops, PO, doctor in 400yd. Overlooking safe, sandy beach. Open April 1-Oct 15.

TAIN

(2m) Dornoch Firth Caravan & Camping Park, Meikle Ferry South, Tain, Highland IV19 1JX. 01862 892292. www.dornochfirth.co.uk. Owner: Will Porter. A9 N from Inverness, past Tain to Meikle Ferry roundabout, A836: Dornoch Firth scenic route, 1st R Meikle Ferry South. Beautiful scenic location, ideal for touring Highlands. Bar/restaurant adjacent to park. New caravan holiday homes for sale. Open March-Nov.

THURSO

(30m) Craigdhu Caravan Site, Bettyhill, Thurso, Highland KW14 7SP. 01641 521273. Owner: Mr & Mrs D M Mackenzie. On A836 Tongue to Thurso. Shop, laundry nearby. Picturesque scenery with golden beaches, popular with

SCOTLAND

botanists and geologists also bird watching. Near new swimming pool. Fishing, PO and fuel pumps available nearby. Open April 1-Oct 31.

(0.5m). Thurso Caravan and Camping Site, Smith Terrace, Scrabster Road, Thurso, Highland KW14 7JY. *01847 894631.* Owner: Highland Council. On A882 Thurso to Scrabster road, in the town boundary. Overlooking Thurso Bay to Orkney Islands in the 4.5-acre grassed park with many facilities including, cafétaria. Area renowned for surfing and sea angling. Open May-Sept.

ULLAPOOL

(3m). Ardmair Point Caravan Site, Ardmair, Ullapool, Highland IV26 2TN. *01854 612054.* sales@ardmair.com. www.ardmair.com. Owner: Mr Peter Fraser. Off A835, 3m N of Ullapool. Small site in beautiful location with panoramic views over the sea. Boat centre on site. Open May 1-Oct 1.

Broomfield Holiday Park, Shore Street, Ullapool, Highland IV26 2SX. *01854 612020/664.* www.broomfieldhp.com. Owner: SM Ross. Turn 1st R after harbour then 1st L. 5 min walk to supermarket, restaurants, bars, cafés, museum, leisure centre. Open Easter- end Sept.

WICK

(0.5m). The Wick Caravan & Camping Site, Riverside Drive, Janetstown, Wick, Highland KW1 5SR. *01955 605420.* wickcaravansite@aol.com. Owner: William Miller. Off A882 into Riverside Drive in 0.5m. River Wick running beside site. Tent campers welcome. Veg prep. MV service point. Information more. Golf, fishing and watersports nearby. Laundry facilities, gas, dog walk nearby. Quiet and peaceful off peak, beach in 3m, good area for walking. Open April-Oct.

INVERNESS-SHIRE
AVIEMORE

(0.5m). Aviemore Touring Caravan & Camping Park, High Range, Grampian Road, Aviemore, Inverness-shire PH22 1PT. *01479 810636.* www.highrange.co.uk. Owner: Mr F Vastano. At south end of Aviemore on the B9152 road, directly opposite the Coylumbridge B970 road leading to the Cairngorm Mountains. In woodland grounds of the High Range holiday complex at the foot of Craigellachie Nature Reserve. 500yd from Aviemore shopping centre. Lodge hotel, chalets, ristorante-pizzeria and bar, playground and launderette on site.

(3m). Dalraddy Holiday Park, Aviemore, Inverness-shire PH22 1QB. *01479 810330.* www.alvie-estate.co.uk. Owner: Mr JDA Williamson. On B9152 (old A9). Launderette. Play area. Licensed shop. Heated facilities block. Fishing, pony trekking and watersports. Quadbikes and 4x4 all in 2m.

YOUR TOP 101 SITES 2009 (7m). Glenmore Caravan & Camping Site, Forest Holidays, Glenmore, Aviemore, Inverness-shire PH22 1QU. *01479 861271.* www.forestholidays.co.uk. Owner: Forest Holidays. From A9 turn on to B9152 S of Aviemore. At Aviemore, turn R on to B970, keeping R at Coylumbridge. In the heart of the Cairngorms. An Area of Oustranding Natural Beauty, close to sandy beaches of Loch Morlich and Scotlands largest ski area. Bookings and brochure requests: 0845 1308221. David Bellamy Gold Conservation Award. Open Dec-Oct.

(1.5m). Rothiemurchus Camping & Caravan Park, Coylumbridge, Aviemore, Inverness-shire PH22 1QU. *01479 812800.* www.rothic.net. Owner: Liz Sangster. From Aviemore take ski road B970, park is situated on R in 1.5m. Touring pitches (hard stand) do vary in size as they are worked in around the trees. All have 16amp and TV hook-ups. New facility block.

LANARKSHIRE
MOTHERWELL

(2m). Strathclyde Country Park, 366 Hamilton Road, Motherwell, North Lanarkshire ML1 3ED. *01698 402060.* www.northlan.gov.uk. Owner: North Lanarkshire Council. M74, J5. Touring site only in 1200-acre Strathclyde Country Park. 4 star site with superb facilities. 24hrs park security and lighting. Watersports and fun boats, guided walks, land train, beaches, play areas. Minutes from site are Innkeepers Fayre and M&D's Theme Park. Open Easter-mid-Oct.

LOTHIAN (EAST)
ABERLADY

Aberlady Caravan Park, Haddington Road, Aberlady, East Lothian EH32 0PZ. *01875 870 666.* Owner: Andrew Dyer. 5m from Haddington on B6137, 3m from Longnddry on A198. Quiet site with a licensed shop selling bread, milk, essentials and wines and beers. Ideal for touring, close enough to 20 golf courses, Edinburgh, Musselburgh Races or the Museum of Flight – home to Concorde. Gosford House. Aberlady village is a small coastal village 1m from the site with 2 hotels, a PO and a shop. Open March-Oct.

DUNBAR

(0.5m). Belhaven Bay Caravan & Camping Park, Edinburgh Road, Dunbar, East Lothian EH42 1TU. *01368 865956.* www.meadowhead.co.uk. Owner: Meadowhead Ltd. From A1 N or S exit at roundabout W of Dunbar. Park about 0.5m down A1087 on L side of road. (From S, do not take first exit to Dunbar.). Peaceful setting located in the John Muir Country Park. Laundry, internet access available on the park. Children's play area. Sandy beaches only a short walk away. Thistle Award. Facilities in 15mins walkling distance. David Bellamy Gold Conservation Award. Open March 1-Jan 4.

(7m). Camping & Caravanning Club Site – Barns Ness, Barns Ness, Dunbar, East Lothian EH42 1QP. *01368 863536.* www.campingandcaravanningclub.co.uk. Owner: Camping & Caravanning Club. Leaving Dunbar E on A1, turn L SP Barns Ness go past cement works and follow signs to site which lies along a stretch of Berwickshire coast. Close to historic town of Dunbar. Beautiful views of the coastline and sea from all pitches. All units accepted. Non-members welcome. Plenty of room for dog walking and childrens ball games. Nearby attractions inlcude 13th century Hailes Castle. Deals for families and backpackers. Open March-Oct.

(4m). Thurston Manor Holiday Home Park, Innerwick, Dunbar, East Lothian EH42 1SA. *01368 840643.* www.thurstonmanor.co.uk. Owner: Dunham Leisure Ltd. S of Dunbar, SP from A1. Close to sea and sandy beaches. Licensed club with entertainment. Family room. Heated indoor pool, fitness centre with sauna, steam room, solarium, spa and gymnasium. Bar meals and takeaway. Private trout lake. Sea fishing and golf in 4m. Open March 1-Jan 8.

LONGNIDDRY

Seton Sands Holiday Village, Longniddry, East Lothian EH32 0QF. *01875 813333.* www.setonsands-park.

130 MOTOR CARAVAN & CAMPING PARKS 2009

SCOTLAND

co.uk. Owner: Bourne Leisure Ltd. Take A1 to A198 slip road. Turn on to B6371 for Cockenzie then R on to B1348. Park is 1m along on R, SP from A1 N and S. Heated indoor swimming pool. Club. Family entertainment. Direct beach access. Mini market. Free kid's clubs. Amusements, pool tables. Play area. Thistle Award. David Bellamy Silver Conservation Award. Open March-end Oct.

MUSSELBURGH

(1.5m). Drum Mohr Caravan Park, Levenhall, Musselburgh, East Lothian EH21 8JS. 01316 656867. www.drummohr.org. Owner: Mr W Melville & AM Brodie. 1.5m E of Musselburgh between B1348 and B1361. 108 mixed pitches. Secluded and well landscaped touring park on edge of beautiful countryside yet only 20mins from Edinburgh to which there is an excellent bus. Open March 1-Oct 31.

NORTH BERWICK

(0.5m). Tantallon Caravan & Camping Park, Tantallon Road, North Berwick, East Lothian EH39 5NJ. 01620 893348. www.meadowhead.co.uk. Owner: Meadowhead Ltd. On the A198 immediately E of North Berwick. Play area, 9 hole putting green. Internet access available on the park. 4 wigwams available for hire. Adjacent to Glen Golf Course. Café/restaurant and takeaway meals available nearby. Holiday homes for the disabled. Close to bus stop. Thistle Award. Open March-Jan, March-Oct for tourers.

(2.5m). Yellowcraig Caravan Club Site, Dirlieton, North Berwick, East Lothian EH39 5DS. 01620 850217. www.caravanclub.co.uk. Owner: The Caravan Club. See website for directions. This is an attractive site with grass covered sandy dunes, shrubs and dog roses creating private pitching areas. Non-members welcome. No tents. Advance booking essential BH and mid-July to mid Aug. Some hardstandings. Toilet blocks with privacy cubicles and laundry facilities. Baby/toddler washroom. MV service point. Play area. Golf nearby. Ideal for families. Veg prep area, gas, dog walk nearby. Quiet and peaceful off peak. Beach in 5m. Open March 27-Nov 2.

LOTHIAN (WEST)
LINLITHGOW

(3m). Beecraigs Caravan & Camping Site, Beecraigs Country Park, The Park Centre, Linlithgow, West Lothian EH49 6PL. 01506 844516. www.beecraigs.com. Owner: West Lothian Council. M9, J3 or J4, follow tourist signs for Beecraigs Country Park from Linlithgow. Set in Beecraigs Country Park, with miles of woodland walks, outdoor pursuit activities, fly-fishing, restaurant and visitor centre. Local shops available in Linlithgow. Good for exploring Central Scotland.

(1m). Loch House Caravan Park, Loch House Farm, Linlithgow, West Lothian EH49 7RG. 01506 848283. From Linlithgow take A706 towards Bo'ness, take first L after motorway bridge. Open April-Oct.

MORAY
ABERLOUR

(1m). Aberlour Gardens Caravan & Camping Park, Aberlour, Moray AB38 9LD. 01340 871586. www.aberlourgardens.co.uk. Owner: Simon & Denice Blades. Midway between Aberlour and Craigellachie off A95. Vehicles over 10'6" high use A941. Quiet sheltered site close to River Spey and Speyside Way on the Malt Whisky Trail. Shop, laundry and dishwashing facilities. 2 luxury centrally heated holiday homes for hire Easter-Oct and disabled/family room comprising shower, toilet, sink, baby changing table. Pets welcome. Small children's play area. Seasonal pitches available. David Bellamy Gold Conservation Award. Open end March-Dec.

(5m). Camping & Caravanning Club Site – Speyside, Archiestown, Aberlour, Moray AB38 9SL. 01340 810414. www.campingandcaravanningclub.co.uk. Owner: Camping & Caravanning Club. On A941 from Elgin towards Craigellachie, turn R on to B9102 for about 3m to site. Walk along the Speyside Way or visit one of the many seaside villages. Salmon and whiskey are the specialities of this area. All units accepted. Non-members welcome. In 7 acres. The surrounding area has historic castles, National Trust properties and gardens to visit. Deals for families and backpackers. Open April-Oct.

BUCKIE

(0.25m). Findochty Caravan Park, Jubilee Terrace, Findochty, Buckie, Moray AB56 4QA. 01542 835303. www.findochtycaravanpark.co.uk. Owner: Moira & Dennis Main. From Buckie 3m E on A942 on west edge of the village by the harbour. Golf, fishing, lawn bowling, pub/restaurant and shops nearby. Situated next to rocky beaches and historic harbour. Open March 1-Oct 31.

(1.5m). Strathlene Caravan Site, Strathlene, Buckie, Moray. 01542 834851. Owner: Kris Fraser. E of town centre on A942. Private caravan site situated by sea on Eastern outskirts of Buckie Open Easter-Oct.

ELGIN

(5m). North Alves Caravan Park, Alves, Elgin, Moray IV30 3XD. 01343 850223. Off A96.Turn N to site at Alves village by the school. Forres 6m, Elgin 6m. North Alves is a well kept park with acres of grassland, 1m from beach. Several golf courses nearby. Open April 1-Oct 31.

(0.5m). Riverside Caravan Park, West Road, Elgin, Moray IV30 8UN. 01343 542813. riversideparks@btconnect.com. Owner: John & Christine Mitchell. On A96 Aberdeen to Inverness road on western outskirts of Elgin. Open April 1-Oct 31.

(7m). Station Caravan Park, West Beach, Hopeman, Elgin, Moray IV30 5RU. 01343 830880. www.stationcaravanpark.co.uk. Owner: David & Angie Steer. On NE coast 7m from Elgin, 10m from Forres follow coast road from Elgin. Launderette and pay phone. 5 golf courses in 10mins driving distance. Shops & doctors' surgery in village, sea and river fishing nearby. Castle & whisky trails close by. Glorious views over Moray Firth. Pubs and take away food in village. Open April-Oct.

FORRES

(3.5m). Old Mill Caravan Park, Brodie, Forres, Moray IV36 2TD. 01309 641244. www.theoldmillbrodie.com/oldmillcaravanpark.htm. Owner: Mr & Mrs Jamieson. On A96 Forres to Nairn. Open April 1-Oct 31.

LOSSIEMOUTH

(1m). Silver Sands Leisure Park, Covesea, West Beach, Lossiemouth, Moray IV31 6SP. 01343 813262. www.travel.to/silversands. Owner: Green Parcs Ltd. On B9040. Lossiemouth to Hopeman road, Elgin 6m. On the Moray Firth with miles of unspoilt beaches. Ideal location to explore whisky distillers, castle and golf course. Excellent facilities for all the family. Open from Feb 15-Jan 15.

SCOTLAND

ORKNEY

KIRKWALL

(0.25m). Pickaquoy Caravan and Camping Park, The Pickaquoy Centre, Muddisdale Road, Kirkwall, Orkney KW15 1LR. *01856 879900.* www.pickaquoy.co.uk. Owner: The Pickaquoy Centre Trust. Turn R off A965 when approaching Kirkwall and follow signs. Situated on the Pickaquoy Centre Campus, licensed for 50 pitches of which 30 have electric hook-up facilities. Utility block includes male and female toilets and showers. Open mid-May to mid-Sept.

STROMNESS

Point of Ness Camping & Caravan Site, Point of Ness, Stromness, Orkney KW16 3DL. *01856 873535.* recreation@orkney.gov.uk. Owner: Orkney Islands Council. Follow signs on leaving ferry. Grass site next to shore. Open May-Sept.

PERTHSHIRE

KILLIN

(1m). Clachan Caravan Club Site, c/o Maragowan Caravan Club Site, Aberfeldy Road, Killin, Perthshire FK21 8TN. *01567 820245.* www.caravanclub.co.uk. Owner: The Caravan Club. See website for directions. Caravan Club members only. No tents. This site is a find, with its several open pitching areas tucked quietly away in woodland ablaze with wild flowers, and with an amazing range of bird life. Own sanitation required. MV service point. Fishing, golf and NCN route nearby. Dog walk on site. Good area for walking. Quiet and peaceful off-peak. Open March-Oct.

(4m). Cruachan Caravan & Camping Park, Killin, Perthshire FK21 8TY. *01567 820302.* www.cruachanfarm.co.uk. Owner: JP & M Campbell. On A827 Killin to Aberfeldy. Quiet, family run park adjacent to farm. Highland cattle. Hill and woodland walks, riding, golf, salmon and trout fishing on Loch Tay. Coffee shop, play area, gas and payphone. Licensed restaurant/takeway meals/packed lunches. Ideal touring centre. Open mid March-Oct 31.

(2.5m). High Creagan Caravan Site, Killin, Perthshire FK21 8TX. *01567 820449.* Owner: Mr A Kennedy. On the A827 Aberfeldy to Killin road. Well SP. Ideal for fishing, birdwatching or to relax. Small family run site, peaceful, elevated with panoramic view of Loch Tay and surrounding countryside. In easy reach of the village of Killin and the famous Dochart Falls. Open March 20-Oct 24.

(0.25m). Maragowan Caravan Club Site, Aberfeldy Road, Killin, Perthshire FK21 8TN. *01567 820245.* www.caravanclub.co.uk. Owner: The Caravan Club. See website for directions. The site is an ideal family holiday base, set on one bank of the river Lochay, and in walking distance of the shops and restaurants of Killin. Hardstandings. MV waste. Toilet block and laundry. Gas. Veg prep. Playframe. Salmon and trout fishing. Non-members welcome. No tents. Advance booking essential BH and June-Aug and advised for Sept. Ideal for families. Privacy cubicles. Dog walk nearby. Quiet and peaceful off peak. Good area for walking, golf and NCN cycle route in 5m, water sports nearby. Open March-Nov.

PERTHSHIRE & KINROSS

AUCHTERARDER

(1m). Auchterarder Caravan & Chalet Park, Nethercoul, Auchterarder, Perthshire & Kinross PH3 1ET. *01764 663119.* www.prestonpark.co.uk. Owner: Stuart & Susie Robertson. Take B8062 (to Dunning). From A824 (between Auchterarder and Aberthven) 1.5m from A9-Stirling/Perth. Ideal for couples and the active retired in the heart of Perthshire's. Golfing country. Lots of wildlife obeservation opportunities and good off-site dog walking facilities. Only 1m from the village of Auchterarder. Chalet for hire.

BLAIRGOWRIE

(9m). Ballintuim Caravan Park, Ballintuim, Blairgowrie, Perthshire & Kinross PH10 7NH. *01250 886276.* www.ballintuimpark.co.uk. Owner: Phil & Karen Clark. A93 to Bridge of Cally then A924 mideay between Bridge of Cally and Kirkmichael. Excellent facilities. Open from 1 March-31 Oct.

(1m). Blairgowrie Holiday Park, Rattray, Blairgowrie, Perthshire & Kinross PH10 7AL. *01250 876566.* www.holiday-parks.co.uk. Owner: Colin & Margaret Wood. Off A93. 1m N of Blairgowrie town centre. Follow international signs. Friendly, family-run park. Excellent heated facilities. Launderette. Adventure playground. Putting green. Pine lodges and caravans for hire and for sale for holidays all year round. Fishing, swimming pool locally. Shops and restaurants in 1m. 6 golf courses in 5m. David Bellamy Gold Conservation Award.

(5m). Corriefodly Holiday Park, Bridge of Cally, Blairgowrie, Perthshire & Kinross PH10 7JG. *01250 876666.* www.holiday-parks.co.uk. Owner: Colin & Margaret Wood. Follow A93, 6m N of Blairgowrie to Bridge of Cally. Turn L to Pitlochry road, at bridge and PO. Corriefodly is about 150yd on L. Rural riverside park set in picturesque valley. Bar, function room and games room. Fishing. Caravan holiday homes for hire and for sale. Riverside and hill walking. Cycling, golf and horse-riding nearby. 20m from Perth & Dundee. David Bellamy Gold Conservation Award.

YOUR TOP 101 SITES 2009

(0.8m). Five Roads Caravan Park, Alyth, Blairgowrie, Perthshire & Kinross PH11 8NB. *01828 632255.* www.fiveroads-caravan-park.co.uk. Owner: Steven Ewart. From Blairgowrie take A926. After 4.5m turn L into site at Blackbird Inn, outside Alyth, an attractive little country town. Park is a small, friendly family run site, just lying on the outskirts of Alyth. There is an inn adjacent to the park and the local shops are 0.5m away. 3 golf courses, 2 driving ranges in 1m. Local walks, fishing, pony treking, bird watching and winter sports at Glenshee. PO, doctor, etc all in 0.5m from park.

(12m). Nether Craig Caravan Park, Alyth, Blairgowrie, Perthshire & Kinross PH11 8HN. *01575 560204.* www.nethercraigcaravanpark.co.uk. Owner: Peter and Pat Channon. At the roundabout S of Alyth, join B954 SP Glenisla, follow caravan signs for 4m. Peaceful, family-run touring park suitable for all country pursuits and near much of historic interest. David Bellamy Gold Conservation Award. Open March 15-Oct 31.

COMRIE

(4m). West Lodge Caravan Park, Comrie, Perthshire & Kinross PH6 2LS. *01764 670354.* www.westlodgecaravanpark.co.uk. Owner: Mr PJ, EL & PP Gill. On A85 Crieff to Comrie. W of Crieff. Quiet, sheltered, family run park with free showers, electricity and good facilities. 10mins walk from village. Good touring centre. Calor Gas and Camping Gaz for sale. Public telephone. Pre book high season. Static vans for hire. Tents, motorhomes and tourers welcome. Winter storage available. Good area for fishing, golf, walking, bowls. Watersports at Loch Earn. Open Easter-Halloween.

132 MOTOR CARAVAN & CAMPING PARKS 2009

SCOTLAND

KINLOCH RANNOCH

■ (3.75m). **Kilvrecht Campsite, Loch Rannoch, Kinloch Rannoch, Perthshire & Kinross PH8 0JR.** *01350 727284.* hamish.murray@forestry.gsi.gov.uk. Owner: Forest Enterprise. Off B846 3.5m W of Kinnloch Rannoch on south bank of Loch Rannach. Woodland setting. Fishing nearby. Woodland walks. Food shop, gas, bar/pub, restaurant 3m. Open Easter-Oct.

PITLOCHRY

(7m). **Blair Castle Caravan Park, Blair Atholl, Pitlochry, Perthshire & Kinross PH18 5SR.** *01796 481263.* www.blaircastlecaravanpark.co.uk. Owner: Blair Castle Estate Ltd. Turn off A9, 6m N of Pitlochry following signs to Blair Atholl (1m). Internet gallery, putting green, extensive recreation areas with adventure playgrounds. Grounds of Blair Castle. Fishing, golf, bowling and pony-trekking nearby. David Bellamy Bronze Conservation Award. Open March 1-Nov 30.

(2m). **Faskally Home Farm, Pitlochry, Perthshire & Kinross PH16 5LA.** *01796 472007.* www.faskally.co.uk. Owner: Mr EMR Hay. On A9 (B8019 Killiecrankie) Perth to Inverness. Bar and restaurant. Indoor heated leisure pool. Sauna, steam room and spa bath. Open March 15-Oct 31.

(17m). **Glengoulandie Country Park, Foss, Pitlochry, Perthshire & Kinross PH16 5NL.** *01887 830495.* www.glengoulandie.co.uk. Owner: Sandy McAdam & Craig McAdam. B846 road, 8m from Aberfeldy toward Kinloch Rannoch, on L. A deer park with Highland Cattle. A fishing lake stocked with brown trout, a coffee shop with small range of gifts and a kids play area. Open Easter-mid Oct.

(5m). **The River Tilt Park, Blair Atholl, Pitlochry, Perthshire & Kinross PH18 5TE.** *01796 481467.* www.rivertilt.co.uk. Owner: Stuart & Marise Richardson. Take B8079 off A9, SP to Blair Atholl. On banks of river Tilt, next to golf course and 100yd from town and Blair Castle. Refurbished heated shower block. Free showers. Gas and Gaz. Calor Best Park Scotland. New indoor heated pool. Sauna. Solarium. Steam room, gym and spa pool. Restaurant. David Bellamy Conversation Award. GS. Open March-Nov (touring), all year (holiday).

(13m). **Tummel Valley Holiday Park, Tummel Bridge, Pitlochry, Perthshire & Kinross PH16 5SA.** *01882 634221.* www.parkdeanholidays.co.uk. Owner: Parkdean Holidays Plc. A9 to Pitlochry B8019 to Tummel Bridge. Indoor pool and toddler's splash pool, solarium and sauna. Kids' club and adventure play area, multi-sports court and amusement. Bar, food, and live family entertainment. Open Feb-Jan.

TAYSIDE

Camping & Caravanning Club Site – Scone, Scone Palace, Scone, Tayside, Perthshire & Kinross PH2 6BB. *01738 552323.* www.campingandcaravanningclub.co.uk. Owner: Camping & Caravanning Club. Follow signs for Scone Palace. Once through Perth continue for 2m and follow signs for racecourse. Site is at R of racecourse car park. Ideally situated for touring Perthshire and central Scotland. All units accepted. Non-members welcome. Trout and salmon fishing is available from the nearby river Tay. There is some beautiful countryside surrounding the site. Deals for families and backpackers. David Bellamy Gold Conservation Award. Open March-Oct.

ROSS-SHIRE
DUNDONNELL

(8m). **Badrallach D, B&B, Bothy, Cottage & Campsite, Little Loch Broom, Croft 9, Badrallach, Dundonnell, Ross-shire IV23 2QP.** *01854 633281.* michael.stott2@virgin.net. www.badrallach.com. Owner: Mick & Ali Stott. 7m along the winding single track road off the A832. 1m E of the Dundonnell Hotel. A lochshore site in a remote highland setting. Bikes, boats, kites, biokarts, kayaks to hire or relax and watch the wild life: otters, easles, red deer, etc.

SHETLAND ISLANDS
LERWICK

(1.5m). **Clickimin Caravan & Camp Site, Clickimin Leisure Complex, Lochside, Lerwick, Shetland Islands ZE1 0PJ.** *01595 741000.* www.srt.org.uk. Owner: Shetland Recreational Trust. From ferry terminal follow signs to Lerwick town centre, then at first roundabout follow signs to Clickimin Leisure complex. Recently refurbished site on outskirts of Lerwick. Exellent location for touring islands. Site is situated next to modern leisure complex with swimming pool, leisure waters, main hall, bowls hall and squash courts. Open May 1-Sept 30.

(18m). **Lerwick Camp Site, Lerwick, Shetland Islands ZE2 9HX.** *01950 422207.* Situated on A970, S of Lerwick, 7m N of Sumburgh Airport SP. Warden: J G Jamieson.

STIRLING
ABERFOYLE

(3m). **Trossachs Holiday Park, Aberfoyle, Stirling FK8 3SA.** *01877 382614.* www.trossachsholidays.co.uk. Owner: John Wrigley & Tracy McNelis. S of Aberfoyle on A81. 40 acre landscaped park with glorious oak and bluebell wood. Shop, games/TV Lounge, play area, enclosed dog walk, use of local leisure club, mountain bikes for hire and sale, fishing 1m, golf 2m. David Bellamy Gold Conservation Award. Open March 1-Oct 31.

BLAIRLOGIE

Witches Craig Caravan & Camping Park, Witches Craig, Blairlogie, Stirling FK9 5PX. *01786 474947.* www.witchescraig.co.uk. Owner: A & V Stephen. On A91, 3m E of Stirling. Graded excellent, Best Park in Scotland finalist. National Loo of the Year awards. Peacefully situated below picturesque Ochil Hills, ideal place to unwind but also a great base for travelling. Superb modern facilities. Also children's play park. Milk, newspapers and rolls sold daily. David Bellamy Gold Conservation Award. Open April 1-Oct 31.

KILVRECHT CAMPSITE KINLOCH RANNOCH, PERTHSHIRE

Quiet and secluded site situated 3.5 miles west of Kinloch Rannoch on the south side of the loch. Woodland walks in the Black Wood of Rannoch nearby. Brown trout fishing and watersports available on Loch Rannoch. 60 touring pitches and 30 camping pitches available. Open Easter to October. Well behaved dogs welcome!

For further information contact: **Forest Enterprise, Inverpark, Dunkeld, Perthshire PH8 0JR**
Telephone: 01350 727384 e-mail: hamish.murray@forestry.gsi.gov.uk

SCOTLAND

CALLANDER

(12m). Balquhidder Braes Caravan & Camping Park, Balquhidder Station, Lochearnhead, Callander, Stirling FK19 8NX. 01567 830293. rwww. balquhidderbraes.co.uk. Owner: Mr & Mrs R Eastland. 1.5 from Lochearnhead take A84 Stirling road, on L from Strathyre towards Lochearnhead 2m. Beautiful scenery. Excellent restaurant beside site. Families welcome. In first National Park in Scotland. Ideal base. Adjacent to route 7 cycleway and Rob Roy Way. Fishing & watersports 1m David Bellamy Silver Conservation Award. Open March 18-Oct 28.

(1m). Keltie Bridge Caravan Park, Callander, Stirling FK17 8LQ. 01327 330606. stay@keltiebridge.co.uk. Owner: Cambusmore Estate. On A84 between Doune and Callander. Quiet riverside location, close to Callander in the scenic trossachs area. Top quality shower block. Golf, sports centre 1m. Open April 1-Oct 31.

FINTRY

(1.5m). Balgair Castle Caravan Park, Overglinns, Fintry, Stirling G63 0LP. 01360 860283. www.balgaircastle.com. Owner: Jason Hartley. Limited facilities for the disabled. Table tennis. Riverside country park. Bar, restaurant, children's play area. Outdoor swimming pool. GS. Open March-Nov.

GARTMORE

(1.5m). Cobleland Caravan & Camping Site, Forest Holidays, Station Road, Gartmore, Stirling FK8 3RR. 01877 382392. www.forestholidays.co.uk. Owner: Forest Holidays. Off A81 Glasgow to Aberfoyle. Set on the banks of the River Forth amist majestic oad trees, Cobeland sits in the heart of the Trossachs. Bookings and brochures: 0834 1308284. Open March-Jan.

ROWARDENNAN

(3m). Cashel Caravan & Camping Site, Forest Holidays, Rowardennan, Stirling G63 0AW. 01360 870234. www.forestholidays.co.uk. Owner: Forest Holidays. Off B837 Drymen-Rowardennan road 3m N of Balmaha. On the shores of Loch Lomond, Cashel is ideal for boating, cycling and walking. The West Highland Way passes the site entrance. No generators on site. Bookings and brochures: 0845 1308224. Open March-Jan.

THORNHILL

(0.25m). Mains Farm, Kippen Road, Thornhill, Stirling FK8 3QB. 01786 850605. gsteedman@lineone.net. Owner: Mr J Steedman. From M9 J10 take A84 for 6m. Then A873 for 3m. In Thornhill village L on to B822, site on R. Five acres with scenic views, ideal touring centre for Stirling, Loch Lomond and Trossachs. Children's play area. Shops, PO, doctor in 0.25m. Golf, tennis, swimming pool, cinema, shopping centre, all in 5-7m. 8 Heated wooden wigwams for hire. Open April 1-Oct 31.

WESTERN ISLES

Isle of Harris

(5m). Laig House & Minch View Caravan Site, 10 Drimshadder, Isle of Harris, Highlands HS3 3DX. 01859 511207. Owner: Ms Catherine Macdonald. 4.5m SE of Tarbert on coast. Turn off A859 down the Golden Road to Drimshadder. Quiet, secluded between loch and sea. Near village shops. Free fishing. Centrally located for touring the isles. Walking and hill climbing. Mobile shop calls weekly. PO in village. Open May-Oct.

ISLE OF LEWIS

Eilean Fraoich Camping Site, North Shawbost, Isle of Lewis, Highlands HS2 9BQ. 01851 710504. eileanfraoich@btinternet.com. 19m from Stornoway. Open May-Oct.

Laxdale Holiday Park, 6 Laxdale Lane, Stornoway, Isle of Lewis, Highlands HS2 0DR. 01851 703234/706966. www.laxdaleholidaypark.com. Owner: Gordon Macleod. From Stornoway ferry terminal take A857 for 1.5m, turn L just before Laxdale river, park is 100yd on L. Quiet, family run park in peaceful tree lined surroundings. Wi-fi available. All modern facilities including bunkhouse. Ideal base for touring the Isles.

ANGLESEY

AMLWCH

(2m). Plas Eilian Caravan Park, Llaneilian, Amlwch, Anglesey LL68 9LS. 01407 830323. Owner: Mr T A Owen. A5025 from Menai to Benllech & Amlwch. Bypass Penysarn. Turn R at filling station. Plas Eilian is next to the church. Site near sea with lovely walks through the farm along the cliffs. Open April-Oct.

(1.5m). Point Lynas Caravan Park, Llaneilian, Amlwch, Anglesey LL68 9LT. 01407 831130. www.pointlynas.com. Owner: Mr P&M Hoyland. From Anglesey Mowers on A5025, 1.5m in seaward direction, 200yd from Porth Eilian cove. Quiet park overlooking the sea by Point Lynas, fishing, walking, swimming. Modern facilites block with launderette, showers etc. Shops 1.5m. Golf course 3m. Open March 1-Oct 31.

(5m). Tyddyn Isaf Caravan Park, Lligwy Bay, Dulas, Amlwch, Anglesey LL70 9PQ. 01248 410203. www.tyddynisaf.demon.co.uk. Owner: Mr & Mrs Hunt. Off A5025 through Benllech up to Brynrefail village, turn R at phone box towards Lligwy beach. Private path to beach. 'Loo of the Year' winner for our superb facilities. Calor Gas 'Finalist' Best Touring Parks in Wales 2003. David Bellamy Gold Conservation Award. Open March 1-Oct 31.

Tyn Rhos Farm, Penysarn, Amlwch, Anglesey LL69 9YR. 01407 830574. llwyfo@aol.co.uk. Owner: HP Hughes. Dogs allowed on leads. Bookings advisable. 4-berth caravan to let. Takeaway, café/restaurant nearby. Open Easter-Oct.

BEAUMARIS

(1.5m). Kingsbridge Caravan Park, Llanfaes, Beaumaris, Anglesey LL58 8LR. 01248 490636/0777484. www.kingsbridgecaravanpark.co.uk. Owner: Mr & Mrs AM Bate. Drive through Beaumaris, past castle, turn third L after 1.5m at first crossroads. A quiet family park in a rural location, close to beaches, golf, fishing, walking. 1.5m from picturesque town of Beaumaris. David Bellamy Gold Conservation Award. Open March 1-Oct 31.

BENLLECH

(1.5m). Ad Astra Caravan Park, Llangefni Road, Brynteg, Benllech, Anglesey LL78 7JH. 01248 853283. www.adastracaravanpark.co.uk. Owner: Mrs I Iddon & Mr B Iddon. Benllech 1.5m, from Benllech take B5108 to California Hotel, turn L park 0.25m on R. Small quiet rural park in open countryside. First class facilities. 10mins walk to pub/restaurant. 0.5m to golf course. 1.5m to shops and all services. Sea and coarse fishing 1.5m. Open March 1-Oct 31.

(0.5m). Bodafon Caravan & Camping Site, Benllech Bay, Amlwch Road, Benllech, Anglesey LL 74 8RU. 01248 852417. www.bodafonpark.co.uk. Owner: Mr & Mrs RGRoberts. Through the village of Benllech on A5025 0.5m on L. Big yellow house. In 0.5m of the village, 1m from the beach, convenient for the local area. Part of a group comprising of three parks. Open

WALES

See page 5 for key to symbols and abbreviations

March 1-Oct 31.

Golden Sunset Holiday, Beach Road, Benllech Bay, Benllech, Anglesey LL74 8SW. 01248 852345. Owner: Mr RJ Hewitt. Site entrance at Benllech Bay off A5025 from Bangor towards Amlwch. At the crossroads in Benllech. Turn R and the park is immediately on the L. Centre of village for shops, PO, doctors, tennis courts, bowls, golf. Elevated cliff side, well drained site with superb views over the bay. Open April-Oct.

Nant Newydd Park, Brynteg, Benllech, Anglesey LL78 7JH. 01248 852266. www.nantnewydd.co.uk. Owner: Mr & Mrs BW Jones. 3m SW. B5108 off A5025 at Benllech. At crossroads after 2m turn L. Site is 1m on R. Hardstanding with hook-up point, mains water and waste disposal. Quiet countryside 3m from coast. Dogs allowed. Fees on application.

(2m). Penparc Caravan Site, Brynteg, Benllech, Anglesey LL78 7JG. 01248 852500. Owner: Mr P Charles. On junction B5110 and B5108, Isle of Anglesey. Unlimited camping. Fishing and golf course nearby. Open March 1-Oct 31.

(2m). Penrhos Caravan Club Site, Brynteg, Benllech, Anglesey LL78 7JH. 01248 852617. www.caravanclub.co.uk. Owner: The Caravan Club. See website for directions. 5mins drive to safe, sandy beach. Close to a farm trail, bird sanctuary and sea zoo. Non-members welcome. No tents. Golf course in 5m. Play area & play equipment. Some hardstandings, part sloping. Toilet block with privacy cubicles. Laundry, gas and gaz, baby and toddler washroom. MV service point, veg prep area. Dog walk nearby. Watersports, good walking NCN cycle route all nearby. Ideal for families. Quiet and peaceful off peak. Open March-Oct.

(0.5m). Plas Uchaf Caravan & Camping Park, Benllech Bay, Benllech, Anglesey LL74 8NU. 01248 763012. Owner: Evans Partnership. Off A5025 SP on B5108. 0.5m from Benllech, SP by fire station. Well sheltered and level park in 1m of beach. Disabled friendly. Hot showers, hairdryers, and dishwashing. Freezers. Play area. Patio seating and tables. Dog walk. Tarmacadam roads with street lights. Tradesmen call. Open March-Oct.

BRYNGWRAN

Tyn Llidiart Camping Site, Tyn Trewan, Bryngwran, Anglesey LL65 3SW. 01407 810678. 106110.521@compuserve.com. Owner: Miss R Hobday. 3m E Rhosneigr A5, sea 3m. Turn L at Bryngwran PO on u/c road for 1m. Turn R at 2nd crossroads at white house. Take R fork, site at bottom of lane on L.

BRYNSIENCYN

(0.5m). Fron Caravan and Camping Park, Brynsiencyn, Anglesey LL61 6TX. 01248 430310. www.froncaravanpark.co.uk. Owner: Mr G&E&M Geldard. On A4080. 6.5m SW of Menai Bridge. Cross Britannia Bridge then first slip road marked Llanfairpwllgwyn, then L on to A4080 to Brynsiencyn. Site is 0.5m beyond village on R. Laundry room. Public telephone. Gas. Hot showers. Heated outdoor swimming pool with dome cover. Adventure playground. Open Easter/April 1-Sept 30.

BRYNTEG

(0.25m). Garnedd Touring Site, Lon Bryn Mair, Brynteg, Anglesey LL78 8QA. 01248 853240. www.garnedd.com. Owner: Mrs S Kirk & Mr M McCann. Take A5025 after Britannia bridge. Go through Pentraeath, turn L on to unclassified road at layby, SP Llanbedrgoch. In 2m turn L on to B5108, 1st L. Site on R in 0.5m at orange signs. Dishwashing and laundry facilities. Winter storage available. Open March 1-Oct.

DULAS

(4m). Melin Rhos Caravan & Camping Site, Lligwy Bay, Dulas, Anglesey LL70 9HQ. 01248 852417. www.bodafonpark.co.uk. Owner: R&S Roberts. Off A5025 Bangor to Amlwch. Turn L at Moelfre roundabout, down hill, first R. Site is at bottom of hill, before bridge. 5m from Benllech. 2m from Moelfre. Close to lovely beach and good walks. 2m from nearest village. Golf course 5m. Medium size town 13m. Open March 1-Oct 31.

HOLYHEAD

(6m). Bodowyr Caravan Park, Bodedern, Holyhead, Anglesey LL65 3SS. 01407 741171. www.bodowyrcaravanpark.co.uk. Owner: CE & MP Hughes. Take the A55 towards Holyhead, turn off J4 direction Bodedern. Follow international camping signs, park on L after 0.5m. Family run touring site in rural countryside. Well located for beaches and ferries to Ireland. Excellent facilities and new licensed restaurant with home cooking. Advance booking advisable. Open March 1-Oct 31.

(9m). Penrhyn Bay Caravan Site, Penrhyn Farm, Llanfwrog, Holyhead, Anglesey LL65 4YG. 01407 730496. www.penrhynbay.com. Owner: E T & O Williams. A55 to Anglesey, Exit 3. A5025 through Llanfachraeth then 1st L, SP Penrhyn. Through farm to caravan park. Coastal park near a sandy beach. Electricity, water and grey waste. Indoor heated swimming pool. Tennis court. Showers. Launderette. Play area. Open Easter-End Oct.

(10m). Sandy Beach Caravan Site, Llanfwrog, Holyhead, Anglesey LL65 4YH. 01407 730302. www.sandybeach.co.uk. A5025 after Llanfacraeth turn L and follow signs for Sandy Beach/Penrhyn. Set in a splendid location adjoining safe, sandy beach. Picturesque views and delightful walks. Ideal for water sports. Licensed café, showers and laundry. Open April-Oct.

(1m). Valley of the Rocks Caravan & Camping Park, Porthdafarch Road, Treaddur Bay, Holyhead, Anglesey LL65 2LP. 01407 765787. Owner: Anglesey Caravan Parks Ltd. Follow A55 across Anglesey to where the road ends at roundabout. Take first L at roundabout then first R between The Foresters and The Angel pubs. 1m to SP for Valley of the Rocks caravan park. Turn L into site then fork R. Reception is on the L at site shop. Licensed club. 10mins walk from beach. Open March-Oct.

ISLE OF ANGLESEY

(1.5m). St Davids Park, Red Wharf Bay, Isle of Anglesey, Anglesey LL75 8RJ. 01248 852341. www.stdavidspark.com. Owner: Mr RS & Mrs LH Davies. Follow A55 and after crossing the Britannia Bridge on to the island take the B5025 and follow for 8m until you see a sign for St David's Park and Red Wharf Bay on your R about 1m after passing through the town of Pentraeth. Private beach, boat park and slipway, tavern, children's play area. Open March-Oct.

(1m). Ty Newydd Leisure Park, Brynteg Road, Llanbedrgoch, Isle of Anglesey, Anglesey LL76 8TZ. 01248 450677. www.tynewydd.com. Owner: Mike & Cathi Monger. Off A5025 Isle of Anglesey. Pass through Pentraeth Village turn L after first lay by, park 1m on R. Club. Swimming pool. Restaurant. Golf course 10m. Fishing 1m. Open March 1-Oct 31.

www.motorcaravanmagazine.co.uk MOTOR CARAVAN & CAMPING PARKS 2009 **135**

WALES

Tyn Rhos Camping Site, Ravenspoint Road, Trearddur Bay, Isle of Anglesey, Anglesey LL65 2AX. *01407 860369.* Owner: Mr D W Williams. 3m from Holyhead. A55 to J3 for Valley A5. L at lights B4545 to Trearddur Bay. L on to Ravenspoint road. About 1m to shared entrance, take L branch. Family run rural site with modern facilities, in minutes of beautiful seaside resort. Coastal walks, bird watching and climbing. Watersports, from fishing to diving, local golf course and horseriding. Ferries to Ireland 3m. Much local history and attractions for all tastes. Open March 1 – Oct 31.

LLIGWY BAY

Creigiau Camping & Touring Site, Dulas, Lligwy Bay, Anglesey. *01248 410897.* Owner: Mr & Mrs RP Williams. On A5025, 1.25m N of Moelfre roundabout. Sheltered touring site. Shops in 1.5m.

MARIANGLAS

Cae Mawr Caravan Club Site, Llangefni Road, Marianglas, Anglesey LL73 8NY. *01248 853737.* www.caravanclub.co.uk. Owner: The Caravan Club. See website for directions. 2m from Benllech. Chemical toilet disposal point. No toilet block. Sea fishing and boating. Safe, sandy beaches. Non-members welcome. No tents. Golf course in 5m. MV waste point, gas, dog walk. Open March-Oct.

(2m). Home Farm Caravan Park, Marianglas, Anglesey LL73 8PH. *01248 410614.* www.homefarm-anglesey.co.uk. Owner: Mr & Mrs GP Jones. On A5025. Amlwch road keep L at roundabout, 1m beyond Benllech, park is 300yd on L after church. Toilets, showers, launderette, indoor playroom, sport games field, tennis court on site. Golf course, fishing 2m. Cinema 13m. David Bellamy Gold Conservation Award. Open April-Oct.

NEWBOROUGH

(0.5m). Awelfryn Caravan Site, Newborough, Anglesey LL61 6SG. *01248 440230.* awelfryncp@aol.com. Owner: Mrs H Dawson. On A4080 about 10m SW of Menai Bridge and 20m from Holyhead. Near Llanddwyn Isle and Newborough Warren (noted beauty spots). Fees on application. SAE. Open March 1- Oct 31.

PENTRAETH

(0.75m). Rhos Caravan Park, Rhos Farm, Pentraeth, Anglesey LL75 8DZ. *01248 450214.* www.rhoscaravanpark.co.uk. Owner: Mr A P Owen. On A5025 on the L after Bull Hotel. N of Pentraeth. Children's play area. Flat sheltered fields (grass & hedges). 10mins walk to Red Wharf Bay. Golf course nearby 2.5m. AA 3 pennants. Open March 15- Oct 10.

RHOSNEIGR

(0.5m). Bodfan Farm, Bodfan, Rhosneigr, Anglesey LL64 5XA. *01407 810706.* www.bodfanfarm.co.uk. Owner: A Pritchard. A55 to A4080, next to school in Rhosneigr. Quiet, family site near lake and sea. Electrical hookups must be prebooked. Showers, shaving points and dryers. 0.5m to shops, PO, pub. Golf course, riding, tennis, bowling green, watersports in village. Open Easter-Sept.

(0.25m). Shore Side Caravan Park, Crigyll View, Station Road, Rhosneigr, Anglesey LL64 5QX. *01407 810279.* www.shoresidecamping.co.uk. Owner: Mr A J Carnall. L off A55 junctions on to the A4080 Rhosneigr road, opposite Anglesey golf club. Children welcome. Panoramic views of Snowdonia. Days visits to Ireland. Local amenities include bowling green, swimming, windsurfing, tennis, plane spotters RAF valley. Restaurants and bars nearby. Park established in 1925. Open March-Oct.

TYNYGONGL

Bwlch Holiday Park, Benllech Bay, Tynygongl, Anglesey LL74 8RF. *01248 852914.* On A5025 then B5108 for 1.5m. Benllech 1m. Mains water and electricity in static caravans. Play area. Launderette. Public phone. Hot and cold showers. Electricity in touring vans. Open March 1- Oct 31.

VALLEY

Pen y Bont Farm, Valley, Anglesey LL23 7PH. *01407 740481.* Owner: Mr E R Parry. From A5 turn S on to B4545 at Valley crossroads. Site is about 1m at Four Mile Bridge. Open Whitsun-Oct.

BLAENAU GWENT

TREDEGAR

(1.5m). Parc Bryn Bach, Countryside Centre, Merthyr Road, Tredegar, Blaenau Gwent NP22 3AY. *01495 711816.* parcbrynbach@blaenau-gwent.gov.uk. Owner: Blaenau Gwent County Borough Council. A465 Tredegar, following signs to Parc Bryn Bach. Caravan and campsite nestling alongside the lake and 100 metre away from the visitor centre with licensed bar and restaurant, gift shop, tourist info. 400 acre countryside park with 9 hole golf course, driving range, bmx track, bike hire, fishing, playground, adventure activities and much more!

CARMARTHENSHIRE

CARMARTHEN

Broadway Caravan Park, Laugharne, Carmarthen, Carmarthenshire SA33 4NU. *01994 427272.* Owner: Mr C Davies. On A4066. 1m from Laugharne. Holiday site on edge of hills, 3m from sea. Dogs on leads allowed. Fees on application. Open March 1-Oct 30.

(1m). Pant Farm Caravan & Camping Park, Llangunnor Road, Carmarthen, Carmarthenshire SA31 2HY. *01267 235665.* Owner: H V & E Jones. Off M4 on B4300. Convenient, flat, sheltered location. Tents welcome. Walking distance to station and town. Near Botanical Garden of Wales. Shops, PO, doctor, golf course, fishing all in 1m.

CLYNDERWEN

(0.5m). Grondre Vale Holiday Park, Clynderwen, Carmarthenshire SA66 7HD. *01437 563111.* accounts@clarach.fsbusiness.co.uk. www.grondrevale.com. Owner: Mr T Scarrott. 2m from Narberth. On A478 Cardigan road, just off A40. Park facilities: pub, pool, shop, showers, launderette, games room. Local

---

ty newydd
LEISURE PARK
Proprietors: Mike & Cathi
Llanbedrgoch, Anglesey, Gwynedd LL76 8TZ
Tel: 01248 450677 Fax: 01248 450711

▶▶▶ This small, select, family-run park is ideally situated for Benllech Bay with extensive views of Snowdonia. Facilities include licensed country club serving meals for the family, well-equipped shop, excellent toilet facilities, free showers, disabled toilet, baby changing room, laundry room, children's playground and games room, heated outdoor swimming pool, health centre with spa, sauna, pool, electric hook-ups and luxury fully-equipped caravans for hire. Dogs on leads are welcomed.
Sailing, water skiing, fishing, climbing, walking, 9-hole golf within 1 mile, pony trekking and safe sandy beaches are available on the island.

WALES

See page 5 for key to symbols and abbreviations

attractions: Oakwood Theme Park, Tenby, Saundersfoot, Folly Farm. Open March-Nov.

KIDWELLY

Carmarthen Bay Touring & Camping Site, Tanylan Farm, Kidwelly, Carmarthenshire SA17 5HJ. *01267 267306*. www.tanylanfarmholidays.co.uk. M4-exit 48 to Kidwelly via Llanelli L at Spar supermarket, coast road to Ferryside 2m. Level site, 200yd from beach. Membership to park resorts available. Free hot water in showers. Open Easter-end Sept.

LLANDOVERY

[101 LOGO]
(7m). Camping & Caravanning Club Site – Rhandirmwyn, Rhandirmwyn, Llandovery, Carmarthenshire SA20 ONT. *01550 760257*. www.campingandcaravanningclub.co.uk. Owner: Camping & Caravanning Club. From A483 in Llandovery take road SP Rhandirmwyn for 7m, turn L at PO, site is on the L before the river. Spectacular countryside in easy reach of the site. The rare red kite can often be seen flying above the site. There are lots of walks in easy reach of site. Non-members welcome. All units accepted. Deals for families and backpackers. David Bellamy Gold Conservation Award. Open March-Oct.

(0.5m). Erwlon Caravan & Camping Park, Llandovery, Carmarthenshire SA20 0RD. *01550 720332*. www.ukparks.co.uk/erwlon. Owner: Messrs Rees & Sons. On A40 Brecon to Llandovery. Set in the beautiful Towy Valley in mid-Wales. An ideal base for touring the beautiful hills and vales of Wales. Luxury amenity block and super pitches. Good access. In 0.5m of Llondovery at the foothills of the Breon Beacons.

(9m). Gellifechan Cottage, Rhandirmwyn, Llandovery, Carmarthenshire SA20 0PF. *01550 760397*. Owner: Mr E Williams. 9m from Llandovery in the beautiful Upper Towy Valley. North of Rhandirmwyn near Llyn Brianne reservoir. Person in charge: Mr D P Jones. 2-3m to shops, PO. Near bird and nature reserves, fishing. Open March-Oct.

LLANELLI

Black Lion Caravan & Camping Park, 78 Black Lion Road, Gorslas, Cross Hands, Llanelli, Carmarthenshire SA14 6RU. *01269 845365*. www.caravansite.com. Owner: Barry G Hayes. Just off A48. Follow brown touring signs from Cross Hands (1m). 4m from Ammanford. Close to National Botanic Garden of Wales. Family owned park, peaceful, well maintained and friendly. Some hardstandings. Children's play area. Caravan storage. Shops 0.5m. Camping & Caravanning Club certificated. David Bellamy Gold Conservation Award. Open April 1-Sept 9.

(6m). Pembrey Country Park Caravan Club Site, Pembrey, Llanelli, Carmarthenshire SA16 0EJ. *01554 834369*. www.caravanclub.co.uk. Owner: The Caravan Club. See website for directions. Set in a large country park with adventure playground and miles of sandy beaches. Non-members welcome. No tents. Advance booking essential bank holidays and school holidays. MV service point. Laundry. Near golf, fishing and watersports. Ideal for walking and families. Some hardstandings, steel awning pegs required. Toilet block with privacy cubicles. Baby and toddler washroom. Veg prep area. Gas and Gaz. Play equipment, storage pitches, quiet and peaceful off peak, good walking area. NCN cycle route in 5m. No tents. Open March-Jan.

LLANGADOG

(1.5m). Abermarlais Caravan Park, Llangadog, Carmarthenshire SA19 9NG. *01550 777868/777797*. www.ukparks.co.ukabermarlais. Owner: Juster & Son. 6m W of Llandovery or, 6m E of Llandeilo on A40. Western end of the Brecon National Park. Hot showers. Ideal for a peaceful holiday in natural surroundings, own woodland. Open March 15-Nov 15.

(6m). Black Mountain Caravan Park, Llanddeusant, Llangadog, Carmarthenshire SA19 9YG. *01550 740217*. www.blackmountainholidays.co.uk. Owner: David Rainsley & Sharon Brooker. A40 from Brecon, follow SP Llandovery. At Trecastle turn L directly before pub Castle Coaching Inn (brown tourist sign) follow road for about 9m, turn R before pub Cross Inn. Fishing & pony-trekking close by. Part of Brecon Beacons National Park, with unique wildlife. Excellent walking country. Good base for touring mid and south Wales. Cycle hire can be arranged locally. Red kite feeding station close to site (50yd), pub with good food adjacent to site.

(7m). Blaenau Farm, Llanddeusant, Llangadog, Carmarthenshire SA19 9UN. *01550 740277*. Owner: Mr P J Dobbs. 6m SE of Llangadog via A4069 to Pontarllechau. Minor roads through Twynllanan to Llanddeusant. Pass church & continue down valley to site. From A40 follow sign W to Llanddeusant at Trecastle. 7m to Cross Inn, L to old vicarage, L and L again, continue down valley towards Llyn y Fan. Isolated mountain farm with basic facilities. Several miles to shops, PO and town. Food sometimes available on site. Open May 1-Oct 30.

(4m). The Pont Aber Inn, Gwynfe, Llanddnesant, Llangadog, Carmarthenshire SA19 9TA. *01550 740202*. Owner: Mrs M Denton. From A40 after Llandovery, turn L to Llangadog. Take Brynaman road for 4m.

LLANWRDA

Maesbach Caravan & Camping Park, Horseshoe Valley, Ffarmers, Llanwrda, Carmarthenshire SA19 8EX. *01558 650650*. admin@maesbach.plus.com. Owner: Kath & Graham Stoddart. A482 Lampeter Road. After Pumsaint, turn R after 1.5m SP for Ffarmers. A tranquil family run peace lovers' retreat in 5 acres with magnificent countryside views. Quiet lanes for walking, cycling, horse riding, bird watching and sightings of Red Kite. Explore West Wales beaches, visit local attractions. Near store/garage with Lampeter's shops, supermarkets, leisure facilities 7m away. Tourist information available from the park. Open March 1-Oct 31.

Penlanwen Caravan Site, Pumpsaiht, Caio, Llanwrda, Carmarthenshire SA19 8RR. *01558 650667*. Owner: Mrs Rosabelle Rees. 7m NW Llandovery take A40, turn R at Llanwrda to A482 past Bridgend Inn, site signs on R. Farm site ideal for children. Pony-trekking, mountain walks, pot-holing. Guided tours of gold mine. Open March-Oct.

Springwater Lakes, Harford, Llanwrda, Carmarthenshire SA19 8DT. *01558 650788*. Owner: M&S Bexon. 4.5m E of Lampeter on A482. Quiet, peaceful, well maintained, garage with convenience shop 500yd. Main shops 4m. No children play facilities. 4 lakes to fish on site: 1x3 acre mixed coarse, 1x3 acre specimen carp, 1 fly only (rainbow & browns), 1 Fly carp. Fishing tackle shop. Open March 1-Oct 31.

NEWCASTLE EMLYN

(2m). Afon Teifi Caravan and Camping Site, Pentre-cagal, Newcastle Emlyn, Carmarthenshire SA38 9HT. *01559 370 532*. www.afonteifi.co.uk. Owner: Mrs S Bishop. Off A484. Quiet, riverside site, an ideal touring base for Cardigan Bay. Family run site with playground and games room.

www.motorcaravanmagazine.co.uk   MOTOR CARAVAN & CAMPING PARKS 2009   **137**

WALES

Shop, pub and restaurant nearby. 18 hardstandings All the usual facilities, well-lit and maintained to a high standard. Open mid March-Oct 31.

(1.8m). Dolbryn Camping & Caravanning, Capel Iwan Road, Newcastle Emlyn, Carmarthenshire SA38 9LP. 01239 710683. www.dolbryn.co.uk. Owner: Mr & Mrs D & B Spencer. Turn off on A484 in Newcastle Emlyn SP Leisure Centre follow camping signs, first R after garage. Peaceful site in sheltered valley. Half hour drive to sea. Licensed bar. Conservation and play area. Fishing on site. Rallies welcome. Shops, pubs, takeaway, leisure centre, restaurant all in 2m. Open from 1 March-31 Oct.

PONTARDDULAIS

(3m). River View Touring Park, The Dingle, Llanedi, Pontarddulais, Carmarthenshire SA4 OFH. 01269 844876. www.riverviewtouringpark.com. Owner: Keith Brasnett. End of M4, J49 take A483 to Ammanford. About 0.5m turn L into Lon-y-Felin. Site at end of road. Golf range nearby. River Gwilli along 2 sides. Plenty of wildlife and wildflowers to enjoy. Quiet site, ideal for visiting beaches, mountains and gardens. Wales Business and Substainability Award winner 2006. 5 Star 'Loo of the Year' award. National Tourism Awards 2007. Winner of Quality & Customer Care – caravan sector AA Campsite of the year 2008 – Wales. David Bellamy Gold Conservation Award. Open March 1-Dec 9.

ST CLEARS

(3m). Afon Lodge Caravan Park, Parciau Bach, St Clears, Carmarthenshire SA33 4LG. 01994 230647. yvonne@afonlodge.f9.co.uk. Owner: Mr W Wiggans. From traffic lights in St Clears take road to Llanboidy in 100yd fork R. 1.75m, 1st R, 0.75m 1st R continue for 0.25m. Beautiful, quiet, secluded park in wooded valley with countryside views. Ideal touring centre for West Wales. David Bellamy Gold Conservation Award. Open March 1-Jan 9.

CEREDIGION

ABERAERON

Aeron Coast Caravan Park, North Road, Aberaeron, Ceredigion SA46 0JF. 01545 570349. www.aeroncoast.co.uk. Owner: Aeron Coast (Holidays) Ltd. On A487 Cardigan to Aberystwyth. Filling station at entrance. Brown SP, northern edge of town. 22-acres of flat, coastal parkland. Club, recreational rooms, heated swimming pool and tennis court. Families only. 500yd from shops and picturesque harbour. Quiet out of high season – good facilities for children in school holidays, including free evening entertainment. Open March 1-Oct 31.

ABERYSTWYTH

(0.25m). Aberystwyth Holiday Village, Penparcau Road, Aberystwyth, Ceredigion SY23 1TH. 01970 624211. www.aberystwythholidays.co.uk. Owner: Mr R Ballard. On A487. 0.25m S of town. Near town and beach. Indoor swimming pool. 10 pin bowling centre. Shop, café, 2 bars, entertainment. Play area. Fishing, fitness centre. Open March 1-Jan 10.

(10m). Aeron View Caravan Park, Blaenpennal, Aberystwyth, Ceredigion SY23 4TW. 01974 251488. www.aeronview.com. Owner: Mr & Mrs T N Bell. 1m off A485 Aberystwyth to Tregaron road, 4m from Tregaron. Quiet, inland site with panoramic views yet only 15mins from the sea. Ideal for fishing, birdwatching and relaxing. Open March 1-Oct 31.

(1.25m). Bryncarnedd Caravan Park, Clarach Road, Aberystwyth, Ceredigion SY23 3DG. 01970 615271. NE of Aberystwyth via A487 for 1m then L on to B4572. Site 0.5m. Overnight stops. Dogs on lead only. Theatre nearby. Motorbikes welcome. Open Easter-Oct.

Devil's Bridge Woodlands Caravan Park, Aberystwyth, Ceredigion SY23 3JW. 01970 890233. www.woodlandsdevilsbridge.co.uk. Owner: R P Davies. On A4120, 12m E of Aberystwyth or 3m S of A44 at Ponterwyd. A peaceful country site adjoining farm. Ideal for walking, birdwatching, touring, fishing and mountain biking. Beautiful scenery. Wales Tourist Board member. Open Easter-Oct 31.

(12m). Erwbarfe Farm Caravan Park, Devil's Bridge, Aberystwyth, Ceredigion SY23 3JR. 01970 890 358. priscilla@erwbarfefarmcaravanpark.freeserve.co.uk. Owner: DB & PM Jones. On A4120 Ponterwyd to Devil's Bridge. Near walking, fishing, bird-watching, Nantyr Arian mountain bike centre (2m). Open March 1-Oct 31.

(2m). Glan-y-Mor Leisure Park, Clarach Bay, Aberystwyth, Ceredigion SY23 3DT. 01970 828900. www.sunbourne.co.uk. Owner: W L Jones Ltd. Off A487 Machynlleth to Aberystwyth. Restaurant and takeaway. Supermarket. Amusements. Bowl and leisure centre. Licensed club. Launderette. Free showers. Fitness gym. Sauna. Steam room. Whirlpool spa. Sunbeds. Entertainment. Dogs not allowed in Bank Holidays and school holidays. Open March 1-Nov 1.

(1.5m). Midfield Holiday and Residential Park, Southgate, Aberystwyth, Ceredigion SY23 4DX. 01970 612542. www.midfieldcaravanpark.co.uk. Owner: Mr & Mrs T B Hughes. On A4120 Aberystwyth to Devil's Bridge Road. Mainly level hilltop site with panoramic views. Public phone. Privately owned park. 0.5m to shops. Touring, holiday & residential sites overlooking Aberystwyth and Cardigan Bay. GS. Open Easter-Oct 31 for holiday vans.

(5m). Morfa Bychan Holiday Park, Llanfarian, Aberystwyth, Ceredigion SY23 4QQ. 01970 617254. www.hillandale.co.uk. Owner: D & D Lloyd Jones Securities Ltd. Off A487 southbound from Aberystwyth, first turning off A487, road unsuitable for caravans, proceed a further 2m to turning alongside radio masts. Set in over 110 acres of pastureland overlooking Cardigan Bay. Superb location from which to explore the area. Heated swimming pool. Cinema and town 3m. Golf 4m. David Bellamy Bronze Conservation Award. Open March 1-Jan 9.

Pantmawr Camping Site, Pisgah, Capel Seion, Aberystwyth, Ceredigion SY23 4NF. 01970 880449. 3m W of Devil's Bridge and 8m from Aberystwyth. On N side of A4120. Farm site overlooking Rheidol Valley.

(9m). Pengarreg Caravan Park, Llanrhystud, Aberystwyth, Ceredigion SY23 5DJ. 01974 202247. www.utowcaravans.co.uk. Owner: Mr C Miller. On A487 S of Aberystwyth, entrance opposite garage. Site situated on beach. Aberaeron 6m. Fishing on site, golf 1m, PO 0.75m. Doctor 6m. Shop on site, laundry, office, licensed club, males, children's room, 2 play areas. Hill walks. Boating ramp. Open March 1-Jan 1.

(3m). Rhoslawdden Farm, Moriah, Capel Seion, Aberystwyth, Ceredigion SY23 4EA. 01974 612585. Owner: H Griffiths. From Devil's Bridge 8m.

138 MOTOR CARAVAN & CAMPING PARKS 2009

WALES

See page 5 for key to symbols and abbreviations

(2m). Riverside Caravan Park, Lon Glanfred, Llandre, Borth, Aberystwyth, Ceredigion SY24 5BY. 01970 820070. Owner: Mr SJ & Mrs JE South. From A487 at Bow Street, turn at Rhydepennau public house on to B4353 Llandre. Turn R 150yd past Llandre PO into Lon Glanfred. Site in 500yd. Quiet, sheltered and secluded site on banks of river Lerri. Hot showers. Open March 1-Oct 31.

(12m). Woodlands Caravan Park, Devil's Bridge, Aberystwyth, Ceredigion SY23 3JW. 01970 890233. www.woodlandsdevilsbridge.co.uk. Owner: Mr & Mrs Davies. 3m off A44 on A4120. A quiet family-run site, 300yd from waterfalls. Fishing and mountain bike trail nearby. Golf, tennis, swimming, horse riding, seaside in 20mins drive. Café/tea rooms and gift shop on site. Take away food on Friday and Saturday evenings. Quiet village pub 5mins walk from caravan park. Spectacular scenery. Open Easter-Oct 31.

(11m). Woodlands Caravan Park, Llanon, Aberystwyth, Ceredigion SY23 5LX. 01974 202342. Owner: Mr I Lampert. From N A487 through Llanon, R at international caravan sign. Level, secluded, tree-lined site with made-up roads. 200yd from sea. GS. Open March 1-Oct 31.

BORTH

(1m). The Mill House Caravan Park, Dol-y-bont, Borth, Ceredigion SY24 5LX. 01970 871481. www.ukparks.co.uk/millhousecp. Owner: Mr OJ Patrick. On A487 turn W at Rhyddapenau Garage Corner (between Talybont and Bow Street) on to B4353 through Llandre. Proceed 1mile. Stop under railway bridge, by white railings, then fork R into Dolybont village, first R before hump-back bridge. Quiet site, close mown grass. Fishing on site, shops, doctor, PO 1m. Golf 2m. Open Easter to mid-Oct.

(3m). Ty Mawr Holiday Home Park, Ynyslas, Borth, Ceredigion SY24 5LB. 01970 871327. Owner: P G & C C Beech. N of Borth on B4353 off A487. Quiet, sheltered, level site with panoramic views of hills, nature reserve and Dovey estuary. Fishing, golf course, shops, PO, doctor near. David Bellamy Gold Conservation Award. Open March 1-Oct 31.

CARDIGAN

Allty Coed, St Dogmaels, Cardigan, Ceredigion SA43 3LP. 01239 612673. Owner: GH Biddyr. Grid Ref: 135-495 –

O.S. sheet 145. Regular visits from dolphins. At start of Pembrokeshire coastal footpath, path goes past camp site. No large tourers or camper vans, narrow road from Poppit Sands.

(2.5m). Brongwyn Caravan & Touring Park, Brongwyn Mawr, Penparc, Cardigan, Ceredigion SA43 1SA. 01239 613644. www.tentsandtourers.co.uk. Owner: Mrs A Giles. On A487 Cardigan-Aberystwyth road, 2.5m N of Cardigan, turn L at crossroads in Penparc signposted Ferwig, carry on over next cross-roads, after 0.5m turn R into lane, opposite blue sign. A small, peaceful park with level pitches. Indoor pool and leisure facilities available (at extra charge), laundry etc. 5mins from the market town of Cardigan and beautiful sandy beaches at Mwnt and Aberporth. Golf course, cinema, theatre, shopping centre all 3m. Ideal location for walking, fishing and golf. Open May-Sept.

Camping Blaenwaun, Mwnt, Cardigan, Ceredigion SA43 1QF. 01239 612165. Owner: D J Davies. 4m NW of Cardigan. Take A487 for 0.25m W of Cardigan. Turn N on to B4548 towards Mwnt. After 0.5m turn R at SP to Mwnt. Follow signs to Mwnt. Site is 300yd from Mwnt beach camp sign. 0.5m from sea. Private coarse fishing lake.

Dolgelynen Holiday Park, Aberporth, Cardigan, Ceredigion SA43 2HS. 01239 811095. Owner: Mr J Price. Located off the B4333, 2m from the A487 coast road. Dolgelynen is situated on closely mown, gently sloping grassland, with panoramic views overlooking Cardigan Bay. Sandy coves of Aberporth 0.75m.

(4m). Ty-Gwyn Farm Caravan Park, Mwnt, Cardigan, Ceredigion SA43 1QH. 01239 614518. Owner: M&MD Evans. Off A487 at Cardigan for Mwnt. Family-run farm site. Mwnt beach 5mins from site. Quiet situation. Dolphins and seals in bay. Open March-Oct.

LAMPETER

Hafod Brynog Caravan Park, Ystrad Aeron, Felinfach, Lampeter, Ceredigion SA48 8AE. 01570 470084. hafod@brynog.wanadoo.co.uk. Owner: Mr & Mrs G Amies. On main A482 Lampeter to Aberaeron road in quiet village of Ystrad Aeron, entrance next to Brynog Arms pub. Well maintained park with plenty of space between caravans and modern shower block. Peaceful with lovely views. Ideal for

coastal and inland touring or just relaxing. Walking distance to village with shops, garage, pubs. Launderette on site. AA 3 pennants. Golf course 6m. Fishing 3m. Open Easter-Oct.

LLANARTH

Llain Activity Centre, Llain Farm, Llanarth, Ceredigion SA47 0PZ. 01545 580127. Owner: Mr & Mrs DK Thomas. Off A487, follow our brown tourist signs just N of Llanarth. Family orientated camping with pool. Activities most days. Hook ups. Camping from £7. Open March-Oct.

Shawsmead Caravan Club Site, Oakford, Llanarth, Ceredigion SA47 0RN. 01545 580423. www.caravanclub.co.uk. Owner: The Caravan Club. See website for directions. This site is only about 4m from the coast which is dotted with lovely bays and beaches ideal for families. Membership on site. Non-members welcome. Some hardstandings. PO in village, garage/shop 1.5m, fishing and golf courses nearby. Laundry, MV service point, veg prep area, gas, watersports nearby. Quiet and peaceful off peak, good area for walking, beach and NCN cycle route in 5m. Open April-Oct.

LLANDYSUL

Brynawelon Touring and Camping Park, Brynawelon, Sarnau, Llangranog, Llandysul, Ceredigion SA44 6RE. 01239 654584. Owner: Mr JG & Mrs SL Brown. N on A487, then turn R at Sarnau Chapel crossroads. 2m from coast. Site 0.25m on L down lane SP. 9m from Cardigan. Small, quiet, family site under personal supervision. Calor Gas available. Open Easter-Sept.

(3m). Camping & Caravanning Club Site – Cardigan Bay, Llwynhelyg, Cross Inn, Llandysul, Ceredigion SA44 6LW. 01545 560029. www.campingandcaravanningclub.co.uk. Owner: Camping & Caravanning Club. On A486, 1m from New Quay. L at Penrhiwgaled Arms, turn R, about 0.75m. Site on R after 250yd. 10m from Cardigan. Well located site in easy reach of New Quay and Cardigan. Good coastal walks nearby. Close to golden beaches. Dolphins and purpoises have been spotted off the coast at New Quay Head. Non-members welcome. All units accepted. Deals for families and backpackers. Open March-Oct.

Maes Glas Caravan Park, Penbryn, Sarnau, Llandysul, Ceredigion SA44 6QE. 01239 654268. www.maesglascaravanpark.co.uk. Owner: Mr &

MOTOR CARAVAN & CAMPING PARKS 2009 **139**

WALES

Mrs T Hill. Off A487 at Sarnau follow road down towards Penbryn Beach. 10m from Cardigan. Peace and quiet. Dry ski slope 3m, golf course 4m, shops 9m. David Bellamy Gold Conservation Award. Open March-Oct.

Manorafow Caravan Park, Sarnau, Llandysul, Ceredigion SA44 6QH. *01239 810564.* manorafow@ukgateway.net. Owner: Susan J Jones. 0.75m from Penbryn beach in wooded valley. From A487 at Sarnau take Penbryn beach signs. Near café and takeaway. Open April-Oct.

Pilbach Holiday Park, Betws Ifan, Rhydlewis, Llandysul, Ceredigion SA44 5RT. *01239 851434.* www.pilbach.com. Owner: Mr Barker. Set in nearly 14 acres of land, this award-winning holiday park is surrounded by stunning countryside and close to Newquay with its picturesque harbour. Modern, refurbished club with live entertainment. Freshly prepared bar food.

(0.5m). Rhydygalfe Caravan Park, Pontwelli, Llandysul, Ceredigion SA44 5AP. *01559 363211.* Owner: DW LAG Davies. S of Llandysul on A486. Good salmon fishing close to site. Local pub and late night shop in easy walking distance. Open March-Oct.

(8m). Talywerydd Touring Caravan Park, Penbryn Sands, Sarnau, Llandysul, Ceredigion SA44 6QY. *01239 810322.* Owner: Mr & Mrs R Milka. From N or S off A487 take second Penbryn turn, site 600yd. Own tap and drain to each tourer. Heated, covered swimming pool, pitch and putt. AA 4 Pennant. Open March-Oct.

Treddafydd Caravan Site, Penbryn Beach, Sarnau, Llandysul, Ceredigion SA44. *01239 654551.* Owner: Mr G&E Griffiths. Off A487 at Sarnau Church into Penbryn Beach Road, 1st L 10m from Cardigan. Washing machine. Tumble dryer & ironing facilities. Open April-Oct.

(2.5m). Brynarian Caravan Park, Cross Inn, Llanon, Ceredigion SY23 5NA. *01974 272231.* www.brynariancaravanpark.com. Owner: Mr & Mrs Weston. Off B4337, turn towards Llanon at Cross Inn second turning on L. 6m from Aberaeron. Quiet secluded family run park, set among mature beech trees. Large touring field, no overcrowding. Play area. H&C showers.Telephone for brochure. Golf, fishing nearby. Shop,

restaurant, PO, garage 500yd from site. Open March 1-Oct 31.

NEW QUAY

(3m). Brownhill Caravan Park, Synod Inn, Llandysul, New Quay, Ceredigion. *01545 560288.* Owner: Mr IL Davies. S of New Quay on A486. 0.5m from Synod Inn. Period of opening and fees on application.

Cei Bach Country Club, Parc-y-Brwcs, Cei Bach, New Quay, Ceredigion SA45 9SL. *01545 580237.* www.cei-bach.co.uk. Owner: Paul & Stephanie Wynne. Off A487. Take B4342 New Quay Road for 1.5m At Cambrian Hotel turn R. Follow signs for Cei Bach 1m. Coastal walks. Open March 1-Jan 9.

(1.5m). Frondeg Caravan Park, Gilfachreda, New Quay, Ceredigion SA45 9SP. *01545 580444.* stevehartley.cbmwc@tiscali.co.uk. Owner: SWH Hartley. From A487 at Llanarth take B4342 to New Quay. Turn R at crossroads after telephone box at Gilfachreda, then L at junction, 200yd on R. 2m from New Quay by road (where harbour, shops, doctor etc) or walk along the beach at low tide. Frondeg is a quiet, secluded site in a wooded valley. Dolphin watching boat trips arranged by site owner. Badger and red kite watching from your caravan window! Open April 1-Oct 31.

(2m). Pencnwc Holiday Park, Cross Inn, Llandyssul, New Quay, Ceredigion SA44 6NL. *01545 560479.* www.pencnwc.co.uk. Owner: IM & Mrs SJ Davies. SP outskirts of village Cross Inn in 2m of New Quay on A486. Club. Open March 1 – Oct 31.

(2m). Wern Mill Camping Site, Gilfachreda, New Quay, Ceredigion SA45 9SP. *01545 580699.* Owner: Mr J B Hand. A487 Aberystwyth to Cardigan road, turn off at Llanarth to Newquay road B4342. Gilfachreda is 1.5m from Llanarth on the B4342. Sheltered level site near two sandy beaches. Ideal centre for touring Mid-Wales. Idyllic walks. family site. Open Easter-Oct 31.

NEWCASTLE EMLYN

(3m). Cenarth Falls Holiday Park, Cenarth, Newcastle Emlyn, Ceredigion SA38 9JS. *01239 710345.* www.cenarth-holipark.co.uk. Owner: Mr & Mrs DHG Davies. On the A484 Newcastle Emlyn to Cardigan road. Luxurious heated indoor pool and health club, bars and restaurant

area. Unheated outdoor pool open beginning June till end of Aug. Excellent caravan holiday homes and cottages for hire and touring facilities. Family-run award winning park. Superb beaches. Lovely walks. Golf. Fishing. Shop 1m. Open March 1-Jan 9.

CONWY

ABERGELE

Gwrych Towers Camp, Llandulas Road, Abergele, Conwy LL22 8ET. *01745 832109.* Owner: MM Dutton. W of Abergele via B5443 and main entrance to Gwrych Castle Park. Office in R-hand tower. Privately owned, family site near quiet beach and golf links. Central for touring and coastal resorts. Fees on application. Open Spring BH, July-Sept.

(2.5m). Henllys Farm, Towyn, Abergele, Conwy LL22 9HF. *01745 351208.* Owner: Mr B Kerfoot. On S side of A548 at Towyn. Level, sheltered site overlooking open farmland. Close to all the amenities and entertainment in Towyn. Open March 27-Oct 18.

(2m). Ty Mawr Holiday Park, Towyn Road, Towyn, Abergele, Conwy LL22 9HG. *0871 664 9785.* www.park-resorts.com. Owner: Park Resorts Ltd. Off A584 Rhyl to Abergele, W of Towyn. Indoor pool. Adventure playground. All weather multi sports court. Free kids club. Free family entertainment day and night. Bar meals. Amusements. Darts. Pool table. Club room. David Bellamy Gold Conservation Award. Open April-Oct.

BETWS-Y-COED

(1m). Hendre Farm Camping and Caravan Site, Betws-y-Coed, Conwy LL24 0BN. *01690 710950.* Owner: Pierce Brothers. On A5 Betws-y-Coed to Capel Curig. Showers, shaving point, washbasins and deep sink for clothes washing. Public telephone. Open March-Oct.

Riverside Caravan Park, Old Church Road, Betws-y-Coed, Conwy LL24 0BA. *01690 710310.* www.morris-leisure.co.uk. Owner: Morris Leisure. Set close to centre of the town, just off the A5. Please follow signs. No entry to park after 9.30pm. Adjacent to golf course and river Conwy for fishing. 2mins walk from shops, restaurants, etc. Open March 1-Jan 15.

140 MOTOR CARAVAN & CAMPING PARKS 2009

WALES

See page 5 for key to symbols and abbreviations

Rynys Farm Camping Site, Betws-y-Coed, Conwy LL26 0RU. 01690 710218. www.rynys-camping.co.uk. Owner: Gareth & Carol Williams. 2m S of Betws-Y-Coed on A5, opposite Conwy Falls. Peaceful, scenic site in the hill of North Wales, close to Snowdonia peaks. Excellent clean facilities. Central for touring North Wales. Open all year for tents, Easter-Oct for caravans.

(3m). Tan Aeldroch Farm, Nr Pont Y Pant, Betws-y-Coed, Conwy LL25 0LZ. 01690 750225. ruegg.peel@virgin.net. www.tanaeldroch.co.uk. Owner: Ms Margrit Ruegg and Dr J Peel. From Betws-Y-Coed (2m) follow A470 to Dolwyddelan, pass under railway viaduct, 0.5m turn L at farm sign. Tranquil family campsite, stunning Snowdonia National Park location amidst wooded rolling hills by River Lledr. Camp fires, well behaved pets allowed, no radios. Contact owners for admission. Open March 1-Nov 30.

COLWYN BAY

[101 LOGO]
(0.5m). Dinarth Hall, Rhos-on-Sea, Colwyn Bay, Conwy LL28 4PX. 01492 548203. Owner: Mr Parry. 2m NW of Colwyn Bay on B5115 to Dinarth Hall Road (opposite college). Touring centre. Golf course across the road. PO, Doctor 15mins walk. Open Easter-Oct.

(3m). Ty-Ucha Farm Campsite Site, Tan-y-Graig Road, Llysfaen, Colwyn Bay, Conwy LL29 8UD. 01492 517051. Owner: Mrs S A Hughes. SE of Colwyn Bay via A55 and A547, turn L on to Highlands road near to hotel. Go up hill to junction then R on to Tan-y-Graig road to site on R. Overnight stop London/N Wales, or longer. 2m from beach. 2.5m from Colwyn Bay leisure centre. Open Easter-Oct.

CONWY

(1.5m). Conwy Touring Park, Trefriw Road, Conwy, Conwy LL32 8UX. 01492 592856. www.conwytouringpark.com. Owner: Conwy Touring Park & Co. 1.25m S of Conwy on B5106. Large slate-roofed sign on L. Sheltered, wooded site with splendid views. Close to beaches and Snowdonia. Special offers available. Storage facilities. Open Easter-Sept.

(5m). Tyn Terfyn Touring Site, Talybont, Conwy, Conwy LL32 8YX. 01492 660525. Owner: G Turner. From Conwy Castle take B5106 for about 5m, first house on L after road sign 'Talybont'. Clean, quiet site on level ground. Hardstandings available. Excellent location for touring N Wales, castle, mountains, beaches, lakes, fishing etc. Butcher, PO, papers milk, groceries etc in 1.5m. Open March 14-Oct 31.

LLANRWST

(0.25m). Bodnant Caravan Park, Nebo Road, Llanrwst, Conwy LL26 0SD. 01492 640248. www.bodnant-caravan-park.co.uk. Owner: Mrs E Kerry-Jenkins. Opposite Birmingham Garage in Llanrwst, turn off A470 for B5427 SP Nebo. Park 300yd on R opposite Leisure Centre. Quiet, relaxed site. Landscaped park with floral features and old farm implements. 26 years winner of 'Wales in Bloom'. Open March 1-Oct 31.

(0.5m). Bron Derw Touring Caravan Park, Bron Derw, Llanrwst, Conwy LL26 0YT. 01492 640494. www.bronderw-wales.co.uk. Owner: Beryl Edwards. Follow A55 on to A470 For Betws-y-Coed and Llanrwst. On entering Llanrwst turn L into Parry Road (SP Llanddoged), at the T junction turn L. Then take first farm entrance, on the R signed 'Bron Derw' and continue up the drive until you reach the site. Secluded family run site on the outskirts of the ancient market town of Llanrwst, with shops, cafés, restaurants, swimming pool and leisure centre. Ideal Snowdonia mountain range and the North Wales coast. AA 3 pennant award and Welcome Host Gold Award. Caravan storage compound. CaSSOA member. Open March 1-Oct 31.

PENMAENMAWR

Trwyn-yr-Wylfa Farm, Conway Old Road, Penmaenmawr, Conwy LL34 6SF. 01492 622357. Owner: E Lloyd Hughes. Leave A55, J16 continue to Penmaenmawr turn L by Mountain view hotel. Site is 0.5m away. In Snowdonia National Park. Open April-Oct.

(1m). Tyddyn Du Touring Park, Conwy Old Road, Penmaenmawr, Conwy LL34 6RE. 01492 622300. www.tyddyndutouringpark.co.uk. Owner: Pam Watson-Jones. Take A55 W of Conwy. Follow Tourist Info signs, 1st L at roundabout at junction 16 immediate L again towards Dwygyfylchi, site entrance 200yd on R after Gladstone Inn. Adults (over 18) only site with superb views across Conwy Bay. Ideal base for enjoying attractions of Snowdonia. Golf, riding, walking, fishing, shops & pubs nearby. Open March 22-Oct 31.

Woodlands Camping Park, Pendyffryn Hall, Penmaenmawr, Conwy LL34 6UF. 01492 623219. Owner: Mr & Mrs K Clarke. Off A55 between Conwy and Penmaenmawr. After Conwy tunnel (under river), pass through Pen maenbach Tunnel (through mountain). Take 1st L SP Dwygyfylchi. 96 acres of private parkland and woods. In Snowdonia National Park. Short walk to beach. Licensed club. Families and couples only.

DENBIGHSHIRE

CORWEN

(8m). Glan-Ceirw Caravan Park, Ty Nant, Corwen, Denbighshire LL21 0RF. 01490 420346. www.ukparks/glanceirw.reserve.co.uk. Owner: Mr & Mrs Parry. Situated between Corwen and Betws y Coed on the A5 bordering Snowdonia National Park. Picturesque site with trout fishing. AA 3 pennants. David Bellamy Gold Conservation Award. Open March 1-Oct 31.

(4m). Hendwr Caravan Park, Llandrillo, Corwen, Denbighshire LL21 0SN. 01490 440210. www.hendwrcaravanpark.freeserve.co.uk. Owner: J&D Hughes. Take B4401 from Corwen (A5) for 4m site on R. The site is SP from A5 at Corwen. Dishwashing room. Limited service during winter. Fishing nearby. Good walking area. Central for touring North & Mid Wales. Open Easter/April 1-end Oct. All year for owner occupied.

(3.5m). Llawr Bettws Caravan Park, Glanrafon, Corwen, Denbighshire LL21 0HD. 01490 460224. david@llawrbetws.go-plus.net. Owner: Mr D M Jones. On A494 off A5. Corwen to Bala road, 2nd R after Thomas Motor Mart. Brochure by request. Gas supplies. Quiet and peaceful, open country. Beautiful walks. Fly fishing available. Open March-Nov.

DENBIGH

(4.5m). Caer-Mynydd Caravan Park, Saron, Denbigh, Denbighshire LL16 4TL. 01745 550302. www.caer-mynydd-park@hotmail.co.uk. Owner: Mrs K Welch. 4m SW of Denbigh off A525 to Ruthin. Past comprehensive school and pool, turn R to Prion and Saron. Delightful, privately-owned park with full services. A family-run park over 40 years. Excellent touring site, Snowdonia Park, fishing, golf and gliding nearby. Static caravans for sale. Parties or groups taken. New play area and toilet block. Open March 1-Oct 31.

www.motorcaravanmagazine.co.uk   MOTOR CARAVAN & CAMPING PARKS 2009   **141**

WALES

LLANGOLLEN

(1m). Eirianfa Riverside Holiday Park, Berwyn Road, Llangollen, Denbighshire LL20 8AB. 01978 860919. On A25N. Fishing on site. White water rafting and canoeing 500yd, golf and others 1m.

(0.5m). Wern Isaf Caravan & Camping Park, Wern Isaf Farm, Llangollen, Denbighshire LL20 8DU. 01978 860632. wernisaf.supanet.com. Owner: Mr & Mrs AC Williams. Turn up hill behind Bridge End Hotel then R into Wern Road. Site 0.5m NE Llangollen at foot of Castell Dinasbran (Crow Castle). Welcome Host Gold Award. Quiet scenic site with views of the Dee Valley and Welsh mountains. Fishing, golf course nearby, horse riding, white water rafting and many more sporting activities 0.75m from town centre. Open Easter-Oct.

PRESTATYN

(0.5m). Nant Mill Touring Caravan Park, Nant Mill Farm, Prestatyn, Denbighshire LL19 9LY. 01745 852360. www.nantmilltouring.co.uk. Owner: K&BL Rowley. On A548 Prestatyn coast road. 0.5m beach and town. Fishing, golf course, swimming, boating and horse riding all nearby. Ideal for sightseeing North Wales. Open April-mid Oct.

(3m). Presthaven Sands Holiday Park, Shore Road, Gronant, Prestatyn, Denbighshire LL19 9TT. 01745 856471. www.presthavensands.park.co.uk. Owner: Bourne Leisure Ltd. A55 then A5151 to Prestatyn. Follow A548 out of Prestatyn towards Gronant. Park SP L at the next set of traffic lights. 2 licensed club rooms and 1 family pub. Playground. Restaurant and takeaway. Go karts. Mini ten-pin bowling. All-weather multi sports court. Heated indoor and outdoor pools. Family entertainment. Direct beach access from park. 2 golf courses in 5-10mins. Shopping town centre 10mins. Rhyl cinema 15mins from park. David Bellamy Gold Conservation Award. Open March-end Oct.

St Marys Touring & Camping Park, Gronant, Prestatyn, Denbighshire LL19 9TB. 01745 853951. Owner: Meldrum Leisure. On A548 coast road Chester to Rhyl, 2m E of Prestatyn. Holiday and overnight site for caravans. Public phone. Hotel with restaurant nearby. Fishing lake on site. Mobile shop, daily pitches available also for tents and camper vans. Open Easter-Oct.

FLINTSHIRE
MOLD

(4m). Fron Farm Caravan Park, Rhes-y-cae Road, Hendre, Mold, Flintshire CH7 5QW. 01352 741482. www.fronfarmcaravanpark.co.uk. Owner: Dylan & Ceri Roberts. Take A541 towards Denbigh for about 5m, take R-hand turn for Rhes-y-Cae. Follow signposts all the way. Working farm with animals and horses. Large playground. Fantastic views and walking. Open April-Oct.

GWYNEDD
ABERDARON

Mur Melyn, Aberdaron, Gwynedd LL53 8LW. 01758 760522. Owner: Mrs JE Evans. 17m SW of Pwllheli and 2m N of Aberdaron. W on B4413, fork R, SP 'Whistling Sands' and turn L at Pen-y-Bont House to site 0.5m. Quiet holiday site near end of Lleyn Peninsula. Grassy level and sheltered. Ideal for ramblers. Just over 1m from several beautiful sandy beaches and the village of Aberdaron. Booking advisable for caravans. Open Whitsun & July and Aug.

ABERSOCH

(1.5m). Beach View Caravan Park, Bwlchtocyn, Abersoch, Gwynedd LL53 7BT. 01758 712956. Owner: Mr F Weatherby. Drive through Abersoch and Sarn Bach over crossroads. Take next L, SP Bwlchtocyn and Porthtocyn Hotel. Continue past Chapel, next L turn follow sign Porthtocyn Hotel. Park is on the L. Only 6mins from beach, fishing and all water sports. Golf course nearby. Doctor 2m; shops, garage in 2m. Open mid March-mid Oct.

(1m). Deucoch Touring and Camping Park, Sarnbach, Abersoch, Gwynedd LL53 7LD. 01758 713293. www.deucoch.com. Owner: Norman & Audrey Winteringham, Andrew & Ruth Pullen. 1m S of Abersoch via the Sarn Bach road. TR at crossroads, school on L, campsite on R. Flat, well-drained site, 10mins from beaches. Families only, children's playground. Dogs on leads. Café/restaurant nearby. Rail station 10m away. Open March-Oct.

(2.5m). Nant-y-Big Caravan Site, Nant-y-Big, Abersoch, Gwynedd LL53 7DB. 01758 712686. Owner: Mr JG Jones. S of Abersoch, through the village of Sarn Bach. Head for Cilan and Porth Ceiriad beach. Shop 1m, golf course 18 hole 1.5m. Fishing on site, beach 150yd. Doctor 2.5m. All water sports at Abersoch. Pony treking 1m. Open Easter-Oct 31.

Sarn Farm, Sarn Bach, Abersoch, Gwynedd LL53 5BG. 01758 713583. Owner: Mr & Mrs G Jones Griffith. Site is near Abersoch village. Golf course. Beaches. Shops. Bus stop. Private road to beach. Hot water. Fridge & freezer. Open March-Oct.

(1m). Seaside Camping Site, Lon Golff, Abersoch, Gwynedd. 01758 712271. Owner: Mr RT Roberts. Off A499 at Lon Golff. Good views. Safe, sandy beach & golf course 450yd. Hairdryers. Plugs. Tarmac road from site to village of Sarn Bach.

Seaview, Sarn Bach, Abersoch, Gwynedd LL53 7ET. 01758 712052. www.tggroup.co.uk. Owner: Mr Griffiths. Through Abersoch to Sarn Bach, then sharp L, site 200yd on R. Holiday site. AA approved. Family site. Short walk down quiet lane to beach. Managers: Arwyn and Catherine Williams. Open March-Oct.

(1m). Tan-y-Bryn Farm, Sarn Bach, Abersoch, Gwynedd LL53 7DA. 01758 712093. Owner: Mr Gwilym Hughes. S of Abersoch via Sarn Bach road. Site is first farm on L. Flat, well-drained site, 1m from sea. Fees on application. Shop nearby. Dogs on leads. Open Easter-Oct.

(1m). The Warren Holiday Park, Abersoch, Gwynedd LL53 7AA. 01758 714100. www.haulfryn.co.uk. Owner: Haulfryn Group Ltd. On A499 Pwllheli to Abersoch. Club. Fun pools and play area. Tennis courts. New leisure centre. Indoor swimming pool, shop. Golf course and Abersoch village 2m. Open March 1st-Jan 17.

(0.5m). Tyn-y-Mur Camping & Touring Park, Lon Garmon, Abersoch, Gwynedd LL53 7UL. 01758 712328. tynymur@abersoch14.fsnet.co.uk. Owner: H Roberts & N Harrison. Turn sharp R at the Land & Sea Garage on the approach to Abersoch. Park 0.5m on L. It has level ground and panoramic views of Abersoch Bay to the south and Hells Mouth. One dog allowed per unit. Open Easter-End Sept.

ARTHOG

Garthyfog Camp Site, Arthog, Gwynedd LL39 1AX. 01341 250338. www.garthyfog.co.uk. Owner: Dora Roberts. From Dogellau, through Arthog then turn L off A493. Turn at end 30mph sign. Site 200yd. Log cabins to let on site.

WALES

See page 5 for key to symbols and abbreviations

Hot water supply to shower only. Mains water, toilets and washbasins.

BALA

(3m). Camping & Caravanning Club Site – Bala, Crynierth Caravan Park, Cefn-Ddwysarn, Bala, Gwynedd LL23 7LN. *01678 530324.* www.campingandcaravanningclub.co.uk. Owner: Camping & Caravanning Club. A5 on to A494 to Bala. Through Bethal and Sarnau villages. Pass Cefn-Ddwysarn sign. R up lane before phone box. Site is 400yd on L. Ideal for watersports. 4m from Bala Lake in Snowdonia National Park. All units accepted. Non-members welcome. Loo Of the Year – champions league, standard of Excellence Award. Barmouth and Welshpool are in easy reach of the site. Enjoy a ride on one of the many narrow gauge railways around Bala. Deals for families and backpackers. Open March-Oct.

(3m). Glanllyn-Lakeside Camping & Caravan Park, & Werngoch Holiday Home Caravan Park, Llanuwchllyn, Bala, Gwynedd LL23 7ST. *01678 540227.* www.glanllyn.com. Owner: Mr E T Pugh & Mrs MW Pugh. SW of Bala on A494 – halfway between Bala and LLanuwchllyn. Plenty of outdoor activities available locally. Launching facilities. Lake side location. Level parkland with extensive views of the Aran, Arenig and Berwyn mountains. Central for touring north and mid Wales. Open mid March-mid Oct.

(0.5m). Penybont Touring & Camping Park, Llangynog Road, Bala, Gwynedd LL23 7PH. *01678 520549.* www.penybont-bala.co.uk. Owner: Mr & Mrs P&C Field. On B4391. Closes park to Bala Town (10mins walk) and the sailing club. Modern shower block to include disabled facility and laundry room. Calor gas available on site. Open April-Oct.

(2.5m). Ty Isaf Caravan Site, Llangynog Road, Bala, Gwynedd LL23 7PP. *01678 520574.* www.tyisafbala.co.uk. Owner: Mr JD & BJ Evans. Off B4391 near telephone kiosk and post box. Quiet, family site with level grass. Camp fires allowed. Gas sales. Free showers. Games area. Fishing, golf course, shops, PO, doctor all in 2.5m Open Easter or April 1-Oct 31.

(4m). Tyn Cornel Camping, Frongoch, Bala, Gwynedd LL23 7NU. *01678 520759.* gates.tooth@talk21.com. www.tyncornel.co.uk. Owner: Mrs J Tooth. Take A4212 from Bala. Drive through Frongoch village, 1m beyond on L. Sharp turn over river bridge. Ideal centre for touring N Wales, water sports and fishing. Hot water to all handbasins. Wonderful riverside walk to the Celyn Reservoir and Dam from site. Open March-Oct.

BANGOR

(3m). Dinas Farm Camping Site, Halfway Bridge, Bangor, Gwynedd LL57 4NB. *01248 364227.* www.dinasfarmtouringpark.co.uk. Owner: ML & LE Jones. J11 on to A5 towards Bethesd, L off A55. For 1m then R towards Tregarth for 0.5m then Dinas Farm site on L. Site is situated on the banks of the river Ogwen and enjoys an entirely sheltered setting amongst woodland. Fishing on site – by permit only. Open March 1-Oct 31.

BARMOUTH

(5m). Benar Beach Camping & Touring Site, Talybont, Barmouth, Gwynedd LL44 2RX. *01341 247001.* Owner: Mr David Powell Jones. 5m N of Barmouth. On the seaward side of A496, mid-way Barmouth to Harlech. Well-equipped family site 100yd from safe beach with miles of golden sand dunes. Satellite & TV hook-ups. Good base for Snowdonia and mid-Wales. Tents welcome. Open March-Oct.

Dalar Farm, Tal-y-Bont, Barmouth, Gwynedd LL43 2AQ. *01341 247221.* 5m N of Barmouth. Leave A496 at Tal-y-Bont on to beach road. Turn R through green gate near station, follow track to farm. Flat, well-drained site near beaches. Fees on application. Shop, café/restaurant in few minutes.

(0.5m). Hendre Mynach Touring Caravan & Camping Park, Llanaber, Barmouth, Gwynedd LL42 1YR. *01341 280262.* www.hendremynach.co.uk. Owner: Mr A R Williams. 0.5m N of Barmouth on the A496 Harlech road. Ideally based for touring mid and north Wales. Heated toilet and shower blocks. Launderette. Café with takeaway. Play area. Mother and baby room. 100 metersfrom a safe, sandy beach. 1 hotel with family rooms 20mins walk. 20mins safe and pleasant walk into Barmouth along the promenade. Awarded 'AA Best Campsite in Wales'. Pets welcome, dog walk provided. Site near to public transport. Open March 1-Jan 9.

Islawrffordd Caravan & Camping Site, Tal-y-Bont, Barmouth, Gwynedd LL43 2AQ. *01341 247269.* www.islawrffordd.co.uk. 4m N of Barmouth via A496. Turn L to beach at Tal-y-Bont. Site is second L. Adjoining safe, sandy beach. Touring centre in Snowdonia National Park. Children's rooms. Amusements and licensed premises nearby.

(5m). Parc Isaf Farm, Dyffryn Ardudwy, Barmouth, Gwynedd LL44 2RJ. *01341 247447.* Owner: Mrs J Edwards. Travel from Barmouth on the A496 through the village of Talybont, then about 0.25m there is a church on the L, few yards on turn R through a pillar gateway. Park is the second farm on R. A lovely spot with a view of Cardigan Bay. Shops, PO, sandy beach, garage in 1m. Golf, fishing, historic castle, caverns in 5m. Woodland walk, lakes and mountain nearby. Open March 1-Oct 31.

(2m). Trawsdir Touring Site, Llanaber, Barmouth, Gwynedd LL42 1RR. *01341 280999.* www.barmouthholidays.co.uk. On A496 200yd N from Wayside Inn. Coastal site N of Barmouth. Touring centre and overnight stop. Separate field for caravans. Advance bookings essential (main weeks). Fees on application. Seasonal pitches available. Open March-Oct.

BEDDGELERT

(0.75m). Beddgelert Forest Camping Site, Forest Holidays, Beddgelert, Gwynedd LL55 4UU. *01766 890288.* www.forestholidays.co.uk. Owner: Forest Holidays. 1m NW of Beddgelert on A4085. In the heart of Snowdonia, in walking distance of Mount Snowdon. Three National Parks and five Areas of Outstanding Natural Beauty in driving distance. Bookings and brochure requests on 0845 1308224

BLAENAU FFESTINIOG

(2m). Coed y Llwyn Caravan Club Site, Gellilydan, Blaenau Ffestiniog, Gwynedd LL41 4EN. *01766 590254.* www.caravanclub.co.uk. Owner: Caravan Club. See website for directions. Caravan Club members only. No tents. Landscaped in the Snowdonia National Park. Toilet blocks. Privacy cubicles. Laundry facilities. Veg prep. MV service point. Play equipment. Fishing and golf nearby. Ideal for families. Open March-Oct.

(4m). Llechrwd Farm, Maentwrog, Blaenau Ffestiniog, Gwynedd LL41 4HF. *01766 590240.* www.llechrwd.co.uk. Owner: Miss N Seears. On A496 between Blaenau Ffestinig (4m) and Maentwrog (1m). Quiet, family-run riverside site in Snowdonia National Park. Excellent centre

www.motorcaravanmagazine.co.uk MOTOR CARAVAN & CAMPING PARKS 2009 **143**

WALES

for walking, mountain biking, slate mines, Ffestiniog Railway and climbing. Portmeirion Italianate village 4m. Safe beach 7m. Porthmadog 9m and Harlech 8m. Open Easter or April 1-Oct 31.

CAERNARFON

■ **(5m). Bryn Gloch Caravan & Camping Park, Betws Garmon, Caernarfon, Gwynedd LL54 7YY.** *01286 650216.* www.bryngloch.co.uk. Owner: I & B Jones. On A4085 Beddgelert Caernarfon. On the bank of river Gwyrfai in the Vale of Betws. All facilities available. Free hot showers. 2m from Mount Snowdon. Award-winning site. AA 4 pennants. AA best campsite in Wales 2005. Golf 5m, pony trekking 3m. Open Jan 1-Oct 31.

Coed Helen Caravan Club Site, Coed Helen Road, Caernarfon, Gwynedd LL54 5RS. *01286 676770.* www.caravanclub.co.uk. Owner: The Caravan Club. See website for directions. See website for directions. Non-members welcome. No tents. A slightly sloping open site 10mins walk from the historic town of Caernarfon. Toilet blocks, laundry facilities, vegetable preparation area, bar and dog walk nearby. Shop adjacent to the site. Fishing, golf, and NCN route 5m. Ideal for families. Open March-Oct.

(0.5m). Cwm Cadnant Valley Park, Llanberis Road, Caernarfon, Gwynedd LL55 2DF. *01286 673196.* www.cwmcadnant.co.uk. Owner: DE & JP Bird. Take A4086 from Caernarfon – Llanberis Road. Campsite next to fire station. Well maintained site in a small peaceful valley. 0.5m walk to town castle. Easy distance Snowdon and Anglesey. Open March 14-Nov 3.

(7m). Dinlle Caravan Park, Dinas Dinlle, Caernarfon, Gwynedd LL54 5TW. *01286 830324.* www.thornleyleisure.co.uk. Owner: Thornley Leisure Parks. SW of Caernarfon. Take A487-A499 Caernarfon and Pwllheli. After 5.5m Dinas Dinlle is SP W past AA phone box. Dinlle Park is SP on beach road. Launderette. Licensed club. Heated swimming pool. Takeaway. Beach 300yd. Open March 1-Nov 30.

(1.5m). Glan Gwna Country Holiday Park, Caeathro, Caernarfon, Gwynedd LL55 2SG. *01286 671740.* www.glangwna.com. Owner: MW Jones and family. Off A4085. Swimming pool. Club. Entertainment. Launderette. Takeaway. Caravan Sales: 01286 671740. Riverside and parkland pitches available. Game and coarse fishing available on the park. Golf courses nearby. Open April-Oct for touring, March-Jan 3 for statics.

(7m). Llyn-y-Gele Farm Caravan Park, Pontlyfni, Caernarfon, Gwynedd LL54 5EL. *01286 660289/660283.* Owner: Mr W Vaughan-Jones. On A499. 7m S of Caernarfon, entrance 1st R by garage in Pontllyfni village. Quiet, family site near beach by private footpath. Ideally situated for touring Snowdonia and the Lleyn Peninsula and Anglesey. Panoramic views of Snowdonia range. Shops & PO 2m, fishing 0.25m, doctor 4m, golf 7m. AA 2* and RAC listed. Open Easter-Oct 31.

(3m). Plas Gwyn Caravan Park, Plas Gwyn, Llanberis Road, llanrug, Caernarfon, Gwynedd LL55 2AQ. *01286 672619.* www.plasgwyn.co.uk. Owner: Robert & Sally Hampton. Entrance off the A4086 on R 3m from Caernarfon, about half way to Llanberis. Gas exchange service. Shop and laundry. Caravans for hire. Bed and breakfast on request. Horse-riding, fishing nearby. Golf course 0.5m, shopping centre 3m, cinema 5m. Open March 1-Oct 31.

(2m). Riverside Camping, Seiont Nurseries, Pontrug, Caernarfon, Gwynedd LL55 2BB. *01286 678781.* www.riversidecamping.co.uk. Owner: Brenda Hummel. 2m from Caernarfon on R of the A4086 (Caernarfon-Llanberis road). Small, sheltered site bordered by river. Ideally in Snowdonia in easy reach of both sea and mountains. Modern toilets and separate disabled facilities. Children's playground. On site: café/restaurant in old mill, launderette, fishing on association water – permits available. General provision shop and chipshop 1m. Indian restaurant in 1/8m. Open Easter-Oct 31.

(5m). Snowdon View Caravan Park, Brynrefail, Llanberis, Caernarfon, Gwynedd LL55 3PD. *01286 870349.* www.nav.to/snowdonview. Owner: Sunnysands Caravan Park Ltd. Off the main A4086 Caernarfon-Llanberis road, 5m from Caernarfon, 2m from Llanberis take the B4547 for 0.75m, park is on R. Playground. Country tavern. Indoor swimming pool. Open March 1-Nov 1.

(3m). Twll Clawdd, Llanrug, Caernarfon, Gwynedd LL55 2AZ. *01286 672838.* www.twllclawdd.co.uk. Owner: Mr PW Dodd. On Caernarfon-Llanberis road. A4086. Quiet, rural surroundings in easy reach of Snowdonia (4m) and Anglesey. Calor Gas stockist. Showers and shaver points. Telephone. Open March 1-Oct 31.

(3m). Tyn-y-Coed Caravan Park, Llanrug, Caernarfon, Gwynedd LL55 2AQ. *01286 673565.* www.hotmail.com-tyn-y-coedfarm. Owner: M&GM Williams. On RHS A4086 road to Llanberis from Caernarfon. Free H&C showers. Razor points. Laundry. Calor Gas. Dogs on lead only. Hotel indoor pool half mile. Fishing, golf course, shops, PO all in 1-3m. Open April-Sept.

(4m). Tyn-yr-Onnen Farm, Waunfawr, Caernarfon, Gwynedd LL55 4AX. *01286 650281.* Owner: Tom Griffith. SE of Caernarfon via A4085 Beddgelert road Turn L at Waunfawr chip shop to lane with 'No Through Road' sign. 200-acre farm site in good walking area. In easy reach of beach, Caernarfon Castle and Snowdon.

(3m). White Tower Caravan Park, Llandwrog, Caernarfon, Gwynedd LL54 5UH. *01286 830649.* www.whitetower.supanet.com. Owner: Mr L Ward. From Caernarfon follow A487 Porthmadog road for about 0.25m go past Tesco supermarket, straight ahead at roundabout take first R, park 3m on R. Super pitches also available. Central heated shower block for tourers. Club.

AA Best Camp Site in Wales within Snowdonia National Park

Breathtaking scenery engulfs this family-run park, nestled between Snowdonian mountain ranges and on the banks of the river Gwyrfai.

Clean, peaceful site, electric hook-ups, luxury toilet/showers, shop & off-licence, games room, spacious play area, fishing, mini golf.

• Static Caravans • Touring Pitches • Tent Pitches • Self-Catering Accommodation

FOR BROCHURE: 01286 650216

Bryn Gloch caravan & Camping Park
Betws Garmon, Caernarfon LL54 7YY
eurig@bryngloch.co.uk www.bryngloch.co.uk

144 MOTOR CARAVAN & CAMPING PARKS 2009

WALES

See page 5 for key to symbols and abbreviations

Games room. TV room. Heated pool, entertainment, and children's play area. Golf course 1.5m. Seasonal touring pitches also available. Open March 1-Nov 30.

CRICCIETH

(1.5m). Cae Canol Camping & Caravan Park, Criccieth, Gwynedd LL52 0NB. 01766 522351. Owner: Mrs EW Roberts. 2m N of Criccieth via B4411. Level site, modern facilities. Electric points, golf, fishing. Lovely riverside walks in 300yd of site. Leading to Lloyd George village of LLanystumdwy. Open April 1-Oct 31.

(3m). Camping & Caravanning Club Site – Llanystumdwy, Tyddyn Sianel, Llanystumdwy, Criccieth, Gwynedd LL52 0LS. 01766 522855. www.camping andcaravanningclub.co.uk. Owner: Camping & Caravanning Club. From Criccieth take A497 W, 2nd R to Llanystumdwy, site on R. 1.5m from the attractive seaside resort of Criccieth. There are scenic coastal views and sandy beaches close to the site. Close to Snowdonia National Park. Pleasant walks just below the village of Llanystumdwy. All units accepted. Non-members welcome. Deals for families and backpackers. Open March-Oct.

(1m). Eisteddfa Caravan & Camping Park, Eisteddfa Lodge, Pentrefelin, Criccieth, Gwynedd LL52 0PT. 01766 522696. www.eisteddfapark.co.uk. Owner: AM & KA Leech. Come to Porthmadog and at roundabout follow the A497 towards Criccieth. Follow road for 3.5m through Pentrefelin take first R after Plasgwyn Eisteddfa. Golf course and PO 1m away. Fishing lake next door. Cinema, swimming pool 3.5m. AA 4 pennants. Open March 1-Oct 31.

(1m). Llwyn Bugeilydd Farm, Criccieth, Gwynedd LL52 0PN. 01766 522235. Owner: Robert Roberts. A487 through Caernarfon, past Bryncir, turn R on to the B4411, site on L 3.5m. From Porthmadog, take A497 then turn R in Criccieth town centre on to B4411, site on R in 1m. Owner's mobile: 07854 063192. 1m walk to beach and shops. Snowdon view. One step to toilets/showers. Shaver and hairdryer points. Deep sinks for laundry and washing-up with free hot water. Senior citizens reduced rate low season. Criccieth golf course 18-hole, and also lake fishing is only 1.5m from the site. Regular bus service from site main entrance. Level site with sea and mountain views, situated away from traffic noise. Dog walking field. AA 2 pennants. Open March 1-Oct 31.

(3m). Muriau Bach Touring Site, Rhoslan, Muriau Bach, Criccieth, Gwynedd LL52 0NP. 01766 530642. Owner: Mr W D Roberts. On B4411. Turn off A487 on to B4411. The site is the 4th on the L over a cattle grid entrance. Between the hills and the sea with splendid views. Quiet and clean modern facilities. Cycle track nearby. Also fishing, golf course and a choice of beaches and walks. Nearest small town is Criccieth, 3m from the site with shops, PO, doctors etc. Ideal for retired people who like peace and quiet – offers for senior citizens during off peak periods. Friendly family site with modern facilities toilets, showers, etc. Dogs strictly on a lead. Open March 1-Oct 31.

(1m). Mynydd-Du Caravan Park, Porthmadog Road, Criccieth, Gwynedd LL52 0PS. 01766 523521. w.owen@btconnect.com. Owner: W&G Owen. On A497. 3m W of Porthmadog, 1m E of Criccieth on the Criccieth side of Pentrefelin. New toilet blocks. Garages, fishing and golf courses in the area. Shops, PO and doctors in 1.5m. Best view in North Wales. Open March 1-Oct 31.

(1.25m). Tyddyn Morthwyl, Criccieth, Gwynedd L552 0NF. 01766 522115. Owner: Mrs Trumper. On B4411 Criccieth to Caernarfon road. Sheltered site with good views and convenient for sea and mountains. Dogs on lead welcome. All amenities in the seaside town of Criccieth. Horse-riding, local attractions nearby. Open March 1-Oct 31.

DOLGELLAU

(3m). Dolgamedd Caravan & Camping Park, Bontnewydd, Brithdir, Dolgellau, Gwynedd LL40 2DG. 01341 450221. www.midwalesholidays.co.uk. Owner: Tom & Mair Evans. Take A494 from Dolgellau, travel 3m towards Bala. Take B4416 for Brithdir, Dolgamedd on L after bridge, beside river Wnion. 11 acre family run park, level and sheltered, set beside a river where camp fires are allowed. Street lights and picnic tables. Well appointed, spacious pitches available to locate your own chosen holiday home. 3 separate fields available for tourers and campers. Swimming and fishing on site. Bird watchers' paradise, excellent base for mountain biking. Rallies & pets welcome. Open: April 1 – Oct 31.

(4m). Llwyn-yr-Helm Farm, Brithdir, **Dolgellau, Gwynedd LL40 2SA.** 01341 450254.. www.llwynyrhelmcaravanpark.co.uk. On minor road 0.5m off B4416 which is a loop road from A470 to A494. Small working farm park in scenic countryside. Toilets, shower block with free hot water/showers. Eggs available. Ideal for walkers, country lovers and the more enthusiastic mountain biker, also for relaxing and enjoying the views. Coast 10m. Open Easter- End Oct.

(6m). Pant-y-Cae, Arthog, Dolgellau, Gwynedd LL39 1LJ. 01341 250892. Owner: Mr & Mrs Thomas. Off A493 Towyn to Dolgellau on road to Cregennan lakes, SP afer Arthog village. We are an organic farm in the foothills of Cadair Idris in the picturesque countryside for bird watching, walking, cycling, fishing and 4m from a sandy beach.

(0.5m). Tan-y-Fron Caravan & Camping Park, Arran Road, Dolgellau, Gwynedd LL40 2AA. 01341 422638. info@tan-y-fron.co.uk. Owner: Mr EP Rowlands. Take A470 from Welshpool, turn L Dolgellau. 0.5m on L by 30mph sign. Small family run quiet park, centrally located for touring. Less than 10mins/ 0.5m into Dolgellau where there are shops, cafés, restaurants etc. Tent prices include showers. No dogs on touring pitches. Open March 1-Dec 20.

(3m). Tyddyn Farm, Islawrdref, Dolgellau, Gwynedd LL40 1TL. 01341 422472. Owner: Mr RD Owen & BM Owen. 0.25m after Gwernan Lake hotel on R. Through two gates first L. Lovely views, 2m from shop, PO, doctors. Fishing, golf, good hotel and pub 1m.

DYFFRYN ARDUDWY

Murmur-yr-Afon Touring Caravan & Camping Park, Dyffryn Ardudwy, Gwynedd LL44 2BE. 01341 247353. mills@murmuryrafon25.freeserve.co.uk. Owner: Mr & Mrs NE Mills. Take A496 coast road from Barmouth to Harlech. Site entrance is 100yd from Bentley's garage in Dyffryn on R. Set in sheltered surroundings 1m from the beach. Shop, Gas & Camping Gaz available in village which has off licence and hotel. Open March 1-Oct 31.

HARLECH

(4m). Barcdy Touring Caravan & Camping Park, Talsarnau, Harlech, Gwynedd LL47 6YG. 01766 770736. www.barcdy.co.uk. Owner: Mrs A L Roberts. On A496 Blaenau Ffestiniog to Harlech. Ideal situation for touring Snowdonia. In quiet, picturesque surroundings. Garage, PO

WALES

1m, golf course 4m. Fishing nearby (10mins walk from park). Open May-Sept 30/March-Jan for caravan holiday homes.

(1m). Min-y-Don Holiday Home Park, Beach Road, Harlech, Gwynedd LL46 2UG. 01766 780286. www.salopcaravans.co.uk. Owner: Salop Caravans (Sites) Ltd. Easily accessible off A596 coast road. Turn into Beach Road opposite Queens Hotel. Central for Snowdonia. Below Harlech Castle. 5mins walk to railway station and bus stop. Near sandy beach and St Davids golf course. Doctor 5mins walk. Laundry facilities on site. Open March-end Oct.

LLANRUG

(3m). Challoner Caravan Park, Erw Hywel Farm, Llanberis Road, Llanrug, Gwynedd LL55 2AJ. 01286 672985. challoner.caravan@tesco.net. Owner: Mrs S Challoner. A4086 4m W of Llanberis and 3m E of Caernarfon. Small friendly camp site, surrounded by mountains and greenery, energetic or relaxing holidays, catered for, by a wealth of activities in the area, from deep water diving to golf. Open March 1-Jan 10.

MERIONETH

(4m). Bellaport Farm, Talybont, Nr Barmouth, Merioneth, Gwynedd LL43 2BX. 01341 247338. Owner: Mrs Beti Roberts. Off A496, turn R at 40mph limit sign leaving Talybont village travelling N to top of lane. Barmouth 4m. 0.5m from village. Adults only. No dogs in static van. Fishing, golf course nearby. Open March-Sept.

NANT PERIS

Snowdon House, Gwastadnant, Nant Peris, Gwynedd LL55 4UL. 01286 870356. Owner: Mr James M Cumberton. On A4086. 3m SE of Llanberis. Ideal for climbing and rambling. Situated at foot of Llanberis Pass. Convenient for Snowdon, The Horseshoe and Glyders.

PORTHMADOG

(3m). Black Rock Camping & Touring Park, Black Rock Sands, Morfa Bychan, Porthmadog, Gwynedd LL49 9YH. 01766 513919. Owner: P Roberts. After coming over toll gate into Porthmadog, turn sharp L by Woolworths. Go through Morfa Bychan to the end, the park is opposite Black Rock café. Adjacent to 7m beach. Shop & PO 1m, leisure centre 3m. David Bellamy Gold Conservation Award. Open March-Sept.

(2m). Garreg Goch Caravan Park, Black Rock Sands, Morfa Bychan, Porthmadog, Gwynedd LL49 9YD. 01766 512210. Owner: Normanhurst Enterprises Ltd. 2m W of Portmadog. Turning for Morfa Bychan. Follow this road – pass BP filling station then turn L into Park. Mainly caravan park but space for tents. Easy reach of beach. Open March 1-Jan 10.

(2m). Greenacres Holiday Park, Black Rock Sands, Morfa Bychan, Porthmadog, Gwynedd LL49 9YF. 01766 512781. www.greenacres-park.co.uk. Owner: Bourne Leisure Ltd. From Porthmadog High Street, turn between Woolworth's and the PO towards Black Rock Sands. Carry on for about 2m. The park entrance is just the other side of Morfa Bychan on L. Welcome Host Award, Investor in People. Heated indoor swimming pool. Mini market. Bakery. Pitch & Putt. Kids' clubs. Access onto Black Rock Sands. Day and evening family entertainment. David Bellamy Gold Conservation Award. Open March-end Oct.

(2m). Gwyndy Caravan Park, Black Rock Sands, Morfa Bychan, Porthmadog, Gwynedd LL49 9YB. 01766 512047. Owner: Mr MS & Mrs J Leech. In Porthmadog turn at Woolworths, 2m to Morfa Bychan, past Spar turn L then second R, SP Gwyndy. Pathway to beach. Launderette, utility room. W.T.B & AA. Golf course nearby. Open March-Oct.

(2.5m). Tyddyn Adi Caravan Park, Morfa Bychan, Porthmadog, Gwynedd LL49 9YW. 01766 512933. www.tyddynadi.co.uk. Owner: Mr Ifor Lewis. From Porthmadoc take Morfa Bycham road u/l large sign on R at end of village 400yd to site. Flat, well-drained site 0.5m from beach. Takeaway meals nearby. Open March 1-Oct 30.

PWLLHELI

(1.5m). Abererch Sands, Pwllheli, Gwynedd LL53 6PJ. 01758 612327. www.abererch-sands.co.uk. Owner: KJ Dunne. On A497 Criccieth to Pwllheli. Heated indoor swimming pool. Fitness room. Play area for children. Open March 1-Oct 31.

(5m). Bodwrog Farm, Bodwrog, Llanbedrog, Pwllheli, Gwynedd LL53 7RE. 01758 740341. www.bodwrog.co.uk. Owner: Mr DR Williams. On Lof B4413, 1m from its junction with A499. Quiet family site. Close to beaches. Superb sea views. Disabled shower and toilet. Electric hook-ups. Open Easter-end Oct.

Bolmynydd Touring & Camping Park, Refail, Llanbedrog, Pwllheli, Gwynedd LL53 7NP. 01758 740511. refail.llanbedrog@ukonline.co.uk. Owner: Christine Evans. A499 from Pwllheli to Llanbedrog. Carry on towards Abersoch for 0.5m. Take first L lane after riding centre. Park 0.5m on L. Secluded park on Llanbedrog headland with glorious views. In 10mins walk of two beautiful sandy beaches, pub and shop. Essential to book in advance. Open Easter-end Sept.

(14m). Brynffynnon Caravan Park, Rhoshirwaun, Pwllheli, Gwynedd LL53 8LF. 01758 730643. Owner: Mr & Mrs EW Jones. Take the 'Whistling Sands' road off B4413. Open March 1-Oct 31.

(6m). Cedfn Caer Ferch, Llangybi, Pwllheli, Gwynedd. 01766 688412. Remote situation, approached off A499 or B4354.

Pen-y-Bont Bach, Llangwnadl, Pwllheli, Gwynedd LL23 7PH. 01758 770252. eai@llwyn78.freeserve.co.uk. Off B4417 8m SW of Nefyn, NW coast of the Lleyn Peninsula. Approaching from Nefyn, do not take the first turning SP to Llangwnnadl, but continue downhill past grocery shop on bridge, to site first on L. Small country site. Open March-Sept.

(5m). Porthysgaden Farm, Tudweiliog, Nefyn, Pwllheli, Gwynedd LL53 8PD. 01758 770206. Owner: JP Owen. SW of Nefyn via B4417 Aberdaron road. Turn R 0.75m beyond Tudweiliog to site 0.75m. Flat, well-drained site 400yd from sea, various coves and beaches along stretch. Good skin-diving area. Slipway for boats. Shops nearby. Open Easter-Oct.

(3.5m). Refail Touring & Camping Park, Llanbedrog, Pwllheli, Gwynedd LL53 7NP. 01758 740511. refail.llanbedrog@ukonline.co.uk. Owner: Mrs C Evans. Follow A499 from Pwllheli. At Llanbedrog turn R on to B4413 (SP 'Refail'). Site 200yd on R. Sheltered family park with glorious views, excellent facilities and easy access. Beautiful sandy beach, shops, pubs, bistro and restaurant all in 5mins walk. Season pitches available. Open Easter-Oct 31.

The Willows Camping & Caravan Park, Mynytho, Abersoch, Pwllheli, Gwynedd LL53 7RW. 01758 740676. www.the-

146 MOTOR CARAVAN & CAMPING PARKS 2009

WALES

See page 5 for key to symbols and abbreviations

willows-abersoch.co.uk. Owner: Mr & Mrs MA James. A499 R at Llanbedrog on to B4085. 30mph sign at Mynytho turn R. Site on L in 0.25m, pass 1st Bryntirion sign. 2m N of Abersoch. 10 acres, lovely peaceful surroundings. 4 acres of level camping fields. Grass & hardstanding pitches. 16amp hook up & tv link, tv room, indoor dishwashing facilities. Free fridge freezers, barrier operated access, boat storage, baby change. Select, quiet site. Shop, PO in 0.25m. Children's play area. Outstanding views of Snowdonia and Cardigan Bay. Pubs, restaurants nearby. Open from 1 March-31 Oct.

(3m). Tyddyn Heilyn Caravan Park, Tyddyn Heilyn Farm, Chwilog, Pwllheli, Gwynedd LL53 6SW. *01766 810441.* Owner: RE & Mrs EA Williams. From A497 to B4354 and at village of Chwilog, before pub turn R opposite butchers. 1.5m, site marked. Beautiful scenic 10m walks passing through this farmland – overlooking Cardigan Bay/ Snowdonia scenery. Ideal birdwatching – coastal and country birds. Easy reach to shops, good eating out places and pubs. Near fishing rivers and lakes, riding school, golf, safe cycle tracks. Site level and shaded. Open Feb-Jan.

(4m). Wern Newydd Tourer Park, Llanbedrog, Pwllheli, Gwynedd LL53 7PG. *01758 740220.* www.wern-newydd. co.uk. Owner: Mrs M L Valentine. Turn R off A499 (Pwllheli-Abersoch) in Llanbedrog on to B4413 (Sp Aberdaron) continue through village, past the PO on the R, then take first turning R on to unclassified road, called Lon Pin. Site entrance on the R in 700yd. Peaceful site. 15mins walk to the beach, 5mins to village. Good eating places, shops, PO, chemist, pubs, sailing, watersports facilities, golf, riding, fishing etc nearby. Mobile shop visits in high season. Doctor's surgery 4m Open March- Oct.

TYWYN

(7m). Cedris Farm, Tal-y-Llyn, Tywyn, Gwynedd LL36 9YW. *01654 782280.* Owner: EE Jones. 7m NE of Tywyn via B4405. 1st farm on L 1m after Abergynolwyn. Quiet valley 7m from beach and close to narrow-gauge railway and Roman bridge. Rock climbing and rambling country. Plenty of interesting walks. Stream few yards from site. Bird watching on farm land (Red Kite). 1m to pub with bar meals. Open Easter-Oct.

Cwmrhwyddfor Camp Site, Talyllyn, Tywyn, Gwynedd LL36 9SR. *01654 761286.* Owner: Mr TD Nutting. On A487 6m from Dolgellau at bottom of Talyllyn Pass. White house on R at foot of Cader Idris mountain. Clean park with hot showers, razor points, flush toilets. Disposal point. Electric Hook-ups. Tents also accepted. Tarmac road from main road to end of site. Touring caravan pitches available for Summer and full season. In easy reach sea. Excellent access. Ideal for walking. Fishing in stream. Craft shops. Pony trekking, golf course, shop nearby. Hotel and café in walking distance. Open March 1- End Oct. Open all year for tents.

Dol Einion, Tal-y-Llyn, Tywyn, Gwynedd LL36 9AJ. *01654 761312.* Owner: M Rees. Situated on the B4405 near junction with A487, at commencement of popular footpath to summit of Cader Idris. A flat 3- acre field with stream near Tal-y-Lyn Lake. Easy access with hardstanding. A superb, quiet location in the Snowdonia National Park, ideal for walking and sightseeing. Pub/restaurant. Narrow gauge railway and trout fishing nearby. Dogs allowed.

(5m). Llabwst Farm, Rhoslefain, Tywyn, Gwynedd. *01654 711013.* N of Tywyn. On A493 coast road. Turn opposite white cottage at Rhoslefain village. Quiet, well-sheltered farm site. Open Whitsun- Oct.

(0.25m). Pall Mall Farm Caravan Park, Tywyn, Gwynedd LL36 9RU. *01654 710384.* Owner: Mr & Mrs ML Vaughan & Mr R Vaughan. Site is 1st farm on L 400yd W of Tywyn on A493. New leisure centre, Play area. Bed and breakfast available. Open Easter-Oct.

■ **(3m). Tynllwyn Caravan & Camping Park,** Bryncrug, Tywyn, **Gwynedd LL36 9RD.** *01654 710370.* www.tynllwyncaravanpark.co.uk. Owner: Mr & Mrs PL McEvoy. Off A493. Small, friendly, family run site with excellent facilities. Telephone, laundry, play area. Talyllyn narrow gauge steam train runs past site. Open March-Oct.

(4m). Waenfach Caravan Site, Llanegryn, Tywyn, Gwynedd LL36 9SB. *01654 710375.* waenfach@aol.com. Owner: Mr & Mrs Davies. Off A493. Beautiful views on working farm. Spacious amenities block with laundry facilities. Public telephone. Deep freeze. Dogs under control. Shops 1m; doctor, hospital, PO in Tywyn. Sea and river fishing, golf course 5m. Open April-Oct.

(1m). Ynysmaengwyn Holiday Park, Tywyn, Gwynedd LL36 9RY. *01654 710684.* www.ynysy.co.uk. Owner: Mr & Mrs Blunden. 1m out of Tywyn on the A493 towards Barmouth. Park is in the grounds of an old manor house, offering excellent facilities for walking, cycling, climbing, fishing and all water sports. Shop van deliveries daily. Open April 1-Oct 31.

MERTHYR TYDFIL

MERTHYR TYDFIL

(4m). Grawen Caravan & Camping Park, Cwm-Taff, Cefn-Coed, Merthyr

---

TYNLLWYN CARAVAN & CAMPING PARK

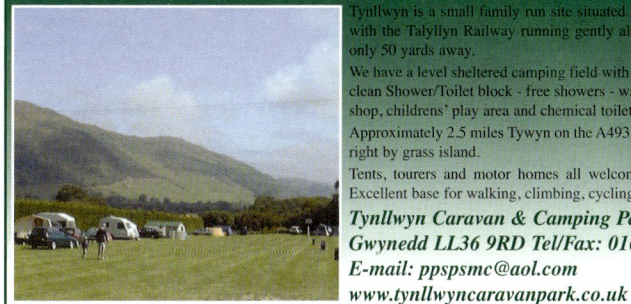

Tynllwyn is a small family run site situated in the picturesque hamlet of Rhdyronnen, with the Talyllyn Railway running gently alongside the site, and Rhdyronnen Station only 50 yards away.

We have a level sheltered camping field with electric hook-ups and water points. Good, clean Shower/Toilet block - free showers - washing-up and laundry facilities, small site shop, childrens' play area and chemical toilet disposal point.

Approximately 2.5 miles Tywyn on the A493, then take a right turn to B4405, then first right by grass island.

Tents, tourers and motor homes all welcome. Also luxury static caravans for hire. Excellent base for walking, climbing, cycling, fishing and all watersports.

Tynllwyn Caravan & Camping Park, Bryncrug, Tywyn Gwynedd LL36 9RD Tel/Fax: 01654 710370
E-mail: ppspsmc@aol.com
www.tynllwyncaravanpark.co.uk

PARC GWYLIAU / HOLIDAY PARK

---

www.motorcaravanmagazine.co.uk MOTOR CARAVAN & CAMPING PARKS 2009 **147**

WALES

Tydfil, Merthyr Tydfil CF48 2HS. *01685 723740*. www.walescaravanandcamping.com. Owner: Mrs F Pugh. On A470. Brecon Beacons road 2m from A465. Picturesque forest, mountain and reservoir walks close to site in clean fresh air with easy access. Also a wealth of history in the town and valleys. Open April-Oct.

MONMOUTHSHIRE
ABERGAVENNY

(5.25m). Pandy Caravan Club Site, Pandy, Abergavenny, Monmouthshire NP7 8DR. *01873 890370*. www.caravanclub.co.uk. Owner: Caravan Club. See website for directions. Level site with views of the Black Mountains. Non-members welcome. No tents. Advance booking essential, some hardstandings. Toilet blocks. Privacy cubicles. Laundry, veg prep. MV service point. Golf, fishing nearby. Good area for walking. Gas, dog walk. Quiet and peaceful off peak. NCN cycle route in 5m. Walkers will love Offa's Dyke path on the border England and Wales. The area is littered with interesting historical buildings. Open March-Nov.

(7m). Pontkemys Caravan & Camping Park, Pontkemys, Chainbridge, Abergavenny, Monmouthshire NP7 9DS. *01873 880688*. www.pontkemys.com. Owner: Bryan & Rose Jones. 4m from Usk. On B4598 to Abergavenny. (M4, J24 N on A449, or from M5/M50/A40, S on A449 to Usk). Pub 300yd, golf course 400yd. Usk Valley walk 300yd. Dog charged for. Dog walk area. Mother and baby room. Booking advisable some hardstandings. Open March-Oct.

(2m). Pyscodlyn Farm Camping & Caravan Site, Llanwenarth Citra, Abergavenny, Monmouthshire NP7 7ER. *01873 853271*. www.pyscodlyncaravanpark.com. Owner: KT Davies. W of Abergavenny on the A40 to Brecon. Ideal area for exploring the Black Mountains and Brecon Beacons National Park. Fishing tickets available for river Usk. Golf and pony trekking nearby. Open April 1-Oct 31.

(5m). Rising Sun, Pandy, Abergavenny, Monmouthshire NP7 8DL. *01873 890254*. Owner: Owen & Mandy Price. 5m N of Abergavenny on A465 to Hereford at Pandy. Bar/restaurant. Hot & cold showers. Children's play area.

MONMOUTH

(3m). Bridge Caravan Park, Dingestow, Monmouth, Monmouthshire NP25 4DY. *01600 740241*. www.bridgecaravanpark.co.uk. Owner: S Holmes. SP from Abergavenny junction of A449 trunk road. In the heart of the Vale of Usk and Wye Valley next to the river Trothy. Fishing available to all visitors. A background of woodland completes the lovely setting of this select park. Open Easter-Oct.

(2m). Glen Trothy Caravan and Camping Park, Mitchel Troy, Monmouth, Monmouthshire NP25 4BD. *01600 712295*. www.glentrothy.co.uk. Owner: H& MY Price. SW of Monmouth off new A40. On edge of Wye Valley & Forest of Dean. Good range of facilities. Play area. Send/phone for free brochure. Open March 1-Oct 31.

(0.5m). Monmouth Caravan Park, Rockfield Road, Monmouth, Monmouthshire NP25 5BA. *01600 714745*. www.monmouthcaravanpark.com. Owner: Mr & Mrs Brown. Family run touring and camping park in easy walking distance of town. New facilities block and club house. Fishing available. 0.25m on B4233 Rockfield Road, just past fire and ambulance station. Open March 1-Jan 5.

Monnow Bridge Caravan Site, Drybridge Street, Monmouth, Monmouthshire NP25 5AD. *01600 714004*. Owner: Mrs M Murray. Small, family-run site in town on banks of river. Caravans for hire. Fishing from site on Offa's Dyke path.

NEWPORT
COEDKERNEW

Tredegar House Country Park Caravan Club Site, Coedkernew, Newport NP10 8TW. *01633 815600*. www.caravanclub.co.uk. Owner: The Caravan Club. See website for directions. This seven acre site is ideally located in 1m of the M4 and is only 7m from Cardiff. Adventure playground ADJ. Toilet blocks. Privacy cubicles. Laundry facilities. Veg prep. MV service point. Fishing and golf nearby. Non-members and tent campers welcome. Some hardstandings, gas, dog walk nearby.

PEMBROKESHIRE
CLYNDERWEN

(0.5m). Gower Villa Touring Park, Gower Villa Lane, Clynderwen, Pembrokeshire SA66 7NL. *01437 562059*. www.gvtp.co.uk. Owner: N & G Featherstone. From Narberth A478 towards Cardigan in Clynderwen village, first R after Farmer Association store. Quiet location off private lane: 400yd to shops, pub and petrol station. Immaculate toilet block. Level grass, some hardstanding, rally field available. Ideal for touring SW Wales. Open March 1st-Oct 31.

(3.5m). Trefach Caravan Park, Mynachlogddu, Clynderwen, Pembrokeshire SA66 7RU. *01994 419225*. www.trefach.co.uk. Owner: O & D Enterprises. 4m E of Maenclochog, 9m N of Narberth via A478 to 1m N of Efailwen, turn L by Cross Inn to site, 1m on R. Well-drained site in good walking area in Preseli National Park. 18-acre country site. Central to all Pembrokeshire, ideal for exploring by foot, car or horseback. Heated swimming pool. Play room. Restaurant. Bar. Fishing nearby. Open March-Jan 6.

FISHGUARD

(3m). Fishguard Bay Caravan & Camping Park, Garn Gelli, Fishguard, Pembrokeshire SA65 9ET. *01348 811415*. www.fishguardbay.com. Owner: C N & L Harries. Take A487 Fishguard to Cardigan road. Turning on your L. Well SP. Games/pool room, children's play area. TV common room. Launderette. Cinema, town and swimming pool 3m. Golf course 5m. Open March-Dec.

(1.5m). Gwaun Vale Touring Park, Llanychaer, Fishguard, Pembrokeshire SA65 9TA. *01348 874698*. www.gwaunvale.co.uk. Owner: Mrs Margaret Harris. From Fishguard take B4313 SP Llanychaer and Gwaun Valley. Park 1.5m on R. Local pub 0.5m. Launderette. Telephone. Play area. Dog walk. Gas. Fishing, boating, swimming, coast and mountain walks and Irish ferry in 2m. Clean, unspoilt beaches. Open March 1-Oct 31.

(1m). Tregroes Touring Park, Fishguard, Pembrokeshire SA65 9QF. *01348 872316*. jch_williams@hotmail.com. Owner: Hugh Williams. S of Fishguard on A40. 1m from coast and ferry port. Attractive farm site. Children's play area. Pets welcome. Late arrivals accepted. Some restricted facilities for the disabled. Takeaways available nearby. Open Easter-Oct.

HAVERFORDWEST

(8m). Brandy Brook Camping and Caravan Site, Rhyndaston, Haycastle, Haverfordwest, Pembrokeshire SA62

148 MOTOR CARAVAN & CAMPING PARKS 2009

WALES

5PT. 01348 840272. Owner: Mr FM Rowe. A487 from Haverfordwest to Roch Motel. SP at the R-hand turn. Secluded and quiet in a remote natural valley. Open Easter-Oct.

Camping & Caravanning Club Site – St Davids, Dwr Cwmwdig Berea, St David's, Haverfordwest, Pembrokeshire SA62 6DW. 01348 831376. www.campingandcaravanningclub.co.uk. Owner: Camping & Caravanning Club. From Fishguard on A487 after Croesgoch, fork R. Follow 'Abereiddy' signs. Site is 300yd W of crossroads. 5m from St David's. Site is set in 4 acres with 40 pitches accepting all units. Chocks will be needed as all pitches are sloping. Near coast, 0.5m by footpath from Aber-eiddy. Site is located in the beautiful Pembrokeshire countryside, just 1m from the heritage coast and close to Britain's smallest Cathedral City. Non-members welcome. Fishing 1m from the site. Special deals for families and backpackers. Open April-Oct.

(5m). Creampots Touring Caravan and Camping Park, Broadway, Broad Haven, Haverfordwest, Pembrokeshire SA62 3TU. 01437 781776. www.creampots.co.uk. Owner: John & Ros Sheppard. From Haverfordwest take B4341 Broad Haven road. At Broadway turn L, follow brown signs for Creampots. Quiet and level with excellent heated facilities including free hot showers. Convenient for touring, beaches, coast path, water sports and bird sanctuaries. Excellent site for couples and young families. 1.5m of Broadhaven beach. Open March-Jan.

(3m). Dunston Hill Farm, Pelcomb, Haverfordwest, Pembrokeshire SA62 6ED. 01437 710525. Owner: Mrs R Jenkins. On A487 St David's road. Touring centre or overnight stop. Peaceful, sheltered site in easy reach of many sandy beaches. Open April-Sept.

East Hook Farm, Marloes, Haverfordwest, Pembrokeshire SA62 3BJ. 01646 636291. Owner: Chetwynd Farmers. From Haverfordwest B4327 towards Dale. First R 2m before Dale and through Marloes, about 1m to farm on Pembrokeshire coast path. 15mins walk to beaches. Scenic views. Small farm site. Cycle hire. Windsurfing nearby.

(2m). Hendre Eynon, St David's, Haverfordwest, Pembrokeshire SA62 6DB. 01437 720474. www.ukparks.co.uk/hendreeynon. Owner: Mr & Mrs I Jamieson. 2m NE of St David's on u/c road to Llanrhigh. Simple style on a working farm with superb facilities. Two perimeter pitching fields with sheltering trees. Ideal for walkers, birdwatchers and botanists. Open April 1-Oct 1.

Howelston Holiday Park, Howelston, Little Haven, Haverfordwest, Pembrokeshire SA62 3UU. 01437 781253. Minor road on coast off B4327 and B4341. From Haverfordwest. Overlooking St Brides Bay and 1m from seaside village of Little Haven. 200yd from coastal path. Open April-Sept.

(12m). Nine Wells Caravan & Camping Park, Nine Wells, Solva, Haverfordwest, Pembrokeshire SA62 6UH. 01437 721809. Owner: ND Bowie. From Haverfordwest take A487 SP St Davids, go through Solva. After 0.5m at Nine Wells turn L at site sign. Fishing, sailing, boating and beaches nearby. PO, village shops, pubs and restaurants in Solva. 5mins walk down National Trust Valley to Pembrokeshire Coastal Footpath, the cove and sea. Open Easter-Oct.

(17m). Prendergast Caravan Site, Trefin, Haverfordwest, Pembrokeshire SA62 5AU. 01348 831368. www.prendergastcaravanpark.co.uk. Owner: Mr A Jenkins. 8m NE of St Davids. Via A487 to Trefin, SP. N for 1m to site. 0.25m from beach. Fees on application Open April-Oct.

(6.5m). Redlands Touring Caravan & Camping Park, Hasguard Cross, Nr Little Haven, Haverfordwest, Pembrokeshire SA62 3SJ. 01437 781300. www.redlandstouring.co.uk. Owner: Trevor & Jenny Flight. On B4327 SW of Haverfordwest, do not approach via Broad Haven. 5 acres of open grassland. Immaculately kept facilities. Pets welcome. Convenient base for Pembrokeshire holidays. Close to beaches and famous coastal path. Open March-Dec.

(5m). South Cockett Touring Caravan & Camping Park, Broadway, Little Haven, Haverfordwest, Pembrokeshire SA62 3TU. 01437 781296/781760. www.southcockett.co.uk. Owner: Mrs E R James. Take B4341 from Haverfordwest, turn L at official caravan & camping sign. Site 300yd on R. Shop 1m. Hot water to basins. Freezer pack service. Gas and Gaz stocked. Clean site with excellent facilities. Disabled facilities. Visit Wales 3 stars, AA 3 pennants. Open Easter-Oct.

Tan-y-Bryn, Whitesands, St David's, Haverfordwest, Pembrokeshire SA62 6PS. 01437 720168. Situated next to Whitesands Beach. Manager: Mr M Pawlik – contact at Whitesands Beach café/shop. Open March-Dec.

(14m). Tretio Touring Caravan & Camping Park, St David's, Haverfordwest, Pembrokeshire SA62 6DE. 01437 781600. www.tretio.com. Owner: Bryn & Phil Rees. Off B3283. St David's 3m. On leaving St David's keep L at St David's R.F.C and continue straight for 3m until sign pointing R. Park 300yd. Park in Pembrokeshire Nationa Park. 0.25m off coast road and 0.5m to coastal path, panoramic views. 4.5-acre 9-hole pitch and putt course. PO, doctors, shops available in St David's, 3m. 1.5m to nearest beach. Open March-Oct.

NARBERTH

Dingle Farm Caravan Park, Narberth, Pembrokeshire SA67 7DP. 01834 860482. Owner: Mrs R Owen & sons. Showers. Clubhouse. Play area. Takeaway facilities, laundry and swimming pool all nearby.

(5m). Little Kings Park, Amroth Road, Ludchurch, Narberth, Pembrokeshire SA67 8PG. 01834 831330. www.littlekings.co.uk. Owner: Mr & Mrs D Jones. From A477 turn L to Amroth and Wiseman's Bridge, take first turn R, SP Ludchurch, park 0.25m on L. Quiet family park in country setting with easy access to explore Pembrokeshire. Residents' bar and restaurant. Indoor pool, shop, 2 amenities block. 2 play areas. Dog walk. Beach 1.5m. Open March-Oct.

(6m). Meadow House Holiday Park, Summerhill, Narberth, Pembrokeshire SA67 8NS. 01834 812438. www.meadowhouseholidaypark.com. Owner: Celtic Holiday Parks Ltd. 6m NE of Tenby. From Tenby take A478. After 3.5m turn R on to A477, turn R again at sign Amroth and Wisemans Bridge. From St Clears on A477 for 10m, after 'Stage Coach Inn' turn L at sign. 1m from beach. Indoor swimming pool. No dogs July 19-Aug 31. David Bellamy Gold Conservation Award. Open March-Oct.

(7m). New Park, Landshipping, Narberth, Pembrokeshire SA67 8BG. 01834 891284. Owner: E&CA Jones. From E turn L off A40 at Canaston Bridge on to A4075, turn R at Canaston Bowls towards Martletwy Landshipping, after 2m turn R, after 200yd turn L. Entrance on L in 0.5m. River Cleddau 1m with fishing, sailing etc.

WALES

Tranquil countryside retreat. Horse riding, theme park and ten pin bowling 3m. Golf course 12m, cinema 14m. Open March 1-Jan 9.

(0.5m). Noble Court Holiday Park, Redstone Road, Narberth, Pembrokeshire SA67 7ES. *0183 4 861908.* www.noblecourtholidaypark.com. Owner: Celtic Holiday Parks Ltd. Off A40 on B4313 road, 0.5m N of Narberth and 0.5m S of A40. Club. Heated swimming pool, coarse fishing. Shops 0.5m. David Bellamy Gold Conservation Award. Open March 1-Oct 31.

(10m). Rosebush Caravan Park, Rhoslwyn, Rosebush, Narberth, Pembrokeshire SA66 7QT. *01437 532206.* Owner: Mr G Williams. On B4313. B4329 1m away. Boating. Coarse fishing. Adults only. David Bellamy Gold Conservation Award. Open March 25-Oct 31.

(2m). Wood Office Caravan Park, Cold Blow, Narberth, Pembrokeshire SA67 8RR. *01834 860565.* On A40, B4315. Close to Oakwood Park A478, Folly Farm and Heron's Brook golf. Central for touring. Flat site, well drained. Oakwood Park, Folly Farm and Heron's Brook all nearby. Restrictions apply on dog breeds. Open Easter-Oct 31.

NEWPORT

Morawelon, Parrog, Newport, Pembrokeshire SA42 0RW. *01239 820565.* Owner: Mrs C Watts. On A487 in Newport turn N on road to Parrog. Site on sea front. Close to sandy beach, safe bathing, good sailing, slipway for boat launching ideal for wind surfers. Sheltered site with beautiful sea views. Open end March-end Sept.

Tycanol Farm Camp Site, Organic, Newport, Pembrokeshire SA42 0ST. *01239 820264.* www.caravancampingsites.co.uk. Owner: Mr Hugh Harris. On A487 near Newport. Sign to Tycanol on milk stand. Level, sheltered pitches, overlooking Newport Bay. By the coastal path with easy access to beaches and town. Free hot showers. Bicycle hire nearby. Nature walk for wildlife. BBQ free nightly.

PEMBROKE

(10m). Castle Farm Camping Site, Angle, Pembroke, Pembrokeshire SA71 5AR. *01646 641220.* Owner: GB Rees & Sons. Enter opposite hotel in Angle or follow directions to Lifeboat station.

Holiday site near entrance of Milford Haven, in National Park (Pembrokeshire). Limited number of touring vans. Site is behind village church, overlooking East Angle Bay. Open Easter-Oct.

(2.5m). Freshwater East Caravan Club Site, Trewent Hill, Freshwater East, Pembroke, Pembrokeshire SA71 5LJ. *01646 672341.* www.caravanclub.co.uk. Owner: The Caravan Club. See website for directions. In the Pembrokeshire Coast National Park. Part sloping, information room, dog walk nearby. 2 toilet blocks. Privacy cubicles. Laundry facilities. Veg prep. MV waste point. Hardstandings. Gas and gaz. Play area. Non-members and tent campers welcome. Do not tow to the beach. Fishing and watersports. Good area for walking. Ideal for families, quiet and peaceful off peak, in 5m of NCN cycle route. Open March-Oct.

(3m). Upper Portclew Touring Site, Freshwater East, Pembroke, Pembrokeshire SA71 5LA. *01646 672112.* Owner: Mrs MA Phillips. Carmarthen – turn L. Milton – Lamphey – 7 E Site on R before village. PO & shops 1.5m, Lamphey. Fishing on beach, rocks. Doctors 3m, Pembroke. Golf course, 6m Pembroke Dock, 10m Tenby. Open May-Sept.

SAUNDERSFOOT

(2m). Mill House Caravan Park, Pleasant Valley, Stepaside, Saundersfoot, Pembrokeshire SA67 8LN. *01834 812069.* www.millhousecaravan.co.uk. Owner: Simon & Amanda Wood. 13m W St Clears A477. Turn L for Stepaside, first L and first L for Pleasant Valley. Site 0.5m on L. Beautiful family site next to old watermill. 15mins walk to beach, coast path and PH. Hardstanding, TV and electricity included. Open March-Oct.

(1.5m). Moreton Farm Leisure Park, Moreton, Saundersfoot, Pembrokeshire SA69 9EA. *01834 812016.* www.moretonfarm.co.uk. Owner: Nixon Ltd. On A478 Kilgetty to Tenby 3.5m. Saundersfoot 1.5m. Set in peaceful surroundings. Modern facilities. Pine lodges and cottages. Bed linen provided. Play area. Open March 1-Nov 1.

(1m). Moysland Farm, Tenby Road, Saundersfoot, Pembrokeshire SA69 9DS. *01834 812455.* Owner: Mrs V Rawson & Mr Humphries. On A478 2.5m S of Begelly roundabout, 1m SW of

Saundersfoot. 4 acres, level. Low level night time lighting, on cycle route Saundersfoot to Tenby. Free hot water and showers, dogs welcome under control. Booking advisable July-Sept. Public transport in 1m. Open July-Sept.

(1m). Sunnyvale Holiday Park, Valley Road, Saundersfoot, Pembrokeshire SA69 9BT. *01834 814404.* www.sunnyvaleholidaypark.com. Owner: Dean Deakin. Take A478 towards Tenby. 3m from Tenby. Enter Pentlepoir. Pass Murco petrol station on R, take next L into Valley Road. Park 150yd down on L. Club. Nightly entertainment. Heated indoor swimming pool. Shop, kiddies play park. Open March-Oct.

ST DAVID'S

(1m). Caerfai Bay Caravan & Tent Park, St David's, Pembrokeshire SA62 6QT. *01437 720274.* www.caerfaibay.co.uk. Owner: D Panton. Off A487 Haverfordwest to St Davids, in St Davids at Visitor Centre near Grove Hotel, park at end of road on the R. Panoramic sea views. Seaside Award. Bathing beach 200yd, adjacent to Pembrokeshire coastal path and numerous local outdoor pursuits. Takeaway. Café/restaurant nearby. Shops 0.75m, golf 2m. No season site pitches available. Pets restrictions in high season. Open March-Nov 11.

Glan-y-Mor Tent Park, St David's, Pembrokeshire SA62 6QT. *01437 721788.* www.divewales.com. Owner: Mr Hayes. Off A487. 5mins walk from beach and St Davids.

(1.5m). Lleithyr Meadow Caravan Club Site, Whitesands, St David's, Pembrokeshire SA62 6PR. *01437 720401.* www.caravanclub.co.uk. Owner: The Caravan Club. See website for directions. A marvellous holiday site nestled by three headlands of the Pembrokeshire coast. Toilet block. Privacy cubicles. Laundry facilities. Veg prep. Information room. Shop adjacent. Gas. MV waste. Play equipment. Non-members welcome. No tents. Fishing, golf and watersports nearby. Good area for walking. Dog walk nearby, beach and NCN cycle route in 5m. Open March-Oct.

(1m). Porthclais, St David's, Pembrokeshire SA62 6RR. *01437 720256.* Owner: Mr Rhys G Morgan. SW of St David's. From Haverfordwest on A487. Keep L at St David's and join Porthclais road. Site is L after 0.5m farm site which adjoins Porthclais Harbour. Open March-Oct.

WALES

See page 5 for key to symbols and abbreviations

Rhos-y-Cribed, St David's, Pembrokeshire Sa62 6RR. 01437 720336. Owner: Mr Williams M Lewis, Mrs Jane Owen. 1m SW via road to Porthclais Harbour, farm is SP. Farm touring site. Fees on application. SAE. Special reduction for deaf children. Healing. Ice pack freezing available.

(1m). Rhosson Farm, St David's, Pembrokeshire. 01437 720255. Owner: Mr W D M Lewis. W of St David's. St Justinian road out of St David's. Site is on S side of road, farm identified by Flemish chimney. Close to good beach and nature survey area. Ice pack freezing service. Fees on application. Special reduction for deaf children. Healing.

TENBY

(5m). Arreton Touring Caravan and Tent Park, Manorbier, Tenby, Pembrokeshire SA70 7SN. 01834 871278. www.arreton.net. On A4139 Pembroke to Tenby. Pass through Penally and Lydstep. After Lydstep straight over crossroads and after 1m turn R at sign to Manorbier Station. Site is 150yd on R. Café nearby. Fees on application. Open Easter-Oct.

(4.5m). Cross Park Holiday Centre, Broadmoor, Kilgetty, Tenby, Pembrokeshire SA68 0RS. 01834 811244. www.newhorizonsholidays.co.uk. Owner: Mr & Mrs MA Whitehouse. Continue on A477 1m W of Kilgetty. Turn R at Cross Inn pub, park 250yd on L. Picturesque family park with excellent facilities, showbar with nightly entertainment, kids club, heated indoor swimming pool, shop, games room. etc, etc. Open March-Dec.

(1m). Kiln Park Holiday Centre, Marsh Road, Tenby, Pembrokeshire SA70 7RB. 01834 844121. www.kiln-park.co.uk. Owner: Bourne Leisure Ltd. Follow A477/A478 to Tenby for about 6m. Follow the caravan/camping signs to Penally. Kiln Park is 0.5m on your L. 2 show bars. Heated indoor fun pool. Outdoor pool. Arcade. Café and takeaway. Mini market. Petrol station. Direct beach access. Family entertainment. Pitch n putt, tennis courts, mini bowling, bouncy castle, play area. 2 golf courses in 5mins drive. Oakwood Theme Park 15mins. Cinema in Tenby. Blue Flag Award, Welcome Host Award, AA Award. David Bellamy Gold Conservation Award. Open March-Nov.

(5m). Manorbier Bay Holiday Park, Manorbier, Tenby, Pembrokeshire SA70 7SR. 01834 871235. www.manorbierbay.com. Owner: Mr & Mrs HB Farr. On A4139 Pembroke to Tenby. 1m from beach. Launderette. Showers. Play area. Park located in Pembrokeshire country park area. Bar on site. Shop, PO 10mins walk in village of Manorbier (0.25m). Open March 1-Oct 31.

(4m). Masterland Farm, Broadmoor, Kilgetty, Tenby, Pembrokeshire SA68 ORH. 01834 813298. www.ukparks.co.uk/masterland. Owner: Mrs Davies. A477 to Broadmoor, turn R at Croos Inn pub, after 300yd turn R for park. Ideal for beaches and touring, all modern facilities. Baby bathroom. Bar and restaurant. TV room. Booking advisable at peak times. Open Feb 28-Jan 9.

(4m). Milton Bridge Caravan Park, Milton, Tenby, Pembrokeshire SA70 8PH. 01646 651204. www.miltonbridgecaravanpark.co.uk. Owner: D Mooney & J Williams. Directly off the A477 at Milton, SP Cosheston. Small, peaceful, family run park set in the National Park on river estuary. Near Pembroke's numerous attractions. Shop over road. Pub and restaurant at entrance to park. Open March 1-Oct 31.

(6m). Park Farm Holiday Park, Manorbier, Tenby, Pembrokeshire SA70 7SU. 01834 871273. Owner: Cramcrest Ltd. Take A4139 W from Tenby about 6m, take second turning for Manorbier after 200yd turn R. Footpath to beach 0.5m, through wooded valley past 14th century castle. Quiet family site. Open March 15-Oct 31.

(1.5m). Red House Farm, New Hedges, Tenby, Pembrokeshire SA69 9DP. 01834 813918. Owner: Mrs J Marden. Situated just off the A478. At Twy Cross, entrance on R, just before roundabout. Quiet small, peaceful adults only site. 0.5m from both Tenby and Saundersfoot. Regular bus service to both Tenby and Saunderfoot. 10mins walk to New Hedges with shop, PO, restaurant.

(2m). Rowston Holiday Park, New Hedges, Tenby, Pembrokeshire SA70 8TL. 01834 842178. www.rowston-holiday-park.co.uk. Owner: Mr D C Ormond. Follow signs for New Hedges through village mini-market on R, park is second turning on L. Flat to sloping park with sea views. Open April-Oct.

(1.5m). The Lodge Farm Caravan Site, New Hedges, Tenby, Pembrokeshire SA70 8TH. 01834 842468. Owner: Mrs K Keedy. On A478 Narberth to Tenby. Flat site. Some touring pitches have sea views. AA 2-pennant award. Sports. Excellent fishing from private beach. Local pub and restaurant nearby. Shops/PO 2yd from site entrance. Garage 50yd from entrance. Animal attractions. Children's play area. Open April-Oct 31.

(3m). Trevayne Caravan Park, Saundersfoot, Tenby, Pembrokeshire SA69 9DL. 01834 813402. www.camping-pembrokeshire.co.uk. Owner: Mr D L Reed. Off A478 Narberth to Tenby. 15mins walk from New Hedges village. We have a newly built block of showers, toilets and washing facilities. Access to Monkstone Bay, one of Pembrokeshire's finest beaches and beautiful scenic walks. Open April 1-Oct 30.

■ **(6m). Tudor Glen Caravan Park, Jameston, Manorbier, Tenby, Pembrokeshire SA70 7SS.** 01834 871417. www.tudorglencaravanpark.co.uk. Owner: V J Stevens & Sons. On A4139 Tenby to Pembroke. Family site, no groups. 1m from Manorbier Beach and Pembrokeshire coastal path. Golf at Tenby with its superb beaches 5m away. Oakwood 10m. Open March 1-Oct 31.

(1m). Well Park, Tenby, Pembrokeshire SA70 8TL. 01834 842179. www.wellparkcaravans.co.uk. Owner: Mr D J Nash. On R of main A478 Tenby road. 1m before reaching Tenby. Excellent facilities – free showers. Holiday caravans and cottages for hire. Family run park convenient for all beaches and touring Pembrokeshire coast. Licensed bar. Wales in Bloom Award. Golf course nearby. 4mins walk to shops, PO. Doctors 1m. 15mins walk to Waterwynch beach. AA 4 pennants. Open March 1-end Oct.

(3m). Whitewell Caravan Park, Lydstep Beach, Tenby, Pembrokeshire SA70 7RY. 01834 871569. Owner: Brian & Diane Kelly. Off A4139 Tenby to Manorbier. Campers' bar. Club. Footpath to Lydstep beach. Theme and adventure park, golf course nearby. Open week before Easter-last w/e Oct.

(0.75m). Windmills Camping Park, Narberth Road, Tenby, Pembrokeshire SA70 8TJ. 01834 842200. camping-tenby.co.uk. 5 acres well-drained, level grass with lovely sea views. Good walking area. Free hot water. Fees on application.

WALES

(1.5m). Wood Park Caravans, New Hedges, Tenby, Pembrokeshire SA70 8TL. 01834 843414. www.woodpark.co.uk. Owner: Mrs E M Hodgkinson. At roundabout 2m N of Tenby take A478 then second R and R again. Friendly, family park with games room, launderette, excellent facilities block. Small dogs only allowed, except Easter week, Spring bank holiday week and school holidays. No dogs allowed in hire caravans at any time. Open Easter-Oct.

WHITLAND

(3m). Pantglas Farm Caravan Park, Tavernspite, Amroth, Whitland, Pembrokeshire SA34 ONS. *01834 831618*. www.pantglasfarm.co.uk. Owner: Joy & Mike Southerton. On A477 to Tenby to Pembroke. Turn R Red Roses to Tavernspite. Take the middle road at village pump, Pantglas 600metres on L. Quiet, family-run, rural park. Play area. New disabled wet room. Near Amroth, Saundersfoot and Tenby. Caravan storage. Shops, doctor, dentist, vets in Whitland 3m away. Golf 4m, fishing 1m. PO in village. Bar on site open Friday/Saturday and weekdays during main school holidays. Games room open daily Open March – Oct.

(6m). South Caravan Holiday Park, Tavernspite, Whitland, Pembrokeshire SA34 ONL. *01834 831451*. Owner: Mr IH James. On B4314. 85 metres SW of St Clears and 2.75m S of Whitland. From St Clears take A477 to Red Roses turn R for 1.25m to Tavernspite. Indoor heated swimming pool. Club. Bar meals. Takeaway food. Coarse fishing on site. Golf course 5m. Open April-Oct.

POWYS
BRECON

(4.5m). Aberbran Caravan Club Site, Aberbran, Brecon, Powys LD3 9NH. *01874 622424*. www.caravanclub.co.uk. Owner: The Caravan Club. See website for directions. On edge of Brecon Beacons National Park. Non-members welcome. No tents. Chemical toilet disposal point. Advance booking essential. Shipping length of outfit required due to size limitation of some pitches. No toilet block. Hardstandings. Gas. Dogwalk. Fishing and golf nearby. Good area for walking. Open March-Oct.

(8m). Anchorage Caravan Park, Bronllys, Brecon, Powys LD3 OLD. *01874 711246*. www.anchoragecp.co.uk. Owner: JA & BM Powell & Sons. Midway between Brecon and Hay-on-Wye in centre of Bronllys village. Nr Brecon Beacons. SAE for brochure. High standard park with panoramic views. Childrens play area, PO, hairdresser's, launderette, TV room. Golf course, cinema 8m. Open all year. Easter-end Oct for holiday vans.

(1m). Bishops Meadow Caravan Park, Hay Road, Brecon, Powys LD3 9SW. *01874 610000*. www.bishops-meadow.co.uk. Owner: HJ & RZ Perry. Situated on the B4602 about 1m from the town centre. With spectacular views of the Brecon Beacons the park was opened in1993 and its Restaurant is open all day. Friendly lounge bar. Heated outdoor swimming pool. Play area. Dogs excercise area. Open March 1-Oct 31.

(1.5m). Brynich Caravan Park, Brynich, Brecon, Powys LD3 7SH. Owner: The Caravan Club. E of Brecon. On A470 200yd from A40-A470 roundabout. Award winning family run park with panoramic views of the Brecon Beacons. Two immaculately clean, fully equipped amenity blocks including baby and disabled rooms. Play area, adventure playground and recreation field. Relaxing brookside walks and dog exercise field. Easy access, large level pitches with short grass. Well stocked shop (inc Off Licence). Restaurant adjoining site (Listed in Good Food Guide). Children's soft indoor play facility next door. Open March 27-Nov 9.

(12m). Genfford Farm, Talgarth, Brecon, Powys LD3 OEN. *01874 711014*. nickygen@yahoo.co.uk. Owner: R G Prosser. 3m S of Talgarth and 12m E of Brecon on A497 (Crickhowell). Edge of Black Mountains, 4m from Llangorse Lake, Brecon Beacons. Gliding, pub, pony trekking 1m. PO, bank, Co-op, takeaways, newsagents, hairdresser, pub & restaurants in Talgarth 3m. Leisure centre in 4m. Direct access to hills for walking.

(6m). Lakeside Caravan Park, Llangorse, Brecon, Powys LD3 7TR. *01874 658226*. www.llangorselake.co.uk. Owner: RPB & WP Davies. Off A40 at Bwlch, then B4560 to Llangorse. SP to Llangorse lake and common. AA 3-pennant site. Excellent club house. Café, activity centre and local pubs nearby. Riding, climbing centres 1m. Indoor swimming pool, golf course, cinema, gliding, shop/market town all in 6m. David Bellamy Gold Conservation Award. Open March 21-Oct 31.

(6m). Llynfi Holiday Park, Llangorse, Brecon, Powys LD3 7TR. *01874 658283*. www.llynfi.com. Owner: B & J Strawford. Off B4560. Park is on flat, secluded and grassy in the Brecon Beacons National Park. LLangorse lake a short walk. Heated pool, licensed bar and all facilities. Open April-Oct.

(3m). Pencelli Castle Caravan & Camping Park, Pencelli, Brecon, Powys LD3 7LX. *01874 665451*. www.pencelli-castle.com. Owner: Mr & Mrs G Rees. On B4558 off A40. 3m SE of Brecon. National Tourism Award for Wales 2005 'Best Place to Stay – caravan park'. AA 'Best Campsite in Wales 2006'. Peaceful, countryside park in the heart of Brecon Beacons National Park. Luxurious shower block. In walking distance of highest peaks. Adjoining Brecon Canal. Village pub 150yd. Bike hire. On bus route. Wifi and internet. David Bellamy Gold Conservation Award. Open all year except Dec 3-28.

(0.5m). Riverside International Caravan & Leisure Park, Bronllys, Brecon, Powys LD3 OHL. *01874 711320*. www.riversideinternational.co.uk. Owner: The Gunning Family. W of Talgarth on A479 opposite Bronllys Castle. Licensed restaurant. Heated indoor swimming pool. Leisure complex, Gym, sauna, jacuzzi. Launderette. Bathroom. Public phone. Takeaway service available. Fishing on site. Ideal site for cycling and

---

LLYNFI HOLIDAY PARK
Llangorse Lake, Brecon Beacons, Wales, LD3 7TR

A flat, well-sheltered camping and caravan park at Llangorse Lake in the Brecon Beacons National Park. An ideal centre for touring South and Mid-Wales. Own boating facilities. All amenities with bar and heated pool. Seasonal sites available for caravans. Holiday homes for sale.

Write for reservation and brochure (SAE please) or telephone
Llangorse (01874) 658 253   Fax: (01874) 658 283
brian.strawford@btinternet.com

WALES

See page 5 for key to symbols and abbreviations

BUILTH WELLS

(4m). Fforest Fields, Hundred House, Builth Wells, Powys LD1 5RT. *01982 570406*. www.fforestfields.co.uk. Owner: Mr & Mrs GT Barstow. Easy access off A481, 0.5m from Hundred House village. Peaceful, level mown site straddling a mountain stream. Hardstandings. Clean, modern facilities with free showers. Laundry. Dogs welcome. Lovely forest and moorland walks direct from site, excellent for bird-watching. Pub 1m. 101 Best Site 2007, Area Winner Wales. David Bellamy Gold Conservation Award. Open April 1-Oct 31.

(6m). Irfon River Caravan Park, Upper Chapel Road, Garth, Builth Wells, Powys LD4 4BH. *01591 620310*. Owner: Pam & Roy. 500yd S of Garth on B4519, W of Builth Wells. Nestling between the Eppynt and Cambrian mountains. A quiet, family run, quality park, on the banks of the river Irfon with trout fishing. Ideal for touring mid Wales. New and used holiday vans for sale. Open Easter-end Oct.

Prince Llewelyn Inn, Cilmery, Builth Wells, Powys LD2 3NU. *01982 552694*. Owner: Ms L Jennings & Ms L Jones. 2m W of Builth Wells on A483. Pleasant position. A pleasant C14th village inn with dining. Children welcome. Also bed and breakfast. Open April-Oct.

(8m). Riverside Caravan Park, Llangammarch Wells, Builth Wells, Powys LD4 4BY. *01591 620465*. Owner: Mr & Mrs B Smith. Peaceful park with surrounding mountain views, many places of interest locally. Modern facilities. Shop nearby. Laundry room, BBQ area with large gazebo. Hard stand, lawned and riverside pitches, all year storage. Large safe play area. Fishing. Open April-Oct.

CHURCHSTOKE

(1.5m). Mellington Hall, Holiday Home Park, Churchstoke, Powys SY15 6HX. *01588 620011*. www.mellingtonhallcaravanpark.co.uk. Owner: Mr Alistair Evans. Fishing on site. Dog exercise area. Peace and tranquility. 1000s rare trees planted around the lush parkland set in 300 acres. Excellent bar and restaurant facilities.

CRICKHOWELL

(4m). Cwmdu Caravan and Camping Site, Crickhowell, Powys NP8 1RU. *01874 730441*. Owner: Mrs OM Farr. On A479. Ideal base for exploring national park. Quiet location. Walking on Black Mountains from site. Open March 1-Oct 31.

(0.25m). Riverside Caravan & Camping Park, New Road, Crickhowell, Powys NP8 1AY. *01873 810397*. Owner: Miss R Price. Between A40 and B4558. Level, grassy site with new improved shower block. Canal nearby. Town 5mins walk. Mountain walks. Restaurant 200yd. No single sex groups, hang or paragliders. Adults only – over 18s. Open March 1-Oct 31.

HAY-ON-WYE

(6.5m). Penlan Caravan Park, Brilley, Hay-on-Wye, Powys HR3 6JW. *01497 831485*. www.penlancaravanpark.co.uk. Owner: Mr & Mrs P Joyce. Site 0.5m from Kington to Whitney on Wye by road, 4.5m SW of Kington. Small, secluded site with magnificent views, peace and space. National Trust farm. Advance notice of arrival essential. Brochure available. 3m to shops. 4.5m to Kington (golf course, market town) Open Easter-Oct 31.

LLANBRYNMAIR

(1m). Cringoed Caravan & Camping Park, The Birches, Llanbrynmair, Powys SY19 7DR. *01650 521237*. cringoedcaravan.park@virgin.net. Owner: Mr Paul & Mrs Sue Mathers. By river Twymyn. New facilities block and laundry room. Ideal for touring castles, slate mines and the Alternative Technology Centre. Machynlleth 5m – golf course, shopping. Idyllic location for escaping the pressures of life. Nestling besides the river Twymyn with breathtaking scenery. David Bellamy Gold Conservation Award. Open March-Jan.

Gwern-y-Bwlch Caravan Club Site, Llanbrynmair, Powys SY19 7EB. *01650 521351*. www.caravanclub.co.uk. Owner: The Caravan Club. See website for directions. A gem of a site in a lovely setting, in Mid Wales between Snowdonia and Montgomeryshire with splendid mountain views and walks Chemical toilet disposal point. Gas and Gaz. Shop 1.5m. Non-members welcome. No tents. No toilet block. Some hardstandings. Dog walk. Open April-Oct.

LLANDRINDOD WELLS

(3m). Dalmore Caravan Park, Howey, Llandrindod Wells, Powys LD1 5RG. *01597 822483*. brianthorpe@tiscali.co.uk. Owner: Mr Brian Thorpe. Off A483, 3m S of Llandrindod Wells and 4m N of Builth Wells, top of the hill. Small, select, well maintained park with level, terrace pitches and panoramic views second to none. 11 hardstandings. All facilities, suitable for retired visitors. Golf, fishing, cinema, bowls, shopping all in 3. 2 Pubs serving meals in 1.5m. Members of Welsh Tourist Board, AA & Camping & Caravan Club + Kleine campings: Adults only. Open March 1-Oct 31.

(3m). Disserth Caravan & Camping Park, Disserth, Howey, Llandrindod Wells, Powys LD1 6NL. *01597 860277*. www.disserth.com. Owner: Mike & Ann Hobbs. 1m off A483 Llandrindod Wells to Builth Wells, by Disserth Church between Howey and Newbridge-on-Wye. Good park with level, sheltered pitches in a peaceful riverside setting. Ideal touring centre. Licensed bar, free hot showers and dishwashing. Fishing on site. Shops, golf 3m. Cinema 6m. AA 3 pennants. Open March 1-Oct 31.

(3m). The Park, Crossgates, Llandrindod Wells, Powys LD1 6RF. *01597 851201*. www.parkhousemotel.net. Owner: Mr & Mrs Barr. On A44 from Kington to Rhayader. 3 acres small exclusive park for over 45 year adults only. Horses kept on park. Licensed restaurant adjacent. Open Nov 14-Jan 11.

LLANGYNOG

(0.5m). Llansent Park, Llangynog, Powys SY10 0EP. *01691 860479*. www.homepage.mac.com/henstent. Owner: Dean & Melanie Morris. Off B4391. From A5 follow signs for Bala, park on R, just before you reach Llangynog. Small peaceful family run park set in the beautiful Tanat Valley, enjoying spectacular mountain views and frontage to the river Tanat. Rural location popular with bird watchers and walkers. Two excellent inns nearby serving meals. Wifi available. Open March 1-Oct 31.

LLANIDLOES

(0.8m). Dol-llys Caravan Park, Dol-llys Farm, Llanidloes, Powys SY18 6JA. *01686 412694*. Owner: Mr OS Evans. From roundabout on A470 in Llanidloes take B4569. Past hospital. Fork R and site is 1st R. Campers kitchen for walkers. Fishing in river Severn. Play area. Golf course, PO, doctor and sports centre all in 1m. Railway station 6m Open April- end Oct.

LLANSANTFFRAED-YM-MECHAIN

Bryn Vyrnwy Caravan Park, Bryn Vyrnwy, Llansantffraed-ym-Mechain, Powys SY22 6AY. *01691 828252*. Main A495 at Llynclys, off main A483 Oswestry

MOTOR CARAVAN & CAMPING PARKS 2009 **153**

WALES

to Welshpool road, on L just outside of village. Quiet park overlooking river Vyrnwy.

LLANWDDYN

(1m). Fronheulog Caravan Park, Lake Vyrnwy, LLanwddyn, Powys SY10 0NN. *01691 870362.* www.fronheulog-caravan-park.co.uk. Owner: Mr & Mrs Neil Jones. Quiet site with breathtaking views. Sorry we do not cater for children, but pets are welcome. Electric hook-ups available on our Caravan Club members site. Static caravans new and used usually for sale. 0.5m local shop, RSPB reserves, tea rooms and gift shops. Walkers and bird watchers paradise. Open April 1-Oct 31.

MACHYNLLETH

(12m). Celyn Brithion Caravan & Camping Park, Dinas Mawddwy, Machynlleth, Powys SY20 9LP. *01650 531344.* www.celynbrithion.co.uk. Owner: Mr & Mrs Turnbull. 4 hotels with bar and restaurant facilities. All a short walking distance of the site. Garage and village shop with adjoining café. Mill shop and café close by. Open March 1-Oct 31.

(5m). Dovey Valley Caravan & Camping Park, no 2 Daulwyn, Llanwrin, Machynlleth, Powys SY20 8QJ. *01650 511501/0771889.* www.pen-y-banc.com. Owner: Mr C Taylor. Small site for walking. Coarse fishing, clay shooting on site. Half hour to beach. Golf 6m. Main shops 6m. village 1m. Barn conversion and 4-bed chalet to let. Open April 1-Oct 31.

(3m). Morben Isaf Touring & Home Park, Derwenlas, Machynlleth, Powys SY20 8SR. *01654 781473.* manager@morebenisaf.co.uk. Owner: Bywater Leisure Parks Ltd. Estuary park ideal for walking, fishing, birdwatching, golf. 10mins to beautiful sandy beach. Open mid-March – end Oct.

(9m). Ty Craig Holiday Park, Llancynfelin, Machynlleth, Powys SY20 8PU. *01970 832339.* Owner: Mr RJ & MB Rhodes. Quiet secluded site. Golf course nearby. Shops, doctors, PO in 3m Open March 1-Jan 10.

(10m). Tynypwll Caravan & Camping Site, Dinas Mawddwy, Machynlleth, Powys SY20 9JF. *01650 531326.* Owner: M&I Pugh. Fishing. PO, shops in 0.5m. Lovely scenery and walks.Takeaway meals, shop, café/restaurant available nearby. Open March-Oct.

PRESTEIGNE

(1m). Rockbridge Park, Presteigne, Powys LD8 2NF. *01547 560300.* dustinrockbridge@hotmail.com. Owner: Mr R M Deakins. On B4356 W of Presteigne. Small, tranquil park in wonderful scenery. Near Offa's Dyke. Open April 1-Sept.

(5m). Walton Court Caravan & Camp Site, Walton, Presteigne, Powys LD8 2PY. *01544 350259.* www.waltoncourtcaravanandcampingsite.co.uk. Owner: Jean & Glyn Price. In beautiful unspoilt countryside. Cottage available. Close to Offa's Dyke, footpath, pub close by. Golf, swimming pool & leisure centre 3m. Hay on Wye, town of books 16m. Open March-Oct.

RHAYADER

Wyeside Caravan Park, Llangurig Road, Rhayader, Powys LD6 5LB. *01597 810183.* www.wyesidecamping.co.uk. Owner: Mr K Brumwell. On the banks of the river Wye. Excellent facilities on site and in town. 3m Elan Valley. Colour brochure available. Open March-Nov.

WELSHPOOL

(5m). Bank Farm Caravan Park, Middletown, Welshpool, Powys SY21 8EJ. *01938 570526.* www.bankfarmcaravans.co.uk. Owner: Mr & Mrs D Corfield. On A458 Shrewsbury to Welshpool. Family run park with beautiful views, part flat, part sloping. Open March-Oct.

(6m). Henllan Caravan Park, Llangyniew, Welshpool, Powys SY21 9EJ. *01938 810554.* www.henllancaravanpark.co.uk. Owner: Mrs Sue Evans. In meadowland adjoining river Banwy. Pitch and putt course. Club. Bottled gas available. Fishing. Club/restaurant on park, play area. Open March 1-Dec 31.

(17m). Riverbend Caravan Park, Llangadfan, Llanfair Caereinion, Welshpool, Powys SY21 0PP. *01938 820356.* www.hillandale.co.uk. Owner: D&D Lloyd Jones Securities Ltd. Level riverside touring field with extensive private fishing. Tranquil and unspoilt area. Shop 200m pub 100m, golf, pony trekking nearby. Short drive to the coast. Open all year.

SWANSEA

GOWER

Three Cliffs Bay Caravan Site, North Hills Farm, Penmaen, Gower, Swansea SA3 2HB. *01792 371218.* www.threecliffsbay.com. Owner: DG & JM Beynon. Fishing, shop on site (basics), PO 1m, golf course 3m, doctor 5m. Open April-Oct 31.

GOWERTON

Gowerton Caravan Club Site, Pont-y-Cob Road, Gowerton, Swansea SA4 3QP. *01792 873050.* www.caravanclub.co.uk. Owner: The Caravan Club. Easy drive to superb Gower Peninsula beaches. Non-members welcome. No tents. Hardstandings. Toilet blocks, privacy cubicles, laundry, veg prep, MV Service point. Gas. Playframe. Information room. Dog walk. Storage, ideal for families, quiet and peaceful off peak. Good walking, NCN cycle route in 5m. Open March-Nov.

LLANGENNITH

(17m). Hillend Caravan Park, Hillend, Llangennith, Swansea SA3 1JD. *01792 386204.* Owner: Hillend Caravan Park Ltd. Adjacent to Rhosilli Bay. 13 acres camping. No bookings. SAE for information. Britain's first Area of Outstanding Natural Beauty. Off licence. Play area. Surfing and canoeing near. Phone for details. Open Easter or April 1-Nov 30.

OXWICH

Greenway Holiday Park, Oxwich, Swansea SA3 1LY. *01792 390220.* Owner: Mr & Mrs Mead. On A4118. Showers. Laundry. Swimming pool. Bars. Children's adventure playground. Open March-Dec.

Oxwich Camping Park, Oxwich, Swansea SA3 1LS. *01792 390777.* Owner: Mrs CA Discombe. A quiet, secluded, family park in the heart of the Gower Peninsula, 8m from Killay. Heated swimming pool, hot showers. Village amenities, shop, restaurant, beach in Oxwich village. Open April-Sept.

PORT EYNON

(14m). Newpark Holiday Park, Port Eynon, Swansea SA3 1NP. *01792 390292.* Owner: Mrs Newland. On A4118. Uninterrupted views over bay. Play area and games room. Open April-Oct.

RHOSSILLI

(1m). Pitton Cross Caravan & Camping Park, Rhossilli, Swansea SA3 1PL. *01792 390593.* www.pittoncross.co.uk. Owner: Mr Roger Button. From Swansea – A4118 to Scurlage 16m, turn R, SP Rhossili, we are 2m on L. Level site 1m from coast. Walking, sea fishing, surfing, bird-watching all nearby. Over 50s from £80 pw off peak season, inc 4 for 3 offer –

154 MOTOR CARAVAN & CAMPING PARKS 2009

IRELAND/NORTHERN IRELAND

Sunday to Thursday, not Bank Holidays. Gower Kite centre and surf hire available.

SWANSEA

(24m). Maes-yr-Eglwys Farm, Pen-y-cae, Swansea, Swansea SA9 1GS. *01639 730849.* Owner: Jeremy Watts. Beautiful mountains, Dan-Yr-Ogof caves. Entrance on wall of church. All welcome. Open May 15-Sept 30.

(4m). Riverside Caravan Park, Ynysforgan Farm, Morriston, Swansea, Swansea SA6 6QL. *01792 775587.* Owner: Mr Brian & Mrs Y Parker. Access from roundabout under M4 J45. Showers, chemical toilet disposal point, laundry, gas, barbecue area. Licensed club. Indoor swimming pool on site. Children welcome. Dogs by arrangement (no dangerous breeds).

VALE OF GLAMORGAN

COWBRIDGE

(3m). Llandow Touring Caravan Park, Llandow, Cowbridge, Vale of Glamorgan CF7 7PB. *01446 794527.* www.llandowcaravanpark.com. Owner: A&S Evans. Sheltered, secluded park set in the Vale of Glamorgan. Seasonal pitches. Caravan storage. Open Feb 1-Dec 1.

LLANTWIT MAJOR

(0.5m). Acorn Camping & Caravanning, Hamlane South, Llantwit Major, Vale of Glamorgan CF61 1RP. *01446 794024.* www.acorncamping.co.uk. Owners: Paul & Nikki Hawkins. 1m from Heritage Coast beach. Hard standings, service pitches. Open Feb-Dec.

PENARTH

(2.5m). Lavernock Point Holiday Estate, Fort Road, Penarth, Vale of Glamorgan CF6 2XQ. *029 20707310.* www.lavernockpoint.com. Owner: Mr S Goodfellow. 2.5m S of Penarth via B4267 Penarth/Barry road. Fort Road to Lavernock Point. Holiday site near beach.

WREXHAM

CHIRK

YOUR TOP 101 SITES 2009

(0.5m). Lady Margaret's Park Caravan Club Site, Chirk, Wrexham LL14 5AA. *01691 777200.* www.caravanclub.co.uk. Owner: The Caravan Club. See website for directions. Caravan Club members only. No tents. A beautiful wooded parkland site adjacent to Chirk Castle – with many other castles and historic sites close by. Some hardstandings. Steel awning pegs required. Toilet blocks. Privacy cubicles. Laundry facilities. Baby and toddler washroom. Veg prep. MV Service point. Gas & gaz. Play equipment. Good area for walking. Ideally suited for families. Open March-Jan.

EYTON

YOUR TOP 101 SITES 2009

(0.5m). The Plassey Leisure Park, Eyton, Wrexham LL13 0SP. *01978 780277.* www.theplassey.co.uk. Owner: Mr JS Brookshaw. Multi-award winning park with many amenities including: 9-hole golf course, swimming pool, badminton courts, table tennis, sauna and sunbed, restaurant, coffee shop, retail shops, craft workshops, adventure playground, garden centre, hairdresser, beauty salon and Craft Centre open all year. David Bellamy Gold Conservation Award.

RUABON

(5m). James' Caravan Park, Ruabon, Wrexham LL14 6DW. *01978 820148.* ray@carastay.demon.co.uk. Owner: Mr Bailey. 0.5m W of the A483/A539 junction to Llangollen. Leisure centre nearby. Fees on application. Golf course, shops, PO, doctor etc 1m.

NORTHERN IRELAND

ANTRIM

ANTRIM

■ **(1m). Six Mile Water Caravan Park, Lough Road, Antrim, Co Antrim BT41 4DQ.** *028 9446 4963.* www.antrim.gov.uk/caravanpark. Owner: Antrim Borough Council. Follow SP for Antrim Forum/Lough Shore Park and turn off Dublin Road (A26) on to Lough Road. Situated close to the shores of Lough Neagh-an area steeped in history and natural beauty with many attractions and activities for the holidaymaker to enjoy. Facilities include modern toilet and shower block, fully equipped laundry and electric hook-up for 20 pitches. The park is an ideal base for touring Northern Ireland and has a TV lounge and a games room. Open Feb 27-Nov 2.

BALLYCASTLE

Silvercliffs Holiday Park, 21 Clare Road, Causeway Coast, Ballycastle, Co Antrim BT54 5DB. *028 20762550.* www.hagansleisure.co.uk. Owner: Hagans Leisure Group. Silvercliffs commands a breathtaking view over Ballycastle Bay. 20mins drive to world famous Giant's Causeway. Facilities include indoor heated pool, play area and a traditional bar with live entertainment. Open March-Nov.

BALLYMONEY

(4m). Drumaheglis Marina & Caravan Park, 36 Glenstall Road, Ballymoney, Co Antrim BT53 7QN. *028 2766 6466.* www.ballymoney.gov.uk. Caravan Club affiliated. Non members and tent campers welcome. This award winning park has access to the lower river Bann. Toilet blocks, laundry, and MV service point. Playground and play area on site. Ideal for families. Fishing, golf and watersports nearby. Facilities for the disabled. Open March-Oct.

CUSHENDUN

Cushendun Caravan Park, 14 Glendun Road, Cushendun, Co Antrim BT44 0PX. *028 21761254.* Open Easter-end Sept.

LARNE

(3.5m). Carnfunnock Country Park, Drains Bay, Coast Road, Larne, Co Antrim BT40 2QG. *028 2827 0541.* www.larne.gov.uk/carnfunnock.html. Owner: Larne Borough Council. On the beautiful A2 Coast Road in parkland. Walled garden, maze, adventure playground, trampolines, 'mini-Silverstone' racetrack, putting and 9-hole golf course, mini railway, mini golf, laser clay pigeon shooting, bungee run, bouncy castle and remote control boats, woodland walks, orienteering, picnic/BBQ areas, gift/coffee shop. Open St Patrick's Day (March) – Oct 31.

Curran Court Caravan park, 131 Curran Road, Larne, Co Antrim BT40 1XB. *028 28273797.* Owner: L Gilpin & S Lowe. 0.5m from ferry terminal and amenities. Near leisure centre, hotel, bowling and putting greens. Town 400yd, 2m to 18-hole golf course. Near sea and river fishing. Open April-Oct.

ARMAGH

LURGAN

(2m). Kinnego Marina Caravan Park, Kinnego Marina, Oxford Island, Lurgan, Co Armagh BT66 6WJ. *028 3832 7573.*

MOTOR CARAVAN & CAMPING PARKS 2009 **155**

IRELAND/NORTHERN IRELAND

kinnego.marina@craigavon.gov.uk. Owner: Craigavon Borough Council, Leisure Department. Off roundabout, 10 M1 Lurgan down embankment road to Oxford Island 0.25m. Based on the shore of Lough and nature reserve. Open April-End Oct.

MARKETHILL, ARMAGH

(1m). Gosford Forest Park, 7 Gosford Demesne, Gosford Forest Park, Markethill, Armagh, Co Armagh BT60 1GD. *028 3755 1277.* Owner: Department of Agriculture & Rural Development (Forestry). Hard standing hook-up pitches. Picnic/bbq areas. Function hall. Horse riding, trails, guided tours, orienteering routes. Heritage, poultry & rare breeds collection.

DOWN
BANBRIDGE

Banbridge Tourist Information Centre, 200 Newry Road, Banbridge, Co Down BT32 3NB. *028 40623322.* www.banbridge.com. On A1/N1 Belfast/Dublin Euroroute. Convenient for ferry ports at Larne, Belfast and Dublin. Electricity included in site fees. Children's play area.

CASTLEWELLAN

Castlewellan Forest Park, The Grange, Castlewellan, Co Down BT31 9BU. *028 4377 8664.* Owner: Dept of Agriculture. 30m S of Belfast SP off the Belfast-Newcastle route. Game fishing on site. Families only. Open Easter-end Oct.

KILKEEL

(4m). Chestnutt Holiday Park, 3 Grange Road, Cranfield West, Kilkeel, Co Down BT34 4LW. *028 4176 2653.* www.chestnuttholidayparks.co.uk. Owner: Chestnutt Holiday Parks. Off A2. Follow signs for Cranfield West. Adjacent to award-winning Cranfield beach. Beside Blue Flag beach, fast food outlet and games room on park. Pitch & putt, golf course. Open Easter-Oct 31.

KILLYLEAGH

(1m). Camping & Caravanning Club Site – Delamont Country Park, Downpatrick Road, Killyleagh, Co Down BT30 9TZ. *028 4482 1833.* www.campingandcaravanningclub.co.uk. Owner: The Camping & Caravanning Club. The site is in an area of outstanding natural beauty with walks, picnic areas, birdwatching, Victorian walled garden and children's playground. Near sea fishing, coarse and game fishing, walking, cycling, golf, riding. Non-members welcome. All units accepted. Some super pitches. Deals for families and backpackers. Loo Of The Year (5 stars). David Bellamy Silver Conservation Award. Open March-Oct.

NEWCASTLE

(2m). Tollymore Forest Park, 176 Tullybranigan Road, Newcastle, Co Down BT33 0PW. *023 4372 2428.* Owner: Department of Agriculture. 0.25m from Bryansford. Woods and parklands. Fees on application. Inquiries to Head Forester. Dogs must be kept under control.

NEWTOWNARDS

(7m). Ballywhiskin Caravan & Camping Park, 216 Ballywalter Road, Millisle, Newtownards, Co Down BT21 2LY. *028 91862262.* www.ballywhiskincaravanandcamping.com. Owner: Roy & Hilda Butler. From Newtownards take B172 E to Millisle, turn R on A2 towards Ballywalter, site on the R. Open weekends during winter. Hard stands and laundry facilities. Situated close to beach. Small animal farm on site. Playing field and play park. Children welcome. In easy reach of many places of interest. Golf, horse riding, tennis, swimming pool, shopping centre, cinema all available in 7m. Open April-Oct.

(15m). Kirkistown Caravan Park, 55 Main Road, Cloughy, Newtownards, Co Down BT22 1JB. *028 42771183.* Owner: Mr Peter Marsden. Off A2. Level, free-draining site with heated facilities block. Sandy beach. Play park. Windsurfing and golf course adjacent. Open March 17-Oct 31.

PORTAFERRY

(4.5m). Silver Bay Caravan Park, 15 Ardminnan Road, Portaferry, Co Down BT22 1QJ. *028 42771321.* info@ardminnan.com. Owner: Mr J Gowan & Mrs I Gowan. On A20. From Belfast to Newtownards, Grey abbey, Kircubbin and take B173 to Cloughey, about 1m on coast road. Beach safe. Bar/restaurant. 50-acre 9-hole golf links. Shop, PO in Cloughey (1m), doctor in Portaferry (4.5m). Open week before Easter-Oct 31.

ROSTEVOR

Kilbroney Caravan Park, Shore Road, Rostevor, Co Down BT34 3DQ. *028 4173 8134.* Owner: Newry & Mourne District Council. About 0.5m from Rostrevor on main A2 road to Kilkeel. Large areas of open space, riverside walks and arboretum. Open April-end Oct.

FERMANAGH
ENNISKILLEN

(8m). Blaney Caravan Park, Blaney, Enniskillen, Co Fermanagh BT93 7ER. *028 68641634.* www.blaneycaravanpark.com. On A46 from Enniskillen to Belleek. Hardstanding and waste hook-ups for touring caravans. 4 star park has a host of amenities with rural activities on its doorstep. Open March-Oct.

Six Mile Water Caravan & Camping Park
Lough Road, Antrim, BT41 4DG

The Six Mile Water Caravan & Camping Park, situated on the beautiful shores of Lough Neagh, is an ideal base for touring Northern Ireland. On-site facilities include: TV lounge, games room, modern toilet and shower block, payphone, fully equipped laundry room, electric hook up for 20 pitches and 24 camping sites. Maximum stay 7 nights. Advance booking advisable. Open March - October.

For bookings or further information:
Tel: 028 9446 4963
Email: sixmilewater@antrim.gov.uk
www.antrim.gov.uk/caravanpark

IRELAND/NORTHERN IRELAND

See page 5 for key to symbols and abbreviations

KESH

(2m). Lakeland Caravan Park, Drumrush, Boa Island Road, Kesh, Co Fermanagh BT93 1AD. 028 68631578. www.drumrush.co.uk. Owner: Joan & Lisa Armstrong. Dogs on leads only welcome. Licensed bar and restaurant on site. 10 bedroomed guesthouse, play park for children, tennis court. On shores of Lough Erne, near watersports centre.

LISNASKEA

(3m). Share Holiday Village, Smith's Strand, Lisnaskea, Co Fermanagh BT92 2EQ. 028 6772 2122. www.sharevillage.org. Owner: Discovery 80 Ltd (Share). From A4 main Belfast to Enniskillin road turn off at Maguiresbridge, go through to Lisnaskea, take B127 to Derrylin, Share Centre is 4m on R. Share Holiday village is a residential outdoor activity centre, all facilities have been purpose built for use by people wih disabilities and able bodied people. Canoeing, sailing, archery, climbing wall and arts activities. Indoor swimming pool with ramped access. Coffee shop and takeaway. Shops, PO doctor 3m from site. Open Easter-end of Sept.

LONDONDERRY

COLERAINE

(1m). Tullans Farm Caravan Park, 46 Newmills Road, Coleraine, Co Londonderry BT5 2JB. 028 70342309. tullansfarm@hotmail.com. Owner: Diana McClelland. Cinema and swimming pool in 2m. Large children's play area. Snooker pool, table tennis (indoors) TV room. Country ambience yet just 1m from Coleraine. "Try the Tullans experience where people matter". Open March-end Oct.

LIMAVADY

(12m). Benone Tourist Complex, 53 Benone Avenue, Magilligan, Limavady, Co Londonderry BT49 0LQ. 028 7775 0555. Owner: Limavady Borough Council. Situated on coast road. 9-hole, par 3 golf course, golf practice range. Outdoor heated splash pool. 4 tennis courts. Bowling green. Modern activity play area. Events and café July/Aug. Seasonal shop. Open April-Sept.

PORTSTEWART

(1m). Portstewart Caravan Park, 30A Burnside Road, Portstewart, Co Londonderry BT55 7SW. 01265 833308. Owner: O'Neills Caravan Sales Ltd. Level ground. Close to beaches and Portstewart Promenade. Open Easter-Oct.

TYRONE

CLOGHER

Clogher Valley Country Caravan Park, 9 Fardross Forest, Clogher, Co Tyrone BT76 0HG. 028 8554 8932. Owner: Sydney Somerville. Forest walks. Birdwatching. Bicycles for hire. Open mid March-end Oct.

DUNGANNON

(1m). Dungannon Park, Moy Road, Dungannon, Co Tyrone BT71 6DY. 028 8772 7327. dpreception@dungannon.gov.uk. Owner: Dungannon & South Tyrone Borough Council. SP off the A29. A 70 acre parkland in the heartland of Ulster. Catering for a wide range of visitor and recreational needs. Open March 1-Oct 31.

FIVEMILETOWN

(0.5m). Roundlake Caravan Park, 20 Murley Road, Fivemiletown, Co Tyrone BT75 0QS. 028 8772 7327. dungannonpark@utvinternet.com. SP from Fivemiletown on the Fintona Road. A tranquil destination in the Lush. Clogher Valley. Short walk to busy Fivemiletown adds to its rural attraction. Open March-end Sept.

IRELAND

CLARE

COROFIN

Corofin Village Camping & Caravan Park, Main Street, Corofin, Co Clare. 00 353 65 6837683. www.corofincamping.com. Owner: Jude & Marie Neylon. From Ennis follow N85 and R476. From Galway City follow the N18 towards Gort, then R460 via Kilmacduagh to Corofin. Well sheltered site with games room and launderette. Ideal for walking and cycling. Fishing lakes nearby Open April 1- Sept 30.

DOOLIN

(0.5m). Nagle's Doolin Camping & Caravan Park, Doolin, Co Clare. 00 353 65 7074458. www.doolincamping.com. Located beside Doolin Pier. Touring site only with 15 hardstands plus grass pitches with electric points. Overlooked by the Cliffs of Moher, a short walk from three pubs, with traditional music nightly. Near excellent restaurants, Seaworld, heated swimming pool, pitch & putt. Shop open from June 1-Aug.31. Open: April 1 – Sept 30.

O'Connors Riverside Camping & Caravan Park, Doolin, Co Clare. 00 353 657074314. www.oconnorsdoolin.com. Owner: Joan & Pat O'Connor. From Lisdoonvarna go towards Cliffs of Moher (N67), turn R for Doolin. Go straight at main crossroads in centre of Doolin. Park is situated over the Aille River Bridge on the L behind O'Connors farmhouse B&B. Well sheltered and supervised. Open May 1-Sept 30.

Riverside Caravan & Camping Park, Doolin, Co Clare. 00 353 65 7074314. www.oconnorsdoolin.com. Owner: Joan & Pat O'Connor. From Lisdoonvarna go towards Cliffs of Moher (N67) turn R for Doolin. Go straight at main crossroads in centre of Doolin. Park is situated over Aille River Bridge on L of road, behind O'Connors B/B. In the centre of Doolin in 5mins walk from pubs, shops & restaurants. Attractions in area include, trips to Aran Islands, coastal walks, pot holing, Ailwee Caves, pony trekking, river and sea fishing, pitch & putt, bicycle hire. Open May 1- Oct 1.

KILLALOE

Lough Derg Holiday Park, Killaloe, Co Clare. 00 353 61376329. From Dublin, Limerick Road, N7, N from Nenagh, follow signs for Killaloe/Ballina. 4.5 acres. Family owned and run, in the scenic Shannon Valley, on the shores of Lough Derg, well sheltered. Open May-Sept.

CORK

BANTRY

(4m). Eagle Point Camping, Ballylickey, Bantry, Co Cork. 00 353 27 50630. www.eaglepointcamping.com. Caravan Club affiliated. Top standard amenities and a relaxing base for touring West Cork/South Kerry. The park situated on a peninsula has a safe and sheltered coastline with pebbled beaches suitable for water sports. Activities include boating, windsurfing, sailing, swimming and fishing. Slipway allows for easy boat launch. Foodstore and petrol station at the park entrance. Open April – Sept.

BLARNEY

(1.5m). Blarney Caravan & Camping Park, Stone View, Blarney, Co Cork. 00 353 21 4516519. www.blarneycaravanpark.com. Owner: C Quill. N25 take N8 towards Cork City. From N8 take sign for north Ring Road/Limerick, N20 then Blarney R617. SP from Blarney filling station. Set in countryside, spacious, well sheltered and well landscaped site, personally supervised giving a high standard of cleanliness and security. 18 hole pitch & putt course on site. Shops, restaurants, pubs in Blarney,

www.motorcaravanmagazine.co.uk   MOTOR CARAVAN & CAMPING PARKS 2009 **157**

IRELAND/NORTHERN IRELAND

coarse/game fishing nearby. Open April 1-Oct 31.

CLONAKILTY

(0.6m). Desert House Caravan & Camping Park, Coast Road, Clonakilty, Co Cork. 00 353 23 33331. desert@eircom.net. Owner: Dorothy & John Jennings. From Cork N71 to Bandon and Clonakilty. Park is SP at roundabout in Clonakilty. Family run park. Small touring park situated on a dairy farm overlooking Clonakilty Bay. Nearby model village, watersports, tennis, golf, pitch & putt, fishing, bird watching, sandy beaches & traditional pubs. Open May 1-Sept 30.

GLANDORE

The Meadow Camping Park, Glandore, Co Cork. 00 353 28 33280. meadowcamping@eircom.net. Owner: Stephen & Helen Keohane. Off N71 at Rosscarbery or Leap take R597 to Glandore. Family run park in a garden setting and the recipient of three environmental awards. It is best suited to people who prefer peace and tranquility. The site is well sheltered surrounded by trees, shrubs and flowers. 7 nights for price of 6 if pre-paid. Special rates for 2 people in camper van including electric. Open May 1-Sept 15.

GLENGARRIFF

(1m). Dowlings Caravan & Camping Park, Castletownbere Road, Glengarriff, Co Cork. 00 353 27 63154. nickydee@eircom.net. Owner: James F Dowling. The park is located just 1m on Castletownbere Road R572 out of Glengarriff. Situated between the mountains and the sea (400yd) from Glengarriff Harbour. Forest walks, angling, swimming, mountain climbing, orienteering, sailing and golf all nearby. On site: shop (June-Sept), play area, games room, TV, laundry service, take away (July-Aug), bar, traditional Irish music and singing nightly. Open 17 March – Oct 31.

SKIBBEREEN

(0.625m). The Hideaway Camping & Caravan Park, Skibbereen, Co Cork. 00 353 28 22254. skibbereencamping@eircom.net. Owner: Stephen & Helen Keohane. On R596 to Castletownsend. Family run park with excellent facilities in an ideal location for touring the southwest. Rural setting only 10mins walk to Skibbereen town. VW, Honda and Hyundai garages in Skibbereen. Bird watching, golf course nearby. Ferries to islands of Cape Clear and Sherkin available from Baltimore. Lidl and Super Valu supermarkets in Skibbereen. April 10-Sept 15.

DONEGAL
CARRIGART

(2m). Casey's Caravan & Camping Park, Downings, Letterkenny, Carrigart, Co Donegal. 00 353 74 55301. 25m N of Letterkenny on the coast. Casey's is situated on the edge of Sheephaven Bay in the fishing village of Downings, 25m from Letterkenny. Shops, pubs and a hotel are all in 200yd. Safe sandy beach near site. Since June 2007: disabled toilet and shower, small laundry and room for camper to make tea; tables and seats + washup. Open April 1 – Sept 30.

PORTNOO

Dunmore Caravans, Strand Road, Portnoo, Co Donegal. 00 353 7545121. Owner: John Gillespie. Flat, sandy site near beach. 9-hole putting green. 18-hole golf course. Open March 10-Nov 1.

DUBLIN
DUBLIN 22

(5m). Camac Valley Tourist Caravan & Camping Park, Naas Road, Clondakin, Dublin 22, Co Dublin. 00 353 1 464 0644. www.camacvalley.com. Owner: Mack Trading International Ltd. M50 motorway, exit at no 9 and take N7 S, direction Cork for 2km ad follow international camping signs off the N7 to Green Isle Road. Award winning park has now established itself as Dublin's premier Caravan & Camping Park with top class facilities. Groups and rallies well catered for in spacious park whilst the individual hardstands are both private and pleasant. The local village of Clondakin has 2 large supermarkets, PO and bars & restaurants. Near golf courses and horse riding.

GALWAY
CLIFDEN

(1m). Shanaheever Campsite & Caravan Park, Shanaheever, Westport Road, Clifden, Co Galway. 00 353 95 22150. info@clifdencamping.com. www.clifdencamping.com. From Galway follow the N59 towards Westport. We are the 1st R (1m) after a lake on the R from Westport, turn off L 1m before Clifden. Sheltered in a valley at the foot of the Twelve Bens but in a few minutes drive of the sea, Shanaheever is ideally situated for the perfect holiday. 15mins walk to Clifden, the capital of Connemara and offers on hand information on the area with O.S. maps on loan. A covered dining area, clean washrooms and showers. Board games to loan out are available on site. Open Easter-Sept.

CONNEMARA

(6m). Acton's Beachside Caravanning & Camping, Gallach, Streamstown Point, Clifden, Connemara, Co Galway. 00 353 9544036. actonsbeach@iol.ie. Owner: Kritoffer Acton. Located 6m W of Clifden, adjacent Omey Island, nr Claddaghduff village. Majestically set on a peninsula in a natural heritage area, 300 degrees of sea and beach frontage. Excellent panoramic views. Riding, golf nearby, diving, water skiing, dolphin watching, fishing, boating, hill and beach walking. Open April-Oct.

Renvyle Beach Caravan & Camping Park, Renvyle Peninsula, Connemara, Co Galway. 00 353 95 43462. renvylebeach@o2.ie. www.renvylebeachcaravanpark.com. Nearest town Clifden. The Park has direct access to the one of the most beautiful beaches on the West Coast. High standard of cleanliness and hygiene. Dogs must be kept on a lead. 15mins walk to shops, pubs and restaurants. Mobile homes for hire. Open April-Sept.

GALWAY

Ballyloughane Caravan & Camping Park, Ballyloughane Beach, Renmore, Galway, Co Galway. 00 353 91 755338. galwcamp@iol.ie. From Dublin/Limerick: 4.5m from Oranmore (N6 West). At first roundabout approaching city take exit 'Galway City East – Merlin Park – docks' the exit is SP 'Merlin Park/Renmore/Mervue'. Second turn L after Merlin Park Hospital/Stores at Dawn Dairies. A quiet family run touring park supervised with high standard of cleanliness and security. Situated beside sandy beach with panoramic views of Galway Bay and less than 3m from city centre. Supermarket, launderette, newsagents in 200yd.

Salthill Caravan & Camping Park, Salthill, Galway, Co Galway. 00 353 91523972. info@salthillcaravanpark.com. www.salthillcaravanpark.com. Owner: Co-operative Enterprises Society. 3m W of Galway on the Salthill road. 0.5m outside Salthill. 2nd park on L. Beautifully positioned site. 0.5m from sandy beach. Well-equipped family site. Boat trips from Galway and many holiday attractions at Salthill Open April

IRELAND/NORTHERN IRELAND

1-Sept 30.

KERRY

BALLYHEIGUE

Casey's Caravan & Camping Park, Main Street, Ballyheigue, Co Kerry. 00 353 66 7133195. Ballyheigue village. 10m from Tralee heading towards Kerry Head. Half-way up the Main Street on R. Family-run park. All amenities. Exit to main street with shops, supermarkets, PO, take-away food and pubs. 9 hole golf course open to Green Fees. Water sports on beach. Hill walking. Open May – Sept.

CAHERDANIEL

(1.2m). Glenbeg Caravan & Camping Park, Caherdaniel, Co Kerry. 00 353 66 9475182/08. glenbeg@eircom.net. Located on the Ring of Kerry Road, about 31m from Kenmare, 18m from Caherciveen. Adjacent to a fine sandy beach. The park fronted by a sheltered cove in the Kenmare bay is an ideal location for water sports enthusiasts. Ideal base for hill walkers, horse riding, visiting historic sites. Restaurants, pubs and a hotel located in walking distance. Open April 15-Oct 1.

DINGLE

(1m). Ballintaggart House Caravan & Camping Park, Racecourse Road, Dingle, Co Kerry. 00 353 66 9151454/08. www.dingleaccommodation.com. Owner: Paddy Fenton. Located on the R as you approach Dingle Town by the Tralee to Dingle Road, the N86. The site is the only camping site located near Dingle Town, located on the grounds of magnificent 1703 hunting lodge, overlooking Dingle Bay. It provides easy access to beaches, rock climbing, archaeological sites, interesting walks and Fungi the Dolphin. Open May – Sept 30.

GLENBEIGH

Falvey's Camping Site, Cahercivéen Road, Glenbeigh, Co Kerry. 00 353 669768238. Take the Cahercivéen Road in Glenbeigh village. Site on main ring of Kerry Road. 0.25m from sea. Well-equipped site with poolroom and children's entertainment. Walking and pony trekking area nearby. Dogs allowed on leads. Open Easter-Oct.

KENMARE

(2m). Ring of Kerry Caravan & Camping Park, Kenmare, Co Kerry. 00 353 64 41648. www.kerrycamping.com. Owner: Catherine Gibbons. From Kenmare take the N70 Sneem/Ring of Kerry road. W of Kenmare. Site established over 20 years with beautiful views of Kenmare bay. Ideally suited for touring the Ring of Kerry, Beara and Dingle peninsulas. Pubs, restaurants, crafts, galleries in Kenmare. Golf, quad biking, diving, walks all available nearby. Open April 1-Sept 30.

KILLARNEY

(2m). Donoghues White Villa Farm Caravan & Camping Park, Killarney-Cork Road (N22), Killarney, Co Kerry. 00 353 6420671. www.killarneycaravanpark.com. Owner: O'Donoghue Family. Located 2m E of Killarney on the N22 Killarney-Cork road. Park entrance is 500yd E of N22/N72 junction. Sheltered peaceful touring park. The park is bordered by a beautiful wood of oak and holly trees. Farm walks to River Flesk (fishing), National farm museum and original traditional Irish cottage. Ideal touring base for Ring of Kerry, Dingle and Beara Peninsulas. Daily coach tours from caravan park arranged. Golf 2m, shopping village 1.2m, pub 0.5m. Taxi and bus service (request bus stop at park entrance). Self-catering apartments for rent. Open April 9-Oct 5.

(1m). Fleming's White Bridge Caravan & Camping Park, White Bridge, Ballycasheen Road, Killarney, Co Kerry. 00 353 64 6631590. www.killarneycamping.com. Owner: Moira & Hillary Fleming. 300yd off N22 Cork Road. E of Killarney. Caravan Club affiliated. GPS: N52:03.37 W09:28.45. 3 modern sanitation blocks, shop open daily (June to end Aug), tourist information, 2 laundries, games room, tv lounge, sports field, fishing on site, bicycle hire and dog walks. Golf, cinema, shopping centre in 1m; 3m. Open 14-30 March, 25 April-5 Oct, 23-27 Oct.

(1m). Flesk Muckross Caravan & Camping Park, Muckross Road, Killarney, Co Kerry. 00 353 64 31704. www.campingkillarney.com. Owner: John Courtney. On N71 road to Kenmare. Follow signs for National Park and Lakes. Next door to Glen Eagle Hotel. 7-acre park is situated at the gateway to 25,000 acres of Killarney's National Parks & Lakes. At the start of the Kerry way walk/cycle path from Caravan Park to National Park and Lakes. Other facilities include takeaway, hotel rooms, bar, restaurant, laundry, bike hire, etc. Open end March – end Sept.

Fossa Caravan & Camping Park, Fossa, Killarney, Co Kerry. 00 353 64 6631497. www.camping-holidaysireland.com. Owner: Brosnan Family. From Cork & Mallow Junction (N22/N72) – continue towards Killarney Town. At the top of the hill take second exit off the first roundabout, follow road till second roundabout – take third exit – (all the time following road signs for the N72 Ring of Kerry/Killorglin/Cahirciveen/Dingle road). Continue for about 3.5m. Fossa Caravan & Camping park is the second park on the R. Family run park set in wooded area, in the village of Fossa, overlooking the MacGillycuddy Reeks and just 5mins walk from Lough Leane. 4 stars under the Failte Ireland scheme. Open from April to end Sept.

RING OF KERRY

Glenross Caravan & Camping Park, Glenbeigh Village, Ring of Kerry, Co Kerry. 00 353 66 9768451. www.killarneycamping.com. Owner: Joan Fleming. From Killarney/Killorglin take the N70 towards Glenbeigh. Park is on the R just before entering village. 10m from Killorglin. Caravan club affiliated. Fine view of Rossbeigh Beach. Ideal touring base for Dingle and Killarney. Popular venue for watersports, fishing, horse-riding, walking, mountain climbing. Bicycle hire. An associate site of Fleming's White Bridge, Killarney, discount for staying at both parks. Open May 3-Sept 24.

Mortimer's Mannix Point Camping & Caravan Park, Cahirciveen, Ring of Kerry, Co Kerry. 00 353 669472806. www.campingkerry.rural-biznet.com. Owner: Mr Mortimer Moriarty. Located on the coast, 300yd off N70 Ring of Kerry road. 15mins walk to restaurants, pubs, shops, cyber café, cycle hire, etc. Impeccably clean facilities include campers' sitting room renowned for impromptu music sessions. Failte Ireland/ICC 2003 The Award of Excellence. The Best Park in Ireland. Overall winner. Open March-Oct.

(1m). West's Caravan Park and Static Caravan Hire & Sales, Killarney Road, Killorglin, Ring of Kerry, Co Kerry. 00353 66 9761240. enquiries@westcaravans.com. Owner: Liam & Linda West. Great location for touring Ring of Kerry, Killarney, Dingle, mountains, Skellig Rock, beaches, golf and peninsulas. Overlooking Ireland's highest mountain, on banks of river. Tennis, game fishing, play area, laundry etc on park. Pubs and food nearby. 8 Golf courses in 8m, sea fishing 15m. ADAC, MCCI. Static caravans for sale on park from 7000 euros. David Bellamy Bronze Conservation

IRELAND/NORTHERN IRELAND

Award. Open Easter-Oct.

TRALEE

(0.5m). Woodlands Caravan & Camping Park, Dan Spring Road, Tralee, Co Kerry. 00 353 66 7121235. www.kingdomcamping.com. Owner: Mike & Martina McDonneill. In a 16-acre parkland setting, 10mins walk from the centre of Tralee town, connected by bridge to the Aqua Dome. Golf, bowling, sea angling, diving, horse riding, sailing, windsurfing all available locally. Irish Park of the Year 2005, Loo of the Year 2006, Alan Rodgers Motorhome Award 2007. Open mid March- end Sept.

KILDARE
ATHY

Forest Farm Caravan & Camping Park, Dublin Road, Athy, Co Kildare. 00 353 507 31231. www.accommodationathy.com. Owner: Mary & Michael McManus. Family run park on 140 acre working farm. Surrounded by mature trees, beech and evergreen. Recently opened and finished to a high standard. Fishing on river Barrow and Grand Canal in Athy. Bicycles for hire.

KILKENNY
BENNETTSBRIDGE

(2m). Nore Valley Caravan & Camping Park, Bennettsbridge, Co Kilkenny. 00 353 56 7727229. www.norevalleypark.com. Owner: Samuel & Isobel Harper. Site on a farm and children are encouraged to assist in animal feeding. River walk through farm and woodland. Crazy golf, poolroom, children's play area, pedal Go-Karts and trailer rides. Indoor two storey maze. Swimming, fishing, canoeing, golf, horse riding all available in 10m. Open March 1 – Oct 31.

KILKENNY

(1m). Tree Grove Caravan & Camping Park, Danville House, Kilkenny, Co Kilkenny. 00 353 56 7770302. www.treegrovecamping.com. Park is ideally located for touring Medieval Kilkenny and the South-east. Horse riding, fishing, golf and other outdoor pursuits are all in easy access of the park. Golf clubs, bikes available for hire. Free and unlimited hot showers, sheltered eating area. Open March – Nov.

LIMERICK
ADARE

(2.5m). Adare Camping & Caravanning Park, Adare, Co Limerick. 00 353 61 395376. www.adarecamping.com. Owner: H&M Doherty. Relaxing atmosphere, sheltered bounderies. Play area for children separate from parking area. Visit for old abbeys, churches, fishing, golf, pitch & putt, horse riding, bicycle hire, restaurants etc. Hot spa on site and campers' kitchen. Open March 12 – Sept 30.

KILCORNAN

Curragh Chase Caravan & Camping Park, Coillte Forest Park, Kilcornan, Co Limerick. 00 353 61396349. www.coillte.ie. The park is in the 242-hectare Coillte Forest Park of exceptional beauty. Open May-Sept.

MAYO
ACHILL ISLAND

Keel Sandybanks Caravan & Camping Park, Keel, Achill Island, Co Mayo. 00 353 9843211. www.achillcamping.com. Owner: Mr John Nestor. Caravan Park is adjacent to Keel Beach, on L as you enter village. Bridged-linked to mainland Mayo, Achill Island offers a variety of scenic beauty and boating, angling, sailboard lessons, surfing, mountain walking and golfing. Plenty of outdoor playing area for the children. ICC member. Rated 4 stars under Irish Failte scheme. Open May 25-Sept 2.

BALLINA

(2m). Belleek Caravan & Camping Park, Belleek, Ballina, Co Mayo. 00 353 96 71533. www.belleekpark.com. Owner: Joe & Phil Lenahan. Sheltered and tranquil location with excellent facilities and high standards. Salmon fishing in River Moy. Nearby historical sites, blue flag beaches, 18-hole golf, deep sea angling and all leisure activities. Amenities in town of Ballina. Open March 1 to Nov 1.

CASTLEBAR

(5m). Carra Caravan & Camping Park, Belcarra, Castlebar, Co Mayo. 00 353 9032054. www.horsedrawn.mayonet.com. From Castlebar follow N84 towards Ballinrobe. Cross the railway bridge and turn L for Belcarra (5m). Horsedrawn caravan holidays and country walks are a speciality from this quiet 'family-run' park in Mayo's award winning "Tidiest Village". Shops, pubs, pub meals, fishery all in 200yd. 2 golf courses, doctor all in 4m. ICC member. Graded 2 stars. Registered with TAMS, Ireland. Open May 4-Sept 22.

(7m). Carrowkeel Camping & Caravan Park, Ballyvary, Castlebar, Co Mayo. 00 353 9490 31264. www.carrowkeelpark.ie. Owner: Alex Peters. Ideally located for walking, cycling, touring and (salmon) fishing. Facilities include an on-site shop with tourist information, clubhouse with open fire, live entertainment in high season. Games room and outdoor play area for children. Open April 1-Oct 1.

CONG

(1m). Cong Caravan & Camping Park, Lisloughrey, Quay Road, Cong, Co Mayo. 00 353 949546089. www.quietman-cong.com. Owner: Gerry & Margaret Collins. A fisherman's paradise with rods and boats available and lakes, rivers and underground streams. Launderette, children's playground, boat rental and shop on site. Bike rental. Mini golf. Film shown to residents in the mini cinema nightly. Pony trekking and falconry nearby. Forest walks, caving.

KNOCK

Knock Caravan & Camping Park, Claremorris Road, Knock, Co Mayo. 00 353 949388100. www.knock-shrine.ie. Caravan Club affiliated site. An excellent base for touring Mayo and the West of Ireland. Toilet blocks, launderette and MV service point. TV rooms and play area. Dog walk nearby. Good area for walking and fishing. Peaceful off-peak. Open March-Oct.

LOUISBURGH

Old Head Forest Caravan & Camping Park, Old Head, Louisburgh, Co Mayo. 00 353 876486885. Site in woodland surroundings, at the edge of Old Head prehistoric woods on the shores of Clew Bay. Old Head has a pier and slipway with lifeguard on duty. Outdoor pursuits at Adventure centres locally. Open June – Sept.

WESTPORT

(3.2m). Parkland Caravan & Camping Park, Westport House & Country Park, Westport, Co Mayo. 00 353 9827766. www.westporthouse.ie. 3m to 18-hole golf course, deep-sea angling on Clew Bay, pony trekking, restaurants, singing pubs, dancing. In easy driving distance: sandy beaches, salmon and sea-trout fishing, sailing and mountain climbing. Open May 12 – Sept 3.

ROSCOMMON
BALLAGHDERREEN

(3.7m). Willowbrook Caravan & Camping Park, Kiltybranks, Ballaghderreen, Co Roscommon. 00 353 949861307. www.willowbrookpark.com. Owner: Dave & Lin Whitfield. Warm, friendly, family run park set in the Lung Valley. Unspoilt and beautiful landscape ideal for a relaxing holiday. Disabled toilet. Tuck shop. On-site archery, coarse fishing, adventure camp (July). Near tennis courts, 9-hole golf

IRELAND/NORTHERN IRELAND

course.

BOYLE

(10m). Lough Arrow Touring Caravan Park, Ballynary, Riverstown, Boyle, Co Roscommon. 00 353 719666018. latp@eircom.net. http://homepage.eircom.net. Owner: Terry & Mary Wilson. Registered with Bord Failte and Irish Caravan Council. Adults only. Shop 3m. Fishing next door and in 5m (lakes). 3 golf courses in 8m. Pub next door. boat hire. Camp site on lake shore. New on-site facilities: boules pitch, golf practice nets. Winner 2 Star Park 2005 (ICC). Open March 13-Oct 31.

(2.5m). Lough Key Caravan & Camping Park, Lough Key Forest and, Leisure Park, Boyle, Co Roscommon. 00 353 719662212. www.loughkey.ie. Owner: Coillte Teo – The Irish Forestry Board. The scenic and historic Lough Key now encompasses a landmark cluster of attractions unique to Ireland. The Adventure House contains challenging activities and puzzles where only teamwork and trial and error allows you to progress. The outdoor Adventure play-zone provides activities for children of all ages. The estate also contains many trails through the woodlands and forest. Open April 1-Sept 15.

SLIGO

SLIGO

Gateway Caravan & Camping Park, Ballinode, Sligo, Co Sligo. 00 353 7145618. gateway@oceanfree.net. Excellent on-site facilities. Shop, pub/pub food across the road. Takeaway deliveries to site.

STRANDHILL

Strandhill Caravan & Camping Park, Strandhill, Co Sligo. 00 353 719168111. sxl@iol.ie. The site is at Strandhill Beach, mecca for surfers from all around the world, while the flat sands of Culleenamore, more suitable for family fun, are just 1m distant. Golf is 500yd, shops, pubs and restaurants in 100yd. Pitches on hardstandings. Open April – Sept.

TIPPERARY

CAHIR

(6m). The Apple Caravan & Camping Park, Moorstown, Cahir, Co Tipperary. 00 353 5241459. www.theapplefarm.com. Friendly site on an award-winning fruit farm. You will be welcome to wander round orchards, try farm-pressed apple juice and help yourself to a few strawberries or raspberries when in season. On site facilities: free access to tennis courts and rackets, free hot water, spring water for drinking and large indoor area. Open May-Sept.

CLOGHEEN

Parsons Green Caravan & Camping Park, Clogheen, Co Tipperary. 00 353 5265290. www.clogheen.com. Small, family-run park, centrally situated for touring the whole of the south of Ireland. Excellent on site facilities include: garden and river walks, pet field, farm museum, coffee shop, playground, pony, boat rides, picnic area, tennis and basketball court. Hot food take-away. Golf, fishing, hill-walking nearby.

GLEN OF AHERLOW

Ballinacourty House Caravan & Camping Park, Glen of Aherlow, Co Tipperary. 00 353 6256559. www.camping.ie. Owner: The Stanley family. Family run park offering facilities of high hygienic standards to those who enjoy holidays away from the crowds in a tranquil surrounding of unspoilt nature. Table tennis, tennis court, children's playground and mini golf on site. Horse riding, fishing, swimming pool all available locally. Graded 4 star Failte Ireland Open May 1-Sept 30.

Glen of Aherlow Caravan & Camping Park, Newtown, Glen of Aherlow, Co Tipperary. 00 353 6256555. www.tipperarycamping.com. Owner: George and Rosaline Drew. Caravan Claub affiliated. Spectacular scenery, top class amenities and a warm welcome await you. Toilet blocks and laundry facilities. TV and games room. Dog walk on site. Good area for walking and golf nearby. Facilities for disabled. Quiet and peaceful off-peak.

ROSCREA

(1.5m). Streamstown Caravan & Camping Park, Streamstown, Roscrea, Co Tipperary. 00 353 50521519. www.tipperarycaravanpark.com. Owner: Keith & Marina Stanley. Park is on a quiet dairy farm, beautifully landscaped. Good amenities and a relaxing atmosphere. 5 nights for the price of 4. Local activities include: horseriding, golf, historical sites, fishing, hill walking. Open April-Oct.

WATERFORD

DUNGARVAN

(2m). Bayview Caravan & Camping Park, Ballinacourty, Dungarvan, Co Waterford. 00 353 5845345. bayview@cablesurf.com. Owner: Dan Barry. Golf and Leisure Centre, restaurant, bar, swimming pool – all 200yd from park. Near angling, sailing, water-skiing, swimming, tennis. Two 18-hole golf courses in 2m. Open April-Sept.

(3.5m). Casey's Caravan & Camping Park, Clonea, Dungarvan, Co Waterford. 00 353 5841919. Follow SP off N25. Direct access to the beach. Top facilities available include playground, TV room, games room, crazy golf, telephone, shop adjacent to park. Top class angling, also sailing and sail boarding. Three golf courses in the area. Cards not accepted as method of payment. Open April 10-Sept 6.

TRAMORE

(2m). Newtown Cove Caravan & Camping Park, Tramore, Co Waterford. 00 353 51 381979. www.newtowncove.com. Owner: John & Sarah Good. Family run park, in a peaceful setting, well sheltered. On site children's playground, TV & Games rooms, shop, laundry. 400yd from sea swimming and fishing. 18-hole golf course. Open April 9-Sept 27.

WESTMEATH

MULTYFARNHAM

Lough Derravaragh Caravan & Camping Park, Multyfarnham, Co Westmeath. 00 353 4471500. camping@iol.ie. Owner: Paul Smith. On N4 between Mullingar and Longford, take road to Multyfarnham and follow signs to Derravaragh/Donore. Set in 38 acres of mature wooded foreshore. Fishing with boat and engine hire. Golf courses, horseriding, dog racing, forest walks, historic sites, castles and pubs are all nearby. Open March-Sept, rest of year by appointment.

WEXFORD

BALLAGHKEEN

(2m). The Trading Post, The Ballagh, Ballaghkeen, Co Wexford. 00 353 539127368.www.wexfordcamping.com. Owner: Patrick Power. Park is just off R741on your L. Designed and opened at the dawn of a new century for the free spirited who like the less beaten track. Facilities include: disabled facilities, TV room, launderette, BBQ area, children's play area, service station deli and forecourt shop. Pub, golf courses, sandy beach all nearby. Open April 1- Sept 30.

ROSSLARE

(1.5m). St Margarets Beach Caravan & Camping Park, Our Lady's Island, Rosslare Harbour, Rosslare, Co Wexford. 00 353 539131169. stmarg@ircom.net. Owner: Kathryn Traynor. Located in an Area of Outstanding Natural Beauty, with an important nature preserve and bird sanctuary, St Margaret's is an attractive quiet place to spend a few days in – adjacent to Wexford coastal parth and miles of safe sandy beach. Family run with

CHANNEL ISLANDS

the owners living on site. Open March-Oct.

WEXFORD

Ferrybank Camping & Caravan Park, Ferrybank, Wexford, Co Wexford. *00 353 44378/43274.* www.wexfordcorp.ie. 5mins walk across bridge on seafront on R741. Situated on seafront overlooking town and harbour. Heated indoor swimming pool and shop attached. Golf, fishing, surfing, sailing, Blue Flag beaches and tennis in easy reach. Open Easter – Sept.

WICKLOW
DONARD

Moat Farm Caravan & Camping Park, Donard, Co Wicklow. *00 353 45404727.* moatfarm@ireland.com. Owner: E&N Allen. Small, quiet, select family run park in a tranquil rural setting, 1min walk from the village. Modern, fully serviced park. Golf, fishing, pony trekking in easy reach. A walking paradise. Open March 15-end Sept.

RATHDRUM

Hidden Valley Holiday Park, Rathdrum, Co Wicklow. *00 353 40446080.* www.irelandholidaypark.com. Owner: Lloyd Williams. Quiet site on the banks of Avonmore river and on the edge of the Wicklow Mountains. 10mins walk away from village pubs, shops and restaurants. Trout fishing on site. Open April 10-Sept 20.

REDCROSS VILLAGE

(3m) River Valley Caravan & Camping Park, Redcross Village, Co Wicklow. *00 353 40441647.* www.rivervalleypark.com. Owner: Mrs V Williams. 30miles south of Dublin on N11 past Beehive Pub on L, then Lil Doyles Pub on R, turn for Redcross beside pub. Site in village. Caravan Club affiliated. In one of the most scenic areas of County Wicklow – an ideal base for tourist attractions, golf, walking, trails, horse riding, water sports, shore and fresh water angling. Restaurant & bar. Dogs allowed in Secret Garden (couples only) in July and Aug). Open March-Sept.

ROUNDWOOD

Roundwood Caravan & Camping Park, Roundwood Village, Roundwood, Co Wicklow. *00 353 12818163.* www.dublinwicklowcamping.com. Situated off N11. A mature modern fully developed park in the heart of the Wicklow Mountains in a quaint village, overlooking Vartry Lakes and Forest. Shops, pubs, restaurants, markets and entertainment - 5mins stroll. Great walking area with mountain and forest walks. Golf, fishing, equestrian sports available nearby. Open May 1-Aug 31.

CHANNEL ISLANDS
GUERNSEY

Fauxquets Valley Farm Camp Site, Castel, St Peter Port, Guernsey. *01481 236951.* www.fauxquets.co.uk. Owner: Mr RO Guille. R from main road at the sign for the German hospital, then fifth L. Families and couples only. Fully equipped tents available for hire. Open Easter-Sept.

La Bailloterie Camp Site, Vale, Guernsey GY3 5HA. *014812 43636.* www.campinginguernsey.com. Owner: Mr Richard A Collas & Caryl D Shaw. Landscaped areas with plenty of room. In easy reach of beaches. Fully-equipped sites available. Dogs welcome at park owners' discretion in one area. AA 3 pennant site. Open May-Sept.

HERM

Seagull Campsite, Herm, Isle of Wight GY1 3HR. *01481 722377.* www.herm-island.com. Owner: Wood of Herm Island Ltd. By launch from St Peter Port, Guernsey. An isolated peaceful site. Lovely beaches. Camping gear and fully equipped tents can be hired. Modern toilet and shower facilities.

ST MARTIN

Beuvelande Camp Site, Beuvelande, Rue de Beuveland, St Martin JE3 6EZ. *01534 853575.* www.campingjersey.com. Owner: Mr De La Haye. 4m from St Helier. Channel Islands only 5 pennant Premier Park. Family run site set in beautiful countryside. Open April 1-Sept 30.

Rozel Camping Park, St Martin JE3 6AX. *01534 855200.* www.jerseyhols.com/rozel. 5m from St Helier on the A6. 0.5m from beach. Children's play area. Package tents and own tents welcome. Free parking near tents. Caravans & motorhomes welcome. Open late May-mid Sept.

ISLE OF MAN
DOUGLAS

Glen Dhoo Farm Camp Site, Hillberry, Onchan, Douglas, Isle of Man IM4 5BJ. *01624 621254.* www.caravanningcampingsites.co.uk. On A18 near Hillberry Corner on TT course. Car ferry 3m. Holiday site in sheltered valley. Fees on application.

KIRK MICHAEL

Glen Wyllin Campsite, Kirk Michael, Isle of Man. *01624 878231.* Owner: Michael Commissioners. Site in National Glen, about 100yd S of Kirk Michael on A3. Adjoins beach. Close to TT course. Brochure and fees on application. Furnished tents for hire. 5mins walk to village.

PEEL

(0.25m). Peel Campsite, Derby Road, Peel, Isle of Man. *01624 842341.* Owner: Peel Town Commissioners. Near Peel Castle and 0.5m from beach. Level, rural site, edge of town, close to all amenities. TT course 3m. Takeaway, café/restaurant available nearby. Fees on application. Open April-Sept.

UNION MILLS

Glenlough Farm Camp Site, Glenlough Farm, Union Mills, Isle of Man IM4 4AT. *01624 852057.* www.glenloughcampsite.com. Owner: Mr Quayle. On A1 Douglas/Peel Road. 1m N of Union Mills, 3m from Douglas. Open April-Oct.

ISLES OF SCILLY
BRYHER

Jenford, Brygher, Isles of Scilly TR23 0PR. *01720 422559.* www.bryhercampsite.co.uk. Owner: Mrs K Stedeford. Off island reached by boat from Hugh Town. Open March-Oct.

ST AGNES

Troytown Farm, St Agnes, Isles of Scilly TR22 0PL. *01720 422360.* www.troytown.co.uk. Owner: Mrs S J Hicks. Unique location on the most remote tip of the beautiful Isles of Scilly. Sensational views across the site's own sandy beach, to uninhabited islands and ocean. Open from 1 March-31 Oct.

ST MARTIN'S

St Martin's Campsite, Middle Town, St Martin's, Isles of Scilly TR25 0QN. *01720 422888.* www.stmartinscampsite.co.uk. Owner: Ben & Caroline Gillett. Ferry, helicopter or plane from Penzance/Lands End. Launch from St Mary's to St Martin's. Level, grassy, sheltered site on quiet, unspoilt island. Booking essential. Open March 15-Oct 13.

ST MARY'S

(0.5m). Garrison Holidays, The Garrison, St Mary's, Isles of Scilly TR21 0LS. *01720 422670.* www.garrisonholidays.com. Owner: Mr & Mrs E W Moulson. From Penzance take ferry (2.45hrs), helicopter or Skybus from Lands End. Short walk from quay. Friendly family run site. Reasonable shelter, small, level fields. Near children's park, beach and places of historical interest. Lovely walking area. Transport and towing of trailers available. Beautiful sub-tropical islands. AA 3 pennants. 18-hole golf course, horse riding and water sports nearby. Open Easter-Oct.

162 MOTOR CARAVAN & CAMPING PARKS 2009